Reprints of Economic Classics

THE ECONOMIC HISTORY OF IRELAND

FROM THE UNION TO THE FAMINE

Also in

REPRINTS OF ECONOMIC CLASSICS

By GEORGE O'BRIEN

The Economic History of Ireland in the Seventeenth Century [1919]

The Economic History of Ireland in the Eighteenth Century [1918]

An Essay on Medieval Economic Teaching [1920]

An Essay on the Economic Effects of the Reformation [1923]

THE ECONOMIC HISTORY OF IRELAND

FROM THE UNION TO THE FAMINE

BY

GEORGE O'BRIEN

[1921]

AUGUSTUS M. KELLEY • PUBLISHERS
CLIFTON 1972

First Edition 1921

(Longmans, Green & Co., *39 Paternoster Row*, 1921)

Reprinted 1972 by

Augustus M. Kelley Publishers

REPRINTS OF ECONOMIC CLASSICS

Clifton New Jersey 07012

. . . .

I S B N 0 678 00816 7

L C N 68 56554

. . . .

PRINTED IN THE UNITED STATES OF AMERICA

by SENTRY PRESS, NEW YORK, N. Y. 10013

TO

SIR HORACE PLUNKETT.

PREFACE.

After this book went to press, my attention was drawn to a review in the Dublin Daily Express of Mr. E. J. Riordan's *Modern Irish Trade and Industry*, in which the historical introduction which I had written to that book was attacked on the ground that I exaggerated the importance of the effects of the repeal of the corn laws on Ireland. The reviewer states that the distress of the Irish farmer in the fifty years following the Union was caused, not by any action of the government, but by the influx of cheap American corn. Anticipating that this criticism may be levelled against the present book, I wish to reply to it in advance. The fact is that the influx of corn from the United States did not begin to assume any considerable dimensions until after 1870, and cannot therefore have materially affected the Irish farmer in the first half of the nineteenth century. The whole subject of the effect of the corn laws and their repeal on the agriculture of the United Kingdom is dealt with in an excellent article by Mr. C. R. Fay in the March number of the Economic Journal, which, I am glad to be able to say, does not contain anything to make me wish to alter any part of the section of the present book devoted to the subject.

I would also like to draw attention to another matter, which occured to me when it was too late to incorporate it in the text, namely the connection between the land system and the rapid growth of population in Ireland, considered in the light of Dr. Havelock Ellis's theory of the effect on the birth rate of the absence of what he calls the ascensional impulse. This theory confirms the view taken in the book that the extremely rapid increase in the population of Ireland after the Union was an effect rather than a cause of the misery of the country. The inability of the Irish tenant to improve his position owing to the evil land system removed the ascensional impulse which would have operated as a prudential check on population.

I wish to acknowledge my indebtedness to the Rev. P. J. Connolly S.J., and Mr. P. S. O'Hegarty who read the MS. of the introductory and concluding chapters; to Mr. F. J. Barnard B. Comm. who read the MS. of the section on the combinations of workmen; and to Miss Mary Mackenzie, who read the revised proofs and compiled the index. I also desire to express my deep gratitude to the Rev. T. A. Finlay S.J. and Mr. Arthur Cox for their kindness in reading the proofs and for making many valuable suggestions.

GEORGE O'BRIEN.

NOTE ON ABBREVIATONS.

The following abbreviatons are used throughout the book:—

DEV. COMM. -	Digest of Evidence taken before Her Majesty's Commissioners of Inquiry into the State of the Law and Practice in respect to the occupation of Land in Ireland (The Devon Commission) Dublin 1847.
F. R. C. - -	Report of the Financial Relations Commission 1896.
PARL PAP. / P. P. -	Parliamentary Papers.
WAKEFIELD. -	An Account of Ireland, Statistical and Political, by Edward Wakefield, London 1812.

TABLE OF CONTENTS.

PART I. AGRICULTURAL RESOURCES.

PART II. NON-AGRICULTURAL RESOURCES.

PART III. PUBLIC FINANCE ETC.

THE ECONOMIC HISTORY OF IRELAND FROM THE UNION TO THE FAMINE.

INTRODUCTION.

IRISH history resembles popular fiction amongst other respects in this, that they both come to an end with the marriage of the heroine. This convention is based on the assumption that in every case the married couple live so happily ever after that there is nothing more to tell of their career, an assumption the truth of which is unfortunately contradicted by the experience of real life. Indeed to the psychologist the years following the wedding bells are more interesting than those which preceded them; and the steps leading up to the divorce are frequently better worth the telling than those leading up to the alliance. The Union was the marriage of Ireland. "The Act of Union" according to Grattan "constituted the marriage articles between the two countries"[1]. As in the case of the heroine of fiction, the prenuptial history of Ireland has been frequently related, but her postnuptial history has on the whole been neglected. While we are all familiar with the steps by which the predominant partner succeeded in leading his reluctant and unwilling bride to the altar, we are less familiar with the events of their lives after the happy ceremony had been completed. The married life of this pair is nevertheless not devoid of interest. Why was it that a bride who had in the popular phraseology "married money" refused to become reconciled to the union she had

[1] *Speeches* vol. iv. p. 360.

contracted? Why did she seek a divorce, or at least a separation, from such an eligible spouse? Why did the beggar maiden tire of King Cophetua? To drop metaphor, why did Ireland express such dissatisfaction at the Union with Great Britain, and seek to have it annulled?

These are questions which have never been satisfactorily answered. As we said, Irish history for the most part ends with the Union; and the sequel, though vitally interesting, has been generally neglected. While we have numerous biographies of Irish politicians, and numerous accounts of particular aspects of Irish life in the early nineteenth century, we have no comprehensive history of Ireland in that all-important period. It is for this reason that the author feels less hesitation in laying the present work before the public than he did in the case of his previous books on the same subject. The seventeenth century had its Carte and Bagwell; the eighteenth its Lecky and Froude; but the nineteenth century has been so far a field untilled even by the minor historian. And of that untilled field—that wilderness of weeds and nettles—that jungle of unindexed bluebooks and undated pamphlets—the most neglected corner is the economic corner; while we are not completely devoid of accounts of the great political events of the early nineteenth century—of the struggle for Catholic emancipation and for the repeal of the Union—we are almost completely in the dark regarding the economic history of the period. The subject that has been so completely neglected is nevertheless of the greatest interest and importance. The economic history of Ireland in the fifty years following the Union is full of the most acute problems and the most embittered controversies.

The period which we have undertaken to review in the present book, though beset with difficulties, which we confess to have but imperfectly overcome, possesses two great advantages; it has a definitely marked beginning and a definitely marked end. The Union is clearly indicated as the date at which we should begin our study, as it was a complete epoch or turning point in Irish affairs, marking, as it did, the disappearance of the old Irish Parliament, and the end of the separate political entity of Ireland. The famine, with which the book ends, was a not less definite turning point in Irish affairs. The potato failure of 1846 drastically solved the perennial problem of the apparent disproportion between the population and the resources of the country, and initiated that great flood of emigration which was to be the dominant feature of Irish economic life in the second half of the century. The famine also did a great deal to hasten the transition of the Irish rural workers from small holders to day labourers, a revolution which had been progressing for thirty years. "The famine" according to a contemporary, "caused the permanent uprooting of the whole social system."[1] Simultaneous with the famine and scarcely less important in its ultimate results was the repeal of the corn laws, which deprived the Irish farmer of his preference in the British market, and tempted him once more to throw his land into pasture. A couple of years later the Encumbered Estates Act was passed, the first of the long line of remedial land measures passed in the second half of the century. Thus the year 1850 marks the middle of the nineteenth century not merely chronologically; it marks the turning point from the increase to the decrease of population, from tillage to pasture, and from a regime of non-interference to one of interference by the state with the landowner. It is therefore a convenient date at which to conclude our study.

The subject will be considered under three divisions, agricultural resources, non-agricultural resources, and public finance. We treat of agriculture first because it precedes all other branches of economic activity both in time and importance in every country and every period,[2]

[1] J. V. Stewart, *A Letter to Lord Clarendon*, Letterkenny 1849 and see *Devon Commn.* p. 523. [2] Adam Smith. *Wealth of Nations* Bk. III ch. i.

but particularly in Ireland in the early nineteenth century. Owing to the policy adopted towards Irish industry in the eighteenth century the vast majority of the population were thrown on the land for their support; and the proportion of the people thus depending on the soil tended to increase rather than diminish after the Union. Sir Robert Kane estimated in 1844 that the percentage of the population dependent on manufactures was 24, and that dependent on agriculture 66.[1] An occupation which took such a prominent place in the economy of the country is entitled to the first and greatest share of our consideration.

In the first part of the book, we shall begin by drawing attention to the actual condition of the Irish agricultural labourers and the state of Irish agriculture, both of which were miserable in the extreme. We shall next inquire into the causes of this anomaly, of a fertile country being disfigured by wretched agriculture and a starving people; and shall direct attention to the remedies for this state of affairs adopted by the landlords and the government respectively. We shall show that the landlords' action was based on two fundamental assumptions—viz. that large farms were more economical than small, and that the country was overpopulated,—and shall demonstrate the error of these assumptions, concluding that the action based on them must therefore have been harmful rather than beneficial. Having next attempted to indicate what, in our opinion, were the real causes of Irish poverty, namely, the unjust distribution of the produce of the land actually cultivated, and the failure to bring the waste land of the country into cultivation, we shall proceed to inquire which course the government of the day pursued; whether it acted on the false assumption of the landlords that Ireland was overpopulated, or on the correct assumption that the resources of the country were not utilized to their full capacity. We shall show that the former rather than the

[1] *Industrial Resources of Ireland* p. 237.

altter assumption was adopted by the government; and that, therefore, while the legislative measures passed for the correction of the inequitable distribution of the produce of the soil and the increase of the land under cultivation were few and negligible, those passed for assisting depopulation were numerous and important. Finally we shall narrate how the disproportion between the population and resources of Ireland was drastically solved by the great famine.

In the second part, that dealing with non-agricultural resources, we shall deal with mines, fisheries, and manufacturing industry. The various reasons put forward to account for the failure of Irish industry to progress will be examined.

The third part is devoted to an account of the numerous public charges with which the population of Ireland was burdened—imperial taxes, county cess, poor rate, tithes and urban tolls,—and of the channels through which millions of Irish money were drained abroad—surplus revenue and the non-residence of the landed proprietor. The subjects of currency and credit and the means of communication will be briefly examined.

PART I

AGRICULTURAL RESOURCES.

CHAPTER I.

THE CONDITION OF THE AGRICULTURAL POPULATION.

IN order that the actual condition of the Irish agricultural labourer may be understood, it is necessary that we should in the first place explain the peculiar method by which he was remunerated. The evidence given before the Devon Commission pointed to a division of the Irish rural labourers into three classes:— "unmarried farm servants who reside with their employers; cottiers who hold, in addition to their cabin, a small lot of ground at a fixed rate, generally payable in labour; and those who hold only a cabin with perhaps a few perches of land as a garden and depend for their subsistence chiefly on potatoes raised on land taken in conacre."[1] There was another class of labourer not mentioned in this classification, namely the families of the small farmers of from five to fifteen acres, who worked their own land. Wakefield drew attention to this class: "The fact is that hiring or going out to labour is unknown in various districts of Ireland and even thought disgraceful. The farms are cultivated by the members of the family, the value of whose labour it would be difficult to appreciate."[2] These however were small holders rather than labourers, for, while they received no pecuniary return for the services they contributed during the lifetime of their parents, they usually received and always expected to receive a part of the holding on their parents' death or

[1] *Devon Commn.* p. 474. [2] Vol. i. p. 511.

on their own marriage. With this class we are not concerned here ; nor need we pay more than passing attention to the first class enumerated above—the unmarried farm servants who resided with their employers. "This class" according to the Devon Commission "seem to be much the most fortunate ; they are provided with food, and their wages, though small, are sufficient to supply them with clothes, and even in some cases to permit them to save some portion of their earnings."[1]

The second and third classes enumerated comprised the vast majority of the Irish rural labouring population. "Of these classes the cottiers with land seem to be the least miserable ; they are in a great measure in the position of subtenants of the allotments which they hold, retaining the same ground in their hands year after year, so as to derive the benefit of the manure which they may be able to apply to it. There is in most districts a customary cottier's "take", which defines the privileges of the labourers so holding ; and these are not utterly inadequate to provide for the support of a family, and are free from the risk of the speculation in conacre. But the third class, holding merely a wretched cabin, or with it only a so-called garden, in general unable to obtain employment even at the lowest rate of wages and dependent for their subsistence on the success of their speculation in conacre, appear to be the most wretched amongst the many wretched classes in Ireland"[2] Two features appear to have been common to both these classes of agricultural labourers—first that they did not live by their wages alone, but were obliged to supplement their earnings in other ways, principally by cultivating a small plot of land ; and, second, that the rent of this plot was frequently paid, not in money, but in labour.

No particular attention need be directed to the distinctive mark of the second class of cottiers, namely the possession of a small holding which they tilled year after year. The

[1] *Ibid.* [2] *Devon Comm.* pp. 474-5.

result of the possession of such a holding was simply to increase the comfort of the cottier, and to elevate him to a higher rank than that of his fellows who had no such holding. What we would direct attention to is the peculiar custom which appears to have been common to both these classes, and which therefore was the distinguishing feature of Irish cottierism, namely the taking of land in conacre. Although this custom was called by different names in different parts of Ireland—"mock ground" in Clare, "dairy land" in the south-eastern counties, "stang" in Wexford, and "quarter land" and "rood land" in other districts [1]—it would appear to have been substantially the same in all parts of Ireland. "The term conacre" again to quote from the Digest of the Devon Commission "appears to mean a contract by which the use of a small portion of land is sold for one or more crops, but without creating the relation of landlord and tenant between the vendor and vendee, it being rather a licence to occupy than a demise. The term is likewise and perhaps more correctly applied to the land held under such a contract. The practice of letting land in conacre appears to be much more prevalent in Munster and Connaught than in Leinster and Ulster. In the latter province it seems that conacre is little known except as potato land, or land let under a conacre contract for a single crop of potatoes; but in the southern and western counties conacre seems to be frequently taken for the purpose of raising crops of oats hay and flax as well as potatoes, although the latter was always the crop for which the conacre was chiefly sought. In the districts in which the practice of conacre is most prevalent, the general arrangement seems to be that the vendor manures the ground, and performs all the labour required to prepare it for the reception of the seed, while the vendee procures the seed, plants it and performs all the subsequent labour. It is stated that in some districts unmanured land is occasionally given for

[1] *Devon Comm.* pp. 532, 537, 542, 1151.

one potato crop without any pecuniary charge in consideration of the taker manuring it, which is esteemed equivalent to rent, from the increased crop of corn yielded to the farmer the following year. Where unmanured land is paid for, the contract is not unfrequently made for the use of the land for two or three crops in order that the taker may receive the benefit of the manure applied with the first crop."[1]

The price paid for this conacre land was generally very high. "The price of conacre varies very much in different districts. Where the land and manure are good, or on rich ley land, it is usually about £10 and not unfrequently as much as £12 or £14 per Irish acre; while on the poorer qualities of land the price comes down to £6 an acre and even less."[2] The amount of the conacre rent was frequently raised by the exactions of a kind of middleman. "It appears that conacre is in general taken by the agricultural labourers for the purpose of securing a certain amount of profitable employment, and also of providing a stock of food for their families; but that other classes speculate in conacre rather from the hope of excessive gain than from absolute necessity. Some, called landjobbers, advance money to necessitous farmers for the purchase at low rates of considerable quantities of conacre, which they afterwards portion out to labourers with large profit to themselves. This however does not appear to be much practised. Another class, for the most part composed of the sons or servants of farmers, take the conacre in the usual manner, but hold over the crop till provisions are scarce and dear, when they sell on credit at exorbitant prices; by which means many of them have realized considerable sums of money."[3] Although the rents were high they were not so high as to preclude the possibility of a good profit being made by the hirer in a good year; the essential evil of the

[1] *Devon Comm.* pp. 519-20. When the skin of the land was burnt, but no manure applied, the contract was called "burnbate" *ibid.* p. 543. [2] *Ibid.* p. 520. [3] *Ibid.* p. 521

system was that the hirer was exposed to the full risk of the year's being bad. He bargained a certainty for a possibility. "The conacre labourer is an indigent speculator who undertakes a *certain* heavy responsibility. If the season is good he derives a considerable profit; if the crop fails he is ruined. He is in the position of a gambler who plays for a stake that he cannot pay if he loses; and he frequently does lose from the uncertainty of the potato crop."[1] The cottier moreover was bound to devote his first attention to his regular employer, and the conacre plots were on this account cultivated irregularly and spasmodically, with the result that they usually did not produce the maximum crop of which they were capable.[2]

The second feature distinguishing the remuneration of the Irish labourer was that he frequently paid the rent of his conacre not in money but in labour—or to put it the other way that he was paid the wages of his labour not in money but in land. "The rent of conacre is sometimes paid in cash, frequently in labour, and sometimes partly in cash and partly in labour."[3] "They try to hire for the season" explained Lord Clements "a quantity of manured ground for potatoes, sufficient, as they calculate, to afford subsistence for their families the whole year round; they bargain for this conacre, as it is called, in money, but, not having sixpence in the world, the farmers allow them 'from charity' to work out the rent in labour; and the nominal rent is worked out in nominal wages; a complex debtor and creditor account is kept of both, and the balance only is settled—if it is settled—in money."[4] In other words, the truck system was in full operation in the case of the Irish agricultural labourer. "The conacre system" according to Professor Hancock "is in agriculture the same as the truck system in the payment of manufacturing labourers."[5] In an excellent pamphlet published in 1850, we read that,

[1] *Ibid.* p. 522. [2] *Report of the Institution Established at Fenagh,* Carlow, 1820.
[3] *Devon Commn.* p. 520. [4] *The Present Poverty of Ireland,* London 1838.
[5] *On Laissez Faire and the Economic Resources of Ireland,* Dublin 1847.

"The crisis which has occurred in the affairs of Ireland gives an opportunity for an effort on behalf of a people reduced to the most degrading serfdom by the most flagitious truck system that ever robbed the labourer of his hire. There never was an instance approaching to it in England, although there the legislature has so often interfered between masters and workmen to prevent that mode of payment. By the conacre system in Ireland the price of land has been artificially raised, and the price of labour unnaturally depressed."[1]

When the conacre rent was paid in labour no money was necessary to settle the account, but when it was paid in money the cottier was confronted with a difficulty. Generally speaking money could not be raised by the sale of any part of the crop produced on the land, as this was almost invariably consumed by the cottier and his family, and some new source of income had to be devised. The solution of this difficulty was found in the pig. In the early years of the nineteenth century the keeping of a pig by the cottiers appears to have been fairly common, but the practice became rarer as time passed, owing to the increasing poverty of the country. "There is scarcely a tenant of any cabin" Trimmer observed "who is not possessed of one hog of a very large kind, and from its being the custom to keep it to the age of two and sometimes three years, it becomes of an enormous size. To the sale of this animal they look for the sum from which they are to pay the rent of their cabin and potato garden, and of course he becomes their chief care. During the day he is suffered to range about at large, and returns when he is in want of food ; his potatoes, and those nearly of as good a quality as the family subsist on, are boiled for him, and with as much care as for themselves."[2] "The treasure of the Irish cottier is his pig. It is his sinking

[1] *Ireland's Hour*, Dublin 1850 App. B ; and see Rogers. *The Potato Truck System of Ireland*, London 1847. Chart, *Ireland from the Union to Catholic Emancipation p.* 89.

[2] Trimmer, *A Brief Inquiry into the Present State of Agriculture in the Southern Parts of Ireland*, London 1809.

fund, the resources for all the changes and chances of the current year."[1] Seasons of distress were always remarkable for an increase in the export of pigs from Ireland ; for the Irish cottier to sell his pig was to fall back on the last trench against starvation.[2]

Another method by which the cottiers obtained a few pounds to pay the conacre rent was by migrating to England for the harvest season. The practice of crossing to England in this way—of "spalpeening", as it was called—was of old standing,[3] and it continued in full force in the early years of the nineteenth century. The poor cottier walked from his home to Dublin, obtained a passage to Liverpool for five shillings, and walked thence to his English destination. A Mayo witness before the Poor Inquiry Commission stated that "those that determine on going are thinking and providing for it perhaps for twelve months before, and many beg from their neighbours at home to make up a little money for it. I sold my pig myself to enable me to go. I thought little of my pig when I had the good English wages before me."[4] The English farmers would have found it impossible to gather in their crops without the aid of these poor migrants, who had the reputation of working hard and conducting themselves very respectably and soberly.[5] The amount which these spalpeens found it possible to bring home with them was on an average about three pounds.[6]

In addition to the care of pigs and the annual migration to England, the cottier increased his income by begging. We do not refer here to begging as practised by the ordinary vagrants, but as practised as an auxiliary mode of livelihood by the peasantry, who did not permit it to interfere with their primary occupation. "In Ireland" we read in 1822

[1] Edwards, *Interests of Ireland*, Dublin 1814.
[2] *Thoughts on the Report of the Committee on Agricultural Distress.* By a Proprietor of Land. Dublin 1820 ; *Poor Inquiry Commission* App. A.
[3] O'Brien, *Economic History of Ireland in the Eighteenth Century* p. 98.
[4] *Appendix* A. p. 206. [5] Nicholls *Second Report* par. 56.
[6] *Devon Commn.* p. 518.

"begging is systematic. As soon as the potato crops are planted in Kerry the men set out for England and other parts in search of work, and the wife and family to beg around the country."[1] "The occupier of a hovel and a rood of land usually leaves his abode of wretchedness in May or June, after he has planted his potatoes, and exercises the trade of a strolling beggar until the harvest, when the produce of his potato ground and the alms which he has collected during his peregrinations are the only sustenance on which he can depend for the coming winter."[2] Sir G. C. Lewis in his invaluable book on *Irish Disturbances* divides the beggars into two classes, those who did nothing else but beg, and "occasional mendicants". The former class comprised four subclasses :— "(1) wandering beggars who go from fair to fair and stand at chapel and church doors and other places of public resort, (2) professional strolling beggars who have no fixed domicile and live constantly by mendicancy, (3) town beggars who live by mendicancy, but have a fixed domicile, and (4) poor housekeepers who are relieved by three or four neighbours to whom their wants are known, but who would not resort to general begging". Of the second class of beggars, with whom we are more particularly concerned here, Lewis remarks "In the summer, when the stock of old potatoes is exhausted, and the new year's crop is not yet fit for food, the country is covered with swarms of occasional mendicants, being labourers' wives and families, who go about from one farmer's house to another, frequently to a considerable distance from their homes, in order to collect potatoes. When the immediate pressure is over, they cease to beg, which they consider as a disgrace, and to which they are only driven by necessity. The father sometimes joins his family at certain places but rarely begs in company with them."[3]

[1] *Report of Committee for Relief of Distress in Ireland.* London 1822 p. 132.

[2] *A Letter on the State of Ireland* by an Irish Magistrate. London 1825.

[3] pp. 310-11 and see Bicheno. *Ireland & Its Economy* p. 251. A vast amount of information on the subject of Irish beggars is contained in Appendix A of the *Poor Inquiry Commission*.

It is obvious that the system of remuneration of labour which we have outlined was unsatisfactory. The rural labourer, unable to live on the wages which he received from his employer, was forced to supplement them by the cultivation of a patch of land, for which he paid a rent, which, if paid in money was onerous if not excessive, and if paid in labour was estimated on the assumption that labour received the lowest possible rate of remuneration; and, consequently, he was frequently driven to the expedients of migration or mendicancy in order to eke out a livelihood. The system of remuneration was bad; and we must next inquire precisely how bad it was. What did a livelihood mean? What was the standard of comfort below which the Irish cottier refused to sink?

In order to answer this question we must first inquire into the rate of wages which prevailed in Irish agriculture in the period under review. According to Mr. Trimmer, who conducted his investigations in 1809, the average rural wage was sixpence a day.[1] In the same year Newenham judged it to be 10½ d[2] and Wakefield one shilling.[3] This apparent discrepancy is probably occasioned by the fact that while the first writer reckoned the average daily wage for the whole year, the others reckoned it for the actual working day. The rural labourer suffered from long periods of unemployment, during which he earned nothing at all, so that there was a serious difference between the average and the actual daily wage. In 1816 the daily wage was said to be 10d;[4] in 1821 it was estimated at 8d in ordinary times, rising to as much as 2/- during the harvest,[5] and in the following year it was stated to be about 8d or 10d for men and about 4d or 6d for women and

[1] *A Brief Inquiry into the Present State of Agriculture in the Southern Parts of Ireland.* London 1809.
[2] *View of Ireland* p. 37.
[3] Vol. ii. p. 234.
[4] Barnes. *A Statistical Account of Ireland founded upon Historical Facts.* Dublin 1821.
[5] Burroughs, *View of the State of Agriculture in Ireland.* Dublin 1821.

children.[1] Daniel O'Connell stated in 1825 that in the poorer and more remote counties the average rate was not more than sixpence a day, and that the cottiers were willing to work for twopence rather than be unemployed.[2] Two years later it was computed that the average wage near Dublin and the large towns was about sixteenpence a day, but that the great majority of the cottiers throughout the country were willing to accept eightpence a day in summer and fivepence a day in winter[3]. The Select Committee of 1830 estimated it at tenpence.[4] The result of the evidence given on the subject before the Devon Commission is summarized in the following table :[5]—

AVERAGE DAILY WAGE OF AGRICULTURAL LABOURERS

District	Winter	Summer
	s. d.	s. d.
Antrim, Armagh, Down, Derry, Tyrone and Carlow	10	1 0
Donegal, Fermanagh, Monaghan, Kildare, Kilkenny, King's Co. Louth, Meath, Queen's Co. Westmeath, Wexford and Wicklow	8	10
Dublin	1 0	1 0
All other districts	8	8

As we said above, these figures represent the sums paid on actual working days, and in attempting to estimate the labourer's annual income, allowance must be made for the long periods of unemployment. "It is not" according to Sir G. C. Lewis "the low rate of wages, but the inconstancy of employment which depresses the Irish labourer.... Only one third of the labourers in the country are employed all the year round, the rest only during the potato digging and the harvest. If every labourer in Ireland could earn

[1] *Impartial Review of the True Causes of Existing Misery in Ireland.* Dublin 1822.
[2] *Select Committee on State of Ireland* 1825.
[3] Burroughs. *Essays on Practical Husbandry.* London 1827.
[4] *Select Committee on Poor of Ireland* 1830 p. 5. [5] *Devon Comm.* p. 476.

eightpence a day for 310 days in the year, we should probably never hear of Whiteboy disturbances. It is the impossibility of living by wages which throws him upon the land; it is the liability of being driven from the land and the consciousness of having no other resource that makes him a Whiteboy."[1] We are probably not far wrong in concluding that the average wage of the Irish cottier in the first half of the nineteenth century was from 8d to 10d a day, and that there were about 200 working days in the year. If this conclusion be correct, the average annual income which the Irish cottier derived from wages was between £6.10 and £8.10.

When we recollect the payments which the cottier had to make it is obvious that this income did not leave him much for luxuries. He had in the first place to pay his employer a rent for the hovel in which he dwelt; he had also to pay a rent for his conacre ground, the whole produce of which was consumed by his own family; during the "meal months" as they were called—that is during the interval between the exhaustion of the old potato crop and the maturity of the new—he had to procure some alternative food; and he had to set aside a certain sum, however small, to procure a few rags to clothe his family. It is a fruitless task to attempt to construct an imaginary budget for a cottier family, as every family was in some respects different both with regard to income and expenditure. A certain insight however into the cottier's mode of life may be gained from the following concrete case given in evidence by a witness before the Poor Inquiry Commission :— I have a wife and five children, the eldest thirteen. I receive from the farmer who employs me a house at a rent of 26/-, 1¼ acres of manured ground at a rent of £5, and the grass of one sheep at a rent of 10/–. I pay the total of these with my labour at the rate of 6½d a day; the amount is made up in 251 working days. After working out the

[1] *Irish Disturbances* p. 313.

amount last year I worked for another farmer, and earned about 9/- or 10/-. I bought a sheep for 7/6 last spring; it will sell at from 14/- to 16/- next spring; it gave a lamb about March which sold for 3/-. I got about four pounds of wool from the sheep. I bought a pig at Christmas for 9/2 and sold it in June for 15/-." This case exhibits all the symptoms of intense poverty; the witness however considered himself to be fortunate to be no worse off, and remarked pathetically: "Only that I have a strong back I would not be so well off as I am."[1] Another witness, whom the commissioners referred to as typical, stated that the total amount available for expenditure on clothes, furniture, and other articles was about 35/- per annum for a man and his wife.[2]

There is no need for us to labour the point that during the first half of the nineteenth century, the condition of the Irish peasantry was miserable in the extreme. If we thought it necessary to do so, we could quote numerous descriptions of the life of the cottier at the time, which would shock and revolt the sensitive or humane reader. Contemporary literature abounds with the most awful accounts of the deep mire of hopeless poverty in which the Irish cottiers were sunk; such descriptions are to be found in the evidence given before numerous government inquiries, in the pamphlets and newspapers of the day, and in the journals of every traveller who visited the country. We do not however feel called upon to reproduce them in a book which professes to be an economic history, and not a guide to a chamber of horrors. We shall confine ourselves to giving a very few typical references to credible contemporary sources.

The houses in which the cottiers dwelt were the merest hovels, unfit for swine to inhabit. They were constructed for the most part of mud, and were sunk in the ground so that the walls of the upper part could be constructed from

[1] *Poor Inquiry Commission App.* A. p. 241. [2] *App. F.* p. 68.

the mud excavated to make room for the lower part.[1] In the not uncommon case where these hovels were constructed by the farmers, the cottiers were forced to pay a most exorbitant rent for their use, often amounting to fifty per cent annually on the capital expended on them, "this rent being generally paid in labour, taken at the lowest rate, and exacted at the most inconvenient or pressing time of the year, when a poor labourer could find employment elsewhere at a higher rate of wages."[2] The clothes of the peasants were of the rudest and roughest description; neither men nor women in general wore shoes or stockings.[3] "There is much less exaggeration" said Sir Walter Scott "about the peasantry than might be imagined. Their poverty is not exaggerated; it is on the extreme verge of human misery; their cottages would scarce serve for pig styes even in Scotland; and their rags seem the very refuse of a sheep, and are overspread on their bodies with such ingenious variety of wretchedness that you would think nothing but some sort of perverted taste could have assembled so many shreds together."[4] It was said that the Irish poor frequently exchanged their garments for those of a scarecrow, and that the latter benefited by the exchange.[5] Light sods skimmed from the surface of the bogs—scraghs, as they were called,—took the place of blankets and other bedclothes.[6]

With regard to the diet of the cottiers, all that it is necessary to say is that they lived principally on potatoes, and on potatoes of a continually deteriorating quality. In the eighteenth century the meal of potatoes had generally been accompanied by milk, but in the early nineteenth century this luxury generally disappeared, possibly on account of the break up of the pasture lands.[7] At the

[1] *The Causes of the Discontents of Ireland*, Dublin 1823. [2] *Devon Commn.* p. 129.
[3] *Select Committee* of 1824-5. Evidence of Daniel O'Connell.
[4] Quoted in Locker Lampson *Ireland in the Nineteenth Century* p. 183.
[5] Monteath, *An Easy System of Draining the Bogs of Ireland*, Edinburgh 1829.
[6] Conner, *A Letter to the Earl of Devon*, Dublin 1843.
[7] *Turnips, Sheep Wool and Prosperity &c.* by an Irish Landlord, Bristol 1824

same time that the condiments of the potato diet were being abandoned, the quality of the potatoes themselves declined. "In many places" we read in 1824 "the poor have been compelled to give up the cultivation of a sound and wholesome potato, because of them the land would not yield a sufficient amount for their support; they have substituted one of a soft watery kind in its stead, and on this inferior food were these poor beings subsisting, and thus they were sinking lower and lower."[1] By the year 1838 the cultivation of "lumpers" was universal. "It could scarcely be thought" reported Drummond's Railway Commission "that their customary diet would admit of any reduction save of quantity alone, yet it has been seriously diminished in quality also". The use of milk had entirely disappeared, and the "lumper" potato was very common.[2] "The potatoes" said Trevelyan "generally used by the people of Ireland were of the coarsest and most prolific kind, called 'lumpers' or 'horse-potatoes' from their size, and they were for the most part cultivated not in furrows but in the slovenly mode popularly known as 'lazy beds'; so that the principle of seeking the cheapest description of food at the smallest expense of labour was maintained in all its force."[3] The following extract from a labourer's evidence before the Devon Commission, which is probably typical, depicts fairly correctly the dietary of the cottier in normal times:—

"How many meals a day have your family generally?"

"Three".

"What have they for breakfast?"

"Potatoes and milk unless we chance to buy a hundred of meal, then they have a stirabout when the potatoes get bad."

"Have you stirabout generally for breakfast?"—

"No, only now and then."

"Do you always have milk?"—

[1] Cropper, *The Present State of Ireland*, Liverpool 1825.
[2] *Second Report*. p. 81. [3] *The Irish Crisis* p. 4.

"No, the cow is sometimes in calf."

"What do you do then ?"—

"Eat them dry."

"Do the children ever get a herring or anything of that kind ?" —

"Yes, when we have a penny to buy it or a sup of gruel to take with the potato."

"Do you ever get any butter ?"—

"No."

"How often in the year do you eat meat ?"—

"We never get meat except a bit at Christmas that would last us for a week. We may chance to buy half a pound of bacon on a market day, and dress a bit of green with it and fry it".

"Do you not have a pig ?"—

"Yes, but it helps to pay the conacre and put clothes on us."

"Have you any vegetables in the garden ?"—

"Yes I sow leeks and a little produce of that kind." [1]

There is no need for us to labour the point that the Irish cottier's lot was extremely miserable. The distress of the lower classes in Ireland in the early nineteenth century is a commonplace not merely of Irish but of world history. We shall conclude simply by quoting two opinions of the general condition of the poor, which put the matter in a strong light. Beaumont the French traveller summed up his impression of Ireland as follows: "La misère nue, affamée ; cette misère vagabonde et fainéante, cette misère qui mendie, couvre le pays entier ; elle se montre partout sous toutes les formes à tous les instants du jour; c'est elle que vous voyez la première en abordant aux rivages de l'Irlande ; et dès ce moment elle ne cesse plus d'être présente à vos regards . . . elle vous suit partout, vous obsède sans relâche ; vous entendez de loin ses gémissements et ses pleurs . . . J'ai vu l'Indien dans ses forêts et le nègre dans

[1] *Devon Commn.* pp. 500-1.

ses fers, et j'ai cru en contemplant leur condition digne de pitié que je voyais le dernier terme de la misère humaine ; je ne connaissais point alors le sort de la pauvre Irlande."[1] The Devon Commissioners record their opinion in almost equally impressive words: "The agricultural labourer of Ireland continues to suffer the greatest privations and hardships ; he continues to depend upon casual and precarious employment for subsistence ; he is still badly housed, badly fed, badly clothed, and badly paid for his labour. We cannot forbear expressing our strong sense of the patient endurance which the labouring classes have generally exhibited under sufferings greater, we believe than the people of any other country in Europe have to sustain."[2]

The agricultural labourers were therefore as miserable as it was possible for any human beings to be ; let us now direct our attention to the condition of the next class in the ascending scale of agricultural employment. The average farmer was but one degree less miserable than the cottier. Of course there were a number of gentlemen farmers and large graziers who were affluent, but the term farmer, as used in Ireland, also included the very smallest cultivator who was not actually a labourer, and it is of these that one generally thinks when the term is used. "The farming class may be defined as those occupying permanently their holdings of whatever size whether with or without leases."[3] Much confusion and misunderstanding has

[1] *l'Irlande Sociale* pp. 201-4.

[2] *Devon Commn.* p. 1116 Those desirous of obtaining more detailed information about the life and customs of the cottiers at the period than it is possible to give in this book may be referred to *A Sketch of State of Ireland Past and Present*, London 1808. Mary Leadbeater's *Cottage Dialogues and Landlord's Friend* published in 1813, the same writer's *Cottage Biography* published in 1822, John Wilson Croker's *Sketch of the State of Ireland Past and Present*, Dublin 1822, "Martin Doyle's" *Irish Cottagers*. Dublin 1830, the same author's *Common Sense for Common People*. Dublin 1835. ("Martin Doyle" was the pseudonym of the Rev. Wm. Hickey of Barrow Glebe, see Berry. *History of the R.D.S.* p. 223). *Hints to Cottagers* by one of the Authors of Cottage Dialogues for the Irish Peasantry. Dublin 1838; A. Nicholson's *Ireland's Welcome to the Stranger*. London 1847, Wm. Bennett's *Narrative of Six Weeks in Ireland*. London 1847. The most voluminous details are to be found in the Appendices to the Report of the Poor Inquiry Commission.

[3] *Devon Comm.* p. 127

been caused by the use of the word farmer to denote two quite different things in England and Ireland, and this confusion has frequently prevented English writers from correctly appreciating Irish economic conditions. "It will be surprising to Englishmen" we read in 1811 "to be told that the farmers in Ireland generally reside in mud cabins and have neither barns nor stables for their use."[1] "In the interior of the south of Ireland" we are told some years later "there are scarcely any persons to be found whom we in England consider to be of the middle rank; for the cultivating classes, whether they pay rent for what they call farms or are labourers, are not in any respect to be distinguished from each other."[2] "I have applied the term 'farmers' to one class, though in truth there is no class which deserves the name, at least according to its significance in England . . . It is hard to find any points of distinction between the farmer and the cottier."[3]

All testimony is agreed that the small Irish farmers were usually exceedingly indigent and miserable. While it is true that many of them found it wise to pretend to be poorer than they actually were, in order to prevent the landlord from raising their rent,[4] it is no less true that their actual condition was in the great majority of cases wretched in the extreme. Wakefield remarked that the houses even of farmers occupying from 50 to 150 acres were remarkably bad and their general standard of living low.[5] Bicheno stated that "the tenant of twenty to thirty acres is but little better accommodated than the cottier; he has probably an additional compartment, hardly divided, for a sleeping place or a dairy."[6] The medium sized farmers lived in low thatched cottages with earth floors;[7] and in their general

[1] *On the State of Ireland* by an Irish Magistrate 1811.
[2] *Turnips Sheep Wool and Prosperity &c.* by an Irish Landlord, Bristol 1824.
[3] O'Flynn. *The Present State of the Irish Poor.* London 1835.
[4] Nicholson, *Report on the General State of Agriculture in the Districts Adjoining the Middle Shannon*, Dublin 1841.
[5] Vol. ii. p. 779. [6] *Ireland and Its Economy* p. 33.
[7] *Letters on the State of Ireland.* London 1831.

mode of living were hardly distinguishable from the cottiers.[1] Although they did not live on an exclusive potato diet, their food was poor and insufficient. Tea constituted one of its main features. "Tea, or an adulterated imitation of it, is in Ireland not the superfluous supplement to the comfortable meal of the poor, but the staff of their life and the support of their existence . . . A quarter of an ounce of this deleterious mixture of leaves called tea, with an ounce of black sugar, a bit of rancid butter, and a loaf made of damaged flour grossly deficient in weight, are the general ingredients of the dinner of a poor family."[2]

[1] Wiggins. *The Monster Misery of Ireland.* London 1844.

[2] *A Word of Advice to the Trading and Monied Interests of Ireland.* Dublin 1804 and see R. H. Price, *Remarks proving the Use of Tea to be against the Interests of Ireland.* Dublin 1812. A certain improvement in the standard of living of the larger farmers was remarked in 1830, caused partly, it was suggested, by the repeal of the Union duties and the consequent cheapness of calico. *Report of Select Committee on State of Poor* 1830 p. 8.

CHAPTER II.

THE CONDITION OF AGRICULTURE.

THE old fashioned and inefficient way in which agriculture was conducted in Ireland aroused the astonishment of many strangers to the country. Arthur Young had described the condition of things in this respect at the time of his visit as being deplorable; and, although in the next thirty years the volume of agriculture had greatly increased owing to the spread of tillage, no improvement in the methods of production was noticeable. "The Irish system of husbandry is defective in the extreme;" we read in 1810 "several essential parts of rural economy are either unknown to or negligently overlooked by the farmers of Ireland; and not one of the various successive improvements of their neighbours within the last hundred years has been as yet generally adopted by them.... An exhausting repetition of grain crops, an injudicious application of natural manures, impoverished lands, ill-fenced fields overgrown with weeds, and clumsy, misshapen, ill-contrived implements of husbandry attract the notice of the traveller in every district of Ireland. Little attention is paid to the quality of the seed committed to the earth; as little to the time of sowing; still less to the accumulation of the manure of cattle. A beast house or foddering yard is scarcely to be met with; compost heaps are far from being common; watered meadows are very seldom seen."[1] This account

[1] *Thoughts on the Expediency and Means of Improving the Agriculture of Ireland.* Cork 1810.

is confirmed by another writer of the same period: "The lower and more numerous class of the farmers are seldom scrupulous with regard to the choice of seed; they rarely clean it sufficiently; they never weed their crops; they prepare their lands very badly and generally sow too late; the consequence of all this is, as might be expected, the inferiority of product."[1] Wakefield complained that the Irish system of agriculture was greatly behind the English, farmyards and out offices being practically unknown; and gave the following description of the chief implement of husbandry commonly in use:—"The Irish plough is made chiefly of wood, and has a very long beam. The breast, which is of wood, has seldom any ground, and when there is one it is not shod. The shock or share has hardly any wing, so that the furrow is forced up by the breast of the plough. The sock in general is of cast iron. The Scotch plough has been introduced of late years; it is a small swing plough, and a most excellent thing of its kind. The many varieties of light ploughs . . . are all unknown."[2] "It is certain" Wakefield concludes "that in Ireland there is abundance of exceedingly rich soil capable of producing the heaviest crops; and yet crops of this kind are seldom seen. This deficiency is to be ascribed to the wretched mode of cultivation and not to the quality of the land. Bad fallows, vile implements, ragwort and thistles, banks without hedges, land saturated with water, meadows mown, and the grass carried off without any return, oats frequently the same, the whole manure of the farm absorbed by the crop of potatoes, are all striking defects which will enable anyone to judge of the state of agriculture in Ireland."[3]

We find occasional evidences of agricultural improvement during the next few years,[4] but the general condition of agriculture appears to have continued extremely backward. "In the midland and southern counties" Lord Bless-

[1] George Barnes. *A Statistical Account of Ireland Founded upon Historical Facts.* Dublin 1811. [2] Vol. i. pp. 360, 468, 501. [3] Vol. i. pp. 579-80.

[4] E. G. Borroughs, *A View of the State of Agriculture in Ireland*, Dublin 1821.

ington wrote in 1822 "there are many excellent farmers, and from the produce of their lands the English market is supplied with fine wheat and oats; but generally speaking agriculture in Ireland is a hundred years behind that in England or Scotland."[1] The Select Committee on the Employment of the Poor in Ireland in the following year reported that, "the want of capital in Ireland is shown by the wretched description of implements used both in domestic manufactures and agriculture, as well as by the general deficiency even of such instruments as the poverty of the people enables them to employ. The plough, carts, and barrows are generally of the rudest description."[2] A French observer remarked that the implements of husbandry in use in Ireland were three hundred years out of date.[3] The one improvement which appears to have taken place at this period was the adoption of the Scotch plough by the larger farmers.[4]

The general condition of agriculture seems however to have remained stationary. "Agriculture" the Railway Commissioners reported "is in the rudest and lowest state. The substantial farmer, employing labourers, and cultivating his lands according to the improved methods of modern husbandry is seldom to be found."[5] Ireland still continued to lag behind other countries in the adoption of improved processes. "The use of foreign manures, the extended application of machinery, and the introduction of steam power to farm purposes has nearly revolutionized the system of those countries where men of skill and capital are engaged on the cultivation of the soil; while the absence of these qualifications in the small tenantry of Ireland has precluded them from their employment."[6] "We can

[1] *Observations on the State of Ireland.* London 1822.

[2] *Report of Select Committee on Employment of the Poor in Ireland* 1823.

[3] *Coup d'Oeil de l'Irlande par* C.H.M.D.C. Paris 1828.

[4] *The Munster Farmers' Magazine* June 1814, Martin Doyle, *Hints to Small Holders on Planting.* Dublin 1830. *Poor Inquiry Commission App.* A. p. 220.

[5] *Second Report* p. 6.

[6] Fitzherbert Filgate, *A Practical Treatise on Through Draining.* Dublin 1840.

scarcely dignify with the name of farming the wretched system of agriculture pursued in a great portion of Ireland, particularly in the south."[1] The Devon Commission was impressed by the evidence of the defective condition of agriculture in Ireland. "The general tenor of the evidence proves that, with the exception of some districts in the north, and some particular localities and estates or individual farms in other parts of the country, the usual agricultural practice throughout Ireland is defective in the highest degree, whether as regards the permanent preparation and improvement of the land essential to successful tillage, the limited selection of the crops cultivated, or the relative succession and tillage of those crops."[2] The absence of suitable farm buildings and out offices was especially remarkable.[3] "To an Englishman journeying westward across Ireland" said Poulett Scrope "it almost seems that he is retrograding from an age of science and civilization to one of ignorance and barbarism."[4] Trevelyan says that "agriculture was carried on in a negligent imperfect manner."[5]

Possibly the respect in which Irish agriculture was most deficient was that of the rotation generally practised. Wakefield complained that "a certain system is pursued, to which the farmers pertinaciously adhere, without the least exception. The first crop is potatoes ; the land is then limed to call forth its productive qualities ; and it is harassed in the most barbarous manner with one crop of white straw after another until it becomes quite exhausted and unproductive for many years after. This is the end and the result of all the exertions of an Irish farmer."[6] Some years later Curwen observed that "their mode of cropping is so unmercifully severe, that if the soil did not possess uncommon

[1] Geale, *Ireland and Irish Questions.* London 1845.
[2] *Devon Commn.* p. 13. [3] *Ibid* p. 128.
[4] *Notes of a Tour in England Scotland and Ireland.* London 1849, and see Napier *An Essay on the Present State of Ireland.* London 1839; Simpkin *A Letter to Earl Grey.* London 1842. [5] *Irish Crisis* p. 4. [6] Vol. i. p. 580.

fertility, a system of such exhaustion as three white crops in succession, without the application of any manure, must soon reduce it to a state of sterility. Yet here the practice is considered a gentle treatment."[1] This was the one feature of Irish agriculture in which time seemed to produce no improvement. "The absence of any important amelioration in the mode of cropping since the days of Arthur Young" remarked Lord Clements "must strike the reader. Improvements of other kinds may be noticed in Ireland—there are better markets—improved breeds of cattle—more mills—better carts and ploughs, &c. but the course of tillage is still the same in its essential features."[2] The evidence given before the Devon Commission showed that the system of rotation practised continued to be most unsatisfactory. "The only crop may be said to be the potato; the ground being manured as a garden every year. On holdings above one acre and not exceeding two to two and a half acres the practice has generally been a two years rotation of potatoes and grain in continued succession. Up to three or four acres, a three years rotation consisting of—1st potatoes, 2nd grain, 3rd grain, and a small portion occupied in what is called grazing. The holdings above these classes are most generally cultivated on a seven or eight years rotation—1st manured for potatoes; 2nd grain; 3rd grain; 4th grain again, or else "left out to rest for grass" and producing little or nothing from the exhausted state of the land, and from no seed having been sown; 5th grass getting a little better; 6th grass still improving; 7th grass on lea, after which the same rotation commences again with potatoes. When the third grass crop is taken, the land is left for the following three years to rest as grazing, and this would extend the rotation to eight years. From this it would appear that there are only about three sevenths of the farm which give something approaching to a tolerable crop, viz. the manured land, the

[1] *Letters from Ireland* vol. i. p. 110. [2] *The Present Poverty of Ireland*, London 1838.

first crop of grain and the lea grain. As to the remaining four sevenths, it may be doubted whether their scanty produce would be sufficient to pay their proportion of the rent and charges of the farm, without bringing any profitable return to the occupiers. Upon the whole this principle of farming consists, first by the application of manure to bring up the land to a certain capability of production, and then, instead of seeking to keep it either in that condition, or in a progressively improving state, the effort is to take everything from it by a continued succession of the same class of exhausting crops, until it becomes incapable of returning the cost of seed and labour; after which it is left to the unaided and gradual operation of nature to recover it from the efforts of this destructive treatment, that it may be again exhausted, and again left for years unproductive to recover."[1]

Another defect frequently complained of was the absence of fences, by reason of which cattle and sheep had to be tethered to prevent their straying and frequently suffered much injury on this account. "As to sheep" observed Curwen "I have seen but few and those truly miserable creatures in a double sense; first in their sorry appearance; and next in the curtailment of the natural use of their limbs by shackles, which fasten their hinder with their fore legs. This practice is resorted to in order to keep the animals within certain bounds, which the fences are insufficient to effect."[2] "In this country of expedients" according to Bicheno "the remedy for bad fences is to tie the legs of each quadruped together with wisps of straw."[3] The paucity of farm buildings drove the farmers to adopt the extraordinary expedient of thatching their cattle with straw to protect them from the weather.[4]

The Irish horse, naturally a very adaptable and useful animal, was treated with such extreme cruelty

[1] *Devon Commn.* p. 14.
[2] *Observations* vol. i. p. 156.
[3] *Ireland and Its Economy* p 15.
[4] Curwen, *Observations*, vol. i. p. 318.

and neglect by the farmers, that its useful qualities tended to become impaired.[1] At the same time the Scotch type of cart horse came to be introduced.[2] The smaller farmers and cottiers relied on the ass for their carrying, and the gradual replacement of the horse by this animal was regarded as a sign of increasing poverty.[3] Asses were very common upon the holdings up to three acres,[4] and were coming gradually to be employed in place of horses even upon larger holdings.[5] A kind of primitive cooperation was practised in the use of these beasts of burthen. Operations requiring the use of several horses at the same time were achieved by the owners of several single horses uniting their efforts, and even the small farmer who owned no horse could obtain the services of his neighbour's by giving a few days' labour in return.[6]

The whole agricultural system of Ireland appears to have been very backward, with the inevitable and necessary result that the produce of the soil was not so great as it should have been. "In point of natural fertility" said Newenham "Ireland is greatly superior to England. Yet owing to an heretofore universal want of capital among the more numerous class of farmers, in addition to habitual negligence and supineness on the part of many, and a lamentable deficiency of agricultural knowledge on that of others, the products of Ireland, which ought unquestionably to be to those of England as at least 6 to 5, are as 4 to 5 only. In other words, the former ought to produce at least one half more than it actually does."[7] "The cottier's gardens throughout the country" complained Borroughs "and even the lands of small farmers do not produce one half of what they could otherwise be made to do if judiciously cultivated."[8] Nassau Senior expressed the opinion

[1] Wakefield vol. i. p. 352. [2] Trimmer, *Further Observations &c.* London 1812.
[3] Gough, *Account of Two Journies Southward in Ireland in* 1817, Dublin 1818.
[4] Nicholson, *Report on the General State of Agriculture in the District Adjoining the Middle Shannon*, Dublin 1841. [5] *Second Repeal Prize Essay* p. 80. *Census of* 1841 p. xxxi.
[6] Curwen, *Letters from Ireland*, vol. i. p. 108, *Poor Inquiry Commission App.* A. p. 198.
[7] *View* p. 82. [8] *Essays on Practical Husbandry*, Dublin 1827.

that "the land of Ireland does not return a fourth, perhaps not an eighth, of what might be obtained from it by fair industry and competent skill."[1] That the superior fertility of Irish to English land is not mere fiction is proved by the experiments of M. Moreau de Jonnes, who prepared the following statistics[2] :

AVERAGE CROP PER HECTARE (2.47 ACRES) IN HECTOLITRES (2.8 BUSHELS)

Crop	England	Scotland	Ireland
Wheat	18	16	20
Rye	10	12	32
Barley	21	12	21
Oats	16	16	16
Mean	16	14	17½

The above animadversion on Irish agriculture must be taken to apply only to tillage. In the region of pasture we find a very different state of things prevailing, and meet with constant accounts of improvement. It must not be forgotten that improvements in the methods of rearing stock did not constitute an unmixed benefit, as every fresh inducement to throw tillage land into pasture tended to increase the unemployment of the people. The more economically and profitably live stock could be produced, the more land was thrown into pasture, the more tenants were ejected. The fact remains that great and extensive improvements took place in the rearing of live stock in the period under review.

"In regard to live stock" said Wakefield "and particularly cattle and sheep, great and most useful improvements have certainly taken place, and every praise is due to those individuals whose exertions have been crowned with success."[3] Whitley Stokes observed in 1821 that both

[1] *Ireland, Journals &c.* vol. i. p. 30.
[2] quoted in Kane *Industrial Resources* p. 243. [3] Vol. i. p. 595.

Irish cattle and sheep had been greatly improved by the introduction of the best English breeds;[1] and the Poor Inquiry Commission was presented with evidence to the effect that the breeds of cattle and sheep had greatly improved.[2]

One obstacle however stood in the way of the full improvement of the live stock, namely the reluctance of the farmers to grow green crops. There was no subject on which Arthur Young waxed more eloquent than this, yet his advice was in the main disregarded. One of the effects of Foster's Corn Law was to concentrate the attention of farmers on the production of food for man, and no attention was directed to the equally important subject of growing food for cattle.[3] The excuse generally put forward by the Irish farmers for their failure to introduce the culture of green crops, was that such crops were generally stolen; and there seems to be some foundation for this plea. An Irish landlord wrote in 1824, "I have been for above twenty five years endeavouring to introduce the cultivation of turnips upon my estate in the south, but cannot accomplish it. As soon as the turnips grow to any size, the common people carry them away as if they were public property."[4] The universality of the custom of stealing crops is vouched for by such excellent authorities as Edward Borroughs and Sir Lucius O'Brien.[5] The evidence before the Devon Commission showed that housefeeding had scarcely progressed at all, and that the growing of green crops was still for the most part unpractised by the Irish farmers.[6]

There was one crop which might have proved a source of substantial profit had its cultivation not been suppressed by the government. By a statute of 1779 the growth of

[1] *Observations on the Population and Resources of Ireland*, Dublin 1821.

[2] *App. H.* pt. 2 p. 26. [3] Fraser, *Gleanings in Ireland*, London 1802.

[4] *The Sun* newspaper, 9th March 1824. [5] Borroughs, *Essays on Practical Husbandry*, Dublin 1827, O'Brien, *Ireland in* 1848, London 1848.

[6] *Devon Commn.* p. 70. The best accounts of Irish agriculture at the time are, for the early part of the period, Trimmer's *Brief Inquiry into the Present State of Agriculture in the Southern Parts of Ireland*, and Wakefield, and for the later part of the period *Appendix* F to the *Report of the Poor Inquiry Commission.*

tobacco, which had since 1660 been forbidden in any part of the British Isles, was permitted in Ireland.[1] The result of this permission was that the Irish farmers engaged in a very extensive cultivation of the tobacco plant, with considerable success. "In the county of Wexford" we read in 1829 "the writer of these pages has seen in the last year upwards of a thousand acres of tobacco, mostly fine and flourishing . . In Wexford the tobacco planters are generally persons of by no means extensive property; they are mostly men who were small farmers and cottiers when they applied themselves to the pursuit . . . . The Wexford peasant who formerly devoted his cottage gardens to a crop of potatoes knew no better fare than those roots moistened with buttermilk; but the profit arising from his tobacco crops has enabled him to become a consumer of tea, sugar, spirits &c."[2] Although the chief centre of the culture was Wexford, tobacco was also grown in other counties, principally Carlow, Waterford, and Kilkenny.[3] The value of tobacco is shown by the very high rate of tithe which was exacted on it; the composition act expressly provided that no account should be taken of "the extraordinary income arising from the tithe of tobacco."[4]

The cultivation of tobacco promised therefore to be a source of prosperity to those who engaged on it. In 1831 it was put down by act of parliament.[5] The statute which suppressed it was bitterly complained of by Irish agriculturalists many years afterwards. "Will the government make any sacrifice for Ireland?" asked Mr. Wiggins. "Will it allow the growth of tobacco, which might be easily and very successfully cultivated by the small farmers?"[6] "When the growth of tobacco" complained a Repeal pamphleteer "was found successful and most productive the British government suppressed it."[7]

[1] 12 Car. II. c. 24, 19 Geo. III c. 35. [2] *Reflections on the Domestic Growth of Tobacco*, Dublin 1829. [3] Brodigan, *A Botanical Historical and Practical Treatise on the Tobacco Plant*, London 1830. [4] 2 and. 3 Wm. IV c. 119 s. 31. [5] 1 and 2 Wm. IV. c. 13.
[6] *The Monster Misery of Ireland*, Dublin 1844.
[7] O'Donoghue, *Irish Wrongs and English Misrule*, Dublin 1845.

There is very little to be said about the timber plantations of Ireland in the period under review. As we have shown elsewhere[1], the Irish woods were almost completely destroyed before the middle of the eighteenth century, and they had not been restored. There was no lack of legislative encouragement of the planting of timber; no less than fifteen statutes dealing with the matter had been passed by the Irish Parliament; but they do not appear to have attained their object to any extent.[2] All observers of Irish affairs in the early nineteenth century agreed that the country suffered from a grievous shortage of timber. "Such is the general scarcity of timber in the south of Ireland" Trimmer remarked in 1812 "that not only the farms are without a comfortable cottage, but in most districts even the fields are entirely without gates. As a substitute large stones are piled up where gates should be.... In the neighbourhood of sea ports what field gates there are are made of foreign fir."[3] Wakefield remarked the same thing:— "Lord Enniskillen remembers being told by his father that a squirrel might have hopped from tree to tree the whole way between Florencecourt and Belturbet, a distance of almost twenty English miles, in which at present not so much as a tree is to be seen; and similar circumstances have been related to me, all which seem to prove that immense woods existed seventy or eighty years ago in places where no other vestiges of them are now to be found than the roots.... Whatever may have been the case formerly, timber speaking generally is now so exceedingly scarce that I have travelled many a dreary mile, crossing whole counties, without seeing so much as a bush. By some cause or other the country has been entirely cleared of wood; and since that time trees have been planted, not on speculation, or with a view to profit; for an opinion has prevailed in Ireland, and I am appre-

[1] *Economic History of Ireland in the Eighteenth Century* pp. 153-7.
[2] *Sketch of the Proceedings of the Society for the Improvement of Ireland*, Dublin 1828.
[3] *Further Observations &c.*, London 1812.

hensive still exists, that the planters of timber seldom reap the benefit of their labour and expense .... The timber of Ireland is confined to the embellishments around family mansions."[1] A few years later Curwen observed "We have not in a circuit of 140 miles met with a single experiment of Irish planting, sufficiently important to entitle the individual to a record of his name as a planter."[2]

One consequence of this great dearth of timber was, as we have seen, to increase the difficulty of erecting proper farm buildings; "Want of timber aggravates the expense of building, enhances the rent of houses, increases the price of all machinery and all utensils, in which wood is employed, obstructs manufacture, agriculture, and commerce."[3] The want of timber was also felt as a serious drawback by those engaged on working the coal mines, as it raised the price of pit props; and by the tanners, as it enhanced the price of bark.[4] The provision trade also suffered through the impossibility of obtaining an adequate supply of casks.[5]

No increase in the amount of timber was noticeable as the century progressed. Indeed in the decade 1841—51 the number of acres under timber actually decreased. In 1841 it amounted to 374,482 acres or 1.8% of the total surface of Ireland, and in 1851 to 304,906 acres or 1.47 %.[6]

We must not leave the subject of agriculture without referring to the efforts made by various public spirited persons and institutions to improve its condition. The Dublin Society had been accustomed during the eighteenth century to encourage good farming by a system of premiums and prizes; and various local farming societies had also

[1] Vol. i. pp. 530-1.

[2] *Observations*, vol. i. p. 258. A good account of the more important plantations in Ireland in 1812 is contained in Wakefield pp. 522-579; and in 1827 in Monteath, *Miscellaneous Reports on Woods and Plantations* and see Hancock. *On the Economic Causes of the Present State of Agriculture in Ireland* pt. V. Dublin 1849.

[3] Finlay, *Letters to the Irish Government*, Dublin 1822 and see Trimmer *Brief Enquiry &c.*, London 1809.

[4] *On the State of Ireland*, by an Irish Landlord 1811.

[5] *Thoughts on the Poor of Ireland* by a Barrister, Dublin 1831.

[6] *Census of Ireland* 1851 *General Report* p. xi.

been formed with the same object. In 1800 there was established the General Farming Society "under the patronage of the Dublin Society". This new society concerned itself with the practical rather than the theoretical aspect of agriculture, and, from the time of its formation until its dissolution in 1828, the Dublin Society discontinued the encouragement it had formerly practised and devoted its attention solely to the theoretical side. Two years later the work of active encouragement was resumed by the Royal Dublin Society. A new special committee "of agriculture and planting" was formed, and the cooperation of local farming societies was invited. Live stock shows were held, and the work of the society took its present form. In addition to the other moneys granted to the Dublin Society a special grant of £5,000 a year was made to the Farming Society, but was discontinued in 1828.[1]

In addition to these central bodies, there were numerous small local societies which had as their aim the improvement of the agriculture of the country. It was in order to create some measure of cooperation and common action amongst these societies that the Agricultural Improvement Society of Ireland was founded in 1840. The number of local societies connected with this body was 23 in 1841, 53 in 1842, 80 in 1843 and 120 in 1850.[2]

The amount of good attained by the efforts of these bodies seems to have been very small. They were criticized first of all on the ground that the amount offered by them in prizes was not sufficient. "The premiums" we read in 1810 "held forth by the Dublin Society and the Agricultural Society, were and are far too trivial to produce the desired effect. Not one in a thousand of the common farmers knows anything about them, and not one in ten thousand thinks it worth his while to be a competitor for any of

[1] Berry, *History of the R.D.S.* pp. 222, 247-8.

[2] *Reports of Agricultural Improvement Society of Ireland*, Dublin 1840 et sq. *Thom's Directory* 1851 p. 232.

them."[4] The principal criticism advanced however was that a disproportionate amount of attention was given to live stock, and not enough to tillage.[2] The justice of this criticism is shown by a table prepared for the Devon Commission from which it appears that of the sums distributed by thirty-two farming societies $^1/_4$ was devoted to cattle as against $^1/_8$ to ploughing, and $^1/_{11}$ to turnips and green crops as against $^1/_{63}$ to farming implements.[3] It was also said that the societies did not help the class that needed them most, namely the small tenants, on account of the lack of any system of personal supervision.[4] Of course there were notable exceptions—for example the Ballinasloe society which did immense good to the district,—but generally speaking the results achieved were disappointing.[5] O'Connell expressed the suspicion that the agricultural societies were designed "to enable the landlords to combine together for the exclusion of Catholic tenants."[6]

Of course the real drawback of the premium system was that it began at the wrong end. It was useless to offer prizes for improved products to a tenantry who were ignorant of how the improvements should be effected. What was really needed was not so much encouragement as instruction. This was clearly perceived by the Devon Commission: "Without wishing to underrate the usefulness of such societies, we must consider as even more important the adoption of such plans as shall best give to the small farmer practical instruction in the best method of cultivation."[7] Ireland was not totally lacking in facilities for agricultural instruction, but they were inadequate. Schools had been opened in connection with the National Board of Education in several counties, but the total amount of land held by

[1] *Thoughts on the Expediency and Means of Improving the Agriculture of Ireland*, Cork 1810.
[2] Lord Clements *The Present Poverty of Ireland*, London 1838.
[3] *Devon Commn.* p. 19.
[4] *Devon Commn.* p. 17. *A Visit to the Glenesk Estate* by a Proprietor, Cork 1844
[5] *Devon Commn.* p. 21.
[6] Fitzpatrick. *Correspondence of Daniel O'Connell* vol. ii. p. 293.
[7] *Devon Commn.* p. 1140.

them was less than 200 acres, and the total number of instructors employed was only 21.[1] The Devon Commissioners were strongly impressed by the necessity of increased agricultural education, but were content to allow it to be provided by individual enterprise.[2]

[1] *Ibid* p. 35. [2] *Ibid*, p 1140

CHAPTER III.

Subdivision and Consolidation.

THE foregoing chapters have been directed to illustrate the fact that while Ireland was a country of great natural fertility its agricultural population was in a state of extreme misery, and its agriculture so defective that the soil was made to produce but a fraction of its full capacity. The existence of the great majority of the people on the very border line of starvation pointed to a disproportion between the population and the resources of the country. The full resources of the country were not exploited, for, as we have seen, the land did not produce its *maximum* product. Ireland thus presented the spectacle of a rich country failing to support its population in comfort. Such an unnatural condition of affairs calls for some explanation. Before entering upon this inquiry however we must first draw attention to the great revolution which took place in the agricultural economy of Ireland in the first fifty years of the nineteenth century. The account of this revolution practically resolves itself into a description of the remarkable swing of the pendulum from large to small and from small to large farms that took place between the Union and the Famine. During the first fifteen years of the century there was a strong tendency operating towards the creation of small holdings; that tendency to some extent ceased, but did not altogether disappear, at the termination of the great war; and from that time forward it was gradually replaced by a tendency in the opposite direction.

In treating of the first swing of the pendulum—that in the direction of small farms—we must carefully distinguish between two categories of subdivision. In the first place we note the tendency in the early part of the century for landlords to demise small holdings, and for tenants to sublet their holdings to more than one subtenant, and in the second place we note the more permanent tendency of the tenants to subdivide their holdings amongst their children and dependents. The former of these tendencies, which is properly known by the name of subletting, grew less and less marked as the century advanced; whereas the latter, properly known as subdivision, remained constant.

The movement towards subletting was the result of several causes, of which the first in point of time was the legislation of the Irish Parliament, culminating in Foster's celebrated corn, law of 1784, which, by raising the price of Irish-grown corn, had the effect of replacing pasture farming to a large extent by tillage, and consequently of decreasing the size of the holding which it was considered profitable to work. The tendency was still further emphasized after 1806, when the last remaining restraints on the importation of Irish corn into Great Britain were removed.[1] The extension of tillage did not however necessitate any diminution in the pastoral products of the country, as the two types of farming are, as is well known, not mutually exclusive but mutually helpful.[2] "Since the year 1784" we read in 1811 "with a home demand one fourth greater than that antecedent to that period, the surplus corn exported after a deduction made for the corn imported is actually twenty times greater than it then was; and there is at present a greater number of acres appropriated to grass than there then were."[3] "From being almost exclusively devoted to

[1] *Edinburgh Review* June 1825 p. 36. [2] *Thoughts on the Expediency and Means of Improving the Agriculture of Ireland* Cork 1806.

[3] Barnes. *A Statistical Account of Ireland Founded upon Historical Facts* Dublin 1811.

pasture" stated Mr. Nimmo "and reduced to the necessity of importing corn to the extent of half a million, Ireland now with a vastly increased population yearly exports to the amount of four millions of tillage produce, without any perceptible diminution of the returns from her grazing system."[1] The high prices of corn of all kinds caused by the great war had the effect of still further emphasizing this tendency. Anybody who was fortunate enough to have become possessed of a large tract of land for a long lease, found that he could derive a substantial income by subletting his holding in small sections to working tillage farmers. In other words, the high prices of agricultural produce which tended to replace pasture by tillage tended to increase the number of the middlemen who lived from rents derived from land, and also to decrease the size of the average farm, as, owing to the general want of capital, it was impossible to find tenants for large tillage farms.[2] In 1810 the movement was apparent to Wakefield who, after complaining of the former extent of large pasture farms, and observing the tendency to divide them up into small tillage farms which was then appearing, remarks that "there is great room for an extension of this system throughout the grazing lands of Ireland, the only fear is the rushing to an opposite extreme, and that instead of the estate being divided into respectable farms, it may be split into the minutest divisions."[3] "To say" wrote Lord Carbery a few years later "that there are now in the maritime districts of the north of Ireland three families for every one that existed there thirty years ago is, I am sure, far short of the fact; in many places double that number might be stated, without a hazard of exceeding the truth."[4] In the same year Mr. Curwen remarked that the movement towards small farms was in danger of being carried to an excessive degree. "The minute subdivision of lands among

[1] *Report and Estimates on Draining and Cultivating the Bogs.* Dublin 1818.

[2] Trevelyan. *Irish Crisis* p. 11. [3] Vol. i. p. 302.

[4] Letter in the *Munster Farmers' Magazine.* 18th Oct. 1818.

the occupants is attended with many serious evils. The rents of these small sub-let parcels become so high to the actual cultivators as to preclude all profitable return from their labour.... The aggregate number of houses is greater than would be required if the estate were distributed into moderately sized farms."[1] "The high prices of agricultural produce during the late continental war, and the consequently increased value of land, appear to have much increased subletting, by enabling the large farmers without personal trouble to derive from their leaseholds considerable incomes in the form of profit rents."[2] All during the Peninsular war large quantities of Irish corn were shipped to Spain and Portugal for the troops at more than the maximum price at which exportation was allowed; and advantage was taken of this opportunity by the corn factors to sell a large quantity to foreign merchants. Great complaints were heard in 1813, when this illegal practice was suddenly stopped by the government.[3]

To this agricultural motive towards subletting, there was added a political motive.[4] The statute of the Irish Parliament in 1793 which had enfranchised the Irish Catholics conferred the vote on freeholders whose interest amounted to the annual value of forty shillings. From the date of the passing of this act it became the interest of Irish landlords to increase as far as possible the number of forty shilling freeholders on their estates. "Parliamentary influence" said Townshend in his *Survey of Cork* "is very much looked to in all leases, consequently every proprietor has an army of freeholders."[5] "The Irish Government" said Mr. Bicheno "in order to attach the proprietors to them were in the habit of distributing divers bounties among them in the shape of places and preferments, civil

[1] *Observations* &c. vol. ii. p. 40. [2] *Devon Comm.* pp. 417-8.
[3] *Official Papers Public Record Office Dublin* 1790 1831. Carton 456 no. 1637.
[4] This classification of agricultural and political motives for subdivision is borrowed from Dr. Sigerson's invaluable book on *Irish Land Tenures* pp. 171-3.
[5] p. 468.

and ecclesiastical. It has been said that everything in Ireland resolves itself into a 'job'. Now in order to tempt by any job it is necessary to possess political influence, and the forty shilling proprietors were created to obtain it."[1] "Till within a comparatively recent period, proprietors do not seem to have taken any active measures to prevent the practice of subletting. It even seems that while forty shilling freeholds conferred the franchise, they, in some cases, rather encouraged subletting for the purpose of increasing their political influence .... The motives towards subletting which we have mentioned ceased to operate in the early years of the nineteenth century. The attention of the proprietors has been latterly more called to the ruinous consequences of this practice; and their exertions, aided by the Subletting Act, have considerably diminished the frequency of its occurrence."[2] The reasons which induced the landowners to change their attitude towards subletting will appear more fully in subsequent sections; all we are called upon to do here is to record that the temptations towards subletting had practically ceased to be effective by the year 1830.

The motives operating to produce subdivision, properly so called, were more enduring and permanent than those which operated to cause subletting. Owing to the lack of industrial development of the country, and to the fact that the landlords neglected to improve and put into cultivation the waste lands on their estates, the only occupation open to the children of the tenants of land was to till part of their parents' farm. This extreme dependence on the land for subsistence led directly to the growth of the custom of a parent's apportioning his land amongst his children, in such a manner that the original family holding grew more and more subdivided in each generation. "Every patch produces a new family;" we read in 1822 "every member of a family a new patch; and so on. Hence a country covered with

[1] *Ireland and Its Economy* p. 140. [2] *Devon Comm* pp. 417-8.

beggars—a complete pauper warren."[1] The evils of the excessive subdivision thus brought about were quite clear to the tenants themselves, who were nevertheless forced to adopt this disadvantageous course through sheer necessity. "Tenants are themselves aware of the evils arising from subdividing very small farms; for they have often told me that if those which they occupy and are splitting up were their own property, they would not subdivide them, as they are already too small to support a family with any degree of comfort and pay a rent."[2] The landlords were quite unable to prevent this kind of subdivision, as the tenants resorted to all sorts of devices to elude their vigilance. "It requires the most careful watch to prevent a subdivision of the farms, and the modes of evading the landlord's refusal to permit it are various; a man will come to beg for leave to divide a farm, already too small for one tenant to live comfortably upon it; his son wishes to be married, and must have a garden, grass for a cow, and a spot for his potatoes; the landlord or his agent refuses, and apparent submission follows; but a room is added to the parental cabin, no second house indeed appears upon the farm, yet the son marries, and occupies that newly made apartment, the landlord's mandate is evaded, two families live upon the farm, in the same house, it is true, but the farm is to all intents and purposes divided between them."[3] "Though" we read in the digest of the Evidence given before the Devon Commission "the practice of subletting is now much less prevalent than it formerly was, it appears that the practice of subdividing farms as a provision for the children of tenants still continues to a very great extent, notwithstanding the most active exertions of proprietors and agents. This evil is one difficult or almost impossible to prevent. The parent possessed of a farm looks upon it as a means of providing for his family after

[1] *The State of the Nation.* London 1822. [2] Nicholson, *Report of the Present State of Agriculture in the District Adjoining the Middle Shannon.* Dublin 1841.
[3] W. R. Anketel. *The Effects of Absenteeism* London 1843.

his decease, and consequently rarely induces them to adopt any other than agricultural pursuits, or makes any other provision for them than the miserable segment of a farm, which he can carve for each out of his holding, itself perhaps below the smallest size which can give profitable occupation to a family. Each son, as he is married, is installed in his portion of the ground, and in some cases even the sons-in-law receive as the dowries of their brides some share of the farm. In vain does the landlord or his agent threaten the tenant; in vain is the erection of new houses prohibited or the supply of turf limited. The tenant relies on the sympathy of his class to prevent ejectment, and on his own ingenuity to defeat the other impediments to his favourite mode of providing for his family."[1]

Many extraordinary instances were cited before the Devon Commission of the extent to which subdivision of this kind had been carried. One witness quoted the case of a holding of 387 Irish acres, of which only 167 were arable, which had passed into the hands of 110 separate tenants.[2] The extent to which this subdivision was carried was not more striking than the manner in which it was effected. The general method of subdividing land between the members of a family was not to apportion the holding into equal shares but to assign strips of the different parts of the land of different quality to the members of the family. These strips were in many cases very small, and were closely intermingled, so that there was created a fruitful source of quarrelling and internecine strife. This method of holding land was distinguished by the name of rundale. "There is a tenure named rundale" we read in 1825 "in which a field is farmed by many persons in common, who are all equally concerned in labouring it. The disadvantages of this mode of tenure do not require to be elaborately set forth. It is a little republic without laws, and therefore cannot prosper. Yet the poorest of the peasantry are

[1] *Devon Comm.* p. 418. [2] *Devon Comm.* p. 419.

favourable to it, because they are thus enabled to cultivate what must otherwise be waste. One lends a plough, another a harrow, and another a horse, which separately would have been useless. Those landlords who wish to discontinue this habit have always experienced difficulty in effecting their purpose, for moneyless cultivators have no other resource than partnership."[1] "The difficulty of getting possession of land" wrote Bicheno "and the poverty of the tenants has upheld to a very great extent the system of partnership farms, frequently consisting of 15 or 20 partners. They are bound jointly and severally to pay the rent, and fulfil the covenants. Each tenant brings in his proportion of stock and labour, erects his own cabin, and shares in the profit and loss according to the terms of the arrangement, which is often extremely difficult to be understood. This system prevailed also in the Highlands, the tenants residing together in what was called a town. The land was held as there expressed 'in runrig', or like common field land in England, only in smaller patches, with the right of intercommoning upon the mountain pastures. A collection of cabins built upon land thus occupied is called 'a village' in Ireland."[2] "The peculiar system" according to the Digest of the Devon Commission" adopted in most parts of Ireland in subdividing land, adds much to the evils necessarily accompanying the existence of holdings so minute as those which the practice of subdivision tends to create. Instead of each sub-tenant or assignee of a portion of the farm receiving his holding in one compact lot, he obtains a part in each particular quality of land, so that his tenement consists of a number of scattered patches, each too small to be separately fenced, and exposed to the constant depredations of his neighbours' cattle, thus affording a fruitful

[1] *A Letter on the State of Ireland* by an Irish Magistrate. London 1825.

[2] *Ireland and Its Economy* pp. 97-8. The same writer in his *Remarks on the Evidence before the Poor Inquiry Commission*, written a few years later, reports that "rundale has almost disappeared from the province of Ulster. It appears that it is rarely met with in Munster.... occasionally in Leinster.... It is most frequent in Connaught" *App. H. part* ii. p. 29.

source of quarrels, and utterly preventing the possibility of the introduction of any improved system of husbandry . . . Lord George Hill records, among other facts relating to rundale, that one person held his farm in forty-two different patches, and at last gave it up in despair of finding it; and that a field of half an acre was held by twenty-two different persons."[1]

The evil effects of rundale on agriculture were universally admitted. Wakefield said that "partnership leases are only compacts for waste and encouraging idleness."[2] "The evidence proves clearly" says the Digest "that these malpractices have produced the results which might naturally be expected, and that subtenants, the tenants of lands much divided, and of lands held in rundale are in general excessively poor, and their lands much exhausted."[3] "The rundale system" wrote Mr. G. L. Smyth some years later "is a lingering remnant of the old cases in which bodies of men took large tracts or divisions of land to cultivate amongst them. This rude custom, and worst form of tenantry, still prevails in Donegal and the wilder regions of the north, where each tenant considers himself entitled to a portion of each various quality of land in his division. The man who has a bit of good land at one extremity is sure to have a bad bit at the other, and bits of other quality in odd corners, each bounded by his neighbours' farms, without any ditch or fence between them; trespasses and fights, and the total impossibility of any improvement are the natural consequences."[4] "There were various refinements I may say" wrote Sharman Crawford "in the cruelty of the rack-renting system. One in particular was the practice of letting in common or copartnership. Never was there a plan so complete for the prevention of prosperity or improvements."[5] "In Mayo and other western counties" according to Trevelyan "the old barbarous Irish tenure called rundale still

[1] *Devon Comm.* p. 419. [2] Vol. i. p. 584. [3] *Devon Comm.* pp. 419-20.
[4] *Ireland Historical and Statistical* vol. ii. p. 433.
[5] *Depopulation not Necessary* London 1849 p. 14.

prevails, which stops short of the institution of private property, and by making the industrious and thriving responsible for the idle and improvident, effectually destroys the spring of all improvement."[1]

We have seen that the movement in the direction of small farms was of two kinds, that of subletting and that of subdivision. The opposite movement in the direction of large farms was also of two kinds. There was on the one hand the attempt at correcting the abuses and inconveniences of the rundale system by rearranging the parcels of land held by each partner, in such a way as to ensure that he would have a single holding instead of a number of scattered patches, and there was on the other hand the attempt to substitute large for small farms.

The former kind of consolidation was altogether commendable, as it did not entail the dispossession of any families, but aimed simply at redistributing the land among the existing holders in a more economical way. "That class of consolidation which consists in giving to each tenant a compact equivalent for lands held in rundale or scattered lots appears to be absolutely necessary, before taking any other steps to improve an estate so circumstanced, or the condition of its occupiers. This however is a most difficult operation, in which the prejudices, the suspicions, the fears of losing by a change, or the desire of obtaining some undue advantage, unite the greater portion of the peasantry in resisting almost any measure of the kind, when proposed to them, although they acutely feel the evils inflicted upon them by the rundale system."[2] Some very interesting examples of successful consolidations of this kind are given in the evidence before the Devon Commission.[3]

The second kind of consolidation was of far more doubtful benefit. We shall not however attempt to criticize it in

[1] *The Irish Crisis* p. 13. [2] *Devon Comm.* p. 453.
[3] *Devon Comm.* pp. 454-5 and see Blacker's *Essay on the Management of Landed Property in Ireland* Dublin 1843.

this chapter, but shall simply give a short account of its actual course. As we have seen, the process of subletting was greatly encouraged by the high prices which prevailed during the war. In 1815 agricultural prosperity had attained to a very high degree. "Every man in Ireland who had for twenty years past any quantity of land for anything like the value is not only comfortable but rich, and this is owing principally to the war, which by causing unusual demand for supplies for the armies and navies had raised the price of all the necessaries of life to a most exorbitant pitch."[1] In that year however the war ended, and a period of severe agricultural decline set in. Within a few months after the declaration of peace, cries of distress were heard from the farmers.[2] The universal fall in the price of corn had the immediate effect of throwing many large tracts of land out of tillage, and the refusal of the landlords to make any corresponding reduction in their rents plunged numerous farmers into insolvency, and drove them to relinquish their holdings. Thus began the process of consolidation, which was destined to be the dominant feature of the agricultural economy of Ireland for the next thirty years. In the very year of the declaration of peace we read complaints of land being thrown into pasture;[3] and the following year it was stated that "since the restoration of peace we have seen a rage for throwing all our arable land under pasture, which has greatly added to the agricultural distress."[4] The movement towards pasture was aided by the introduction of steam navigation, which rendered easier the conveyance of live stock by sea.[5] The replacement of tillage land by pasture was remarked on by a parliamentary committee in 1823: "Since the depression of prices of agricultural produce, the necessity of consolidating many

[1] *An Address to the People of Ireland* by a Compatriot. Dublin 1815.
[2] *View of the Agricultural State of Ireland.* Cork 1815.
[3] Major. *Observations Demonstrative of the Necessity to Ireland's Welfare &c.* Dublin 1815.
[4] Parker, *A Plea for the General Improvement of the State of the Poor in Ireland.* Cork 1816 and see *View of the Agricultural State of Ireland* Cork 1816.
[5] Lord Clements. *The Present Poverty of Ireland* London 1838.

small into one great farm seems to be generally admitted and acted on; and much of arable land has been laid down for the purpose of rearing and fattening cattle as well as for dairy."[1] By 1830 the land of Ireland was about equally divided between pasture and tillage;[2] and a few years later Lord Clements remarked that tillage was practised only by the poorest class of farmer.[3]

The operation of transforming small farms into large was greatly facilitated by a statute passed in 1816 to which we shall refer in more detail in another place. This statute aimed at making eviction a cheap and rapid process. "It was hoped by some, graziers and the like", Dr. Sigerson says "that they might sweep clear their pasture grounds of that industrious and improving population they had planted when it had suited them, now that they wanted them no longer, and that cattle might perchance be more profitable. From this time recommenced the specious theorizing concerning the advantage of large farms, the superfluity of population, the inaptitude of the soil to produce cereals or textile crops . . . These excuses for eviction were simply ornate repetitions of those heard during the previous eviction period from 1768 to 1793."[4] Consolidation, accompanied by clearances, advanced very rapidly during the twenties. "On many large estates" we read in 1822" there has not been any reduction; the consequences have been such as might be expected; the pounds of the country were filled with the cattle of the tenantry, with little profit to the landlord; the poor peasantry were harassed by drivers, whose fees on the seizure and sale were a large addition to the debt. Their time was wasted in bringing fodder to their cattle in the pound to preserve their existence, and many beasts perished there by want and cold. Oh! what scenes

[1] *Select Committee on Employment of the Poor in Ireland* 1823.
[2] Morris. *A Demonstration that Great Britain and Ireland have Resources* &c. London 1830.
[3] *The Present Poverty of Ireland* London 1838 Attention must be directed to a source of confusion in discussing this subject. In Ireland the term "arable" meant useful or cultivable land, and in England land in tillage only. Wiggins. *The Monster Misery of Ireland* London 1844. [4] *Irish Land Tenures* p. 171.

of misery were witnessed in Ireland in this way during the years 1818-20; by that time the people were left without cattle; after this their potatoes and corn were seized and sold, and in some cases their household furniture, even to their blankets."[1] Having reduced the tenants to this state of poverty, the landlords then evicted them for non-payment of rent.[2] Numerous families were thus dispossessed and turned out on the roads. Lest they might return to the land their houses were razed. Lord Stradbrook deprived fifty families of their homes in this way.[3] The practice of consolidation grew yearly.[4] "This operation has now a particular term to express it," wrote Sadleir in 1829 "and is called 'clearing'—a very emphatic phrase in connection with the consequences. Hume somewhere says 'the comparison between the management of human beings and cattle is shocking', but what terms can convey the natural disgust one feels when the comparison is between human beings and vermin. The rage however is for 'clearing' estates in Ireland from their human vermin."[5] The injury inflicted by the clearances was aggravated by the conacre system; the conacre holder's potato crop was simply preparatory to a corn crop by the farmer, and the result of the latter's abandonment of tillage was that no more land was offered in conacre.[6]

The desire of the landlords to clear their estates was counteracted to some extent before 1829 by their eagerness to possess the political influence which could only be obtained by the presence of a large number of forty shilling freeholders on their lands. The rebellion of the tenants against slavishly voting as their landlords directed decreased the weight of this consideration, and the disfranchisement of the forty shilling freeholders removed

[1] *Lachrymae Hiberniae.* Dublin 1822.
[2] Lewis. *Irish Disturbances* p. 67; see O'Driscoll. *Views of Ireland* vol. i. p. 63.
[3] *Select Committee on State of Ireland* 1824 p. 21.
[4] Fry and Gurney *Report.* London 1827.
[5] *Ireland and its Evils* p. 104.
[6] *Thoughts on the Poor of Ireland* by a Barrister, Dublin 1831.

the last barrier which restrained the landlords from wholesale ejectment. "The disfranchisement of the forty shilling freeholders has confirmed the landlords in their previously existing notions of the benefit to be derived from it."[1] "It is a mistake" we read in the report of the Select Committee on the State of the Poor in Ireland 1830 "to assume that the clearances of estates have originated with the Subletting Act or with the statute that raised the franchise. On the contrary they existed ten years before these measures were adopted ; but it is undoubtedly true that both statutes have given motives or afforded facilities for pursuing a course previously adopted on the grounds of private interest."[2] "The act of 1829" according to the Devon Commission "destroyed the political value of the forty shilling freeholder, and to relieve his property from the burden which circumstances had brought upon it the landlord in too many cases adopted what has been called the clearance system."[3] After 1830 the process of eviction progressed very rapidly, and was prevented from depopulating the whole country only by the widespread fear of the Whiteboys. "But for the salutary dread of the Whiteboy Association" wrote Poulett Scrope in 1834 "ejectment would desolate Ireland and decimate her population, casting forth thousands of families like noxious weeds rooted out of the soil, on which they have hitherto grown, perhaps too luxuriantly, and fling them away to perish in the roadside ditches. Yes, the Whiteboy system is the only check on the ejectment system ; and weighing one against the other, horror against horror, and crime against crime, it is perhaps the lesser evil of the two."[4] Drummond in his famous letter to the Tipperary Magistrates remarked the great eagerness of the landlords to clear their estates :—"If from political changes or the improvements in modern husbandry, these objects are not any longer to be obtained by a continuance of such a state

[1] Bicheno, *Ireland and Its Economy* p. 142.
[2] p. 8 and see Fagan *Life and Times of Daniel O'Connell* vol. i. p. 540.
[3] p. 1110. [4] Poulett Scrope *Letter to Lord Melbourne* 1834

of things, His Excellency conceives that it may become matter of serious question whether the proprietors of the soil are not attempting in many instances too rapidly to retrace their steps, when he finds the fact to be that the number of ejectments in Tipperary in 1837 is not less than double the number in 1833. The deficiency of a demand for labour, and the want as yet of any legal provision against utter destitution, leave this humble class when ejected without any protection against absolute starvation."[1]

The fate of the evicted tenants was terrible in the extreme. Great numbers flocked to the country towns, on the outskirts of which they congregated in the most miserable cabins imaginable; others migrated to Dublin in the fruitless search for employment.[2] "Numbers" said Bicheno "resort to the cities towns and villages. Some settle on waste lands, mountains or bog in their neighbourhood, sometimes with their own means, and sometimes with the assistance of the landlord. This seems to be the case chiefly in Connaught. Some emigrate with the aid of the proprietors, but more by their own resources; and some become dealers, little shopkeepers, or the keepers of shebeen houses. But after all there is a great residue of homeless wanderers!"[3]

The effect of the poor law as an incentive to eviction will be discussed on a later page; it is sufficient to say here that it was intended by its authors to aid the process, and that in fact the number of evictions increased greatly after its enactment. The evidence before the Devon Commission demonstrated that ejectments were still being pursued with as much energy as ever, and that, even if the consolidation of farms were justified, the methods by which it was being obtained were oppressive. "The error appears to have been not in the principle of seeking to bring back the condition of the property to a state which

[1] Barry O'Brien, *Life of Drummond.* p. 283.

[2] *Third Report of Select Committee on Emigration* 1826. White *Report and Observations on the State of the Poor of Dublin.* Dublin 1833.

[3] *Poor Inquiry Commission* app. H. part 2. p. 21.

would enable the land to support in comfort the population living upon it, but rather in doing this without sufficient reference to the future fate of the people removed. Admitting that the previous situation of the latter was very wretched, still they had something to depend upon; but their ejectment, even when a few pounds may have been given to them, caused absolute destitution. The money must soon become exhausted, and they would find themselves in an overstocked labour market, without the power of obtaining employment. Every reform of a property should distinctly regard the interests of the parties removed, and should provide a fair opportunity by which they might be enabled, with industry, to establish and maintain themselves for the future. This latter consideration has rarely been sufficiently attended to."[1] "The natural and necessary consequences of the system of clearance" according to the Repeal Association "have been that large numbers of the ejected peasantry have been driven into miserable dwellings along the dykes, and in the ditches adjacent to the public roads; or to the filthy lanes of small neighbouring towns; so that multitudes have perished, and are daily perishing, from sheer want of the common necessaries of life; the clearance system being the natural and necessary propagator of disease and death."[2]

The great famine was made the occasion of still further clearing the land of its inhabitants. "The perishing of the potato was at once laid hold of as an auxiliary argument for the consolidation of farms"[3]. At the very height of the famine, many landlords were most energetic in evicting their starving tenants. "In every direction" reported an English traveller "the agents of the landlords, armed with the full powers of the law, are at work; everywhere one sees the driver or bailiff canting the small patches of oats or potatoes, or keepers placed over the crop. Even the pro-

[1] *Devon Comm.* p. 831. [2] *Repeal Report* vol. ii. p. 297.
[3] Mackey. *Depopulation Illegal and a Crime.* Dublin 1850.

duce of seed distributed through the agency of the benevolent associations has been totally swept away. To add to the universal distress caused by this system of seizure, eviction is in many places practised, and not a few of the roofless dwellings which meet the eye have been destroyed at the instance of the landlords."[1] The clearance of the land was greatly facilitated by the ingenious clause of the poor law act of 1847 which precluded from relief all who occupied more than a quarter of an acre. "The fact" said Poulett Scrope "notoriously is that the present policy being still to leave to the landlord the task of carrying the country through the perils of this crisis, or of being ruined by the poor rate, the first and readiest and simplest mode of saving themselves from the threatened penalty that suggests itself to their minds is to get rid of the poor altogether by clearance. Why risk capital, even if they could borrow it, for the purpose of employing the poor on their estates, when by ejectment and pulling down of houses they can get rid of them for good? Therefore clearance and eviction are the order of the day. There were difficulties in former times to get the people to go. They clung to their little farms and their houses with a desperate tenacity, which made it dangerous to attempt to remove them. But the famine has made a wonderful difference in this respect. They are starving. They cannot even get admittance to the workhouse till they have given up their land—so says the Gregory clause of the poor law—in many cases it seems not until the driver of their landlord certifies that they have given up possession of their house also."[2]

The landlords appear to have been ruthless in the exercise of their power to evict. "In each day's drive" said Poulett Scrope, writing of county Clare, two years after the famine "I passed the sites of many habitations unroofed or levelled with the ground. In some of these ruins, a

[1] Tuke, *A Visit to Connaught* London 1847. [2] *The Irish Relief Measures.* London 1848.

faint smoke, rising from one corner, showed where a family formerly dwelling there still crouched under a few sticks and sods propped against the broken wall."[1] In the three years 1847-8-9, no less than 35,416 ejectment decrees were granted, but this figure gives no idea of the number of evictions that actually took place, as it does not include the numerous cases where the tenants were forced to quit their holdings through sheer inability to pay the rent, or when suits were begun and not brought to judgment.[2]

It must not be forgotten that the year that witnessed the famine was also marked by the repeal of the corn laws, a measure calculated to strengthen the existing tendency to convert tillage land into pasture. The abolition of the corn laws tempted the landlords to turn their attention from agriculture to grazing pursuits and to make extensive pastures on their estates, and the tenants on them possessing small tracts of land were ejected wholesale.[3]

The following table shows how far the process of consolidation advanced in the ten years 1841-51 :-

Size of Holdings*	Number of Holdings	
	1841	1851
Not exceeding 1 acre	134,314	37,728
Exceeding 1 but not exceeding 5 acs. ..	310,436	88,083
„ 5 „ „ „ 15 „ ..	252,799	191,854
„ 15 „ „ „ 30 „ ..	79,342	141,311
„ 30 ..	48,625	149,090

* *Census of Ireland* 1851 p. xxiii.

The extent to which the cottier had been cleared is also shown by the decrease in the number of "fourth class" houses in the same period, which amounted to 355,689 or about 70 per cent.[4] During the same period the population per square mile decreased from 217 to 164.[5]

[1] *Notes of a Tour in England, Scotland and Ireland.* London 1849.
[2] Marmion *Maritime Ports* p. 58.
[3] *Ibidem* p. 50.
[4] *Census of Ireland* 1851 *General Report* xxiii.
[5] Ibid. p. xii.

CHAPTER IV.

THE ASSUMPTIONS OF CONSOLIDATION.

Section I. The Advantages of Large Farms over Small.

THE dominant feature of Irish agriculture in the early nineteenth century was the consolidation of holdings, and the consequent evictions. We may say that this constituted the landlords' remedy for the distress of the agricultural population of Ireland. The problem, as we have already stated, which had to be solved was an apparent disproportion between the population and resources of the country; and the landlords' method of adjusting this disproportion was by decreasing the former rather than by increasing the latter. The wisdom of the consolidation campaign can be rightly estimated only by examining the justice of the two assumptions on which it rested. These were, first that large farms were preferable to small, and second that Ireland was overpeopled in relation to its resources. Let us examine these assumptions in turn.

With regard to the former assumption, namely that large farms were preferable to small, we find it was not admitted by the best opinion. The question was frequently examined by agricultural and economic experts, and the almost unanimous conclusion reached was that *ceteris paribus* the small farm system of cultivation was preferable to the large. Of course there is no doubt that many farms in Ireland had been subdivided to a point where the separate parcels were no longer capable of maintaining the cultivator and his family, and it is obvious that such "uneconomic holdings"—as they came to be called at a later date—were undesirable. Incidentally we may remark that it appears somewhat unreasonable to attempt to solve the problem of the uneconomic holding by depriving the possessor altogether of his land, and that it would appear more rational to increase the holding rather than to diminish it to vanishing point. This however raises the question of whether there was enough land to go round, to which we shall return later. We have referred to the uneconomic holding here simply in order to make it clear that, in contrasting the merits of large and small farms, we assume that the latter are at least of sufficient extent to support the cultivator and his family.

Trimmer, in his valuable book on Irish agriculture, indicated the many disabilities under which the small farmer laboured, but pointed out that there was not one which could not be surmounted by the practice of cooperation. In this respect Trimmer was almost a century ahead of his time, and his writings display a knowledge of the fundamental principles of that great movement which has done so much in recent years to advance the agricultural prosperity of Ireland.[1] A few years later Dr. Whitley Stokes expressed his approval of small farms. "The great step to relieve the peasantry, to secure the landed interest, to multiply all the products of the earth, and to restore general activity in every department of society, is to convince both landlords and tenants that smaller farms would answer better for all parties, under the circumstances of Ireland. I know the general opinion of the agricultural writers of England is favourable to large farms. Some intelligent men begin to see that even in England many leading errors have taken place. . . .; large farms may be the best for England yet small the most convenient for Ireland. Very important differences must be admitted to exist in the fertility

[1] Trimmer. *A Brief Inquiry into the Present State of Agriculture in the Southern Parts of Ireland.* London 1809. *Further Observations &c.* London 1812.

of the soil, the capital of the cultivators, and the state of the market. Two arguments seem to me to go far towards proving the advantages of smaller farms in Ireland; first it is generally allowed that the value of farming stock per acre requisite for profitable occupation increases with the number of acres. In a poor country where labour is cheap and capital scanty, small farms are more likely to bring the whole surface into good profit; nor does it much concern the farmer, if his return is sufficient, whether a certain sum is expended in rent or in labour. I also appeal to those who know the tenantry of Ireland whether in fact they are not oftener distressed by too much than too little land. These observations are branches of the first, that farming stock should increase in a greater proportion than the number of acres; or, to speak somewhat more accurately, than the annual rent of the farm. The second argument on which I confidently rely in favour of the subdivision of land is this, that the cottier can always afford more than double the farmer's price for a few acres of land. . . . The small farmer has many advantages—his flocks and herds lose less by accident, in proportion to their number; he has less labour in laying out manure, and drawing home produce; suffers less loss of time and labour in going to and returning from work; suffers less pillage, less waste, and receives more assistance from his family; has more friendly zeal with him; less eye service; he has the retailer's and consumer's advantages on a greater proportion of his produce".[1]

Mr. Michael Thomas Sadleir also took the view that small farms were more economical than large, and held that the process of consolidation had been detrimental, not only to the public, but to the landlords as well. "The plan of accumulating farms has not answered. The inducements held out to the proprietors have been falsified; and in these

[1] Whitley Stokes, *Observations on the Population and Resources of Ireland.* Dublin 1821 and see *The Causes of the Discontents of Ireland.* Dublin 1823..

trying times they will appear more fallacious every day. With the exception perhaps of the better preservation of game, in all other respects they have been prejudicial to the owners. Smaller rents are invariably paid for the larger farms, and those rents, in bad times, are paid with far less punctuality and certainty. . . ." Mr. Sadleir then proceeds by quoting examples from other countries to demonstrate that small scale cultivation was generally speaking more productive than large. His book is a noteworthy indictment of the process of consolidation.[1]

The classical treatise in favour of small farms is that of Mr. Wm. Blacker, published in 1834. This gentleman was no mere theorist; on the contrary, he put his theories into practice with the most striking success, not alone on the estate of Lord Gosford in County Armagh, which he managed as agent, but also in several other parts of Ireland. Mr. Blacker's essay on the subject is of such importance that we feel justified in quoting from it at length. The essay first draws attention to the fact that the reason why the Irish farmer did not derive the proper amount of benefit from his holding was the defective method of agriculture which he practised. "The general defect in the management of small farms in Ireland is the constant succession of grass crops, which are continued until the land is unfit to produce anything, when it is let out to *rest* as it is termed, in which unprofitable state, nearly one third, or in many cases one half, of the small farms are allowed continually to remain; this arises from the want of *manure* to restore such portions to cultivation, and the want of green crops to support sufficient cattle to produce it. The business of the agriculturist is first to point out where drainage is required, how the land is to be cleaned, and to point out how manure may be acquired, and how green crops may be raised, and house feeding the cattle may be establis-

[1] *Ireland Its Evils* &c. pp. 119-50.

hed."[1] Mr. Blacker then proceeds to point out the manifold advantages that would result from a proper manuring of the land, and the cultivation of green crops. He had already insisted on this in a pamphlet which he had printed and distributed, first to the tenants on the estate which he managed, and afterwards to the tenants in other parts of Ireland.[2] He found however that, however willing the cultivators were to apply the system which he advocated, they were unable to do so owing to their inability through want of capital to procure the requisite manure. The first thing therefore was to suggest a method by which the manure could be obtained. The solution suggested by Mr. Blacker was that which he had himself successfully put into practice, namely, the advance by the landlord of a loan for that purpose, and the superintendence by a skilled agent of the application of the money so advanced. "All difficulties on the subject of manure are at an end if it is a country where lime can be procured, and this is generally to be met with in almost every part of Ireland. With the assistance of it mixed with soil, a most abundant crop of the cup potato of excellent quality may be raised, by putting on about twenty-five barrels to the English acre, and if the tenant is so far impoverished as to be unable to buy this, it is the province of an intelligent landlord to advance the amount either as a gratuity or a loan, or by giving security to the lime burner until the return of the crops may enable the farmer to pay him".

Mr. Blacker made various other proposals for the more economical management of land in Ireland, all of which assume that the landlord or his agent must be expected to take an intelligent interest in his property. The following is his own summary of the suggestions which he made for the improvement of agriculture: "A statement of the existing errors in the present mode of cultivation pract-

[1] *Essay on the Management of Landed Property in Ireland.* Dublin 1834 p. 8.
[2] *An Essay on the Improvement to be made in the Cultivation of Small Farms.* Dublin 1834.

ised by the generality of small farmers, circulated amongst them to direct their attention to the subject; an active intelligent agriculturist to give the necessary instructions and practically teach a better; a landlord who will advance the necessary quantity of lime to render those instructions available, and an agent willing to take the trouble of seeing the experiment fairly tried. The first shows the necessity of a change, the second supplies the necessary skill to correct what is amiss. The third affords the capital wanted, and provides an additional inducement by the known gain arising from the crop which follows it; and the lime being used only on the certificate of the agriculturist, this gives him the power of insisting on the ground being properly drained and properly cleaned to which it is to be applied. And lastly the influence and personal attention of the agent keeps up the spirits and energy of the tenantry, and makes all things work together, and cooperate towards the successful issue of the undertaking".

Mr. Blacker then proceeds to state his opinion that, if his system of improved methods of agriculture were adopted by the tenants, and encouraged by the landlords, the small farms of Ireland would amply support the whole population of the country. Believing this, he set his face resolutely against consolidation. "The consolidation of farms I understand to mean the conversion of sundry small holdings into others of larger dimensions. In this I have had some experience, and my opinion is decidedly against it, in all cases where the object can only be accomplished by turning out the unfortunate occupants without making provision for their future support. In Ireland I apprehend we are too apt to be carried away by the ideas and practices of our English fellow-subjects, without considering the differences of circumstances between the two countries. In England, large farms, large fields, straight fences &c. have long been the favourite theme of English landlords and English writers, and no doubt, where there is capital and no very redundant population, such arrangements are very desirable; but it should be remembered that to these large farms and these large fields England owes the necessity of poor laws. But with increase of population the rates have increased until at length the demands of pauperism in England alone mount to about one sixth of the entire revenue of the empire; and the evil is becoming so great that people are beginning now to try back, and in many districts are returning in principle to the very identical state of things which formerly met with so much reprobation; I allude to cottage allotments of land, which, so far as they have been tried, have immediately been found to mitigate the evil. Does not this at once speak volumes on the subject?.... Land and land only can afford to the labouring population of a country constant materials to work upon, and to it recourse must eventually be had for the employment of those who have no other means of earning a livelihood. Urgent necessity is now beginning to force these truths upon the minds of most reflecting people in England, and even with the short experience now derivable from the partial change of the existing system to cottage allotments there made, will anyone be bold enough to say that if England was now like Ireland covered with an agricultural population, settled in small farms over the entire face of the country, that these poor and contented families should be ejected, to introduce the consolidation of their lands? Surely none would have the folly to think of such a thing, and, if so, why should we, with the bad effects of the system fully before us, be led to adopt the practice, which those who have tried it are obliged now to counteract?" Mr. Blacker reinforced the conclusion he had reached by pointing out that, as the result of experience, he had found that spade husbandry was far superior to horse husbandry on small farms.[1] In a later treatise Mr. Blacker repeated this opinion,

[1] *Essay on the Management of Landed Property in Ireland* pp. 10-26.

and drew attention to the remarkable paradox that, while the Irish landlords were endeavouring to increase, the English landlords were endeavouring to diminish, the size of the farms on their estates. "The small farms of Ireland which are so often instanced as the cause of our miseries, are coming back to in England by way of a cure."[1] The same view was taken by Mr. Poulett Scrope[2], and Lord Dufferin expressed the opinion that "the greatest gross produce is obtained from *la petite culture* as practised under short leases in East Flanders, though at a cost of labour in excess of what is required in England and Scotland to obtain almost equally large returns."[3]

That Mr. Blacker was not a mere theorist is proved by the following concrete examples of the improvement effected in the condition of tenants on the estate in Armagh which he managed, and to which he applied his methods in practice:- "James Mulholland of Carrickgollaghy, near Beleek, holds six English acres, upon which he has three cows, one calf and one pig. Formerly he was only able to keep one cow. Thomas Alexander, Corlust, near Clare, holds five English acres, which he lately purchased from a man who was only able to keep one cow; but by sowing green crops he is now able to keep two cows, one heifer, two calves, and two pigs. John Hogg of Drumgaw, near Armagh, keeps now in the house four cows, one calf and two pigs. He was formerly only able to keep one cow. Patrick Farrell, Garvagh, on the road from Markethill to Hamilton's Bawn, has now two cows upon five English acres and one pig. Formerly he had no cow at all. Widow Brannigan, near Hamilton's Bawn, holds two and a half English acres; keeps by means of housefeeding one cow and one pig, and has oats flax and potatoes for herself and daughter. She had no cow whatever formerly".

[1] *An Essay on the Best Means of Improving the Condition of the Labouring Classes of Ireland* London 1846. [2] See *The Irish Relief Measures* pp. 75-8.
[3] *Irish Emigration &c.* p. 339.
[4] *Essay on the Improvement to be made in the Cultivation of Small Farms.* p. vi.

Time and further experience failed to shake Mr. Blacker's conviction on this subject. "I shall notice" he remarked in a pamphlet written some years later "one assertion:- 'It is impossible that agriculture as a system can be carried on in Ireland until the farms are consolidated, and provided with buildings necessary to the successful management of land'. I positively deny the fact asserted, having proof to the contrary every day before my eyes. The small farmer of four to eight acres requires no buildings or granaries. He sells his crop when he threshes it out, perhaps in the open air or in a mud walled farm; and a simple cowshed is all that he wants besides; and nine times out of ten he realises as good a price for his grain in this way as by holding it over".[1]

The next most important treatise dealing with this question, after that of Mr. Blacker, was that of Mr. Sharman Crawford, published in 1849. The principal point which Mr. Sharman Crawford made was that the most prosperous part of Ireland was precisely that in which the farms were smallest. This is shown in the following table:

County	Average area of farms
	acres
Down	19½
Armagh	13¼
Galway	35¼
Mayo	29¼
Roscommon	22¼
Clare	30¼
Kerry	46
Cork	39

These figures are striking, in view of the fact that Down and Armagh were admitted on all sides to be amongst

[1] *Review of C. Shaw Lefevre's Letter* London 1837. The merits of small farms were advocated also in Revans *Evils of the State of Ireland.* London 1837; Lord Clements *The Present Poverty of Ireland*, London 1838; Lambert *Agricultural Suggestions*, Dublin 1845; Tuke, *A Visit to Connaught.* London 1847; Anketel, *The Effects of Absenteeism* London 1847; and Digwell, *Modern Agriculture as Peculiarly Applicable to Ireland* Dublin 1848.

the most prosperous counties in Ireland. Yet the average size of the farms in those counties was not greater but smaller than that in the admittedly distressed counties of the south and west. This fact must certainly give pause to those who are inclined to argue that the cause of the distress of the Irish farmers was the excessive subdivision of their holdings. Mr. Sharman Crawford strikes the true keynote of the situation when he points out that the reason for the superior prosperity of the north-eastern counties was the better system of husbandry pursued in them, and that the reason for that superior system of husbandry was the better system of land tenure that there prevailed. He quotes the evidence of Mr. Griffith before the Devon Commission in support of his conclusion. "I am inclined to hope" he continues "that any person who shall take the trouble of reviewing the facts I have stated will join me in the following conclusion, namely, that, whilst in the south and west of Ireland immense poverty and suffering occur in connection with dense population and minute subdivision of land; nevertheless a like denseness of population and subdivision of land occur in the parts of Ulster I have referred to, connected with a very high degree of peasant-prosperity and absence of pauperism. I trust the foregoing conclusion is incontrovertible from the facts I have stated; and, if it be established, another conclusion follows of the highest practical value. If those economists be correct who say that no amelioration of the Irish people can be produced except by a reduction of their number, and by the consolidation of their small holdings into an aggregate of large farms, then there is no remedy but the extermination, new location, or transportation of the people. The former is that which is now resorted to by the landed proprietors of the distressed districts, which progresses with a refinement of cruelty disgraceful to any civilised country, and which the ruling powers permit to go on with a seemingly placid assent, impressed as it would appear by the detestable doctrine of the Malthusian economists. My object then is, by the first conclusion I have established, to controvert this doctrine; to prove by facts that extermination is not necessary for the amelioration of the condition of the people; and that, instead of resorting to this heartless expedient, it is our duty to investigate by what means the prosperity of the north-east of Ulster has been created, and then to devise the means of conducting our western and southern Irish fellow creatures on the same track which has led to the prosperity of the north-eastern portion of our island."[1] On a later page in the same pamphlet Mr. Sharman Crawford shows that the consolidation of the small farms into large could not possibly succeed in giving employment to the persons displaced.

To these valuable expressions of opinion, we must add those of Sir Robert Kane,[2] and of John Stuart Mill. The latter great economist, after examining the system of land tenure in every European country, reached the conclusion that the most efficient agriculture was obtained in a system of small farms, worked by a peasant proprietary.[3]

Thus we see that the best agricultural and economic opinion of the time was of the view that Ireland could be developed more profitably by small than by large farms. If that opinion was correct, then the first of the two assumptions on which the process of consolidation was based falls to the ground. We postpone the consideration of the reason why the actual cultivation of the small farms was so unprofitable until a later page; we wish to emphasize however that, whatever were the causes for that uneconomical state of affairs, the smallness of the farms was not one of them. That being so, consolidation was no remedy for the economic evils of Ireland, but rather an aggravation of the disease. We now pass to the second

[1] *Depopulation not Necessary* and see *Repeal Reports* vol. i. p. 231 and *Second Report Railway Commissioners* 1838 p. 5. [2] *Industrial Resources* p. 298.

[3] Mill. *The Irish Land Question* pp. 51 and 100. *Political Economy*. I. IX. 4 and see Poulett Scrope *Extracts of Evidences on the Waste Lands Reclamation* London 1847.

assumption underlying consolidation, namely that the country was overpopulated.[1]

Section 2. The Overpopulation of Ireland.

Complaint that Ireland was overpopulated was repeatedly heard in the first half of the nineteenth century. "Touching Ireland" said Sadleir "the greatest unanimity prevails; Ireland must be depopulated to be enriched."[2] It must be remembered that this was the age of Malthus, and that all economic evils were assumed by the economists to flow from a superabundant population. The doctrines of Malthus were held to be peculiarly applicable to Ireland, as nowhere did there seem to be a greater disproportion between the population and the resources available for its support. The destiny of Ireland in the early nineteenth century was very largely moulded by the ideas of two great economists, Adam Smith and Malthus, and of the two the latter was probably the more influential.

The growth of population in Ireland in these years was certainly remarkable. The population, which was calculated at about 5,000,000 at the time of the Union, was estimated by Newenham in 1805 at 5,395,456,[3] and by the incomplete census of 1813 at 5,395,856. Obviously one of these calculations was wide of the mark. In 1821 it was said to have risen to 6,801,827, in 1831 to 7,767,401, and in 1841 to 8,175,124. The population probably attained its maximum in 1846, after which, as a result of the famine, it began to decrease, and it was estimated at 6,552,385 in the census of 1851.

We need not enter in detail into the causes which produced this extremely rapid increase in the population of Ireland, as they were mainly the same as those which

[1] It could not be denied that the landlords sometimes derived certain benefits from consolidating their estates. We have discussed the matter however from the point of view not of the landlords but of the public. In cases where a conflict occurs between national and private interests, the former must be made to prevail.

[2] *Ireland Its Evils* &c. p. 4. [3] *Essay on Population.*

prevailed in the eighteenth century, which we have treated elsewhere.[1] The existing motives operating to produce a rapid increase were however strengthened by some additional motives which first appeared about the time of the Union. These were mainly identical with those which, we have seen, operated in favour of the subdivision of farms. In the first place the high war prices decreased the area of the holding upon which a family could live. "We are inclined to think" said O'Driscoll "that the war had much to do with the evil of an excessive population in Ireland. The war acted in that country as a bounty upon population, not in the case of the peasantry only, but greatly also in the middle classes. The war acted in various ways; the army the navy and the civil department were a resource of every family, rich or poor; and the stimulus which agriculture received called for additional hands and gave occupation to all."[2] Moreover the new franchise, and the eagerness of the landlords to obtain "an army of freeholders" operated in the same direction. "Among the causes which have produced increased population in Ireland the minute division of land for the purpose of making freeholders ought to be dwelt upon"[3] These new causes must have become apparent quite early in the century, as we find the prediction made in 1803 that in twenty years Ireland would be the most densely populated country in Europe[4]. This prediction was verified; in spite of a most exceptional rate of infantile mortality, the population of Ireland increased by leaps and bounds.[5]

If we were to analyse the causes which produced this great increase of population we should find that they ultimately resolved themselves into the low standard of com-

[1] *Economic History of Ireland in the Eighteenth Century* pp. 10-14.
[2] *View of Ireland* vol. i. p. 193.
[3] Wakefield vol. ii. p. 690.
[4] *Essays on the Population of Ireland and the Character of the Irish* by a Member of the Late Irish Parliament. London 1803.
[5] *A Letter on the State of Ireland* by an Irish Magistrate. London 1825.

fort that prevailed. In a country where the diet had been reduced to the simplest compatible with the maintenance of life, there were to be found no prudential checks to a reckless multiplication of the race. The general standard of subsistence was so low that it could not be further reduced except by actual starvation. In such a state of affairs there was no motive which could operate to discourage early marriages and the propagation of an abundant offspring. "They say of marriage", said Dr. Doyle, the famous Bishop of Kildare, "as of other changes in life, that it cannot make them worse, but it may give them a helpmate in distress, or at least a companion in suffering."[1] In such a condition of affairs a strong child was looked on as a source of income rather than of expense. "In various parts of the country I found that children are thought a valuable acquisition, on account of the labour which they can perform when they grow up. A son's enlisting into the army is considered therefore as a great misfortune."[2] With this opinion in their minds, the orthodox economists who considered the state of the country emphasized the necessity of increasing the standard of life of the people with a view to checking population—an aim which Sadleir characterized as a wish "to give the people a taste for good living in preference to matrimony; or practically speaking to induce them to exchange chaste living for good eating."[3]

It is frequently a matter of difficulty in dealing with two closely related phenomena to say which is the cause and which the effect of the other. Thus it was constantly asserted by the contemporary economists that the excessive subdivision of land in Ireland was caused by the remarkable increase of population. The opposite however was

[1] *Letters on the State of Ireland* by J. K. L. p. 110.

[2] Wakefield vol. i. p. 513.

[3] *Ireland Its Evils* &c. p. 167. See Wakefield vol. ii. p. 691; Ricardo, *Letter to Malthus* pp. 138-9. It was remarked that the problem of population in Ireland was different from that in any other country, because in Ireland the population was found to be most dense in the poorest localities. *The Irish Difficulty Addressed to His Countrymen* by an Englishman London 1848.

nearer the truth. We have in the previous chapter pointed out many causes quite sufficient in themselves to account for the great subdivision of farms which took place in the early years of the nineteenth century; and, we suggest, the manifold advantages to be derived from subdivision at the time formed one of the reasons which induced the tenantry to increase their families. No doubt the large families thus produced tended still further to subdivide the holdings. In other words, this, like many other phenomena of Irish life, worked in a vicious circle. But the primary cause of the whole movement was, we suggest, the temptation to subdivide holdings afforded by the high price of corn and the forty shilling franchise. The motive for subdivision having been supplied, the tenantry were not slow to act upon it. Their method of putting it into effect was by increasing their families as rapidly as possible.[1]

The population of Ireland therefore increased very rapidly in the first half of the nineteenth century. Are we entitled to conclude from this fact that the country was overpopulated? The answer to this question must depend upon whether the population increased to a point at which it exceeded the resources of the country. In attempting to estimate the resources of the country, we must have regard, not only to the amount of wealth produced under the existing system of cultivation, but also to the amount which might have been produced if the resources of the country were developed to their full capacity. A disproportion between the needs of the people of a country and the wealth available to satisfy them may arise through the neglect of those responsible for the cultivation of the soil to perform their duty. In such a case it would be incorrect to allege that the ensuing distress is the result of overpopulation; it is caused rather by underproduction. The question before us, then, is whether the apparent

[1] It is interesting to notice that one of the apparent results of the great tendency towards increased population was a remarkable decrease of the pains of childbirth. See Wakefield vol. ii. p. 781 and Curwen, *Observations* vol. ii pp. 343-4.

insufficiency of the wealth of Ireland to maintain its inhabitants was the result of underproduction or of overpopulation.[1]

There were four main directions in which the wealth produced in Ireland might have been increased. In the first place the system of agriculture might have been improved so that a greater quantity of food would be raised in a given area. To this we have referred in a previous chapter, and shall return later; and we need only remind the reader here that the land of Ireland did not in fact produce the maximum of which it was capable. In the second place, manufacturing industry might have been developed, so as to afford employment for the surplus agricultural population. This will be discussed in a later part of the book. In the third place, the wealth actually produced might have been distributed so as to produce a greater benefit to the population than it actually did. In this way the disproportion between resources and population would have been amended just as if a real increase of production had taken place. In the fourth place, the amount of land under cultivation might have been increased; it is this branch of the subject which we propose to examine in the present section.

There is no subject upon which there prevailed such unanimity amongst all conversant with Irish affairs in the early nineteenth century as that of the possibility of greatly increasing the resources of the country by the reclamation of waste land. The classical authorities on the subject were the four reports which were issued in the years 1810-14 by the Commissioners on Bogs, whose conclusions were never seriously controverted. The Commissioners, who acted largely on the expert opinion of Mr. Richard Griffith,

[1] This distinction was insisted on by many contemporary economists. "Ireland is suffering from underproduction, not overpopulation." Hancock *On Laissez Faire and the Economic Resources of Ireland*. Dublin 1847; "The overpopulation of Ireland so often declared has really no existence. There is no overpopulation but enough of underproduction." Lawson, *The Overpopulation Fallacy Considered*. Dublin 1849.

reported that the draining of the bogs would be quite practicable, and that, far from interfering with the supply of turf, more turf than ever would be available, as the cutting would cease to be confined to the edge of the bogs. They reported further that an expenditure of from £1 to £10 per acre on reclamation would secure a permanent return of from 10 to 15 *per cent.* on the outlay. This advantageous work, it was pointed out, was not undertaken by the tenants because their interest in the land was too uncertain, nor by the landlords because they could not reconcile the claims of the different tenants to their respective patches of the bog. The commissioners recommended the appointment of commissioners to fix boundaries, and the granting of additional powers of leasing to tenants for life; and stated in conclusion, that they estimated the peat soil in Ireland to amount to 2,830,000 English acres, of which 1,576,000 consisted of red bog, which was easily reclaimable, and 1,255,000 of mountain bog, which might be rendered suitable for pasture and plantations.[1]

As we said, the opinion of this commission was never seriously controverted; and its four reports remained for many years the classic authority on reclamation, and were accepted as correct by the majority of later economists and public inquiries. When the matter was investigated anew by the Royal Dublin Society in 1821, similar conclusions were reached. "Although differences of opinion exist as the best mode of draining the bogs, there exists perfect unanimity as to the important fact that every description of bog is capable of being reclaimed and converted into profitable land, which would adequately, nay liberally, remunerate the outlay of the capital necessary to accomplish that object.... In the reclaiming of 3,000,000 acres now waste the skilful capitalist will have ample scope for pursuing agriculture on a large and profitable scale, and, so far from being under the necessity of unhousing

[1] *Reports of Commissioners on Bogs* 1810-4.

the humble cottager, will have an opportunity of greatly improving his condition by affording constant employment".[1] "That Ireland" wrote an Irish magistrate in 1825 "is too populous for her present circumstances is a fact which cannot be denied. But that she is too populous for the means which nature has given to her is an assertion which cannot be proved.... It therefore appears that instead of restraining by law the multiplication of the human species it would be advisable to provide support for those who exist.... Let us colonize Ireland rather than the Antipodes."[2] Robert Owen was of opinion that Ireland could support 50,000,000 inhabitants if her waste lands were put into cultivation.[3]

That these views were not the opinion of mere theorists was proved by the success of the few actual attempts which Irish landlords made at reclaiming the waste land on their estates. In every such case, the process of consolidation ceased; the standard of life of the occupiers rose; and the spirit of agrarian disturbance gave place to one of industry and contentment. The most notable example of reclamation was that of the Glenbegh estate of Lord Headley. "Your committee" reported a select committee of 1830 "cannot close this branch of the inquiry without calling the particular attention of the House to the satisfactory results stated to have been obtained at Glenbegh. In that experiment there has been shown an example worthy of imitation by the other landed proprietors."[4] Valuable experiments of the same kind were carried out by the Irish Improvement Society, and by the monks of Mount Melleray.[5] Wherever the reclamation of

[1] *Report of the Committee of the R. D. S. on Drainage.* Dublin 1821 and see Whitley Stokes, *Observations on the Population and Resources of Ireland* Liverpool 1825.

[2] *A Letter on the State of Ireland* by an Irish Magistrate. London 1825 and see *Commentaries on National Policy and on Ireland* Dublin 1831.

[3] *Report of Proceedings at a Meeting in Dublin held by Robert Owen.* Dublin 1823.

[4] *Select Committee on State of Poor in Ireland* 1830 p. 9; see on the Glenbegh experiment *Hints to Irish Landlords* by a Land Agent London 1824; and Wiggins Report on *Three Cases of Successful Improvement in Ireland*, London 1836.

[5] *Visit to Glenesk Estate* by a Proprietor, Cork 1844.

waste lands was attempted, the happiest results followed.

The findings of the Devon Commission on this subject are of the greatest importance. They were founded largely on the evidence of Mr. Richard Griffith, who saw no reason for departing from the opinion which he had expressed thirty years earlier. We quote from Mr. Kennedy's invaluable digest of the evidence given before the Commission.[1] "There is scarcely any subject investigated by the commissioners upon which the evidence is so concurrent as that of waste land reclamation, with a view of increasing remunerative employment for the labouring population. Mr. Griffith's valuable report exhibits the amount of waste land in the different counties according to the different degrees of capability for improvement. It shows that Ireland contains:-

Waste land improvable for tillage	1,425,000 acres
" " " " pasture	2,330,000 "
Total improvable	3,755,000 acres
Waste land unimprovable	2,535,000 acres
Total	6,290,000 acres

The method in which this waste land might be rendered available for the colonization of the occupants of uneconomic holdings is shown in the following table, in which it is postulated that the minimum holding on which a man can support his family is one of eight acres:-

[1] *Devon Comm.* p. 564.

APPENDIX TO LAND COMMISSION EVIDENCE, No. 95. (2).

A table framed from the data contained in the Summary of Classified Returns of Holdings in Ireland, to determine the Number of Occupiers of Land at present living on Holdings too small for their support and the corresponding quantity of Improvable Waste Land required to supply such a number of additional Holdings as would accommodate those removed by a Consolidation of the old Holdings into eight-acre Tenements, taking this to be the lowest size that would support a Family in comfort.

Classification of small holdings, assumed to be insufficient to enable them to support the families occupying them.	Number of Holdings in each Class.	Mean area of separate Holdings in each Class in Acres.	Aggregate area of Holdings in each Class in Acres.	Number of Holdings which each Class would furnish, supposing a consolidation effected, bringing the size up to 8 acs. & assuming that sized Holding adequate to support a family.	Number of Families of each Class to be otherwise provided for, supposing Consolidation contemplated in col. *e* to be effected.	Number of Acres of Improvable waste Land required to be provided & reclaimed, in order to supply Occupiers of each Class removed, as contemplated in cols. e and f. Supposing each New Holding to contain.			
						8 acres.	10 acres.	15 acres.	20 acres.
a.	b.	c.	d.	e.	f.	g.	h.	i.	k.
Under 1 acre for tillage	39,290	$\frac{3}{8}$	24,556	3,069	36,221	289,768	362,210	543,315	724,420
Proportionate number of tillage farms under 1 acre not separately returned	25,539		15,968	1,996	23,553	188,424	235,530	353,392	471,060
Over 1 to 2 acres	50,355	$1\frac{1}{2}$	75,532	9,441	40,914	327,312	409,140	613,710	818,280
" 2 " 3 "	35,951	$2\frac{1}{2}$	89,877	11,235	24,716	197,728	247,160	370,740	494,320
" 3 " 4 "	45,363	$3\frac{1}{2}$	15 ,770	19,844	25,519	204,152	255,190	382,785	510,380
" 4 " 5 "	50,281	$4\frac{1}{2}$	226,264	28,283	21,998	175,984	219,980	329,970	439,960
" 5 " 6	36,630	$5\frac{1}{2}$	201,465	25,183	11,447	91,576	114,470	171,705	228,940
" 6 " 7 "	42,665	$6\frac{1}{2}$	277,322	34,665	8,000	64,000	80,000	120,000	160,000
Total	326,084		1,069,754	133,720	192,368	1,538,944	1,923,680	2,885,520	3,847,360

From the above table it appears that the first quality of improvable waste land in Ireland would have been very nearly sufficient to afford eight acre settlements to all those whom it might be desirable to remove from the overpopulous districts, with a view to consolidating minute holdings of old productive land up to eight acres; and that the first and second qualities of improvable waste land taken together would have supplied holdings averaging about twenty acres to those whom it might be desirable thus to remove. "And the evidence tends to the conviction" proceeds Mr. Kennedy "that this result can be obtained not only without any permanent loss, but with a very large permanent gain; as it appears that 3,755,000 acres of waste land, now not giving a gross produce exceeding on the average four shillings per acre, may be made to yield a gross produce of £6 per acre, being a total increase from £751,000 to £22,530,000 and that the first three or four years crop would return the cost requisite to bring about this change." Mr. Kennedy then shows that the evidence proved that the reclamation of waste lands would be a more profitable and less expensive undertaking than either the encouragement of emigration, or the drainage of the lands already in cultivation. It had the particular advantage over the latter that it afforded a course of permanent rather than temporary employment. He next proceeds to discuss the best method to be pursued for the reclamation of the waste lands. "The practice hitherto adopted may be classed under three distinct methods; first, by leaving the whole operation to the unassisted exertion of the tenant; second, by the proprietor reclaiming at his own cost, and then letting the land at the full improved value; third, by locating the tenant on the unimproved land and assisting him in those operations which are beyond his own means, or which tend to bring the land more rapidly forward to a perfect state of tillage. . . . It is probable that the third would be the most practicable mode of accomplishing the object." Mr. Kennedy then discusses at length the advantages of the respective methods of reclamation, and the means by which the difficulties may be surmounted.[1]

The commissioners adopted to a large extent the views of Mr. Griffith. "Connected with many of the largest estates in Ireland, there are extensive tracts of land thinly populated, and affording opportunities for easy reclamation. Without going the length of supposing that employment for the people upon bringing such lands into a profitable cultivation is to furnish a cure for the evils of Ireland, we concur in the opinion so strongly expressed in former reports that very great advantages may be expected from judicious arrangements for that purpose. . . . It may be worthy of serious consideration whether the State might not very usefully make for these purposes, at a moderate rate of interest, some advance regulated, within such limits as Parliament may prescribe, by the amount which companies or individuals may advance in aid of such operations. . . . The funds which would be so required would not practically be large in any one year, and yet a great public benefit would be attained in increased employment for labour, in the progressive extension of productive land, and in the opportunity thereby afforded for the location of industrious families who may have been from unavoidable circumstances compelled to quit their former holdings. . . . We are desirous of stating our opinion that, under proper arrangements, the reclamation of waste lands, whilst it gives useful and permanent employment to the labouring population, will at the same time produce a fair return for the capital employed upon it."[2]

The necessity for the reclamation of the waste lands was urged by all enlightened Irish opinion. "The great, the all-important question," wrote Sharman Crawford

[1] *Devon Comm.* pp. 563-75. Mr. Griffith's estimate of the quantity of improvable waste land in each county is given in *Devon Comm. App B* p. 585.

[2] *Devon Comm.* pp. 1142-4.

"is how the cottier system is to be abolished. The grand panacea of English political economists is the consolidation of the lands into the hands of capitalist farmers, and the converting the cottier tenantry into labourers at wages without land. But this necessarily involves the reduction of the numbers of the working people; and this thinning, if not produced by natural means, must, in order to carry out this object, be produced by some other means. There are three modes. One by subjecting the population to circumstances which will create disease and death. This I call extermination. The second the more humane, and I believe impracticable mode with reference to large masses of population, is emigration. The third, that which I contend for, is the removal of the surplus tenants from overpopulated districts to unoccupied waste or unimproved lands, dividing the same into such size as will support a family. This mode of what may be called 'home colonization' has been advocated by, among other able writers, Mr. Mill, Mr. Thornton, and Mr, Poulett Scrope."[1]

It would appear therefore that a comparison between the amount of unemployed land and unemployed labour led to the conclusion that the one would have about balanced the other. There was plenty of potential employment in Ireland for all the inhabitants, if the resources of the country were properly developed. It was a remarkable fact, which may be cited in confirmation of this view, that there was more unemployment in the neighbourhood of the waste lands than elsewhere. "Waste population and waste land are generally found in the same district."[2] Moreover, as we stated in the previous section, the most thickly populated counties of Ireland were the most prosperous. This point was made very well by Mr. Blacker: "It appears that the county of Armagh contains 212,755 acres and a population of 220,653 souls, and that the entire

[1] *Depopulation not Necessary*. London 1849. [2] *Letters to Lord John Russell on the Further Measures* &c. by Poulett Scrope. London 1847 and see the *Census of* 1851 p. ix.

kingdom contains 17,190,726 acres and 7,839,469 souls; now, in the county of Armagh, more than one seventh of the surface is taken up by lakes and unprofitable land, and the remainder is for the greater part but indifferently cultivated, and the peasantry are better clothed lodged and fed than they are in most other counties in Ireland. I cannot therefore be accused of taking away from the comforts of the rest of the kingdom by taking the county of Armagh as a standard, and its proportion of unprofitable surface is not very remote, I believe, from the average of the others; if then 212,755, the number of acres in Armagh, gives a population of 220,653 souls, 17,190,726 acres, the entire contents of the kingdom ought to give a population of 17,828,888, in place of 7,839,469, the population at present. It therefore appears that, supposing the other parts of Ireland to be as well cultivated as Armagh, it would support two and a half times the number of its present inhabitants, and be able to export provisions largely besides, for Armagh, notwithstanding the population, exports pork, butter, and grain in great quantities. But before deciding finally upon the population which the kingdom could support, it ought to be examined how far the county of Armagh has arrived at its full complement; and in regard to this I would say, from a pretty general knowledge of it, that, under an improved system of agriculture and a regular rotation of crops, the produce would be treble of what it raises at present; but supposing it only to yield double as much, it would follow that the population of Armagh, if that beneficial change became general, would be doubled also, without in any degree lessening the comforts of its inhabitants; which increase being taken as the basis of the calculation, and applying it to the whole of Ireland, would make it adequate to the support of more than thirty-five million souls."[1] Mr. Blacker proposed therefore that every effort should be made to ensure that

[1] *Essay on the Management of Landed Property in Ireland.* Dublin 1834 pp. 30-31.

the natural resources of the country should be used to their full advantage, and that, in particular, the waste lands should be reclaimed. "I would therefore propose that the State should assume the right of taking to itself those tracts of reclaimable land which the owners continue to let remain uncultivated, and, after giving fair compensation, should make a practical experiment whether they could not be colonized to advantage."[1]

So far, we have combated the suggestion that Ireland was overpopulated by the single argument that the productive resources of the country were capable of a large increase. There were many other arguments however which could be urged in the same direction. Possibly the most effective of these was that the very evils from which Ireland suffered had been attributed by a previous generation of economists to precisely the opposite cause, underpopulation. This point was made extremely well by Mr. Sadleir, who examined one by one the symptoms urged as evidence of a condition of overpopulation. These symptoms were, first, the wretchedness and degradation of the people, second, the numbers out of employment, third, the periodical appearance of famine and epidemics. With regard to the first of these evils, Sadleir reminds us, that the people were almost as miserable in the seventeenth as in the nineteenth century, but that the general complaint at the former period was that Ireland was too thinly populated. He deals in similar fashion with the second symptom, the want of employment, which he shows, by quotation from Petty and other old writers, to have been quite as great an evil in an age when the population of the country was extremely small. With regard to the third and fourth symptoms—famines and epidemics—he demonstrates likewise that they were both quite as common when the population of Ireland was one million as when it was five. He concludes his argument by the following striking obser-

[1] *Ibid* pp. 33–4.

vations:- "It forms indeed a most singular feature of the present argument, not only that the whole train of evils which have long afflicted Ireland, now ignorantly attributed to her overflowing numbers, existed long before the alleged cause had any being; but that persons fully as competent to observe and decide on the subject as any of those who now dogmatize upon it, unhesitatingly attributed them to a diametrically opposite reason, namely, the fewness of the people. Amongst them were Sir Wm. Temple, Lord Clarendon, Dean Swift, Sir William Petty &c. From the latter I shall quote a single passage, referring for a comment upon it to the whole of some of his principal works. The following passage closes his *Political Anatomy of Ireland*: 'The greatest and most fundamental defect of this kingdom is the want of people.' I add another only; half a century afterwards we find an authority equally competent to the subject, Arthur Dobbs, asserting that the improvement of Ireland depended upon 'the increase of the people'."[1]

It would appear from the above that the population of Ireland could have been easily supported by the annual produce, even had the country remained purely agricultural, if the obvious measures had been adopted of increasing the amount produced per acre on the land already in cultivation by introducing improved methods of agriculture, and of reclaiming the bogs and waste lands. We must not however forget the importance of the additional employment which would have been afforded if the industrial resources had been developed as well. The question of the neglected development of manufacturing industry is one which we must relegate to a later part of the book; all we wish to do here, is to remind the reader of the obvious fact that the pressure on agricultural employment would have

[1] *Ireland Its Evils* &c. pp. 12-31 and see *Speech of Poulett Scrope in the House of Commons* 27th March 1849; and *The Irish Difficulty and How it must be Met*. Westminster and Foreign Quarterly Review Jan. 1849.

been greatly relieved, if the manufactures of the country had been prosperous.[1]

The second assumption underlying consolidation seems therefore to have been as fallacious as the first. Neither the subdivision of land, nor the rapid increase of population was the cause of Irish distress, and therefore neither consolidation nor depopulation was the proper remedy for that distress.

[1] See Sigerson. *Irish Land Tenures* p. 165. Parker. *A Plea for the Poor and Industrious*. Cork 1819; *On the State of Ireland* by an Irish Landlord 1821.

CHAPTER V

The Real Causes of Irish Agricultural Distress.

Section 1. The System of Land Tenure.

IF the conclusions arrived at in the previous chapter be correct, it would appear that the distressful condition of Ireland was not caused by the smallness of the farms or by the excess of the population, and that the attempted remedy by way of consolidation was therefore bound to fail, as it did in fact fail, to achieve any good result. In order to arrive at a correct conclusion regarding the proper measures which should have been applied to ameliorate the condition of the country, we must endeavour to ascertain what were the real causes of its distresses. Diagnosis must always precede treatment. We shall find on examination that the real causes of the economic distress of Ireland were the manner in which the land was cultivated rather than the size of the holdings into which it was divided, and the under-development of the resources of the country rather than the over-development of its population.

We are here faced with a difficulty. In order fully to explain the causes of Irish agricultural distress, it would be necessary to enter at length into the history of the Irish land system, a course which we are reluctant to adopt, because we have already done so to some extent in our books dealing with the seventeenth and eighteenth centuries, because it has been fully treated in many special treatises, and because it would swell the present volume to undue length. On the other hand it is impossible altogether to omit some reference to this all-important subject. We have decided therefore to take a middle course; to assume that the reader is familiar with the main features of the Irish land system; and to confine our reference to it to an examination of the particular problem before us, namely, how it was that a rich and fertile country failed to support its population in comfort. In doing so we shall refrain from encumbering the argument by quotations from the host of contemporary publications on the matter, and shall quote from none but the authorities which are most generally accepted as reliable—for example the Devon Commission. Fully to enter into the Irish land system, illustrating our conclusions from contemporary sources, would entail the publication of a volume of at least twice the size of the present, which can devote only one section to the subject.

The distress of the Irish rural population arose from two causes, first, the retardation of the improvement of the methods of agriculture pursued on the land already in cultivation, by reason of the inequitable distribution of the produce of the soil, and second, the fact that a large part of the potentially productive land in the country was suffered to remain waste. Under the first heading we shall discuss the division of the produce of the land between the owner and the occupier, or in other words between the landlord and the tenant; and shall refer to the payments which the tenant had to make other than to the landlord, namely to the clergy of the Established Church, to the county, to the corporate towns where he marketed his produce, and to the poor law unions. Under the second head we shall call attention to the failure of the tenants and of the landlords to increase the quantity of land available for cultivation.

The discussion of the respective shares of the produce of the soil enjoyed by landlord and tenant may be conveniently divided into two parts, first, a consideration of the amount of the tenant's produce which the landlord took at the commencement and during the continuance of a lease, and second, a consideration of the advantages which the landlord enjoyed at the end of the lease, as the result of the tenant's exertions. The first head practically resolves itself into a discussion of the amount of the rents paid, and the second into a discussion of the landlord's confiscation of the tenant's improvements.

That rents were much too high in Ireland under the old land system will not be seriously disputed at the present day. In many cases the rent was so high that it was absolutely impossible for the tenant to pay it even after a prosperous year. One of the principal causes of this injustice was the evil practice of letting land by auction, or "cant" as it was called. In England, when a lease was about to be made, an interview between the landlord and the prospective tenant usually resulted in their agreeing upon a reasonable rent. In Ireland, on the other hand, the land was put up to public auction, the highest bidder being accepted. The eagerness of the tenants to obtain land—without which they could not exist—tempted them to offer rents which they could not possibly pay. The result of course was that they had to give to the landlord almost the whole produce of the land, in order to pay as large a portion of the rent as they could, and were themselves forced to live on the very margin of subsistence. All these consequences flowed directly from the system of canting. This vicious practice was continued on the great majority of Irish estates throughout the first half of the nineteenth century. "The whole business of letting an estate" Wakefield wrote "is conducted in a manner that must excite the astonishment of an Englishman, who has been accustomed to make the strictest inquiries respecting those who solicit for farms. Regard to present gain, without the least thought of the future, seems to be the principal object which the Irish landlord has in view. The highest bidder, whatever be his character or connection, is invariably preferred; and if he can pay his rent no inquiries are made whether he cultivates the land in a proper manner, or ruins and exhausts it by mismanagement."[1] The practice of canting was said in 1815 to be less common than formerly.[2] Curwen however found it in full force when he visited Ireland three years later. "The rents are very high, being regulated not by the worth of the tenant but by the wants of the people."[3] "In the south and west of Ireland" to quote from the Devon Commission "the rent is commonly determined by proposals made by those who wish to obtain a vacant farm; the highest solvent bidder is in most cases accepted. It might be thought that there would be little danger to the tenant from such a mode of letting the farm; that no one would offer for land more than its value to himself; and that the person about to engage in such an undertaking would be well qualified to judge the probable capabilities and productive powers of the land. It is however asserted that this mode of determining rent is replete with evil; that, from the excessive competition for land, the tenant to obtain possession is tempted to offer a higher rent than can be paid for the farm under his unskilful management; that when making the offer he has no intention of fulfilling his part of the bargain, but trusts that the difficulty of enforcing repayment will ensure him a reduction of the rent afterwards. It appears that, though this mode of letting land is most common in the south and west of Ireland, it occasionally occurs in other districts, especially on estates under the courts, where it is almost invariably adopted. Well-managed estates are generally let by private contract or valuation, even in the districts where the practice of letting by proposal is most frequent."[4] Nassau Senior remarked that "the treaty between landlord and tenant is a struggle like the struggle to buy bread in a

[1] Vol. i.p. 304.
[2] *An Address to the People of Ireland* by a Compatriot Dublin 1815.
[3] *Observations &c.* vol. i. p. 105.
[4] pp. 753-4.

besieged town or to buy water in an African caravan."[1] This custom of canting, according to John Stuart Mill, was the distinguishing feature of a cottier tenure. "By the general appellation of cottier tenure I shall designate all cases without exception in which the conditions of the contract, especially the amount of rent, are determined not by custom but by competition."[2]

It was inevitable that under such a system rents should tend to reach the highest point consistent with the continued existence of the occupier, or in other words that the landlords should come to receive the whole surplus produce of the soil. And such in fact was what happened. The great majority of the witnesses examined before the Devon Commission agreed that "rents are in general too high, and that much of the misery prevalent in Ireland arises from this fact." Although the actual money rent paid per acre might be shown to be lower than that paid in England, Scotland, Belgium, or other countries, still it was proportionately higher when allowance was made for the inferior condition of Irish agriculture and the consequent small produce per acre.[3]

The evil of high rents was worst on the estates of middlemen, a class which increased in number as a result of the high price of land caused by the war.[4] "I shall suppose the case" wrote Wakefield "that a middleman, such as one of those who abound in every town of Ireland, obtains a lease of land, and that this person takes it without the least intention of ever laying out upon it a single shilling, or of occupying an acre of it. This man relets it at a considerable rack rent, and, whatever success attends the occupiers, the whole fruit of their labour finds its way

[1] *Ireland Journals* vol. i. p. 28. [2] *The Irish Land Question* p. 71.

[3] *Devon Comm.* p. 756. The worst example of canting was met with on estates managed by the Court of Chancery of which the Devon Commission remarks "The destructive tendency of lettings by auction at intervals of seven years forcing tenants to take leases at heavy charges for such short terms exhibits an incredible degree of ingenuity in the production of evil". p. 1032.

[4] On the way in which the war swelled the number of middlemen see *Strictures on Bankruptcy Insolvency and on the State of the Nation* Dublin 1815.

into the pockets of this petty despot. There are various ways by which persons of this description have it in their power to ruin and destroy the real tenantry of an estate; such as that of binding them by an oath to pay their rent on a certain day, or to drive their cattle to the pound, and it is extremely difficult to counteract this system. I have known estates offered at a fair but highly increased rent to the occupiers, who to a man refused to take them. They have then been let to one of the 'land-sharks' as they are called; and I have seen the occupiers, rather than quit, give a pound an acre more than the rent at which they had rejected the same land a few weeks before. This singular change is effected partly by fear and partly by persuasion and encouragement. Many advantages are held out by way of lure. One strong inducement is that the middleman, not being in want of money, engages to take promissory notes at a long date in payment of the rent; but these poor deluded people soon find to their cost that their confidence has been most shamefully abused; for when the day of payment comes the middleman has nothing to do but to drive away their cattle. Middlemen of this kind are a disgrace to a country; they are real pests of society; as great tyrants in Ireland as the farmers-general were in France; and while they excite the detestation of the honest part of society, they are loaded with curses by the poor whom they oppress."[1] "The middleman" we read "was apparently a fine jovial fire-eating fellow, certain to have the best gun and dogs in the barony; and as to his horse no man living was allowed to lead him at the foxhunt. Steeped to the eyes in the very purple of orangeism he hated sincerely what he called the bloody papists."[2] The number of middlemen continued to grow until the end of the war: "The times were very bad for the farmers, and there was a peculiar kind of gentry, a kind of middle order between the rich gentry of the country and the peasantry; persons

[1] Vol. i. pp. 287-88. [2] *Suggestions for Checking the Repeal Agitation* Dublin 1843.

who were generated by the excessive rise of the agricultural produce during the war, and got the education of persons above their rank";[1] and much injustice was perpetrated by them after the peace by their refusal to reduce the rents in spite of the fall in prices. This we have dealt with already.[2] Although at the date of the Devon Commission the number of middlemen was tending to decrease, the oppression of those who survived was as severe as ever. "The general management of estates of middlemen is stated to be very bad; the term middlemen being chiefly applied to those who, holding short terminable leases, or as tenants from year to year, sublet their lands. Many of the cases of oppression brought before the notice of the Commissioners seem to have been perpetrated by individuals of this class. Most of the proprietors in Ireland seem to struggle violently to overthrow this system, and their efforts have been in a considerable degree successful. It appears that as one means of abolishing the class of middlemen, proprietors in many cases on the expiration of a lease set the land to the occupying tenants, letting to the middleman that part only of the farm which he retained in his own possession. And to avoid the operation of this system many middlemen have sought to remove the competitors for a renewal, and have ejected all their subtenants previous to the lapse of their own interest. This has not unfrequently caused much suffering and outrage."[3] The Devon Commissioners say in their report:— "The practice of letting land to middlemen is now rare; but the system has entailed upon the country the most injurious consequences, and has been a fruitful source of the difficulties which embarrass those who endeavour to place the land of Ireland upon a safe and wholesome footing."[4]

[1] *Select Committee of* 1825. p. 401.

[2] A good description of the different classes of landlord is contained in Ryan *Essay on Improvement* London 1824. The middlemen were frequently the leaders of the Whiteboys *A Letter on the State of Ireland* by an Irish Magistrate London 1825).

[3] p. 1029. [4] p. 1121.

Of course it must not be forgotten that there were a certain number of middlemen who managed their property well. This is admitted by the most violent opponents of the middleman system—such as Wakefield and Blacker.[1] But generally speaking the system produced the evil consequences we have described, and cannot escape condemnation on account of a few exceptions to the rule. Lord Dufferin pronounced the middlemen to be the real curse of the Irish land system.[2]

In attempting to ascertain what the Irish tenant paid for his land, it is not sufficient merely to enquire as to the amount of his annual money payments. There were many additional payments which must be taken into account. One important item was the payment which frequently had to be made to the landlord's agent before a lease was granted. "I must observe also" wrote Wakefield "that the most barefaced bribery and corruption are practised by this class of people (agents) without the least sense of fear or of shame. I have known instances where the first question asked, on a person applying for a lease, was 'and how much do you propose to give to myself?' Wives, daughters, kept-mistresses, all receive money, and the same infamous system prevails even among some resident landlords. Nay I have known instances where the tenant, after feeing the agent in this manner, could not have his lease executed without having recourse to the proprietor's lady, who was to be moved only by weighty arguments of the same kind, and to whom it was necessary for the fleeced tenant to present a similar fee before he could succeed in his application."[3] Voluminous evidence of the continued existence of this extortion could be produced, but we shall content ourselves with quoting the digest of the Devon Commission on the matter:- "On much the greater number of estates agents are paid by the landlords directly, but on a few

[1] And see O'Driscoll *Views of Ireland* vol. ii. p. 157; Parker, *Observations on the Intended Amendment of the Irish Grand Jury Laws* London 1816.

[2] *Irish Emigration &c.* pp. 93-96.

[3] vol. i. pp. 297-8.

they are paid by the tenants, and on many the practice has been for the tenant to pay a fixed fee to the agent for the grant of a lease, out of which fee the agent defrays the conveyancing expenses. Allegations of bribery and favouritism, in consequence of presents given by particular tenants, were made by many of the witnesses; but in few cases were such allegations founded on personal knowledge of the facts alleged. A few charges of bribes received by agents were however brought before the commissioners under circumstances which rendered it extremely probable that they were well founded; and these were generally cases in which such sums were given on the grant of a lease or the appointment of a tenant. In a few instances it appeared that the agents were in the habit of receiving gratuitous labour from the tenants under their charge, but this practice has generally ceased."[1] The widespread success of such practices forced the honest agents to raise rents as high as possible, as an agent who let at a low rent was suspected of taking a bribe.[2]

The reference to gratuitous labour leads us on to the second of the additional payments which we must take into account. Wakefield remarked the existence of this "duty labour." "Though few leases contain clauses by which the tenant is bound to cultivate the ground in a particular manner, there are some which oblige him, when called upon, to labour for his landlord at an inferior rate of wages. The common price in these cases is eightpence a day, in some instances only sixpence; and in consequence of the service required by this clause being neglected, I have seen a poor man's cattle taken from his door, and driven away without the least feeling or regret."[3]

"Besides the rent the tenant had to pay certain 'dues' in kind, and perform certain 'duties'. Contributions of poultry, eggs, etc., were required as 'duty fowl', 'duty eggs' and so forth. The 'duty work' to be performed con-

[1] pp. 1026-7. [2] Curwen *Observations &c.* vol. ii. p. 135. [3] vol. i. p. 245.

sisted in labour given to plant, reap, and gather the landlord's crops, to thresh his corn, draw home his turf, or like agricultural services. A rate of payment was occasionally fixed, but this payment was always less than the market value of the labour. The tenants had to neglect their own occupations in order to perform this labour. A receipt was passed for its performance, as well as for tithe rent payment, and for non-performance a penal sum was reserved in the lease to be recoverable in the same manner as rent."[1] The practice of extorting these "duties" appears to have become less frequent with advancing years. According to the Devon Commission, "suits and services seem to be seldom reserved in modern leases, although common in those granted forty or fifty years since."[2] These duties, however, added to the other payments we have mentioned, must have operated greatly to enhance the real, as distinguished from the nominal rent, paid by the occupiers. "Leases were no protection to the tenant" wrote Sharman Crawford "who from the extravagant rent he was bound to pay—extravagant more particularly as regards his means to pay it—was always in arrear and in the power of the landlord. Such was the position in which these poor people had been placed; subject to the grinding process in every petty form which such a system must give rise to—fees to agents—to bailiffs and drivers—free labour on the lands of those imperious slave-masters—and even duties and fees to the landlords' wives; so that under this system of extortion, the rent was no index of the claims which the poor tenant was bound to meet."[3] The last additional payment that we shall mention was that of the stamp duty on the lease, to which we shall return later.

While it is clear, therefore, that the landlord and his agent derived an inequitably large share of the produce of the tenant's labour, it is useless to attempt to arrive

[1] Sigerson *Irish Land Tenures* pp. 152-3. Wakefield vol. i. pp. 507, 511, 513. [2] p. 237.
[3] *Depopulation not Necessary*. London 1849.

at an estimate of the actual average rent of Irish land. Too many disturbing factors are present to allow a satisfactory calculation to be reached. Wakefield estimated the average rent in 1810 at £1.7.1 per acre, but this figure can only be taken as roughly approximate.[1] Cairnes estimated that many rents in Ireland rose between 1760 and 1815 in the proportion of 4 to 1.[2] In 1807 the Duke of Bedford estimated the average rental of Ireland at 20/- or 21/- per acre.[3] Nor is it possible to compare the rents of land in England and Ireland. In order to do so, one would have to make allowance for the different degrees of agricultural development in the two countries; one would also have to allow for the different nature of the farms leased; and one would make constant errors—especially in drawing conclusions from figures relating to the early years of the century—on account of the difference between the English and Irish currencies and method of mensuration.[4] It was a favourite apology of Irish landlords that the high rents they obtained compared with rents in England were due to the superior fertility of Irish soil. We must remember however that in judging the amount which the owner of land is entitled to receive for its occupation the important factor to be taken into account is not the natural fertility of the soil but the amount which it is made to produce; and, as we have already seen, the amount produced in Ireland per acre was less than in England.

Although, therefore, we cannot arrive at any definite figure for the rent of Irish land per acre at the period, nor at any satisfactory comparison between the rents paid in England and Ireland, we have sufficient evidence to justify the conclusion that the rents of Ireland were unreasonably high in the circumstances of the country at

[1] Vol. i. p. 305. [2] *Political Essays* p. 170. [3] *Fortescue MSS* vol. ix. p. 94.

[4] The last error s warned against in *Letters to a Friend in England on the Actual State of Ireland.* London 1828. The middlemen were sometimes known to let land by "the acre", which was understood by the tenant to be an Irish acre, but which was afterwards insisted to be an English acre. Thus the rent was most unjustly raised. Trimmer, *Further Observations &c.* London 1812.

the time. In other words, the landlords took too great a share of the total wealth produced. "The sole object of the landlord is how to improve his rent; that of the tenant how to pay it."[1] Mr. Wiggins, a most experienced English agriculturist, reached this conclusion as the result of prolonged inquiries:- "In tracing the present state of the relation of landlord and tenant in Ireland, we must admit, however reluctantly, that too high rents, or in other words too large a share of the produce of the soil, is exacted of the occupier of land."[2]

So much for the distribution of the produce of the soil, between landlord and tenant during the continuance of the lease; we must now discuss in what proportions they shared any additional value which the land might have acquired at the end of the tenancy. In other words, to whom did the improvements belong? The great importance of this question with regard to land in Ireland can be realized only by a clear understanding of one of the characteristic features of the Irish contract of tenancy, namely, the practice of letting unimproved land. In England the general practice was that the landlord should construct the farmhouse and offices, and otherwise put the holding into good order, before letting it; but in Ireland nothing was let but the naked unimproved land. Obviously therefore the question of the ownership of improvements was of far greater importance in the latter than in the former country. In England it was possible for a tenant to work his holding economically and profitably, and restore it to the landlord at the end of his term in very much the same condition as that in which he received it; in Ireland on the other hand, it was necessary for the tenant to lay out a certain amount of capital on his holding before it could be made to produce anything at all, and it was almost inevitable under such a system that the land would have

[1] *Letters on the State of Ireland.* London 1831.
[2] *The Monster Misery of Ireland.* London 1844.

acquired an additional value in the course of the tenancy.

We need not labour a point so well known as this difference in the mode of letting the land in the two countries. "It is well known" reported the Devon Commissioners "that in England and Scotland, before a landlord offers a farm for letting, he finds it necessary to provide a suitable farmhouse, with necessary farm buildings for the proper management of the farm. He puts the gates and fences into good order, and he also takes upon himself the burden of keeping the buildings in repair during the term. In Ireland the case is wholly different. The smallness of the farms as they are usually let, together with other circumstances, render the introduction of the English system extremely difficult, and in many cases impracticable. It is admitted on all hands that, according to the general practice in Ireland, the landlord builds neither dwelling-house nor farm offices, nor puts fences, gates &c. into good order, before he lets his land to a tenant. The cases in which a landlord does any of these things are exceptional. The system however of giving aid in these matters is becoming more prevalent. In most cases, whatever is done in the way of building or fencing is done by the tenant, and in the ordinary language of the country, dwellinghouses, farm-buildings, and even the making of fences, are described by the general word 'improvements', which is thus employed to denote the necessary adjuncts to a farm, without which in England or Scotland no tenant would be found to rent it. Under the same common term of improvements, are also included various agricultural operations, such as draining, deep trenching, and even manuring, which ought to stand upon a very different footing from buildings."[1] "An Irish farmer" according to Wakefield "may be said to commence without any capital. He has not to pay taxes or poor rates; the county cess he discharges by labour, that is by working with his car on

[1] pp. 1122-3.

the roads; and, as he begins his agricultural career in want, and continues it amidst poverty, it may readily be perceived that cultivation under such untoward circumstances must be wretchedly bad."[1]

The landlord thus gave nothing to the tenant at the beginning of the tenancy except the bare land. The next question is, what did he take away at its termination? Here, again, we need not reinforce our answer by references and quotations, as it is well known that the landlord at the termination of the letting received back from the tenant not merely the land which he had let, but in addition all the improvements which the tenant had made. Indeed this fact constituted the central pivot of the Irish land question. "The importance and absolute necessity of securing to the occupying tenant of land in Ireland some distinct mode of remuneration for the judicious permanent improvements that he may effect upon his farm is sustained by a greater weight of concurrent evidence than any other subject which has been brought under the consideration of the Commissioners."[2] Naturally, as soon as the landlord became possessed of this property of enhanced value, he was able to let it again at an increased rent. If the old tenant refused to take it at the increased rent it was let to somebody else. Thus the tenant was placed in the dilemma of having either to pay a rent for the fruits of his own labour, or to submit to eviction and all the dreadful consequences which it entailed. Nobody today would deny that this method of distribution was unjust and indefensible. Let us now see how it affected the production of wealth in the country.

If there was one subject on which all the competent agriculturalists and economists who studied the condition of Ireland were agreed, it was, that the confiscation of the tenant's improvements operated as a great discouragement to the development of agriculture. Opinions dif-

[1] Vol. i. p. 428. [2] *Devon Comm.* p. 155.

fered widely as to how this evil could best be remedied, but as regards its existence there was only the one view. "The cultivator" wrote Trimmer early in the century "from having so short a time in the land, has had little inducement to preserve the fences, where there are any, or to make and plant them where there are none. Neither can he afford to run any risks in attempting improvements in husbandry. His whole concern during the time he occupies the land is to obtain the most he can from it, however disadvantageously to the estate, in that way which his experience teaches him will just enable him to pay his rent and gain a scanty subsistence. It is not my purpose to enumerate all the pernicious effects of this system. It is the very pest of the country, the cankerworm of its prosperity."[1] "So surely as the tenant showed any symptoms of improving means" wrote Sharman Crawford "that moment he was pounced upon, he was ejected for arrears, and his farm offered to the highest bidder, without regard to any improvements he might have made. The certain consequence of improvement was ejectment; a man to obtain a continuance of occupation must avoid the semblance of the common comforts which human beings ought to enjoy, and still more any exhibition of improved cultivation."[2] John Stuart Mill pointed out the evil consequences of this practice, namely that "any increased value given to the land by the exertions of the tenant would have no other effect but to raise the rent against himself and so to afford an inducement to the landlord for his dispossessment. The consequence is that there can be no improvement, and therefore there can be no employment; that the population are indolent, apathetic and apparently lazy; that they have not the sufficient means to support life, although those means could be procured from the soil by proper cultivation;

[1] *A Brief Inquiry into the Present State of Agriculture in the Southern Parts of Ireland.* London 1809 and see *Further Observations* etc. by the same author, Dublin 1812, and John Edwards *The Interests of Ireland* Dublin 1824 and Fraser *Gleanings in Ireland* London 1822. [2] *Depopulation not Necessary.* London 1849.

and that amidst accumulating pauperism, overwhelming rates, and non-payment of either rents or rates the people are starving."[1] "It is a prevalent opinion in England" said Bicheno "that the Irish cultivators are what they are in consequence of their not being allowed the same share of produce as the English farmers. The truth is the Irish tenantry are not entitled to the same proportion of profit as the English, for the peasants bring nothing to the cultivation of the soil but their own labour, and get nothing out of it but their own subsistence; whilst the farmers invest in agriculture no capital, which is made to fructify like the seed they grow, but conduct their husbandry by the means of persons who draw their wages immediately from the land at their own risk and charge."[2] "Until the landlords of Ireland" said no less an authority than Richard Griffith "can be persuaded that it is their interest to allow the small farmer some portion out of the fruits of his labour, the country must be for ever disturbed; because until that happens the people can never feel an interest in upholding the law, as any change to them affords a prospect of improving their condition."[3] "In Ireland there are few persons who, either in manufacture or agriculture, conduct their operations on such a scale as to admit of much surplus for accumulation. The tendency from various causes to subdivision of farms and the general practice of throwing the expense of buildings and repairs on the tenants, countered the accumulation of profit in the hands of the farmer, and the application thereof to beneficial enterprise in agriculture."[4]

The whole trend of the evidence before the Devon Commission went to prove that the confiscation of improvements was attended by the most ruinous consequences

[1] Quoted in Sharman Crawford *op. cit.*

[2] *Remarks on the Evidence. Poor Inquiry Comm.* App. H. part ii p. 25, and see Poulett Scrope *A Letter to the Landed Proprietors of Ireland* London 1847.

[3] *Practical Domestic Politics* London 1819.

[4] *Second Report of Select Committee on the Condition of the Labouring Poor in Ireland* 1819.

to agriculture. "The want of some measure of remuneration for tenants' improvements has been variously stated as productive directly or indirectly of most of the social evils of this country. It has been shown that the master evil, poverty, proceeds from the fact of occupiers of land withholding the investment of labour and capital from the ample and profitable field for it that lies within their reach on the farms they occupy; that this hesitation is attributable to a reasonable disinclination to invest labour or capital on the property of others, without a security that adequate remuneration shall be derived from the investment; that no such security at present exists in regard to the vast mass of cases, including tenancies from year to year and leases with short unexpired terms; that the characteristic tillage of the country is most barbarous and unprofitable; that the introduction of the more profitable courses of cultivation must be impracticable until the requisite preparatory improvements of the soil shall have first taken place; that this preparatory or permanent improvement of the soil offers the most profitable return for money or labour invested in it that can be imagined, varying from about 15 to 100 per cent. on the outlay; that, so far as the small working farmer is concerned, these lucrative operations may be effected without the investment of money capital, but merely by the judicious application of the time and labour of his family, which are now wasted while he is complaining that employment cannot be had; that the more extensive farmers have the same ample opportunity of employing the labourers in their immediate neighbourhood on similar works, calculated to bring back a return varying from 15 to 100 per cent. upon the money they invest in certain classes of work; that notwithstanding these evident means, afforded by the circumstances of almost very district, of giving ample employment to the people and of deriving a return unparalleled in other pursuits, no effort is made by the farmer—1st because he is not certain of being permitted to reap a remunerating benefit from his exertions; 2nd because, if a tenant at will, he may be immediately removed from the improved lands after having invested his labour or capital without receiving any compensation for what he has done, or his rent may be immediately raised to the full value of the improvements; 3rd because, if a tenant with a lease, the unexpired portion of his term may be insufficient to remunerate him, and at its termination he may either be removed without receiving the balance of his investment, or his rent may be raised so as to deprive him of the power to repay himself from the lands. . . . Many persons of the most upright intentions are surprised that a tenant at will should hesitate to expend large values in labour or money for the permanent improvement of land or building, which it may require several years to draw back from the land, although the following year this outlay might legally be appropriated by the landlord. They would be much more surprised at the folly or indiscretion of a man, not being a tenant, who would place his money at the arbitrary control of any other party, without requiring either bond or security for its repayment with interest."[1]

One point which emerges clearly is the intimate connection between the payment for improvements and the duration and certainty of the tenancy. Indeed this connection is obvious. A tenant with fifty or sixty years still to run may well consider it worth his while to lay out money on his holding which would be withheld by a tenant with only ten years to run, or still more by a tenant from year to year or a tenant at will. Again, a tenant with twenty years certain to run will be more inclined to improve his

[1] *Devon Comm.* pp. 156-8. According to Professor Hancock the six legal impediments that prevented the application of capital to land by tenants were (1) the old feudal principle that the ownership of inprovements followed the land (2) the law of agritural fixtures (3) restraints on leasing powers (4) restraint on the power of making tenant right agreements (5) stamps on leases and (6) the remnant of the usury laws which still operated for land loans. *On the Economic Causes of the Present State of Agriculture in Ireland* Dublin 1848. Poulett Scrope attributed the backward state of agriculture in Ireland to(1) the crippled condition of the landlords and (2) that of the tenant under the existing law of land tenure. *A Plea for the Rights of Industry in Ireland* London 1848.

holding than one whose tenancy is for the life of another person, who may live for fifty years, or who may die tomorrow. The shorter or the more uncertain the tenancy, the less will the holding be improved. Thus, in a country where short or uncertain leases are general, the evils resulting from the non-remuneration for improvements will certainly be more acute than in one where long and certain leases are the general rule. In order then fully to realize the extent of the evil which Irish agriculture experienced from this cause it is necessary for us to inquire what were the usual conditions of leases in Ireland.

The general answer to this inquiry is contained in a short passage from the digest of the Devon Commissioners: "Some writers seemed to think that leases for a short term of years do not give a sufficient security to induce tenants to invest their labour or capital in the improvement of the ground; and several mentioned sixty-one years or three lives and thirty-one years as the shortest remunerating periods. *The greater portion of the occupiers of land in Ireland hold as tenants from year to year.*"[1] Thus, with regard to the evils likely to arise from the short duration of tenancies, Ireland occupied the worst possible position. With regard to the evils arising from the uncertainty of the tenancy, things were not much better, as life leases were very common. This was accounted for by the anxiety of the proprietors in the early years of the century to increase the number of freeholders on their estates for political purposes, and, as is well known, it is one of the principles of English law that a tenant for life is a freeholder, while a tenant for a fixed period—however long—is but a leaseholder. Wakefield found that the leases most common in his time were for 61 years and lives, 31 years and lives, 31 years, 21 years and lives, and 21 years.[2] As was natural, the leases of uncertain duration made for bad agriculture. "I have endeavoured" wrote Wakefield "on various occasions

[1] p. 234. [2] Vol. i. p. 285

to convince an occupier that it was not his interest to run so many crops, and that a greater weight of corn could be raised under proper management in a less number of years, but my logic was of no use; the invariable answer was 'I hold the land only during such a person's life, he is advanced in years, and how do I know when he may drop?' "[1]

There was one species of tenancy common in Ireland which would appear at first sight to have been ideal both as regards duration and certainty, namely the lease for lives with a covenant for perpetual renewal. In practice however the anxiety of the landlords to recover possession of lands which their predecessors had granted, possibly at a time of distress or financial necessity, on these very favourable terms, led to incessant litigation, and the informality with which the original documents had been prepared frequently led to decisions adverse to the tenants. These leases were therefore open to the objection of uncertainty. "It is our duty" observed the Devon Commissioners "to observe upon one species of tenure, scarcely known elsewhere, which prevails very extensively in Ireland. We allude to the tenure by lease for lives with a covenant for perpetual renewal, on payment of a fine, sometimes merely nominal, on the fall of each life. . . . This tenure though manifestly intended to be perpetual has proved a source of frequent litigation. Various constructions have been put upon the covenant for perpetual renewal. We cannot more clearly exhibit the extent of this evil than by quoting . . . . a judgment of the late Sir M. O'Loughlin, when Master of the Rolls, in reference to the subject:- 'Every day's experience shows how very uncertain the duration of an interest under such a tenure is. Forfeitures of the right to enforce a renewal daily occur through the neglect of tenants, or the dexterous management of landlords. Covenants treated in some cases for more than a century as entitling tenants to renewal for ever have been construed

[2] Vol. i. p. 303.

in courts of justice as not conferring that right. Any person who is much engaged in the investigation of titles under leases of lives renewable for ever will find , in almost every abstract of such titles, a statement of the result of one or more suits in equity for enforcing the right."[1]

The tenure of land in Ireland thus suffered in a peculiar degree from the circumstances, which, as we have said, tended to exaggerate the evils attendant upon the confiscation of improvements—namely leases of short or of uncertain duration. The introduction of the practice of granting leases for a fairly long term of years was therefore highly desirable. Much stress was laid by the landlord witnesses before the Devon Commission on the fact that tenants frequently refused to take leases, even when they were offered by the landlords. The explanation of this apparent anomaly is that the leases the landlords were willing to grant often contained clauses and covenants, the disadvantages of which were sufficient to outweigh the advantages of the possession of a lease. "Perhaps by comparing the forms of leases which landlords are ready to grant with those which tenants are anxious to obtain, these apparent contradictions may be in some degree reconciled. Many tenants asserted that leases reserving the present rents were not to be desired; that leases for a very considerable time were necessary to remunerate the occupiers; and several adverted with strong disapprobation to the covenants and conditions commonly contained in leases. It does not appear probable that the proprietors would willingly reduce their rents merely for the sake of giving leases to their tenants. Many landlords disapprove of long leases, and they generally require the insertion of strict covenants, for the sake of protecting their property from injury. It may therefore be the case that not infrequently those who assert the unwillingness of landlords to grant, and the anxiety of tenants to obtain, leases, and those who

[1] *Devon Comm.* pp. 232-3.

contradict them, may in a great measure refer to different subjects."[1] The need of the tenants was not for leases simply, but for leases of reasonable length, reserving a fair rent, and free from oppressive covenants.

There was another cause which operated to make tenants hesitate before executing a lease, namely the high stamp duties. "Many witnesses asserted that the stamp duties, by increasing the expense of leases, have frequently caused tenants to avoid rather than seek them. This as well as other evil consequences of the stamp laws were vehemently denounced by several witnesses, amongst others by Mr. O'Connell."[2] The stamp duties on leases were substantially reduced as a result of the report of the Devon Commission.[3]

Assuming however that these initial difficulties were surmounted, and a lease granted, there were many unwritten customs attached to it which tended to counterbalance the good effect it should normally have had on the agriculture of the country. The chief of these was the custom of allowing a certain amount of rent to fall into arrear, so that the landlord's remedies for non-payment of rent could be immediately exercised at any moment. Wakefield had condemned the practice of the "hanging gale" as an oppressive custom. "This is one of the great levers of oppression by which the lower classes are kept in a kind of perpetual bondage, for, as every family almost holds some portion of land and owes half a year's rent which the landlord can exact in a moment, this debt hangs over their heads like a load , and keeps them in a continual state of anxiety and terror."[4] "In many districts a considerable amount of rent in arrear is by the practice of the country or of particular provinces allowed to accumulate. The custom of having a running gale or hanging gale seems to be very prevalent; where this is the case the tenant is not

[1] *Devon Comm.* p. 235.
[2] *Devon Comm.* p. 239.
[3] 9 and 10 Vict c. 112.
[4] Vol. i p. 244.

called on or expected to pay one half year's rent till he owes two. In some cases it appears that even greater arrears are habitually allowed to accrue. In addition to these customary arrears of rent, the tenants, from inability to pay, or from a wish to defraud, frequently incur further arrears to a very considerable amount; and though old arrears are seldom pressed for, they are even less frequently forgiven. It is asserted that in all cases the existence of an arrear operates most injuriously, that it gives a feeling of insecurity to the tenant, and prevents his attempting to improve his farm."[1]

Thus we see that, whether the Irish tenant held as a tenant from year to year, a tenant for life, a tenant for lives renewable for ever, or under a lease, he was in every case without an adequate motive to improve his farm. "In Ireland" we read in a pamphlet written in 1822, "tenure at will is indefinite oppression; tenure by lease, oppression by lease. The peasant and the land alike are neglected, impoverished, and starved."[2] Beaumont records that he had visited districts in England where both long and short leases were the custom, but that the population of these districts was always better off than they would have been in Ireland—"La lettre de l'engagement sera toujours stérile, sans l'esprit qui seul peut la féconder."[3]

We have adduced sufficient evidence to justify the conclusion that one of the principal causes of the impoverishment of the country was the law which denied to the cultivator the value of his improvements. Beaumont perceived this clearly; the reason that Ireland was as poor in 1839 as in 1739 was that the landlords took the whole surplus of the wealth produced in both years.[4] If any confirmation were needed of this opinion we should find it by the appli-

[1] *Devon Comm.* pp. 757-8, where other objectionable practices between landlord and tenant are also instanced.

[2] Wesley Doyle. *Ostensible Causes of the Present State of Ireland* Scarborough 1822.

[3] *L'Irlande Sociale* vol. i. p. 229 and see Wakefield vol. i. p. 599.

[4] *L'Irlande Sociale* vol. ii. p. 126.

cation of the maxim *exceptio probat regulam.* The conclu sion that the confiscation of the tenant's improvements was the main cause of Irish poverty would be strengthened if we could point to any particular part of the country, where the rule did not apply, which was more prosperous and contented than the regions in which it did apply; or if we could show that in any case where the rule was temporarily relaxed, the condition of affairs immediately improved. Luckily we are able to produce instances of both these cases; the former is illustrated by the Ulster custom, and the latter by Ralahine.

It is not necessary to discuss the origin of the so-called Ulster custom, or why it was that the practices in the northern and in the other provinces of Ireland were different; it is sufficient that we should describe the custom as it existed in the early nineteenth century. The Ulster custom may be defined as the recognition of tenant right by the landlords. Tenant right was the name given to the equitable claim which a tenant was deemed to possess to some remuneration at the end of his tenancy for his goodwill and for the improvements he had effected. In the south of Ireland this right was everywhere understood and recognized by the tenant class, but it was not recognized by the landlords or the law courts.[1] The result was that the tenantry, being denied the legal protection of a custom which was unanimously recognized to be just, endeavoured to protect it by illegal action. Such in a word was the explanation of the so-called agrarian outrages of the time. "It was not easy for a man when building a house, and thereby investing his property permanently in the land, to imagine that he had still in equity only a year's title; that he might with justice be removed at the end of that year, leaving his investment behind him, and that he was to think no more

[1] It is interesting to observe, as evidence of the universal prevalence of tenant right in the south, that the legislature admitted payment for it in the case of the compulsory acquisition of land for railways. See Alcock. *The Tenure of Land in Ireland Considered* London 1848.

of the matter. As the principle affected the great mass of the people, all were interested in inventing a remedy. The remedy was a simple one. Failing that equitable settlement which was neglected by the land proprietor, it was only requisite to appeal to Lynch law, and to extort a payment by intimidation from the incoming tenant with great injury to the latter, and, through him, to the proprietor. This court of appeal did not feel bound to measure the payment in reference to the extent of improvements effected, but as deciding on a case affecting their own interests; and in the determination to maintain 'fixity of tenure' the sum was calculated to discountenance such proceedings, whether improvements were made and unliquidated investments left behind, or on the contrary much arrear had accrued on the outgoing tenant, and much injury had been done by him to the premises."[1]

Such was the method in which tenant right was enforced in the south of Ireland, a method obviously pregnant with injustice and fraud. In the northern counties, while the claims put forward by the outgoing tenant were identical with those advanced elsewhere, the method of their enforcement was entirely different, because the northern landlords recognized and acted on the assumption that the claim of tenant right was just and reasonable. It was therefore not the existence of the right but its recognition that distinguished Ulster from the rest of Ireland. "In most of the northern counties, the incoming tenant thinks it preferable to make his arrangements methodically with the person going out, and to insure his life by the payment of a considerable sum of money, varying from five to ten, and in many cases to a much larger number of years' purchase of the rent; and this on farms not only where no improvement may have been effected, but where much injury may have been done by the outgoing tenant."[2] The last mentioned case may be reckoned as a payment for

[1] *Devon Comm.* 159. [2] *Devon Comm.* p. 160.

goodwill. "The tenant right of Ulster" wrote Professor Hancock "when considered economically is only a recognition by long established custom of the right of the tenant to the fair profit of the capital invested by him, by purchase or expenditure, on the permanent improvement of the land, or to the inherited profit arising from such improvement, when made by some of his ancestors."[1] "The peculiarity of the province of Ulster" according to Poulett Scrope "consists simply in the fact that both landlords and tenants have thought it wiser and more for their common advantage to eschew Lynch law and maintain voluntarily in place of it that system of tenant right which preserves the peace, encourages the agriculture, and secures the full payment of the rental of the province, making it so strong a contrast to the disorganization and neglected agriculture of the south."[2] One result of this recognition was that the sums paid for tenant right were more substantial in the north than in the south.[3]

The rights which were thus recognised by custom were (1), the right of the tenant to continue in possession of the farm, until for non-payment of rent or for some other reason the landlord had a good and sufficient cause to eject him, (2), the right of the outgoing tenant to receive a sum of money from the incoming tenant on a change of tenancy, and (3), the right of the tenant, subject to the approbation of his landlord, to transfer to his assignee or to leave to his personal representatives or heir all the interest in the farm which was recognized by custom to be in him.[4]

The Ulster custom was attended with great blessings to the agriculture of the district where it prevailed. "On

[1] Hancock. *The Tenant Right of Ulster Considered Economically*. Dublin 1845.

[2] *A Plea for the Rights of Industry in Ireland* London 1848. On the tenant right of Ulster at a later date see Dufferin. *Irish Emigration* pp. 116 sq. 308 sq.

[3] *Devon Comm.* p. 291 and see Dobbs *Some Observations on the Tenant Right of Ulster* Dublin 1849.

[4] Hancock *The Tenant Right of Ulster Considered Economically*. Dublin 1845. A good account of the Ulster custom is to be found in Sigerson's *Modern Ireland* p. 92.

the estates" according to Sharman Crawford "which adopt the tenant right principle the rent charged is always considerably below the rack rent. It is calculated so as to leave the tenant his fair proportion of all profits deduced from the culture of the soil; to afford him the means of a comfortable living, and the means for the improvement and cultivation of the farm, and at the same time allowing to the landlord a fair proportion for the use of that which he supplies, namely, the land itself and that alone—as the landlord supplies nothing but the land itself in its bare unimproved state, without housing or farming appurtenances of any kind. The lands are never put up to what in the west is called cant, meaning thereby a kind of auction bidding; they are never subjected to competition; the rent is fixed from time to time by valuation, according to the custom of the estate. On these grounds I have called the connection produced between the landlord and tenant under this system, a partnership; which cannot be dissolved without an adjustment of the claims of the working partner, and under which the payments by the latter, which are termed rent, are settled on the basis of the fair consideration of mutual interests. . . . The tenant feels himself secure in the permanent occupation of the premises, and in this confidence, whether he has a lease or no lease, he proceeds with his improvements and his buildings, and applies his industry in every form by which his comforts or his profits can be increased. And hence springs that very industry which has caused the production of superior crops from bad land. But although the rent is regulated on the most moderate principles of valuation, nevertheless it is a full rent as compared with the intrinsic value of the land. The industry of the people, excited by moderate rents and security of possession, creates a value far beyond the productive power of the soil from its natural qualities. To define tenant right in the fewest possible words, it is practically a letting in perpetuity, subject to a revaluation of the rent from time to time. Thus every tenant holding under this custom may be considered as a peasant proprietor; and from hence, it appears to me, arises that same prosperity in this portion of Ireland, which is found to exist in other countries where the occupier of the soil has all those advantages which the interest of ownership creates."[1] "Anomalous as the custom is", the Devon Commission reported, "if considered with reference to all ordinary notions of property, it must be admitted that the district in which it has prevailed has thriven and improved, in comparison with other parts of the country; and although we can foresee some danger to the just rights of property from the unlimited allowance of this tenant right, yet we are sure that evils more immediate and of a still greater magnitude would result from any hasty or general disallowance of it."[2]

The best evidence of the good effect of the Ulster custom on agriculture is that of the population maintained per acre in the northern countries. We have already quoted William Blacker's remarks on this subject. The same thing was observed by Sadleir. "The farmers of Downshire, of ten acres each, are fairly dealt by, and hold directly from the proprietors; their situation consequently is this: they eat animal food; build slated houses—a great distinction in Ireland; their furniture is decent and abundant; and finally, many of them have saved very considerable sums of money. As to the labourers, they are represented to be in regular employment, and as paid in money. In the county of Down there are 367 souls to the square mile; in Galway, incontestably the most wretched and least populated part of Ireland, just one third that number. It is erroneous then to attribute the misery and distress of the country to the density of its population."[3] The connection between the Ulster custom and agricultural prosperity was well put by Sharman Crawford:- "The points

[1] *Depopulation not Necessary.* London 1849.
[2] *Devon Comm.* p. 1120.
[3] *Ireland Its Evils &c.* pp. 150-1.

I have established are the following:- 1st; that in the northern parts of the province of Ulster, the density of the population in proportion to the area is greater than it generally is in the southern and western counties of Ireland.

2nd; that there is great prosperity in these districts combined with that density and subdivision of the soil.

3rd; That in connection with these circumstances there is a security of tenure created by the tenant right custom.

4th; That in the southern and western districts great distress exists, where the density of population and subdivision of the soil are less than in the prosperous districts I have quoted.

5th; That in these districts there is no security of tenure."[1]

Thus the difference in the system of land tenure in Ulster and the other provinces produced a complete difference in the state of agriculture and the prosperity of the tenants. Lest however it should be suggested—as it sometimes is—that the prosperity of Ulster was due to the superior character of the people, it is important to be able to give an instance of the same cause producing the same effect in the south of Ireland. This brings us to the second exception with which we are endeavouring to prove the rule—the famous Ralahine experiment.

Although the hand to put this experiment into effect was that of Mr. Vandeleur, a county Clare landlord, the brain which inspired it was that of Robert Owen, who was an enthusiastic advocate of the solution of all the difficulties of Ireland by the application of his theory of cooperation. Owen held three meetings in Dublin in 1823. At the first meeting the discussion began on economics, but drifted away to religion, whereupon the meeting broke up. The two other meetings however confined themselves to a discussion of Owen's scheme for congregating the people into communistic and self-supporting

[1] *Depopulation not Necessary*, London 1849.

villages, by which means, it was contended, a vastly increased population could be maintained at a high standard of comfort. Owen urged that the scheme should be carried through by the government, a suggestion which was ignominiously flouted by the select committee of the following year. "When it is considered that Mr. Owen's plan" reported the committee "is founded upon a principle that a state of equality can be produced, and can lead to beneficial consequences, your committee consider this position so irreconcilable with the nature and interests of mankind and the experience of all ages that it is impossible to treat the scheme as being practicable."[1]

These plans of Mr. Owen so greatly impressed the imagination of Mr. Vandeleur that he endeavoured to put them into practice on a small scale on his estate. He accordingly procured the services of Mr. E. T. Craig, one of Owen's collaborators in Scotland, and these two gentlemen went down to Clare, amidst the ridicule of the other Irish landlords, to make their great experiment. Mr. Vandeleur's decision to take such a step shows him to have been a man of remarkable courage and intelligence; his own estate was one of the most disturbed in the country; his steward had recently been violently done to death; and the members of his household had hastily fled from his mansion, around which a reign of terror prevailed.

The first step was to found the nucleus of a cooperative association of the workers on Mr. Vandeleur's estate. The association was to take a lease of six hundred and eighteen acres, of which about one half were under tillage, at a fixed annual rent which was to be paid not in money but in kind. The advantage of this arrangement was that the value of the rent would not be liable to be varied from year to year by the fluctuations of the market prices of farm produce; the landlord would justly suffer by any diminution and benefit by any increase in the value of the produce of his

[1] *Report of Select Committee on Employment of Poor in Ireland* 1823.

lands. In this the arrangement resembled the *métayer* system. All the capital employed on the farm, other than the land itself, was to belong to the association; an annual payment equivalent to six per cent on its value was to be paid to Mr. Vandeleur, who had provided it; and, between the members of the association, all the stock was to be held in common, without any individual rights of ownership. The cost of living was to be reduced by the adoption of large scale domestic arrangements; refectories and dormitories were to be erected for the unmarried members of the association; and all the necessaries of life were to pass direct from the producer to the consumer, without affording a profit to any middle, or unproductive class.

No member of the society was to be in any way superior to any other. The direction of the agricultural operations of the farm was entrusted to a small committee, elected by, and composed of the workers themselves. Each evening this committee allocated certain duties to each member of the association for the following day. This arrangement worked remarkably smoothly; in the whole career of the association there was not a single instance of a member refusing to perform the work assigned to him by the committee; and the possibility of a conflict between the committee and the members at large was minimised by the practice of each member being at absolute liberty publicly to state his views on the behaviour of the committee in a suggestion book.

Although the capital of the association was held in common, each member was paid for the labour which he actually performed. Payment was made at the rate current in the district, namely, eightpence a day for men and sixpence for women, and payment was made not in money, but in labour cards, which passed current in the stores of the association. These cards could be cashed into money on demand at any time.

Whatever surplus remained after payment of the rent,

interest on capital, wages, and working expenses, was the absolute property of the association. This was the most significant feature of the society in its Irish surroundings, as it established the very principle, the denial of which constituted the fundamental injustice of the Irish land system. The association thus embodied the most advanced ideas of tenant right.

Admission to the association was by the ballot of all the members, the original ballot being conducted by all the labourers who resided on the lands of Ralahine. All those who applied for membership were admitted, and the constitution of the society when it commenced operations was as follows:-

Single men	21
Married men	7
Single women	5
Married women	7
Boys under 17	4
Girls under 17	3
Children under 9	5
Total	52

From the very beginning the career of the association was attended with success. The district changed in a few months from the most disturbed to the most peaceful in Ireland. Agrarian outrages completely ceased; and it was remarked that the most industrious and amenable members of the association were those who, the year before, had been the most conspicuous "Terry-alts" in the county. The whole attitude of the workers towards their labour was transformed. Formerly it was the aim of every labourer to get through the day with a minimum of exertion, but now all exerted themselves to the utmost, knowing that they would themselves reap the fruits of their own industry. A higher standard of living began to be adopted, and wheaten bread took the place of potatoes as the staple food of the people.

The fame of the association spread far and wide. Many

travellers and students of social questions repaired to Ralahine to witness the wonderful changes which had taken place; other Irish landlords eagerly sought to learn the secret of pacifying their tenantry without injuring their income; one enthusiast walked from London to Liverpool and from Dublin to County Clare to offer himself as a citizen of Ralahine. But what was still more important, the fame of the "new system", as it was called, began to spread among the cottiers of the adjoining districts, and many applications were made for admission to the membership of the association. Every applicant was subjected to the ballot of all the existing members, and was tested by a week's probation before election. At the end of two years the membership of the association had grown from 52 to 81, made up of 35 men, 23 women, 7 youths and 16 children. The necessity for this increased membership was caused by the fact that much unprofitable land had been reclaimed, and that the cultivation of the farm was becoming more intensive. The members showed a remarkable wisdom in their attitude towards the introduction of machinery, which they welcomed, contrary to the general practice of the time. The first reaping machine used in Ireland was at Ralahine.

Indeed there is no doubt whatever that this remarkable experiment was an unqualified success, and there is no reason to doubt that it would have continued to succeed, had it not been broken up by causes completely outside the control of the members. In 1833, the third year of the association's existence, Mr. Vandeleur fled the country to escape from the consequences of his gambling debts. Most unfortunately, the lease granted in the first instance was only for one year, but the tenants had continued in possession after the year was up, and the lease for a long term of years, which was in contemplation, was never actually executed. So long as Mr. Vandeleur managed the estate this was a matter of no importance, as he was far too interested in the experiment to think of bringing it to an end, but after his departure the tenants lost that guarantee of security. The other members of his family refused to regard the association, in the absence of a legal lease, as more than a tenant at will, and took possession of the stock and buildings on the farm. The association was thus broken up by a purely unavoidable accident, which incidentally illustrated the impossibility of effecting any permanent reform in Ireland under the existing land system. The important thing about Ralahine was not its ultimate failure, but its initial success. So long as it was dependent upon the exertions of its own members it surpassed all expectations; its breakdown was not to be attributed to any defect in its organization or its members, but was the result of an outside and independent event.

The cause of the failure of the Ralahine experiment is important as indicative of the cause of its success at first. It was nothing more or less than the absence of security of tenure. So long as the people of Ralahine were assured of the enjoyment of the fruits of their own labour, so long did they continue industrious and improving agriculturalists; in other words, so long as the Ulster custom prevailed in county Clare, the Ulster character and prosperity prevailed there also. But the moment the flourishing community became exposed to the operation of the ordinary Irish land law it collapsed. Ralahine has been frequently quoted as a triumph of communism,[1] but in our opinion it is much more correctly to be considered as a triumph of fixity of tenure. The mode in which the tenants shared the produce of the land between themselves was an interesting but irrelevant factor; the main factor was that the amount of the produce available for division increased. That produce would not have increased by an ounce if the most perfect communist colony in the world had cultivated it in the full knowledge that their improve-

[1] e. g. by Connolly, *Labour in Irish History*, p. 130.

ments would have been confiscated by an outsider at the end of the year. No doubt the superior division of labour obtainable by reason of many workers working together under central direction helped to increase the amount of the wealth produced on the land—a dangerous argument, since, if pursued to its logical conclusion, it would favour large farms and clearances—but the animating motive which made possible any increase in the volume of production arose not from communism but from fixity of tenure.[1] Another example of the benefits of fixity of tenure is that of the Palatines in County Limerick, who had been granted exceptionally favourable terms on their arrival,[2] and were still remarked as late as 1830 to be in advance of the native Irish in agriculture.[3]

We cannot overemphasize the importance of these two exceptions—the Ulster custom, and the Ralahine experiment—which we have quoted in order to prove the rule, that the backwardness of Irish agriculture was due in a great measure to insecurity of tenure and confiscation of improvements. Wherever the distribution of the produce of the land between landlord and tenant was equitable, agriculture tended to improve; wherever it was inequitable, agriculture was backward.

The evil of this unjust distribution was intensified by the fact that so many landlords resided in England, and that such a large sum was remitted abroad in rents. We shall postpone the treatment of absenteeism until a later chapter, as it was a loss which affected the nation as a whole rather than the tenantry. In many cases the estates of absentee landlords were extremely well managed, while many of the worst cases of oppression and neglect occurred on the estates of residents. The evil results of absenteeism therefore did not fall necessarily on the tenants on the

[1] The best account of Ralahine is Mr. E. T. Craig's book, which was reedited with notes by Mr. Diarmid O'Coffey in 1920.
[2] O'Brien *Economic History of Ireland in the Eighteenth Century* p
[3] Bicheno *Ireland and Its Economy* p. 101.

absentee estates, but rather on the community as a whole, and we think that the subject will be more properly treated in the chapter dealing with public burdens.

The landlord was not the only person who robbed the tenant of the fruits of his labour. In addition, the tenant was subject to heavy burdens in respect of tithes, grand jury cess, tolls in the corporate towns, and, after 1838, poor rate. These burdens, when added to the crushing rent he had to pay, conspired to impoverish the tenant, and to diminish the proportion of his produce which he retained for his own use. John Leslie Foster giving evidence before a select committee of the House of Lords in 1825 stated that the burdens complained of by the Irish tenants were (1) rent (2) tithes (3) county rates (4) parochial rates, and (5) the support of the Catholic clergy.[1] We do not however intend to deal with these burdens in the present chapter, because, although they pressed on the tenantry, they were not imposed on the tenantry alone. Tithes were payable by the owner of a fee simple farm as well as by a tenant under a lease; grand jury cess was payable by persons other than tenants; tolls in the corporate towns were payable by persons who did not rent a rood of land; and the poor rate was payable by urban as well as rural occupiers. It is more proper therefore to deal with these matters in the section devoted to public burdens than in the present chapter. We mention them here simply to remind the reader that, in calculating the proportion of his produce which the Irish tenant was allowed to retain for himself, rent is not the only payment which has to be taken into account.

To summarize the conclusions of this section: the main cause which tended to impede the cultivation of Irish land to its best advantage was the inequitable distribution of the produce between the owner and occupier; that inequality operated at the beginning and during the continuance

[1] Lewis's *Irish Disturbances* p. 75.

of the lease under the guise of too high rents, and at the end of the lease under the guise of the confiscation of the tenant's improvements. Added to these exactions of the landlord the tenant had to pay onerous sums to the county, the towns, and the Churches.

Section 2. The Failure to Reclaim the Waste Lands.

We now pass from the discussion of why the land already in cultivation was not worked to its maximum advantage to discuss why the land not already cultivated was not brought into cultivation— in other words from a discussion of why the resources of the country were not developed in quality to a discussion of why they were not developed in quantity. We need not labour the point with which we have dealt in an earlier section, that the waste lands of Ireland were capable of being reclaimed at a comparatively moderate expense, and, if reclaimed, they were capable of supporting the whole population in comfort. The question now before us is why was this not done; why was this excellent opportunity of making a remunerative investment neglected? The answer to this question is different in the case of the two classes of persons who might have been expected to make this investment—the tenants and the landlords.

The reason that the tenants did not lay out money on the reclamation of the waste land on their holdings was precisely the same as that which prevented them from improving the system of agriculture on the land actually in cultivation. The only result of reclaiming any portion of their holding would be to raise the rent on themselves, or else to tempt the landlord to eject them without compensation, to make way for some other tenant who was willing to pay an increased rent. The tenants moreover had no capital to invest in reclamation. The only chance they had of creating capital was by increasing the produce of their lands, but they were unable to save any part of such increase, as the immediate result of such improvements was the increase of their rents. It is obvious that in such a state of things they could have nothing to lay out on reclamations, which in their turn would raise the rent still more. The vicious customs of insecurity of tenure and confiscation of improvements thus wrought evil in more ways than one; they prevented the tenant from improving his cultivated land, and the neglect of such improvement rendered it impossible for him to accumulate the capital necessary for the reclamation of his wastes. "There is an absolute deficiency of capital amongst the farming classes for the profitable cultivation of their lands; and this deficiency is increased by disinclination, especially amongst the small farmers, to invest on their farms such money capital as they possess."[1] The reason therefore why the tenants did not engage on reclamation is plain; let us next see why the landlords did not do so.

In the first place, a great many of the landlords were absentees, and took no interest whatever in their estates beyond the collection of the rent. Many resident proprietors were guilty of the same inattention. This attitude was not unnatural, however culpable. Why should a landlord, who could derive a considerable and constantly increasing income from his estate without any exertion, trouble to reclaim the wastes upon it or otherwise to improve it? So long as the tenants were forced to pay exorbitant rents for utterly barren holdings, why should the landlord risk the outlay necessary for reclamation? It is true that as the result of a course of improvement his property would ultimately become much more valuable. But then the Irish landlord was notoriously improvident. Wakefield remarked that the landlords never thought it worth their while to spend a penny on drainage or other improvements,[2] and many years afterwards Poulett Scrope

[1] *Devon Comm.* p. 193. [2] Vol. i. p. 471.

drew attention to:- "the indolent reckless spendthrift and unbusinesslike habits of the proprietors of Ireland, as a class, owing to the long course of partial government and legislation by which they were encouraged to believe that their territorial rights were independent of all duties towards the persons inhabiting their estates, and would be enforced at all hazards and to the utmost extent by the overwhelming power of Britain.... Under such a system the tenants could scarcely be expected to accumulate or expend capital. The landlord never for a moment thought of such a thing"[1].

The landlords, though undoubtedly blameable to a large extent for their failure to expend capital in the improvement of their waste lands, were not wholly to blame, as they suffered under many disadvantages over which they had frequently no control. They were often frustrated in their attempts at improvement by the tenacity with which the tenants resisted any encroachment upon their prescriptive rights of grazing and turbary. A more serious and insurmountable difficulty was that many of the landlords lacked the means of raising the necessary capital. A great part of the land of Ireland was held under strict settlements, with the result that the landlord was frequently only a tenant for life or the possessor of some other limited interest. In the existing state of the law it was almost impossible for the owner of such an interest to raise money on the security of the land. "A very large proportion of property in Ireland is strictly settled. It is asserted that this mode of tenure is injurious; that the proprietor is unable to raise money for the improvement of his estate on the security of the land; and that he is unwilling to invest his capital or to burden his life interest for the sake of improving a property for an eldest son already thus amply provided for. Although the improvements, if judiciously effected, ought to repay the proprietor in a very short time; yet, as the

[1] *A Plea for the Rights of Industry in Ireland.* London 1848.

duration of his interest is uncertain, he does not willingly incur the risk."[1] One of the recommendations of the Devon Commission was that tenants for life should under certain conditions have the power of burdening the inheritance for the amount expended in effecting the improvement of the estate.[2]

Another very important obstacle in the way of improvement was the extent to which Irish land was encumbered. This not only rendered it difficult for the owner to raise capital on the security of his estate, but it also hindered the sale of the land to a solvent and improving purchaser. "At present the sale of estates, especially of encumbered estates, is frequently attended with great difficulty and expense, and is sometimes even impossible from the embarrassment of the title, caused by the existence of encumbrances and settlements. Judgments, by binding lands in the hands of purchasers, frequently cause great difficulty in the sale of estates, and the tendency of modern legislation has been to extend the lien of judgments upon lands, and thus to increase the difficulty of selling lands."[3] The attempts made by the Government to improve lands in Connacht during the famine were frequently frustrated by the hopelessly encumbered condition of the estates.[4] "The master evil of the agricultural system of Ireland" according to Trevelyan "is the law of entail, and the encumbrances which seldom fail to accumulate upon entailed estates."[5] "The land" said Poulett Scrope "is in the hands of nominal and embarrassed proprietors, who either cannot or will not themselves improve their estates, nor allow such terms of tenure as will induce others to improve them and carry on a spirited course of cultivation."[6] It was the im-

[1] *Devon Comm.* pp. 231-2.

[2] And see Pim *Observations on the Evils Resulting to Ireland from Insecurity of Title* Dublin 1847.

[3] *Devon Comm.* pp. 863-4.

[4] Tuke. *A Visit to Connaught.* London 1847.

[5] *The Irish Crisis.* p. 13.

[6] *The Irish Difficulty and How It must be Met.* Westminster & Foreign Quarterly Review Jan. 1849.

portance attached to this evil by the commissioners that led to the passing of the Encumbered Estates Act.[1]

Thus, we see that the failure of the landlords to carry out reclamation operations was not always culpable. We are not however concerned here to assign blame or praise, but simply to describe the actual situation as it was. The main fact in that situation which emerges is that, from one cause or another, avoidable or unavoidable, the waste lands of Ireland were not reclaimed, although their reclamation would have been a source of great benefit to the country. The tenants could not, and the landlords either could not or would not, invest the capital necessary for the undertaking. The only question that remains is whether there was not some other agency whose duty it was to undertake this important national work on the failure of the proprietors and tenants to do so. We reply that such an agency did exist—namely the government. The duty of the government in this respect is admirably stated in an excellent pamphlet from which we have already quoted: "The land pines for the husbandman and the husbandman sighs for the land. What hinders the espousals? Whose acres are these that lie uncultivated by millions—whose subjects are these that stand idle or lie starving with the means of plenty within reach of honest industry? The soil is owned by the landlords of Ireland; the people are subject to British government. What curse hangs over that country? Do the people live under bad laws, or under hard masters?.... The blame lies between the landlords and the government.... The last man who should throw a stone at the Irish landlord is the British minister or legislator....[2]

We shall therefore next examine how far the government helped to make up the deficiencies of the proprietors and tenants in this respect. It is our duty therefore to inquire

[1] As to the extent of the encumbered estates in Ireland see *Devon Comm.* p. 1030.

[2] *Ireland's Hour* Dublin 1850 pp. 47, 54, 68.

how far the government adopted the objectionable policy, pursued by the landlords, of righting the apparent disproportion between the population and resources of Ireland by diminishing the population, and how far they adopted the preferable policy of increasing the resources of the country.

CHAPTER VI.

Governmental Remedies.

Section 1. Directed towards Increasing Production. *(a) Improving the Quality of Agriculture.*

AS we have seen, the problem which Ireland presented in the first half of the nineteenth century was an apparent disproportion between the population and the resources of the country. In a country, the resources of which have already been exploited to the utmost, such a situation is of extreme consequence, as it indicates a condition of absolute overpopulation. So long however as a country still retains undeveloped sources of employment the overpopulation is only relative and not absolute. This, we have proved, was the case in Ireland, the misery and distress of which were caused by underproduction rather than by overpopulation. Two remedies for this distressful condition of affairs were therefore possible, namely the increase of the available resources of employment or the diminution of the number of the people. "There are but two remedies.... One is the sudden importation and diffusion of a large capital; the other the exportation of a large portion of the population."[1] The former was obviously the preferable course, as it did not entail the same amount of suffering and privation as the latter. The method by which the former course could be best pursued can be arrived at by a consideration of the causes which operated to prevent these resources from being exploited. These were, as we have seen, first the inequitable distribution

[1] *Lord Carbery's Letter to the Munster Farmers' Magazine* 20 Oct. 1818.

of the produce of the land actually in cultivation, which operated as a discouragement to the tenantry to introduce improved methods of farming; and second the failure of the owners and occupiers of land to bring into cultivation the waste and unreclaimed lands. The method by which the alternative course—of diminishing the number of people in the country—could have been best pursued was by facilitating the process of eviction. The one course was as obviously desirable as the other was objectionable. Let us see which the government pursued.

The measures taken by the government towards increasing the resources of the country can be best considered by following the same classification that we adopted in the last chapter—by considering first those directed to correct the existing inequality of distribution, and secondly those directed to encourage reclamation. Of course these two classes of measures were largely interdependent. Neither could have been wholly successful without the other. No widespread attempt at reclamation could be expected until the tenants were assured of being granted some fixity of tenure in the land they reclaimed ; and, on the other hand, legislation simply directed to providing compensation for improvements and fixity of tenure would only solve the problems of those already in possession of farms ; the landless men could only be accommodated by the encouragement of reclamation.[1]

With regard to the measures directed to the correction of injustice in the distribution of the produce of the land, we must refer in the first place to the opposition of the classical or orthodox economists to any legislation which interfered with the sacredness of private property. This was one of the inevitable consequences of the doctrine

[1] These points are made, and the whole question discussed in a host of contemporary publications, amongst the most able of which are Poulett Scrope's *Letter to Lord John Russell* London 1846, the same writer's article *The Irish Difficulty and How it must be Met*, in the Westminster and Foreign Quarterly Review Jan. 1849; Sharman Crawford's *Depopulation not Necessary* London 1849; and an anonymous pamphlet, *Ireland's Hour* published in Dublin in 1850.

of *laissez faire*, which reigned predominant in the early years of the nineteenth century. "If, by the fundamental principle of our constitution" we read in a publication of 1822 "every individual is the uncontrolled master of his own person, except when the State requires his service under an obligation common to all classes of subjects, still more is he master of his own property. A particular law against personal liberty, or a particular statute against the unqualified dominion of a proprietor over his own property would be alike an invasion of the first principles of our constitution. Under these principles the complaints of absenteeship and high rents belong to manners and not to laws ; to the native local gentry, and not to the United Parliament."[1] "Is it within the province of government" exclaimed the Chief Secretary for Ireland in the same year "to interfere between landlord and tenant? Or would it be proper that legislative enactments should prescribe to the landlord the conduct which he ought to pursue in that relation? In this respect, as in many others, our appeal must be made to the landed gentry of Ireland."[2] "The obvious source of the miseries under which this country at present labours" wrote a Protestant clergyman a few years later "is perhaps beyond the region of direct legislative interference. I allude to the system adopted in letting land. To regulate the management of private property is not the province of a wise government."[3] Thus, we may take it that during the early years of the nineteenth century the claim of the legislature to interfere with the right of a landlord "to do what he wished with his own" was not generally admitted.[4]

It is interesting to note in passing that the sacredness

[1] *The State of the Nation* London 1822.

[2] *Speech of the Rt. Hon Charles Grant in the House of Commons on 22nd April* 1822 London 1822.

[3] *A Letter to Wilmot Horton Esq., M. P. on Emigration* by the Rev. M. I. Keating, rector of Ventry, Limerick 1827.

[4] This principle did not fail to meet with numerous opponents, see, for instance, Wiggins, *The Monster Misery of Ireland*, London 1844. Generally speaking however it was unchallenged.

of private property was a doctrine of particular novelty in Ireland. It did not apparently apply in the time of Queen Elizabeth, or of Cromwell, or of William III, during whose reigns it was frequently ignored. Nor, strangely enough, did it apply, even in the nineteenth century, with the same rigidity in the case of the owners and the occupiers of land. While the rights of the former were held to be above and beyond the interference of the legislature, those of the latter were more than once altered by *ex post facto* legislation. "The law as it stands at present" said Poulett Scrope in 1848 "is the result of innumerable interferences in favour of the landlord and against the tenant. Some sixty acts of this one-sided legislation stand catalogued in the statute book. If all these were repealed, there would be something to be said for non-interference."[1] "The whole code relating to landlord and tenant in this country" said Lord Chief Justice Pennefather "was passed with a view to the interests of the landlord, and to enforce the payment of rent by the tenant. The interest of the tenant never entered into the contemplation of the legislature."[2] It is important to remember that the government entrusted with legislation for Ireland was essentially representative of the landlords; prior to 1828 no Catholic could sit in Parliament; and after 1828 the franchise was raised so as to minimize the voice of the ordinary tenantry.

In spite however of all this opposition the demand for the interference of the legislature in the relations of landlord and tenant in Ireland never wholly died out. Various select committees of the House of Commons, to which we shall more particularly refer in a later part of this chapter, reported that much of the distress of the country arose

[1] *A Plea for the Rights of Industry in Ireland* London 1848.

[2] Smyth, *Ireland Historical and Statistical* vol. ii. p. 42, and see Whitley Stokes *Observations &c.* 1821 p. 20, Sharman Crawford *Depopulation not Necessary* London 1849, p. 16. We may mention in passing that the supreme culmination of *laissez-faire* as regards Irish land was Deasy's Act of 1860. As this brings us outside our period we shall not refer to it further. See Cunningham, *Growth of English Industry and Commerce* vol. ii. pp. 848-9. Montgomery, *Land Tenures in Ireland* p. 126.

from the system of land tenure, and the obvious inference from this finding was that that system should be altered. Proposals were made in 1824 for the appointment of commissioners for each district to settle rents, with reference to current prices of agricultural produce.[1] In the following year it was proposed that a joint stock company should be founded with the object of converting the occupiers of land into fee simple tenants.[2] The great advocate of land reform was William Conner, who was prosecuted for a speech which he delivered on the subject. His suggestions were, (1), that every person having the possession of any portion of the soil as tenant at will or on lease should have a fair valuation of his land by a jury of sworn men; and that neither tithe, rent-charge, county cess, poor rate, nor any other acreable assessment, should be added to that valued rent; (2), that each tenant should have a perpetuity of his farm, the landlord having no power to turn him out, even at the expiration of his lease. This plan differed from that of Sharman Crawford, the next most important advocate of land reform, in that the latter suggested that the landlord should have the right to resume possession on the expiration of the tenancy, but only on payment of a sum in respect of the tenant's goodwill and permanent improvements.[3] It was not by Irish writers alone that land reform was demanded; it was urged by the Frenchman Gustave de Beaumont,[4] the German Von Raumer,[5] and the Englishman John Stuart Mill.[6]

The British government and parliament however, which still remained under the joint influence of the orthodox economists and the Irish landlords, were not impressed

[1] *Turnips Sheep Wool and Prosperity* by an Irish Landlord, Bristol 1824, *Hints to Irish Landlords* by a Land Agent (John Wiggins) London 1824.

[2] *Statement of Some of the Causes of Disturbances in Ireland* by a Friend. Dublin 1825.

[3] Conner *The Prosecuted Speech etc.* Dublin 1842; *Two Letters to the Editor of the Times* Dublin 1846. Mr. Conner, who was the author of many other publications on the land question was described by Mill as "the earliest, most enthusiastic, and most indefatigable apostle" of land reform, *The Irish Land Question* p. 88, and see Elliott *Letters of J. S. Mill* vol. i. p. 147. [4] *L'Irlande Sociale.* [5] *England im Jahre* 1835 vol. ii. p. 404.

[6] *The Irish Land Question* p. 88.

by these demands; commissions and committees were appointed, only to see the result of their labours committed to the waste paper basket; and any attempt to raise the matter in the House of Commons was met with hostility, tempered with indifference and ridicule. Such was the reception accorded to Poulett Scrope's motion on the reform of Irish land tenures in 1834; and a similar greeting was given to a bill introduced by Sharman Crawford in 1835 to secure the Irish tenant some compensation for his improvements and a limited degree of security of tenure. In the following year Sharman Crawford reintroduced his bill with the like result.[1]

In 1843 the famous Devon Commission was appointed. The Commission, which sat for two years, made a very full and exhaustive examination of the whole subject of Irish land tenures. The report, delivered in 1845, though it did not go so far as Gladstone afterwards went in redressing the grievances of the Irish tenant, was a comparatively progressive document in view of the date and *personnel* of the Commission. Various recommendations of minor importance were made—for instance that the stamp duties on leases should be reduced, and that the law of distress should be amended—but the most important and most revolutionary recommendation was that the right of the tenant to some compensation for his improvements should be admitted. We had better give this part of the report *verbatim*:—"Although it is certainly desirable that the fair remuneration to which a tenant is entitled for his outlay of capital, or of labour, in permanent improvements should be secured to him by voluntary agreement rather than by compulsion of law; yet, upon a review of all the evidence furnished to us upon the subject, we believe that some legislative measure will be found necessary in order to give efficacy to such agreements, as well as to provide for those cases which cannot be settled by private arrangement.

[1] Locker Lampson, *Ireland in the Nineteenth Century*, p. 257.

We earnestly hope that the legislature will be disposed to entertain a bill of this nature, and to pass it into law with as little delay as is consistent with a full discussion of its principle and details. We are convinced that in the present state of feeling in Ireland no single measure can be better calculated to allay discontent, and to promote substantial improvement throughout the country. In some cases the existence of such a law will incline the landlord to expend his own capital in making permanent improvements. In others he may be called upon, on the eviction or retirement of tenants, to provide the amount for which their claims may be established under the Act.

"We do not express these opinions, without having come to the conclusion from a careful examination of the whole subject, that a satisfactory enactment may be framed for this purpose, which should contain some such provision as the following:—

(1) A power to register with Clerk of the Peace an agreement between landlord and tenant, relative to improvements on farms by draining, or otherwise, and on farm buildings &c. with a power to the assistant barrister, to enforce same, with an appeal to judge of assize.

(2) In cases where parties do not agree, a power to tenant to serve notice on landlord of any proposed improvement in farm buildings, offices, or exterior fences, the suitableness thereof to be reported on by mutually chosen arbitrators, with power to the assistant barrister, on such report, and after examination, to decide and certify the maximum cost, not exceeding three years' rent.

(3) If tenant be ejected, or his rent raised within thirty years, the landlord to pay such a sum, not exceeuirg the maximum fixed, as work shall then be valued at.

(4) Provisions for the registration of such adjudications—Work to be completed within a limited time from date thereof—and landlord to have power to execute, charging five per cent, on outlay, not exceeding estimate stated therein."[1]

One recommendation of the commissioners bore important fruit, namely that the sale of encumbered estates should be facilitated. "As an encumbered estate must at all times be managed at great expense and at much disadvantage under the courts, we recommend that every

[1] *Devon Comm.* pp. 1124 5.

facility consistent with safety should be given for bringing such estates to an early sale, rather than allowing them to remain for years the subject of expensive litigation". This recommendation was in accord with the best economic opinion of the time. Trevelyan stated that "the master evil of the agricultural system of Ireland is the law of entail and the encumbrances which seldom fail to accumulate upon entailed estates";[1] and in 1849 Lord Clarendon wrote to Sir R. Peel: "The landlords are the real obstacle to improvement, and their condition generally is deplorable. As a body they are insolvent. Many of them lack the first necessaries of life, and, though still exercising the rights of property, they can perform none of its duties."[2] The writings of Poulett Scrope and Professor Hancock are full of complaints that the development of Irish land was retarded by the hopelessly encumbered condition of the estates. These writers did not however suggest that the transfer of encumbered estates would alone be sufficient to give an impetus to improvement; they insisted on its being accompanied by other reforms in the land system. So also, as we have seen, did the Devon Commission, whose recommendations must be read as a whole. The mistake that the government made was that they adopted one part of the report and rejected the other; they passed a measure to aid the sale of encumbered estates, but neglected to reform the Irish land system in other respects.

In 1845 a land bill, founded upon the report of the Devon Commission, was introduced by Lord Stanley in the House of Commons. It provided for the appointment of a commissioner of improvements, to whom a tenant desirous of improving his property was to apply for a decision as to whether the proposed improvements were desirable; and, if the commissioner approved of them, the tenant, on eviction within a certain period, was to be entitled to compensation. The three classes of improvement recognized

[1] *The Irish Crisis* p. 13. [2] Parker. *Sir Robert Peel* vol. iii. p. 517.

by the bill were building, fencing, and draining. The tenant who built on his farm was entitled to compensation for thirty years after the completion of the building, one thirtieth of the cost of the improvement being deducted for every year during which he enjoyed the improvement; the tenant who fenced his farm was entitled on a similar principle to compensation for twenty years; and the tenant who drained his farm for fourteen years. This bill pleased no party. The Repeal Association, speaking on behalf of the tenants, denounced it because of "the insurmountable difficulties interposed between the tenant's claim to the fruits of his industry, and the miserable, transitory instalment of that right delusively promised;"[1] and the landlords objected to the admission of the tenant's right to any compensation at all. The parliamentary opposition of the latter was so strong that Stanley withdrew the bill. A similar fate awaited a private bill introduced by Sharman Crawford in the same year.[2]

In the following year Lord Lincoln introduced a bill providing for the payment of compensation in certain cases by the landlord to the tenant for his unexhausted improvements, but the passage of this bill was interrupted by the resignation of Peel's government. In 1847 and 1848 two bills introduced by Sharman Crawford were summarily rejected; and in the latter year a bill was introduced by the Chief Secretary, Sir Wm. Somerville, but was finally dropped. In the following year the Encumbered Estates Act was passed.[3]

This act[4] set up a court for the express purpose of selling out embarrassed landlords. It entitled every creditor, except the petitioner who was forcing the sale, and even the latter, if he obtained the leave of the court, to bid for the encumbered property, and to become its owner with an absolutely indefeasible title. No provision of any kind

[1] *Report of Repeal Association and the Tenants Compensation Bill* 1845.
[2] Locker Lampson *op. cit.* p. 261. [3] Locker Lampson *op. cit.* p. 262.
[4] 12 and 13 Vict. c. 77.

was made for the allocation of any part of the purchase money to the old tenants in respect of their improvements, so that, as regards the tenants, the act operated simply to substitute one master for another. As this act was passed at the very end of the period with which we are dealing in the present book, an examination of its results would bring us outside the scope of our subject; suffice it to say that its results were as highly praised by some writers as they were deeply condemned by others.[1]

The only thing which it is necessary for us to say about the act is that it was passed purely for the benefit of the landlords, and showed no consideration for the tenants. As to effecting a more equitable distribution of the proceeds of agriculture in Ireland the act did nothing at all. We must therefore conclude this section, which has been devoted to an inquiry as to what the government did to remedy the first great cause of Irish backwardness and misery—the inequitable distribution between the owner and occupier of the soil—by stating that the government did absolutely nothing. Let us now pass to the second section of our inquiry namely, what the government did to increase the quantity of land under cultivation.

(b) *Increasing the Quantity of Agriculture.*

In considering the action of the government in the matter of the reclamation of the waste lands of Ireland, it is important to consider how far that action may have been the result of ignorance. We shall therefore in the first place inquire to what extent the process of reclamation had been recommended by the advisers of the

[1] See Cairnes, *Political Essays* p. 179; Barry O'Brien, *Fifty Years of Concessions* vol. ii pp. 150-1; Locker Lampson, *Ireland in the Nineteenth Century*, p. 263; Montgomery *Land Tenure in Ireland* p. 112, *The Encumbered Estates of Ireland*, London 1850. Pim. *A Letter to Sir John Romilly M. P.* London 1850 Hancock, *Statistics Respecting the Sale of Encumbered Estates in Ireland* Dublin 1850. John Bright clearly perceived the futility of the Encumbered Estates Act as a remedy for Irish agrarian ills. "Our territorial system" he wrote in 1849 "is one which works a wide and silent cruelty, beggaring, demoralizing and destroying multitudes". Trevelyan *Life of John Bright*, p. 164.

government, and how far it had been advocated by the economists of the time. We have already referred to the four reports delivered by the Commissioners on Bogs in the years 1810-14, in which attention was drawn to the practicability of cultivating with profit an immense area of waste land in Ireland. The proposals of the commissioners were in no sense revolutionary; they simply suggested that the government should remove the existing obstacles to improvement, principally arising from the uncertainty prevailing with regard to the boundaries of contiguous estates, and from the existence of various rights upon them, which were claimed by the neighbouring tenantry. Even these moderate and eminently reasonable proposals were neglected by the government.

The Select Committee of 1819 referred to the reports of the Commissioners on Bogs, and commented on "the small extent to which their recommendations have been acted on". This committee professed the same anxiety as the Commissioners on Bogs not unduly to interfere with the rights of the owners of property, but it nevertheless felt it a duty to indicate how the full development of the land could be aided by legislation. It recommended that, while the reclamation of bogs should be in the main left to private enterprise, a general Enclosure and Drainage Act should be passed; and that the improvement of the mountain districts should be to a large extent undertaken by the government, in connection with the development of the fisheries.[1] The report of this committee was also consigned to the waste paper basket. "It is much to be lamented" we read in 1822 "that, notwithstanding the recommendations of this committee, no legislative measure has been adopted to facilitate the reclaiming of those extensive tracts. This is the more to be regretted, as it appears in the evidence that Mr. Alexander Nimmo, one

[1] *Second Report of Select Committee on the State of Disease and the Condition of the Labouring Poor in Ireland* 1819.

of the engineers, had drawn up the heads of a bill for this purpose, and placed it in the hands of Mr. Secretary Grant nearly three years ago, and no parliamentary proceedings have taken place as yet thereupon."[1]

In 1823 another select committee urged that the measures recommended by the committee of 1819 should be introduced on the ground that no real improvement could take place in Ireland until the tranquillity of the country was restored, and that tranquillity could not be restored except by the active encouragement of industry.[2] The committee of 1830 strongly urged the same view. "When the immense importance of bringing into a productive state 5,000,000 acres now lying waste is considered, it cannot but be a subject of regret and of surprise that no greater progress in the undertaking has as yet been made. If this work can be accomplished, not only would it afford a transitory but a permanent demand for productive labour, accompanied by a corresponding rise in wages, and an improvement in the condition of the poor. Opportunities would also be afforded for the settlement of the peasantry, now superabundant in particular districts, on waste lands .... This change would be alike advantageous to the lands from whence the settlers are taken, and to those on which they may hereafter be fixed. The severe pressure of the system of clearing farms and ejecting subtenants may thus be mitigated and the general state of the peasantry improved."[3] The committee animadverted on the negligence of the government as follows:—"The following conclusions may be drawn:—(1) That in the experience of fifteen years from 1802 to 1817 a system of public works appears to have been adopted in the Highlands of Scotland which has improved the habits and excited the industry of the people, and has advanced the country one hundred years; (2) that successive parliamentary committees in the years 1819,

[1] Fraser, *Sketches and Essays on the Present State of Ireland* Dublin 1822.
[2] *Report of Select Committee on Employment of the Poor in Ireland* 1823.
[3] *Report of Select Committee on the State of the Poor* 1830. p. 45

1823 and 1829 have recommended the application of an analogous system to Ireland; (3) that public works have been carried on in Ireland since the year 1822, which, though not conducted upon any permanent or well digested system, have in all respects confirmed the recommendations of the select committees; and (4) that the effects produced by these public works appear to have been extended cultivation, improved habits of industry, a better administration of justice, the reestablishment of peace and tranquillity in the disturbed districts, a domestic colonization of a population in excess in certain districts, the diminution of illicit distillation, and a very considerable increase to the revenue."[1]

The report of the Select Committee of 1835—possibly the most important of all authorities on the subject—draws attention to the undoubted benefits which would result from the adoption of a system of improvements, and proceeds to make the following concrete recommendations:

"1. That the Board of Public Works in Ireland have power to undertake, on the requisition of the proprietors of two thirds of the property to be improved, drainage of bogs, embankments, and the removal of obstacles in rivers which cause inundation.

2. Juries to be formed for valuing well sites and fish weirs, and also to ascertain the increased value of lands drained, freed from inundations, or otherwise improved, and apportion the outlay to the several proprietors, according to the benefit derived to each estate or interest.

3. The outlay apportioned to be a charge upon the estate or interest benefited.

4. The Board of Works to be compensated in money or a sufficient portion of the waste lands improved, and powers to be given for that purpose, and also either to sell or mortgage a sufficient portion of the whole estate, any portion of which shall be benefited.

[1] *Ibidem* p. 40.

5. Tenants for life to have power to charge the inheritance with an outlay, to the amount of three years value, under the direction of the Board of Works, for the drainage, embankment, or other permanent improvement, save buildings; the Board in the first instance to make a report in which the feasibility of the improvement, when projected shall be certified . . . .

6. Tenants for life paying any portion of the outlay with their own moneys, or out of the rents and profits, to be entitled to the charge of that amount on the inheritance, but to be bound to keep down the interest of such charge.

7. When lands are mortgaged the wastes to be valued, and the encumbrances to have operation on such portions as liens to the amount only of the value ascertained anterior to the improvement, that is, if the wastes prove worth £200, the mortgagor to have a lien on them only to that amount, and the enhanced value to be susceptible for new encumbrance for the purpose of improvement.

8. Mortgaged lands, when the rent to be received in respect of which will not exceed 2/6 an acre, to be let by the proprietor under the approval of two arbitrators.

9. Enlarged powers of leasing to be given to the Board of Trinity College, Dublin, and the Board of Commissioners of the schools founded in Ireland by Erasmus Smith.

10. Reclaimed wastes which shall be conveyed to the Board of Works, to be sold in small lots of not less than ten acres or more than 200 acres statute measure."[1]

The Poor Inquiry Commission, to which we shall hereafter more particularly refer, recommended the appointment of a Board of Improvement, with wide powers for the drainage and reclamation of uncultivated and partially cultivated lands. They recommended that the functions of this new board and of the existing Board of Public Works

[1] *Second Report of Select Committee on Amount of Advances made by the Commissioners of Public Works in Ireland.* 1835.

should be to some extent combined, and that the obstacles in the way of improvement of waste lands by their proprietors should be removed.[1] The same recommendations were reiterated in the reports of Drummond's Railway Commission. "We humbly represent the necessity of affording peculiar encouragement to the promotion of public works in Ireland . . . It would appear just and reasonable, whether regarded as a question of policy or of duty, that every possible aid and facility should be extended to public undertakings, the utility of which has been clearly established."[2] The commissioners repeated this view in their final report:—"The policy of rendering such assistance is unquestionable. It is acknowledged to be necessary towards a colony, and must be considered more so in the case of part of the United Kingdom, when neither the land nor the population can continue to be useless without being hurtful at the same time."[3]

The Devon Commission also insisted on the vital necessity of reclaiming the waste lands. "Without going the length of supposing that employment for the people upon bringing such lands into a profitable cultivation is to furnish a cure for the evils of Ireland, we concur in the opinion, so strongly expressed in former reports, that very great advantages may be expected to result from judicious arrangements for that purpose . . . . It may be worthy of serious consideration whether the State might not very usefully make for these purposes, at a moderate rate of interest, some advances regulated within such limits as parliament may prescribe for the amount which companies or individuals may advance in aid of such operations. The funds which could be so required would not probably be large in any one year, and yet a great public benefit would be attained in increased employment for labour, in the progressive extension of productive land, and in the opportunity

[1] *Third Report of the Poor Inquiry Commission* 1835.
[2] *First Report of Railway Commissioners* 1837.
[3] *Second Report of Railway Commissioners* 1837 p. 85.

thereby afforded for the location of industrious families who may have been from unavoidable circumstances compelled to quit their former holdings."[1]

We postpone for a moment the consideration of how far the government acted on these recommendations; all we wish to point out here is, that the reclamation of waste lands was indicated over and over again as a proper subject for government action by royal commissions and parliamentary committees. We now pass to a consideration of how far the same course of action was recommended by the acknowledged agricultural experts of the period. An examination of the works of those who devoted the greatest attention to Irish agricultural affairs shows us that it was their unanimous opinion that the reclamation of waste lands was a project which should be encouraged by the government in every possible way. A citation of all the extracts from contemporary writings on this subject would fill a large volume. We must therefore confine ourselves here to the quotation of a few typical examples. Lord Blessington in 1822 strongly urged the adoption of some measure of improvement by the government: "In short, make gradually all those improvements which individual wealth creates in England, but which can at present only be done in Ireland by parliamentary aid."[2] "Relief by emigration should not be attempted" wrote the able pamphleteer "Hibernicus" "while there is one improvable acre of land found uncultivated. The sum allowed in the last session of parliament for the emigration of a single family— £100—would make three or four very comfortable at home". An invidious comparison was drawn by the same writer between the treatment accorded by the legislature to Scotland and Ireland: "The condition of the two countries is so analogous, both in their wants and in their resources, that much useful information must be obtained by reference

[1] *Devon Comm.* pp. 1143—4.

[2] *Observations on the State of Ireland* London 1822.

to the system of improvement adopted in either. I apprehend that the material distinction will be found to consist in that systematic gradual improvement which was provided for Scotland, and which appears much more rational than those occasional irregular ebullitions which are exhibited in Ireland. In Scotland the public works are conducted under a responsible parliamentary board, whose attention is continually directed to the object. In Ireland we have no such advantage."[1] In the following year the need for government interference was emphasized by an Irish landlord:—"The extensive plans of public improvement which it is said the landlord ought to devise and carry into effect are not to be accomplished except by the assistance of government."[2]

Even John Ramsay McCulloch, the arch-evangelist of *laissez faire*, admitted that some legislative action was called for in this matter. When asked before the Select Committee of 1824-5, "Are you of opinion that it is possible for the efforts of individual landlords to do anything considerable towards overcoming this difficulty?" he replied:—"No; unless the landlords were all to cooperate, or a very considerable proportion of them to cooperate, I should think that the isolated efforts of individuals would have very little power to increase the ratio of capital to population."[3] "Here it is" exclaimed Mr. Lambert, the eminent agriculturalist, a few years later "that I would throw out a hint to the *able* advocates for emigration on the other side of the water, who must lose sight of the vast tracts of unreclaimed land in Ireland .... Let the encouragement recommended be applied at home, and let Pat be encouraged to emigrate some five or perhaps twenty miles to his unreclaimed native hills and moors .... We are not unmindful that we must be content to learn from and follow our neighbours at an humble distance in the way of improve-

[1] *Practical Views and Suggestions* by Hibernicus, Dublin 1823.
[2] *Turnips, Sheep, Wool, and Prosperity*, by an Irish Landlord, Bristol 1824.
[3] p. 811.

ments; but as one good practical experiment would be worth one hundred theoretical speculations for benefiting us, why do not some of those politicians propose to cultivate and drain our waste lands?"[1] "I would propose" said Mr. Wm. Blacker, possibly the most reliable authority on Irish agriculture in the first half of the nineteenth century, "that the state should assume the right of taking to itself those tracts of reclaimable land which the owners continue to let remain uncultivated ; and after giving fair compensation, should make a practical experiment whether they could not be colonized to advantage."[2] An admirable scheme was devised by Lord Cloncurry, the least selfish and most far-seeing of the Irish landlords of the time, wherein he proposed that commissioners should be appointed to carry into effect a wide course of improvement, under which loans should be advanced for the erection of farm buildings and other public works, including the drainage of waste lands. Lord Cloncurry, who in this, as in other matters, was considerably in advance of his time, founded his suggestions upon two incontrovertible assumptions—that those unable to work were entitled to public support, and that those able to work were entitled to employment.[3]

The Repeal Association strongly approved of reclamation, but despaired of any step being taken in that direction by the United Parliament. "The construction of public works, and the drainage and reclamation of waste lands are most useful propositions; but what hope is there of any such extensive undertakings being entered upon under the auspices of the British Parliament? Experience shows there is none."[4] Even Martin, the pro-Union pamphleteer, advocated the energetic pursuit of works of this kind. "We ought not" he remarks "to be behind the Chinese in this

[1] *Observations on the Rural Affairs of Ireland* Dublin 1829.
[2] *Essay on the Management of Landed Property in Ireland* Dublin 1834.
[3] *The Design of a Law for Promoting the Pacification of Ireland* Dublin 1834.
[4] *Report of the Loyal National Repeal Association on the Woollen Cotton and Silk Manufactures* Dublin 1840.

work of civilization."[1] Possibly the most able advocate of government measures for the drainage of the Irish bogs was the Englishman, Mr. Poulett Scrope. "On the one hand" he observes "hundreds of thousands of the people of Ireland are asking for food in return for their labour. On the other hand millions of Irish acres only require labour to produce food. Can there be question that the first and most urgent of all measures demanding the attention of the government and legislature must be one to apply the unemployed labour to the unemployed land?"[2]

The government did not therefore suffer under the disadvantage of insufficient advice on this important matter; the voice of many important observers was joined to that of its own commissions and committees in the demand for legislation dealing with the waste lands of Ireland. Let us now investigate how far these urgent recommendations were heeded.

Before giving an account of the actual measures undertaken by the government, we may state generally that the legislation introduced fell very far short of that recommended by the government's own committees of inquiry. Between 1800 and 1833 no less than 114 commissions and 60 select committees had investigated the state of Ireland, but, in spite of all this inquiry, very little was done in the way of actual remedial measures.[3] The literature of the time is full of bitter complaints of the government's inaction, "A large sum was granted many years since" we read in 1827 "to ascertain the capability and expense of draining the bogs of Ireland, and experienced men were appointed for this undertaking. The measure was feasible enough,

[1] *Letters to Lord John Russell on the Further Measures Required*, London 1847, and see *A Plea for the Rights of Industry in Ireland*, London 1848, by the same writer, and an article by him in the *Westminster and Foreign Quarterly Review* of January 1849,and see Beaumont *l'Irlande Sociale*, vol. ii. p. 805, Kennedy, *Instruct, Employ, Don't Hang Them*, London 1835, and Sharman Crawford *Depopulation not Necessary* London 1849. Muggeridge *Notes on the Irish Difficulty*, London 1849, Butt, *The Famine in the Land* p. 52.

[2] Wiggins *The Monster Misery of Ireland* London 1844.

[3] *Ireland Before and After the Union* p. 88.

yet to this day nothing further has been effected."[1] "The neglect of Ireland in the Imperial Parliament amounts to a violation of the constitutional trusts delegated by the nations. Year after year from 1800 the sufferings of Ireland were made known, and remedies were devised, but never adopted."[2] "Assuredly no one can complain" John Pitt Kennedy remarked some years later "that a sufficient portion of time has not been devoted to the consideration of Irish affairs ; but has it been devoted to the right points, in the right spirit, has it produced beneficial results? Many people quote the long list of parliamentary committees that have sat during the last twenty years upon Irish affairs, as a proof that the British Government has done all that was required upon the subject, without however stating how far the evidence produced before those committees and the reports drawn up from that evidence have been acted upon, and how grossly they have been neglected."[3]

The government not only did not itself attempt to carry into effect the proposals of the committees, but it put obstacles in the way of private individuals doing so. In 1824 a large number of Dublin capitalists proposed the formation of a joint stock company to drain the waste lands. Legislative sanction was required for this undertaking; but it was refused on the ground that the government was itself about to introduce a bill for the purpose. Of course no such bill was introduced, but the government had succeeded in stopping the private project. It is remarkable that the same parliament extended its legislative sanction to schemes for the drainage of Canada and Australia.[4]

The recommendations of the early committees were

[1] Burroughs, *Essays on Practical Husbandry* Dublin 1827.

[2] *Commentaries on National Policy and on Ireland* Dublin 1831.

[3] *Instruct, Employ, Don't Hang Them.* London 1835.

[4] *A Letter from Lord Cloncurry to Lord Downshire* Dublin 1826, Staunton *Hints for Hardinge* Dublin 1830. *Sketch of the Proceedings of the Society for the Improvement of Ireland* Dublin 1828. The formation of a similar joint stock company was suggested in 1834. *A Plan for the Improvement of Ireland* London 1834.

reiterated with great emphasis by the Poor Inquiry Commission and the Railway Commissioners. But the same fate awaited these reports. An arterial drainage bill, to which we shall presently refer, was passed in 1842, but it was still the general opinion that the government was not serious in its intentions to reclaim the waste lands. "Another large measure," complained Nassau Senior "that for partitioning and improving the waste lands of Ireland, has not been acted on, though it cannot be said to have been totally neglected. As is too often the case in Irish matters, it has been talked about, admitted to be useful, and dropped."[1] "The true history of the bogs" we read in one of the Repeal Prize Essays "is that, though there were surveys and reports which cost £21,556, the whole work has been almost useless to the present hour, through the neglect of parliament and the executive government."[2] The later history of the government's neglect to press on measures for reclamation falls more naturally into the section dealing with the famine. It is sufficient to state here that when the distress was at its height Lord John Russell admitted publicly that measures for this purpose were necessary, but no such measure was actually introduced.[3]

Let us now pass to a consideration of the steps actually taken by the government for the reclamation of waste lands. This subject is complicated by the fact that the legislation dealing with it formed part of the general code of legislation dealing with public works, and it is difficult to deal with one without dealing with the other. The different items of the expenditure on public works are more properly to be considered in connection with the particular subjects to which they relate; and we shall therefore postpone our consideration of

[1] *Ireland, Journals &c.* vol. i. p. 160.
[2] *Second Repeal Prize Essay* p. 89 and see Lord Shrewsbury, *Hints towards the Pacification of Ireland* London 1844.
[3] O'Rourke *Great Irish Famine* p. 323, and see Poulett Scrope, *Extracts of Evidence on the Waste Lands Reclamation.* London 1847, Smyth, *Ireland Historical and Statistical* vol. ii. p. 452.

the public money devoted to the erection of piers and harbours until we come to deal with the subject of fisheries, of that devoted to canals until we discuss inland navigation, and so on. All that we are concerned with here is the public aid which was granted to the reclamation and draining of waste land. Of course we do not deny that the opening up of new methods of communication was an important contribution to increasing the productive powers of the country. We fear however that to deal with such matters in the present section would obscure the issue before us, namely how far the government assisted *directly* in the increase of Irish resources by the method which had been recommended by so many high authorities.

The United Parliament, following the example of the Irish Parliament, never ceased to allocate a certain amount of public money, either by way of grant or loan, to the development of the resources of the country. The method of management of these grants was wasteful in the extreme and was strongly commented on by many governmental inquiries. "During a period of twelve sessions" observed the select committee of 1830 "there have been repeated admissions made by parliamentary authorities that the present system of carrying on public works in Ireland has been open to serious objections, and in 1819, 1822, 1823 and 1829, specific recommendations were given, all concurring with respect to the remedy that could be relied on. And yet, whilst the evil is recognised and undeniable, both the law and the practice have been allowed to continue without alteration or amendment."[1] We need not delay however to consider these early measures for the promotion of public works in Ireland, as none of them dealt with the reclamation of waste land, the particular subject of the present inquiry.

The first measure introduced in parliament for the

[1] *Report of Select Committee on the State of the Poor* 1830 pp. 35—37.

further encouragement of the process of reclamation was that proposed in 1824. In that year a bill to encourage Irish drainage was laid on the table of the House of Commons, but no further step was taken in regard to it.[1] In 1829 a further attempt was made to pass a measure, authorizing every person possessed of a portion of bog or waste land to raise money for its improvement; but, although this bill passed the House of Commons, it was held up in the House of Lords, and was allowed to lapse.[2] Two years later an act was passed constituting the Board of Public Works in pursuance of the recommendations of the Spring-Rice Committee.[3] While this act[4] dealt more particularly with the advance of money for the construction of piers, harbours, roads and other public works in the strict sense of the term, it contained provision for the advance of money to landowners for the reclamation of their wastes. One section (s.32) provided that advances by way of loan might be made upon the security of freehold or leasehold interests in land, for the draining, embanking, reclaiming, or otherwise improving land; but it was required that money so advanced should be repaid within three years after the work was completed, with interest at five per cent. The act further provided that none but a full owner could obtain a grant for the purpose of improvement. Provision was made for making advances to life tenants and other holders of limited interests for building roads and bridges, but not for reclaiming waste land. (s. 66).

Both the rate of interest and the terms of repayment laid down by this act were unduly onerous. The result was that but a negligibly small number of the landowners of Ireland availed themselves of its provisions. The Select Committee of 1835 reported that, of a total

[1] *Sketch of the Proceedings of the Society for the Improvement of Ireland* Dublin 1828.

[2] Barry O'Brien, *Fifty Years of Concessions* vol. ii. p. 36. Locker Lampson, *Ireland in the Nineteenth Century* p. 256.

[3] *Report of Select Committee on State of Poor in Ireland* 1830 p. 40.

[4] 1 and 2 Wm. IV. c. 33.

amount of £497,170 advanced under the Act, only £2,200 had been advanced for the purpose of reclamation and drainage.[1] This committee made many important suggestions as to how the law could be improved, the principal being that the repayment of loans should be spread over a period of fifteen years. These recommendations however were not acted on, and the act continued to remain practically inoperative as far as grants for the improvement of waste lands were concerned. In the whole period of fourteen years during which the act continued in force we can find only two instances of advances being made under it for this purpose, one of £200 to a Mr. O'Gowan of Tipperary in 1832, and the other of £2000 to Lord Bessborough in the same year.[2] Thus the total sum lent by the government for this all-important purpose before 1845 amounted to the miserable total of £2,200. "This part of the act," the Devon Commissioners reported "which was evidently intended to promote agricultural improvement, has totally failed of its purpose."[3]

The Devon Commissioners devoted much attention to the possibility of increasing the resources of Ireland by means of the advance of public money, and reported on the subject as follows:—"Two important principles have been recognized by the legislature with respect to advances of money for the improvement of Ireland, (1st) that it is desirable and proper to give assistance by way of loan towards the agricultural improvement of that country.. and (2nd) that in cases in which the property of individuals is to derive a permanent benefit from the execution of such works, it is just and proper to give power to persons having limited interests or being under legal disability to charge such property with the repayment of money advanced in aid of such improvements.

[1] *First Report of Select Committee on the Amount of Advances made by the Commission of Public Works in Ireland* 1835.
[2] *Thirteenth Report of the Commissioners of Public Works* 1845 p. 9.
[3] *Devon Comm.* p. 1147.

"We believe that the soundness of the view thus taken by the legislature will be admitted by all those acquainted with the actual state of Ireland, and who are enabled therefore to appreciate the very great importance to the public interest of the improvement of that country, and the employment of her people; and we believe also that the advance of money from the public treasury in aid of these objects under proper guards and restrictions is consistent with the truest economy . . .

"It appears to us that the two provisions of the Public Works Act to which we have particularly referred require amendment, so as to make them more extensively useful, and in order to carry out the apparent intention of the legislature.

"We think that the advances authorized in aid of agricultural improvements ought to be made upon the same terms which are prescribed by the act in other cases of advances by way of loan, as to the rate of interest and the time and manner of repayment.

"We recommend also that the provision of Section 66 (relating to advances to limited owners) should be extended, so as to be applicable to all cases of advances by way of loan under the act."[1]

The recommendations of the Devon Commission were adopted by the legislature. A couple of acts were passed in 1846 increasing the provision of money for the purposes of agricultural improvement;[2] and the whole law on the subject was consolidated by a comprehensive statute in 1847.[3] By this act the treasury was authorized to advance £1,500,000 by way of loan to the proprietors of estates for the improvement and reclamation of their lands. Full provision was made for the making of advances to tenants-for-life and other holders of limited interests, and it was provided that the repayment of the sums thus advanced

[1] *Devon Comm.* pp. 1149-50.
[2] 9 and 10 Vict. cc. 1 and 101.
[3] 10 and 11 Vict. c. 32.

should be made by twenty-two annual payments at the rate of 6 per cent. The purposes included under the term agricultural improvement were enumerated as follows:—

1. The drainage of lands by any means which might be approved by the commissioners.

2. The subsoiling, trenching, or otherwise deepening and improving the soil of lands.

3. The irrigation or warping of lands.

4. The embankment of lands from the sea or tidal waters or rivers.

5. The enclosing or fencing, or improving the fences, drains, streams, or watercourses of land.

6. The reclamation of waste or other land.

7. The making of farm roads.

8. The clearing land of rocks or stones.

To these purposes the construction of farm buildings was added in 1849.[1]

This legislation was a great advance on any that had preceded it, and it was availed of to a very large extent by the landed proprietors. Before the end of 1849 the total sum applied for was £3,501,776, of which £1,617,529, was sanctioned, and £788,238 actually advanced. The number of acres drained amounted to 73,660, and the average number of labourers employed was 20,000.[2] "It is very gratifying to note" observe the Census Commissioners of 1851 "the progress made in the conversion of waste into arable land, more especially in some of the mountainous districts of the country. Thus in 1841, Donegal, Kerry, Mayo, Galway and Wicklow had the largest proportion of uncultivated land to the entire area of each; in 1851 the proportion though still high was considerably reduced."[3] It is doubtful however if the legislation went far enough. It must be remembered that it was passed at a time of

[1] 10 and 11 Vict. c. 32, 12 Vict. c. 23; 12 and 13 Vict. c. 59, Trevelyan, *Irish Crisis* pp. 82-3; *Ireland's Hour*, Dublin 1850 p. 6.

[2] *Thom's Directory* 1851 p. 224.

[3] *Census of Ireland* 1851 p. xi.

unexampled misery and unemployment, and that, w id as it was, it did not prevent the starvation of thousands during the famine, nor did it, to any appreciable extent, stem the growing tide of emigration. This is a matter which will be more properly dealt with in our section on the famine. It is sufficient here to note that the legislation was very severely criticized at the time on the ground that it did not make the reclamation of waste lands compulsory, and that the landlords were inclined to neglect their duty in the matter. "Millions of acres were in a wretched half barren condition for want of being drained; the money for the purpose, already granted by parliament, was in the coffers of the Board of Works, and more would have been supplied; the return for the outlay would have been quick and remunerative; but the money remained unused and sterile; the land was not drained, and the people in myriads died of hunger."[1] We are not called upon to discuss the relative merits of public and private enterprise; nor how far the government was well advised in leaving the process of reclamation to the initiative of the landlords, rather than of undertaking it itself.[2] What we are concerned with is the behaviour of the government in the matter throughout the whole period under review. Let us assume therefore that the legislation of 1846-7 was wise and beneficial. Even on this assumption, there is no getting away from the conclusion that it came too late; that the dramatic natural solution of the apparent discrepancy between Irish population and resources was already upon the country; and that it was impossible at the eleventh hour to stem the tide which might easily have been stemmed at the first. Let us give the government full credit for the benevolent intentions and practical utility of its measures for the reclamation of waste land in 1846-7; let us nevertheless not be blinded to the fact that the damage was already

[1] O'Rourke *Great Irish Famine* p. 187.
[2] This is admirably discussed in Trevelyan, *Irish Crisis* pp. 84 sq.

irreparable, and that whatever praise must be conceded for that belated measure of justice is more than outweighed by the censure which must attach to the previous forty-five years of neglect and indifference.

In considering the efforts of the legislature to increase the quantity of profitable land under cultivation we must not leave out of account the Arterial Drainage Act of 1842,[1] which aimed at the reclamation of whole districts rather than of particular estates. The idea underlying this act was admirable, but it was so badly drawn as to remain to a large extent inoperative. Many districts were surveyed under the provisions of the act, but nothing further was done, and the operation of the act was brought to a standstill by the famine.[2] "The drainage bill" complained Poulett Scrope "was so cautiously drawn as to exclude the owners of entailed estates—that is the great bulk of the proprietors, and that portion of them especially whose land is in most need of improvement—from the power of taking advantage of it. The terms likewise on which loans were proposed to such landlords as were in a position to borrow money under the act were so little attractive, that of a sum of £1,000,000 only £ 170,000 had been applied for up to the 1st Jan. 1847."[3] A parliamentary return of 1849 recites a depressing litany of drainage works, "not commenced", "not followed up", and "suspended for want of funds."[4] The Arterial Drainage Act must be pronounced to have been an undoubted failure.

It would appear therefore that the measures taken by the government to deal with the pressing causes of Irish distress were half-hearted and quite inadequate. Neither was there any legislation passed to correct the abuses of distribution that characterized the existing land system,

[1] 5 and 6 Vict. c. 89.
[2] *The Times* 28th Oct. 1849.
[3] *The Irish Relief Measures* London 1848 p. 15 and see Kinahan and McHenry, *A Handy Book on the Reclamation of Waste Lands* p. xii, and Blackwood's Magazine Dec. 1848.
[4] P. P. No. 174 of 1849.

nor was any serious attempt made to increase the area of land under cultivation. Thus the government failed to pursue the first of the alternative means of providing for the population of the country from its resources—namely the increase of the latter; let us now see how far it pursued the other alternative, namely the reduction of the former.

Section 2. Directed Towards Decreasing the Population.

(a) The Ejectment Acts.

We now pass from the consideration of the measures passed by the government to increase the productivity of the country to the consideration of those designed to decrease the population. We propose to call attention to six distinct measures or groups of measures which, we suggest, were passed with no other object than to aid the landlords in their policy of consolidation, ejectment, and depopulation.

The first of such legislative aids to eviction were the Ejectment Acts. It is significant that the first of these acts for facilitating the recovery of possession of land by landlords was passed in the year following the peace, when the fall in prices, which, as we have seen, was one of the early causes of consolidation, first began to make itself felt. This act enabled a landlord to evict an obnoxious tenant in two months at a cost of two pounds, whereas a similar process by an English landlord would take at least twelve months and cost eighteen pounds. The act further empowered the landlords in Ireland to distrain the growing crops of their tenants, to keep them until they were ripe, and to save and sell them when ripe, charging upon the tenant the accumulation of expense. This act was amended in the direction of still further augmenting the landlords' powers in 1818 and 1820.[1] The power of distraint was pregnant with great evil to the tenants, whose beasts were frequently destroyed through confinement in

[1] 56 Geo. III c. 88, 58 Geo. III c. 39, I Geo. IV. c. 87. A good account of the Irish law of ejectment and distraint is to be found in the evidence of Serjeant Howley before the Devon Comm. p. 853.

one of the evilly constructed pounds of the country towns. "I never saw a pound in Ireland, the floor of which was made of flagging or pavement or kept clean; and but very few, certainly not half a dozen in my life, the walls of which were sufficiently raised to provide shelter for the shivering animals.... It happens not only generally but almost universally, that the cattle are much injured, often depreciated a third or more in value, whereby the poor peasant is made a serious sufferer."[1]

Dr. Sigerson suggests that these acts were secured by the landlords in anticipation of the granting of Catholic emancipation, when it might become desirable to clear their estates of refractory voters. "It seems probable that the act for facilitating evictions was obtained partly as a prudential political measure, for although it preceded the concession of the Catholic Relief Act it did not precede the agitation for it. Two years before the peace, a Catholic relief bill was lost by only four votes; the year after the peace, when the ejectment act was passed, a Catholic relief bill was rejected by a majority of 202."[2]

This one-sided legislation was the instrument of much possible injustice. Daniel O'Connell pronounced the power of distraining growing crops as "the fruitful source of murder and outrage,"[3] and stated before the Select Committee of 1824-5 that the power was responsible for some of the worst agrarian outrages of the south.[4] "In legislating upon this subject" O'Connell told the House of Commons, "two evils have been inflicted on Ireland. The first was by the act which then for the first time enabled landlords to distrain the growing crops of their tenants, and the second by that which afforded to the landlord a cheap and expeditious mode of ejecting his tenant. These two measures I may truly describe as measures by which a landlord can

[1] *Practical Views and Suggestions* by Hibernicus Dublin 1823.
[2] *Irish Land Tenures* p. 174.
[3] *Collected Speeches* vol. ii. pp. 201-2.
[4] *Select Committee on State of Ireland* Ev. of D. O'Connell.

first ruin a tenant, and then turn him out without expense."[1] The acts were the subject not only of political but of judicial comment. Chief Justice Pennefather went so far as to say that they constituted a code of law made solely for the benefit of the landlord and against the interest of the tenant, and that it was upon this principle that they must be administered and interpreted;[2] and Judge Blackburn described the remedies of the Irish landlord as "the most powerful that the law can create."[3]

The Devon Commission took into consideration the Ejectment Acts. "The civil bill jurisdiction in ejectment is denounced by several witnesses as injurious to the tenant from the increased facilities of recovering possession given by it to the proprietors. They assert that the cheapness of the remedy in many cases causes the proprietor to eject tenants against whom he would much less readily have commenced proceedings in the superior courts, and that the notice of trial is insufficient."[4] The commissioners refused however to recommend any radical change in the law although they suggested several amendments, on the ground that it had proved beneficial to the tenants on account of the power of pleading equitable defences. Yet it is difficult to say how far the equitable defence provision was of real value to the tenants; Daniel O'Connell thought it practically valueless on account of the great difficulty found in sustaining it.[5] Moreover, if the landlord carried the suit by way of appeal to the superior courts, the equitable defence was disregarded, unless the tenant was in a position to launch a bill in chancery. The commissioners recommended that the power of distraining growing crops should be altogether abolished.[6]

[1] *Speech of Daniel O'Connell in the House of Commons on the 11th November* 1830. London 1830.
[2] Locker Lampson. *Ireland in the Nineteenth Century* p. 255.
[3] *Parl. Pap.* vol. VII of 1825 p. 36.
[4] *Devon Comm.* p. 828.
[5] *Devon Comm.* p. 835.
[6] *Devon Comm.* p. 1132.

(b) *The Subletting Act.*

The legislative prohibition of subletting was strongly urged by John Ramsay McCulloch as the sovereign specific for the too rapid increase of population in Ireland.[1] In the year following the report of this committee the famous Subletting Act was passed. This act provided that after June 1826 no assignment or sublease was to be valid unless the landlord became a party to the instrument, if in writing; or, if not in writing, gave his written consent; and it was made unlawful for the lessee to devise by will to more than one person.[2] The effect of this act was to insert in every lease a stringent non-alienation clause. No doubt the motive of fear of a hostile electorate appearing after the grant of Catholic emancipation, which as we have seen, was active on the passing of the Ejectment Act, was also present on this occasion. "As the Subletting Act was not enacted until the undertenants became the political opponents of the chief tenants and the proprietors, the opprobrium of a sinister political design has been attached to it. The law has already been used as an instrument of vengeance, and the poor families who were despoiled under it have been dispersed and their doom is irrevocable."[3]

The Subletting Act was productive of much suffering. The pressure of eviction became much more intense than before, and the suffering resulting from it was intensified because the tenants could not get other lands, as the landlords refused to take poor people as tenants, and it was impossible to obtain land as under-tenant to another on account of the act.[4] The act was repealed in 1832, save as to prior leases and agreements.[5]

[1] *Select Committee on State of Ireland* 1825 p. 819.
[2] 7 Geo. IV. c. 29.
[3] *Commentaries on National Policy and on Ireland* Dublin 1831.
[4] *Letters to a Friend in England on the Actual State of Ireland.* London 1828 ; *Speech of Daniel O'Connell in the House of Commons on 11th Nov.* 1830, *Report of Select Committee on State of Poor in Ireland* 1830 p. 8. Lewis, *Irish Disturbances* pp. 77-84.
[5] 2 Wm. IV c. 17.

(c) *The Raising of the Franchise.*

The process of clearing the estates could never have been carried to its ultimate conclusion so long as the small tenants continued to be of political value. The supposed superiority of large over small farms was more than counterbalanced by the value of an army of freeholders. "Having encouraged tillage before the war" said Dr. Sigerson "they now fancied that pasture would pay better; and their next step was to take means to rid themselves of those of the tenant-tillers who might cumber soil fit for pasturage. No time was lost. The following year saw the first act passed for making evictions more easy. The tenants however had one thing still in their power; they were voters."[1] As long as the tenants continued to exercise their votes agreeably to the landlord's wishes, this advantage was suffered to continue, but, when they showed their determination to use the vote as they themselves wished, it was immediately decided that their franchise must be abolished. "The forty shilling freeholders" according to Lord Anglesea "were first created for electioneering purposes. As long as they allowed themselves to be driven to the hustings like sheep to the shambles, without a will of their own, all was well; not a murmur was heard. But the moment these poor people found out the value of their tenure, the moment they exercised their power constitutionally, that moment they were swept out of political existence."[2]

There can be no doubt that the disfranchisement of the forty shilling freeholders had an important effect in helping on the process of clearing the land. "It is a mistake to imagine that these clearances of estates have originated with the Subletting Act, or with the statute that raised the franchise. On the contrary they existed more than ten years before those measures had been adopted; but

[1] *Modern Ireland* p. 84, and see *Irish Land Tenures* p. 139.
[2] Walpole, *History of England* vol. ii. p. 519.

it is undoubtedly true that both statutes have given motives or afforded facilities for pursuing a course previously adopted on the grounds of private enterprise."[1] "It was not until the forty shilling freeholders were abolished" says Mr. Barry O'Brien "that the landlords became very actively alive to the evils of subdivision, and applied themselves to the promotion on a large scale of the system of clearances and consolidation."[2] "It is curious" we read in a pamphlet of 1843 "that after the abolition of the forty shilling franchise, many of those who had encouraged or compelled their tenants to divide their farms, and who had risen to rank, as well as in many cases to power, through their support, were the most indefatigable supporters both in theory and in practice of the clearance system."[3] "The act of 1829" reported the Devon Commission "destroyed the political value of the forty shilling freeholders, and, to relieve his property from the burden which this chain, of circumstances brought upon it, the landlord adopted, in too many instances, what has been called the clearance system."[4]

(*d*) *The Poor Law.*

Although there was, previous to 1838, no general poor law in Ireland, several acts of the Irish and the United Parliaments had made provision for the relief of particular classes of poor. Apart from certain penal acts directed against vagrancy and begging, the first enactment of the Irish Parliament dealing with the poor was passed in 1703, providing for the erection of a workhouse and for the maintenance and apprenticing out of foundling children in the city of Dublin. The expenses of these objects were to be defrayed out of a tax on hackney coaches and sedan chairs, and a rate of threepence in the pound on every

[1] *Select Committee on State of Poor in Ireland.* 1830 p. 8.
[2] *Fifty Years of Concessions* vol. ii. p. 141.
[3] Anketel. *The Effects of Absenteeism.* London 1843.
[4] *Devon Commn.* p. 1110.

house within the city and liberties.[1] This act is important as it marks the earliest recognition by the Irish Parliament of the principle that the poor should be supported by compulsory taxation. In 1735 a similar act was passed applying to the city of Cork.[2]

In 1715 an act was passed which applied to the whole of Ireland, giving power to ministers and churchwardens, with the consent of a justice of the peace, to apprentice out helpless children to "any honest and respectable protestant housekeeper."[3] Many years later provision was made for the care of foundling and deserted children in cities by means of a rate assessed on the inhabitants, and shortly afterwards the provisions of this act were extended to country districts.[4] About the same time the workhouse and foundling branches of the Dublin institution were separated.[5]

An important act was passed in 1771 making provision for the establishment of a house of industry in each county. Corporations were to be established in every county with power to purchase land for the purpose of erecting houses of industry, "as plain, as durable, and at as moderate expense as may be", to be divided into four parts, one for such poor helpless men, and another for such poor helpless women, as should be judged worthy of admission, a third for the reception of men able to labour and committed as vagabonds or sturdy beggars, and the fourth for idle, strolling and disorderly women committed to the hospital and found fit to labour. It was expected that the greater part of the money required for these establishments would be provided by private contributors, but in addition grand juries were required to present annually in every city a sum between £100 and £200, and in every county a sum between £200 and £400 for their support.[6] If this act had been carried out by the local authorities, something resembling a general system of poor relief might have come to exist before the

[1] 2 Anne c. 19 Ir. [2] 9 Geo. II. c. 25 Ir. [3] 2 Geo. I. c. 17 Ir.
[4] 11 and 12 Geo. III c. 15 ; 13 and 14 Geo. c. 24 Ir.
[5] 11 and 12 Geo. III c. 11 Ir. [6] 11 and 12 Geo. III c. 30 Ir.

Union, but, as we shall see, it was put into operation in only a few counties.

The following is Nicholls' summary of the poor relief legislation of the Irish Parliament:—"Houses of industry and foundling hospitals, supported partly by public rates and partly by voluntary contributions, were established at Dublin and Cork, for the reception and bringing up of exposed and deserted children, and the confinement of vagrants; parishes were required to support the children exposed and deserted within their limits, and vestries were organized and overseers appointed to attend to this duty; hospitals, houses of industry, or workhouses were to be provided in every county and city; severe punishments were enacted against idle vagabonds and vagrants; while the deserving poor were to be lodged or licensed to beg, or if infirm and helpless were to be maintained in the hospitals or houses of industry, for the building and upholding of which reliance was chiefly placed on the charitable aid of the humane and affluent, assessments for the purpose being limited to £400 in counties at large and to £200 in counties of cities or towns."[1]

No statute of the United Parliament dealing with the relief of the able-bodied poor was passed before 1838, though various acts were passed making provision for the sick and lunatic poor. An act of 1805 provided that, in counties where the county infirmary was unavailable to the poor of any district on account of distance, the grand jury might raise a sum by presentment equal to the amount already raised by private subscription to establish local dispensaries.[2] In the following year the amounts which the grand juries were authorized to present for the erection of houses of industry were slightly increased.[3] In 1814 an act was passed providing that, when any fever hospital had been established in a county, the grand jury might

[1] *History of the Irish Poor Laws* pp. 57—8.
[2] 45 Geo. III. c. 111. [3] 46 Geo. III. c. 95.

raise a sum not exceeding £250 for its support;[1] and four years later a further act provided for the creation in every county of a corporation, charged with the duty of erecting fever hospitals and authorizing grand juries to present sums for their support not exceeding double the amount raised by voluntary subscription.[2] In the following year provision was made for the appointment of officers of health to supervise the carrying into effect of the last mentioned act.[3] An act of 1817 empowered the Lord Lieutenant to direct the erection of lunatic asylums in districts where they were needed, the cost to be defrayed by grand jury presentments.[4] In 1825 the provision for deserted children was slightly extended.[5]

Such were the principal measures directed to the relief of the Irish poor, and it now remains for us to inquire how far they were effective. The Select Committee of 1804 on the Poor of Ireland reported that "the acts directing the establishment of a house of industry in every county have not been complied with, nor any presentment made by grand juries to assist in the support of such establishments for relief of the aged or infirm poor and the punishment of vagrants and sturdy beggars, except in the counties of Cork, Waterford and Limerick." The committee drew attention to the fact that the house of industry in Dublin being open to the admission of the poor from all parts of Ireland, may have led the other counties and cities to consider it sufficient. It must be remembered that the Dublin house of industry, alone of all the institutions of the kind in Ireland, received public assistance. In the year 1776 the parliamentary grant towards its support amounted to £3,000, in 1786 to £8,600, in 1796 to £14,500, in 1806 to £22,177, in 1814 to £49,113 and in 1827 to £23,000.[6] The spectacle of this specially favoured institution doubtless operated to tempt

[1] 54 Geo. III. c. 112. [2] 58 Geo. III. c. 47.
[3] 59 Geo. III c. 41. [4] 57 Geo. III c. 106.
[5] 6 Geo. IV c. 102.
[6] Nicholls *op. cit.* p. 84.

the grand juries of the other counties to neglect their statutory functions for the relief of the poor.

The Spring Rice Committee of 1830 found that there were then in existence thirty-one county infirmaries—one in every county except Waterford, where the provisions of a local act had prevented one from being erected; and that the entire cost of their maintenance amounted to £54,000 per annum, all of which was derived from local subscriptions and grand-jury presentments, except £3,000 furnished by government. The committee recommended that the grand juries should be enabled to provide more than one infirmary in the large counties, and that their presenting powers should be extended. The committee reported that, with the exception of some minor amendments, "the county infirmaries of Ireland may be considered as adequate to the purposes for which they were intended." The committee next devoted its attention to fever hospitals, which it found had been established in most parts of Ireland. "No county is said to be without one in Munster, and the county of Cork has four and Tipperary eight; but many counties in the province of Ulster and Connaught have omitted to provide fever hospitals." The committee further found that nearly 400 dispensaries had been established, affording relief annually to upwards of half a million of persons. It was recommended that the optional power of grand juries in respect of dispensaries and fever hospitals should be rendered compulsory. The provision for lunatics wasf ound to be sufficient and satisfactory; "as regards one of the most painful afflictions to which humanity is exposed, there has been provided within a few years a system of relief for the Irish poor as extensive as can be wished, and as perfect and effectual as is to be found in any country." The committee recommended that curable and incurable cases should be segregated.

The committee then proceeded to deal with the houses of industry, and reported that the number of those institutions in Ireland did not exceed twelve, "including the great establishment bearing that name in Dublin, which is supported exclusively by votes of parliament." There were eight houses of industry in Munster, three in Leinster, but none in Ulster or Connaught. The committee was of opinion that the system might prove more effective if the criminal were separated from the distressed poor, and that compulsory work would be more successfully insisted on in houses of correction than in houses primarily intended for old age and infirmity.

Attention was also drawn to the great volume of private charity in Ireland, of which the foremost example was the Dublin Mendicity Institution. Dublin has always been remarkable for the extent of its charities supported by voluntary contributions. In 1815 they numbered about fifty, including dispensaries, hospitals, schools, asylums, penitentiaries, infirmaries and loan societies. About 16,000 pounds was said to be raised annually by charity sermons alone.[1] Two years later the Mendicity Institution was founded. The famine of 1817 had flooded the streets of the city with more than the usual number of beggars, for whose assistance subscriptions were raised; the committee appointed for this purpose led processions of beggars through the streets, and taught them to howl outside the doors of those who would not subscribe to the fund; as a result of which campaign about £9,000 was collected, and the Mendicity Institution founded.[2] Among the charitable associations which the committee of 1830 observed in Dublin may be mentioned, "schools, hospitals, Magdalen asylums, houses of refuge, orphan establishments, lying- in hospitals, societies for relief of the sick and indigent, mendicity associations, and charitable loans."[3]

The second report of the Poor Inquiry Commissioners, published in 1836, was devoted to the existing establish-

[1] *An Address to the Public on Behalf of the Poor*, Dublin 1815.
[2] Douglas, *Life and Property in Ireland*, London 1846.
[3] Nicholls, *op. cit.* p. 105.

ments for the relief of distress in Ireland. It was stated that there were in existence 31 county and 5 city and town infirmaries, 452 independent dispensaries, and 42 more united with fever hospitals, and 28 fever hospitals. The total cost of the upkeep of these institutions in the year 1833 was calculated to amount to £109,054, of which £55,065 was furnished by grand jury presentments, £37,563 by subscriptions, £6,661 by parliamentary grants, and £9,766 by petty sessions fees and miscellaneous funds. With regard to these institutions the commissioners remarked:— "The medical relief at present afforded throughout Ireland is very unequally distributed. In the county of Dublin, containing exclusive of the city about 176,000 inhabitants, and about 375 square miles, there are 19 dispensaries, or one for every 9,306 inhabitants. In the County of Mayo, containing 311, 328 inhabitants, and about 2,100 square miles, there is only one dispensary supported at the public expense." In spite of these inequalities of distribution, however, the sick poor of Ireland would seem to have been reasonably well provided for: "the sick poor of Ireland are better attended than even the sick poor of England"[1] While however the existing system was sound in principle, it was vitiated by many practical abuses, amongst others, (1) the total omission of an efficient superintendence and control exercised by properly qualified persons, whether over the working of the whole system or its subordinate machinery, (2) the authorizing of a sort of partnership in charity between the public purse and private individuals, thereby placing it within the power of designing persons to impose a permanent tax upon the community for their own or their friends' private advantage, (3) the leaving it discretionary with grand juries to diminish or extinguish the funds of a charity capable of much usefulness, and (4) the dispensary acts requiring no specific medical qualifications of any kind.[2]

[1] Stanley, *Ireland and Her Evils.* Dublin 1836. [2] *Poor Inquiry Commission App. B.* p. 3.

Passing from medical charities to the institutions for the general relief of the poor, the commission found that there were in existence nine houses of industry, and two large foundling hospitals, one in Dublin, the other in Cork, and a small one in Galway. These institutions, according to the commissioners, were utterly indefensible, in view of the large cost of their upkeep. In addition to these institutions there were also eleven lunatic asylums in Ireland. The total cost of these institutions in 1833 was as follows :

	£
Infirmaries, Dispensaries, Fever Hospitals	109,054
Lunatic Asylums	26,247
Houses of Industry	32,967
Foundling Hospitals	36,628
	204,896

Of this sum upwards of £50,000 was furnished by parliamentary grants, the remainder being derived from grand jury presentments, voluntary contributions, and other local sources.[2]

Such was the provision made for the Irish poor when the famous Poor Inquiry Commission embarked upon its labours. Let us next inquire into the nature and source of the demand for the extension to Ireland of some system corresponding to the English poor law. For many years previous to the setting up of the Poor Inquiry Commission in 1833, constant complaints had been made in England of the ruinous effects of the increasing immigration of Irish labourers. It was alleged that this influx had the result of depressing the rate of wages of English labour, and of further adding to the burden of the English poor rates. While the latter of these allegations was no doubt well grounded, the former was quite erroneous. Sir George Cornewall Lewis, in the lengthy and able report on the Irish

[1] *Second Report of Poor Inquiry Commission* 1836.

poor in Great Britain which he prepared for the Poor Inquiry Commission, stated that in his opinion the presence of the Irish labourers did not lower the current rate of wages in England, but simply enabled a greater output to be attained. He went further, and said that the Irish immigration actually succeeded in raising wages in England in the long run, as it furnished a constant supply of mobile labour, without which the great industrial changes of the time could not have proceeded. "We ought not to overlook" he added "the advantage of this demand for labour in England and Scotland being amply and adequately supplied, and at a cheap rate, and at very short notice, simply because they are a potato-fed and disorderly population .... They came in the hour of need, and they afforded the chief part of the animal strength by which the great works of our manufacturing districts have been executed."[1] "We must not condemn too precipitately" wrote Sir R. Peel "the incursion of Irish labourers into England. We must bear in mind the advantages as well as the disadvantages of cheap labour."[2] The Poor Inquiry Commission drew attention to the fact that wages were highest in those districts of Great Britain where the Irish were most numerous.[3] In reply to the allegation that the Irish immigration caused unemployment, Lewis answered that there were other causes operating, quite sufficient to account for the prevalence of unemployment. English labour was not mobile on account of the settlement laws, and could not therefore present itself where the demand appeared; and the English rural classes showed a certain indisposition to migrate to the towns, nor were they so versatile and adaptable as the Irish.[4]

Lewis's opinion may have been, and probably was, correct, but it was useless to attempt to fight against a popular sentiment by scientific arguments. The feeling that the

[1] Lewis's *Report* p. xxxvii.
[2] Parker *Sir Robert Peel* vol. ii. p. 117.
[3] *Third Report* p. 24.
[4] Lewis's *Report* p. xxxvii.

hordes of Irish labourers did tend to depress wages and increase unemployment in Great Britain was deep-rooted and widespread. "The returns lately called for by the House of Commons as to the number of deck and steerage passengers which in the last three years have migrated from Ireland to Great Britain is the best proof of the alarm felt by our fellow-subjects in that country as to this increasing migration, which tends to fill the factories and the poorhouses of Great Britain with Irish artisans."[1] The question of how Irish paupers could best be removed from the English parishes, in which they were felt as an intolerable burden, was considered by two select committees of the House of Commons in the course of a few years. The committee of 1828 reported that the number of these paupers was growing annually, and the expense of their removal was assuming large proportions. "If the present system is continued unchecked" the report stated "the effects of its operation will inevitably be to throw upon England, and that in no very distant period, the expense of maintaining the paupers of both islands." The committee recommended an alteration of the law by which the removal of the Irish poor was made a charge on England.[2] Five years later the question was considered by another committee, which reported that the evil of Irish vagrancy had greatly increased. The number of vagrant orders made in the county of Middlesex, for example, had increased from 1,892 in 1828 to 2,026 in 1829, 2,163 in 1830, 2,648 in 1831, and 2,977 in 1832. The committee expressed the opinion that the only real remedy for the evil would be to exclude Irish paupers from all right to poor relief in England, but that this measure would be too drastic if immediately introduced, and that it might be postponed until after the enactment of an Irish poor law. The committee recommended that in the mean-

[1] *Sketch of the Society for the Improvement of Ireland.* Dublin 1828.
[2] *Select Committee on Irish and Scotch Vagrants* 1828.

while removals from the south and east of England should be made by sea and not by land, as the former method of travelling was cheaper.[1]

While the attention of parliament was thus being directed to the problem of the Irish in England, the British public and press were loudly demanding the extension of the poor law to Ireland, as the only thorough remedy for the evil. "We must always keep in mind" we read in 1829 "that the great and undisguised motive on the part of the English journals and British members of parliament is that a poor rate should be established in Ireland, not so much for the purpose of alleviating the miseries of the poor Irish, as to protect them, the English, from the visitation of the Irish labourer."[2] "The advocates for this measure" wrote Sir John Walsh "rest their arguments upon two distinct bases. They maintain that it will benefit Ireland, but they likewise hold it up as a sovereign remedy for the evils with which England is menaced by the migratory tribes of pauper Irish. This latter view seems indeed considerably the more important in their eyes; at least it is more prominently advanced and more frequently dwelt upon."[3] Mr. G. Poulett Scrope addressed an open letter to the landowners of England urging them to use their influence to have the poor law extended to Ireland "in justice to themselves, their tenantry, and the labouring classes of Britain."[4] "There was rather a mournful expression of countenance in the cabinet" Peel wrote to Lord Francis Gower in 1829, "at the mention of these Irish subjects .... first the state of the Irish poor, particularly in their relation to the English poor law and the maintenance in comfort of the English labourer."[5]

[1] *Select Committee on Irish Vagrants* 1833.
[2] G. H. Evans, *Remarks on the Policy of Introducing the System of Poor Rates into Ireland.* London 1829.
[3] *Poor Laws in Ireland* London 1830.
[4] *Plan of a Poor Law for Ireland,* London 1833 and see Barnett Smith *Life of John Bright* vol. i. p. 252.
[5] Parker *Sir Robert Peel* vol. ii. p. 116.

The importance of the part played by English public opinion is fully admitted by Nicholls. "An impression had long prevailed, and was daily becoming stronger, of the necessity for making some provision for the relief of the destitute poor in Ireland. The perpetually increasing intercourse between the two countries brought under English notice the wretched state of a large proportion of the people in the sister island; and the vast numbers of them who crossed the channel in search of the means of living, and became more or less domiciled in the large towns and throughout the western districts of England, made it a matter of policy, as it assuredly was of humanity, to endeavour to improve their condition; and nothing seemed so equitable or so readily effective for this purpose as making property liable for the relief of destitution in Ireland, as was the case in England, in other words, establishing some description of poor law."[1] In view of this volume of contemporary evidence, it is impossible to resist the conclusion that the Irish poor law was proposed by the government largely with the object of facilitating the expulsion of the Irish immigrants from England. It is interesting to observe that, while the poor law as passed contained ample provisions for this purpose, no corresponding powers were conferred on Ireland with regard to the repatriation of the English paupers.[2]

English opinion was therefore altogether in favour of an Irish poor law. Irish opinion, on the other hand, was, with a few important exceptions, such as that of Dr. Doyle, unanimous against it. The Select Committee of 1804 reported that "the adoption of a general rate of provision for the poor of Ireland, by way of parish rates as in England, or in any similar manner, would be highly injurious to the country, and would not produce any real or permanent advan-

[1] *Op. cit.* p. 153.

[2] This fact is commented on in the Report of the Vice-regal Commission on the Irish Poor Law 1906 p. 13. On the state of the law regarding the removal of the Irish poor from England see *Repeal Reports* vol. i. pp. 17 sq.

tage even to the lower classes of people who must be the objects of such support."[1] Mr. Curwen in his excellent book on Ireland remarks: "It has been a question with some whether an extension of the English poor laws to Ireland might not greatly relieve and highly benefit the lower classes—God forbid the attempt should be made."[2] The Select Committee of 1819 took the view that "a system of poor laws would produce incalculable evils to every class of the community."[3]

In the literature of the next decade we meet constant references to the unsuitability of the English poor law if applied to Ireland. "The introduction" wrote an Irish magistrate "of poor laws like those of England would produce the most ruinous consequences."[4] "Were poor houses to be erected, the country's existing distresses would run rapidly into absolute pauperism."[5] Mr. Lambert, whose opinions on Irish affairs were always valuable, wrote that "the English system of poor laws is not adapted to us for many reasons .... Those who are thoroughly acquainted with the peculiar state of the country will be found opposed to their introduction under existing circumstances."[6] In view of this widespread feeling of opposition, it is not surprising that the Spring Rice Committee of 1830 refused to recommend the introduction of a poor law, and uttered the following warning: "It is impossible to overestimate the importance of a correct judgment on this subject; involving, as it does, if decided affirmatively, an entire change in the domestic economy of upwards of eight million people. A false step may here be of such fatal consequences that it greatly behoves the legislature to proceed cautiously, to investigate closely, and to weigh accurately before any final decision is made."[7]

[1] *Select Committee on Poor of Ireland* 1804. [2] *Observations* vol. i. p. 207.

[3] *First Report of Select Committee on State of Disease and Condition of Labouring Poor in Ireland* 1819. [4] *A Letter on the State of Ireland by an Irish Magistrate*, London 1825.

[5] John Beere, *A Letter to the King on the Practical Improvement of Ireland*, London 1827.

[6] *Observations on the Rural Affairs of Ireland.* Dublin 1829.

[7] *Select Committee on State of Poor*, 1830 p. 55.

This was an exceedingly grave warning; and it will be interesting to observe how it was acted on by the government. There was a clear divergence of opinion between the committees whose advice had been sought for the remedying of evils affecting England and evils affecting Ireland. The former had recommended the introduction of an Irish poor law, the latter had reported against it, or had advised that such a step should be taken only after the most mature consideration. The correct thing to do in the face of such conflicting advice was what the government actually did; it constituted a commission of the most representative Irishmen whom it could assemble, and instructed them to report on the advisability of introducing a system of poor laws into Ireland. It is not sufficient however to establish a commission of inquiry, if one is determined to ignore its advice should it prove unpalatable. A commission, whose recommendations are only to be carried into effect provided they agree with the preconceived opinions of the government, can achieve no purpose except the waste of a certain amount of public money. That such was the nature of the Poor Inquiry Commission will, it is suggested, appear from the following pages.[1] The commission, the *personnel* of which was calculated to command respect, fulfilled its duties in an exceptionally able and thorough manner. The evidence which it took fills several massive volumes, and the appendices to its reports are models of erudition and orderly arrangement. It would not therefore have been too much to expect that the recommendations of such a body would have been, if not followed, at least listened to with profound respect by the government. Far other, however, as we shall see, was the case.

The commission presented three reports. The first deals with "the modes in which the destitute classes in Ireland

[1] That the government had its mind made up to introduce a poor law for Ireland, regardless of the findings of the commission, appears from Whately *Life of Whately* vol. i. p. 199 and pp. 394 sq.

are supported, to the extent and efficiency of these modes, and their effects upon those who give and upon those who receive relief." Full details are given of the existing facilities for the relief of deserted and orphan children, illegitimate children, widows, the sick poor, and the able-bodied out of work. The report complains of the great difficulty of the inquiry on account of "the extensive and complicated nature of the subject and the peculiar social conditions of the Irish people," and explains that it was not yet possible to make recommendations with regard to remedial measures. The commissioners complain in particular of the number of theorists, who offered them panaceas for every Irish evil:—"One party attributed all the poverty and wretchedness of the country to an asserted extreme use of ardent spirits, and proposed a system for repressing illicit distillation, for preventing smuggling, and for substituting beer and coffee. Another party found the cause in the combination among workmen and proposed rigorous laws against trade unions. Others again were equally confident that the reclamation of the bogs and waste lands was the only practical remedy. A fourth party declared the existing connexion between landlord and tenant to be the root of all the evil. Pawnbroking, redundant population, absence of capital, peculiar religious tenets and religious differences, political excitement, want of education, the maladministration of justice, the state of prison discipline, the want of manufactures and of inland navigation, with a variety of other circumstances were each supported by their various advocates with earnestness and ability, as being, either alone, or jointly with some other, the primary cause of all the evils of society; and loan funds, emigration, the repression of political excitement, the introduction of manufactures, and the extension of inland navigation were accordingly proposed, each as the chief means by which the improvement of Ireland could be promoted."[1]

[1] *First Report.*

It is not surprising that, in the midst of such confusion of counsel, the commissioners should have sought further time in which to come to an opinion.

The second report of the commission dealt with "the various institutions at present established by law for the relief of the poor." These were stated to consist principally of medical institutions, lunatic asylums, houses of industry, and foundling hospitals. This report is purely statistical in nature, and does not contain any recommendations for the future.[1]

The third report of the commission is the most important, as it contains the considered scheme of a number of the most representative Irishmen that could be consulted on the economic regeneration of their country. It is possibly the most important document in existence for the student of Irish economic history. The report in the first place draws attention to the fact that there were in Ireland about five agricultural labourers for every two that there were for the same quantity of land in Great Britain; and describes the miserable condition of the Irish agricultural population. The report then proceeds to show that the English poor law was quite unsuited to Ireland, as the problems of poverty in the two countries were fundamentally different. "The difficulty in Ireland is not to make the able-bodied look for employment, but to find it profitably for the many who seek it."

It is then pointed out that workhouses in Ireland, in order to be effective, would have to be on a colossal scale. "We cannot estimate the number of persons out of work and in distress during thirty weeks of the year at less than 585,000, and the number of persons dependent on them at less than 1,800,000, making in the whole 2,385,000. In this condition of affairs, a workhouse system could not be recommended. In the first place the cost would be prohibitive, probably about £5,000,000 annually, "whereas

[1] *Second Report.*

the gross rental of Ireland (exclusive of towns) is estimated at less than £10,000,000, and the net income of the landlords at less than £6,000,000." Moreover the Irish poor would probably be hostile to any such system. "We believe that the able-bodied in general and their families would endure any misery rather than make a workhouse their domicile." The commissioners therefore stated that they had arrived at the conclusion: "We cannot recommend the present workhouse system of England as at all suited to Ireland." They further expressed the opinion that the establishment of out-door relief would be equally pernicious, as it would eat up the rental of the country, and prevent the accumulation of capital.

Having thus advised against a system of poor law on the grounds of practicability and policy, the commissioners next proceed to their positive proposals for the alleviation of the misery of the country. The general scope and trend of these measures are outlined as follows: "Considering the redundancy of labour which now exists in Ireland, how earnings are kept down by it, what misery is thus produced, and what insecurity of liberty, property, and life ensues, we are satisfied that enactments calculated to promote the improvement of the country, and so to extend the demand for free and profitable labour, should make essential parts of any law for ameliorating the condition of the poor. And for the same reasons, while we feel that relief should be provided for the impotent, we consider it due to the whole community, and to the labouring class in particular, that such able-bodied as may still be unable to find free and profitable employment in Ireland should be secured support only through emigration or as a preliminary to it. In saying this, we mean that those who desire to emigrate should be furnished with the means of doing so in safety, and with intermediate support, when they stand in need of it, at emigration depôts . . . ." "We do not look to emigration" the commissioners add, "as an object to be permanently pursued upon any extensive scale, nor by any means as the main relief for the evils of Ireland, but we do look to it for the present as an auxiliary essential to a commencing course of amelioration." The last words are very important, as they strike the keynote of the whole report of the commissioners ; what they aimed at was not temporary measures, but a "course of amelioration".

The report next outlines the concrete measures of improvement of which the commissioners approved. The first of such measures was an act modelled on the Bedford Level Acts for the "enforced improvement of property at the expense of the property improved." It was suggested that a board should be created charged with the duty of improving unreclaimed and waste lands, and that the Board of Works should be authorized to construct main drains and roads at the expense of the property benefited. The commissioners next recommended that, with regard to land already in cultivation, a general drainage act was required. They further recommended that the funds at the disposal of the Board of Works should be increased; and that some provision should be made for the better housing of the working classes. "We consider it advisable that the Board of Improvement should be enabled as far as possible to make provision for the occupants of cabins which may be nuisances, and, when such provision is made, to cause the cabins to be taken down; and that landlords should be required to contribute towards the expense of removing the occupants and providing for them." Other recommendations included the provision of agricultural model schools, the grant of increased powers to tenants for life, and the reform of the grand jury system.

The commissioners then passed to a discussion of what measures of direct relief were needful. The substance of their recommendations is as follows;—"We think that a legal provision should be made and rates levied . . . . for the relief and support of incurable as well as curable lunatics, of idiots, epileptic persons, cripples, deaf and dumb and blind poor, and all who labour under permanent bodily infirmities—such relief and support to be afforded within the walls of public institutions; also for the relief of the sick poor in hospitals, infirmaries, and convalescent establishments, or by extern attendance, and a supply of food as well as medicine, when the persons to be relieved are not in a state to be removed from home; also for the purpose of emigration, for the support of penitentaries to which vagrants may be sent, and for the maintenance of deserted children; also towards the relief of aged and infirm persons, of orphans, of helpless widows with young children, of the families of sick persons, and of casual destitution." With a view to carrying these recommendations into effect, the commissioners advised that poor law commissioners should be appointed; that the country should be divided into relief districts with local boards of guardians ; that national establishments, supported by a national rate, should be founded for lunatics, the deaf, dumb, and blind, penitentiaries for vagrants, and emigration depôts; that one half of the expense of emigration should be borne by the general imperial funds, and the other half, in the case of urban tenants, by the national rate, and, in the case of rural tenants, by the landlords from whose lands they had been evicted within the previous twelve months; that the poor law commissioners should have power to borrow for emigration depôts, and to repay such loans out of the national rate ; and that a loan fund should be established. The commissioners further recommended the immediate provision of accommodation for the relief of aged and infirm, of helpless widows, and of destitute people. There was a difference of opinion as to whether such establishments should be supported by voluntary or compulsory contributions, the majority being in favour of the former, aided by such grants as the poor law commissioners should think proper. It was recommended that the holders of land of less than £5 valuation should be exempt from the payment of rates for any of the above purposes, and that encumbrancers of land should be made to pay an equitable share of the rate. After making various minor recommendations, the commissioners concluded the report by an appeal to the patriotism of the Irish landlords:—"The efficacy of remedial measures, under Providence, must depend mainly upon those who possess power and influence in the country. In proportion as such persons are raised high, they have high duties to perform."[1]

The recommendations of the commission were quite clear and consistent. They aimed at giving employment to the able-bodied and relief to the disabled, and embraced a complete scheme for the industrial regeneration of the country. It was the best exposition of the policy of increasing resources as contrasted with that of decreasing population that had yet been made. Nor could it be said to be impracticable, as almost every one of the recommendations has since been more or less put into effect after many years delay. It therefore deserved the government's most serious consideration.

No such consideration was however accorded to it. On the contrary it was immediately set aside as being undesirable, and a fresh investigation, this time conducted by a more pliable instrument, was established. This new arbiter, whose finding was destined to overrule the three years' labour of the commissioners, was Mr. George Nicholls, one of the English poor law commissioners. This gentleman had, prior to the presentation of the commissioners' third report, drawn up a series of suggestions upon the matter for the consideration of the government. "He did not pretend to any personal knowledge of the state of Ireland, but considered that the information provided by the evidence appended to the commissioners' first report showed that destitution and wretchedness prevailed to such an extent

[1] *Third Report.*

among the poorer classes in that country, that legislative interference could no longer be delayed." Mr. Nicholls recommended the extension to Ireland of the English poor law system.[1] Even at this stage, the ideas of Mr. Nicholls seemed to be shared by the government, for the royal speech opening parliament stated that, "a further report of the Commission of Inquiry into the condition of the poorer classes in Ireland will shortly be laid before you. You will approach this subject with the caution due to its importance and difficulty; and the experience of the salutary effect produced by the act for the amendment of the laws relating to the poor in England and Wales may in some respects assist your deliberations."[2] It would appear from this that the ministers distinctly favoured the extension of the English poor law to Ireland, quite apart from the recommendations of the commission, which indeed they had not yet seen.

The third report, which was shortly afterwards presented, appears to have been distasteful to the government, who refused to embody any of the recommendations contained in it in a bill, and allowed the session to pass without taking any action on it. Two days after the prorogation of parliament, the government directed Mr. Nicholls to proceed to Ireland to inquire into the practicability and advisability of introducing the English poor law. This step definitely marks the rejection of the advice of the commissioners, as is evident from the letter of instructions which Mr. Nicholls received from Lord John Russell:—"You will carefully weigh the important question whether a rate might be usefully directed to the erection and maintenance of workhouses for all those who sought relief as paupers .... Your attention need not be very specially given to the plans for the general improvement of Ireland contained in the report of the commissioners of inquiry."[3]

[1] Nicholls *op. cit.* p. 130. [2] Nicholls *op. cit.* p. 154.
[3] *Vice-Regal Commission on Irish Poor Law* 1906 p. 4.

Mr. Nicholls accordingly paid a flying visit to Ireland, and, after a six weeks tour in the country, proceeded to prepare his first report, which completely reversed the conclusions which the commissioners had reached as the result of three years' close investigation. This report is divided into three parts: the first, giving the general result of inquiries into the condition, habits, and feelings of the people, especially with regard to the introduction of a law for the relief of the poor; the second, dealing with the question whether the workhouse system could with safety be established; and the third, considering the chief points requiring attention in the framing of a poor law for Ireland.

In the first part of the report Mr. Nicholls deals with the objections usually put forward against his favourite scheme: "The objections usually urged against the introduction of poor laws into Ireland are founded on an anticipated demoralization of the peasantry, and on the probable amount of the charge. The first objection derives its force from the example of England under the poor law, but the weight of this objection is destroyed by the improved administration under the new law, which is rapidly eradicating the effects of previous abuse .... With respect to the second objection, founded on the probable amount of expenditure, it may be remarked that the Irish population, like any other, must be supported in some way out of the resources of the country, and it does not follow that the establishment of such a system of relief will greatly increase the charge, if it increase it at all." Having thus answered the principal objections to his scheme, Mr. Nicholls next proceeds to make a statement, which we find it hard to credit: "Notwithstanding these objections, I found everywhere, after quitting Dublin, a strong feeling in favour of property being assessed for the relief of the indigent."

The conclusion that a poor law was desirable in Ireland having been reached, the next question was the form it should take. "There are two points for consideration under this division of the subject, which are of primary import, first, whether the workhouse system can be safely and effectively established in Ireland, and secondly, whether a machinery can be there established for their government, such as exists in the English unions." Both these questions are answered in the affirmative. "In the course of my inquiries I soon found reason for concluding that there was no ground for apprehension, either as to the applicability of the workhouse for the purpose of relief, or as to any danger of resistance to such a system of classification and discipline within it, as would make it a test of destitution." The cost of erecting sufficient workhouses was estimated at £700,000; and the opinion was expressed that the English system of unions, with certain modifications, could be successfully applied.

The third part of the report is concerned with the chief points deserving of attention in the framing of an Irish poor law. This section is prefaced by an interesting remark, which throws much light on the spirit in which Mr. Nicholls conducted his inquiries. "The governing principle to be observed is that the poor law of Ireland should assimilate as nearly as possible to that established in England." Starting from this cardinal assumption, Mr. Nicholls recommended that no outdoor relief should in any circumstances be granted, that the poor rate should be borne in equal shares by the owners and occupiers of land, that the English law of settlement should not be extended to Ireland, that the English poor law commissioners should be entrusted with the administration of the scheme in Ireland, and that provision should be made for emigration in certain cases.[1]

It appears from every line of this report that Mr. Nicholls went to Ireland with his mind quite made up to recommend the poor law. "He set about his task under the greatest possible disadvantages; first, he was unacquainted with

[1] Nicholls *op. cit.* pp. 160-187

the nation for which he was selected to lay the basis of a most important law; second, he was, according to his own statement, imbued with partial and erroneous notions concerning the inhabitants; and, third, he was extremely limited as to the time given him to assess that knowledge by which the opinion of the rest of mankind was to be corrected .... It seems a question whether he was not seeking to shape the wants and conditions of the Irish people to his act, rather than to frame an act suitable to their real needs and condition."[1] "It would appear from the published reports of Mr. Nicholls that he went to Ireland for the purpose of discovering reasons for introducing there the workhouse system, and the means of accomplishing that object; and he seems to have seen nothing but what he had previously made up his mind to see ... He came to Ireland with his whole soul full of English workhouses, so full that nothing else could gain access to it. From the moment that he landed in Ireland, five minutes conversation with him on the subject was sufficient to enable anyone to determine what would be his report."[2]

In spite of the disadvantage of insufficient knowledge and experience under which Mr. Nicholls laboured, his report was immediately adopted by the government, and he was instructed to prepare a bill embodying its recommendations.[3] This bill was rushed through the House of Commons, but its progress was temporarily delayed by the death of the king. Advantage was taken of this delay to send Mr. Nicholls to Ireland again, to visit the counties which he had neglected to visit on his first journey. On his return he prepared a second report, answering certain objections which had been suggested against his first, and concluding that, "the investigations I have just concluded have not afforded ground for any material

[1] J. P. Kennedy. *Analysis of the Projects proposed for the Relief of the Poor in Ireland.* London 1837.
[2] *Strictures on the Proposed Poor Law for Ireland.* London 1838
[3] Nicholls, *op. cit.* p. 188.

change of opinion. I may perhaps estimate the difficulty of establishing a poor law in Ireland somewhat higher than I did before, but of the necessity for such a measure I am, if possible, more fully convinced."[1] This report was also adopted by the cabinet, and a measure embodying its recommendations was framed and rushed through parliament with the utmost possible speed. With the exception of certain minor amendments insisted upon by the House of Lords, the bill received the royal assent in its original form on the 31st of July 1838.[2]

The main provisions of this act, which still remains the basis of the Irish poor law, were as follows:—

(1) The division of the country into unions, composed of electoral divisions, which in turn were made up of "townlands."

(2) The formation of a board of guardians for each union—the board consisting of elected and ex-officio guardians.

(3) The establishment of a central authority, viz., the Poor Law Commissioners for England and Wales.

(4) A compulsory rate for the relief of the poor.

(5) The relief to be at the discretion of the guardians, and accordingly no poor person, however destitute, to be held to have a statutory right to relief. A preference to be given to the aged, the infirm, the defective, and the children; after these had been provided for, the guardians to be at liberty to relieve such other persons as they might deem to be destitute, priority to be given to those resident in the union, in the event of the accommodation in the workhouse being insufficient for all.

(6) The relief to be limited to relief in the workhouse.

(7) The relief to be subject to the "direction and control" of the Poor Law Commissioners, who, however, were prohibited from interfering in individual cases for the purpose of ordering relief. The Commissioners to make orders for

[1] Nicholls, *op cit.* p. 196. [2] Nicholls, *op. cit.* pp. 209-21.

the guidance and control of guardians, wardens, officers, the auditing of accounts, and for carrying the act into execution in all other respects as they might think proper.

This act which, as we have seen, was passed in complete defiance of the report of the Poor Inquiry Commission, also ran counter to the best public opinion in Ireland. Of course we must remember that a good deal of the Irish opposition was purely selfish, as it originated with landlords, anxious lest their estates should be charged for the support of the poor; neverthless there was a strong body of opinion which opposed the measure on the more statesmanlike grounds that it began at the wrong end, in aiming at cure rather than prevention, and that it was not calculated even to cure. In parliament the majority of the Irish members in both houses were opposed to the bill ; and between the second and third readings 86 petitions with 31,221 signatures were presented against the bill, and only 4 petitions with 593 signatures in its favour.[1]

Public opinion in Ireland on the matter, which was at first indifferent, gradually became inflamed against the bill. Isaac Butt, lecturing in Trinity College in December 1837, complained that, "at this moment legislators are preparing for Ireland a measure, which, whether wise or unwise, is an experiment of the most fearful magnitude and perilous character—and yet public opinion appears as perfectly indifferent to its introduction, as if it were only a turnpike bill that were passing through parliament." Six months later, according to Butt, this indifference no longer existed; but the public interest in the matter came too late, when the bill was half way through parliament.[2] Butt was himself violently opposed to the bill: "Anyone acquainted with Ireland must feel upon perusing this bill that it has not grown naturally out of a knowledge of the wants and circumstances of the country.... It is a piece

[1] *Viceregal Commission* 1906 p. 6. [2] Butt, *Rent, Profit and Labour*, Dublin 1838.

of forced legislation; and in every clause you can discern that it is erected, more from the impression that as much of an article called legislation must be produced, than from any *a priori* conviction that a particular provision is of itself expedient.... Mr. Nicholls' great and fatal mistake is this—he started on the assumption that he must deal with destitution in Ireland, as if it were the accident of individuals, instead of considering it as the essential and general condition of a class. It is this which has led him to propose, as a remedial measure, workhouses where one out of every hundred of the population might be occasionally relieved; instead of suggesting some measure by which we might endeavour to find sufficient food for one-third of the population who have not enough to eat."[1] Even Nicholls admitted that, "In Ireland especially the recommendations of the inquiry commissioners were more popular than the government bill."[2]

It was remarked that the advocates of the poor law were in the habit of supporting their case by inconsistent and contradictory arguments. "Its agricultural supporters assume that it will cause the inhabitants to consume their own wheat, and therefore leave less to export; whereas other advocates insist that by forcing landlords to employ the population all the Irish wastes would be reclaimed, and of course a much larger exportation would follow,"[3]

Why, we are tempted to inquire, had the government its mind so bent on the passing into law of a measure so ob-

[1] *The Poor Law Bill for Ireland Examined.* London 1837.

[2] *Op. cit.* p. 210.

[3] Blacker, *Review of C. Shaw Lefevre's Letter.* London 1837. One of the most determined opponents of the measure was Beaumont. *L'Irlande Sociale*, p. 143. Those who wish to study the contemporary discussion on the poor law will find the following among the most valuable of the pamphlets of the time:—In favour of the bill; Wm. Stanley, *Remarks on the Application of the Workhouse System to the Irish Poor* by an Assistant Commissioner, London 1837; against the bill; Philohibernus. *Remarks on the Bill &c.* London, 1837. J. P. Kennedy, *Analysis of the Projects Proposed for the Relief of the Poor in Ireland*, London 1837; Isaac Butt, *The Poor Law Bill for Ireland Examined* London 1837; *Irish Poor, A Word to Mr. Nicholls by a Looker on* London 1837; W. T. McCullagh, *Letter to the Representative Peers of Ireland.* Dublin 1838; *Strictures on the Proposed Poor Law for Ireland* London 1838 Maunsell. *A Letter to Viscount Morpeth* Dublin 1838.

viously distasteful to the majority of those whom it was meant to affect? Of course there was the pressure from England, which we have noticed, directed towards the relief of the English unions from the pressure of the Irish poor. This is however scarcely sufficient to account for the strong government action on this occasion, as the grievances of the English unions could have been met by some measure falling far short of the far-reaching poor law act. We suggest that the true reason which impelled the government to rush through its measure for the establishment of an Irish poor law was that it was hoped that such a law would operate as an aid to depopulation. It is for this reason that we have included the treatment of the Irish poor law in the present chapter.

Bicheno, in his excellent book on *Ireland and its Economy*, observed that the condition of Ireland was parallel to that of England in the sixteenth century, in so far as the cottiers were being cleared; and consequently the need for a poor law was similar.[1] In other words, Ireland was going through a period of transition, when special measures were called for on behalf of the dispossessed. This point was strongly put by Mr. Nicholls in his report, on which, as we have seen, the action of the government was based: "A system of poor laws, if established in Ireland, must not be expected to work miracles. It would not immediately give employment or capital; but it would, I think, serve to help the country through what may be called its transitional period; and in time, and with the aid of other circumstances, would affect a material improvement in the condition of the Irish people. The English poor laws in their earlier operation contributed to the accomplishment of this object in England; and there seems nothing to prevent similar results in Ireland. Facilities now exist in Ireland for helping forward the change, and for shortening its duration as well as for securing its benefits,

[1] p 237.

which England did not possess in the time of Elizabeth or for a century and a half afterwards. By the term 'transition period', which I have used above, I mean to indicate that season of change from the system of small holdings, which now prevails in Ireland, to the better practice of day labour for wages, and to that dependence on daily labour for support which is the present condition of the English peasantry. This transition period is, I believe, generally beset with difficulty and suffering. It was so in England; it is and for a time will probably continue to be so in Ireland, and every aid should be afforded to shorten its duration and lessen its pressure."[1]

After Nicholls, possibly the most influential adviser of the government was Sir George Cornewall Lewis. It is interesting to note therefore that in his remarkable book on *Irish Disturbances*, published in 1836, Lewis stated that the consolidation of farms could never be carried sufficiently far without the passing of a poor law. "The remedy is to alter the mode of subsistence of the Irish peasant; to change him from a cottier living upon land to a labourer living upon wages; to support him by employment for hire instead of by a potato ground.... But the landlords cannot consolidate farms because they cannot clear their estates.... The tenant cannot quit his holding; he has not the means of emigrating, and he cannot get regular employment, there being no large farmers. On the other hand the landlord cannot eject his cottier tenants in order to make large farms; he exposes the ejected parties to the risk of starvation, and the new tenant to the risk of being murdered by the Whiteboys."[2] All these difficulties would disappear, if there were a convenient workhouse to receive the evicted tenant. "The law alone can furnish a remedy; by its insistence alone can the transition of the peasantry from the cottier to the labourer state be effected. What is wanted is to give the peasant some third alternative

[1] Nicholls, *op. cit.* p. 166. [2] p. 319.

besides land and starvation, by which he may be induced to relax that desperate grasp with which he clings to his potato ground. This alternative—as it seems to me—can alone be furnished by a legal provision for the poor".[1] Torrens in his pamphlet advocating emigration remarked, "Considered as a final measure the poor law is not worth its cost; regarded as the beginning of the end it is of inestimable value."[2] Mr. Bicheno, who was one of the Poor Inquiry Commissioners, expressed the opinion that "a poor law would furnish an excuse for ejectment"; and stated that "the prospect of it has already been made a plea for dispossessing many of the poor."[3] The following is the comment of the Viceregal Commission of 1906 on the motives influencing Nicholls and Lewis, and through them, the government. "It appears that the bringing about of a transition period was the object of the principal promoters of the workhouse system in Ireland.... To paraphrase the recommendations briefly, the landlords were to be enabled to evict their small tenants by the provision of workhouses, into which the evicted tenants could be received.... The community of sentiment between Mr. Nicholls and Mr. Lewis is obvious, and the former was the draughtsman of the bill."[4] It is interesting to note that, in Lewis's confidential opinion to the Chancellor of the Exchequer on the report, the following passage occurs: "In the present condition of Ireland I can conceive no other means except a strongly guarded poor law of restoring to the landlords the power of doing what they will with their own...." Of course all this reasoning was based on the obviously false assumption that there was employment to be found for the evicted cottiers, and that the latter were competent to earn high wages.[5] The influence of the poor law and the consolidation of farms worked in a vicious circle. The poor

[1] *Irish Disturbances* p. 321.
[2] *A Letter to Lord John Russell.* London 1837.
[3] *App. H. Part* 2 p. 20, and see Sigerson *Irish Land Tenures* p. 185.
[4] pp 8-9.
[5] Clements. *The Present Poverty of Ireland.* London 1838.

law was not only directed to assist the process of consolidation ,but was to some extent rendered necessary by the length to which consolidation had already advanced.[1]

There can be found no better example of the conflict between the British and Irish suggestions for remedying the economic ills of Ireland than the introduction of the poor law. This is well put in the report of the Viceregal Commission: "Mr. Nicholls in his second report remarks: 'many sanguine persons appear to consider it as the purpose of a poor law not only to relieve destitution but to eradicate poverty'. This was undoubtedly the desire so far as practicable of the Irish Royal Commission, and it was the precise point of divergence between British and Irish opinion in 1838. The Irish Commission aimed at making the country gradually prosperous through the judicious development of its resources. The British promoters of the act of 1838 were, on the contrary, prepared to hazard the fortunes, such as they were, of the tenantry of Ireland, in a 'transition period', during which they were to be turned from small tenants into day labourers after an interval 'beset with difficulty and sufferings'. The act passed; the difficulties and sufferings arose, but the small tenants did not turn themselves into day labourers."[2]

In so far as the act was designed to aid eviction it was a great success, as the number of evictions greatly increased after its passing.[3] "The influence of the new poor law has accelerated immensely the clearances of estates," wrote Mr. G. Poulett Scrope.[4] "The measure" according to Dr Sigerson "was so different from that passed for England, so aptly imperfect, that it has constantly held out inducements to the prosecution of a war of eviction. The system of parish settlement was not extended to Ireland, a scheme of electoral division rating was established in place of union

[1] Blacker, *Essay on the Management of Landed Property in Ireland* Dublin 1834. [2] p. 10.
[3] *Cases of Tenant Evictions from* 1800 *to* 1846. Dublin 1848.
[4] *A Plea for the Rights of Industry in Ireland*, London 1848.

rating. The Irish upper tenants, by means of this cunning change, enabled themselves to expel all who had grown nigh exhausted in producing rent for them from their estates, and to thrust the burden of their support upon the adjoining towns."[1]

The process of eviction does not seem to have been advancing rapidly enough to satisfy the government, as a few years later they devised another provision calculated to facilitate it further. This was the famous Gregory clause, which provided that no person in possession of more than a quarter of an acre of land could be deemed to be destitute, and that it was not lawful for the guardians to relieve such persons.[2] The significance of this clause is obvious; passed, as it was, at the height of the famine, when small holdings had completely failed to be productive, it held out to the peasant the clearly defined alternatives of quitting his holding or starvation. Many of the poor families chose the latter. Although great numbers surrendered their holdings, many others clung desperately to them. "The class of poor and destitute occupiers, who are debarred by law from receiving relief unless they give up their land, struggle, notwithstanding their great privations, to retain it, and endeavour by every effort to pass through the season of difficulty, beyond which they see the prospect of their former mode of subsistence returning, provided they continue in the possession of their land. The use for a long time of inferior food has in such cases sometimes induced disease fatal to the occupier himself or one or more members of his family."[3] "A more complete engine" stated Father O'Rourke "for the slaughter and degradation of a people was never designed. The previous clause offered facilities for emigrating to those who would give up their land; the quarter-acre clause compelled them to give it up or die of hunger".[4] Lord John Russell's bio-

[1] *Irish Land Tenures* p. 186. [2] 10 Vict. c 31. [3] *First Report of Irish Poor Law Commissioners* 1847 p. 18. [4] *Great Irish Famine* p. 331.

grapher admits that "the extension of the poor law furnished Irish landlords with a new reason for evicting their tenantry"[1]. John Mitchell described the quarter-acre clause as "the cheapest and most efficient of the ejectment acts."[2] So many persons perished from starvation in this way that the government wished to prosecute heads of families under the Vagrancy Act for neglecting to maintain them, but this course was advised against by the law officers. So great had the evil become, that ultimately the grant of relief to the families of such persons was authorized during the period of crisis.[3] By an act of 1848 special provision was made for granting relief to families evicted from their dwellings.[4]

The only other important amendments to the Poor Law Act which we need mention here were the establishment of an Irish Poor Law Commission in 1847,[5] and the authorizing of the grant of outdoor relief to the old and infirm and to poor widows, with two or more children depending on them, in all cases, and to others when the workhouse was full.[6] The progress of the poor law during the first seven years of its operation is shown by the following table:

Year*	Number of Unions in operation	Expenditure £	No. in Workhouses on Dec. 31	Total number relieved in year
1840	4	37,057	5,648	10,910
1841	37	110,278	15,246	31,108
1842	92	281,233	31,572	87,604
1843	106	244,374	35,515	87,898
1844	113	271,334	39,175	105,358
1845	123	316,026	42,068	114,205
1846	130	316,026	94,437	243,933

* Nicholls *op. cit.* p. 323.

The dissatisfaction which Irish public opinion had expressed at the passing of the poor law was continued against its operation, and the measure remained extremely unpo-

[1] Walpole *Life of Lord J. Russell* vol. i. p. 450. [2] *Apology for British Government.*
[3] *Second Report of Irish Poor Law Commissioners* 1848 p. 4. [4] 11 and 12 Vict. c. 47.
[5] 10 and 11 Vict. c. 90. [6] 10 Vict. c. 31.

pular in the country. For one thing it was complained that, although the act was said to be modelled on the English law, many of the best features of the latter were omitted. Poulett Scrope decribed it as a "fragment only of the English poor law; a poor law only in name and pretence, the mere skeleton of what such a law should be."[1] "The present law is perhaps the greatest failure of modern legislation. It has cost an enormous sum of money, and has in no sensible degree lightened the pressure of distress or the claims of charity by its operation and effects."[2] "The present Irish poor law—as is now universally admitted—has turned out a complete failure."[3] Far from relieving the distress, the act simply succeeded in adding to the already heavy burdens which oppressed the country. "All the expectations from the minute examination of the Poor Inquiry Commission ended in a tax, whereas the general inquiry amongst the people was 'what have the gentlemen come to do for us?' "[4] Complaints were levelled not only against the amount of the tax, but also against its incidence and the method in which it was expended. The system of valuation was unsatisfactory, some districts being assessed much more heavily than others.[5] "The poor law valuation is denounced by many witnesses as very inaccurately, sometimes even as fraudulently, made."[6] The method of administration was felt to be unduly extravagant. "I know of many districts where each pauper has hitherto cost £100 per annum, as few as 5 or 6 being in the poorhouse from districts paying £500 or £600 each."[7] "The poor rate" Mr. Wiggins tells us "is at present felt as a great grievance in Ireland on the ground that so large a portion of it goes to the staff

[1] *The Irish Relief Measures*, London 1848.

[2] Smyth, *Ireland Historical and Statistical.* vol. ii. p. 444; and see Butt *The Famine in the Land* pp. 35—55.

[3] *Observations and Strictures on the Present Irish Poor Law* by an Irish Magistrate Dublin 1843.

[4] Wiggins. *The Monster Misery of Ireland*, London 1844.

[5] *Report of Grand Jury Commission* 1842 p. xxviii.

[6] *Devon Commn.* p. 704.

[7] *Observations and Strictures on the Present Irish Poor Law* by an Irish Magistrate. Dublin 1843.

or officers, and to the support of the union houses, leaving what is considered but a small share of the rate applicable to the actual relief of the poor."[1] The grievance of the rate was increased in 1849, when a rate in aid was added to the existing burdens.[2]

But the real objection felt to the poor law arose less out of the financial burden it imposed, than out of the realization that it did not ameliorate the condition of the country. We shall see in a later chapter that it broke down in the face of acute distress, but even in normal years it did not succeed in suppressing mendicancy. Although there were 3,722 inmates in the Dublin workhouses in 1841, the number of destitute to be seen in the streets had scarcely diminished at all,[3] and the Mendicity Association was found as necessary as ever.[4] Generally speaking the act was felt to have been a complete failure. "Ten years ago" wrote G. L. Smyth "the hope prevailed with many that the operation of the poor law would have put an end to the existence of such a state of distress. But that hope was soon dispelled.... The law is one of the greatest failures in modern legislation. The number of the poor has not diminished, while the poor themselves and every other superior interest in the country stand compactly arrayed against its administration."[5] Nothing is more indicative of the failure of the act than the innumerable suggestions which were constantly being made for its reform.[6]

(e) *The Repeal of the Corn Laws.*

Our inclusion of the repeal of the corn laws amongst the legislative measures which we have classified as aids to depopulation may at first sight surprise some of our

[1] *The Monster Misery of Ireland.* London 1844.
[2] 12 and 13 Vict. c. 24, Nicholls *op. cit.* p. 359. Butt, *The Rate in Aid,* Dublin 1849.
[3] 23*rd Report of Mendicity Association* 1841.
[4] 28*th Report of Mendicity Association* 1846.
[5] *Ireland Historical and Statistical* vol. iii. p. 41.
[6] These suggestions are classified in a pamphlet entitled *What is to be Done?* Tralee 1849.

readers, and, indeed, it is undeniable that this measure is not precisely in the same class as those we have already mentioned. The ejectment acts, the subletting act, the raising of the franchise, and the poor law, were measures deliberately designed to encourage the clearance of estates, and the consequent depopulation of Ireland; the repeal of the corn laws on the other hand was passed primarily with the object of reducing the price of bread for the English manufacturer. Its effect nevertheless was undoubtedly to hasten the process of clearance, and, as we shall show, that effect was, or ought to have been, clearly foreseen by its proposers. In law, wilful recklessness and a blind disregard of other people's interests are held to be equivalent to positive negligence. If this be so, we are surely not overstepping the mark in suggesting that, in passing a measure—primarily designed, it is true, to attain other ends—the inevitable consequence of which was to aid the process of clearing estates, the government must be held responsible for the passage of another calculated aid to depopulation.

Nothing was more clearly grasped in the early nineteenth century than the proposition that Ireland was England's granary—in other words, that England was to provide a preferential market for Irish corn, in return for the abandonment on Ireland's part of all pretence to become an industrial country. In 1806 Irish cereals were admitted free from restrictions into England. This concession, which was often subsequently cited as an instance of the tender regard of England for Ireland's economic welfare, was, of course, dictated by purely selfish motives. If Irish corn had not at the time had access to the British market, the absentees would have found it difficult to obtain payment of their rents, and the English consumer, on account of the war, would have found it impossible to obtain food.[1]

[1] Fraser. *Sketches and Essays on the Present State of Ireland.* Dublin, 1822; Ensor, *An Address to the People of Ireland.* Dublin 1822.

Whatever its motive, however, this action of parliament had the effect of crystallizing the idea that Ireland was entitled to some preference in the British market; and Irish agriculturalists continued to direct their operations on this assumption. When the corn bill was introduced in 1815, Grattan emphasized the duty which England lay under to buy Irish corn; and exhorted parliament that, having already driven Ireland out of manufacture, it should not then drive her out of tillage. "Do you propose" Grattan exclaimed on this occasion "that Ireland should prefer the British manufacturer, and that the British manufacturer should prefer the French husbandman? . . . . If you go out of tillage, what will you do with the population of Ireland?"[1] Peel, who afterwards repealed the corn laws, remarked on this occasion that "among measures likely to be productive of practical benefit, I consider those which are calculated to secure to the productions of Ireland a just preference over the productions of foreign countries."[2] "The advantages of this protection" said Francis Wyse "offered to the people of this country some partial atonement for the complete or near annihilation of every kind or species of manufacturing industry."[3] "The cry since the Union" according to John O'Connell "has been, that we ought not to think of *any* manufacture, but to devote ourselves to the supplying of Great Britain with our agricultural produce."[4] "Dazzled" wrote Sir Robert Kane "by the wondrous facilities for industrial activity which the structure of the sister kingdom presents, we had gradually sunk under a stupefying impression that Ireland was unsuited for any manufactures; and the phrase currently ran: 'we are an agricultural people; our soil and climate fit us for producing corn and cattle, whilst her union of coal and iron make her the workshop of the world. The position of the two islands is therefore correlative and mutually

[1] *Grattan's Speeches*, vol iv p. 370 and see Grattan *Life of Grattan*, vol v. p. 512.
[2] Parker *Sir Robert Peel* vol i p. 232. [3] *A Letter to Lord Stanley*. Dublin 1846
[4] *An Argument for Ireland*. Dublin 1847.

advantageous; she sends us clothing and we send her food; from her crowded factories we receive all the products of complex manufacture, and in return she takes our corn and cattle, the raw productions of our soil.' "[1]

This understanding was analagous to that which had prevailed at the end of the seventeenth century with regard to the woollen and linen trades. It will be remembered that the consideration offered for the destruction of the former was the encouragement of the latter. The two understandings were not alone similar but similarly observed. As soon as the destruction of the woollen industry had been safely accomplished, the British parliament proceeded to discourage the linen; and, now, as soon as Ireland had become definitely an agricultural and tillage country in consideration of receiving a preference in the British market, that preference was taken away. The same type of argument was put forward, and the same type of excuse offered on each occasion. As, in the eighteenth century, specious arguments were based on the alleged unsuitability to Ireland of the particular industry the destruction of which was contemplated; so, in the nineteenth, it was said that Ireland was not suited for tillage. Acccording to Professor Cairnes, the arch-freetrader, the movement from pasture to tillage in the first half of the nineteenth century was "a violent diversion of Irish industry from its natural source—a diversion from which have directly flowed no small part of all the most serious evils which Ireland has since endured."[2] If however this were so, and if Ireland had become a tillage country only by reason of strong artificial encouragement, this would surely make it all the more incumbent on the legislature to watch carefully that this encouragement was not suddenly withdrawn. If the staple industry in a country is one which springs naturally from its resources, the sudden withdrawal of public encouragement from that industry will probably be innocuous, if not beneficial; but, when a

[1] *Industrial Resources* p. 250. [2] *Political Essays* p. 128.

country has been forced into a new and unnatural economic life by the action of the legislature, it behoves the legislature to guard against the sudden subversion of an artificial condition which it has itself established. The argument of Professor Cairnes therefore merely strengthens the case against the government that repealed the corn laws.

We must not be taken as expressing any opinion about the wisdom of Peel's measure at the time it was passed. Probably the admission of cheap food into England was very beneficial, and aided the development of English industry. The only point we wish to make is, that the repeal of the corn laws, like so many other measures of the United Parliament, was carried purely in the interests of England, and that the special circumstances of Ireland do not appear to have engaged the attention of the government or parliament. The difference between the effects of the measure on the two countries is well put by Professor Cairnes:—"It is, I hold, indubitably true that the cultivation of cereals in Ireland on the scale on which it prevailed anterior to 1846 depended upon Ireland's being secured in the monopoly of the English markets; and this condition free trade forbade. Whether England was on this account bound to exclude her own people from procuring their food where they could get it cheapest —bound to set limits to her own development in order to find a market for products unsuitable to the Irish soil—is a question which free traders have to meet. For my part I meet it by denying the obligation."[1] This was precisely the problem which faced Sir Robert Peel in 1846, and he solved it as Profesor Cairnes would have done. The interests of the smaller must give way to those of the larger country ; minorities must suffer. That Peel was quite alive to the possible consequences of his measure is proved by a passage in his speech, where he said, "If there be any part of the United Kingdom which is to suffer by the withdrawal of protection,

[1] *Political Essays p.* 137.

I have always felt that it is Ireland."[1] "It seems strange" we read in a contemporary publication, "that amidst all that has been spoken and written on the subject of a repeal of the corn laws, scarcely an allusion has been made by the contending interests to the effect it would have on Ireland."[2] The repeal, when it came, exactly bore out the startling prediction uttered by Sheil ten years before, that "if the safety of the empire were placed in one scale and a quartern loaf in the other, there was no doubt which scale would sink at the impulse of the political economist."[3]

We shall refer further in a later section to the pretended reason for the immediate repeal of the corn laws, namely, the desirability of admitting cheap food into Ireland during the famine, and shall simply remark in passing that it rested on the assumption that what Ireland lacked in those terrible years was food. Nothing however could be further from the truth; what the country lacked was not food but the means of purchasing it. If any measure had been desirable for increasing the supply of foodstuffs in the Irish market, surely it would have been wiser to place an embargo on the exportation of Irish corn than to give facilities for foreign farmers to flood the country with cereals of an inferior description to those which it itself produced. So long as the Irish peasantry suffered from the evil of unemployment, they were not concerned as consumers in the price of corn, as they were equally unable to purchase it whether it was cheap or dear; they were vitally interested on the other hand as producers in its price, as the higher the price of corn, the more employment would be available. The interest of Ireland was thus diametrically opposed to that of England in this matter. The latter was naturally as anxious to buy its corn cheap as the former to sell it dear. This was clearly perceived by Newenham quite early in the century:—"In consequence of the inferior

[1] Hansard 3rd Ser. vol 83 Col. 273.
[2] Philip Reade, *Whig and Tory Remedies for Irish Evils.* Dublin 1844.
[3] *Debate on the Repeal of the Union.* Dublin 1834. p. 138.

orders of the Irish people subsisting chiefly on potatoes, the corn of Ireland cannot with propriety be viewed in the same light as that of other countries. There, it is a mere necessity of life; here, it is rather an exportable manufacture by the foreign vent whereof those who labour in preparing it for market are enabled to purchase that article of food which they have been in the habit of using. Some part of the Irish community may no doubt experience distress in the event of any great rise in the price of corn; but by far the greater part would be nowise affected thereby, and many might be thereby benefited."[1] The truth of Newenham's observations increased rather than diminished in later years.

The best writers on Irish economic affairs during the first half of the nineteenth century were unanimous in insisting on the importance of the corn laws to the prosperity of Ireland. "Evil as the present system is," the Rev. Henry Major wrote in 1815 "who can tell what the consequence may be if hereafter, on the return of a general peace, Irish corn shall be denied in the British market that preference to which it is indubitably entitled? The tradesmen and manufacturers of England will object to purchase corn at a higher price from Ireland than they shall be able to procure it from different parts of the continent; nor in all probability will the legislature compel them to do so. Under this circumstance, the specie we receive for our exports becoming still less than the specie we are necessitated to part with for our imports, the virtual balance of trade will be turned against Ireland more fatally than we find at present; and we shall probably behold the approach with accelerated pace of the impoverishment and depopulation of Ireland."[2] Sadleir also insisted on the vital necessity for the continuance of the corn laws. "Other propositions in favour of Ireland I shall waive at present in favour

[1] *View of Ireland* p. 211.
[2] *Observations Demonstrative of the Necessity to Ireland's Welfare*, &c. Dublin 1815.

of one which can neither be overlooked nor hastily dismissed; involving as it does without a figure of speech the remaining vital interest of a country deserted and degraded; that interest which gives the limited measure of employment and food which is still afforded to the mass of the community, and in the due support of which the best hopes of their future improvement are founded. But this proposition is strictly speaking of a negative character, and goes to the continuation of an advantage which has now been for many years enjoyed, rather than the bestowment of any new or additional benefit; it implores that, if no new policy shall be pursued to serve and assist Ireland, none shall be adopted that shall injure her interests or complete her ruin. It is almost needless to explain that I refer to a continuation of a free and exclusive access to the markets of Great Britain for her agricultural products; or in other words that the legislature shall still continue to protect her almost only branch of national industry by efficient corn laws .... Withdraw the last protection, and the wish expressed by one of the interlocutors in Spenser's *View of Ireland* that we could set our foot upon it and sink it to the bottom of the Atlantic Ocean, would, if accomplished, be an act of kindness."[1] "If the corn laws were to be repealed," we read a few years later "before Irish husbandry shall be improved, so as to meet foreign competition, the agricultural interests of Ireland would be overwhelmed with difficulties producing most fearful results."[2] The great danger threatened to Ireland by such a measure was emphasized by the Dublin Chamber of Commerce.[3]

Petitions were presented to parliament from every part of Ireland protesting against the proposed repeal of the corn laws.[4] William Blacker was to the fore in resisting the suggested measure: "The importation of foreign corn

[1] *Ireland Its Evils &c.* pp. 318-9.
[2] A. H. Lynch, *Address to the Electors of Galway.* London 1838
[3] *Report of the Dublin Chamber of Commerce* 1838.
Bermingham. *A Letter on the Corn Laws.* Dublin 1841.

is more likely to deteriorate than to improve our agricultural labourers' condition, and even the cheap provision which it promises seems to me likely to last no longer than until the present race of farmers are driven out of the field."[1] A very well-attended and representative meeting of the Society for the Improvement of Ireland adopted the following resolution. "That, though we approve of the policy of Sir Robert Peel, and the present ministry in their general principles of free trade, and striking the shackles from commerce, yet, as Ireland may suffer from losing the advantage of supplying corn and provisions to the sister country, we feel that Ireland is now entitled to an ample equivalent."[2] The agitation for the repeal of the Union received much stimulation from the general fear of the repeal of the corn laws.[3].

In repealing the corn laws, therefore, the government must have been fully aware of the injury that the measure would inflict upon Ireland. We need not labour the point that such injury was in fact experienced, as on this all the available testimony is unanimous. Professor Cairnes, who, as we have seen, was a vigorous supporter of repeal, nevertheless fully admitted the evil effects which repeal had entailed. "The famine of 1846" he writes "is commonly taken as the turning point in the industrial history of Ireland. In fact it has proved so, because the famine precipitated free trade; but it is not less true that free trade would of itself have entailed, though without the frightful aggravations incident on the sudden failure of a people's food, all the consequences of a permanent kind which we trace to that calamity. All the leading incidents of the industrial economy of Ireland as it stood in 1846 were identified with the maintenance of the tillage system; and of

[1] *An Essay on the Best Means of Improving the Condition of the Labouring Classes in Ireland.* London 1846, *Pro Corn Law Tracts* London 1850. and see H. Geale. *Ireland and Irish Questions.* London 1845.

[2] *Report of General Meeting on the* 18*th Feb.*, 1846. *Haliday Pamphlets*, vol. 1914.

[3] Reade, *Whig and Tory Remedies for Irish Evils* Dublin 1844; *The Constitutional Rights of Landlords.* Dublin 1844.

that system free trade sounded the inevitable doom.... The shock, of the famine, rude as it was, extensively deranging, as it could not fail to be, to the entire territorial system, might possibly not have been fatal, had not the famine been the occasion of free trade, but free trade effectually and for ever sealed its doom."[1] "The Irish famine" according to Dr. Cunningham "was the direct occasion of breaking down the policy of agricultural protection; the importation of foodstuffs was temporarily encouraged for the sake of the starving peasantry; but the complete abandonment of the corn laws proved to be a very serious blow to the more energetic elements in the population."[2] "I suppose," said Lecky addressing the House of Commons, "that England under free trade has advanced her prosperity far beyond any other country; but in Ireland the effects of free trade were totally different. Ireland was almost exclusively an agricultural country, and the effects of free trade were first of all to depreciate the article she produced, and then to deprive her of the monopoly which she had for her goods."[3] Mr. Childers expressed the same view:—"The change is usually considered to have been advantageous to a population, the great bulk of which had come to depend not upon agriculture but upon manufacturing industry and commerce. It is, we think, evident that the change has not been so advantageous to Ireland as it has been to England, and although, as consumers, the Irish population may have gained in some cases by the abolition of duties on food stuffs, yet that on the other hand, as producers, chiefly dependent upon agriculture, they have lost in a far greater degree by the cheap prices in the British markets."[4]

The first noticeable effect of the repeal of the corn laws

[1] *Political Essays* pp. 136, 171.
[2] *Growth of English Industry and Commerce* vol. iii p. 848 and see Murray *Commercial Relations* p. 384.
[3] Quoted in Shaw Mulholland, *The Predominant Partner* p. 29
[4] *Financial Relations Commission* p. 159.

was a decrease in the value of Irish agricultural produce. "Free trade" complained Isaac Butt in 1849 "has very much declined the value of what is raised;"[1] and in the same year we read that, "the staple commodity of Ireland free trade has entirely annihilated; nor could that able financier Sir Robert Peel have considered Ireland as an integral part of the United Kingdom when he inflicted on her this last most fatal blow."[2] From 1850 onwards a diminution in the area under tillage was to be remarked.[3] The discouragement of tillage inevitably led to more rapid consolidation and to further clearances. "The enormous decrease in the number of small holdings" said J. S. Mill "and increase in those of a medium size is attested by the statistical returns . . . It is probable that the repeal of the corn laws, necessitating a change in the exports of Ireland from the products of tillage to those of pasturage, would of itself have sufficed to bring about this revolution in tenure."[4] "Let us glance at a few of the consequences of free trade," wrote Professor Cairnes, "and, first and most important of all, free trade imperatively prescribed a large reduction in the number of the Irish people; for it struck at the root of the large cereal cultivation by which those numbers were sustained . . . Free trade in Ireland thus of necessity involved as its consequence a diminution in the number of its people."[5] In view of the above, can it be suggested that we are straining language when we include the repeal of the corn laws amongst the legislative aids to depopulation?

One result of the repeal of the corn laws was that the prosperous milling industry experienced a reverse. One of the provisions of Foster's Corn Law was the prohibition of the importation into Ireland of corn ground into meal or flour, with the result that the number of mills was greatly

[1] *The Rate in Aid.* Dublin 1849. [2] R. B. Mosse, *Ireland, Its State, Its Evils & Its Remedies.* London 1849 and see *Ireland's Hour* Dublin 1850. [3] Marmion *Maritime Ports* p. 152. [4] *The Irish Land Question* p. 92. [5] *Political Essays* p. 140.

increased. Wakefield states that mills for grinding wheat had been erected in almost every county, and that mills for grinding oats were common.[1] A few years later we are told that "mills are being established in every part of the kingdom."[2] A great part of the corn exported to England was ground at Liverpool or Bristol in the early part of the century, but it became more and more the custom to grind in Ireland.[3] In 1835 there were 1882 registered corn mills and 2296 corn kilns in Ireland. Naturally the repeal of the corn laws inflicted serious damage on this flourishing industry. "Previous to the repeal of the corn laws" Marmion complained in 1856 "Clonmel had the most extensive flour mills in Ireland, on the erection of which large capitals were expended. The legislature, so tenacious on other occasions of interfering with vested interests or individual enterprise, particularly in English, admitted foreign flour duty free, without affording the slightest compensation to those whose investments were thus in a great measure rendered a nullity."[4]

(f) *Emigration.*

In one sense it may be said to be out of place to treat of emigration in the present chapter, as the exodus from Ireland was an indication rather than a cause of the depopulation of the country. Moreover, there were with a few trifling exceptions no legislative measures passed in the period under review directly designed to aid emigration out of public funds. But in another sense it is strictly logical to treat of emigration in this place. The other measures which we have mentioned conspired to clear the land of its tenants, who, in the absence of manufactur-

[1] Vol i. p. 759.
[2] *Official Papers Public Record Office Dublin* 1790-1830 carton 456 no. 1924.
[3] *Second Report of Railway Commissioners* 1838 p. 9.
[4] *Maritime Ports* p. 559. An account of the quantities of grain flour and meal exported from Ireland between 1801 and 1828 is to be found in *Parl Pap* no. 180 of 1828.

ing industry, were left but two alternatives, starvation or emigration, of which the latter was naturally the more popular. The volume of emigration that took place in the period was thus the inevitable consequence of the government's general policy, and, this being so, we suggest that we are justified in stating that the encouragement of emigration formed part of that policy. The policy of the government had the inevitable and easily foreseen result of increasing the volume of emigration; and a government, like an individual, must be credited with intending the results which must flow immediately from its actions.

It is a by no means uncommon error to think that Irish emigration dates from the famine. Of course, as we shall see, the famine caused great numbers to emigrate, but there was also a considerable volume of emigration previous to 1846. It is with the latter that we are exclusively concerned in the present section, as the post-famine emigration falls more naturally into the next chapter.

In the early years of the nineteenth century, emigration was practically confined to the northern counties. Wakefield says that it had very materially diminished in the other parts of Ireland in the years preceding 1810,[1] but it seems to have continued in Antrim, Down, Armagh and Derry.[2] While the emigration from Ireland never totally ceased, it seems to have been confined to comparatively reasonable dimensions before 1820.[3] It must not be forgotten however that the drain caused by ordinary emigration was swollen by the great numbers of Irishmen who joined the British army and navy in these years. "The country since 1792" we read in 1810 "has been largely drawn on for soldiers and sailors, who to the amount of

[1] Vol, ii, pp. 712-3.

[2] De Salis, *Considerations on the Propriety of a General Drainage Bill.* Armagh 1813.

[3] Major. *Observations Demonstrative of the Necessity to Ireland's Welfare etc.* Dublin 1815; *Hints to Irishmen who Intend with their Families to Make a Permanent Residence in America.* Dublin 1817.

some hundreds of thousands have perished in the service of their country;"[1] and Wakefield stated that Ireland was the great *officina militum* of the empire.[2] The enlistment of Irish Catholics was encouraged by the government. "The enlistment of Catholics" Lord Grenville wrote in 1806 "is recommended by every consideration. We greatly want the supply which Ireland might afford to our recruiting; and Ireland wants such a vent for its population, being exactly in that stage of society which increases population without an adequate increase of the means of employment."[3] A further drain was caused by the system of "indentured apprentices." When American merchantmen touched at Irish ports, it was the common practice to get young Irish boys to sign agreements to serve on board for a number of years, to use them for the voyage, and then to turn them adrift. "This traffic in Irishmen has been of long continuance, and to a very great extent; as lately as last year I witnessed an American vessel freighted with nearly three hundred of these poor deluded self-sold men."[4] Generally speaking however the great tide of emigration from Ireland did not set in until about 1823.

The impetus which emigration received in that year was caused by the severe famine, as a result of which thousands of homeless families were driven from the country in search of a living. The emigrants however betook themselves less to America than to Great Britain. From this time onwards we meet with the constant complaint of the flooding of the English labour market by Irish emigrants. Doubtless a certain amount of emigration to England had taken place before that date; in 1819 it was stated that large numbers of the poor in London were Irish;[5] and the 1821 Census showed that Glasgow contained 25,000 natives of Ireland;[6] but generally speaking it is correct to say

[1] *The State of Ireland Considered* Dublin 1810. [2] Vol. ii. p. 713.
[3] *Fortescue MSS.* vol. viii. p. 486.
[4] Trimmer, *Further Observations Etc.* London 1812.
[5] Parker, *An Essay on the Employment of the Labouring Classes.* Cork 1819.
[6] *Select Committee on State of Ireland* 1825 p. 823.

that the great flood of Irish emigrants did not appear in England until after the famine of 1822.[1] From that date onwards we meet incessant complaints of the way in which the English labour market was flooded with cheap Irish labour, to the detriment of the English working class. We have already examined how far this complaint was justified; the only thing for us to remark here is that it was persistently made, and that it produced an intense desire in England to get rid of the Irish emigrants. Hence arose the cry in favour of colonial emigration as the panacea for Irish ills. What was not apparently perceived was that, as far as the interests of Ireland were concerned, the destination of the emigrant was a matter of indifference; that the overpopulation of the country was equally relieved by the departure of a family for Liverpool and for New York; and that, if emigration from Ireland was desirable, it might just as well be to England as to the American colonies or the United States.

Of the extent of the Irish immigration into England at this time there can be no question. "I feel certain" Sir Henry Parnell predicted in 1824 "that there will be a great emigration of labourers from Ireland to England; not of labourers coming over for the harvest, and returning to Ireland, but of young able labourers who will settle permanently in England. The practice is already becoming very general."[2] "There is a vast surplus of Irish labourers at this season in the west riding of Yorkshire", we are told three years later. "At Huddersfield the number is so great that it is with difficulty they can find shelter during the night; the farmers all the way from the western to the eastern coast are quite annoyed with applications for employment from these half-famished people."[3] "Females continually proceed to the different manufacturing districts in England, and are enabled to earn weekly wages even higher than what men

[1] O'Rourke, *The Great Irish Famine* p. 483.
[2] *Speech of Sir Henry Parnell in the House of Commons on May* 11*th*1824. London 1824
[3] *Yorkshire Gazette* 23rd May 1827.

earn in this country in agricultural labour, but it is to be observed that it often happens that when they are reduced to poverty from continued want of employment, or from ill health, they are sent back to this country under the poor law system."[1] Enormous numbers of Irish workers were employed on public works in the lowlands of Scotland and in the textile trade in Lancashire.[2] The migration of Irish labourers to England was greatly encouraged by the introduction of steam transit. "Every hour" exclaimed O'Driscoll in 1825 "throws its multitudes of Irish poor on the English shores. All the powers of steam labour to cast the living burden upon Britain."[3] The owners of steamships were accustomed to convey the Irish poor to Great Britain free, in expectation of the passage money they would receive on their return journey, when the migrants were repatriated under the poor law.[4]

The best account of the Irish immigrants in Great Britain is to be found in the report drawn up on the subject by G. C. Lewis for the Poor Inquiry Commission. Lewis divided the Irish poor to be met in England into two classes—temporarily and permanently resident. The former were of three kinds, harvest labourers, cattle drovers, and mendicants. The latter class however was exclusively the subject of Lewis' investigations. They were principally engaged in the textile industries of Lancashire and Scotland, on coarse unskilled labour. "The kind of work on which they are employed is usually of the roughest, coarsest and most repulsive description, and requiring the least skill and practice; and their mode of life is in general on a par with that of the poorest of the native population, if not inferior to it. . . . The emigration from Ireland to England and Scotland is of a very remarkable character, and is perhaps nearly unparallelled in the history of the world. It has

1 Kinahan. *Outline of a Plea for Relieving the Poor of Ireland.* Dublin 1829.
2 Fay, *Life and Labour in the Nineteenth Century* pp. 104., 171, 217, 220.
3 *Review of the Evidence before the Irish Committees.* Dublin 1825.
4 *Thoughts on the Poor of Ireland* by a Barrister Dublin 1831.

usually happened that emigrations have taken place from more civilized to less civilized nations; but the Irish emigration into Britain is an example of a less civilized population spreading themselves as a kind of substratum beneath a more civilized community." Lewis estimated the number of Irish in Lanarkshire at 50,000, in Edinburgh at 10,000, in Dundee at 5,000, in Aberdeen at 3,000, in Lancashire at 100,000 and in Birmingham at 6,000. Many were employed in factories, others engaged in a small retail trade, but the greater number were navvies and the like. The first generation of settlers did not, generally speaking, raise their standard of life in proportion to the increased wages they received; but the second generation generally did so, and became indistinguishable from the native English. Lewis pays a remarkable tribute to the high industrial character of these poor Irish settlers: "The introduction of so large a number of Irish into Great Britain has been influenced by the qualities which the Irish brings into competition with the English or Scotch workman. The most valuable of these, and those to which the employment of the Irish has been mainly owing, are willingness, alacrity, and perseverance in the severest, the most irksome, and most disagreeable kinds of coarse labour. . . . In these departments of work it has been found by contractors and others more advantageous to employ Irish than native labourers; and, though in Ireland a labourer perhaps does not perform half so much work in a day for 8d as an English labourer for 16d, yet when he is stimulated by high wages he is found to exert an energy and zeal which cannot easily be surpassed."[1]

While the emigration to England thus continued to increase considerably, no material augmentation of the colonial and foreign emigration was noticeable. The movement in this direction was retarded by the high cost of

[1] Lewis *Report.* p. xxxi. A good account of the early Irish emigration is to be found in O'Rourke *The Great Irish Famine* pp. 483 sq.

passage abroad—about £20 per head from Dublin to New York[1]—, and by the merchant shipping regulations which subjected the owners of emigrant ships to many severe restraints.[2]

As we said above, the influx of cheap Irish labour into Great Britain aroused considerable anxiety amongst the English working classes, and the desirability of the Irish being encouraged, or compelled, to betake themselves elsewhere came to be frequently discussed. Numerous pamphlets were issued on the subject; amongst them a genuinely Swiftean modest proposal for the compulsory transportation of four millions of people from Ireland to the colonies.[3] The orthodox economists were unanimously of opinion that the only possible remedy for Irish ills was a wholesale system of emigration. "I certainly think" said Mr. J. R. McCulloch "that in the circumstances in which Ireland is actually placed, it would be most proper and advisable for the government to lay out a very large sum of money on carrying away such tenants as might be ejected or deprived of the means of subsistence by the consolidation of farms, provided the landlords gave the government unquestioned security that the place which these tenants now fill would not be occupied for some considerable number of years."[4] Malthus advocated, as one of the prime steps towards the regeneration of Ireland, "a judicious system of emigration."[5] Mr. Nicholls strongly advocated emigration as an absolute necessity for Ireland: "As long as the labourers exceed the number required, so long will their competition for employment tend to depress their condition, and to counteract any efforts that may be made

[1] Cairnes *Political Essays* p. 149.

[2] *Select Committee on State of Ireland* 1824-5. Evidence of John Astle; Buchanan. *Emigration Practically Considered.* London 1828.

[3] John Wheatley, *A Letter to the Duke of Devonshire on the State of Ireland*, Calcutta 1824; *The Means of Improving the Condition of the Unemployed* by a Retired Officer, Dublin 1822; Watson. *The Immigrants Guide to the Canadas.* Dublin 1822. A. C. Buchanan. *Outline of a Practical Plan, etc.* Brighton 1837.

[4] *Select Committee on State of Ireland* 1825 p. 830.

[5] *Third Report of Select Committee on Emigration* 1826.

to improve it. The only alternative therefore in such case is either to increase the amount of employment or to decrease the number of labourers depending upon it. Now to effect an artificial increase in the amount of employment may under certain circumstances be practicable for a time, I believe only for a short time, but this would merely mitigate the symptoms; it would not destroy the seeds of the disease."[1] George Cornewall Lewis concurred in this opinion: "As we cannot make more land for the inhabitants, we must make fewer inhabitants to the land."[2] Torrens also recommended an extended system of emigration, and approved of the poor law as a necessary preparation for such a scheme.[3] Nassau Senior regarded it as the one certain means of Irish regeneration.[4] Thus all the leading English economists looked with favour on a scheme of emigration. "Of all the systems" said Beaumont "which for the past twenty years have been proposed for the salvation of Ireland, there is none perhaps which has had in England more favour than that of emigration practised on a large scale."[5]

The government was advised in this direction not alone by the economists, but also by several official committees of inquiry. In 1823 an experiment on a small scale was carried into effect, and it was generally admitted that it proved successful. The total number transported to America under this scheme was 2,592.[6] The select committee on emigration of 1826 strongly recommended emigration. "Very important evidence by Mr Leslie Foster and Mr. Nimmo will be found with respect to the cultivation of the bog lands of

[1] *Nicholls' Report p.* 111.

[2] *Irish Disturbances* p. 332.

[3] *A Letter to Lord John Russell.* London 1837 ; and see *Plan of an Association in Aid of the Irish Poor Laws.* London 1838.

[4] *Ireland Journals &c.* vol. i. p. 262.

[5] *L'Irlande Sociale* vol. ii. p. 121. See Barry O'Brien *Fifty Years of Concessions to Ireland* vol. ii. p. 143 and see Dufferin, *Irish Emigration etc.* p. 23.

[6] O'Rourke *The Great Irish Famine* pp. 483-4. Lord Cloncurry complained bitterly of the encouragement given to emigration by this experiment. *A Letter from Lord Cloncurry to Lord Downshire.* Dublin 1826.

Ireland; but, whatever may be thought of the advantages which might arise from such an application of capital, they would in no degree supersede the benefits to be derived from a contemporaneous and systematic principle of emigration." The committee made it quite plain that emigration to Great Britain would not satisfy its desires. "The question of emigration as connected with Ireland has been already decided by the population itself; and that which remains for the legislature to decide is to what points the emigration shall be directed, and whether it shall be turned to the improvement of the North American Colonies, or whether it shall be suffered to deluge Great Britain with poverty and wretchedness.... The question whether an extensive plan of emigration shall or shall not be adopted resolves itself into this simple point, whether the wheat-fed population of Great Britain shall or shall not be replaced by the potato-fed population of Ireland."[1] The Spring Rice Committee of 1830 also insisted on the necessity for emigration, and recommended that facilities should be afforded by the government to such peasants as were disposed to emigrate, and who could, either by themselves or their landlords, provide funds to defray the expense of their passage to and location in America.[2] It was pointed out that, whereas emigration from Great Britain, by tending to raise the rate of wages, encouraged the migration of Irish labourers from Ireland to England, emigration from Ireland, by tending to raise the rate of wages there, operated to check such migration. The important committee on public works of 1835 on the other hand viewed emigration with disfavour: "While the empire is loaded with taxation to defray the charges of its wars, it appears more politic to use its internal resources for improving the condition of the population, by which the revenue of the Exchequer must be increased, than to encourage emigration,

[1] *Third Report of Select Committee on Emigration* 1826.
[2] *Select Committee on Irish Poor* 1830.

by which the revenue would suffer a diminution."[1] The Poor Inquiry Commissioners, as we have seen, looked on emigration as "a purely temporary expedient, and in no sense as a permanent remedy." The Devon Commissioners took a similar view:—"We desire to express our own conviction that a well-organised system of emigration may be of very great service, as one amongst the measures which the situation of the occupier of land in Ireland at present calls for. We cannot think that either emigration or the extension of public works or the reclamation and improvement of land can singly remove the existing evil. All these remedies must be provided concurrently, and applied according to the circumstances of each case."[2] A select committee of the House of Lords in 1846 recommended "that increased facilities for the emigration of poor persons should be afforded, with the co-operation of the government."[3]

In spite of these many recommendations, no legislative assistance was given to emigration until the passing of the Irish poor law in 1838, one section of which enabled the majority of the ratepayers in any union to strike a rate of not more than one shilling in the pound to aid the emigration of any of its paupers.[4] An amending act of 1843 provided that two-thirds of the guardians in any union might assist any person who had been in the poorhouse for three months to emigrate to a British colony, and might charge the expenses on the union or on the electoral division on which such poor person had become chargeable, the rate to be levied not to exceed sixpence in the pound.[5] A further amending act of 1847 enlarged the powers of guardians in this respect. "If any occupier of land within any union valued under £5. is willing to give up land to his landlord, and to emigrate with all persons dependent upon him for support, and if he shall be approved of by the Secretary

[1] *Second Report.* [2] *Devon Comm.* p. 1142.
[3] *Parl. Pap.* No. 24 of 1846. [4] Sec 51.
[5] 6 and 7 Vict. c. 92 s. 18.

for the Colonies, and if the landlord is willing to release him from all claim for rent, and to provide two-thirds of the sum required for emigration, then the guardians may charge the electoral division of the occupier with one half of the sum contracted to be paid by the landlord, in aid of the emigration of such occupier and his family."[1] The power of guardians was further increased in 1849.[2] These acts were however availed of to but a very limited extent[3]

The amount of assistance given by the government directly to emigration was not great; but emigration nevertheless continued to progress. We have no figures of the number of emigrants to Great Britain, but the extracts which we have quoted from Lewis's report show that it was considerable. We are however in possession of approximate figures relating to the colonial and foreign emigration, which show that, in spite of the expense of the passage, this kind of emigration constituted a substantial drain on the manhood of Ireland. The figures from 1832 to the famine are as follows:-

YEAR*	Number of emigrants from Irish ports to colonies and foreign countries.
1832	33,007
1833	20,417
1834	30,165
1835	10,315
1836	20,800
1837	25,382
1838	4,424
1839	11,835
1840	28,148
1841	29,554
1842	89,686
1843	37,609
1844	54,289
1845	74,969
1846	105,955

* *Devon Commn.* p. 701. *Thom's Directory* 1851 p. 173. *Census* 1851. p. lv.

[1] 10 Vict. c. 31 s. 13.
[2] 12 and 13 Vict. c. 104.
[3] Nicholls *Irish Poor Law* p. 370.

Although the emigration previous to 1846 was insignificant compared with what came afterwards, it was nevertheless substantial when considered absolutely. The strange thing that first strikes us about it is the fact that it did not appear to benefit the country in the very least; while the tide of emigration became greater and greater, the misery of those who remained at home became worse and worse. This was undoubtedly accounted for to some extent by the fact that the people who emigrated were precisely those who were most needed in Ireland. Owing to the cost of the passage none could emigrate to the colonies or foreign countries, unless possessed of a small capital. We have abundant evidence that it was the small artisan class and middle farming class who composed the bulk of the emigrants. In 1801 Lord Enniskillen complained that great numbers of emigrants were leaving Derry, "and they are all the well-affected people that are going."[1] In 1816 Peel complained that the majority of the emigrants were from the north, and remarked: "I think this diminution of the Protestant population very unfortunate."[2] In 1823, the Bishop of Down and Connor was much alarmed by the drain on the Protestant population.[3] About 1823, large numbers of Protestants engaged in the linen manufacture went to America.[4] The owner of an emigrant ship told a committee of inquiry that it was mostly respectable agriculturalists and artisans who went, and that more Protestants went than Catholics in proportion to their numbers.[5] Mr. Nicholls insisted that there should be government assistance for emigration provided in the poor law bill, because "the individuals who now spontaneously emigrate are for the most part possessed of more means, and more mental and physical energy than their neighbours. They

[1] *Official Papers Public Record Office Dublin* 1790-1831, carton 333 no. 579.
[2] Parker. *Sir Robert Peel* vol. i. p. 234. Yonge. *Life of Lord Liverpool* vol. ii. p. 279.
[3] *Official Papers. Public Record Office* Dublin 1790-1831. carton 333.
[4] *Causes of the Discontents of Ireland.* Dublin 1823.
[5] *Select Committee of* 1824-5. *Evidence of John Astle.*

are in fact forced into it by the growth of a lower class at home. The best go—the worst remain."[1] Mr. Muggeridge found that the emigrants from the Ulster ports were "with very trifling exceptions all Protestants, and many of them were small capitalists, and exactly the sort of persons it was most desirable to keep at home."[2] The evidence before the Devon Commission established "that the present emigration does not relieve us from those classes that it would be most desirable to part with; that the voluntary emigrants for the most part consist of families possessing capital, whilst our paupers remain at home; and that the young, the strong, the enterprising and the industrious individuals of families leave us, whilst the old, the impotent, the idle and indolent portions stay with us."[3] "Emigration" according to William Blacker "so far from being a remedy for the evils of Ireland may fairly be considered as one direct and influential cause of their continuance. It is the wealthy, the industrious, and the well-doing, or the young and the healthy and strong who swell the emigrant list."[4]

The actual emigration which took place was thus a source of weakness rather than of strength. The mass of the poor peasantry who constituted the so-called surplus population were unable to emigrate through poverty. We must therefore inquire whether, assuming that their removal was advisable, it could have been effected by government aid as economically as the other measures for the regeneration of Ireland which we have discussed. This question was fully investigated by the Devon Commission, when the conclusion was reached that the expense of a state-aided emigration on a sufficiently large scale would have been considerably more than that of a thorough reclamation of the waste lands. We have not space here to follow the calculations

[1] *Second Report* 74.
[2] *Report on the Handloom Weavers* p. 722.
[3] *Devon Commn.* p. 567.
[4] *Essay on the Best Mode of Improving the Condition of the Labouring Classes in Ireland.* London 1846; and see Trevelyan *The Irish Crisis* p. 66. Butt, *The Rate in Aid.*

in detail; it is enough to state that the cost of the passage to, and location of an emigrant in Upper Canada was taken to be £21. 5s. per head, or £106. 5s. for an average family; that it was estimated that £30 of this could not be expected to be repaid, and must therefore be regarded as a dead loss; and that the number of families which it would be necessary to transport would be 192,368. The minimum dead loss thus incurred would amount to £5,771,040; and the return on the capital which would be ultimately repaid could not exceed 3%.[1] This scheme would therefore prove more costly than the alternative scheme of reclaiming the waste lands, which involved a greater initial outlay, but which was calculated to produce a handsome return by way of interest.

The dilemma therefore was that, if the government left emigration to take its own course, the best and not the worst elements of the population went, and the country was thus weakened instead of strengthened, whereas it could interfere only at colossal public expense. Nor was it at all certain that the good results expected would follow. The place of those who emigrated would probably soon be filled by an increase in the rate of the growth of the population. Moreover it was pointed out that the periods of the greatest emigration in the past had synchronized with those of the greatest possible misery in Ireland.[2] The arguments against emigration were well summarized by Sadleir[3] as follows:- "(1) It is but a temporary expedient on the acknowledged principles of those who would adopt it; (2) It is demonstrably a totally worthless remedy, having been tried largely and long and having totally failed, and (3) the disposable revenue of the country would not suffice to carry the scheme into effect on a scale sufficiently large to answer the purposes contemplated."

The government, while not directly encouraging emigra-

[1] The reader is referred for the full figures to *Devon Comm.* pp. 567 sq.
[2] This is well put in Sadleir's *Ireland Its Evils* &c. p. 79.
[3] *Op. cit.* p. 80.

tion by the assistance of the emigrants from the public funds, nevertheless indirectly assisted it by passing other measures which rendered it inevitable in the ordinary course of things. The result of this policy was that the emigration that took place was productive of the greatest possible damage to the country and of the greatest possible suffering to the emigrants.

CHAPTER VII.

The Great Famine.

Section 1. Earlier Famines.

THE previous chapters have been devoted to a discussion of the great problem of Irish economic life in the first half of the nineteenth century, the apparent disproportion between the population and the available resources of the country. We have seen that there were two possible solutions of the problem, the one to increase the resources, and the other to decrease the population; and that while all the best opinion of the time, including that of many public commissions of inquiry, was in favour of the adoption of the former course, the latter was in fact adopted, both by the landlords, who pursued their policy of consolidation regardless of consequences, and by the government, which passed a series of measures designed to facilitate the progress of the landlords' policy. The fundamental problem however was no nearer solution in 1845 than it was in 1800; because, in spite of the long campaign of state-aided clearances, the agricultural population of Ireland remained as poor as ever—or rather grew poorer from year to year. The problem therefore not only remained unsolved, but became more acute. Further discussion on the best means of solving it was however saved by the interposition of a great natural catastrophe, which solved it completely and beyond all discussion. The importance of the great famine of 1845-7 in the economic history of Ireland arises from the fact that it cut the Gordian knot of the question of disproportion between resources and population by drastically reducing the latter. While the economists and the politicians were discussing what should be done for Ireland, the potato blight provided a complete and unanswerable solution.

The famine of 1845-7 is frequently spoken of as if it were an isolated phenomenon in Irish history. Though often referred to as "the great famine", it is more frequently referred to simply as "the famine." Though not unintelligible, this description is apt to be misleading. While it is perfectly natural that the unprecedented magnitude of the calamity of 1845-7 should distinguish it in a special way from all previous misfortunes of the same nature, we should not lose sight of the fact that the calamity, though unprecedented in extent, was not unique in kind. The truth is that, throughout the whole of the eighteenth and the first half of the nineteenth centuries, Ireland had been living on the very border of famine, and that the border was not unfrequently crossed.

As we have seen, the outstanding feature of the economic condition of Ireland in the early nineteenth century was the dependence of the vast majority of the people on a single article of food. Naturally the fewer the commodities to which a people look for subsistence, the more dangerous becomes a failure of the supply of any one of them; and, when one article alone is depended upon, any failure of that article becomes a matter of vital importance. The danger of such a situation is aggravated when that single article is one which is in its very nature peculiarly liable to fail in certain seasons. The potato is an article of this kind. The many diseases to which this plant is liable to fall a victim are thus described in the census of 1851:— "It appears that the potato dies in the ground by what is termed the "Dry Rot", without ever vegetating, as was frequently the case from the year 1832 to 1836; that it suffers from extremes of wet at all periods of its development after vegetation has commenced, but especially during the latter end of summer and beginning of harvest; that at a later period it is liable to sour and rot, both before being dug and also when in the pits, by inundations and excessive moisture saturating the ground, as occurred in the memorable autumn of 1821; that it is subject to partial blight by arrest of growth at the most critical period of its progress, from the slight frosts which sometimes occur in spring and early harvest; and to complete destruction of the tuber itself, by the direct influence of those very severe and premature frosts which have occasionally occurred so early even as October and November (as in 1739) and, which, by converting the starch of the potato into sugar, make it unfit for present use, and render its preservation impossible. To these ordinary and accidental means of destruction may be added the distemper in the leaves, denominated the *Curl*, which appears chiefly in summer; and finally the *Blight*, that mysterious disease, which fatally affected leaves, stalks and tubers in rapid succession, and to which the recent wide-spread calamity is to be attributed."[1]

The dependence of a large population upon so delicate a root was fraught with danger. Since the beginning of the eighteenth century Ireland had been subject to recurring periods of famine, owing to the failure of the potato crop. The history of these famines before 1845 is admirably summarized in the census of 1851:"The following resumé will show how little dependence can be placed upon the stability of the potato crop, and how frequent have been the warnings given of its liability to decay. As already stated, the potato was introduced into Ireland at the end of the sixteenth century; but we have no proof that it was so extensively planted as to become a staple article of human food, and to displace corn to any extent, until towards

[1] *Census of, Ireland* 1851 pt. V. p. 241. The defects of the potato as the staple food of a country are well stated in John Revans' *Evils of the State of Ireland* London 1837, and in Sandham Elly's *Potatoes Pigs and Politics the Curse of Ireland* London 1848.

the end of the seventeenth century. The first great destruction of the potato crop occurred in the winter of 1739-40, and was attributed to the early, very severe, and long-continued frost of that period. There had been a very wet summer and autumn in 1739; and although the frost, no doubt, was one of the chief causes of its destruction, yet we are inclined to think that the potato failures in 1739, 1740, and 1741, were not altogether attributable to the severity of the winters. A century ago, improvidence and bad agriculture were more marked than in the present day ; and thus, when the great frost broke out in the November of 1739, and which increased in intensity during the following month, it found all the potato crop not already used, in the ground, either undug, or in pits with such a loose covering of earth as was penetrable to the frost; and thus it was said that the potato crop was destroyed in one night. Three hundred thousand people are stated to have perished of famine resulting from this failure. Even in 1741 the people were cautioned against eating potatoes, which were believed to be diseased, and likely to produce disease in man.

"In 1756 a new epidemic constitution commenced, and the seasons were characterized by extreme wetness, yet it does not appear that the potato suffered. There had been a series of unusual wet seasons preceding the year 1765, which was memorable for the quantity of rain which fell in the early part of it, and the excessive drought in the commencement of summer—an amount of heat and dryness so great that the trees dropped their leaves for want of moisture, and cattle were unable to supply milk;—the potatoes were scarce and small, as occurred again, under like circumstances in 1826. In 1770 there was a potato failure, attributed to the *curl*, or disease in the leaves; and this is the first year in which we read of an epiphytic to any degree in Scotland, because, in all probability the potato only then began to be cultivated to such an extent there as to attract attention in case of failure. The earliest date assigned by writers for its cultivation in Scotland, except in gardens, is 1728.

"In 1775 the disease denominated *curl* destroyed the potato crop in Flanders to such an extent that its cultivation was for a time almost abandoned. From this we may suppose that the potato was then in general use in the Low Countries. 'The disease,' says Van Adbrock, 'increased from year to year to that degree that the root was threatened with total destruction; and fresh seed was introduced from Virginia.' The Royal Academy of Brussels gave a prize for the best treatise on the cause of the malady.

"Although we do not read of any special failure in the potato crop about the year 1779, yet that philosophical writer, Arthur Young, informs us that in some of the northern counties, the people sprinkled their potato land with lime, in order to prevent the *Black Rot.* And now again we read of symptoms of degeneracy in the plant in Scotland, where the *curl* prevailed for the first time; and the deterioration of the plant continued in so marked a degree that in 1784 or 1785 the whole crops of the Lothians were affected by it. In 1784 we are led to believe that the intense frost injured the potato in Ireland. In later years the people seemed aware of the deleterious effects of the frost, and denominated the potato so injured, "*spuggaun,*" expressive of its softness. The year 1795 was one of unusual character, both in Europe and America. The weather here was uncommonly severe, the spring cold and late, the summer suffocatingly hot, damp, and rainy, while south winds were prevalent. The fruits perished from mould, and there was a disease among vegetables, especially potatoes and cabbages. The latter part of the year 1798 was unusually wet in Ireland, and 1799 was particularly cold; general bad harvests ensued, but we do not read of any special destruction of the potato crop, although there is reason to believe that it suffered materially, together with the wheat and oats.

"In 1800 there was a partial failure of the potato, owing to excessive drought; the disease appeared in the stalks, but science has not informed us what the specific nature of the epiphytic was; and the harvest generally was a bad one. Great scarcity and distress succeeded this time. The potato also failed in England, and for some years afterwards the *curl* injured many of the best varieties there. In 1801 there was a very general potato failure in Ireland, attributed to obstructed vegetation, consequent upon the heat and drought, while the roots were yet in the ground. Again, in 1807, the frost, which set in about November with unusual severity, destroyed about one-half of the potato crop. In 1809 the *curl* again injured the potatoes, though not to such an extent as to deserve the name of a failure; but in 1811, the spring and early summer of which year were excessively wet, a partial failure of the potato crop was again reported. At this time, as on subsequent occasions, the loss of the potato was not much felt during the year in which it occurred; as, even in the worst of times, there is a sufficient amount of food derived from the year's crop to suffice for the wants of the community until the following spring. In 1812 some of the early planted potatoes likewise failed, but not sufficiently as to affect human life.

"The memorable frost in the winter of 1813-14 did not in any way affect the food of men in this island, although it was the forerunner to other calamities of a character no less remarkable; but a new and memorable pestilential constitution now commenced. In 1816—the spring being unusually backward, the summer and autumn also very late, and the whole year characterized by far more than the average amount of rain—the potato again failed very generally throughout the kingdom. At this time the stalk was the part chiefly affected, and the disease was attributed to the excessive wet and extreme cold of the seasons. The potato crop, in England as well as Ireland, was especially defective, which shows how wide-spread and malignant were the peculiar atmospheric influences which characterized that well-known period. The accounts of this epidemic in England state that early in September the potatoes were 'blackened and spoiled; they smell at a distance the same as after a frosty night late in October'—symptoms which indicated a similarity between the epidemic of that period and the one with which we have lately become so familiar.

"The end of 1820 was distinguished for the great quantity of snow which fell; heavy and extensive inundations followed, which produced remarkable telluric phenomena early in the following year. May and June, 1821, were dry, cold, and frosty; but the autumn was one of unusual moisture; the rain accumulated upon the surface of the ground, the rivers rose, the lakes swelled, and the floods spread far and wide over the face of the land, while the rain continued to pour in torrents during November, December, and part of the following January. It was scarcely possible, and generally unprofitable, to dig out the potato crop—it soured and rotted in the ground; and although a sufficiency was obtained in the dry and upland districts to support human life for some months, it was expended early in the ensuing spring; and then destitution, famine, and pestilence in quick succession followed. Fortunately these effects were not general throughout the kingdom, but occupied a district which might be defined by a line drawn from the bay of Donegal, upon the north side, at the junction of the counties of Sligo and Leitrim, to Youghal harbour, where the counties of Cork and Waterford border on the south—thus including the whole western seaboard of Sligo, Mayo, Galway, Clare, Limerick, Kerry, and Cork; all exposed to the full force of the Atlantic, the influence of which though mild is moist. A failure of the potato crop was reported in Scotland in 1823.

"In 1825 the seasons were mild, yet we read of a partial

failure of the potato crop; the test of which in this, as well as in previous and subsequent years of failures, may be instanced by the rise of the price of potatoes. Epidemic diseases prevailed to a great extent during the excessively dry summer of 1826, yet the potato, although stunted in growth, was free from any epiphytic; and the same remark holds good with respect to that crop in America; but in parts of Holland and Germany there was an unmistakable failure of the potatoes, especially in Holstein. The year 1829 was wet, and the month of August particularly so; the crops were beaten down by the heavy rains and severe storms, and in all the low grounds the water overran the potatoes, and so remained for many weeks; thus a great quantity of the potatoes were lost this year also. The great arterial drainage in many parts of the country, that has taken place since that period, the lowering of the waters of some of our principal lakes and rivers, and in several places the consequent drying-up of the great turloughs and callows must to a large extent prevent the recurrence of calamities similar to the foregoing.

"In 1830, we read 'that violent storms and heavy rains brought upon the West of Ireland another failure of the potato, with its usual accompaniment of famine and pestilence,' but it was principally confined to the coasts of Mayo, Galway, and Donegal. This blight was common to parts of America, and to Germany, where it continued for two years. In 1832, and for several years following in succession, an unmistakable epidemic attacked the potato in spring throughout Ireland, and also extended to other parts of Europe and to America. In 1833 it presented not only the appearance of the *curl*, but likewise attacked the potatoes in the pits. In 1834 the failure was chiefly observed in the early-planted potatoes, but having been discovered in spring, was to a certain extent susceptible of remedy. Although there was an intermission in 1835, a partial failure of the potato was observed in several parts of Ireland in 1836, which had been wet, and July and August unusually so; and the price of food rose to a height almost unparalleled. Both in 1835 and 1836 failures of the potatoes were noted in Scotland. We have no recorded account of any special failure of the potato crop in Ireland in 1838, which was also a wet year, but the 'inherent constitutional weakness' of that esculent was observed, and the deterioration in the best kinds of the potato formed the theme of public remark at the time. In 1839 there was an unmistakable failure of that crop, attributed to the incessant rains, and the extensive inundations in the latter part of the year. In New England, at the same time, the potato found a formidable enemy in the *Black Rust*, which 'struck universally on the 27th of August.'

"The year 1839 was characterized by an amount of moisture unparalleled, according to modern observations; the quantity of rain that fell near Dublin being nearly 10 inches beyond the average; and the potatoes failed throughout the western and midland counties. Part of 1840 was likewise characterized by excessive moisture; although there was less rain than in the previous year, yet it came down at an unpropitious period;—the potato crops failed again in Leinster and Munster; and upon both occasions great distress followed. The Scotch islands of Arran, and the Highlands, are said to have suffered from partial potato failures yearly from 1839 to 1842 inclusive. In 1840 the potato disease prevailed to such a degree in Germany as to threaten the total extinction of that esculent there; and in the following year the crop was extensively affected in that country with a disease called "*Dry Gangrene*". In 1841 excessive rains occurred in August, causing a partial destruction of crops, especially in the south of Ireland; the year was cold and frosty, and although not specially characterized for its wetness, the number of days (246) upon which rain fell was very great. As much as 10.58 inches of rain fell in July, August, and October. In 1842, which was more than unusually unfavourable to vegetation, we read that 'although the harvest generally was good, the potato crop was injured by the inundations.' 1843 was more fatal to animal than vegetable life, epizootics largely predominating over vegetable diseases in Ireland; but in other countries, and especially in North America, the potato crop suffered severely from the *Dry Rot*—evidently the commencement of that great *Blight* which prevailed during the ensuing five or six years. In 1844, the severity of the seasons again acting prejudicially upon vegetable life, there was a partial failure of the potato, and destitution again followed in its wake. The failures were noted soon after the seed was planted; and in the beginning of summer, even as early as the month of June, the first symptoms of that vegetable pestilence which laid the foundations of the late misery appeared; and although the crop was reported generally a good one, acute observers remarked the degeneracy of the tubers, and prognosticated that the future crop would either fail entirely when any additional predisposing causes ensued, or would send up a puny and diseased stalk. The disease likewise showed itself, late in the autumn of this year, in England, especially in Kent and Devonshire. In America, also, although the weather was dry, the potato crop was very defective, having suffered much from *Blight*."[1]

In view of this melancholy recital, it is not too much to say that Ireland had been in a chronic state of famine for many years previous to the great calamity of 1845. This conclusion was arrived at by the census commissioners: —"We have thus seen, that during the hundred years previous to this date, repeated failures in the potato crop of Ireland were noted. Public aid was afforded, and private benevolence largely contributed, to save, year by year,

[1] *Census of Ireland* 1851, pt. V. pp. 238-41; and see Wilde *An Inquiry into the Time of the Introduction and the General Use of the Potato in Ireland* Dublin 1856. "Tous les ans" according to Beaumont "à peu près à la meme époque, on annonce en Irlande le commencement de la famine, ses progrès, ses ravages, et son déclin." *L'Irlande Sociale* vol. i. p.207.

from absolute starvation, those who were reduced to want by the failure of their favourite and prolific esculent; but which, for upwards of a century, in all weathers, during the extremes of heat and cold, in dryness and in moisture, whether planted early or late, was destined to fail, either in whole or in part, leaving those who trusted to its support for food and maintenance nearly destitute for months together previous to the ensuing crop arriving at maturity; so that a state of chronic famine had existed in many districts on the west coast of Ireland for several years antecedent to the late great potato failure. This may be seen from the newspapers and other public records of the day, and receives confirmation from the number of parliamentary grants made to relieve the frequent distress of these districts."[1]

Section 2. The Course of the Famine.

It was the conditions under which the potato was cultivated rather than any inherent defects of the plant itself that caused its failure to be attended by such disastrous consequences. It was not uncommon for contemporary writers to contend that, had the staple article of Irish diet been wheat or oats, the famine could not have occurred. Thus Trevelyan says: "A population whose ordinary food is wheat and beef, and whose ordinary drink is porter and ale, can retrench in periods of scarcity, and resort to cheaper kinds of food, such as barley, oats, rice and potatoes.

[1] *Census of Ireland* 1851, pt. V. p. 242. For further particulars of famines previous to 1845 see *Report of the Committee Appointed to Distribute Relief to the Poor of Dublin*, Dublin 1814, *View of the Agricultural State of Ireland* London 1822. Freeman Bindon, *Suggestions on the Best Mode of Relieving the Present Prevailing Distress in Part of the South of Ireland* Dublin 1822, *Report of Select Committee on Disease and the Labouring Poor in Ireland* London 1819, Francis Rogan, *Observations on the Condition of the Middle and Lower Classes in the North of Ireland* London 1819, *Report of the Proceedings of the Committee of Management for the Relief of Distressed Districts in Ireland held at the Mansion House, Dublin.* Dublin 1822, *Practical Views and Suggestions* by Hibernicus, Dublin 1823, *Report of Select Committee on the Employment of the Poor in Ireland* 1823, *A Letter on the State of Ireland* by an Irish Magistrate. London 1825, Dr. Doyle, *Letter to Thomas Spring-Rice* Dublin 1831. *Report of the Western Committee for the Relief of the Irish Poor* 1831. *On the Failure of the Potato Crop* Dublin 1835.

But those who are habitually and entirely fed on potatoes live upon the extreme verge of human subsistence, and, when they are deprived of their accustomed food, there is nothing cheaper to which they can resort. They have already reached the lowest point in the descending scale, and there is nothing beyond, but starvation or beggary."[1] Trevelyan, in common with many of his contemporaries, seems to have fallen into error on this point. It is true that the potato is the cheapest and lowest of all foods; that it is, as we have insisted above, peculiarly unsuitable as the staple article of a people's diet, because it is a plant peculiarly subject to disease and decay. There is therefore not the slightest doubt that a peasantry engaged in the production of corn is in a happier position than one engaged in the production of potatoes, so long as the produce is intended for the market. The peasant who produces corn cultivates a crop which is fairly constant from year to year, and which is certain to fetch a reasonably high market price; while the peasant who is engaged on potato culture is the victim of low prices and of much uncertainty. This distinction however ceases to carry weight when the crop is produced not for the market but for the peasant's own consumption. In this case, whether the crop be of potatoes or of corn, a total failure spells ruin for the producer. In Ireland the peasant's crop was produced not for the market but for domestic consumption; not for money but for food. It is difficult to see how in such a state of affairs the producer of potatoes was any worse off in the event of a total failure than the producer of corn. In either case the failure would entail the total annihilation of the peasant's means of subsistence. It may be said that corn can be kept from one year to another, whereas the potato cannot be kept for more than a few months, and that therefore a corn-growing people may make provision against bad years in advance. No doubt this is generally true, but we must remember that, whatever

[1] *The Irish Crisis*-p. 5.

crop is cultivated, no provision can be made for future years, when, as was the case in Ireland, each family has barely sufficient to support itself during the current season. Even were the potato as easily preserved as wheat or oats, no store could have been put aside by the Irish peasantry, who were reduced to the cultivation of the smallest holding upon which life could be supported.

Isaac Butt thus described the absolute dependence of the Irish peasantry on the potato:—"The destruction of the potato crop entailed a double misery upon the poor. It destroyed their food, and at the same time it took from them their income. Let the corn of England fail, and you have indeed the distress among her population that a scarcity of the means of subsistence will occasion, but the capacity of the great mass of the people to purchase that subsistence, were it offered at the accustomed price, is left unimpaired. Far different however was the effect of the withering of the potato gardens and the conacres of Ireland. The poor man's store was altogether gone; a purchaser of provisions he never had been—the means of purchasing them he never had. Send the potatoes into the market at the usual price, and the cottier who never had the wherewithal to purchase, if unsupported by the charity of others, must still starve. His whole wealth has perished in his potato-ridge; not only was the usual quantity of provisions removed from the country, but his power of commanding a share of those that were, or might be in it, was gone."[1]

In Ireland the potato, in addition to being grown on this unsatisfactory system, was cultivated to an extent unequalled elsewhere, so that a failure of the potato crop would naturally affect a greater proportion of the families of Ireland than of any other country. Whenever the staple food of a community perishes the community is bound to suffer; and in Ireland the staple food happened to be the potato. It must not be forgotten that the failure of 1845-6 was not

[1] *The Famine in the Land* p. 7.

confined to Ireland; the crop also failed in the Highlands of Scotland and in parts of England, particularly in Wiltshire, Somersetshire and Devonshire.[1] Yet these British failures have not been remembered to the present day as among the most appalling calamities recorded in history, simply because the number of people in Great Britain who depended on the potato for their sustenance was but small. The blight was equally virulent in both countries; but its evil effects were proportioned to the number of the population who were supported by the plant which it attacked.

It must also be borne in mind that the calamity was so unprecedented in its severity, as to have been practically incapable of being foreseen. "Sometimes the failure occurred in a single year, sometimes during two in succession; but in no other period have we had to deplore its loss in five consecutive years."[2] Even assuming that the Irish people had been living on corn instead of potatoes, and that they had exercised the utmost possible providence in accumulating reserves of grain for a period of scarcity, it is hardly likely that they would have laid aside sufficient to carry them through a succession of several years of total failure. However we regard the matter, we are driven to conclude that no blame for the sufferings of the famine should be attributed to the Irish people simply because they engaged to such a degree in the cultivation of the potato. That they depended upon a plant that proved so unreliable in the result was their misfortune and not their fault.

The actual facts of the course of the potato disease are well known and do not require any elaboration. They can be briefly narrated in the words of Trevelyan: "The potato disease, which had manifested itself in North America in 1844, first appeared in these islands late in the autumn of 1845. The early crop of potatoes, which is generally

[1] *13th Annual Report of Poor Law Commissioners* 1847. Nicholls, *History of the English Poor Law* vol. ii. pp. 391-3. *History of the Scotch Poor Law*. p. 199.

[2] *Census of Ireland* 1851 pt. v. p. 241.

about one-sixth of the whole, and is dug in September and October, escaped; but the late, or what is commonly called the 'people's crop', and is taken up in December and January, was tainted after it arrived at an advanced stage of maturity. When the disease had once commenced, it made steady progress, and it was often found, on opening the pits, that the potatoes had become a mass of rottenness. Nevertheless, this year the attack was partial; and although few parts of the country entirely escaped, and the destruction of human food was, on the whole, very great, a considerable portion of the crop, which had been a more than usually large one, was saved. The wheat crop was a full average; oats and barley were abundant; and of turnips, carrots, and green crops, including a plentiful hay harvest, there was a more than sufficient supply. On the Continent, the rye crops failed partially, and the potato disease was very destructive in Holland, Belgium, France, and the west of Germany.

"In the following year (1846) the blight in the potatoes took place earlier, and was of a much more sweeping and decisive kind. 'On the 27th of last month (July), I passed,' Father Mathew writes in a letter published in the parliamentary papers, 'from Cork to Dublin, and this doomed plant bloomed in all the luxuriance of an abundant harvest. Returning on the 3rd instant (August), I beheld with sorrow one wide waste of putrefying vegetation. In many places the wretched people were seated on the fences of their decaying gardens, wringing their hands, and wailing bitterly the destruction that had left them foodless.' The first symptom of the disease was a little brown spot on the leaf, and these spots gradually increased in number and size, until the foliage withered and the stem became brittle, and snapped off immediately when touched. In less than a week the whole process was accomplished. The fields assumed a blackened appearance, as if they had been burnt up, and the growth of the potatoes was arrested when they were not larger than a marble or a pigeon's egg. No potatoes were pitted this year. In many districts where they had been most abundant, full-grown wholesome potatoes were not to be procured; and even in London and other large towns, they were sold at fancy prices, and were consumed as a luxury by the wealthy, rice and other substitutes being had recourse to by the body of the people. The crop of wheat this year was barely an average one, while barley and oats, particularly the former, were decidedly deficient. On the Continent, the rye and potato crops again failed, and prices rose early in the season above those ruling in England, which caused the shipments from the Black Sea, Turkey, and Egypt, to be sent to France, Italy, and Belgium; and it was not till late in the season, that our prices rose to a point which turned the current of supplies towards England and Ireland. The Indian corn crop in the United States this year was very abundant, and it became a resource of the utmost value to this country. In the third year (1847) the disease had nearly exhausted itself. It appeared in different parts of the country, but the plants generally exerted fresh vigour and outgrew it."[1]

The years 1845-7 were characterized by failures other than those of the potato. They constituted a period of disease of many other plants, the crops of which proved considerably less abundant than usual. "To the deficiency in vitality in vegetable life may be mainly traced the calamities of this memorable period. It was not the potato alone which was attacked; wheat, oats, and in time turnips, beans, and onions etc. were affected; even the hardy race of the pines suffered and large tracts of larch trees and other coniferae decayed."[2] The animal kingdom experienced a simultaneous period of disease. "An epizootic of pleuro-pneumonia had spread extensively over the cattle pastures of Europe, and proved remarkably fatal to the bovine

[1] *The Irish Crisis* pp. 19-21. On the scientific aspect of the blight see Niven *The Potato Epidemic*. Dublin 1846. G. W. Johnson. *The Potato Murrain and its Remedy*. London 1846.

[2] *Census of Ireland* 1851 pt. v. p. 236.

species, especially in Holland and Germany, for a number of years antecedent to 1840. This disease invaded Ireland about 1839 and for the ten years period following that date largely affected the horned cattle in the country, especially the modern improved breeds—thus seriously damaging the interests of the grazier and stock farmer.... During the epidemic period animal life among all descriptions of cattle was more or less affected, with the exception of horses. .... Sheep perished from the rot, and even domestic fowl decreased under the mortal influence of the prevailing atmospheric constitution."[1] The potato failure moreover tended to decrease the stocks of some other kinds of food much in use in Ireland. "With its failure those valuable animals the pigs were almost extinguished in many districts; which was also to a great extent the case with the poultry."[2] It will thus be seen that the period of the famine was one of shortage in many directions. The value of the produce destroyed by the blight was estimated to amount to sixteen million pounds.[3]

We do not intend to harrow our readers with any detailed description of the misery produced by the failure of the potato crop. We could fill page after page with the most horrifying accounts of the sufferings of the Irish people. We forbear from doing so however, because the tale has been told so often before and because we are concerned with the causes and results of the calamity, rather than with its actual details. We shall content ourselves with the quotation of a single passage, which is eloquent on account of its detachment. It is to be found in an appendix to the Census of 1851, and was therefore written some years after the actual famine, so that its author cannot be accused of the hysteria produced by the spectacle of horrifying sights. "Agriculture was neglected," we read in this cold unimaginative blue book, "and the land in many places remained untilled. Thousands were supported from day

[1] *Ibid.* [2] *Ibid.* [3] *Ibid.*

to day upon the bounty of outdoor relief; the closest ties of kindred were dissolved; the most ancient and long-cherished usages of the people were disregarded; food the most revolting to human palates was eagerly devoured; the once proverbial gaiety and light heartedness of the peasant people seemed to have vanished completely; and village merriment or marriage festival was no longer seen or heard throughout the regions desolated by the intensity and extent of the famine; finally, the disorganization of society became marked and memorable by the exodus of above one million of people, who deserted their homes and hearths to seek for food and shelter in foreign lands, of whom thousands perished from pestilence and the hardships endured on shipboard. It is scarcely possible to exaggerate in imagination what people will and are forced to do before they die from absolute want of food, for not only does the body become darkened, the feelings callous, blunted, and apathetic; but a peculiar fever is generated, which became but too well known to the medical profession in Ireland at that time, and to all those engaged in administering relief. In this state of what may almost be called mania, before the final collapse takes place, when the victim sinks into utter prostration through inanition, some instances may have occurred at which human nature in its ordinary healthy condition revolts. Thus a stipendiary magistrate stated in Galway in extenuation of the crime of a poor prisoner brought up for stealing food, that to his own knowledge before he was driven to the theft, he and his family had actually consumed part of a human body lying dead in the cabin with them. Generally speaking the actually starving people lived upon the carcases of diseased cattle, upon dogs, and dead horses, but principally on the herbs of the field, nettle tops, wild mustard, and watercresses, and even in some places dead bodies were found with grass in their mouths. The shamrock or wood sorrel, mentioned by Spenser as forming part of the food used by the starving people in his time, does not now, owing to the extirpation of woods, exist in sufficient quantity to afford any nutriment; but along the coast every description of seaweed was generally devoured, often with fatal consequences; even the dillisk or "salt-leaf", though a safe occasional condiment, became the cause of disease when used as the sole support of life."[1]

The patience of the poor people under this heavy load of oppression excited the admiration of all who witnessed it. "No such amount of suffering" we read in the Census of 1851 "has been chronicled in Irish history since the days of Edward Bruce; and yet, through all, the forbearance of the Irish peasantry and the calm submission with which they bore the deadliest ills that can fall on man can scarcely be parallelled in the annals of any people . . . The slight amount of crime of a serious nature which prevailed throughout Ireland during the years of extreme destitution was remarkable."[2] This aspect of the Irish peasant's character had also impressed Sir George Cornewall Lewis: "It may be remarked that some active interference either actual or apprehended with the ordinary state of the peasantry is required in order to rouse them to aggressive measures; some positive ill usage, or infliction of evil, such as ejectment from land, driving for rent etc; to the mere passive state of suffering produced by scantiness of food or the failure of the potato crop the Irish peasants, a class remarkable for their patient endurance, are willing to submit, and hence we find that at times when a large part of the population are hanging over the verge of starvation, the country is nevertheless for the most part tranquil."[3]

[1] *Census of Ireland* 1851 pt. V. p. 243. Those who wish for further particulars of the sufferings of the famine will find them *ad nauseam* in O'Rourke's *Great Irish Famine* and Tuke's. *A Visit to Connaught.* London 1848.

[2] Pt. v. p. 243.

[3] *Irish Disturbances* p. 91.

Section 3. The Cost of the Famine.

As we said above, the problem of population *versus* resources was tragically solved by the famine. The period preceding 1845 had been remarkable for a steady and continuous growth of population; and the period after that year was equally remarkable for its steady and continuous decrease. The immediate decrease in the population consequent on the famine was the result of two causes, emigration and death.

As we have already seen, the system of eviction and clearances was strengthened and reinforced during the famine years, partly by the action of the landlords in their desire to rid their lands of paupers, and partly as a result of the famous Gregory or quarter-acre clause. Innumerable families were turned out on the roads; and, as it was impossible to obtain a new holding in another part of the country, or to find employment in manufacturing industry, there were no alternatives but starvation or emigration. The number of emigrants consequently swelled to an unprecedented degree. "The annual emigration from the 30th June 1846 to the end of 1845 averaged 61,242. Such however was the effect of the potato blight and the warning voice of the pestilence that the number rose to 105,955 in 1846, after which the emigration seemed to partake of the nature of an epidemic, and in 1847 the numbers who left the country more than doubled those who departed in the previous year. Owing to a slight mitigation of the potato blight, and a consequent improvement in the harvest of 1847, there was an arrest of the exodus at the beginning of 1848, when the numbers who emigrated only amounted to 178,159; but in the following year they again rose to 214,425. In 1850 the amount of emigration was 209,054. The emigration reached its highest point in 1851 when the numbers amounted to 249,721."[1] Two features besides

[1] *Census of Ireland* 1851 pt. V. p. 243.

its magnitude distinguished the emigration following from that preceding the famine. One was that the greater part of the emigrants proceeded to the United States instead of to British colonies; and the other was that those who went materially aided the departure of those who remained by the remittance of large sums of money. The contributions so made, either in the form of prepaid passages, or of money sent home, were estimated to amount to £460,000 in 1848, £540,000 in 1849, £957,000 in 1850, and £990,000 in 1851.[1] Besides those who emigrated to the colonies and the United States, large numbers emigrated to Great Britain, "Many have reached Manchester and the other manufacturing towns of Lancashire, as well as of the West Riding and Cheshire .... Large numbers of Irish have also landed at Newport and Chepstow, and have thence moved on to Cheltenham and other towns in the Midland counties. A considerable number of Irish poor (estimated at about a thousand within a week) have recently been landed in London by steamer from Cork and Dublin. In addition to these some Irish have reached the metropolis from Bristol and Newport."[2]

The losses suffered by the population on account of the abnormally high death rate were even greater than those incurred through emigration. The growth in the death rate during the famine can best be realized by considering that, of all the deaths recorded in the decennial period 1841-51,5·1 per cent. took place in 1842,5·2 per cent. in 1843, 5·6 per cent. in 1844, 6·4 per cent. in 1845, 9·1 per cent. in 1846, 18·5 per cent in 1847, 15·4 per cent. in 1848, 17·9 per cent. in 1849, and 12·2 per cent. in 1850.[3] The first and most immediate cause of this increased death rate after 1845 was simple starvation. "In every country," we read in the excellent and exhaustive report on the table

[1] *Census of Ireland* 1851 p. lvi.

[2] *13th Annual Report of Poor Law Commissioners* 1847. On the appalling sufferings endured by the emigrants see O'Rourke *Great Irish Famine* pp. 497 sq.

[3] *Census of Ireland* 1851 p. l.

of deaths published by the census commissioners "even in England, deaths from starvation are annually recorded. The deaths registered in England from privation of food were for many years above 100 annually; and even in the year 1853 as many as 78 persons perished there from want. In the Irish returns prior to 1841 only 117 deaths were registered from starvation for the two years prior to that period; but from thence, according to the registration made in 1851, deaths from this cause began notably to increase; from 187 in the year 1842 to 516 in 1845. After that date deaths attributed to starvation increased rapidly so as to amount to 2,041 for the year 1846; in 1847 they reached the great height of 6,058; and in the two following years 1848 and 1849 taken together they amounted to 9,395. In 1850 they were even more than in 1846; and during the first quarter of 1851 as many as 652 deaths attributed to starvation were recorded. The total deaths returned to us under the head of starvation amounted to 21,770. As many as 383 of these occurred in workhouses, being persons received in a dying state as a result of previous privation. Large, therefore, as the total deaths from this cause returned to us on the census forms appear, a review of the past circumstances of the kingdom will, we think, strengthen the belief that many more must have perished from disease remotely induced by privation during the years of famine and pestilence."[1]

Next in number to the deaths from starvation were those resulting from pestilences which accompanied the famine. The most fatal of these diseases was that known simply by the name of fever.[2] "Up to the end of the year 1845 the annual average mortality from fever in Ireland was but 7,249 .... According to the information with which we have been supplied, the disease increased gradually from 1840 to 1846, when the deaths reached 17,145

[1] p. 253. [2] Full medical particulars of this disease are to be found in the *Census of Ireland* 1851 pt. v. pp. 246-7.

in the latter year. In 1847 there were 57,095 deaths from fever; in 1848 there were 45,948; in 1849 as many as 39,316; and in 1850, 23,545."[1] These figures, appalling though they are, do not represent the whole toll which the fever exacted. "The Irish typhus of this period was of a highly contagious nature, and was carried by those who fled in dismay from the famine and the pestilence to the sister kingdom—where it spread rapidly throughout Glasgow, Liverpool, Birmingham, Manchester and other towns and districts in which the Irish emigrants worked. It was also carried on board the emigrant vessels, in which the crews and passengers were in several instances decimated by it, even before they reached the destined ports; while at Quebec and New York it spread its pestilential influence among those sufferers, who, wasted by previous destitution in Ireland, and the hardships and privations induced during the time they were cooped up between the decks of a closely packed plague-ship, became, even when allowed to breathe the pure air of the shore, ready victims for its fury."[2] The census commissioners, taking everything into account, reached the conclusion that 250,000 people perished from fever between 1845 and 1851.[3]

Besides the fever, many less deadly pestilences raged in Ireland during the famine. Scurvy appeared in county Kildare in 1845, spread to parts of the west in 1846 ,and was general throughout the country in the next year. "Under the head of Purpura and Scurvy" we read in the census "were registered 167 deaths; and of these the greater bulk was returned from hospitals and work-houses, upon medical authority, during the years from 1846 to 1850 inclusive. These deaths form however but a small proportion of those which absolutely occurred throughout the country, either directly or indirectly as the consequence of scurvy; and we have introduced the subject here, not

[1] *Census of Ireland* 1851 pt. v. p. 247.
[2] *Ibid.* pp. 247-8.
[3] *Ibid.* p. 249.

so much because of the fatality of the disease, as on account of its forming so remarkable an illustration of the peculiar pestilential period from which the country suffered."[1] Dysentery, the habitual companion of famine, also accounted for many deaths. "The first manifest increase of dysentery occurred in 1846; it then rose rapidly to its climax in the succeeding year, the numbers being 5,492 in the former, and 25,757 in the latter. In 1848, the deaths from dysentery amounted to 18,430, and from diarrhoea to 7,264; in 1849 both these diseases occurring on about the same proportions, produced death in 29,446 instances; and in 1850 the mortality from both these causes was 19,224."[2] At the end of 1848 an epidemic of cholera broke out, producing 30,156 deaths in the following year.[3]

Death was not the only evil result of the epidemics of this terrible period. From the economic point of view, permanent incapacity is even more detrimental than death; and we must therefore draw attention to the great increase of blindness resulting from ophthalmia, and to the growth of insanity during the famine years. At the time of the 1851 census Ireland presented the largest proportion of blind of any country in Europe, with the exception of Norway; and the number of inmates in Irish lunatic asylums greatly increased in the year following the famine.[4]

The figures which we have quoted do not give any real idea of the loss which the population of Ireland suffered during these years. An attempt to ascertain the real extent of this loss was made by the census commissioners, who aimed at calculating what the population of Ireland would have been, had the famine not occurred. The following is the result of this attempt:- "Supposing the immigration and emigration to have been equal, and that the increase of population by an excess of births over deaths was in a similar ratio to that which had taken place in England and Wales during the last sixteen years, viz. 1·0036 per cent.

[1] *Ibid.* p. 250. [2] *Ibid.* p. 251. [3] *Ibid.* p. 252. [4] *Ibid.* pp. 253-4

per annum, the number of people in Ireland would have been 9,010,798 on the 30th March 1851. But, as the last census returns have only afforded a population of 6,552,385, it is important to account (as far as is possible in the unfortunate absence of any general registration of births and deaths) for the deficiency in the population of nearly 2½ millions, independent of the emigration. Inevitable deficiencies must result from any retrospective inquiry derived from the remnant of a population upon a certain day subsequent to the events to which it has reference. It is manifest that the greater the amount of disruption of the population in any walk of life, so much the more difficult will be the attempt to acquire subsequent information, and consequently the less will be the amount of recorded deaths derived through any household form,—for not only were whole families swept away by disease, and large districts depopulated by emigration, or the inhabitants driven to seek a refuge in the workhouse, but whole villages were effaced from off the land. Yet notwithstanding these difficulties in the way of a complete enumeration of deaths, and with a great decrease of population from non-births, owing to the diminution of marriages, and other causes which during some portion of the period sensibly affected the question— the recorded mortality for the last five years of the decennial period 1841-51 was as great as 985,366, or very nearly one million."[1] In O'Rourke's book on the famine the number of deaths is calculated at 1.240.000.[2]

Section 4—The Relief Measures.

Having dealt briefly with the causes, the course, and the effects of the famine, let us next consider the measures which were taken to alleviate its ravages. This subject falls naturally into two divisions, the private and the public relief measures.

[1] Pp. 245-6. [2] *The Great Irish Famine* p. 499.

It is impossible to speak too highly of the magnificent efforts made by private charity, not only in Ireland, but in Great Britain and abroad, to minimize the sufferings caused by the potato failure. As early as November 1846 the English Society of Friends opened a subscription and sent a deputation to Ireland. In January of the following year was founded the British Association for the Relief of Extreme Distress in Ireland and the Highlands and Islands of Scotland, which collected and distributed funds amounting to £263,251. Shortly afterwards a Queen's Letter was issued, in response to which £171,533 was collected. Of these large sums one-sixth was allotted to Scotland and five-sixths to Ireland.[1]

Innumerable smaller bodies also exerted themselves to relieve the Irish distress to the best of their ability. "Besides the great stream of charity" says Trevelyan "there were a thousand other channels which it is impossible to trace, and of the aggregate result of which no estimate can be formed. There were separate committees which raised and sent over large sums of money. There were ladies' associations without end to collect small weekly subscriptions and make up clothes to send to Ireland. The opera, the fancy bazaar, the fashionable ball rendered tribute, and above all there were the private efforts of numberless individuals, each acting for himself and choosing his own almoners, of which no record exists except on High....

"In the contemplation of this great calamity the people of the United States forgot their separate nationality and remembered only that they were sprung from the same origin as ourselves. The sympathy there was earnest and universal, and the manifestation of it most generous and munificent. The contributions from this land of plenty consisted principally of Indian corn and other provisions .... The freight and charges on the supplies of food and clothing sent to Ireland by charitable societies and individuals.

[1] Trevelyan *The Irish Crisis* pp. 57-8.

as well from the United States and Canada on the one side, as from England on the other, were paid by the government to an amount exceeding £50,000; all customs dues were remitted . . . ."[1]

In Ireland itself private charity was no less active than abroad. A large committee, known as the General Central Relief Committee for all Ireland, was founded in Dublin, and collected subscriptions amounting to £50,000, many of which were contributed by the colonies and foreign countries. The Irish Relief Association for the Destitute Peasantry which had been established in 1831 was revived, and distributed large sums. The Irish Society of Friends was conspicuous for its charitable activity; and the Ladies' Relief Association for Ireland and the Ladies' Industrial Society for the Encouragement of Remunerative Labour among the Peasantry of Ireland did excellent work. Innumerable other associations and individuals lent their aid in the good work, and nobody can deny that private charity did all it could to alleviate the misery of the terrible period.[2]

The calamity was however of such a magnitude that private charity alone could not deal with it; and public action became imperative. We shall here describe the measures taken by the government in their order, and shall reserve our comments and criticisms until later.

One of the first steps taken by Sir Robert Peel was the lowering of the import duties on corn, with the object of increasing the supply. On the 27th January 1846 he proposed his measure for the relaxation of the duties on the importation of foreign corn, by which the scale of duties payable on wheat was to range from four to ten shillings per quarter, and Indian corn, which had previously been charged with the same duty as barley, was to pay only one shilling a quarter. This was to last till February 1849 when a uniform duty of one shilling a quarter was to be charged on every description of grain. The bill passed the

[1] *Ibid* pp. 60-1. [2] *Ibid.* pp. 61-5.

House of Commons in June. In the following January Lord John Russell introduced bills to suspend until the 1st. of September 1847 the duties on foreign corn, and the restrictions imposed by the navigation laws on the importation of corn in foreign vessels. The suspension of the corn and navigation laws was subsequently extended to the 1st. March 1848.[1]

The government's next step was to order from the United States £100,000 worth of Indian corn. Owing to the prohibitory duty, Indian corn was unknown as an article of consumption in the United Kingdom, and private merchants therefore could not complain of interference with a trade which did not exist. Thus the government continued to adhere to the sacred principle of *laissez faire*, and, in order still further to adhere to the principle, the transaction was kept secret as long as possible. In order to distribute this food, central depôts were established in various parts of Ireland under the direction of officers of the commissariat, with sub-depôts under the charge of the constabulary and coast guards; and, when the supplies in the local market were insufficient, meal was sold through these depôts at reasonable prices. In the time of the heaviest pressure one sub-depôt retailed as much as twenty tons of meal daily. Relief committees were formed for the purpose of selling food to those who could buy it and giving it to those who could not, the requisite funds being obtained from private subscriptions aided by the government.

These arrangements were very good as far as they went, but they rested on the fundamentally false assumption that what was needed was to procure a supply of food in the famine-stricken areas. As a matter of fact the provision of such a supply did not tend materially to relieve the situation, for the simple reason, to which we have already referred, that the Irish peasantry had not been in the habit of purchasing their food, and therefore

[1] *Ibid.* p. 22.

when their home grown stocks failed, they had no money wherewith to purchase food. It was therefore imperative that purchasing power should be provided for the peasantry; and the method by which this end was attained was by the provision of public works on which the poor could be employed and earn a wage.

These public works, which were authorised by a statute of 1846,[1] were to be undertaken on the application of the magistrates and principal cess-payers of the district, the expenses of executing them to be defrayed by an advance of public money, half of which was a grant, and half a loan to be repaid by the barony. It was made a fundamental condition of grants for these works that they should be beneficial purely to the public and should not benefit any private landowners. The result of this limitation was that most of the works undertaken were completely useless, as, for example, roads constructed for miles into the bog. The largest number of persons employed under this act was 97,000. The existence of a large and unprecedented source of employment at which substantial wages could be earned for comparatively light work had a pernicious effect on the ordinary agriculture of the country, as the labourers were drawn away from tillage. The relief works were consequently brought to an end on the fifteenth of August 1846. The total amount of money expended by the government on Irish relief up to this date was £753,372, of which £368,000 was in loans and £365,372 in grants.

The failure of the potato crop in 1846 called for further measures of relief, and a new system of public works was inaugurated in the autumn of that year. A statute[2] was passed making the whole expense of public works authorised a local charge, and the deficiencies were directed to be repaid by a rate levied according to the poor law valuation, which made the landlords liable for the whole amount on tenements under £4 yearly value, and for a proportion,

[1] 9 and 10 Vict c. 1. [2] 9 and 10 Vict. c. 107.

generally amounting to half, on tenements above that value, instead of according to the grand jury cess, the basis of the repayments under the previous act, which laid the whole burden upon the occupier. It was also determined that the wages given on the relief works should be slightly below the average rate of wages in the district; that the persons employed should as far as possible be paid by task or in proportion to the work actually performed; and that the relief committees, instead of giving tickets entitling persons to employment on public works, should furnish lists of persons requiring relief which should be carefully revised by the officers of public works.

The provision of employment for the people was thus ensured and the other problem of the provision of food had next to be considered. It could not be expected that private traders would adapt themselves sufficiently rapidly to supply the totally new demands of the Irish market, and the government therefore were faced with the difficulty of having to insure that a double supply of food would be available, when required, without unduly interfering with the operations of the private trader. It was therefore announced, (1) that no orders for supplies of food would be sent by the government to foreign countries, (2) that the interference of the government would be confined to those western districts of Ireland in which, owing to the former prevalence of potato cultivation, no trade in corn for local consumption existed, and, (3) that even in these districts the government depôts would not be opened for the sale of food while it could be bought from private dealers at reasonable prices. The relief committees of the preceding season were reorganised, and inspecting officers were appointed to superintend their proceedings.[1]

The successful working of the new scheme of public works depended largely on the active cooperation of the local gentry, but that cooperation was unfortunately not

[1] Trevelyan, *op. cit.* pp. 35-6.

forthcoming, and the whole labour of working the scheme devolved upon the officers of the Board of Works, who obviously were not in a position to detect frauds, or to observe economy, so completely as administrators with local knowledge. "The resident gentry and rate-payers, whose duty it was to ascertain, as far as possible, the probable amount of destitution in their neighbourhood, the sum required to relieve it, the works upon which that sum could best be expended, and who had the necessary local knowledge, in almost every case devolved these functions upon the Board of Works, who could only act on such information as they could obtain from naval and military officers and engineers, most of whom were selected from among strangers to the district, in order to prevent undue influence being used. After that, to advance funds; to select the labourers; to superintend the work; to pay the people weekly; to enforce proper performance of the labour; if the farm works were interrupted, to ascertain the quantity of labour required for them; to select and draft off the proper persons to perform it; to settle the wages to be paid to them by the farmers, and see that they were paid; to furnish food, not only for all the destitute out of doors, but in some measure for the paupers in the workhouse; were the duties which the government and its officers were called upon to perform. The proprietors and associated rate-payers, having presented *indefinitely*, said it was the fault of the government and its officers if the people were not instantly employed, and these officers were blamed even by persons of character and understanding, if they were not at once equal to execute the duties which in this country are performed in their respective districts by thousands of country gentlemen, magistrates, guardians, overseers, surveyors, &c., resident throughout the country, and trained by the experience of years to the performance of their various functions. The Board of Works became the centre of a colossal organization; 5,000 separate works had to be reported upon; 12,000 subordinate officers had to be superintended. Their letters averaged upwards of 800 a day, and the number received on each of the following days was:

January 4th—3,104	April 19th—4,340
February 15th—4,900	May 17th—6,033

"The strain on the springs of society from this monstrous system of centralisation was fearful in the extreme. The government, which ought only to mediate between the different classes of society, had now to bear the immediate pressure of the millions, on the sensitive points of wages and food. The opposition to task-work was general, and the enforcement of it became a trial of strength between the government and the multitude. The officers of the board were in numerous instances the objects of murderous attacks, and it became necessary, for the preservation of the whole community, to have recourse to the painful expedient of stopping the works whenever cases of insubordination or outrage occurred."[1] Not only did the gentry neglect to work the scheme, but they actually increased the burden which it imposed, by endeavouring to get as many of their own tenants and labourers as possible employed on the public works. The average number employed in October was 114,000, in November 285,000, in December 440,000, and in January 1847,570,000. It was generally known that vast numbers were employed on relief works who were in no sense destitute. The works, moreover, extensive though they were, had not succeeded in grappling with the problem of destitution, inasmuch as the wages given, although high, were not high enough to enable a labourer to support his family at the existing price of food.[2] The pressure on the works nevertheless continued to increase, and the number of persons daily employed became in February 708,000, and in March 734,000,

[1] Trevelyan, *op. cit.* pp. 29-30. [2] *Ibid* p. 32.

representing at a moderate estimate of the number of each family, upwards of three million persons. The government, having become alive to the abuse of which the works formed the subject, and the neglect which the ordinary agricultural operations of the country were experiencing, determined to reduce the numbers employed as rapidly as possible; and successive reductions were made, beginning in March and ending in August, whereby the whole system of public works was brought to an end.

We drew attention above to the fact that the operations under the first Labour Rate Act were strictly confined to public works which could not possibly benefit any private landholder. This condition was again insisted on in the second act, but it proved so unpopular in Ireland that it was relaxed by the government in October 1846. The announcement of this relaxation was made in a communication known as Labouchere's letter, which authorised presentments for the drainage and subsoiling of the estates of individuals, provided that their estates were charged with the repayments of the sum advanced. Owing to the hampering conditions and unsatisfactory terms which accompanied this offer, no substantial benefit was derived from it. The aggregate amount presented was but £380,607, of which presentments were acted on to the gross amount of £239,476. The sum actually expended was about £180,000; and the largest number of persons at any one time employed was 26,961, in the month of May 1847. Trevelyan says that "some incidental good was done by the example of the advantages of thorough draining, and of the proper mode of executing it; but as a remedy for the wide-spread calamity, the plan totally failed."[1] Baronial presentments were also authorised at a later date for the construction of railway earthworks, but advantage was taken of this permission only in two baronies.

The government's commissariat operations were less

[1] Trevelyan *op. cit.* p. 34.

objectionable than the public works. Upwards of 300,000 quarters of corn were purchased from time to time to supply the government depôts in the west of Ireland, and large supplies of biscuits and salt-meat were applied to the relief of the people. In order to facilitate grinding, hand mills were distributed in the distressed districts. Thirty-four large depôts were established in the west of Ireland, from Dunfanaghy to Skibbereen, and every available steamer was utilised for the carriage of food to the distressed districts. Care was however taken that private trade should be interfered with as little as possible, with the result that, simultaneously with the government importation, the importation of corn by private traders developed to an unprecedented extent. 1097 relief committees were established under the superintendence of the commissariat; while £199,470 was subscribed by private individuals, and £189,914 by the government (making together £389,384) in support of their operations.

One of the functions of the relief committees was to distribute gratuitous food to those who were unable to earn the means of purchasing it, and it was found that the distribution of cooked food proved an excellent test of destitution. It was the general experience that the distribution of food in this way was accompanied by fewer abuses than attended the provision of employment by the relief works, and the government therefore determined to alter its whole system of relief by substituting the distribution of food for the provision of employment. Effect was given to the government's determination by the passing of an act[1], known as the Soup Kitchen Act, by which a relief committee, composed of the magistrates, one clergyman of each persuasion, the poor law guardian, and the three highest rate-payers, was constituted in each electoral division the unit of Irish poor law administration. A finance committee, consisting of four gentlemen, carefully selected

[1] 10 Vict. c 7.

for their strength of character and knowledge of business, was formed to control the expenditure in each union. Inspecting officers were appointed, and a commission sitting in Dublin superintended the whole system. The expense was to be defrayed by payments made by the guardians out of the produce of the rates, and when this fund was insufficient—as it always proved to be—it was supplemented by loans, to be repaid by rates subsequently levied. Free grants were also made in aid of the rates in those unions in which the number of destitute poor was largest, compared with the means of relieving them, and, when private subscriptions were raised,donations were made to an equal amount. The check principally relied on to insure economy was that the expenditure should fall either immediately or ultimately on the local rates. No loan was to be made to any board of guardians until the inspecting officer had certified that they had passed a resolution to make the rate upon which it was to be secured, and that, to the best of his belief, they were proceeding with all possible despatch to make and levy that rate. Generally speaking this check proved effective, as those engaged in the administration of the act were most anxious not to overburden their district with the repayment of large advances. The cooked food test also prevented abuses. The temptation of the poor people to sell their rations was overcome by the fact that the food provided was of no use except for immediate consumption. The soup kitchen system reached its highest point in the month July, 1847, when, out of 2,049 electoral divisions, 1,826 had been brought under the operation of the act, and 3,020,712 persons received separate rations. The season of harvest rendered available new and abundant supplies of food, and the relief under the act entirely ceased at the beginning of October. The expense of the act was comparatively moderate. The amount at which it was originally estimated by the commissioners was £3,000,000; the sum for which parliament was asked to provide was £2,200,000, and the sum actually expended was £1,557,212.[1]

Another measure undertaken by the government for the relief of the famine was the importation of turnip and flax seed, whereby the foundation was laid for an improved system of rotation. An act was passed[2] appropriating a sum of £50,000 to be granted in aid of public works of acknowledged utility—half of the expense was to be provided by a loan, and the other half to be contributed in cash by the persons principally interested in the works. No application was made to participate in the advantage of this arrangement, and the £50,000 was therefore transferred in the next session of parliament to the erection of fishery piers and other useful objects.[3] We must also mention that towards the end of the famine the Irish poor law was amended in some important particulars, principally by the authorisation of outdoor relief. We have considered this in another section. The entire amount advanced by the government towards the relief of the Irish people during the famine was £7,132,268, of which £3,754,739 was to be repaid within ten years, and the remaining £3,377,529 was a free grant. Of the sums lent, a large part was remitted between 1847 and 1852, when a select committee of the House of Lords recommended the remission of the whole amount, and in 1853 the total loans made to meet the famine were remitted by Gladstone, in consideration of Ireland's assuming the burden of the income tax. To comment on this bargain would take us outside our period; it is sufficient to state that it ultimately proved very beneficial to England.[4]

In discussing the wisdom of the measures adopted by the government for the relief of the Irish famine we do not

[1] Trevelyan *op. cit.* pp. 42-45. On the question whether the rations dispensed were sufficient to support life see a discussion in O'Rourke *Great Irish Famine* pp. 428 sq.
[2] 9 and 10 Vict. c. 109.
[3] Trevelyan, *op. cit.* 49-51.
[4] Nicholls *History of the Irish Poor Law* p. 320. *F. R. C.* App. vol. i. p. 253.

propose to make more than a passing reference to those administrative abuses which are inevitable in the conduct of an elaborate system of emergency legislation. It is necessary however to draw attention to the fact that such abuses existed, and did much to lessen the possible benefits which the government's measures might otherwise have produced. One inevitable accompaniment of the expenditure of public money on so large a scale was widespread jobbery. "The torn-up roads" a contemporary complains "are crowded with miserable creatures, lorded over by hosts of well paid officials, who continue to secure no regularity in work or pay. The sums disbursed, however large, are thrown away, because the whole is in truth a jobbing expenditure."[1] "Millions of public money" wrote Poulett Scrope "were flowing into that country from the Treasury, and there arose a general scramble to obtain a share of it. Though distributed chiefly in payment of wages to the destitute, much of it could not fail to find its way into other pockets directly or indirectly; an army of overseers and other agents, some twelve thousand in number, were to be appointed to places worth a guinea or two at least per week; jobs without end of every grade and character thus sprang into activity."[2] Enormous sums of public money were squandered in useless projects. "In every district that was proclaimed" according to Isaac Butt "the gentry and the farmers vied with each other in voting away money with a reckless prodigality."[3] The farmers in particular encouraged every kind of public works as a safeguard against the pillage of their own stocks of wheat and oats.[4]

Another abuse which lay in the administration of the system, rather than in the system itself, was the unnecessary strictness with which some of the directions were enforced.

[1] Mulock. *Three Letters on the Present Destitution of the Irish Peasantry.* Dublin 1846.
[2] *The Irish Relief Measures.* London 1848 p. 17.
[3] *The Famine in the Land* p. 14.
[4] Parker. *Sir Robert Peel* vol. iii. p. 466 and see Walpole *Life of Lord John Russell* vol. i p. 438.

Thus, for example, it was made a rule that no stores should be sold from government depots until it was proved to the satisfaction of the assistant commissary-general of the district that no other means for obtaining food existed. This rule was in some instances kept to so stringently that people died of starvation within easy distance of these depôts, with money in their hands to buy the food that would not be sold to them.[1] Another serious error of administration was the interval which was allowed to intervene between the cessation of the public works and the opening of the soup kitchens, during which the people were without either form of relief.[2] The administration of the soup kitchen act was not free from many abuses. "Cases occurred in which more rations were demanded than there were individuals in the whole district. Hundreds of names were struck off by the inspecting officers, including servants and men in the constant employ of persons of station and property; the latter were frequently themselves members of the committees; and in some cases the very chairmen, being magistrates, have sanctioned the issue of rations to tenants of their own of considerable holdings."[3]

As we have said, however, it is not our intention to dwell upon these abuses which were inevitable in the administration of measures so complex and so novel. What we are more concerned with is the question how far the measures themselves were calculated to serve the interests of the country, in the first place by alleviating the immediate distress, and in the second place by minimizing the possibility of such a calamity in the future. In criticizing the government's action in this matter, we are not unmindful of the extreme difficulty of the situation with which it was faced. The account which we have given of the extent of the potato failure and the magnitude of the relief operations will sufficiently convey to the reader that we do not regard the relief of the Irish famine as a matter which could have

[1] O'Rourke, *op. cit.* p. 225. [2] *Ibid.* p. 447. [3] *Ibid.* p. 459.

been attained by any but the most careful consideration. In estimating however to what degree the complexity of the problem should be taken into account in discussing the adequacy of the government's actions, two important considerations must not be left out of account, first that the government had received frequent and ample warnings of the danger which would arise in the event of a potato failure in Ireland, and second that it was itself to some extent responsible for the extreme gravity of the situation which such a failure would produce.

We need not labour the point that frequent and ample warnings had been received of the dangers of a potato failure. As we have seen above, such failures were so common that it was possible to speak of Ireland being in a condition of chronic famine; and the failure of 1845 differed simply in degree and not in kind from innumerable failures in previous years. But the government had not alone the spectacle of former famines to warn it; it had been gravely warned by commissions of its own appointment of the danger which would arise in the event of a general potato failure. To quote but one of such monitions, the Select Committee of 1835 on the Advances for Public Works in Ireland had solemnly reported that, "if the potato crop be a failure, its produce is consumed long before the peasantry can acquire new means of subsistence, and then a famine ensues. . . . Thus the present system not only creates poverty and rapidly augments the population, but also entails on the country all the horrors of famine." Nor need we labour the further point that the government was itself in some measure responsible for the gravity of the situation produced by a potato failure. Commission after commission, and committee after committee, had recommended specific measures calculated to enable Ireland to support its large population on a sounder basis than that of reliance upon this single and highly perishable food; but, as we have seen, such advice was habitually ignored by the governments to whom, and at whose invitation, it was tendered. We do not suggest that this foreknowledge of, and partial responsibility for, the situation created by the failure of the potato in 1845 in any way rendered the problem presented to the government of the day less difficult; we do however suggest that they are relevant considerations which must be taken into account when attempting to arrive at a sound opinion on the wisdom of the action of the government.

As we have already said, of the two questions which must be answered before we can arrive at a just estimate of the action of the government in the famine, the first is how far did it succeed in alleviating the immediate distress. The answer to this question is to some extent contained in the preceding pages which record the appalling suffering, mortality, and emigration which Ireland experienced between 1845 and 1850. Certain apologists of the government at the time spoke of the relief measures as though they had been completely successful. Thus Trevelyan's excellent account of the period drops no hint that the measures were not completely successful; and Poulett Scrope remarks, with justice, of Trevelyan's essay that "a stranger to the real events of the last two years might read through the whole hundred pages without even finding out that during the 'Irish crisis' several hundred thousand souls perished in Ireland of want, through the inefficiency of those 'colossal' relief measures."[1] No doubt more people would have perished of hunger and pestilence, had there been no relief works and no soup kitchens; but this is simply to say that the measures were not entirely abortive. But it would be as absurd to suggest that they were entirely successful as that they were entirely abortive, in view of the terrible facts and figures which we have stated.

In the twentieth century however, looking at the matter

[1] *Op. cit.* p. iii.

from a distance, and regarding it rather as part of the general economic history of the period than as an isolated incident, we are more concerned with the second question, how far the relief measures tended to render impossible the recurrence of such a misfortune. How far did they attempt to provide a solution of the great economic problem of the time, the apparent disparity between the population and the resources of Ireland? Did they show that the government proposed to increase the resources rather than decrease the population? Did they point in the direction of depopulation or of development?

The first measure adopted by the government was the repeal of the corn laws. Now, there can be no question that in a state of affairs like the Irish famine, when there was a total failure of one of the great staple commodities of life, it was a wise and obvious step to encourage the supply of all other kinds of food at the lowest possible price. It is difficult to say however how far the repeal of the corn laws was calculated to increase the supply of alternative foodstuffs in the Irish market sufficiently soon to meet the immediate demands of the situation. For one thing the proposal to repeal the corn laws took many months to pass through parliament, and proved one of the most contentious and vigorously combated measures ever debated in that assembly. On this O'Rourke justly remarks, "So early as the end of October 1845 Dr. Playfair expressed to Sir R. Peel his opinion that fully one half of the potatoes in Ireland were perfectly unfit for human food . . . Sir R. Peel knew this in October 1845, admitted its truth more than once during the session of parliament that followed, and yet the bill which he persisted in regarding as the only panacea for such a national calamity did not become law until the 25th of June 1846, eight months afterwards; but of course four millions of foodless Irish must battle with starvation until the premier had matured and carried his measure for securing cheap food for the artisans of England; and further those same famishing millions had, day by day, to submit to be insulted by his false and hollow assertions that all this was done for them."[1]

Moreover, even when the measure was passed, it showed an unwarranted confidence in the operation of the ordinary law of supply and demand to assume that the Irish market would immediately be inundated with quantities of cheap American corn. No doubt in time the supply would have adapted itself to the demand; but the Irish demand was immediate, and could not afford to wait upon the attainment of the politico-economic equilibrium. This was excellently put by Isaac Butt: "There can be no doubt that if any change in the circumstances of Ireland were to cause Ireland permanently to need an importation of Indian corn, and if the same change of circumstances were to endow her people with the means of paying for it, in a few years trade would accommodate itself to this new market, so as to afford the required supply. Shipping, probably, would be built to carry on the new transit—capital would be gradually withdrawn from other occupations, to be embarked in the trade—merchants would build stores, and carriers establish conveyances, to distribute the imported produce through the country; retail dealers in the towns and villages would gradually spring up, and in the course of a few years the new social machinery which the altered habits of the people demanded would be called into existence. But all this must be, in any event, the work of time, and it could only be the work of time where there was a market existing, and people with the means of purchase known to exist in their hands; but to expect all this to be done as if by magic, to meet a sudden emergency, and this to supply the wants of a people known not to have the means of purchase in their hands, whose ability to pay must depend upon the successful application of the provisions of a questionable statute—to expect this economic

[1] *Op. cit.* p. 128.

miracle to be wrought, would indicate the most miserable misapprehension of every principle and law that regulates the system by which the wants of mankind are supplied. The process by which extraordinary demand produces within certain limits additional supply is one not very difficult to understand. The retail dealer of an article finds the calls of his customers for that article increasing; he correspondingly increases his orders to the merchant, who again, if the article be one of importation, gives larger orders to his correspondents abroad. By what delusion could any man persuade himself, that by the natural operation of this process, Indian corn could find its way to the wilds of Mayo, or the village of Carberry? There were neither dealers nor merchants in the article required. The people whose food was gone were, in fact, beyond the pale of all mercantile system—they had lived upon the produce of their potato gardens, and had been customers of no shop. To trust to mercantile enterprise to supply a country so circumstanced, was to expect men suddenly to embark in the trade of supplying Ireland with food, not by any of the ordinary processes by which merchants are led into the affording of additional supplies, by orders coming in the usual way of trade, but upon some vague and uncertain speculation that a country of which they knew nothing would have a demand for corn, and the still more uncertain speculation that the pauper inhabitants of that country would have the means of paying for that demand. We say nothing of the difficulty, upon such a sudden emergency, of finding in the ordinary way of trade the shipping necessary for the additional transit; from what other branch of commercial marine were they to be withdrawn? what trade was to have all its contracts disturbed—its promised freights retarded—its orders for importation disregarded? and all this to meet an emergency for which no calculation had prepared men."[1]

[1] *The Famine in the Land* pp. 9-10.

But, even assuming that the maxims of orthodox political economy were to be allowed to govern the situation, at least those laws should have been allowed to operate in the most favourable conditions. If the free flow of demand and supply were to be relied on, at least the flow should have been allowed to be free. The government did not apparently take this view, for, while professing their unbounded confidence in the Irish markets being supplied by the action of foreign producers, they delayed for many months in taking a necessary step to allow those foreign producers to import their goods in the obvious and natural way. In other words, they refrained from repealing the navigation laws for many months. "The refusal or neglect to suspend the navigation laws" wrote Butt "was the climax of infatuation. While food was deficient in the country, and the freight of corn from America had risen to three times its ordinary rate, not a vessel of any foreign nation would have been permitted to unload a cargo of grain in any one of our ports. If ministers resolved to trust the lives of the Irish people to private enterprise, was it not common sense and common justice to them that private enterprise should be unencumbered by any restrictions in the execution of the task of supplying, at the notice of a few months, provisions to five millions of people; yet, during the months in which food might have been imported into the country, the ministry left the importation of corn impeded by the restriction of the navigation laws, and subject to a duty on importation which an order in council might have removed."[1] "If those laws were suspended in time" says O'Rourke "food could be carried to British ports in the ships of *any* nation; and in fact, while a great outcry was raised by our government about the scarcity of food, and the want of ships to carry it, Odessa and other food centres were crowded with vessels, looking for freights to England, but could not obtain them, in consequence

[1] *Op. cit.*

of the operation of the navigation laws. The immediate effect was a great difficulty in sending food to those parts of Ireland where the people were dying of sheer starvation. But a second effect was the enrichment to an enormous extent of the mercantile marine of England; freights having nearly doubled in almost every instance, and in a most important one, that of America, nearly trebled. The freights from London to Irish ports had fully trebled."[1]

A further criticism directed against the government's action in repealing the corn laws was that, if the end aimed at by that measure was, as was suggested, the provision of an abundant supply of corn in the Irish market, the same end could have been much more certainly attained by prohibiting the exportation of corn from the country. In any event, it was argued, the latter measure should have accompanied the former. The relaxation of the duties on the importation of corn was a remedy frequently adopted in other countries in time of famine, but such a relaxation was invariably accompanied by a prohibition of the export of grain. Such was the precedent of England itself in 1793; and in the very years of the Irish famine, as soon as the cereal crops on the continent showed signs of shortage, Belgium and Portugal stopped the export of grain, and Russia that of rye.[2] In the years of the famine, the exportation of food was forbidden in every country in Europe where the potato blight was threatened, except Ireland.[3] In the case of Ireland the prohibition need not even have been complete; it would have been quite sufficient to place some limitation on the amount exported. Captain Larcom's agricultural census showed that the value of the produce of Ireland in 1847 amounted to £44,958,120, and was sufficient to feed more than twice the population of the island.[4] We need not labour this point, which must be obvious to present day readers.

[1] *Op. cit.* pp. 375-6.
[2] Mitchell *Apology for the British Government.* O'Rourke *op. cit.* p. 96.
[3] Gavan Duffy. *My Life in Two Hemispheres* vol. i. p. 197.
[4] *Thom's Directory* 1851 p. 226.

It was admitted that it was most desirable that a cheap and plentiful supply of corn should be rendered available in the Irish market; in order to attain this end it was no doubt expedient that the greatest possible liberty should be given to the foreign importer; but, as it was certain that the supply would take some time to adapt itself to the new demand, and, as that demand was urgent, it is difficult to see what argument could be advanced against the obvious measure of meeting the Irish demand by the Irish supply. The extraordinary spectacle of Irishmen starving by thousands in the midst of rich cornfields was thus witnessed. One case, typical of many others, is recorded of a man's dying of starvation in the house of his daughter, who had in her haggard a substantial stack of barley, which she was afraid to touch, as it was marked by the landlord for his rent.[1] We may remark in passing that the underlying reason that this obvious precaution was not taken was that Ireland was not regarded as a separate entity. It is impossible to believe that any self-governing nation would have allowed its people to perish in the midst of plenty; and the extraordinary spectacle of a famine that was not a famine was to some extent explicable by the fact that for certain purposes Ireland was simply regarded as a geographical division of a larger political unit.

Thirty years earlier, in a similar famine, Sir R. Peel had expressed himself as opposed to an embargo on exportation, on the ground that such a measure would tend to weaken the unity of the United Kingdom.[2] In the very beginning of the famine Peel explained his opposition to a prohibition of export, "I have no confidence in such remedies as the prohibition of export, or the stoppage of the distilleries. The removal of impediments to import is the only effectual remedy."[3] In previous famines attempts had been made to prevent the export of food by force, and the canals

[1] O'Rourke, *op. cit.* p. 252.
[2] Parker. *Sir Robert Peel* vol. i. p. 241.
[3] Ibid. vol. iii p. 223.

had been cut to prevent corn being conveyed to Dublin.[1]

The prohibition of the exportation of corn from Ireland should therefore have preceded or at least accompanied the suspension of the corn laws. But even assuming that the latter measure was called for by the immediate needs of the situation, it cannot be suggested that it was beneficial to Ireland that the suspension should have been permanent. We have dealt with this matter in another chapter, where we pointed out that the repeal of the corn laws could be classed as one of the legislative aids to depopulation, and it is not necessary for us to discuss the matter again here. Suffice it to say that the spectacle of Ireland's immediate necessity was made the excuse for hurrying through parliament a measure, which, however it may have helped to alleviate the immediate needs of the moment, proved ultimately detrimental rather than beneficial to Ireland. John Mitchell put the matter in a nutshell. "The repeal of the duties on foreign corn and provisions was a measure for cheapening that commodity which the English buy and which the Irish sell."[2] We are thus driven to the conclusion that whatever temporary benefit the repeal of the corn laws may have produced was more than counterbalanced by its ultimate harmful results.

If we turn to the next method of relief employed by the government, we shall find it open to the same objection. While the public works undoubtedly did a great deal to mitigate the immediate suffering caused by the famine, they did nothing to extend the permanent means of employment in the country. This was owing altogether to their unproductive nature. It is unnecessary for us to repeat what we have already said with regard to the benefits which Ireland would have derived from the investment of a large sum of public money in the reclamation of waste ands and the drainage of bogs. As we have already stated,

[1] *Official Papers Public Record Office Dublin* 1790-1831 carton 324 no. 1451.
[2] *Apology for British Government.*

such an investment had been recommended by countless commissions and committees as the true solution of the apparent conflict between the population and the resources of Ireland. In the famine the government had an unprecedented opportunity of carrying that policy into effect; the necessity for the expenditure of public money to provide employment for the Irish people was admitted on all sides; and the sole question was whether that expenditure should be productive or unproductive. The government, in the face of widespread public opinion in Ireland, decided in favour of the latter alternative.

We need not emphasize the magnitude of this error. Not only did it result in hundreds of thousands of pounds being squandered on works from which nobody did or could derive any possible benefit, but it actually tended to diminish the amount of productive work already being carried on in the country. "The consequence" wrote Poulett Scrope "was that the wages were necessarily placed high enough to allow of even the weakest labourer maintaining from his earnings the largest possible family; otherwise these large families must have been starved; or, when wages were not placed as high as this, it became at least necessary to employ on the roads old people, women, and children, to help to eke out the maintenance of the family, through which their health was much injured and their lives in many instances destroyed. The comparatively high rate of pay thus rendered necessary made it easy for a strong man, single or with few incumbrances dependent on him, to earn wages far beyond what any farmer would give. And hence the relief works drew and kept this class of labourers from the land."[1] Not only did the act tempt the labourers to desert their ordinary agricultural employment; it also discouraged landlords from undertaking improvements on which they would otherwise have embarked. "The Labour Rate Act" we read in a well-informed contemporary

[1] *Op. cit.* p. 34.

pamphlet "to a great extent paralysed the exertions of improving landlords. Those who lamented the effects of the law could not take upon themselves the responsibility of declining its provisions. They could not encounter the risk of leaving a large population of destitute poor to the precarious support to be obtained from private employment; and, with diminished means, they could not reserve their funds to meet heavy taxation, and at the same time expend those funds in carrying on measures of improvement upon their properties."[1] "Not only" writes O'Rourke "did the Labour Rate Act exclude productive labour from its own operations, but its direct tendency was to discourage and put a stop to improvement on the part of others. This is manifest enough. The baronies were to be taxed for all the works undertaken to give employment to the starving people. No one could foresee when or where that taxation was to end. There could be no more effectual bar to useful improvements."[2]

It was no doubt to the unproductive nature of the works that was attributable the neglect of the gentry to administer the act, which formed the subject of so much complaint on the part of the government. While the landholders would probably have taken an active interest in the administration of public works from which they could expect to derive some benefit to their estates, it was too much to expect them to interest themselves actively in operations which were notoriously and intentionally futile. It was the same knowledge of the utter futility of the task on which they were engaged that rendered the workers idle and lazy. "The Irish are an acute people" observes Isaac Butt "and they understood as well as their employers that the works upon which they were set were valueless; the inference was not an unnatural one, that the less labour they could bestow upon them the better. They knew that the labour was but a pretence for giving them wages, and they made

[1] John Ball. *What is to be done for Ireland* London 1849. [2] *Op. cit.* p. 177.

as little of the pretence as could possibly suffice. Hence the public works became schools of idleness, in which men met to teach each other how little it was possible to do in a day's work."[1] Poulett Scrope remarks "Set an Irishman to dig holes only to fill them up again, and he will loiter over his task or shirk it altogether. He looks upon it as—what it is—a sort of treadwheel task employed as a penalty or at the best only a roll call. Employment of this description—and such was the general character of the relief works—is as demoralizing as gratuitous relief to the idle. But set them to work on draining a bog, or reclaiming waste land, or making a really useful road or a bridge, or any other obviously productive work—and none will labour more rapidly or harder than an Irishman."[2] "I am inclined to think" Sir T. Fremantle wrote to Peel, "that encouragement given by the government at a very small expense would induce proprietors at this time to carry forward very extensive operations."[3]

We have referred to the neglect of the gentry to administer the Labour Rate Act, and the loud complaints of the government on this score; and have suggested that that neglect was partially caused by the unproductive nature of the works. It must also be remembered that the conduct of the gentry, far from being an excuse for inaction, was a compelling reason for action on the part of the government. For many years the Irish gentry had failed lamentably in their duties towards their tenants, and in this failure they had met with the uniform approval and encouragement of the government. It therefore ill suited the government, which from time out of mind had condoned the landlords' behaviour, and which had passed numerous measures to facilitate them in their selfish conduct, to complain that they were guilty of a dereliction of duty in the famine years. Was it not the government's duty to see that the Irish gentry should do their's ? As Poulett Scrope observes,

[1] *Op. cit.* p. 15. [2] *Op. cit.* p. 49. [3] Parker. *Sir Robert Peel* vol. iii. p. 228.

"This lamentable state of things was too clearly owing to the too great reliance placed by government on the voluntary exertions of the gentry of Ireland, and the practice still pursued in spite of the warnings of all past experience of merely *exhorting* and *urging* them to the fulfilment of those duties—in which their real ultimate interests were involved—instead of *compelling* them with that strong hand of authority, which in so serious a crisis as the present, should have compelled the owners of land to that which of their own motion they had so culpably neglected."[1]

It cannot we suppose be suggested by the most enthusiastic supporters of the government, that it was ignorant of the measures best calculated, not alone to relieve the pressure of the famine, but in addition permanently to improve the country. We have repeatedly referred to the recommendations of the commissions and committees in favour of expenditure on productive purposes; and in addition to this source of information, the government had the benefit of the expression of much well informed opinion at the time of the famine itself. Lord George Bentinck's Railway bill would, in the words of Butt, "have given relief to all grades and classes of the Irish nation without costing the British Treasury one penny. It would have employed our destitute labourers; it would have stimulated our stagnant trade; developed the resources of our soil, about to be subjected to novel and unprecedented burdens ; and poured into Ireland rapidly and naturally an amount of capital productively employed, that would have arrested the evil effects of the present calamity upon her commerce and her trade."[2] Yet this bill was opposed and defeated by the government. Lord John Russell himself admitted the great benefits which would have flowed from a measure designed to reclaim the waste lands; indeed he proposed to introduce such a measure, which however never saw the light.[3] Innumerable bodies of representative

[1] *Op. cit.* p. 187. [2] *Op. cit.* p. 38. [3] O'Rourke, *op. cit.* p. 436.

Irishmen pressed upon the government the necessity of some measure for the draining of the bogs and the reclamation of waste lands.[1] The famine was as acute in the Highlands of Scotland as in Ireland; yet the sufferings endured in the former region were incomparably less than in the latter, principally because the same government that refused productive works in Ireland adopted them in Scotland.[2]

But the most conclusive proof of the government's knowledge of the futility of the Labour Rate Act was the Labouchere letter, by which the very productive works, which had theretofore been denounced as impracticable and impolitic, were approved and authorized. As we have already seen, the actual amount of benefit derived under the Labouchere letter was insignificant; and this disappointing result was attributable to the conditions and limitations with which the government's proposal was hampered. "The cry for productive employment" writes Poulett Scrope "produced no other result than Labouchere's letter, which proved almost wholly abortive in consequence of the conditions which it imposed on those who desired to act under it. This letter, in language so guarded as not to be clearly intelligible, and to take two months' correspondence to explain it, *permitted* reproductive works to be substituted for the roads, only in cases where individual landowners chose to sign a contract to repay the expense. It was at once seen that few or none would do this, by reason of the absence and incapacity of many, and the unwillingness of the rest to take on themselves exclusively the repayment of what the employment act justly made a common burden . . Hence it proved almost a complete failure, and gave rise to universal complaints, as holding out a false expectation of aid, while imposing conditions that prevented its acceptance. The mistake clearly lay in making the repro-

[1] *Reports of the Society for the Improvement of Ireland* Dublin 1846.
[2] Poulett Scrope. *Notes of a Tour in England, Scotland and Ireland*, London 1849.

ductive employment optional; allowing it only as a favour on conditions of a very hard and generally unacceptable nature—impossible indeed in a moiety of the cases perhaps, unlikely to be accepted in any but a very few—instead of making it compulsory wherever the Board of Works judged the circumstances of the district to require it."[1]

The Royal Agricultural Society in a memorial presented to the Lord Lieutenant pointed out that reproductive works under Labouchere's letter could not be undertaken for the following reasons:—

"1. Because it was scarcely possible to find works in any electoral division of such universal benefit as would render them profitable or reproductive to all owners and occupiers in such divisions.

"2. Because, by the terms of the letter, drainage in connection with subsoiling appeared to be the only work of a private character allowed as a substitute for public works, whereas, in many districts this class of work was not required, whilst others, such as clearing, fencing, and making farm roads, were.

"3. Because, in case of works the cost of which was to be made an exclusive charge on the lands to be improved, as specified in the letter, it was necessary for the just operation of the system, that each proprietor should undertake his own portion of the sum to which the electoral division would be assessed, and unanimity, so essential on this point, was seldom attainable. For instance, townlands were chiefly in the hands of separate proprietors, of whom many were absentees, whose consent it would be almost impossible to obtain; others were lunatics, infants, tenants for life, in which cases impediments existed to the obtaining of the required guarantee; others again were embarrassed; some, too, might prefer the work on the public roads to private works, and their opposition could counteract the wishes of the majority.

[1] *Op. cit.* pp. 22-25.

"4. In practice it could not be expected, that a proprietor would submit both to the direct charge incurred for drainage or other improvement of his property, and likewise to that proportion of the general rate, which would be cast upon him by the refusal of other proprietors to undertake their own portion. Such a state of things would not only involve the enterprising proprietor in a double expense, but would, in precisely the same proportion, relieve his negligent neighbours from their allotted share of the burthen." The Royal Agricultural Society concluded its memorial by various suggestions as to amendments which would render the government's scheme more practicable; but these suggestions were ignored.[1]

In addition to the objection arising out of its unproductive character, the Labour Rate Act was objected to on the ground that, by making labour the sole test of destitution, and by prohibiting the grant of gratuitous relief for the first few months of its operation, the act deprived of any relief the old and infirm who were not able to labour. "The result was a vast mortality among the infirm poor—the class to which above all others the care and protection of the state would seem due. Painful reports arrived day after day of the numbers of old people, of cripples, beggars, single women, widows and children, whom the famine swept off. This is the class of the population who were found to have suffered most, when the sad reckoning was made up of the frightful loss of life which had taken place. Indeed it is said that the class of habitual beggars consisting chiefly of the impotent has been wholly annihilated .... Within many of the relief districts comfortable farmers, with both corn and cattle in their yards, were allowed to earn a large amount of the public money at the relief works, or to place their sons upon them, while they sat idly smoking their pipes at home; while at the same time and in the same

[1] O'Rourke *op. cit.* p. 254. For a landlord's objection to the Labouchere Letter see G. W. Blackhall, *Labour on the Land* Dublin 1846.

neighbourhood, many and many a wretched cripple or poor widow with her fatherless orphans—nay many an entire family struck down by the sickness of their bread-earner—were suffered to die unknown."[1] We are therefore driven to the unpleasant conclusion that, not alone were the relief works unsound in principle and not calculated permanently to improve the country and to provide employment for the population, but that they did not even succeed in achieving their immediate purpose of relieving the distress and of preventing starvation during the period of crisis. As O'Rourke says:—"Everything connected with the public works tends to impress one with their gigantic proportions . . . Notwithstanding, the famine was but very partially stayed; on it went, deepening, widening, desolating, slaying . . . . The numbers applying for work without being able to obtain it were fearfully enormous."[2] At the height of the famine John Stuart Mill wrote to John Austin:—"You ask what I think of the Irish measures. I expect nothing from them but mischief, or if any good, only through excess of evil."[3]

It was the realization of the fact that the public works were largely ineffective and productive of great abuses that prompted the government to drop the labour test principle and to adopt the soup kitchen system. It does not however always follow that the reverse of wrong is right, and it would seem that the new system erred in the opposite direction. As the essence of the first system was payment for labour only, the essence of the new system was the provision of food for all without requiring work from any. Both systems offended equally against the excellent maxim which stood at the base of the English poor law: "Relief to the impotent poor gratuitously; to the able bodied only in return for work." Of course the soup kitchen system did not pretend to do anything towards permanently

[1] Poulett Scrope *op. cit.* pp. 37 9. [2] *Op. cit.* p. 219.
[3] Elliott *Letters of J. S. Mill* vol. i. p. 132. For a good criticism of the government policy see Moore. *An Irish Gentleman* ch. 7

ameliorating the condition of the country; it was a pure emergency measure; and from the point of view of providing permanent employment for the Irish people was quite as futile as the Labour Rate Act.

The large sums of public money spent at the time of the famine were therefore devoted purely to the alleviation of the immediate distress, when they might have been much more usefully employed in laying the foundations of a better condition of things for the future. A great opportunity was thus thrown away. It is no exaggeration to say that the public money spent at this time was for the most part wasted. A Select Committee of the House of Lords in 1852 complained of "the uselessness of a great portion of the works executed, their incompleteness, and the enormous waste of labour and capital which they have produced."[1]

We are now in a position to attempt to give an answer to the question which we proposed at the beginning of this section—how far did the government's relief measures attempt to provide a solution of the great economic problem of the time, the apparent disproportion between the population and the resources of Ireland? Did they show any evidence that the government wished to increase the resources rather than decrease the population? Did they point in the direction of depopulation or development? There can be no doubt that they pointed towards depopulation.

In the first place, as we have said repeatedly in the foregoing pages, there were only the two possible paths for a government to follow; and, if it deliberately refused to follow one, it must be taken to have inclined towards the other. The famine, with the vast expenditure of public money that it entailed, gave an unequalled opportunity for pursuing a policy of development, but that opportunity was deliberately missed. As we have seen, it was an essential feature of the public works promoted by the government

[1] *F. R. C.* App. vol. i. p. 253.

that they should be unproductive, and should not help to increase the amount of employment in the country in future years. The policy of development was thus rejected; and, as the only alternative solution of the problem was depopulation, we may say that the policy of depopulation was adopted.

This is the negative method of arriving at the answer to the question; but there are positive considerations also. As we mentioned in another chapter, eviction and clearances never assumed such dimensions as during the famine and in the years immediately following it; and the quarter acre clause of the Poor Law Amendment Act of 1847 was one of the most effective legislative aids to ejectment ever devised. But eviction in Ireland meant depopulation, as the evicted family had but two alternatives, starvation or emigration. Those who could escape the former chose the latter; and the country was depopulated in either case.

It may be suggested that the fact that the government lent no direct aid to emigration proves that it did not view it with favour. This is however fallacious for the simple reason that the evicted tenants were obliged either to emigrate or to starve, and that no state aid was needed to stimulate a man to fly from starvation. Besides we stated above the fact that the powers possessed by public bodies to assist emigration were extended in 1847, and these powers were widely acted on in the years following the famine.[1] It is true that Lord John Russell refused to give the government's support to the gigantic scheme organized by a group of Irish landlords to assist large numbers of Irish to emigrate; but there was no need for him to do so, as the tide of voluntary emigration had already set in, and the starving people were flocking abroad as rapidly as they could have been transported by any public scheme.[2]

We are driven to the conclusion therefore that even the

[1] *2nd Annual Report of Irish Poor Law Commissioners* 1849.
[2] On this gigantic proposal see O'Rourke, *op. cit.* pp. 488-95.

great famine did not succeed in awakening the government to a proper sense of its responsibility towards Ireland. The measures it passed to stem the tide of the calamity were purely emergency measures, passed with no regard to the future. This was admitted by Lord John Russell, who, in his reply to a question regarding his attitude towards the great emigration scheme, remarked, "I deny on the part of the government the responsibility of completely, still less suddenly, resolving the question of the great excess of labour existing in Ireland. What we can do, and what we have endeavoured to do is to mitigate present suffering."[1] Nassau Senior put the matter well when he said, "The English resolved therefore that the Irish should not starve. We resolved therefore that for one year we would feed them. But we came to a third resolution, inconsistent with the first, that we would not feed them for more than a year."[2] In other words the policy at the time of the famine was to look to immediate and to ignore ultimate problems. The policy of the government, which we have traced throughout the previous fifty years, of favouring depopulation rather than development suffered no alteration.[3]

The failure of the government to change its Irish economic policy at this time is the more to be regretted because the great changes brought about by the famine rendered the policy of development in after years far more difficult than before. The tide of emigration that set in at that time could not be easily stayed; it was cumulative in its results; and depopulation had come to be accepted as the normal solution of the problem. "We lost that opportunity" exclaimed John Stuart Mill twenty years after, "and we lost it for ever, because since that time fully one half of all the

[1] O'Rourke, *op. cit.* p. 495.

[2] *Ireland Journals* &c. vol. i. p. 209.

[3] On the interesting question of the extent to which the relief of the famine was considered a party question in England, and how political capital was made out of the sufferings of the Irish people see Butt. *The Famine in the Land* p. 3. and O'Rourke, *The Great Irish Famine* pp. 71 and 299. The government case is well presented in Trevelyan *The Irish Crisis*, and in Walpole's *Life of Lord John Russell* vol. i. pp. 441-2.

reclaimable waste land has been reclaimed—that is it has been got hold of by the landlords.... Therefore it is no longer possible to produce those great results in Ireland merely by reclaiming the waste lands."[1]

[1] *Speech in the House of Commons* 12th March 1868.

PART II

NON-AGRICULTURAL RESOURCES

CHAPTER VIII

MINES.

IN the first part of the book we discussed the agricultural resources of Ireland, and we now pass to a consideration of the non-agricultural resources, which we propose to treat of in the order of mines, fisheries, and manufacturing industry. In the first chapter, which is devoted to the subject of mines, we shall not mention the coal mines, which will be more properly included in the chapter dealing with manufactures.

We need not delay long in describing the mining industry in Ireland, as that industry did not attain to any considerable dimensions in the period under review. Iron ore was present in the neighbourhood of the coal fields, and had been worked as long as the supply of timber lasted; on the cessation of that supply however the works ceased to be carried on except on the very smallest scale [1] One of the principal measures recommended by Sir Robert Kane for the industrial regeneration of Ireland was the introduction of the practice of smelting iron ore by means of turf. This suggestion was not carried into effect.[2]

The metal most extensively raised in Ireland in the early nineteenth century was copper. Wakefield describes the flourishing condition of the copper mines at Ross Island, Killarney, where five hundred men were employed. Copper

[1] Wakefield vol. i. p. 136. Thomas Guest. *Report of the Arigna Iron Works in Ireland.* Dublin 1805. *Report of the Committee of Investigation &c. of the Arigna Ironworks,* London 1827. [2] Kane, *Industrial Resources* pp. 150-3. *Thom's Directory* 1851 p. 162.

mines were also worked at Cronebane near Arklow, but the once prosperous mines of Ballymurtagh had fallen into disuse. Although many copper mines had been discontinued in other districts before Wakefield's time, the mines that had remained open were so prosperous that the exports of copper ore increased considerably between 1783 and 1810.[1] Sir Robert Kane, thirty years later, divided the copper mines then working into three divisions, the first in county Wicklow, occupying the valley of the Ovoca, the second in county Waterford, occupying the district of Knockmahon, and the third in the southern portions of Cork and Kerry. The output of the mines of the first division may be judged by the following figures:-

Mine*	1826		1836		1840		1843	
	tons	value	tons	value	tons	value	tons	value
		£		£		£		£
Ballymurtagh		3373	4659	19,943	3,274	6,956	1,385	4,866
Connoree			2158	10,960	3,017	12,889	654	2,512
Cronebane & Tigroney		12354	4691	23,497	158	1,250	1,160	5,438
Ballygahan			305	1,417	198	346	28	100

* *Industrial Resources* p. 177.

The following figures illustrate the condition of the mines in the second division:-

Year*	output	
	tons	value
		£
1836	3588	33,166
1840	7875	63,087
1843	9101	62,956

* *Ibid.* p. 181.

The mines in the third district were on a smaller scale, the principal undertakings having failed through overspeculation.[2]

The total amount of ore sold at Swansea is the only figure we have to guide us as to the quantities of copper

[1] Wakefield vol. i. pp. 131-4. [2] *Ibid.* pp. 184-8.

raised in Ireland, and these figures are not altogether conclusive, as a good deal of ore was exported to Lancashire as well as to South Wales.[1] The following are the amounts sold at Swansea from 1845 to 1849;

Year*	tons	value
		£
1845	18,430	97,122
1846	17,471	106,078
1847	14,857	96,330
1848	12,808	82,039
1849	10,425	68,794

* *Thom's Directory* 1851 p. 162.

The output of copper from the Wicklow mines in 1850 was very small, and the enterprises could not have been carried on but for the profits derived from the sulphur which they produced.[2]

Next to copper, lead was the most important metal raised in Ireland. In Wakefield's time ten hundredweight was daily smelted at the Glendalough mines, but no other mines appear to have been worked.[3] Sir Robert Kane found lead mines in operation at Glendalough, and Glenmalure, county Wicklow, Ballycorus county Dublin, Caime co. Wexford, and Kilbricken and Ballyhickey co. Clare. The quantity of dressed ore obtained in Glendalough was about 600 tons annually, and in Caime about 300 tons.[4] Small lead mines were also worked at Clonligg and Newtownards county Down, Bond and Newry co. Armagh, Castleblaney co. Monaghan, Kenmare co. Kerry, and Bantry co. Cork.[5]

The Wicklow gold mines which had been worked at the end of the eighteenth century ceased to be productive early in the nineteenth, and in 1807 Foster opposed the

[1] *Ibid.* p. 178.
[2] Alfred Webb, *Recollections of a Three Days Tour in County Wicklow* Dublin 1851.
[3] Wakefield, vol. i. pp. 134-5.
[4] *Industrial Resources* pp. 196-207.
[5] *Thom's Directory* 1851 p. 163.

outlay of any further public money on them, remarking that "the whole. . . . was an experiment worthy of trial but it has now completely failed." In 1814 various parties endeavoured to obtain a lease of the mines from the government with a view to working them again, but the negotiations seem to have fallen through. In 1809 a labourring man discovered some gold deposit in Queens County, but refused to indicate the spot until he received a payment which was considered excessive.[1]

The total volume of mining in Ireland was thus very inconsiderable. Many attempts were made by bodies concerned in the development of Irish industrial resources to awaken interest in the mines of the country, but without success. In 1812 the Dublin Society appointed Richard Griffith Junior as their mining engineer, and he prepared a series of most valuable reports upon the mining resources of Ireland.[2] In the years 1823-1828 four companies, the Mining Company of Ireland, the Hibernian Mining Company, the Royal Irish Mining Company, and the Imperial Mining Company, were formed to work the Irish mines, but the greater number of the works undertaken by them were soon abandoned.[3] One thing that helped to impede the progress of mining in Ireland was the disrepute cast upon the Irish mines by their failure in the hands of English speculators. "During the last fifty years", wrote Richard Griffith, "wandering English miners of the lowest order and worst character have in many parts made rude attempts to reopen some of our ancient mines; but, possessing no capital of their own, and little dependence being placed either on their skill or honesty by the inhabitants of the country, as might be expected, they failed in every trial. By these means the character of many of our mines has been injured, though no trial, at least none deserving the name, has

[1] *Official Papers Public Record Office Dublin* 1790-1831. Carton 388 nos. 1155, 1213, 1610 and 1756.
[2] Berry, *History of R. D. S.* pp. 162-8.
[3] R. Griffith. *Report on the Metallic Mines of Leinster*. Dublin 1828.

been made."[1] Many years later Sir Robert Kane made a similar complaint; speaking of the Audley Copper Mines, he remarks that "they, like the Arigna Mining Company, are an example of the bringing into disrepute Irish industrial enterprises through the fault of jobbing speculators in London."[2] The most important reason however why the Irish mines were not worked to their full capacity was probably the same as that which prevented the Irish soil from being worked to its best advantage—the shortage of capital, and the reluctance of those who possessed it to sink it in Irish land; as Professor Hancock expressed it: "limited or encumbered estates on the side of the landlords, and insecurity of tenure on the part of the tenants."[3] The statute of 1815 which facilitated the granting of loans to landowners for the working of mines and mineral properties remained to a large extent a dead letter, so far as Ireland was concerned, as it applied only to the case of existing mines, and did not extend to the opening of new undertakings.[4]

[1] *Report on the Metallic Mines of Leinster*, Dublin 1828.
[2] *Industrial Resources* p. 183, where a full account of the frauds practised in connection with the Audley mines is given.
[3] *On the Economic Causes of the Present State of Agriculture in Ireland* pt. VI. Dublin 1849.
[4] Beere, *A Letter to the King on the Practical Improvement of Ireland*, London 1827. Full statistics of the condition of the Irish mines in 1836 and 1849 will be found in *Thoms Directory* 1851 p. 163.

CHAPTER IX

Fisheries.

THE principal Irish fishery—that of herrings—appears to have declined after the Union. "The herring fishery" we read in 1811, "has declined greatly since 1785; but cod, ling and hake are in as great abundance as ever."[1] Wakefield stated "the herring fishery in Ireland is at present in a very declining state. The assertion that these fish have deserted the coast seems to admit of considerable doubt; perhaps the Irish fishermen from their unskilfulness, and the boats in use, are not enabled to proceed to that distance from the land where it is likely they would be found."[2] Wakefield estimated the total number of men engaged on the fishery to amount to 9,911, and attributed the backward condition of the industry to the primitive manner in which it was conducted. "The only boats used at present," he writes, "consist merely of a wooden frame, covered with a horse's or a bullock's hide."[3] He also drew attention to the fact that the majority of the fishermen divided their time between fishing and agriculture—"It appears that there is one impediment in Ireland to the success of the fishery. This obstacle is so striking that it will readily be perceived, I allude to that minute division of land which has been so injurious in other respects. The employment of the fisherman and that of the farmer are so unlike that

[1] George Barnes. *A Statistical Account of Ireland founded upon Historical Facts.* Dublin 1811. [2] Vol. ii. p. 102. [3] Vol. ii pp. 97, 117.

the same person cannot be expected to be proficient in both.[1]" There were other reasons besides those mentioned by Wakefield why the Irish fisheries were backward and unprogressive. The British fisheries were entitled to substantial bounties on the construction of vessels engaged on the deep sea fishing, and on herrings properly cured and packed, which the Irish were denied; the tax on salt was heavier in Ireland than in Great Britain; the security required to be given against smuggling before a fishing licence could be obtained was prohibitive; the duties on foreign timber, taken in conjunction with the destruction of the Irish woods, operated to discourage boat-building; and, finally, Ireland suffered from a grievous want of suitable piers and harbours on the southern and western coasts.[2] It was alleged that the Irish were very adverse to the introduction of improved methods and processes;[3] but it is probable that the failure of the Irish in this respect was due, not so much to conservatism, as to lack of capital. Whatever the cause, it is beyond dispute that the Irish fisheries declined seriously in the twenty years following the Union, so that Ireland soon became a fish-importing instead of a fish-exporting country. "The failure of the existing system may be proved by the fact, established in the public accounts, that, while in the last year herrings were imported to the value of £58,197, the export trade within the past three years has fallen to a twentieth part of its former amount."[4]

In consequence of the strong recommendations made by the select committee from whose report we have just quoted, an act was passed for the purpose of encouraging the Irish fisheries. This act provided that a sum of £5,000 *per annum* should be appropriated for bounties on the

[1] Vol. ii. p. 129.

[2] Stokes, *Observations on the Population and Resources of Ireland.* Dublin 1821, Mac Dougall. *A Treatise on the Irish Fisheries.* Belfast 1819.

[3] *A View of the British and Irish Fisheries* by an Old Sailor, Dublin 1820.

[4] *Second Report of Select Committee on State of Disease and Condition of Labouring Poor in Ireland* 1819.

building of suitable fishing boats and on the curing of fish. Provision was also made for grants for the construction of piers and harbours.[1] Although this act was the object of a certain amount of adverse criticism on the ground that no person could obtain the bounties which it offered for boat building unless he was possessed of a fairly substantial capital,[2] it nevertheless succeeded in greatly stimulating the fishing industry. As early as 1823 an increase in the number of vessels employed and an improvement in the quality of fish landed was remarked;[3] and the number of persons employed in the fishery increased from 36.000 in 1819 to 64.771 in 1830.[4] The objection that the poor fisherman, possessed of no capital, was excluded from the benefits of the act was met in 1824 by the passing of an amending act allotting £500 *per annum* for the repairing of the boats of poor fishermen.[5] The total amount granted between 1819 and 1830 was £163.376.[6]

In 1830 this encouraging legislation was allowed to lapse, and the only help extended to the fisheries after that date was the grant of an annually diminishing sum for the completion of the piers and harbours commenced under the act of 1819. The administration of this sum was at first entrusted to the Board of Inland Navigation, but afterwards transferred to the Board of Public Works.[7] The result of the withdrawal of the former encouragement was that the Irish fishery experienced a fresh period of decline. "Under the operation of the system (under the Act of 1819)" the Fishery Commissioners reported in 1836 "a great increase in the activity of the trade was experienced, much capital was drawn to it, and large sums were circulated amongst the fishermen and curers. When the bounties were discontinued, the trade began to fall back into languor and exhaustion."[8] "The fishery continued to prosper until

[1] 59 Geo. III c. 109. [2] *Repeal Reports* vol. i. p. 317. [3] *Report of the Fishery Commissioners* 1823. [4] *First Report of Commission on Irish Fisheries* 1836. [5] 5 Geo IV c. 64, 7 Geo IV c. 34. [6] *First Report Fishery Commissioners* 1836. [7] 1 and 2 Wm. IV. c. 33. [8] *First Report.*

the year 1830," we read in the Report of the Repeal Association "when the acts were suffered to expire; and since that period the Irish fisheries have been annually decreasing, the condition of the fishermen deteriorating, the boats and gear wearing out and going to wreck."[1] The number of men and boys employed decreased from 64.771 in 1830 to 54.119 in 1836.[2]

The decay of the fisheries was so apparent in 1835, that the government appointed a commission to enquire into the subject. This commission, having heard voluminous evidence, reported in favour of the granting of such pecuniary aid for the construction of piers and harbours as was thought necessary, that the Board of Works should be authorized to advance one half of the cost of the construction of roads leading to fishing centres, that the Board should be further authorized to advance, by way of loan to be repaid by the baronies, one half of the cost of erecting curing stations, salt houses, and fishermen's houses, and that educational facilities in matters relating to the fisheries should be provided by the government.[3]

The usual course in respect of the recommendations of its own commissions was pursued by the government of the day. No action of any kind was taken for six years, and even then when tardy legislation was introduced the suggestion for expending public money on the fisheries was ignored. In 1842 an act was passed constituting the Board of Public Works the commissioners for the regulation and control of the fisheries; but no grant of public money for their encouragement was authorized.[4] "The charge of the Irish fisheries" the Repeal Association reported "is committed to the Commissioners of Public Works, and

[1] *Repeal Reports* vol. i. p. 318.

[2] *First Report of Irish Fishery Commission* 1836.

[3] *First Report of Commission on Irish Fisheries* 1836. A Select Committee of the previous year had recommended grants for deep sea harbours which would encourage the deep sea fisheries. *Select Committee on Advances for Public Works in Ireland* 1835.

[4] 5 and 6 Vict. c. 106, amended by 7 and 8 Vict. c. 108, 8 and 9 Vict. c. 108, 9 and 10 Vict. c. 114, and 11 and 12 Vict. c. 92.

the act is in most of its clauses penal and prohibitory—in no one instance offering encouragement or aid to the poor deep sea fisherman, while it gives abundant protection to the wealthy owners and farmers of the inland fisheries."[1] It was only under the pressure of the crisis brought about by the famine, that the government was induced to sanction the outlay of public money for the encouragement of this most important industry. An act passed in 1846 authorized the grant of £50.000 by the Treasury for the erection of piers and harbours, provided that one-fourth of the expenditure was repaid by the county, district, or proprietors on whose lands the improvements were effected;[2] and a further act of the following year authorized a further advance of £40.000 for the same purposes.[3] In 1850 the amount granted under these acts amounted to £68.636, and the loans to be repaid by the districts benefited amounted to £25.390; while the sum guaranteed by the landed proprietors amounted to £6.981.[4]

In spite of this legislative encouragement, the herring fishery experienced a severe decline in the decade 1840-50. The whole Irish fishing industry went through a period of revolution in these years owing to the increased facilities of transport, which tended to substitute a fresh for a salt fish industry.[5] Under the powers conferred by the act of 1846, the government opened seven model curing stations-at Roundstone, Baltimore, Castletown, Inniscoe, Valentia, Belmullet, and Killybegs—all of which were closed down within two years from their commencement.[6] The opening of these curing stations was not, however, unattended with good results, as it encouraged private capitalists to embark on the same business.[7] The progress of the fishing industry during the years 1830-50 is shown in the following table:—

[1] *Repeal Reports* vol i.; p. 319. [2] 9 Vict. c. 3.
[3] 10 and 11 Vict. c. 75. [4] *Thom's Directory* 1852 p, 235.
[5] *Ibid* p. 234. [6] *Ibid.*
[7] *Sixteenth Report of Commissioners of Public Works* 1847.

	Vessels & Boats*	Men & Boys
1830 — System of bounties and loans ..	15,119	64,771
1836 — After withdrawal of bounties ..	10,761	54,119
1844 — No assistance	17,955	84,708
1845 — Before famine	19,883	93,073
1848 — After famine	15,932	70,011
1851 —	14,756	64,612

* *Thom's Directory* 1852 p. 233.

The above figures demonstrate how severely the Irish fishing industry felt the results of the famine. This is explained by the fact that, in Ireland, fishing and agriculture were closely inter-dependent, and that any adverse influence affecting the one could not be without its results on the other; in other words, the division of labour was not carried very far. "The fishermen of Ireland" said the commissioners of 1836 "usually depend more on the land than on the sea; and their condition is mainly determined by the local circumstances of agriculture."[1] The Commissioners of Public Works reported that no industry had suffered so severely through the famine as the fishery, partly because there was a prejudice among the country people against the use of fish unless they could obtain potatoes to use with it, and partly because the fishermen had been compelled to pawn or sell their tackle to meet their immediate needs.[2] The normal progress of the fishery was interfered with in the year of its greatest need by the government's prohibition of the use of the trammel net.[3]

It was the very backwardness of the Irish fisheries that constituted their strongest claim to public assistance. As we have already seen, the progress of the industry was impeded by lack of capital, and it would have been a very profitable investment for a far-seeing government to provide the capital for an industry calculated not alone to

[1] *First Report* p. vii. [2] *Sixteenth Report of Commissioners of Public Works* 1847.
[3] *Facts from the Fisheries.* Waterford 1848.

create a large volume of employment, but also to furnish an inexhaustible "nursery for seamen" who would prove useful in time of war. The Irish fishermen were in no way inferior to the English as regards skill; it was capital alone that they lacked. "It was purely lack of capital that prevented the Irish from developing fisheries; they were very skilful; no men could understand the hook fishing better than the west coast fishermen."[1] "The number of boats," it was complained in 1822, "and of fishermen on the coasts of the distressed districts are very considerable, but from the poverty of the fishermen they are not able to refit the boats they have at present or to build new ones."[2] As we have seen, the small attempt that was made to repair this deficiency in 1824 was discontinued in 1830, before it had time to produce any permanent good result. Six years later the Irish Fishery Commission recommended the application of public money to help to put the fisheries on a footing on which they could compete with the Scotch, but the government did not take action on this part of the commission's report. The Devon Commission found that the fishermen on the Irish coast were still without the means of furnishing themselves with the proper boats for going out to sea, and that such boats would cost about £300 each. "Much good" we read, "was done by loans to fishermen made by the late Fishery Board when it was in existence, and if proper encouragement were given, much benefit and employment might be expected to arise from the fisheries generally."[3] The urgency of such encouragement was increased by the fact that a great part of the population of the maritime counties depended on the fisheries for subsistence.[4] One thing in particular should have been provided by the government, namely curing stations. The people were unable to erect them themselves, and, owing to the absence of any properly regulated market,

[1] Brabazon, *The Deep Sea and Coast Fisheries of Ireland*, Dublin 1848.
[2] Fraser *Sketches and Essays on the Present State of Ireland*. Dublin 1822.
[3] p. 936. [4] *Fourth Report of Bog Commissioners* 1814.

the price of salt tended to soar when it was most needed. Although the salt tax was repealed in 1825, the price was frequently run up by the retailers to seven or ten pounds a ton.[1] On the coast of Galway the herrings were often used as manure in consequence of the fishermen being too poor to obtain salt at the proper moment.[2] Yet this very necessary work was completely neglected for many years; and, when it was attempted, was done in a half-hearted manner and discontinued in two years.

Indeed the behaviour of the government with regard to the fisheries was strictly in accordance with its general Irish policy. It is interesting to compare the treatment of the Scotch and Irish fisheries. The principle of encouraging the fisheries in Scotland with public money was admitted in 1802-3, whereas it was not admitted in Ireland till 1819, on the urgent recommendation of the select committee of that year. "In the case of Scotland in 1802-3 the Treasury adopted the principle of applying the public money for the great ultimate public object of encouraging the fisheries. . . . Of the signal success of that scheme your Committee have the most satisfactory evidence. On every ground of policy as well as of justice your Committee earnestly recommends the application of the precedent of Scotland to the Highland districts of Ireland. . . . To all the natural claims to similar encouragements, those districts of Ireland add the very serious one that, from the non-residence of a majority of the proprietors, they do not possess within themselves the means of effecting those objects by private enterprise."[3] The recommendations of the committee in this respect were adopted; but the encouragement so given was discontinued in 1830, while that given to the Scotch fisheries, which by that time stood in far less need of it, was continued. "The treatment which the Irish

[1] *First Report of Irish Fishery Commission* 1836 p. xv.
[2] *Devon Commission* p. 936.
[3] *Second Report of Select Committee on State of Disease and Condition of Labouring Poor in Ireland* 1819.

fishery received entirely arose from Ireland not being sufficiently strong to protect her own interests; for every effort which was then made in favour of Ireland was counteracted by Scotch influence, of which we need not look for stronger evidence than that the very act which deprived Ireland of the encouragement which her fisheries received, has continued to Scotland a Fishing Board, officers, and grants of money."[1] As a result of this differential treatment the Cork export trade in herrings almost entirely disappeared in a few years;[2] and the Irish markets, even in the sea coast towns, were flooded with Scotch herrings.[3] In 1850 Ireland was Scotland's best customer for fish.[4]

This unfair treatment was the subject of perpetual complaints in Ireland. "Fisheries are eight times mentioned in the catalogue of commissions and committees; but there is nothing better now to be told of them than that the bounties were withdrawn, and they languish; while the Scotch fisheries are still carried on with vigour under a pecuniary encouragement, existing, in part, ever since the remote period of the Scottish Union."[5] The Earl of Glengall wrote as follows to the Devon Commission:- "The truth is, an intrigue to destroy the Irish deep sea fisheries was too successful, in order that (as I believe) the Scotch fisheries might not be interfered with; and this just at the moment that the Board had seen their way through their difficulties."[6]

[1] *Report of Repeal Association on Fisheries.* Dublin 1840.
[2] Marmion, *Maritime Ports* p. 537.
[3] *Irish Fishery Commission* 1836 p. ix.
[4] *Thom's Directory* 1851 p. 240.
[5] *Second Repeal Prize Essay.* Dublin 1845 p. 90.
[6] *Devon Commission* p. 938. Those wishing to acquire fuller information regarding the fisheries should consult, in addition to the authorities referred to above, the following—*An Account of the Present State of the Fisheries for the Year* 1823. Dublin 1825; T. Knox Fortescue *Remarks on the Deep Sea Fisheries of Ireland.* Dublin 1846; Sir T. D. Lauder, *Instructions for the Curing of Fish.* Dublin 1846; *Prospectus of the Irish Fishery and Fishing Boat Company*, London 1847; James Ward, *How to Regenerate Ireland, or Facts from the Fisheries.* London 1850; *The Second Report of the Royal Irish Fisheries Co.* 1851; and the annual reports of the Fishery Board 1819-30.

CHAPTER X

MANUFACTURING INDUSTRY.

WE now pass to a consideration of the manufacturing industries of Ireland in the fifty years following the Union. The method we propose to adopt in dealing with this subject is to give a short account of each of the most important manufactures in the period; and then to pass to a consideration of the causes which impeded their development. We may preface the first part of the subject by reminding the reader that, although the eighteenth century was generally speaking a period of excessive manufacturing depression in Ireland, the eighteen years of Grattan's Parliament had witnessed the beginning of an important industrial revival.[1]

Section 1. The Condition of the Industries.

(a) The Woollen Industry.

The woollen industry provides the most famous example of English oppression of Irish manufacture. Owing to the hostile legislation of 1698 this industry continued under a cloud during the greater part of the eighteenth century; and made but a partial and tardy recovery in the eighteen years of liberty which preceded the Union. During the latter period the industry increased to some extent, as was admitted even by those most opposed to bounties

[1] O'Brien. *Economic History of Ireland in the Eighteenth Century* pp. 269-289.

and other artificial encouragement. "From all the information which we have collected upon the subject" stated the Revenue Commissioners of 1822 "we are led to believe that in the thirty years which preceded the Union the manufacture gradually but not very materially increased."[1]

By the Act of Union the duties on the importation of woollen goods, included under the categories of old and new drapery, were reduced to ten per cent. for twenty years, subject to revision at the end of that period. This limited measure of protection did not succeed in restoring the decayed industry to anything approaching its former prosperity; but it did succeed in preserving it from complete decay. Various circumstances operated to retard the progress of the industry. In the first place there was the fact that Ireland was not a mutton-consuming country, and that the export of sheep was consequently encouraged. "In considering the disadvantages" said Wakefield "which this manufacture has to encounter, I shall observe in the first place that Ireland is by no means a country favourable to the consumption of mutton. The consequence is that a great number of her sheep, when fit for the butcher, are sent to England."[2] Another great impediment to the development of the Irish woollen industry was the prevalence of the domestic manufacture of woollen goods. "The worst consequence arising from the conduct of England towards Ireland has been, that it has prevented the exportation of wool in a manufactured state. This, and the minute division of land, which renders every man an artificer, making the women become the manufacturers of their own clothing, has been attended with the worst consequences to the woollen trade of Ireland, in every part of the country except among the northern manufacturers. . . All the wool that is shorn is made into frieze and linsey by the proprietors of the stock, who card, spin, weave, dye and consume

[1] *Fourth Report* and see O'Brien *Economic History of Ireland in the Eighteenth Century* p. 273.
[2] Vol. i. p. 729.

it. . It may be estimated that, except in the eastern part of the province of Ulster, the domestic manufacture of woollen goods is everywhere prevalent without that due division of labour which can render it of any benefit to the country".[1]

In spite of these drawbacks, the industry increased in extent during the years following the Union. On account of the protection afforded by the Union duties, English manufacturers were unable to find a market in Ireland for their coarser cloths, and were consequently induced to open factories in Ireland. Two large Yorkshire manufacturers, Houghton and Willans, opened factories in Dublin, and at the same time another Yorkshire manufacturer, Atkinson, opened a large factory at Celbridge. This last firm, it is interesting to note, transferred its operations to Ireland because of the more progressive attitude of the Irish workers in regard to machinery. "Within these few years" says Wakefield "a Yorkshire firm has been driven to Celbridge where they have established the shearing machinery which the Yorkshire manufacturers would not permit to be employed in their own country."[2] On the whole, the industry flourished during the ten years following the Union. "Though the manufacture may have decreased at Midleton, Carrick, and Kilkenny, it is evidently upon the increase."[3]

In 1810 the woollen industry passed through a period of severe distress. One of the government contractors failed in that year, and his failure was followed by the bankruptcy of almost the entire woollen trade of Dublin. No less than twenty-two firms stopped work; and the credit of the whole industry was seriously affected owing to the refusal of the bankers to discount the woollen manufacturers' bills. "A week or a fortnight before that crash" said one of the witnesses before the Handloom Weavers

[1] *Ibid.* vol. i. pp. 729 and 758.

[2] Vol. i. p. 717 It is interesting to compare this with George Cornewell Lewis's tribute to the progressiveness of the Irish worker twenty years later, supra p. 170.

[3] Wakefield vol. i. p. 718.

Commission thirty years later, "the weavers were better able to pay 1/10d and 1/11d for the loaf of bread than they are now able to pay 8d."[1]

Although most of the smaller firms were driven out of business by this crash, some of the larger ones survived, and from that time onwards the woollen industry tended to change in character, and to become concentrated more and more in the hands of a few large employers. Of course the old domestic spinning and weaving continued still, and probably supplied most of the needs of the peasantry. An effort was made by the farming societies and the Dublin Society to improve the quality of Irish wool through the introduction of the Merino breed. This attempt was not unsuccessful. "In Ireland" Lord Sheffield observed in 1813 "the growth of Spanish wool is cultivated with great spirit, sells at very high prices, and the cloths made of it are excellent"[2]. The principal locality where the Merino breed was introduced was county Kilkenny, where it was greatly encouraged by the proximity of the Merino factory. In 1820 there was in that county one flock of six hundred pure Merinos; and there were also large flocks kept by Lord Lismore at Shanbally, county Tipperary.[3] Outside Dublin the most active centre of the industry during this period was Kilkenny. Curwen noticed in 1813 that "a considerable manufactory of coarse woollens is established here, and blankets are also manufactured of extraordinary lightness and fineness of quality."[4] In 1810 the Merino Factory, to which we have already referred, was established in Kilkenny to give employment to the children of the peasantry. In the year after its foundation this factory gave constant employment to nearly four hundred operatives. In 1820 the factory turned out 40,000 pieces of cloth. Although the factory was admittedly productive of the greatest economic and moral benefit to the district, it was not a

[1] *Otway's Report* p. 664. [2] *Of the Trade in Wool and Woollens*, Dublin 1813.
[3] Rev. Thomas Radcliff *Reports on the Fine Woolled Flocks of the Messers Nolan*, Dublin 1820. [4] *Observations* vol. ii. p. 53.

financial success; and the promoters petitioned the government more than once between 1817 and 1820 for an advance out of the public works fund, in which demand they were supported by a resolution of the Kilkenny grand jury.[1] Generally speaking, outside Dublin and Kilkenny the industry tended to decline, largely on account of the growing taste for English and Scotch productions. "The unfortunate predilection which we have for the manufacture of every country but our own has almost ruined that of the woollen, not only here (in Carrick-on-Suir) but in many other considerable towns in Ireland."[2]

The worsted manufacture also made some progress in Dublin. "Worsted yarn is very extensively employed in the manufacture of tabbinets, bombazeans, stuffs, etc. and the manufacture of these articles, particularly of the first, has for a long series of years been almost exclusively confined to Ireland, and being one in which this country particularly excels, has furnished and is likely to furnish a source of considerable employment to its industrious poor. Extensive as is the employment afforded by the manufacture of tabbinets, bombazeans, etc., it falls far short of that furnished by the manufacture of the worsted yarn itself in the proportion of at least twenty to one."[3] In 1820 an industry was established for the spinning of worsted yarn by hand in Dublin, which gave employment to hundreds of the worst beggars in the city.[4]

The Revenue Commissioners of 1822 devoted considerable attention to the woollen industry, and much important information regarding it is contained in the report of their proceedings. They concluded that the industry had increased from the time of the Union, from the facts that the Irish woollen manufactures consumed the whole of the raw

[1] *Official Papers Dublin Record Office* 1790-1831 carton 456 no 1924 and carton 457 nos 2135 and 2228. *Sketch of the Origin and Progress of the Merino Factory, County Kilkenny* Dublin 1817. *Sketch of the Merino Factory*, Dublin 1818, Radcliff, *Reports on the Fine Woolled Flocks of the Messers Nolans*, etc. Dublin 1820.

[2] Gough, *Account of Two Journies Southward in Ireland in* 1817, Dublin 1818.

[3] *Report of a Committee of the Dublin Society*, Dublin 1820.

[4] *Ibidem.*

material produced in Ireland,that the amount of the imports of wool and yarn had increased during the same period,[1] and that there was no ground for believing that the quantity of wool produced in Ireland had diminished. "There can be no doubt" they state "that the quantity of woollen goods manufactured in Ireland since the Union is very greatly increased." Statistics prepared for the commissioners showed that the number of billies at work on the manufacture of old drapery was 92, that the number of persons employed was 6,069, and the average annual value of the products amounted to £535.600.[2]

The cloth produced in Ireland satisfied about two-thirds of the demand of the home market, the other third being supplied by imports from England. The cloth imported was all of a fine quality, as the duty of 8½d a yard was not sufficent to stop the importation of highly priced goods, but only that of cheap and coarse goods. "Under these circumstances", the commissioners state, "the manufacture in Ireland is confined to the production of the lowest description of goods; and as yet no fabric of superfine cloth to any extent has been successfully established." The wages paid to woollen weavers in Ireland were considerably higher than in England.[3]

With regard to the manufacture of new drapery, the commissioners made a curious error, owing to their acting on insufficient evidence. In their fourth report they stated that the growing importation of worsted yarn enabled the poor country weavers to engage in the industry; that the business was thus passing out of the hands of the large manufacturers; and that the only kinds of new drapery manufactured in Ireland were plain worsted stuffs, and

[1] Statistics of the importation of wool and woollen yarn into Ireland in this period are printed in Appendix 8 to the Fourth Report of the Commissioners.

[2] *Fourth Report of Revenue Commissioners* 1822, App. 23. Mr. Willans thought these figures rather an overestimate. *Second Report Railway Commission* 1836 App. A. No. 8. The exports of woollen goods from Ireland 1800-23 are printed in appendix B of Miss Murray's *Commercial Relations.*

[3] *Fourth Report of Revenue Commissioners* 1822. *Select Committee on Artisans and Machinery* 1824, pp. 283-6.

woollen and worsted flannels. After the publication of the report however they learnt that their information was defective, and they issued a supplement, in which they stated that "establishments of considerable magnitude have been recently formed in Ireland for the manufacture of woollen and worsted stuffs, figured, twilled, and printed, serges, calamancoes, shaloons, moreens and camlets."[1]

We shall see in another section that the outcome of the recommendations of the Revenue Commissioners was the repeal of the Union duties. The effect of this repeal on the woollen manufacture was very serious. The inability of the Irish manufactures to compete with the English in a free market was predicted by all the Irish witnesses before the commissioners, but, as we shall see, these expressions of opinion were ignored. The effect of the repeal on the industry cannot be better told than in Mr. Willan's words addressed to the Handloom Weavers Commission many years later :—"The protecting duties ceased in 1823; but it is remarkable that their withdrawal was hardly felt, if at all, until the spring of 1826. This may be accounted for, first by the trade in England being good up to Nov. 1826, and no surplus stock on hand; therefore no active competition from them in this market; secondly a gradual reduction in the high rate of wages previously paid...... The panic in November and December 1825 in England was severely felt in Ireland. In the spring of 1826 the distress arising from accumulated stocks induced English manufacturers to throw their goods into this market in large quantities, and at such low prices that no solvent person could attempt to compete with them. Irish manufactures had not only to contend with a glutted market, but a reduction in the price of wool; and, such was the reduction from these causes as seriously to affect the stock on hand, solvent manufacturers refused to sell at the ruinous price then offered, and in general their manufacturing operations were discontinued.

[1] *Supplement to Fourth Report of Revenue Commissioners* 1823.

This cause was attended with great loss to them in another respect. Naps and coating for women's wear, being the principal articles manufactured, were by the low price of English cloth put out of fashion, cloths being generally substituted for them."[1] Mr. Willans gave similar evidence before the Railway Commissioners: "Competition under such circumstances" he stated "was utterly impossible for the Irish manufacturers, and their business was at a complete standstill for many months. The effect was destructive to nearly all the small manufacturers."[2] In 1829 many woollen operatives were driven to rely on alms for subsistence.[3] The woollen industry was ruined in Roscrea as a result of the removal of the duties.[4]

The decline of the industry had become an unquestionable fact in 1831. "The flannel trade of Wicklow and Kilkenny declined, and the serge trade of Limerick, which gave employment to a number of men and women. The woollen cloth trade in Ireland was long in a sinking condition, though it is now improving in Dublin and its vicinity, but it has sunk totally in other parts of Ireland. The trade requires a division of labour, to perfect the manufacture, which only an extensive trade will bear; and when the trade has sunk, such a division of labour could not be accomplished."[5]

One branch of the trade which totally disappeared after the repeal of the duties was the once flourishing flannel manufacture of county Wicklow. Although Wakefield noticed that the trade was not increasing at the time he wrote, it nevertheless was not declining, and maintained a considerable magnitude.[6] In the next few years the manufacture would seem to have increased; it was stated that in 1816 there were twelve fairs held, and as many as 1200 pieces of flannel were offered for sale at a single fair;[7]

[1] *Otway's Report* p. 663.
[2] *Second Report* App. A no. 8.
[3] *Report of the Mansion House Relief Committee* Dublin 1830.
[4] *Poor Inquiry Commission* App. A p. 266.
[5] *Commentaries on National Policy and on Ireland*, Dublin 1831.
[6] Vol. i. p. 712. [7] *Otway's Report* p. 665.

and in 1822 it gave employment to three thousand people, and attained an annual output of 7,800 pieces of flannel of the value of £54,600.[1] From that time onwards the trade rapidly declined; in 1830 the flannel hall at Rathdrum was closed, and the fairs came to an end.[2]

The Railway Commissioners of 1837 found that the industry had declined very considerably since 1824, and that the value of the manufacture in Dublin was only about £90,000 *per annum*; in Cork, Kilkenny, Moate and Carrick on Suir, £20,000; and that the flannel trade of Wicklow and Wexford was extinct. The manufacture of worsted and stuff articles was carried on at Mountmellick and Abbeyleix. The greater part of the wool produced in Ireland was exported to England, and "three fourths of the frieze generally worn by the peasantry throughout Ireland is now an article of import." The Commissioners were impressed by the fact that the Dublin manufacturers had adopted every new improvement in machinery.[3]

In view of the unanimous evidence on the subject, it is difficult to understand how Mr. Otway could have committed himself to the following *obiter dictum*. "The woollen trade, from the negligence and extravagance of its manufacturers, the want of an extensive home market, from the poverty of the peasantry, and the absence of a middle class, notwithstanding its monopoly of clothing all the Irish regiments, no matter where quartered, almost expired before the protecting duties were withdrawn, and it is only now beginning to revive and advance towards a healthy condition."[4] This passage is typical of the school of economists to which Mr. Otway belonged. It is also characteristic that Mr. Otway rather welcomed than regretted the changes

[1] *Fourth Report of Revenue Commissioners* 1822 App. 23.
[2] *Otway's Report* p. 665.
[3] *Second Report of Railway Commission* 1837 pp. 8. 14. Striking figures illustrating the decline of the woollen, serge, hosiery and carpet manufactures in Dublin, Cork, and other towns are contained in *The First Repeal Prize Essay* 1845; and in the *Repeal Dictionary*, tit. Manufactures.
[4] *Otway's Report* p. 599.

which had taken place, because they had resulted in the triumph of the stronger over the weaker industry. "I am led to believe" he says in his report "that this crisis (of 1827) produced many beneficial effects; it swept away all the establishments supported by a fictitious credit, and it led to the examination of the rate of wages, . . . What the woollen trade lost in extent it gained in real stability"; and again, in another part of his report: "Let the extent of the woollen manufacture have been what it may, let it have been established when it may, I consider it now only in its infancy, and for the first time containing the germs of life within itself". In other words, a manufacture of small extent under free trade is preferable to one of large extent under a protective system—the logical conclusion of *laissez faire.* The contentment of the classical economists at the contemplation of the sufferings endured by the unemployed manufacturers during the displacement of small scale by large scale industry was precisely parallel to the satisfaction with which they regarded the consolidation of the farms. Truly, periods of transition seem to have been pleasant spectacles for the orthodox.[1]

We are in possession of full figures relating to the industry so far as it was conducted in factories during the years 1839-50, as we have the detailed returns of the factory inspectors made at various dates. From these figures we learn that the condition of the industry in 1839 was as follows:—In the whole of Ireland there were 31 mills engaged on the woollen manufacture, containing 5 steam engines and 39 water wheels; the total horse power engaged was 581, and the total number of persons employed 1231. The industry was distributed as follows:

[1] The gradual decay of the hand loom weavers in country and city respectively is described in *The Causes of the Discontents of Ireland,* Dublin 1823, and *A Letter to Sir John Newport Bart.* by Hibernicus, Dublin 1821.

County*	No. of Mills	Number of operatives employed
Dublin..	12	580
Kildare	2	32
Wicklow	2	13
Kilkenny	3	87
Cork	5	188
King's	2	56
Queen's	5	275

* *Parl. Pap.* No. 41 of 1839.

Eight years later the industry had declined, the statistics for the year 1847 disclosing the following results:

County	No. of persons employed
Cork	181
Dublin..	402
Kildare	32
Kilkenny	211
Queen's	105
Tipperary	16
Waterford	135

In the same year the number of operatives employed in the woollen industry in Scotland amounted to 9,637, and in England to 62,687. The worsted industry employed 238 persons in the same year, as compared with 143 in Scotland and 51,797 in England.[1] Three years later the Irish woollen industry had decreased by almost fifty per cent. The returns of 1850 present the following particulars:—

Counties	No. of Factories	No. of spindles	No. of power looms	No. employed
Factories for spinning				
Cork	1	5,638	—	187
Dublin	2	3,170	—	57
King's	1	500	—	25
Queen's	3	2,784	—	177
Factories for spinning & weaving				
Kilkenny	1	800	10	57
Waterford	1	1,566	12	50
Total	9	14,458	22	553

[1] *Parl. Pap.* No. 294 of 1847.

In the same year there were employed in Scotland 9,464, and in England 64,426, operatives. The statistics for the worsted manufactures in this year show that there were at work 2 factories, with 1552 spindles, and employing 76 operatives in Ireland; whereas the number employed in Scotland anounted to 746, and in England to 78,915.[1] It is important to note that these figures relate only to the woollen industry as carried on in factories, and do not throw any light on its extent as a domestic industry. They are however conclusive as to the fact that the Irish woollen industry had before 1850 become very insignificant compared with the English and Scotch industries.

(*b*) *The Cotton Industry.*

The cotton industry was the one branch of manufacture which received special consideration in the Act of Union. Owing to the strong representations made by those engaged in the manufacture in Ireland, the general principle of the ten *per cent* duties on the channel trade was abandoned in this one case, and the existing high duties retained until 1808, when they were to be diminished annually until 1816, from which date until 1821 they were to stand at ten *per cent.*

At the date of the passing of the Act of Union the Irish cotton industry employed about 13,500 people;[2] and in the following ten years the manufacture showed every sign of progress. The average annual importation of the raw material of the industry trebled in the decade 1800-10, and in the latter year Wakefield remarked that "the industry is now fully established in Ireland, and holds out strong hopes of its future success and prosperity."[3] In 1816, the cotton manufacture was placed on the same footing with regard to protection as the other industries of Ireland, but

[1] *Parl. Pap.* No. 745 of 1850.

[2] Marmion, *Maritime Ports* p. 74; for the early history of the industry in Ireland see Horner, *The Linen Trade in Europe* p. 132.

[3] Vol. i. p. 705; on the distress of the industry in Prosperous in 1810 see *Official Papers Public Record Office Dublin* 1790-1831 carton 457 no. 1287.

its progress continued till many years later. Its advance in the twenty years following the Union may be gauged by two criteria—the amount of raw material imported into Ireland, and the amount of the finished product exported. With regard to the former, we learn that the imports of cotton wool during the three years 1802-4 were 42,993 cwt, and during the period 1819-21, 91,448 cwt; and that in the same years the imports of cotton twist and yarn were 2,291,388 and 5,230,812 lbs. respectively.[1] With regard to the latter, we may state that the exports of finished cotton goods increased during the period.[2]

All accounts agree that, at the date arranged for the termination of the Union duties, the Irish cotton industry was in an exceedingly flourishing condition, particularly in the north. "The cotton mills and print works of Messrs Grimshaw (at Whitehouse) are very extensive, there being nearly 500 persons employed on the different processes of engraving, painting, cutting, dyeing, drying and the like; they finish on the weekly average 1500 pieces."[3] In 1825 there were 10,700 weavers employed in the trade, and a very large number of spinners.[4] The Irish calico printers were able to compete successfully with their English rivals in foreign and colonial markets.[5]

Why was it that, in a period marked by the industrial decay of Ireland in other directions, the cotton industry not only did not recede, but advanced? It is impossible not to believe that the retention of the high protecting duties had some connection with its success. Even the Revenue Commissioners, who were prejudiced in favour of free trade and were hostile to all forms of protection, did not dare to attribute its progress to the gradual lowering of the Union duties. "While the duty was diminishing

[1] *4th Report of Revenue Commrs.* 1822. Full figures for each year are given in Appendix 8 to the report.
[2] Full figures are given in appendix B of Murray's *Commercial Relations.*
[3] C. Hannah, *An Excursion in Antrim, Down and Derry.* Belfast 1821.
[4] Marmion, *Maritime Ports* p. 74.
[5] *Fourth Report of Revenue Commissioners* 1822.

the manufacture continued to increase in so steady and regular a manner as almost to point to the conclusion that the increase was actually produced by the reduction of the duties. As this reduction was not carried so far as to throw open the British market to the Irish manufacturers, that opinion cannot be justly entertained."[1] The fact that the one industry that progressed in the years following the Union was the one protected by high duties is too remarkable to be dismissed as a mere coincidence.

Another reason why the cotton industry proved an exception to the general Irish industrial decay of the time was that it was the one industry in which improved processes and methods of production had been adopted by the Irish manufacturer. "It may be considered a fortunate circumstance that the cotton manufacture was not established in Ireland, till it had been brought to such a state of perfection in England that the whole process was divided into a certain number of distinct branches. It is the division of labour that gives to the English manufactures that perfection to which they have attained. The same method will of course be adopted by workmen in Ireland."[2] "Very much higher wages were paid than in the linen manufacture, and much more advanced methods were used. Instead of the weaver bringing his yarn and selling it in a manufactured state, the yarn was given to the weaver by the master manufacturer, who paid him so much for his labour, or it was woven on looms erected within buildings belonging to the manufacturer. While linen yarn was still being spun by hand, cotton yarn was being spun by machinery."[3]

The rapid progress of the Irish cotton industry after the Union must not lead us to exaggerate its importance. In the first place, it did not advance nearly so rapidly as the British industry in the same period. Whereas the latter was quickly overcoming all competition in the markets

[1] *Fourth Report.* [2] Wakefield vol. i. p. 708.
[3] Murray, *Commercial Relations* p. 349.

of the world, the Irish industry aimed principally at the supply of the home market. Even in the Irish market, moreover, its supremacy was not unchallenged; and, although the imports into Ireland of calicoes and muslins were insignificant, there continued to be a substantial importation of other cotton goods—quilts, counterpanes &c. The severe results moreover of a glut in the home market—a condition which prevailed about every third year—emphasize the narrow limits of the Irish cotton industry. In 1820, the Revenue Commissioners could not help contrasting the comparative progress of the cotton and linen manufactures to the advantage of the latter, which they described as "the most prosperous one in Ireland, and perhaps the only one which can deserve the description of 'prosperous' in comparison with those of Great Britain."[1]

The advance of the Irish cotton trade came to an end in 1825, when it was severely affected by the prevailing industrial depression. About the year 1828 the linen trade again definitely became the staple industry of Ireland owing to the introduction of improved methods of production. "In 1828 the cotton trade was obliged to give way, and the linen trade was once more revived by the invention of machinery for spinning flax."[2] In the succeeding ten years the Irish cotton industry experienced a period of genuine decline. The principal cause of this was that it encountered for the first time the full competition of the English firms. "After 1826" said Mr. Otway "the cotton trade had greater difficulties and more powerful competition to contend against . . . . The cotton trade suffered more than any other industry during the panics of 1825 and 1837. It has had to compete with the extensive and long established cotton manufacturies of England, her power looms and spinning factories, her direct market for the raw material, and all that capital and skill could accomplish to cheapen production and enlarge a market. Some large cotton mills have been

[1] *Fourth Report of Revenue Commissioners* 1822. [2] Marmion *Maritime Ports* p. 74.

lately established in Ireland, and intelligent manufacturers have embarked in the trade; . . ."[1] The calico-printing industry was most seriously injured by the repeal of the protecting duties, as had been predicted by the witnesses before the Commission of 1822.[2] "Printing cotton is carried on to a considerable extent in Ireland, and the persons employed in this trade represent in the most decided terms their inability to continue it in competition with the English printers."[3] One result of the opening of unrestricted competition between Great Britain and Ireland was that the manufacturers of the latter country found themselves quite unable to keep pace with those of the former, through lack of capital, in the adoption of improved methods of production. "The cotton weaving of England is conducted on a very superior system to that which generally prevails in Ireland. It is carried on with power looms . . . . In Ireland there have been some improvements . . . but still the Irish weaver generally works with the old cumbrous loom, which stands in a separate edifice, as it were, within his cabin; and the delivering out of yarn, and the taking in of work is conducted as in the linen trade."[4]

Certainly a few years later there was no doubt that the cotton industry was on the decline. "This branch of manufacture" reported the Poor Inquiry Commission in 1836" is nearly extinct, and the few surviving weavers are in a state of extreme indigence;"[5] and the Railway Commissioners reported in the following year that "the only town in Ireland in which the cotton trade has been established to any extent is Belfast; and it is represented as declining even there. Several of the mills originally designed for the spinning of cotton are now employed in spinning flax."[6] The export of cotton goods from Ireland fell from 10,567,458

[1] *Otway's Report* pp. 599-600.
[2] *Fourth Report of Revenue Commissioners* 1822.
[3] *Ibid. App.* 33 and 34.
[4] *Considerations on National Policy and on Ireland* Dublin 1831 pp. 105-6.
[5] *App.* C pt. 1. p. 87.
[6] *Second Report* p. 7.

yards in 1825 to 1,039,038 in 1835; while in the same period the imports increased from 3,384,918 yards to 7,884,000 yards.[1] The progressive decline of the industry in the years 1839-1850 is shown by the following figures:—In 1839 there were 24 mills containing 19 steam engines and 22 water wheels, with a total horse power of 1089, and employing 4622 persons. The distribution of mills was as follows.

County	Dublin*	3	mills employing	342	persons
„	Kildare	1	„ „	247	„
„	Wexford	1	„ „	91	„
„	Waterford	1	„ „	1011	„
„	Cork	1	„ „	55	„
Queen's	Co.	1	„ „	50	„
County	Antrim	10	„ „	2000	„
„	Armagh	2	„ „	210	„
„	Down	3	„ „	587	„
„	Mayo	1	„ „	29	„
		Total		4622	

* Parl. Pap. no. 41 of 1839.

In 1847 the number of persons employed in the cotton industry had shrunk to the following:—

County	Antrim	1018
„	Armagh	195
„	Down	799
„	Dublin	387
„	Kildare	103
„	Louth	165
„	Queen's	41
„	Waterford	1223
„	Wexford	95
„	Wicklow	157
	Total	4183

In the same year the total number employed in Scotland was 35,116, and in England 277,028.[2]

In 1850, the volume of the Irish cotton industry had still further diminished, as is shown by the following table—

[1] *Second Report of Railway Commissioners* 1838 App. B no. 10
[2] P. P. No. 294 of 1847.

Counties	No. of factories	No. of spindles	No. of power looms	Employed
Factories for spinning				
Antrim	3	63,224	—	616
Dublin	1	576	—	22
For spinning & weaving				
Armagh	1	4,332	122	143
Dublin	2	9,372	296	343
Kildare	1	8,000	150	180
Louth	1	4,896	143	165
Waterford	1	26,055	626	1362
Wexford	1	3,500	1100	106
Total	11	119,955	2437	2937

In this year 292,862 persons were employed in the English, and 36,325 in the Scotch, cotton industry.[1]

These figures demonstrate three things; that the Irish cotton industry declined during the decade 1840-50; that it became of ever diminishing importance compared with the gigantic industry of Great Britain; and that it tended to become localized in the neighbourhood of Belfast. In the early part of the century, although Belfast was always the most important centre of the cotton trade, the manufacture showed signs of prosperity in the south and west; but in 1850 it had become quite definitely localized in north east Ulster. The causes of this change, which were probably the same as those which produced the same result in the linen industry, will be discussed in a later section. Special causes operating to localize the cotton industry in north-east Ulster were the facilities which Belfast offered for the importation of the raw material, and the proximity to the seat of the Scotch cotton manufacture.[2] Of ten thousand weavers employed in Belfast in 1840, no less than 5100 were employed by Scotch houses, on account of the low rate of wages they would accept.[3]

The only places outside Ulster where the industry presented any signs of prosperity were Limerick, Clonmel, and Port-

[1] *Parl. Pap.* no. 745 of 1850. [2] *Otway's Report*, p. 655.
[3] *Muggeridge's Report* p. 785. This report contains much information about the condition of the industry in Belfast.

law. The Limerick industry was founded in 1836 by a Mr. Buchanan, who was tempted to open there by reason of the great cheapness of labour which he found to prevail. In 1840 the whole industry was conducted on a handloom basis, and it was found impossible to compete with the British machine-made goods, except by means of very low wages and very long hours. The wages paid to the weavers ranged from two to four shillings a week, and the working day consisted of twelve hours in summer and nine hours in winter. The factories at Clonmel and Portlaw were conducted on a large scale, with improved methods of production, and were very successful.[1] All traces of the cotton industry in other parts of Ireland were rapidly disappearing. In 1829 two thousand weavers had found employment in Bandon; in 1840 they had been reduced to 150. Nobody attempted to earn a living from weaving except the aged and infirm who could not emigrate. The young either left the country or joined the army. "Bandon" we read "is one of the best recruiting depôts in the South of Ireland."[2]

The fact seems to be that the old Irish cotton industry was practically completely destroyed by the competition which it had to face after 1825, and that a new industry arose quite independently. The new trade was practically confined to north-east Ulster; and, with the exception of the isolated instances we have mentioned, no attempt was made to revive it in the south.

(c) *The Linen Industry.*

It is impossible to understand the progress of the linen industry in the first half of the nineteenth century unless one bears in mind the great change which took place in the

[1] *Otway's Report.* Marmion *Maritime Ports* p. 558.

[2] *Otway's Report* p. 658. *Report of Repeal Association on Woollen, Silk and Cotton Manufacturers* 1840. An interesting account of the cotton industry in Bandon in 1820 is to be found in Official Papers 1790-1831. Public Record Office Dublin, carton 304 no. 2220.

condition of the industry between the beginning and end of the period. Indeed it is scarcely too much to say that the revolution that took place was not so much the introduction of improvements as the substitution of a new industry in place of the old. At the beginning of the century the manufacture was essentially domestic, and carried on largely in conjunction with agriculture; fifty years later, the domestic manufacture, both in the spinning and weaving branches, had almost entirely disappeared, and the functions of weaver and agriculturalist had become entirely distinct. "Forty years ago" we read in 1840, "almost the entire weaving of the country was done by or on account of weavers. Each man bought, or raised and prepared, his own materials, from which he made his linen web, and sold it in the public market or by private contract, to agents or travellers who went round the country to make purchases. Those weavers who had more than one loom, entrusted them either to other members of their families, or to apprentices or journeymen, under their own personal inspection. The latter were frequently remunerated by a scale now almost exploded, which was termed the 'fourth penny'; that is, each man received as his wages for weaving a piece of cloth, one fourth part of the gross sum such cloth sold for. At this period, many weavers who were small farmers also, had three to six or eight looms in their houses. The spinning and various preparatory processes which the flax underwent were chiefly performed by the female branches of the family. The owner, his apprentices and journeymen worked either at the loom or in the field, as interest prompted or the seasons dictated;. . . ."[1]

The linen when manufactured was sold in the brown linen markets which were under the regulation of the Linen Board. There is a vivid description of the proceedings at one of these markets in Young's *Tour in Ireland,* which we have

[1] *Handloom Weavers Commission. Muggeridge's Report* p. 704.

quoted elsewhere.[1] The markets continued to be conducted in the manner described by Young until their abolition in 1840, although the quantities of linen brought in to be sold decreased greatly in later years.[2]

Another feature of the linen industry which we must not fail to notice was that in the earlier period it was not localized in Ulster to nearly the same extent as it was in later times. The statistical surveys of the Irish counties, made at the beginning of the century by the Dublin Society, show that, while the manufacture was undoubtedly most flourishing in Ulster, it did not fail to show signs of healthy vigour in the other provinces. The manufacture of coarse linens formed the principal industry of county Galway; large quantities of cloth were exhibited in the linen hall of Sligo; the farmers of King's County supplemented what they earned from agriculture with the profits of the loom; four bleach greens existed in county Leitrim; large quantities of the coarse fabrics were manufactured in Meath; and the presence of the manufacture to a greater or less degree is mentioned in many other southern counties.[3] "The linen manufacture" Wakefield wrote "flourishes most in Ulster, but it is established also in Galway, Mayo and Sligo, and towards the south in the whole neighbourhood of Drogheda; it is found also in the King's County, Kerry, and along the coast of Cork; in a word it may be said in some measure to extend to every part of Ireland except Wicklow and Wexford, where it is almost unknown."[4]

The report prepared in 1817 by Peter Besnard, Inspector General under the Linen Board of Munster Leinster and Connaught, discloses a similar state of affairs. The linen goods made in county Louth exceeded in value those made in any other counties except Armagh, Tyrone, and Antrim;

[1] *Economic History of Ireland in the Eighteenth Century* p. 205.
[2] *Muggeridge's Report* p. 709.
[3] Horner, *Linen Trade of Europe* pp. 111-3.
[4] Vol. i. p. 758.

in Longford the trade was very considerable; and many of the other counties of Leinster did a fairly considerable amount of spinning, though weaving was less frequently pursued. The manufacture of coarse linen employed thousands of persons in south county Cork; and considerable quantities of coarse linens were made in Limerick and Clare. In Mayo the operations both of spinning and weaving were conducted on an extended and increasing scale, and in the other counties of Connaught, though the weaving was inconsiderable, large quantities of yarn were spun for export.[1]

The following passage from Wakefield shows how widespread the manufacture was throughout Ireland:— "Narrow linens . . . are made in Donegal, Derry, Tyrone and Antrim. In the neighbourhood of Belfast, Lisburn and Lurgan, the fine yard-wide or cambrics, lawns and diapers are made; and in Armagh coarser yard-wide cloths. Cavan produces a thin linen . . . Fermanagh and Sligo manufacture 7/8; and in these counties are found most of the bleach greens. A strong kind of dowlas, some sheetings made in the counties of Louth, Meath, and Dublin, are sold in the market of Drogheda. A coarse cloth, very much like Scots Osnaburgs, is manufactured in Kerry and Cork . . ."[2] In 1818 the industry was thought to be growing in the south. "Manufacture of linens and the several branches of trade connected with it is making its way from the north to the south parts of the island . . . The cultivation of flax is extending towards the south of Ireland, a large quantity of linen is now manufactured in Kerry."[3]

Of course it is not suggested that the linen trade of the south of Ireland approached that of Ulster at any time in magnitude or importance; all that we wish to point out is that there was not, in the first twenty years of the nineteenth

[1] Horner, *op. cit.* pp. 114-27.
[2] Vol i. p. 690.
[3] Curwen, *Observations*, vol. i. pp. 344, 385.

century, the complete absence of the manufacture from the southern provinces which was observed in 1840. The following figures, which show the relative pre-eminence of the north, illustrate at the same time the absolute magnitude of the industry in the south:—

I. FIGURES FOR 1817*

Value of linen goods produced in	Ulster	£ 2,500,000
" " " " " "	Munster, Leinster & Connaught	" 651,752
		£ 3,151,752

* Horner, *op. cit.* p. 169.

II. FIGURES FOR 1821*

Value of goods sold in brown linen markets in	Ulster ..	£ 2,073,122
" " " " " " " " "	Leinster ..	" 285,358
" " " " " " " " "	Munster ..	" 68,870
" " " " " " " " "	Connaught	" 117,664
		£ 2,545,014

* Horner, *op. cit.* p. 199.

Parallel to the contrast between the relative positions of Ulster and the other three provinces at the two periods is that between the different counties of Ulster itself. As we shall see, in 1840, the industry was becoming more and more centralized in Armagh, Down and Antrim; but the following figures for 1821 show that, twenty years earlier, that centralization, though undoubtedly noticeable, was not so complete:—

Value of goods sold in brown linen markets in	Cavan*	£ 116,626
" " " " " " " " "	Monaghan	" 142,952
" " " " " " " " "	Fermanagh	" 23,386
" " " " " " " " "	Tyrone	" 33,076
" " " " " " " " "	Londonderry	" 231,219
" " " " " " " " "	Antrim	" 345,504
" " " " " " " " "	Down	" 214,199
" " " " " " " " "	Armagh	" 570,348

* Horner, *op. cit.* p. 198.

The exports of Irish linen did not increase after the Union — "the first period in the history of the Irish linen industry, when the exports did not increase."[1] This was probably mainly attributable to two causes, the growth of the cotton industry, and British competition. As we have seen above, the superior wages which it was possible to earn in the cotton trade had the effect of attracting many weavers away from the linen; and, at the same time that the industry was suffering from this drain, it also experienced in some branches severe competition from Great Britain. The prohibition of the export of yarn from Great Britain in 1784 had the effect of turning the attention of British manufacturers to the weaving of coarse linen; and, from that time onwards, the Irish manufacturers were driven to depend more and more upon their fine linen products. The decrease of the quantity of the exports of Irish linen goods after the Union was however probably more than compensated for by the increase in their quality. It must also be remembered that the population of Ireland was growing very rapidly, and that the home demand must have considerably increased, so that we are not justified in concluding a diminution of production from the diminution of export.[2]

If the absolute extent of the Irish linen industry was still maintained, it was becoming year by year of less relative importance compared with the manufacture of Great Britain. This is shown by the following figures:—

Export in 1822 of linen goods from Ireland to foreign countries*	£	200,314
Export in 1822 of linen goods from Gt. Britain to foreign countries, Irish goods	,,	661,630
British goods	,,	1,933,152
Bounties on export of Irish goods from Ireland	£	17,112
,, ,, ,, ,, ,, ,, ,, Great Britain	,,	74,393
,, ,, ,, ,, British goods from Great Britain ..	,,	208,355

* *Practical Views and Suggestions* by Hibernicus Dublin 1823.

[1] Murray, *Commercial Relations* p. 348. [2] *Otway's Report* pp. 620-1.

Thus, the industrial superiority of Great Britain over Ireland was manifest even in the case of the leading Irish industry. The day of the Irish supremacy in the linen trade had passed away. Nor was the Irish trade conducted on methods so improved as those generally prevailing in England. "The different branches of the trade in Great Britain" reported a parliamentary committee in 1825 "are divided among different persons, each of these branches becoming a separate business in itself; and this division of labour necessarily leads to a better economy of time and the production of more even and better fabrics, all which advantages might be gradually introduced into Ireland."[1]

The decade 1820-30, which was notable in the case of the other Irish industries for the repeal of the Union duties, also marked a turning point in the history of the linen industry on account of the changes which took place with regard to its public regulation. These changes were part of the general policy of the time, which aimed at the attainment of complete absence of state interference as far as it was possible.[2] The artificial stimulus which the manufacture received from protective duties was quickly abolished. The transit duties on foreign linen, which had been retained in 1823 only by the spirited action of the Belfast Chamber of Commerce, were repealed about 1830.[3] The bounty on the export of linen to foreign countries, the continuance of which had been strongly recommended by the select committee of 1822, was nevertheless brought to an end in 1832.[4]

The most important change however which this decade witnessed in the public regulation of the manufacture was

[1] *Select Committee on Linen Trade* 1825.

[2] As early as 1802 Lord Hardwicke had urged the repeal of all statutory protection of the linen industry as "the manufacture was no longer in its infancy". *Official Papers Public Record Office Dublin* 1790-1831 carton 372 no. 813; and see a letter from Lord Grenville in the same sense in *Fortescue MSS* vol. vii p. 469.

[3] *Letter to the Marquis of Downshire on the Proposed Repeal.* Belfast 1817, *Report of the Belfast Chamber of Commerce* 1823. Warden *The Linen Trade* p. 670.

[4] *Select Committee on Linen Trade of Ireland* 1822. Marmion, *Maritime Ports* p. 76.

the dissolution of the Linen Board. The Board had been the subject of a certain amount of hostile criticism for many years; but the surprising thing is that, composed as it was of country gentlemen, with no technical knowledge of the trade, who could attend the meetings of the Board at but infrequent intervals, it attained a certain efficiency and success. Wakefield complained that the administration by the Board of the money at its disposal was wastefully conducted, and that the Board was made the victim of many fraudulent applicants for aid.[1] The Board was also criticized on the ground that it entertained an unreasonable preference for spinning wheels at a time when spinning could be much more economically carried out by machine mills.[2] It is probable, however, that, in devoting its attention to hand wheels rather than machine mills, the Board was doing what was more practically useful, as the former were found to be more economical than the latter in Ireland-on account of the cheapness of labour.[3] On the whole the Board seemed able to meet any criticism directed against it, and it came triumphantly through the inquiries conducted by the select committees of 1822 and 1825. The former committee reported that, "although the present constitution of the Linen Board may be open to some objections, yet nevertheless it appears to your committee to secure to the linen trade so many advantages that they do not feel justified in recommending any alteration. Your committee are however of opinion that frequent intercourse should be held with those concerned in the trade, on these various subjects of application, which ought to receive more prompt attention and decision than has been under present circumstances afforded." The committee commended the Board for its endeavours to introduce improved processes and machinery, on which it could afford to make experiments on a more extended scale than would be pos-

[1] Vol. i. pp. 695-7.
[2] Horner, *op. cit.* pp. 118-9.
[3] Wakefield vol. i. p. 684.

sible for private traders.[1] The Select Committee on Employment of the Poor in Ireland, which reported in the following year, also laid stress on the necessity of fostering the linen industry by the continuance of public encouragement: "This may in the south and west require some artificial encouragement, or rather it may require a removal of those difficulties, which poverty and ignorance produce, and which at present check its introduction and extension. The want of implements is peculiarly felt; the want of scutching mills, and a defective system of preparing the flax, yarn, and linen for the market. Aid might be given in these respects to the people, not substituting public for private effort, but assisting and encouraging the latter."[2] The Select Committee on the Linen Trade of 1825, while recommending some minor changes in the existing law, again emphasized the necessity for a public superintendence and support of the manufacture. The committee resolved "that Ireland has claims undoubtedly strong upon the Parliament of the United Kingdom for every aid and encouragement necessary to the maintenance and support of the linen manufacture, at least to the extent of the annual parliamentary grant"; and further, "that the laws which relate to this important branch of the public industry of Ireland require revision and amendment, and many of them that were wise and necessary at the time of their enactment would, if now enforced, produce much inconvenience, if not a serious injury in many particulars, to the interests of the manufacture, and such laws ought therefore to be repealed." The committee then proceeded to recommend, among other things, laws to enforce the use of clean flax, for the encouragement of scutch mills for dressing flax and of mill machinery for dressing yarn, that the existing laws relating to the sale of brown linens should be continued, that the distribution of mill utensils by the Linen Board

[1] *Select Committee on the Linen Trade of Ireland* 1822.
[2] *Report of Select Committee on Employment of Poor in Ireland* 1823.

should be stopped; and concluded by expressing the opinion that some superintending authority was needed in Ireland for the regulation of the manufacture.[1] An act was rapidly passed embodying these recommendations; the Linen Board was continued; and many regulations were made regarding the sealing and stamping of yarn and linen.[2]

The government soon determined however that the whole existing machinery for the encouragement of the linen industry must be abolished. We find accordingly that the bounty granted to the Linen Board was reduced to £10,000 in 1827, and completely discontinued in 1828. The views of the trustees and of the trade generally were taken as to whether the dissolution of the Board was desirable; and it was ultimately resolved by the Board; "(1) that legislative provisions continue to be essentially required for the protection and regulation of some branches of the linen trade of Ireland, particularly with reference to the sealing and measuring of linen cloth brought to market, and for detecting and punishing frauds in the manufacture and making up of linen cloth and yarn, and in the preparation and manner of exposing flax for sale; (2) that such parts of the act of 1825 as relate to the foregoing resolution ought to be retained or re-enacted as law, together with such additions as may be deemed necessary for the protection of the trade."[3]

An act was accordingly passed by which the Linen Board was dissolved; the brown sealmasters were retained, and provision was made for the appointment by the Lord Lieutenant of county committees of twelve for their regulation and direction. The linen and yarn halls were vested in the Lord Lieutenant with power to lease them to factors in the linen, yarn, and cotton trades.[4]

These provisions for the regulation of the trade were declared to continue only for three years. They were however continued by subsequent statutes until 1842,

[1] *Select Committee on Linen Trade of Ireland* 1825.
[2] 6 Geo. IV c. 122.
[3] Smith. *Irish Linen Trade Handbook* pp. 72-4.
[4] 9 Geo. IV. c. 62.

when they were allowed to lapse, principally on account of the strong report presented to the Handloom Weavers Commission by Mr. Muggeridge, who stated that the seal-master system had been the subject of constant abuse.[1]

The second great revolution which the Irish linen industry underwent in the decade 1820-30 was the change of the processes employed. The introduction of improved methods of production in the linen industry was hastened by the growing public taste for cotton fabrics, which threatened ultimately to annihilate altogether the demand for linen goods. "When in process of time the unprecedented growth and rivalry of the cotton manufacture forced down still lower the prices of linen, it became obvious that cheaper production was essential, not alone to the permanency, but to the prolonged existence of the trade."[2] One method of cheapening production resorted to was the introduction of a new material called unions, composed of cotton warp and linen weft.[3] The two great branches of the linen manufacture were spinning and weaving; changes in the methods of conducting both were adopted after 1825; but the changes in the former were far more radical and were introduced earlier than those in the latter. The invention of the wet spinning process in 1825 completely revolutionized the whole spinning industry, and sounded the death knell of the spinning wheel. Henceforward hand-spun yarn was at a hopeless disadvantage, and no locality could hope to become a flourishing centre for weaving unless it had access to plentiful supplies of mill-spun yarn. In the weaving branch of the industry the change which the period witnessed was not so much one affecting the actual process as the manner in which it was conducted. Handloom weaving still continued the order of the day, but the old independent weaver, who himself performed all the operations of the manufac-

[1] 2 and 3 Wm. IV. c. 77; 5 and 6 Wm. IV c. 27; 1 and 2 Vict. c. 52, *Muggeridge's Report* pp. 686-7.

[2] *Muggeridge's Report* p. 704.

[3] Riordan *Modern Irish Trade and Industry* p. 117.

ture, was rapidly displaced by the new class of employee-weavers who worked on materials, and in many cases on looms, provided by a capitalist manufacturer. At a later stage, these employee weavers came to work in factories belonging to their employer instead of in their own homes. These were the principal changes which the industrial revolution wrought in the linen manufacture; and, as in the case of every other manufacture, where they were adopted the industry not alone survived but increased, whereas, where they were not adopted, it waned and ultimately disappeared. The former was the case in north-east Ulster, and the latter in the rest of Ireland.

The wet spinning process was introduced into Belfast by the great firm of Mulholland. "The first spinning factory was established in 1829. This industry, having the raw material on the spot, rapidly gained ground, and finally has become more flourishing than in the English and Scotch branches of the trade, forced to purchase their flax abroad."[1] In 1840 Belfast was the "great linen yarn market for Ireland. The amount of the value of the hand spun yarn sold *per annum* in Belfast is stated to be £100,000 . . . There are fifteen mills in the town and four in the neighbourhood established for spinning yarn . . . One-fourth of the flax used is imported."[2] The unemployment caused by the substitution of mill-spun for hand-spun yarn was to a large extent made good by the increased employment of women in weaving.[3]

The great growth of the spinning industry in Ulster before 1850 is shown by the following figures:—

[1] James Macadam, *An Economic Review of the Linen Industry*, Belfast 1847.
[2] *Otway's Report* pp. 632-3.
[3] *Ibid.* p. 595.

FIGURES SHOWING NUMBER OF FACTORIES, NUMBER OF SPINDLES AND NUMBER OF PERSONS EMPLOYED IN FACTORIES ENGAGED ON THE MANUFACTURE OF LINEN IN 1850.*

County	No. of Factories	No. of spindles	No. of persons employed
Factories for spinning			
Antrim	36	234,576	10,974
Armagh	4	15,786	1,064
Donegal	1	2,604	185
Down	11	61,462	4,335
Derry	2	5,144	251
Monaghan	2	4,124	349
Tyrone	5	21,320	1,341
Factories for weaving			
Antrim	1	power looms 34	138
Factories for spinning and weaving			
Antrim	1	11,394 power looms 24	545

* *Parl. Pap.* no. 745 of 1850.

The corresponding changes in the weaving branches of the manufacture were also adopted in Ulster. As early as 1825 it had been noticed that "the assimilation of Irish methods of weaving to the English has already begun in the north."[1] In the next fifteen years this assimilation continued without interruption. "Already the advantages of concentrated capital, and ingenuity and enterprise, over the isolated efforts of the lonely and industrious rural weaver are rapidly developing themselves in Ireland, and day by day are transplanting the loom from the cabin of the cottier to the factory or weaving shop of the manufacturer. Throughout the counties of Down, Antrim, Derry and Armagh many thousand weavers, formerly weaving for the market, are now in the regular employ of manufacturers, and though they still retain their looms, have no property in the materials in them. Almost all of them

[1] *Select Committee on Linen Trade of Ireland* 1825.

who yet continue weaving on their own account, combine the character of small farmers, and retain the loom as an auxiliary to their agricultural operations."[1]

Banbridge was the principal centre in which the improved method of conducting weaving was introduced. It was in this district that the manufacturers first realized that, "unless the linen trade should be placed on a new foundation, and conducted on the improved principles that were being applied in the other parts of the United Kingdom, Ireland would lose its trade altogether." The linen manufacture in the neighbourhood was consequently "placed on a new foundation, and men of extensive capital and skill became engaged on it."[2] The old system of the farmer-weaver conducting all the processes in his own home was rapidly displaced by the new system in which the master manufacturers provided the weavers with mill-spun yarn. Of course, remnants of the old system still survived even in the most advanced parts of Ulster, notably in the neighbourhoods of Ballymena, Lurgan, and Tandragee. Those engaged on it however found themselves placed at a hopeless disadvantage, as the day for making use of hand-spun yarn had passed away, and they could not obtain mill-spun yarn except in large quantities, which of course they had not the capital to buy. Generally speaking the farmer-weaver was being rapidly replaced in Ulster by the employee-weaver.[3]

In Belfast the revolution had progressed a step further, as the employee-weavers were being gradually congregated in factories, instead of being allowed to work in their own houses. "The congregating together of weavers in weaving shops or factories is of comparative recent introduction into Ireland, and at present seems to have taken firmer root in Belfast than in any other part of the country which I visited. This system, which is exceedingly distasteful to the operatives, is nevertheless said to possess many

[1] *Muggeridge's Report* p. 711. [2] *Otway's Report* p. 637. [3] *Otway's Report* pp. 640-6.

peculiar advantages. It is represented (1) as ensuring regularity of employment and production, (2) as attaining comparative uniformity of quality, (3) as preventing embezzlement or abstraction of materials, and (4) as stimulating, and to some extent enforcing, regular and continuous labour."[1] It was the general experience throughout county Down that weavers working on their own account earned less than those working in factories.[2]

It appears, therefore, that the north-east of Ulster succeeded in adapting itself to the changed conditions of the industry. Unfortunately, the other parts of Ireland failed to do so, and consequently lost the small share of the trade they had previously enjoyed. A decline in the southern linen manufacture had been observed in the years 1820-1830.[3] By 1840 the predominance of the neighbourhood of Belfast had become unquestionable. The one time flourishing linen markets of Dungannon and Strabane had practically come to an end owing to the overwhelming competition of mill-spun yarn. In county Donegal the independent weavers were quite extinct, and the sole survivors of the trade were those weavers who wove for the farmers, and these were plunged into a condition of extreme poverty. Sligo presented only a few traces of the former prosperity; the linen hall had been leased for other purposes; and the only evidence of the trade to be observed on market days were a few hawkers with hand-spun yarn.[4] In Dublin the manufacture was restricted within very narrow limits, and was practically confined to one or two manufacturers. One of these firms—Messers Crosthwaite—employed 138 looms, and a sail cloth manufactory at Glasnevin, 13 looms. The wages of the linen weavers were lower than those of any other class of workers.[5]

In no town had the decay of the industry produced so much distress as in Drogheda, where the condition of the

[1] *Muggeridge's Report* p. 717. [2] *Otway's Report* p. 636.
[3] *Commentaries on National Policy and on Ireland*, Dublin 1831.
[4] *Otway's Report* pp. 648 sq. [5] *Otway's Report* pp. 623-6.

weavers was shocking. The total number continually or casually employed in 1840 amounted to 1890; wages were very low, and supplementary employment almost impossible to obtain. By means of begging and of planting a few potatoes on patches of ground given to them by neighbouring farmers for the sake of the manure, they managed to "supply themselves with the lowest species of vegetable food, and provide a place of shelter, if shelter it can be called..... The cabins that the weavers live and work in are fearful specimens of what habit will enable a human being to endure; I am persuaded that no part of Europe, or I might add of the world, presents such a specimen of dwellings for human beings as part of Drogheda."[1] The cause of the decay of the manufacture in Drogheda was in the first place the competition of England and Scotland in the coarse linen trade. The leading master manufacturers migrated to Ulster to carry on the fine linen trade, but the weavers did not accompany them, and were plunged into unemployment. The introduction of mill-spun yarn helped to complete their ruin, as they had to import their yarn. It was not unusual for flax to be exported from Drogheda to England, where it was spun into yarn, and returned to Drogheda. This gave the English manufacturer an advantage amounting to 6 or 8 *per cent* in the cost of his raw material. In order to ward off the ruin which they saw approaching, the weavers formed combinations, and the resulting strikes and disturbances only hastened the inevitable disaster.[2]

In so far as the manufacture survived at all in the south, it was only in the rudest form. The peasantry still continued to make a certain amount of coarse linen cloth for their own use. "The poor farmer finds it more convenient to grow a small bit of flax, and employ the otherwise unavailable labour of the female and younger portions of his family

[1] *Otway's Report* p. 627.
[2] *Poor Inquiry Commission* app. C. pt. 1 pp. 45 sq; *Otway's Report* p. 630.

in the several processes required for converting it into yarn or linen, than to go into the town and purchase shop goods."[1] In some districts small quantities were manufactured for sale. "Linen weaving is chiefly confined to the making up webs for the use of the peasantry, except in a few districts where the almost total lack of employment for the great mass of the people has rendered hand loom labour so cheap as to afford a profit to the few jobbers who still continue to frequent the linen markets."[2] But even this remnant of the industry was rapidly disappearing; the quality of the products was bad; many of the looms were out of repair; and great difficulty was experienced in procuring supplies of suitable yarn.[3]

The following table, in conjunction with those we have given for the years 1817 and 1821, shows that north-east Ulster tended more and more to become the centre of the Irish linen manufacture:—

NUMBER OF PERSONS EMPLOYED IN FACTORIES ENGAGED IN THE LINEN MANUFACTURE IN 1839, 1847 AND 1850*

County	No. of persons employed		
	1839	1847	1850
Antrim	5,986	9,246	11,630
Armagh	518	577	1,064
Donegal	—	174	185
Down	752	3,449	4,336
Dublin	297	297	422
Kildare	205	406	480
Londonderry	214	384	251
Louth	589	920	869
Meath	168	173	167
Monaghan	129	338	349
Tyrone	159	1,124	1,341

* *Parl. Pap.* nos. 41 of 1839, 294 of 1847 , and 745 of 1850.

We shall not discuss here the causes which operated to produce this marked centralization of the linen industry in Ulster, as we shall discuss the question of Ulster's rise to

[1] *Otway's Report* p. 610. [2] *Ibid.* p. 611. [3] *Ibid.*

industrial pre-eminence in the next section. The causes which affected the linen industry were in the main identical with those which affected every other industry, for instance, the superior position which that province enjoyed in regard to the accumulation of capital, owing to the prevalence of the Ulster custom, and the comparatively light incidence of the penal laws.

It must also be borne in mind that the Irish linen industry passed through the period of transition with less strain than the other Irish industries, because it was the one last affected by the changes of the industrial revolution. "There is one trade" we read in 1831 "that is an exception to general rules regarding manufacture. The linen trade is a rural manufacture, carried on in the cabin of the peasant by his wife and daughter."[1] The Railway Commissioners noted the slowness of the introduction of improved methods in the weaving branch of the industry:—"The number of weavers who manufacture on their own account is diminishing; but, as the power loom has not yet been so extensively applied to the manufacture of the linen as machinery is to the spinning of the yarn, the handloom weaver is enabled to stand his ground."[2] "I regard" wrote Mr. Muggeridge, three years later "the linen manufacture of Ireland as now being in a transition state. It is just ceasing to be a domestic manufacture and is becoming a national one. The change is natural and analogous to that which has already passed over the cotton, the silk, the woollen, and the hosiery."[3] "The manufacture of flax" according to Mr. Jonathan Pim "has more slowly adapted itself to the factory system than either of cotton or wool. Linen is still woven by hand, and flax continued to be spun by hand until recently; the machinery for spinning flax by power not having been invented until long after that for spinning cotton had been brought to nearly its present state of perfection. When

[1] *Poor Laws the Panacea for Ireland,* London 1831.
[2] *Second Report of Railway Commrs.* 1837 p. 7.
[3] *Muggeridge's Report* p. 725.

the contest between the spinning wheel and the flax mill commenced, the linen trade of Ulster might have experienced the same fate as the cotton and woollen trades of the south, but that it was still necessary to weave by hand."[1] "With free trade" said Nassau Senior "handloom weaving has prospered. Those whom you found, when you made your handloom weavers inquiry fourteen years ago, in misery, are now all employed and at good wages."[2]

We noticed above that in 1820 the English and Scotch linen manufactures were outdistancing the Irish, and we must call attention to the continued relative insignificance of the Irish industry in later years. This is shown by the following figures:—

NUMBERS EMPLOYED IN LINEN FACTORIES IN 1847 AND 1850.*

	Year 1847	Year 1850
Ireland	17,088	21,121
England	19,840	19,001
Scotland	21,330	28,312

* *Parl. Pap.* nos. 294 of 1847 and 745 of 1850.

"The extent of this manufacture" said Sir R. Kane "stands in such relief from the usual absence of all manufacturing industry in Ireland that we frequently attach to it a degree of importance, and an idea of absolute magnitude, that it does not really possess. Thus we often hear the linen manufacture spoken of as being the staple industry of this country. In reality however Ireland is almost as much behind in this as in every other branch of industry. The town of Dundee alone is considered to manufacture as much linen as the whole of Ireland."[3]

Before passing from the linen industry, we must say a word about the Irish supply of the raw material. The Irish Parliament acting through the Linen Board had made it the practice to encourage the growth of Irish flax by premiums and bounties on the importation of flax seed,

[1] *Condition & Prospects of Ireland* 1848 p. 153. [2] *Ireland Journals* vol. i. p. 53.
[3] *Industrial Resources* p. 320.

and this encouragement was continued after the Union. Wakefield strongly disapproved of this system, and condemned it in forcible language.[1] The encouragement however had the desired effect, as the amount of flax grown in Ireland increased during the twenty years following the Union. The amount of rough flax exported increased from 4 cwt. in 1801 by a steady progression to 65,293 cwt. in 1821.[2]

The cultivation of flax did not progress with the same rapidity in the next twenty years. No doubt the abolition of the Linen Board removed a certain degree of encouragement. Moreover the preference still given to Irish cereals in the English market probably induced the farmer who was inclined to practise tillage to cultivate those crops which enjoyed a favoured market, rather than one which was exposed to the full pressure of foreign competition. There seems to be no doubt that Irish flax growing was subject to many of the same defects as the other branches of Irish agriculture, and the product was consequently not of the standard which it should have been. The Select Committee on the Irish Linen Trade reported in 1822: "The natural excellent quality of Irish flax as contrasted with foreign or British, has been admitted; yet at market it is found to bear a deteriorated price when compared with either of these."[3] "The flax of Ireland" we read in the following year "in consequence of the frauds practised on damping it, and the dirty condition in which it is brought to market, is not so valuable by 25 or 30 per cent as the Scotch and English flax. It is likewise ill assorted, and its sale in England and Scotland, as well as that of the spun yarn, is in consequence almost entirely precluded."[4] Another committee on the linen manufacture shortly afterwards reported that, "English manufacturers of mill-spun linen

[1] Vol i pp. 701-3. [2] Horner *Linen Trade of Europe* p. 206. Parker. *A Plan for the General Improvement of the State of the Poor in Ireland.* Cork 1816. A table showing the imports of flax seed and the exports of hackled and rough flax between 1801 and 1821 is given in Horner *op cit.* p. 206. [3] *Select Committee on Irish Linen Trade* 1822.
[4] Henderson, *Observations on the Great Commercial Benefits which will result from the Warehousing Bill.* London 1823.

yarn supply themselves to a comparatively small extent with Irish flax, in consequence of the dirty imperfect state in which it is offered for sale, to the injury of the growers and vendors of the article to the amount of from 25 to 30 per cent in its value."[1] Mr. Besnard found in 1823 that the method of cultivation practised in Ulster was very defective.[2]

It was with a view to the correction of these evils, and the extension of the growth of flax in the south and west of Ireland, that the Royal Flax Improvement Society was founded in 1841. This society procured experienced instructors from Belgium, who endeavoured to improve the existing imperfect methods of the Irish farmers. The repeal of the corn laws, which, as we have seen, lessened the inducement to grow wheat and other cereals, turned the attention of the farmers to the cultivation of flax. The Flax Improvement Society sought to popularize the new American method of steeping the plant, and erected model apparatus at Newport and Ballina, Co. Mayo, Drimoleague and Kildinan, County Cork, Ballybay and Grasslough, Co. Monaghan, Craigie, Co. Down, Limerick, Toome, Co. Antrim, Omagh, and Abbeyleix. Scutching mills were also erected in several counties.[3] The society received annual government grants of £1000 per annum after 1847. The result of this encouragement was not so great as might be expected. While the amount of flax grown in Ulster tended to increase slightly, and the method of its cultivation to improve, the good results in the other provinces were negligible. This is shown by the following table:—

ACRES UNDER FLAX*

	1847	1848	1849
Ulster	53,701	49,549	57,651
Munster	1,156	1,249	937
Leinster	1,644	1,239	741
Connaught	1,811	1,826	985

* *Thom's Directory* 1851 p. 229.

[1] *Select Committee on Linen Manufacture* 1825.

[2] *Report of a Tour though the Province of Ulster* Dublin 1823 and see *Commentaries on National Policy and on Ireland* Dublin 1831 p. 102.

[3] Marmion *Maritime Ports.* pp. 78-9 ; *Thom's Directory* 1851 p. 232.

(*d*) *The Silk Industry.*

The duties on the importation of silk goods into Ireland from Great Britain before the Union were as follows:-

	£.	s.	d.	
Silk ribbands*		11	8 3/5	the lb.
" stockings		4	8 4/5	" pair
" manufactured		8	10 3/20	" lb.
" and cotton goods	12	14	1	*per cent.*
" and worsted goods	12	14	1	*per cent.*

* *Fourth Report of Revenue Commissioners* 1822.

By the Act of Union these duties were all reduced to a uniform *ad valorem* duty of ten *per cent.* which was to be revised at the expiration of twenty years.

Obviously this decrease in the duties very seriously diminished the protection which Irish silk goods enjoyed in the home market. The reduced duty however would seem to have sufficed in some measure to exclude the productions of English competitors, for, although the industry declined somewhat in the twenty years following the Union, it did not decline very seriously, and its lack of success may be accounted for by causes other than the reduced protection. The finer branches of the industry suffered severely on account of the increase of absenteeism which the Union brought about; and many of the manufacturers in these branches consequently emigrated to England.[1] In 1809 the Berlin decrees raised the price of raw silk to a point that proved prohibitive to the Irish merchants; and at the same time that the Irish manufacturers were contending against these disadvantages, the English silk manufacture was advancing considerably and competing seriously for the first time in the Irish market.[2] The general distress and failure of markets which followed upon the peace produced serious reactions in the industry.[3]

All during this period we find recurring complaints of

[1] *Select Committee on Petitions of Ribbon Weavers* 1818 p. 87.
[2] *Otway's Report* p. 606.
[3] Webb, *Industrial Dublin since* 1698 p. 156.

the unsatisfactory condition of the Irish silk trade. "I believe" said Wakefield "that this branch is now very much on the decline."[1] A memorial presented to the Dublin Society in 1815 stated that, "although the consumption of silk fabrics in Ireland has increased for many years past, yet the character of the Irish silk manufactures has progressively declined. For, as the appearance of new improved and beautiful works evinced the progress of the manufactures abroad, the comparison of disgracefully imperfect imitations, and the want of interesting variety, proved the derogation of home-made works, and induced a decided preference of British and foreign productions." The memorialists then proceed to state the cause of this decay. "Nothing has more materially injured the silk manufacture than the irregular mode of rearing apprentices in the ribband branches, which originated in the uncertainty of employment for them, occasioned by a regulation made in 1805, that placed so high a value on works made in single looms, in comparison with the same made in engines, as effectually to discourage the one (giving extensive employment to numbers) and encourage the other (giving employment to a few, who are aided by machinery)." The memorial sets out many other abuses which had arisen in the trade on account of, it was suggested, the inefficient supervision exercised by the Dublin Society; and concludes by recommending the appointment of "a permanent committee of direction of the Silk Manufacture."[2] Not alone the weaving but the throwing of silk declined during this period, as is shown by the changed proportions between the raw and the thrown silk imported.[3]

The Revenue Commissioners gave the following account of the industry in 1822:—"The Irish manufactures of silk are stated to have been gradually declining for several years, and the accounts with which we have been furnished

[1] Vol. i. p. 722.
[2] *Memorial of Silk Manufacturers of the City of Dublin to the Dublin Society* 1815.
[3] Webb, *Industrial Dublin since* 1698 p. 155.

from the Custom House confirm this statement. In the first six years which immediately followed the Union the total quantity of silk, both raw and thrown, imported in Ireland amounted to 445,713 lbs; in six years ending 5th Jan. 1822 the amount was 387,290 lbs. Dublin is the chief seat of the manufacture. One establishment lately erected at Tullamore is the only one not included within its limits. There are said to exist 1500 looms, the whole of which are not believed to be at constant work.... From 3000 to 4000 persons are employed in the silk manufacture in Ireland.... It appears, from a reference to the accounts of the quantities of silk goods imported, that the general consumption increases rather than diminishes in Ireland; it cannot therefore be to a decreased demand that the decline of the manufacture should be attributed." The Commissioners then expressed the opinion that the manufacture could not be said to be suffering from the defects of infancy, as it had been established many years; nor had it lacked the benefits of protection, as it had been protected in varying degrees ever since its establishment.[1]

The Commissioners next proceeded to discuss how far the industry required the continuance of the Union duties, and referred to a memorial which had been presented to the government in 1819 by the Irish silk manufacturers, in which it was stated that they could not hope to compete with England if the duties were removed. This memorial explained that the disadvantageous position of the Irish manufacturer arose principally from two causes, the expense of importing the raw material through English ports, and the absence of a poor law, which, it alleged, supplemented the low wages of the weavers in England. The Commissioners refused to attach importance to the former reason, at any rate as regards the Irish market for manufactured silk, on the ground that the expense of importing the raw mate-

[1] *Fourth Report.* Statistics of the importation of raw and thrown silk into Ireland from 1800 to 1820 are to be found in Appendix 8 to this report.

rial was no greater than that of importing the finished product; but they were inclined to admit the second reason. They went on however to state that in their opinion these disadvantages were not such as to entitle the Irish manufacturer to any protection. "These are arguments for perpetual and not for temporary restraint. We can see no time in which these circumstances are less likely to exist than at present; and if it is an object on other grounds to complete the union between the two countries, we can look forward to no period at which these obstacles will not equally remain to be overcome." The report next proceeds to state what, in the opinion of the Commissioners, was the real cause of the decline of the manufacture in Dublin, namely the existence of the so-called Spitalfields Acts, The Dublin Society apparently always fixed the wages of the Dublin weavers at precisely the figure prevailing in London, without any regard to the needs of local circumstances; and no reduction had taken place since 1814 in spite of the fall in the cost of living. The existence of the Spitalfields Acts had driven the English industry away from London to Manchester and Macclesfield, and the report states that "unless these acts are repealed, or establishments are founded in some places not subject to their influence, the silk manufacture in Ireland will fall into decay." The report concludes by recommending the immediate repeal of the Union duties on poplin, their reduction on other kinds of silk goods, the repeal of the duty on thrown silk exported from England, and an increase of the drawback on the export of tabinets and poplin to foreign countries.[1] It is interesting to note that, while the recommendation of the Commissioners that the protecting duties should be repealed was immediately carried into effect, their other recommendation that the drawback on the exportation of Irish tabinets should be increased was ignored[2].

The Union duties came to an end in 1824. In the following

[1] *Fourth Report.* [2] Sisson, *Second Letter to Earl Grey.* London 1832.

year the Spitalfields Act was repealed.[1] This was an obviously beneficial change, as the act only operated to favour one locality at the expense of another. A select committee in 1818 had recommended the extension of the act to the whole United Kingdom,[2] but the measure ultimately adopted was preferable, as the act undoubtedly impeded the industry. In 1824 the Dublin Chamber of Commerce complained of "the serious injury which the silk manufacture of this city has sustained from the operation of the laws that subject the wages of the weavers to the regulation of the Dublin Society, and upon the repeal of which the very existence of the manufacture in fact depends."[3] Of course such a radical change could not but produce some temporary inconvenience, but the good results would ultimately have outweighed the bad, had not the industry at the same time been subjected to the full pressure of English competition.[4]

The effect of the repeal of the duties on the silk industry was immediate and unmistakable. "When the duties began to expire" according to a committee of the Dublin silk manufacturers "and the drawback on home manufactured goods was taken off, and steam communication opened with England, the market was inundated with goods during the panic of 1825, at a price less than the cost of the raw material; and thus the loss of the silk trade was rendered inevitable. At this period the weavers made a reduction of fifteen *per cent* on the price of weaving whole silk. Yet after all the sacrifices that were made, the effort proved unavailing to preserve the trade in whole silks. The English were able to pour their silk goods into Ireland at a price below that for which they could be manufactured in Dublin."[5] Any ray of hope for the preservation of the industry which

[1] 5 Geo. IV. c. 66.
[2] *Select Committee on Petition of Ribbon Weavers* 1818.
[3] *Report of Dublin Chamber of Commerce* 1824.
[4] *Report on State of Poor* 1830 p. 16.
[5] *Otway's Report* p. 607.

succeeded in surviving the repeal of the duties was extinguished by the admission of French silks in 1826, and the reduction of the duties on them in 1829, in spite of the spirited protests of both English and Irish manufacturers. "The Irish manufacturers had then a twofold difficulty to contend with in both English and French manufactures; and the result has been the almost total extinction of the silk manufacture in Dublin save a remnant of the tabinet fabric."[1] In the course of seven years from the repeal of the duties, the Tullamore factory and another factory seven miles from Dublin had closed down, and the number of looms working in Dublin had been reduced from 2196 to 150.[2]

A few years later the industry had declined still further. Mr. Otway found the number of silk weavers in Dublin in May 1838 amounted only to 400. Many of these obtained but the scantiest and most precarious employment, and were idle for many weeks or months in the year. The earnings of the weavers during the period when they were working were very uncertain; some families earned as much as £1 19s. a week, while others could not earn more than 8s or 4s. The working day averaged from 14 to 17 hours. Generally speaking, the trade was exceedingly depressed. "It is evident" says Otway "that the silk trade of Dublin has decreased, and, whatever may be the exaggerations as to its former state, it is now confined to the manufacture of one fabric, the tabinets. There can be no doubt that the trade in weaving whole silk is extinct, and that the manufacture of velvets, handkerchiefs and ribbons is reduced to a few looms." Outside Dublin the industry was non-existent.[3]

Many reasons were suggested for the decline of the manufacture. Some said it was the absence of a poor law. There may have been an element of truth in this suggestion, but it must be recalled that the absence of the poor law did not cause the decay of the industry previous to 1824. Others

[1] *Select Committee on the Silk Trade* 1831-2 p. 931. [2] *Ibidem*, p. 837.
[3] *Otway's Report* pp. 601-8 *Report of Repeal Association on Woollen Silk and Cotton Manufactures* 1840.

thought that the combinations had done a great deal to injure the industry. This was the cause upon which Mr. Otway laid most stress. A careful perusal of the evidence offered on the subject shows conclusively that the combinations in this, as in every other Irish industry, were defensive rather than offensive; that they aimed far more at the prevention of the disimprovement than at the attainment of any improvement in the status of the workmen; and that their marked activity about 1830 was an effect rather than a cause of the decay of the industries which they influenced. This is a matter to which we shall return later. It is sufficient here to draw attention to an inconsistency in Mr. Otway's report, which ought to make us pause before accepting without question his conclusions. In one place he states that the combinations helped to cause the ruin of the silk industry by driving many workers to migrate to Macclesfield, where they were willing to work at a lower rate of wages than they received in Dublin;[1] yet a few pages earlier he had stated that the cause of the migration of the Irish weavers to Macclesfield was the higher wages which they could obtain there.[2] It is impossible to reconcile these two statements. There seems to be little doubt that the real deciding factor in the decay of the Irish silk industry in the years 1825-40 was the repeal of the protecting duties; such was the unanimous opinion of all the witnesses examined on the subject before the select committee of 1831-2.[3] The committee of silk weavers who gave evidence before the Handloom Weavers Commission expressed the same opinion.[4] In attempting to arrive at a conclusion on a question of this kind it is safer to follow the opinion of the actual business men of the time than that of a government official, whose one

[1] p. 611. [2] p. 607. [3] Messrs Jonathan Sisson, Barrett Wadden, and John Scott. The second and third of these witnesses quite frankly averred that they had transferred their business from Ireland to England on account of the repeal of the duties, and for no other reason. They did not suggest that they had been annoyed by combinations. The evidence of Mr. Wadden is exceptionally clear and outspoken, and contains a remarkable account of the attitude of the government in 1822. [4] *Otway's Report* p. 609.

guiding principle in life was the infallibility of a particular economic theory. Mr. Otway, true to the principle of his school, strongly recommended against any government intervention to restore the decaying Irish silk industry, on the ground that it is better to let a man die than to endeavour to retain life by artificial respiration.

After 1840 the decay of the Irish silk industry continued without interruption. The lot of the handloom weavers grew worse and worse; and not a single factory was opened to afford them employment.[1]

(e) *The Brewing Industry.*

Although the brewing industry was one of the few manufactures that flourished in Ireland in the fifty years following the Union, it is, curiously enough, one about which it is difficult to obtain any definite statistical information. One cause of this is the fact that the Irish Parliament took off all taxes on beer in 1794, with a view to the discouragement of spirit drinking. Accounts of the amount brewed in Ireland were however kept until 1809, and of the amounts exported until 1823. The former of these accounts shows that the nine years after the Union was a period of increasing prosperity for the Irish brewing industry :

Year *	Ale and beer brewed in Ireland. Barrels.
1800	449,790
1801	398,746
1802	402,942
1803	561,438
1804	695,100
1805	770,688
1806	760,371
1807	750,307
1808	751,146
1809	960,300

* Morewood, *Inebriating Liquors* p. 727.

The legislative attempt to encourage and foster a taste

[1] *Parl. Pap.* No. 294 of 1847; no. 745 of 1850.

for beer in preference to spirits was continued by the United Parliament. In 1810 a statute was passed giving a bounty to retailers of spirits who also retailed beer, provided that they sold at least one barrel of the latter for every four barrels of the former.[1] This bounty was however repealed two years later by a statute, the preamble of which recited that "the provisions of the act have not proved beneficial."[2]

Newenham, in his *View of Ireland*, published in 1809, expressed the opinion that the official estimates of the quantity of beer brewed fell far short of the truth, and stated: "It is obvious to everybody that the number of breweries in Ireland has been augmented since the year 1792; that the additional ones are on a much more extensive scale than the former ones; and that their proprietors resort to every expedient to induce the people to prefer their liquor to whiskey."[3] Three years later Wakefield gave the following account of the industry: "It is not many years since public breweries were introduced into Ireland, but at present they are pretty general; there are establishments at Cork, Fermoy, Limerick, Waterford, Roscrea, Dublin, Belfast, Navan, Armagh, Donoughmore and Dungannon. Formerly beer was imported from England, but there is every reason to conclude that this beverage may be made in sufficient quantity in the country, as there are many circumstances favourable to the success of breweries in Ireland. In the first place the whole duty is levied on the malt, and therefore no encouragement is held out for housekeepers to brew their own beer, as is the case in England; in the next place the brewers are not under the necessity of purchasing public-houses, which proves a heavy tax on their trade in England; and as the publicans have no cellar room to enable them to lay in a large stock, they are served as occasion

[1] 50 Geo. III c. 46. [2] 32 Geo. III c. 46. Although hops were exempt from excise duty in Ireland, the Irish brewing industry did not thereby enjoy any advantage over the English, as no drawback was allowed on the importation of English hops, and no hops were grown in Ireland. *Digest of Excise Commissioners* 1837 p. 80. An account of the quantity of hops imported to Ireland from Great Britain is contained in app. 20 to the Fourth Report of the Revenue Commissioners. [3] p. 227.

requires, and by these means there is no loss of casks, which are articles of the greatest expense to an English brewer..... Malt is prepared by the brewers themselves, and not purchased from maltsters who follow the business exclusively as in England. When the distillers worked from corn ,there were large malting houses at Wexford and at Monasterevan ; but at the time I was in Ireland the malting houses were entirely stopped...."[1]

The brewing industry seems to have grown steadily. In 1818 the firm of Crawford & Beamish, in Cork employed nearly five hundred workmen.[2] The following table, which shows that during the years 1800-23, the quantities of beer imported into Ireland greatly diminished, while the quantities exported remained almost constant, proves that the industry must have progressed during that period :

QUANTITIES OF BEER AND ALE IMPORTED TO AND EXPORTED FROM IRELAND

Year*	Import barrels	Export barrels
1800	19,709	444
1801	17,972	363
1802	10,495	2,108
1803	9,884	5,782
1804	3,209	6,775
1805	3,143	9,707
1806	2,160	5,797
1807	2,449	4,510
1808	2,188	4,630
1809	1,708	5,713
1810	1,101	4,098
1811	1,378	5,393
1812	528	8,727
1813	338	6,266
1814	215	6,814
1815	173	8,022
1816	220	8,556
1817	163	5,480
1818	194	1,153
1819	162	679
1820	317	4,128
1821	235	3,185
1822	—	5,483
1823	—	6,096

[1] Vol. i. pp. 744—5. [2] Curwen, *Observations* vol. ii. p. 9. There is an interesting MS. in vol. 15 of the large pamphlets in the National Library of Ireland containing a list of the brewers in Dublin and their output in 1825. * Morewood, *op. cit.* p. 727.

After 1823 we have no reliable figures of the Irish import or export of beer. The following figures however which show the quantities of malt used by brewers prove that the industry did not decline in the period following the repeal of the protecting duties, which was marked by the decay of almost every other Irish industry.

Year*	Amount of malt used for brewing. bushels
1826	1,336.992
1827	1,410,797
1828	1,512,612
1829	1,402,654
1830	1,343,240

* *Parl. Pap.* no. 187 of 1830.

The attempt to impose a taste for beer on the Irish in place of their taste for spirits does not seem to have been successful. "Since 1796", Morewood complained in 1838 "the year in which the beer duty was rescinded, there has been on the whole a falling off in the consumption of malt, notwithstanding the immense increase in the population, clearly showing that the abolition of the beer duty did not answer the intention, and proving that the Irish people preferred spirits."[1] It must not however be concluded from this that the brewing industry had declined; on the contrary it had developed a flourishing export trade. It was noticed in 1834 that porter was coming to be an article of export rather than of import.[2] The quality of Irish beer had moreover greatly improved. "The quality of the Irish malt drink has of late, through the conduct of some spirited individuals, been greatly improved, and is getting into greater repute not only at home but in the sister kingdom and even in foreign countries."[3]

Morewood gives the following account of the industry

[1] *Op. cit.* p. 623.
[2] *Debate on the Repeal of the Union* Dublin 1834 p. 60.
[3] Morewood, *op. cit.* p. 623.

in 1838: "In Cork, Limerick, Fermoy, Bandon, Waterford, Clogheen, Clonmel, Kilkenny and Carlow are the principal establishments of the south.... In the north there are many highly respectable breweries, viz. Drogheda, Castlebellingham, Dundalk, Newry, Armagh, Monaghan, Dungannon, Donoughmore, Lurgan, Belfast and Derry. The ales of Drogheda, Castlebellingham, Lurgan and Belfast have attained a high character, while the porter and ales of Dublin are accounted equal to any brewed in the empire.... The house of Guinness was the first to open the trade of exportation, and it has been successfully followed by several other respectable houses in Dublin."[1] "The Irish brewing trade" we read in 1852 "is recovering from the serious injury which it sustained from the temperance movement; its home consumption is very little interfered with by English importation; and the Irish brewers on the contrary do a large and increasing business in England and with foreign countries."[2]

(*f*) *The Distilling Industry.*

The distilling industry continued to increase after the Union. It is impossible to quote any statistics that will give an accurate idea of the extent of the industry, as the published figures refer only to the amount of spirits on which duty was paid, and leave out of account the far larger quantity of spirits which was illicitly distilled. If this be kept in mind, and if it be also assumed that—as was undoubtedly the case—the volume of spirits on which no duty was paid tended to increase with every increase of that duty, the following table will show that the amount distilled in Ireland, both for home consumption and for export, tended to increase in the twenty-three years following the Union:

[1] *Op. cit.* p. 629. In 1835 there were 236 registered breweries and 388 maltsters in Ireland. *Second Report of Railway Commissioners* 1838 app. B, no. 14.

[2] Maguire *Guide to Cork Exhibition.*

GALLONS OF IRISH SPIRITS CHARGED WITH DUTY 1801-23.*

Year	Manufactured for home consumption	Quantity exported
1801	1,565,380	1,319,717
1802	1,032,713	1,951,931
1803	4,805,196	1,130,019
1804	4,426,085	930,800
1805	3,611,312	196,569
1806	3,756,671	1,044,548
1807	3,931,829	531,648
1808	5,704,158	648,706
1809	3,643,751	512,098
1810	1,386,381	76,990
1811	4,818,876	136,955
1812	6,500,361	793,140
1813	4,085,913	411,843
1814	3,219,040	144,351
1815	5,496,778	942,038
1816	4,406,466	580,559
1817	3,625,172	196,268
1818	3,655,473	48,260
1819	4,367,396	43,833
1820	3,747,782	236,713
1821	3,363,611	516,885
1822	3,375,652	415,912
1823	2,966,901	656,979

* 5th Report of Revenue Commissioners 1823 app.35; Morewood, *Inebriating Liquors*, p.729.

The increase during this period was attributable in a great measure to the improved processes introduced by various Scotch distillers who had settled in Ireland.[1] Unlike other industries however the increase in distillation was not the subject of universal congratulation, as the benefits arising out of the employment that it gave were, in the opinion of many, more than outweighed by the pernicious effects of the growth of drinking which it evidenced. "Everything" wrote O'Driscoll, "was favourable to the growth of this manufacture; the very dissoluteness of the people—the very villainies of the tradesmen—all the habits and propensities which would have choked and destroyed any other manufacture nourished and promoted this. Accordingly under all the weight and discouragement of a burdensome and unsteady excise, the manufacture has

[1] Morewood, *op. cit* p. 633.

attained a height of towering prosperity, and created for itself a plenteous and splendid capital; and now, in the day of its triumph, it feeds and fosters those vices from which it drew its early aliment."[1]

The widespread practice of illicit distillation had always been a matter of grave anxiety in Ireland, both on account of the serious injury which it inflicted on the revenue, and of its deplorable moral effects on the people. "Illicit stills" according to Wakefield "are completely established in all the north-western counties, and afford a striking proof that a branch of industry may be extended and flourish without the aid of premiums. I am convinced that, whatever penal laws or regulations may be made, it is almost impossible to extirpate illicit distilleries from the mountains. It has been represented to me, and I believe with truth, that they are erected in the kitchens of baronets and in the stables of clergymen. The mountains are covered with them, and they are to be met with in the very last places where an English excise officer would expect to discover them."[2] "The manufacture of illicit stills " says Morewood "has long been a favourite beverage in Ireland, being made from malt without adulteration, and possessing a flavour which habit has rendered most agreeable. This, combined with the high duties on legally distilled spirits, and the want of a ready market for the disposal of the grain of remote and mountainous districts, induced the people to embark on this illicit traffic to an extent which was not only injurious to the revenue and manufacture of the country, but to the morals and peaceful habits of the community. To such an extent was it carried that in 1808, out of 11,400,030 gallons, 3,811,000 gallons were allowed to be the produce of illicit manufacturers; and in 1811, 1812 and 1813 there were no less than 19,067 illicit stills destroyed by the revenue and military."[3] It was well known that far more "Queen's"

[1] *Views of Ireland* 1823 vol. i. p. 243 [2] Vol. i. p. 729.
[3] *Op. cit.* p. 673. Morewood gives many remarkable instances of the manner in which the excise officers were misled and defrauded.

spirit than "King's" spirit was sold in Ireland;[1] complaints were general that the morals of the inhabitants of remote districts were being completely destroyed by the prevalence of cheap spirits;[2] and the evil was greatly increased after 1815 on account of the fall in the price of corn sold for legitimate purposes.[3]

The government was much concerned with the widespread prevalence of illicit distillation, and devised numerous measures for its repression. There is possibly no one subject which engaged the attention of parliament more frequently in the twenty years following the Union than the Irish distilling laws. Wakefield complains that "it is impossible for the most rapid writer or printer to keep pace with the progress of the distillery laws in Ireland. Those made in one month are seldom those of the next."[4] The Irish Parliament had conceived the idea of giving all the inhabitants of a district a direct interest in the enforcement of the excise law, by providing that the whole townland in which an illicit still was discovered should be penalized by a fine. This plan does not seem to have produced the desired result. "The law which imposes a fine of £50 on the townland, parish, or county according to circumstances, on the discovery of an illicit still at work therein, instead of answering the purpose for which it was intended, has produced a contrary effect, and acted as an encouragement to the erection of new ones. Many a still which was purchased originally for three guineas has been sold, when burned out, for £50. Had a reward been offered to the parish-officers for the discovery of stills, instead of subjecting them to a fine for one being taken within their jurisdiction, they would have been as anxious to search for them as they are now careful to conceal them from the officers of the revenue. It is a well known fact that the latter receive a

[1] Parker, *Observations on the Intended Amendments of the Irish Grand Jury Law*, Cork 1816. [2] C. Hannah, *An Excursion in Antrim, Down and Derry* Belfast 1821.
[3] *Impartial Review of the True Causes of Existing Misery in Ireland* Dublin 1822.
[4] Vol. i. p. 729.

more regular rent while the still is at work, than any landlord does for his land, and they often divide with the proprietor half the value of its sale by the receipt of the fine."[1]

The system of fining the district was nevertheless continued in default of a better remedy. The fine was increased in 1809 to £100 in the case of a second or third offence.[2] The whole system was abolished in 1819, and three years later a revenue police was established. This force was distributed in parties, each to watch a separate district. The number of parties in 1826 was 32, in 1833, 57, and in 1838, 70; but, in spite of very great exertions, they succeeded only in partially suppressing illicit distillation.[3]

In 1831 a further act was passed giving to a single justice of the peace or to the owner or occupier of the land on which a still was found power to seize the still and to hand it over to the revenue authorities.[4] The effect of these penal measures was however small, compared with that produced by the lowering of the duty on spirits in 1823. Obviously, the smaller the duty, the less becomes the temptation to evade it; and there is no doubt that the lowering of the duty in 1823 did more to render the business of illicit distillation unattractive than all the punishments on townlands and powers of magistrates that parliament could devise. "To the vigorous measures of government" Morewood wrote in 1838 "aided by the gentry of the country, but still more to the lowering of the duty and the encouragement given to small stills, the present decrease of illicit distillation may be mainly attributed; and though it still exists its prevalence is comparatively partial."[5]

The government resorted to another device to discourage illicit distilling, namely the encouragement by means of preferential taxation of stills of a certain size. Strangely enough, the government seems never to have been quite certain whether more beneficial results would follow from

[1] Wakefield, vol. i. p. 729. [2] 49 Geo. III c. 99.
[3] Morewood *op. cit.* p. 676. On the history of the Irish Revenue Police see Digest of Excise Commissioners 1837 p. 38. [4] 1 and 2 Wm. IV. c. 55. [5] *Op. cit.* p. 677.

the encouragement of large or of small stills. On the one hand it was argued that if none but large stills were licensed, the task of the excise officers in tracing down and suppressing illicit stills would be facilitated; while on the other hand it was replied that, if small stills were to receive public recognition and favour, the temptation to work them in opposition to the law would be minimized. We find therefore the strange inconsistency that almost simultaneous statutes were passed for the encouragement of large and small stills. In 1806 an act was passed providing that no still holding less than 500 gallons should be licensed, and that a bounty should be awarded to stills of more than 1500 gallons capacity.[1] The following year another act was passed, allowing stills of 200 gallons to be licensed, but not within five miles of any 500 gallon still.[2] Two years later the minimum capacity of a still that might receive a licence was reduced to 50 gallons, but the protection of a monopoly of a five mile radius for 500 gallon stills was still retained.[3] In the following year the minimum capacity was reduced from 50 to 44 gallons, at which it remained until the important consolidating act of 1823.[4] These acts obviously aimed at the encouragement of large stills; but at the same time there was a movement in favour of the encouragement of small stills. Two select committees of the House of Commons had recommended that the only way to put an end to illicit distillation was by encouraging small stills; and accordingly a preference was shown to them in calculating the number of charges at which they should be assessed.[5]

As we have said above, none of these measures had as great an effect in discountenancing illicit distillation as the lowering of the excise. The duty in Ireland prior to the Union, and until 1858, was always lower than in England.

[1] 46 Geo. III c. 88. [2] 47 Geo. III Sess. 2. c. 17.
[3] 49 Geo. III c. 99. [4] 50 Geo. III c. 15.
[5] *Select Committee on Illicit Distillation* 1812-3; *Select Committee on Illicit Distillation* 1816; *Fifth Report of Revenue Commissioners* 1823 app. 42.

At the time of the Union it amounted only to 2/4¼d per gallon, but it was raised by successive steps to 2/10¼ in 1802, to 3/6¼ in 1803, and to 4/1d. in 1804.[1] In 1808 it was fixed at four shillings per gallon, and in the following year an additional duty of ten shillings per six gallons was imposed.[2] In 1810 the duty was reduced to 2/6 per gallon[3]; but it was raised to 5/0 in 1812,[4] and to 5/6 in 1813[5].

The same acts that regulated the amount of the inland excise on Irish spirits also settled the amount of the countervailing duties to be paid on the import of British spirits into Ireland and of Irish spirits into Great Britain. After the Union, complaints arose because the Irish exporter to Great Britain obtained a drawback without reference to the discount he had received on account of owning a large still, and had thus received in some cases a positive bounty. This was corrected in 1804[6]. The export of Irish spirits to Great Britain was frequently suspended for various reasons, but in 1814 the law on the matter was consolidated and reformed. By an act passed in that year, the following countervailing duties were fixed to be paid on the exportation of Irish spirits to Great Britain and *vice versa*— British spirits exported to Ireland 6/0½d per gallon, Irish spirits exported to England 9/10½d per gallon, Irish spirits exported to Scotland 7/8¼d per gallon.[7] The result of the lax manner in which the duties were collected in Ireland, as compared with Great Britain, was that the Irish distillers were tempted to export the greater part of their spirits on which they had paid duty, and to meet the home demand with illicitly distilled spirits.[8]

The Revenue Commissioners consequently recommended that Irish distillers should be permitted to distil for export to Great Britain only by observing the same regulations that applied to distillation in Great Britain itself. The

[1] Morewood *op. cit.* p. 730. [2] 48 Geo. III c. 78; 49 Geo. III c. 73.
[3] 50 Geo. III c. 15. [4] 52 Geo. III c. 46.
[5] 53 Geo. III c. 94. [6] 44 Geo. III c. 104. [7] 54 Geo. III c. 149.
[8] *Fifth Report of Revenue Commissioners* 1823, *Supplement*.

following table shows the quantity of spirits exported from Ireland to Great Britain and from Great Britain to Ireland in the years 1801-22.

QUANTITIES OF SPIRITS EXPORTED FROM GREAT BRITAIN TO IRELAND AND FROM IRELAND TO GREAT BRITAIN.

Year*	Export from Ireland to Great Britain. Gallons.	Export from Great Britain to Ireland. Gallons.
1801	227,410	0
1802	1,085,907	0
1803	883,486	0
1804	1,156,993	14
1805	1,035,267	38
1806	526,618	23
1807	643,745	5,164
1808	510,996	127,776
1809	75,713	239,938
1810	0	225,711
1811	47,911	0
1812	27,679	0
1813	0	0
1814	291,042	2
1815	373,021	0
1816	32,249	0
1817	1,268	0
1818	13,339	60
1819	120,940	2
1820	436,947	0
1821	370,039	0
1822	605,392	0

* *Supplement to Fivth Report of Rev. Commrs.* 1823. app. 14 and 18.

While the government was perplexed with the problem of the illicit stills, and was at pains to devise methods to suppress them, the very regulations designed with this aim were found oppressive by the landowners and legal distillers. Owing to the provision that the excisemen should receive part of the fines imposed for breaches of the excise laws, the regular distillers were harassed and impeded in the legitimate conduct of their business;[1] and the landlords complained of the discouragement to tillage which the incessant interference of the excisemen produced.[2]

[1] Chichester, *Oppression and Cruelties of Irish Excise Officers* London 1818.
[2] *An Address to the Nobility and Gentry of Ireland on the Subject of Distillation*, Dublin 1819.

The agricultural interests were also dissatisfied at the constant prohibitions of the export of Irish spirits to England.[1] Altogether the state of the law regarding distillation gave universal dissatisfaction. "The regulations of the Board of Excise" complained Lord Blessington, "are such as to render it impossible for the licensed distillers to make good whiskey; consequently they either buy from the private stills, or themselves distil in private for the purpose of mixing the purer spirit with that run off according to the direction of the Excise."[2] No doubt this widespread dissatisfaction was one of the reasons which caused the Revenue Commissioners to devote so much attention to the distillery laws.

The first thing that attracted the attention of the Commissioners was the prevalence of illicit distillation. "Parts of the country" they observe "have been absolutely disorganized and placed in opposition not only to the civil authority but to the military forces of the government." They estimated that the amount of spirit on which duty was paid in 1822 amounted to but 29 *per cent* of the spirits actually distilled in that year. The Commissioners came to the very sensible conclusion that the principal reason for the prevalence of illicit distillation was the high duty on spirits. "It is obvious" they remark, "that unless the licensed distiller can bring into the market spirits not inferior in quality at a price nearly equal to that at which the unlicensed distiller can afford to sell, he cannot hope to succeed in competition with the latter." They recommended therefore that the duty on spirits should be reduced to half a crown or three shillings per gallon.[3]

The Revenue Commissioners further came to the conclusion that the existing method of collecting the duty was oppressive and ineffective, and recommended that the Scotch system should be applied to Ireland. The basis of this system was the use of the saccharometer, an instru-

[1] *A View of the Agricultural State of Ireland* Cork 1816.
[2] *Observations on the State of Ireland* London 1822.
[3] *Fifth Report of Revenue Commissioners* 1823.

ment by which the excise officers were enabled to ascertain the density of the wort extracted from the grain, and therefrom to infer the quantity of spirits it was capable of producing. The advantage of this method over the old method was that it left the distiller free to distil at whatever rate he pleased, and did not set a premium on rapid distillation, which was frequently the cause of inferior spirits.

The next matter to which the Commissioners devoted their attention was the oppressive incidence of the malt duty, which tempted distillers to distil from grain rather than from malt. "It was of the utmost importance to observe the discouragement given to the use of malt in distillation, and the injury which is in consequence done to the quality of the spirit, without any corresponding advantage to the revenue. The use of raw grain for distilling spirits, to the extent to which it at present prevails, is of modern origin, and appears to be entirely the consequence of the high duty imposed on malt." It was pointed out that this evil was to some extent remedied in Scotland by an act which gave a drawback on malt used in distillation,[1] and it was recommended that a similar drawback should be granted in Ireland.[2]

The oppressive nature of the malt tax was more particularly dealt with in a later report of the Commissioners, in which they pointed out that the maltsters' licence was much higher in Ireland than in England, and that, while the duty could only be collected in one way in the latter, it could be assessed on four different *bases* in the former country. "The evident operation of such a duty" the Commissioners observe "is to prevent persons from commencing or from continuing the trade .... and the result has been that, whilst in England the number of maltsters exceeds 12,000, in Ireland only 246 were at work in 1822".[3] The following table demonstrates how the successive increases

[1] 1 and 2 Geo. IV c. 82.
[2] *Fifth Report of Revenue Commissioners* 1823.
[3] *Eighth Report of Revenue Commissioners* 1824.

in the duty on malt had operated to diminish the amount used, and to induce distillers to replace malt by grain:—

DUTY PAID ON MALT.*

Year ending	Quantity, barrels	Duty	Rate of duty
		£. s. d.	s. d.
25 Mch. 1793	1,191,854	148,981 15 0	2 6
25 ,, 1798	1,190,875	312,604 17 3	5 3
5 Jan. 1803	920,382	299,124 8 11	6 6
5 ,, 1808	604,561	327,470 18 11	10 0
5 ,, 1813	562,234	304,543 18 1	10 0
5 ,, 1818	353,981	171,931 1 3	9 4
5 ,, 1823	417,928	241,523 13 1	10 0

* *Eighth Report of Revenue Commissioners* 1824, app. 45.

The recommendations of the Commissioners were at once put into effect by Parliament. By a statute passed in 1823 the duty on spirits was reduced to two shillings per gallon, permission was given to license stills of 40 gallons content, and the Scottish method of collecting the duty was applied to Ireland. At the same time the duty on malt was reduced from 28/10 to 20/9 per quarter.[1] The duty on spirits was slightly raised in 1826 and 1830, and was not again raised until after 1850.[2] The drawback on malt used in distillation recommended by the Commissioners was also carried into effect, but it had not the desired result. Indeed the amount of malt used in distillation diminished after 1824, as is shown by the following figures:—

AMOUNT OF MALT USED BY DISTILLERS IN IRELAND.*

Year ending 5th Jan.	Amount. Bushels
1826	1,047,592
1827	888,348
1828	837,645
1829	753,445
1830	684,148

* *Parl. Pap.* no. 187 of 1830.

[1] 4 Geo. IV c. 94. [2] Morewood, *op. cit.* p. 720

The excise commissioners found in 1836 that there was scarcely any distillation from malt in Ireland at that date.[1]

The drawback seems to have been imposed contrary to the advice of the Irish distillers, and was never popular with them. In later years there were many complaints of illicit malting, and it is interesting to observe that the Excise Commissioners thought that this was largely due to the change in the law which took place at this time. The following extract from their report is a curious commentary on the passion for assimilation: "The old law is stated to have worked well, and without any complaint on the part of the fair and legal maltsters; and its repeal took place, not because of any faults belonging to it, but solely in order to carry the law of assimilation in England and Ireland into effect."[2] A select committee of the House of Commons in 1842 reported that "the repeal of the malt drawback in Ireland will not be prejudicial either to the trade in spirits or to the revenue of the country." The drawback was accordingly discontinued.[3]

It is difficult to say how far the legislation of 1823 succeeded in suppressing illicit distillation in Ireland. On the one hand we have the evidence of certain distillers before the Poor Law Commissioners in 1836, who stated that "if the Government would take some measures to prevent illicit distillation the fair trader would do very well; two large concerns now in Dublin are preparing to turn their distilleries into breweries, as they are unable to contend with the illicit trader."[4] Moreover the Commissioners on the Excise referred to "the universal and alarming extent to which illicit distillation has prevailed in Ireland, especially in the years 1831 and 1832, and to the openness with which it has been publicly sold in that country as low as

[1] *Digest* p. 34 See a memorial from the distillers of Dublin on this subject in *Parl. Pap.* no. 395 of 1826-7.

[2] *Digest.* p. 43.

[3] *Select Committee on Spirit Trade in Ireland* 1842. The malting business was subjected to numerous regulations in 1827 by 7 and 8 Geo. IV c. 52.

[4] *Evidence on Combinations, Poor Inquiry Commission* app. C. part 2.

3/- a gallon, the price of the legal spirits being from 7/- to 7/2 a gallon; the consequence having been ruinous to the legal distillers, and the accumulation in their hands of an immense stock of unsaleable spirits. Another almost inevitable consequence has been the evasion of duty to a considerable extent on the part of many of the legal distillers . . . The increases of the duty in 1826 and 1830 are distinctly pointed out as the primary causes of the lamentable state of things . . . The abolition of the townland fines appears also to have been adduced as a contributory cause."[1] On the other hand Mr. John Jameson stated in 1842 that the act of 1823 had completely put an end to illicit distillation, except in the more remote country districts, and that at a later date it tended to decline even in the west.[2] Possibly the best criterion by which to judge the fortunes of the illicit distillers is to enquire to what extent legitimate distillation prospered; on this we have definite statistics, which enable us to conclude that the legitimate distillery trade of Ireland prospered exceedingly in the years following the remedial legislation. The falling off about 1840 disclosed by the following table is accounted for by the success of Father Mathew's temperance campaign, and this decline was doubtless felt by the illicit stills as well—

AMOUNT OF SPIRITS WHICH PAID DUTY, 1824-49.*

Year ending 10 Oct.	*gallons*
1824	8,158,046
1825	9,208,618
From 10 Oct. 1825 to 5 Jan. 1826	4,325,649
Year ending 5 Jan.	
1827	6,837,408
1828	8,260,919
1829	9,937,903
1830	9,212,223

* *Parl. Pap.* no. 186 of 1830; *Select Committee on Spirit Trade of Ireland* 1842 p. 63; *Thom's Directory* 1851 p. 248 *Parl. Pap.* no. 369 of 1851.

[1] *Digest of Excise Commissioners* 1837 p. 34.

[2] *Select Committee on Spirit Trade in Ireland* 1842 pp. 3 and 43.

Year	gallons
1832	8,710,672
1833	8,657,756
1834	8,168,956
1835	9,708,416
1836	11,381,223
1837	12,248,772
1838	11,235,635
1839	12,291,342
1840	10,815,709
1841	7,401,050
1842	6,485,443
1843	5,290,650
1844	5,546,483
1845	6,451,137
1846	7,605,196
1847	7,952,076
1848	5,737,687
1849	8,126,507

The export trade also increased steadily, although it was widely complained that the export to England was discouraged by the fact that the English duty was payable on the full quantity shipped without any allowance for wastage, and by the prohibition of the export of compounds.[1]

(g) *The Glass Industry.*

Although the duties on the importation of British glass were substantially reduced by the Act of Union, the glass industry does not appear to have suffered any injury on that account. This is probably owing to the fact that the raw materials required could be obtained as cheaply in Ireland as in England, and that the slight advantage that the English manufacturer possessed, by reason of the cheaper coal which he could obtain, was more than outweighed by the disadvantage which he suffered by reason of the excise duty to which he was subject. In view of the later evidence one cannot help thinking that Wakefield took an unduly pessimistic view of the state of the industry in 1812, when

[1] *Digest Excise Commissioners* 1837 p. 34.

he stated that "glass manufactories are established at Dublin, Waterford, and Belfast; but the use of English glass in Ireland is very prevalent, and the reason assigned for it is the want of fuel."[1]

A few years later, at any rate, the Revenue Commissioners found the Irish glass industry in a very flourishing state. "The manufacture of glass is carried on to a considerable extent in Ireland and is at present stated to be increasing. There are four established in Dublin, two in Belfast, two in Cork, and one in Waterford, and one lately established in Derry. They are all employed in making white glass and bottles; neither plate nor window glass are at all manufactured in Ireland. All the necessary materials for making glass are said to be obtained in Ireland on nearly as reasonable terms as in England, coals only excepted . . . Coals affect the value of bottles more than of white glass; and if the import duty was removed, the supply from England would be more likely to interfere with the manufacture of bottles than with that of white glass". The Commissioners then drew attention to the absence of excise duties on Irish glass—"No excise is imposed upon glass (except a small duty of 3d per gross on bottles) . . . Ireland is not only exempt from the vexation and inconvenience of the excise regulations, but, in consequence of the mode in which the countervailing duty and drawback are arranged on the importation of British glass into Ireland, an important advantage is obtained by the Irish manufacturer." The Commissioners concluded by recommending the gradual abolition of the Union duties on glass.[2]

The duties were completely abolished in 1824; and in the following year the excise duties on flint glass manufactured in Great Britain and Ireland were assimilated.[3] Two years later the duties on all other kinds of glass

[1] Vol. i. p. 755.
[2] *Fourth Report*. Statistics of the export of glass from Ireland 1800-23 are printed in appendix B of Murray's *Commercial Relations*.
[3] 6 Geo. IV. c. 117.

were likewise assimilated.[1] The Irish manufacturer thus lost all the advantages which he previously enjoyed.

As a result of these changes the Irish glass industry was not only exposed to the full pressure of English competition, but was subjected to a very vexatious and annoying course of official interference. The Commissioners of Excise Inquiry in their thirteenth report stated that "no tax can combine more objections, or be more at variance with all sound principles of taxation than this duty on glass", and further, "that unless some material change shall take place, the persons who carry on the manufacture must either be driven out of the trade or left to carry it on at a ruinous loss." The commissioners found that the number of glass houses in Dublin had diminished from 5 to 2, in Cork from 2 to 1, in Belfast from 3 to 1, in the period 1825-36, during which period the only glass house in Waterford had closed down.[2] The Repeal Association complained bitterly of the oppression of the duties: "The regulations of the Excise with regard to the manufacture of glass are penal in the extreme. The manufacturer cannot be said to be the master of his own concern; as, by the existing state of the excise laws, his business and premises are placed under the control of a class of men, to whose will and caprice it is most irksome to submit. Parts of the premises cannot be extended without the permission of these officers; and no one act can be done in the conduct of the manufacture without having previously notified one of the officers . . ."[3]

Whatever the reason, it is certain that the repeal of the protecting duties and the imposition of the excise coincided with the beginning of a period of depression in the industry. "The trade was making rapid progress till

[1] 7 and 8 Geo IV c. 53: 9 Geo IV v. 48.

[2] *Digest* p. 61. They added that "the whole of the evidence paints in strong colours the depressed state of the manufacture since the imposition of the duty in 1825" *Thirteenth Report* p. 48.

[3] *Repeal Reports* vol. i. p. 276.

the year 1825, when the excise duty was first put on; a gradual decay shortly after took place. There were four manufactories at that time, three were dropped off, and there is now only one in Dublin."[1] The Railway Commissioners reported that there were only six glass works in Ireland.[2] The factories at Waterford, Newry, and Derry closed down.[3] The eleven glass houses at work in 1825 had been reduced to three, twenty years later.[4]

One result of the excessive tax on window glass was that many of the cottages of the peasantry were forced to remain unglazed. "The duty on window glass is extravagant, and most oppressive on the poor. It is nominally about 8d *per lb*; but from the manner in which it is charged, it cannot be less than 1/- *per lb*. Hence it is that in all poor localities and in the cabins throughout the country there is almost a total absence of window-glass, giving to the wretched abodes even a more dismal and squalid appearance than they otherwise would have, if glass were at such a price that it could be purchased by the poor; but in consequence of the high rate of duty a small pane of glass will cost 1/- or 1/6d, a sum amounting to nearly a total prohibition of the use of the article."[5] The same observation was made by the Devon Commissioners:—"The duty on glass, as it is now enforced and levied, operates injuriously on the poorer classes, with respect to the comfort of their habitations, and, by enhancing the price upon the lowest quality of glass, virtually prevents its use, even among the occupiers of small farms."[6] These obnoxious duties were repealed in 1845.[7] The only figures we can adduce to show the extent of the glass industry in the later portion of our period are the quantities of glass on which excise was paid in Ireland

[1] *Evidence on Combinations, Poor Inquiry Commission* app. C pt. 2.
[2] *Second Report* app. B no. 14.
[3] Westropp, *Glass Making in Ireland* Proc. R. I. A. vol. xxix C p. 34.
[4] *Repeal Reports* vol. i. p. 275.
[5] *Repeal Reports* vol. i. p. 278.
[6] *Dev. Comm.* p. 1162.
[7] 8 and 9 Vict. c. 6.

during the five years before the abolition of the duties:

Year*	Quantity of glass on which duty paid	
	flint, cwts.	bottle, cwts.
1841	6,268	10,712
1842	5,570	9,375
1843	5,355	7,417
1844	4,070	—
1845	6,249	2,471

* *Thom's Directory*. 1845 p. 215 and 1850 p. 179.

(*h*) *The Pottery Industry.*

The manufacture of pottery had never attained to any large dimensions in Ireland, probably on account of the difficulty of obtaining coal; and the Union cannot be said to have had any effect, either beneficial or harmful, on the industry. The industry appears to have been practically non-existent in 1811;[1] and Wakefield in the course of his exhaustive explorations could find but few traces of it. "About Fintona good flooring and ridge tiles are made, also garden pots, and a great variety of earthenware for country use. The best pottery in the county, and perhaps in Ireland, is within a mile of Coalisland. All sorts of coarse crockery ware, fire bricks, and tiles for malt and oat kilns, of as good a quality as any imported, are manufactured here."[2] Wakefield attributed the absence of potteries to the shortage of coal: "To the want of fuel I ascribe the want of potteries for earthenware, similar to those which have succeeded in such an astounding manner in Staffordshire, from their contiguity to the coal pits of that county. Ireland possesses abundance of clay well adapted for the purpose, but, till veins of bituminous coal are discovered in the country, such works cannot be contemplated with any hope of success."[3]

[1] Joseph Hamilton, *Proposals for the Establishment of a Pottery in Ireland* Dublin 1811.
[2] Vol. i. p. 113. [3] Vol. i. p. 723.

It is difficult to form an opinion as to the extent of the pottery industry in 1820, as we are faced with a certain amount of contradictory evidence. On the one hand Mr. James Donovan, a leading glass manufacturer, gave the following evidence before the Revenue Commissioners, from which it would appear that the industry was practically non-existent:—

"You have no manufactory of china in this country, have you ?

"No, we enamel a little. We import the china and pottery in a white state and decorate it here; the object is principally to match sets.

"Are you aware of any china manufacture in Ireland?

"There is none.

"Is there any manufactory of pottery in Ireland?

"No, there are some garden pots of a very coarse description, nothing beyond that."[1]

This evidence is corroborated by the statement in a contemporary pamphlet that "we have not a single pottery in this country."[2] As against these statements, we have the fact that pottery of the coarser kinds appears to have been not only made in, but exported from, Ireland at this period, as the Custom House books contain entries of exports from Ireland of earthenware of native manufacture. These exports were chiefly from Cork and Dublin, and the annual amounts for the year 1820-3 varied in value from £100 to £500.[3] We have the further evidence that in 1818 a firm in Limerick advertised that it was engaged on "the manufacture of kiln, ridge and pan tiles, garden pots, crockery ware suitable for domestic purposes, and chimney tops, all of which will be of the best manufacture, having gone to considerable expense to procure good workmen."[4] Between these conflicting statements we leave the reader

[1] *Fourth Report* app. 42.
[2] *A Letter to Sir John Newport, Bart.* by Hibernicus, Dublin 1821.
[3] Westropp. *The Pottery Manufacture in Ireland* Proc. R. I. A. vol. xxxiii C. p. 1.
[4] *Ibidem.*

to decide for himself, but we suggest that the probable solution is that, though the Revenue Commissioners acted, as they did in the case of the manufacture of new drapery, on insufficient evidence, the pottery industry in Ireland was very small and insignificant, and cannot therefore have been seriously injured by the repeal of the Union duties. It certainly did not grow to the extent of using up all the raw material which Ireland produced, for we learn that some of the finest clay employed in the English pottery districts was imported from Ireland.[1]

The evidence regarding the condition of the Irish potteries in the later part of our period is scanty in the extreme—so scanty, indeed, as to lead us to the conclusion that they must have been practically non-existent. All we know is that in the decade 1840-50 small quantities were manufactured in the neighbourhood of Cork and Youghal.[2]

(i) *The Shipbuilding Industry.*

During the whole of the first half of the nineteenth century the volume of the shipbuilding industry in Ireland was so small as to be almost negligible. The great modern shipbuilding industry of the north did not begin to develop until after 1850. Immediately after the Union, there was a decrease in the number of ships built in Ireland, as the following figures show:

NUMBER AND TONNAGE OF VESSELS BUILT AND REGISTERED IN IRELAND.*

	vessels.	tons.
12 years 1788-1800	515	23,550
12 years 1801-1811	346	18,362

* Wakefield vol. ii. p. 63.

During the next forty years the number of ships built in Ireland increased only to the small extent disclosed by the following table:

[1] *The Case of Ireland* London 1823. [2] Westropp, *op. cit.*

NUMBER AND TONNAGE OF VESSELS BUILT AND REGISTERED IN IRELAND.*

Year	vessels	tonnage
1794	32	1,441
1804	38	1,611
1814	46	1,973
1824	35	1,376
1834	39	2,521
1844	38	3,564
1849	25	2,147

* Wakefield, vol. ii. p. 65; *Statistical Illustrations of the British Empire* London 1825. *Thom's Directory* 1849 p. 199, and 1851 p. 253.

The principal change which took place in the industry during the period under review was its shifting away from Dublin to other centres. We shall refer on a future page to the currently accepted theory that the decay of the industry in Dublin was the result of the action of the trade unions. It is certain however that the industry did decay in that city. While Dublin was the principal centre of Irish shipbuilding in 1800, no ships at all were built there in 1838, and the industry was showing signs of becoming established in Waterford, Cork, Drogheda, and Belfast.[1] It is interesting to observe that the great pre-eminence of Belfast had not yet appeared. Although a steam vessel had been completely built there in 1824, and an iron vessel in 1838, the industry continued very small and unimportant until after 1850.[2]

(*j*) *The Paper Industry.*

Until 1798 paper manufactured in Ireland had been free from taxation. In that year however a small excise duty was imposed by the Irish Parliament.[3] In 1807 a duty was imposed of 3d per pound on first class paper, 1d per lb. on second class, £1 per cwt on third class, and 5/- per cwt. on paper used for hot pressing.[4] Some years later paper

[1] *Select Committee on Combinations of Workmen* 1838 vol. ii. pp. 119-121.

[2] Benn, *History of Belfast* vol. ii. pp. 124-5. On the importance of the Waterford shipbuilding yards see Marmion *Maritime Ports* p. 559. [3] 38 Geo. III. c. 5. [4] 47 Geo. III c. 18.

makers were made liable to a charge of 12/6 per calendar month for every cubic foot of the contents of their engines used to reduce the rags or other materials into the pulp from which the paper was made, unless the duty chargeable by weight should exceed the amount of the duty chargeable on the engine.[1] Similar duties were levied on paper hangings.[2]

The Revenue Commissioners found fault with the system of taxation because it tempted the manufacturers to speed up production to a point at which quality was sacrificed to quantity, and because it encouraged the manufacture of coarse rather than of fine paper.[3] The English method was consequently introduced, and the amount of the duties in the two countries assimilated in 1824.[4] This change was not popular with the Irish manufacturers who preferred the old method of levying the tax.[5] The tax on paper was productive of injurious effects to the industry, and while the amount of paper manufactured in Great Britain increased between 1814 and 1823 that in Ireland diminished. "The paper manufacture particularly belonging to counties engaged in the flax and hemp manufactures was rapidly advancing in Ireland until the tax on the paper mills was imposed."[6] In 1822 there were 42 registered paper makers in Ireland and 57 in 1835.[7] In 1828 the manufacture employed 20,000 people.[8]

The printing industry suffered severely as a result of the Union. "At the time of the Union" according to the Revenue Commissioners "the copyright act was extended to Ireland, and the Irish publisher was thus deprived of the power of reprinting British publications for the supply of the home market. The extension of the law, however

[1] 56 Geo. III c. 78, 58 Geo. III c. 41. [2] 47 Geo. III c. 18, 55 Geo. III c. 106.

[3] *Eighth Report* 1824. [4] 5 Geo. IV c. 55. [5] *Digest of Excise Commissioners* 1837 pp. 66-7.

[6] *The Causes of the Discontents of Ireland*, Dublin 1823.

[7] *Fourth Report of Revenue Commissioners* app. 58. *Second Report of Railway Commissioners* app. B. no. 14. On the state of the industry in 1850 see Riordan *Modern Irish Trade and Industry* p. 168.

[8] *Sketch of the Proceedings of the Society for the Improvement of Ireland*, Dublin 1828.

just in principle, has had the effect of nearly destroying the trade of publishing in Ireland; and the press, at this time, affords no supply beyond that of a few tracts of local interest and some school books."[1]

(*k*) *The Provision Industry.*

The provision industry is so closely connected with agriculture that it is difficult to decide whether it should be treated in the agricultural or industrial section of the book. We have decided however to include it in the latter, as any process which involves the working up of the produce of the soil into a condition different from its native state is properly regarded as an industry. The provision industry differs from most other industries in that its presence on an extensive scale in any country is not necessarily a sign of national prosperity, but is very often on the other hand a sign of economic backwardness. In order to furnish the raw material of a provision trade large areas must be given up to the grazing of cattle, which entails as an almost inevitable consequence the unemployment of a large part of the rural population.

The provision industry, which had flourished throughout the eighteenth century,[2] showed no sign of decay in the years immediately following the Union. Wakefield found the industry largely centralized in Cork: "The principal part of the provision trade is confined to the city of Cork, whence most of the beef, pork, and butter produced in the southern districts of Ireland is exported. The average number of oxen slaughtered is calculated at 10,000, and that of cows at 8,000. The beef cured is divided into three different sorts; planters' beef, India beef, and common beef...... The merchant purchases the carcase of the graziers by weight; cows and small lean cattle bring the least price,

[1] *Third Report* 1822.
[2] O'Brien. *Economic History of Ireland in the Eighteenth Century* pp. 217-23; 288-90.

and fat oxen of six years old the greatest...... The meat is suffered to remain seven or eight days in salt before it is packed. The expedition with which the animals are slaughtered, the meat cut up and salted, and afterwards packed, is astonishing. As the people employed in this business have acquired great expertness by habit, every part of it is conducted with the utmost regularity and dispatch. When the animals are killed the hides are returned to the grazier for sale...... Pork is packed in the same manner. St. Ubes' salt, on account of the coarseness of the grain, is preferred to any other...... The wood of which the barrels and tierces are made is imported from America."[1]

Although the trade was so prosperous in Cork, Wakefield thought that it was rather declining in the country as a whole. "The number of bullocks slaughtered in Ireland is much decreased since the American war. This diminution is ascribed by the merchants to the increased consumption of meat at home, and the extension of tillage."[2] Nevertheless other centres besides Cork showed considerable progress. Dublin was rather gaining on Cork, and a very extensive trade in bacon and hams was conducted in Limerick, Clonmel, and Waterford.[3] The quality of the Irish beef was in general excellent, whereas that of the pork was not so good, principally on account of the pernicious effects of the pigs having been fed on a continuous potato diet.[4]

The great market for cattle was Ballinasloe, where the annual fair was an event of great importance. "Ballinasloe" stated Curwen, "is a considerable town; at its autumnal fair it is calculated to receive ten thousand visitors, the price of whose beds varies from sixpence to a guinea per night. The Farming Society of Ireland have a very good house here with admirable accommodation for the company and ample convenience for the reception and exhibition

[1] Vol. i. p. 750.
[2] Vol. i. p. 751.
[3] Vol. i. p. 752.
[4] Trimmer, *Further Observations* &c. London 1812.

of stock. The arrangement of the prize cattle is perfectly well conducted."[1]

The prosperity of the provision trade in the early nineteenth century was due largely to the practical monopoly which Ireland enjoyed of supplying the British colonies, the navy, the army, and the mercantile marine.[2] The following figures show the exports of the principal articles of Irish provisions from 1802 to 1826, the last year for which separate records were kept:

Year ending* 5th Jan.	Beef barrels	Pork barrels	Bacons and Hams cwt.	Butter cwt.
1802	79,239	81,601	21,161	304,666
1803	80,161	59,528	86,643	396,353
1804	79,347	119,049	61,146	334,251
1805	79,531	82,193	47,505	320,155
1806	111,673	110,425	95,073	294,415
1807	120,588	113,376	119,151	338,508
1808	110,218	170,289	153,343	333,998
1809	122,064	168,603	144,033	346,656
1810	126,176	136,568	167,122	385,953
1811	95,498	110,806	171,730	390,833
1812	136,713	177,250	227,776	433,714
1813	144,597	156,685	249,982	435,408
1814	139,732	141,771	234,606	461,514
1815	110,510	165,056	234,561	432,154
1816	81,270	154,719	236,349	428,193
1817	60,344	103,585	227,668	391,118
1818	129,510	133,095	191,025	397,965
1819	103,872	118,345	214,956	432,438
1820	70,504	120,334	224,134	501,163
1821	62,604	142,431	262,736	556,366
1822	77,955	141,211	366,209	472,944
1823	59,643	115,936	241,865	441,158
1824	84,556	120,046	343,675	521,465
1825	77,373	106,543	313,788	482,964
1826	73,135	108,141	362,278	474,161

* *Parl. Pap.* no. 180 of 1828.

We have no precise figures for the period after 1826, but we are able to state that the exports of beef and pork,

[1] *Observations* vol. ii. p. 229. Full statistics of the number of cattle sold in the Ballinasloe fair from 1800 to 1848 are given in Smyth. *Ireland Historical and Statistical* vol. iii. p. 53. [2] Keating Trenor, *An Inquiry into the Political Economy of the Irish Peasantry* London 1822.

which amounted to 604,253 quarters in 1825, had sunk to 370,172 quarters in 1835.[1]

The principal cause of the decay of the provision trade in the middle of the nineteenth century was the growth of the export of live cattle. Wakefield noticed as early as 1812 that "our blockading system renders necessary a very great supply of live cattle for the use of war fleets and ships of war in the European seas. This circumstance no doubt has tended to increase the exportation of fat cattle, in a live state, from Drogheda, Dublin and Waterford."[2] This tendency towards the exportation of live stock is shown in the following table:

EXPORTS OF LIVE STOCK FROM IRELAND 1802-26*

Year ending 5th Jan.	Cows and oxen	Swine	Sheep
1802	31,664	1,968	2,891
1803	42,680	11,728	4,470
1804	28,522	12,976	7,482
1805	16,003	4,750	5,502
1806	21,941	6,383	10,988
1807	27,764	11,458	14,851
1808	26,351	17,345	14,442
1809	14,122	7,433	8,653
1810	18,335	4,712	7,596
1811	45,185	35,876	21,029
1812	68,426	57,345	24,634
1813	79,285	34,853	15,891
1814	49,592	14,521	7,690
1815	17,502	45,392	11,721
1816	33,941	127,577	26,512
1817	31,815	83,629	34,483
1818	45,322	24,418	29,478
1819	58,185	24,328	25,152
1820	52,243	61 763	19,710
1821	39,030	99,114	24,164
1822	26,759	104,556	25,354
1823	34,680	65,041	35,753
1824	46,363	82,793	55,370
1825	62,393	73,031	61,226
1826	63,524	65,919	72,191

* *Parl. Pap.* no. 180 of 1828.

[1] *Second Report of Railway Commissioners* 1838 app. B. no. 10.
[2] Vol. i. p. 751.

After 1826, we are not able to give annual statistics; we are able however to state that in 1835 the number of cows and oxen exported had increased to 89,150, and the number of swine to 125,452.[1] Ten years later they had increased still more:

EXPORTS OF LIVE STOCK FROM IRELAND 1847-50

Year ending* 5th Jan.	Oxen, bulls and cows	Calves	Swine	Sheep
1847	186,483	6,363	480,827	259,257
1848	189,960	9,992	106,407	324,179
1849	196,042	7,086	170,787	255,682
1850	201,811	9,831	68,053	241,061

* *Parl. Pap.* no. 423 of 1850.

Undoubtedly the export of live cattle was encouraged by the increasing facility of exporting cattle across the sea after the introduction of steam navigation.[2] Other causes were also in operation, the joint result of which was to injure the provision industry. "The salt provision trade" we read in 1836, "has fallen to one fourth the amount it was in war time. The causes are obviously the reduction of the navy and the army ,the equalization of the salt duty, and the quantity of live stock now taken to England by steam vessels."[3] Between 1825 and 1830 many of the duties excluding foreign provisions from the British Colonies were repealed, and Irish provisions thus lost one of their most valuable markets.[4]

One branch of the provision industry which attained large dimensions was the making of butter. Wakefield had remarked that "a much greater extent of country is covered by dairy than by grazing farms; large tracts in Kerry, Cork, and Waterford, also part of Kilkenny, Carlow, Meath, Westmeath and Longford, the mountains of Leitrim and Sligo, and a considerable portion of Fermanagh."[5] An

[1] *Second Report of Railway Commissioners* 1838 App. B. no. 10.

[2] *Thoughts on the Poor of Ireland* by a Barrister. Dublin. 1831; Lord Clements, *The Present Poverty of Ireland*, London. 1838.

[3] *Poor Inquiry Commission* App. C. part 1 p. 27.

[4] Riordan *Modern Irish Trade and Industry* p. 31.

[5] Vol. i. p. 323.

act passed in 1812 to regulate the Irish butter trade caused much dissatisfaction amongst those engaged on it, but does not appear to have inflicted any serious injury on the industry.[1]

One of the principal causes of the prosperity of the Irish provision industry in the early nineteenth century was the absence in Ireland of the excise tax on salt, by reason of which this most important commodity could be obtained cheaper than in Great Britain. The bulk of the salt used in the Irish provision trade was imported. "In Ireland," stated Wakefield, "there are few salt manufactories. Those of Waterford only purify the Cheshire rock salt, and bring it into a state fit for use...... There are salt works at Sligo. When I was in Ireland in the summer of 1808 the French were in possession of Portugal, and great alarm was spread among the provision merchants about St. Ubes' salt, which they consider as superior in curing beef and pork to any other. In the preparation of bacon and ham the Cheshire salt is found to answer exceedingly well...... The St. Ubes' salt, being longer in dissolving, is preferable; and as the provision merchants reckon the Cape de Verd next in quality they had it in contemplation to employ it, had they been debarred by the events of the war from the use of the former."[2] The passion for assimilation which became prominent about 1820 did not fail to take account of the discrepancy between the duty on salt in Ireland and Great Britain, and a proposal was made that it should be equalized in the two countries by reducing it in the latter and imposing it in the former. The Dublin Chamber of Commerce however offered such a strenuous opposition to this proposal that it was amended into a simple reduction of the duty in Great Britain.[3] The following extract from the report of the Chamber for 1823 gives a good account of the proceeding. "At the Union—the union of a rich commercial country

[1] Parnell, *Observations on the Irish Butter Acts* London 1825. Berry. *History of the R. D. S.* p. 235. *Report of Select Committee on Butter Acts* 1826, 46 Geo. III. c. 59: 52 Geo. III c. 134; 7 and 8 Geo. IV. c. 61. [2] Vol. i. pp. 757-8. [3] 3 Geo. IV. c. 82.

with a poor and agricultural one—it was recognized as not only reasonable in itself, but essential to the well being of Ireland, mainly dependent on the export of her produce, that the article of salt, so necessary to render a large portion of that produce exportable, should be exempt from the weight of taxation, to which, as an article of domestic consumption in an opulent country, it was subjected. On this equitable principle were the salt duties in the two countries then regulated. The consequent inequality in the price of salt in Great Britain and Ireland became the means of conferring important advantages on the latter—it served as a protection to her weakness, and an encouragement to her industry. The prosperity of the provision trade in all its branches it essentially contributed to promote, while her landed interests largely participated in that prosperity—thus the sources of national wealth were augmented and profitable occupation given to multitudes. It is obvious that the equalization of the salt duties in depriving Ireland of such advantages must in itself be deeply injurious to her interests...... If Ireland had only been exposed to the evils inseparable from the diminution of the burdens of England, however they might have lamented the effects, no murmur on their part would have been heard. But conjoined with the negative cause of injury, other and positive measures were proposed, which to your council did appear not only impolitic in themselves, but peculiarly inapplicable at a juncture when Ireland would have to contend with other and great disadvantages...... In Ireland, whose chief commerce arises from the export of her produce, and whose chief manufacture is its preparation for export, few are the branches of industry, to which salt is not vitally necessary, and to whose prosperity the contemplated measures must not have proved either destructive or deeply detrimental...... Sensible that the projected measures in their bearing upon the general interests of Ireland assumed an importance to which the unaided powers and limited influence of a local institution were wholly inadequate, they invited the assistance of all whose cooperation might contribute to avert impending mischief. The call was promptly complied with; meetings comprising individuals of various classes and from distant places were held; a perfect accordance of opinion and sentiment prevailed; and a petition, setting forth the evils that were deprecated, was passed and presented to Parliament...... The declaration of public opinion led to a renewed investigation. The obnoxious resolutions were recommitted, and, except as they related to the repeal of the duties in England, were abandoned."[1] Sir Robert Kane advised the Irish merchants to continue to import salt from England, and not to attempt to manufacture it in Ireland, as the Irish salt would inevitably cost more.[2]

The decay of the provision trade entailed the decay of many allied industries. Thus, the coopering trade was severely affected by the growing practice of exporting live cattle.[3] The most important of these allied industries was that of tanning. Wakefield stated that about one half of the hides produced in Cork were exported and the other half tanned there.[4] The tanning industry however did not progress with time. The evidence given before the Revenue Commissioners in 1822 established that the use of imported leather was on the increase, and that the manufacture of leather in Ireland was stationary if not retrogressive. This was attributed to the high price of bark in Ireland owing to the shortage of native oak trees, and to the recently introduced method of assessing the excise on the capacity of the vessels employed instead of on the output, a method which, it was alleged, made for hasty and careless workmanship.[5] The small protecting duties on the importation of

[1] *Report of Council of Dublin Chamber of Commerce.* Dublin 1823.
[2] *Industrial Resources* p. 273.
[3] *Poor Inquiry Commission* app. C. part 1. p. 27.
[4] Vol. i. p. 751.
[5] *Fourth Report of Revenue Commissioners* 1822. pp. 316-20.

leather goods into Ireland were removed in 1824, and the immediate result was a further diminution of the industry. "The tanneries of Ireland" we read in 1828, "are now almost totally extinct...... This loss has been occasioned by the total failure of native oak bark, and the increasing export of live cattle."[1] In 1836 there were only 60 master tanners in Dublin, and from 300 to 350 journeymen.[2] Thenceforth the leather industry steadily declined.[3] The following table shows the export of hides and leather from Ireland from 1802 to 1821:—

Year ending* 5th Jan.	Tanned hides no.	Untanned hides no.	Manuftd. leather lbs.	Unmanuftd. leather lbs.
1802	643	42,048	26,886	210
1803	1,607	32,364	3,352	2,232
1804	172	28,304	6,358	—
1805	217	36,996	3,485	565
1806	1,279	33,308	4,493	1,224
1807	1,397	23,108	5,579	1,224
1808	744	39,319	9,698	—
1809	1,263	54,396	10,538	3,578
1810	973	34,895	19,272	2,514
1811	8,245	54,846	27,524	390,818
1812	1,167	21,841	15,317	75,332
1813	594	35,254	19,579	88,456
1814	2,712	16,425	11,465	30,324
1815	82	21,131	26,176	47,003
1816	135	24,773	28,506	99,739
1817	1,236	50,758	24,928	115,883
1818	485	101,052	27,377	205,498
1819	310	53,186	34,705	196,319
1820	added to leather unmanufac- tured	11,300	28,280	120,839
1821		3,353	11,061	91,489

* *Fourth Report of Revenue Commission* 1822 App. 7.

The following table shows the quantity of leather goods imported into Ireland from Great Britain during the same period:

[1] *Sketch of the Proceedings of the Society for the Improvement of Ireland.* Dublin 1828
[2] *Poor Inquiry Commission* App. C. pt. 2.
[3] Maguire *Guide to Cork Exhibition* 1852; Riordan *Modern Irish Trade and Industry* p. 177.

Year ending* 5th Jan.	Saddlery value £	Tanned hides no.
1802	8,314	5,606
1803	7,053	9,353
1804	9,915	4,337
1805	10,628	4,704
1806	9,679	8,997
1807	10,374	15,560
1808	10,925	19,920
1809	13,183	19,418
1810	15,142	14,943
1811	12,462	12,445
1812	12,480	20,758
1813	17,837	45,259
1814	22,746	76,223
1815	17,444	38,309
1816	11,752	30,743
1817	7,284	18,8[illegible]0
1818	7,939	19,283
1819	11,977	17,811
1820	10,487	
1821	8,917	

* *Fourth Report of Revenue Commrs.* 1822 App. 13 and 20.

Section 2. The Causes of Irish Industrial Depression.

It appears from the foregoing section that manufacturing industry did not develop at all normally in the first half of the nineteenth century. The backward condition of Ireland in this respect is even more striking when it is compared with that of Great Britain in the same period. The early nineteenth century was in Great Britain a period of unprecedented industrial development, which enabled an ever-increasing population to be supported independently of agriculture. In Ireland, on the contrary, the problem of the pressure of the population on agricultural resources was more acute than in England; yet it was not solved except in the very smallest degree by the growth of non-agricultural employment. If Irish industry had developed in the fifty years after the Union at the same rate as British, the problems with which we were concerned in the first part of this book would have been much less difficult of solution and much less disastrous in their consequences. As we have said, the great problem of Irish economic life at this time was the apparent disproportion between population and resources; and the absence of any degree of manufacturing industry was a vital factor in that problem. It is therefore of the utmost importance that we should form some opinion as to whether the non-development of Irish industry was the result of avoidable or unavoidable causes ; whether it was the outcome of some inherent defect in the Irish people or in their country, or of the human institutions under which they were destined to live. Five principal causes have been suggested as accounting for the industrial decay of the time: (1) the character of the people, (2) the combinations of the workmen, (3) the scarcity of fuel in Ireland, (4) the fiscal policy of the government, and (5) the difficulty of accumulating capital under the existing land laws. Of these, the first three refer to some inherent defect in the people or the country, and the last two to some defect in the institutions under which the people lived. Let us examine what part each of these causes played in retarding the industrial development of Ireland.

(a) *The Character of the People.*

It is a common experience to come across statements to the effect that the Irish did not make an industrial success of their country because they were idle and dissolute; and that manufactures would have progressed to the same extent as in England, had not the Irish been a naturally depraved and slothful race. It is important to examine this suggestion, because, if true, it is sufficient to account for the whole industrial backwardness of Ireland without any other explanation. We shall examine the question in two parts, first inquiring whether the Irish were in fact lacking in the industrial virtues, and then inquiring whether, assuming that they were, their deficiency was the cause or the consequence of the industrial failure of the country.

We need not quote examples of the sort of vilification which was commonly cast on the Irish character at the beginning of the nineteenth century, as its nature is perfectly familiar to the readers of English newspapers at the beginning of the twentieth. We may draw attention to the fact however that the majority of the best informed observers of the period refused to endorse the opinion of the popular scribes. It cannot of course be denied that one of the evils of the Irish land system was the existence of an unusually large number of idle and unproductive people, principally recruited from the middlemen and smaller gentry.[1] The toleration of such a swarm of drones must have produced a very bad example; it would not have been surprising if the tenant class had grown to regard as a virtue the idle habits of their social superiors. Such however does not appear to have been the case. While on the one hand we find that the landlord class grasped at every opportunity to escape laborious occupation, the tenant class eagerly sought every opportunity to obtain it.

The popular fiction of the indolence of the Irish working classes is contradicted by the evidence of numerous contemporary observers. "It were injustice to say that they are not industrious," said a Belfast writer in 1819, "they labour like galley slaves. The wretchedness of their habitations and the want of certain comforts about them often induce careless and superficial observers to pronounce them idle."[2] The Select Committee on the Employment of the Poor in Ireland reported in 1823, "Your Committee have every reason to conclude that, so far from being uniformly inactive and idle, the peasantry of Ireland have a considerable anxiety to procure employment." A few years later Mr. J. E. Bicheno, a most trustworthy witness, expressed the same opinion: "The potato crops are large; the utmost

[1] Wakefield vol. ii. pp. 808-9.
[2] Mac Dougall, *A Treatise on the Irish Fisheries* Belfast 1819.

pains are taken to cultivate them; and the industry and care the people display in this business completely contradicts the charge of inherent and unconquerable indolence.... I have never seen any field cultivation in England, except perhaps hops, where more diligence is discovered."[1] " I maintain" wrote Wm. Blacker "that there is no unwillingness in an Irishman to work when sufficient remuneration is held out—but he will not work for nothing, and he would be a great fool if he did."[2] "The Irish peasantry are charged with being indolent, improvident, and factious . . . But the Irish are not indolent. If they were they could not obtain employment in England or London where they are considered to be most industrious. Neither could they prosper in America . . . It is not however necessary to travel out of Ireland for evidence of their industrious disposition, for in it industry exists wherever encouraged."[3] "If the Irish peasant" said Sir George Cornewall Lewis "were as utterly reckless and improvident as he is said to be, he would not commit crimes in order to protect the occupant of the soil; he would not see that his own interest was bound up with that of his class in preventing the ejection of tenants. It is his foresight which prompts him to crime; it is his wish to obtain some guarantee for his future subsistence which drives him to Whiteboy disturbances."[4] Sir John MacNeill, the famous engineer, gave the following evidence before the Devon Commission:—"An Irishman is the most active fellow possible if remunerated for his work; there is no idleness among them if they can turn their work to a fair remuneration . . . No man will do more, or undergo more hardship for the sake of his children, than an Irishman."[5] John Bright referred to the fact that the Irish labourers in Lancashire worked as well as, if not better than the English;[6] and W. N.

[1] *Ireland and Its Economy* p. 21. [2] *Essay on Improvement &c.* 1834.
[3] *Commentaries on National Policy & on Ireland* Dublin 1831 p. 193.
[4] *Irish Disturbances* p. 313. [5] P. 506.
[6] Barnett Smith. *Life of John Bright* vol. i. p. 250.

Hancock, the professor of political economy in Trinity College, remarked upon the same trait:—"The migrations of labourers afford the strongest proof of the energy, industry, and foresight of the Irish labourers. They are willing to undergo every toil for good pay. The self denial which they practise while in England, in order to save all they can of their wages in order to provide for their families during the winter, is the strongest proof of their providence."[1]

If the evidence of the important authorities we have cited is not to be completely overlooked, we must hesitate to pronounce the Irish labourer as being indolent. We must always bear in mind the distinction between industry and skill; the most well-meaning and assiduous workman may find himself at a disadvantage on account of the inferior opportunities of developing his faculties that he enjoys. In this sense, the Irish working classes may have been inferior to those in other countries. Indeed it would be surprising if it had been otherwise. The whole policy of the government during the eighteenth century had been to rob the Irish workman of his industrial character. The penal laws had condemned the vast majority of the people to a life of idleness and poverty; the land system had deprived the agriculturalist of all inducement to exercise the virtues of industry and thrift; and the commercial code had compelled the best of the Irish manufacturers to emigrate, if they were not to starve at home. Is it matter for wonder that this disastrous policy was attended with disastrous results? The whole aim of the government during a period of over a hundred years had been to render the Irish Catholic a degraded and impotent serf. If that policy succeeded, who should incur the blame of its consequences—the party who put it into operation, or the party against whom it was directed? The demoralizing effect of the land system on the tenantry was well summa-

[1] *On the Condition of the Irish Labourer* Dublin 1843; and see *Statement of some of the Causes of the Disturbances in Ireland* Dublin 1825.

rized by J. S. Mill:—"In such a condition what can a tenant gain by any amount of industry or prudence, or what lose by any recklessness? If the landlord at any time exercised his full legal rights the cottier would not be able to live. If by extra exertion he doubled the produce of his land or if he prudently abstained from producing mouths to eat it up, his own gain would be to have more left to pay to his landlord; while, if he had twenty children, they would still be fed first, and the landlord could only take what was left. Almost alone amongst mankind the cottier is in this condition, that he can scarcely be any better or worse off by any act of his own. If he were industrious or prudent, nobody but his landlord would gain; if he is lazy or intemperate, it is at his landlord's expense."[1]

It may be said that the penal laws had been repealed and the commercial restraints relaxed before the Union, and that to refer to these causes as the reason for the industrial weakness of the Irish character—if such weakness did in fact exist—is far-fetched. It must be remembered that it is far easier to wound the human character than to heal it; and that the characteristics which the Irish people had acquired as the result of long years of deliberate oppression were not to be removed by the mere passing of an act of parliament. As we shall see in a later chapter, the penal laws were repealed in letter rather than in spirit, and the worst evils of the Irish social system still survived. The practice of rack rents had not ceased with the mere repeal of the laws which made them compulsory in the case of Catholic tenants; and the commercial oppression of Irish industry had not passed away, but had merely assumed a new form. The whole method of working the land tended to foster idle habits in the peasantry, as was observed by Otway:—"The want of work .... operates fatally to the industrious habits of the Irish labourer; it destroys industry and encourages sloth. The habits

[1] *The Irish Land Question* p. 77.

of idleness thus engendered are by no means inconsistent with occasional laborious exertion of the most extraordinary kind. Under strong exciting circumstances the Irish peasant will work harder than the labourer of any other country; but this toil is neither steady nor continuous. The season of total inactivity comes as regularly as the seasons of violent exertion, and the character of the peasant is rendered all the worse by the striking magnitude of the vicissitude."[1]

One factor constantly cited as evidence of the inherent idleness of the Irish people is the number of public holidays that were observed. The Irish were said to lose one or two days a week in holidays.[2] It was generally deemed indecorous to work in a townland where a death had taken place till the day after the funeral.[3] Wakefield's language on this point is very emphatic. "The state of the prevailing religion in Ireland, and the manner in which the affairs of the Catholic Church are conducted, have a very powerful tendency to diffuse a spirit of idleness among the people; as the priest depends for an income on the gratuitous donations of his parishioners, and as he has the power of commanding as many holidays as he chooses . . ." Wakefield, it must be observed, admits that the evils of excessive holidays were as prevalent in Ulster as in the south, and that an additional waste of time was caused by the yeomanry. "Even in Ulster, which abounds so much with Presbyterians, the idleness created by the yeomanry corps is greater than can well be conceived, but by those who have actually seen it; the lieutenant is sometimes a tenant of the captain, and frequently keeps a whiskey shop where the men receive their pay, and, unless they spend on that intoxicating liquor a considerable part of what is due to them, they are not considered as good fellows."[4] The more reasonable view of the great number of holidays is that it

[1] *Otway's Report* p. 595.
[2] Steven. *Remarks on the Present State of Ireland* London 1822.
[3] *A Letter on the State of Ireland* by an Irish Magistrate London 1825.
[4] Vol. i. pp. 518-9.

was largely caused by the prevailing low wages, and that it was rather a symptom than a cause of the industrial depression of the country.[1]

On the whole we do not think that sufficient evidence is forthcoming to warrant us in the conclusion that the industrial depression of Ireland was caused by any defect in the character of the Irish people. Indeed all the evidence points in the contrary direction; the majority of unbiassed contemporary observers denied that the Irish were tainted with an indolent or slothful character; and, in so far as the Irish character lacked the industrial virtues, the deficiency was the result, and not the cause, of the underdevelopment of the country.

The next great defect of character urged against the Irish, after idleness, was drunkenness. It is quite true that spirit drinking was exceedingly prevalent in Ireland in the early nineteenth century, until a temporary stop was put to it by Father Mathew's temperance campaign. We need not labour a point on which all testimony is agreed.[2] To admit that the Irish lower classes drank heavily is not however to admit that this evil habit was an operative cause of Irish underdevelopment. We must remember for one thing that the Irish character was always vilified by contemporary English writers, and that all the vices of the people were painted in the blackest colour possible. We cannot refrain from suspecting therefore that the accounts of Irish drinking were somewhat exaggerated. At least one case is recorded in which a large brick works was carried on for two years during which only one case of intoxication arose. It was suggested that similar results might follow in many other industries if the employers would pay their men on Saturday morning instead of on Saturday night in a public house, as was the general custom.[3] "The Irish peasant" an Irish

[1] *Muggeridge's Report* p. 726. [2] See e. g. Wakefield, vol. ii. p. 787; *An Address to the Public on Behalf of the Poor* Dublin 1815; Edgar, *An Address to the Temperate* Dublin 1829; Haliday, *Observations on the Habits of the Labouring Classes in Ireland* Dublin 1836.

[3] Trimmer, *Further Observations &c.* London 1812.

magistrate wrote "is accounted lazy and dissipated; but I doubt the truth of both of these accusations. When he has an interest in his work, he labours most diligently, and I think that the lower orders of Englishmen are as much addicted to drunkenness as the same class of the Irish. The Irishman however is more noisy when he is drunk."[1]

It must also be remembered that the temptation to drink spirits was aggravated by the very low spirit duty, and the prevalence of illicit distillation.[2] The period of twenty months in 1810-1 during which distillation from grain was prohibited was marked by a noticeable falling off in the amount of drunkenness, which was attributed to the rise in the price of spirits.[3] Twenty years later it was complained that a man could get "dead drunk for two pence".[4] In addition to the increased temptation under which the Irish suffered by reason of the cheapness of spirits, we must also bear in mind the fact that, owing to their extremely low standard of living, they were probably more affected by excessive or even moderate drinking than they would have been had they been able to afford the same diet as the English labouring classes.

(b) *The Combinations of Workmen.*

While the subject of the combination of workmen is really a subdivision of the subject last treated, it is sufficiently important to merit a separate section. To produce evidence to prove that the Irish urban workers, especially those of Dublin, were highly organized in trade unions would be pushing an open door. Mr. and Mrs. Webb describe the Dublin trades in 1830 as the "best organized in the Kingdom".[5] It is sufficient for us to state that in

[1] *A Letter on the State of Ireland* by an Irish Magistrate, London 1825.

[2] Wakefield vol. i. p. 737.

[3] *A Letter to the Rt. Hon. Henry Grattan on the Deplorable Consequences resulting to Ireland from the Very Low Price of Spirituous Liquors* Dublin 1811.

[4] Nicholls. *First Report on Poor Law* 1837.

[5] *History of Trade Unionism* p. 93.

Dublin every trade possessed a "body" or union, which insisted on certain regulations being observed with respect to apprentices, wages, and hours; and that the "bodies" or unions of the different trades were themselves united in some larger body, the precise nature of which it is difficult to ascertain. The supreme authority of the trades seems to have been the Board of Green Cloth "whose dictates became the terror of the employer".[1] This Board exercised jurisdiction over no less than nineteen trades.[2] Associations similar to those in Dublin existed in the other towns of Ireland.[3]

How far the Irish unions were connected with the English it is impossible to say. It has been, and is frequently asserted that the bond of union between the workers in the two countries was very close, and that the Irish workers were used as a tool to ruin Irish industry in the interests of English rivals. It must be confessed however that evidence in support of this charge is not forthcoming. The committees which investigated trade unionism endeavoured to gather some enlightenment on this point, but the information they elicited was very vague and unsatisfactory. The following evidence of Mr. Robert Hutton, a Dublin coachbuilder, is typical:—"Does the union which exists in Dublin hold any correspondence with similar associations in England ?—I believe it does.—With London or with Liverpool ?—I have been told with both.—With any other places ?—I have been told they have a general correspondence".[4] The evidence of Mr. Farrell, chief constable of the Dublin police, was more definite, but it does not enlighten us as to the nature of the correspondence

[1] *Ibid.* [2] *Select Committee on Combination Laws* 1825 p. 9.

[3] Those who desire full information on the Irish trade unions will find abundant details in the Reports of the Select Committees on *Artisans and Machinery* 1824, on the *Combination Laws* 1825, and on *Combinations of Employers and Workmen* 1838. The evidence given before these committees is summarized in Ryan, *The Irish Labour Movement* pp. 46 sq. There is also much valuable information in the *Evidence on Combinations* contained in Appendix C of the Poor Inquiry Commission's Report. Some information is also to be found in the *Official Papers Public Record Office Dublin* 1790-1831 subhead *Combinations*, particularly with regard to combinations on the Grand Canal, in Limerick, and in Bandon. [4] *Select Committee on Combination Laws* 1825 p. 14.

between the English and Irish unions:—"Do you know whether or not the Dublin clubs are connected by correspondence with the English clubs?—There are a few trades; the ironmoulders and foundrymen, that have a general correspondence throughout the empire.—The tailors?—No, not the tailors; the curriers, hatters, and thickset cutlers."[1] The best conclusion at which one can arrive is that there was no general rule in the matter. While some of the Irish workers, for example the carpenters and bricklayers, were enrolled in the same union as the English, others, such as the printers, had "no pecuniary connexion but communication by correspondence only", and others again, such as the painters, had no correspondence of any kind.[2] Cases were not unknown where the English unions supplied funds to the Irish to enable them to maintain a strike, and the Irish unions frequently supported each other in the same way.[3]

It is also frequently stated, as a commonplace that admits of no dispute, that the combinations were the principal cause of the decay of Irish industry. Of course there is no doubt that an industry which is constantly harassed by strikes is at a disadvantage compared with one where perpetual harmony prevails between masters and men, and it is indisputable that many individual employers in Ireland did discontinue business on account of the incessant stoppages of work which occurred and the high wages which were enforced. There is abundant evidence of a close connexion between the prevalence of combinations and the decay of industry in Ireland.

The calico-printing trade of Belfast was very injuriously affected by strikes in 1835 as a result of which three hundred men permanently lost their employment.[4] Many years before, the woollen industry in Kilkenny had been completely

[1] *Select Committee on Artisans and Machinery* 1824 p. 295.
[2] *Select Committee on Combinations of Workmen* 1838 vol. ii. pp. 99, 104, 139, 145.
[3] *Ibid.* p. 108. *Evidence on Combinations, Poor Inquiry Commission App. C.*
[4] *Select Committee on Combinations of Workmen* 1838 vol. i. p. 237.

destroyed by the same cause.[1] The collieries in the same county were kept unworked for long intervals by reason of strikes.[2] The Dublin hat industry was said to have been ruined by combinations.[3] The once flourishing business of housepainting was allowed to pass into Scotch hands, as the Scotch workers did not obey the mandates of the Dublin union.[4] But the classical example cited to prove the injurious effects of combinations was that of the Dublin shipbuilding industry. It was generally asserted as quite beyond dispute that it was combination, and combination alone, that drove this important industry away from Dublin about 1820.[5]

We find the view expressed repeatedly in contemporary publications that it was combinations which caused the ruin of Irish industry. "That spirit of combination" we read in a pamphlet of 1817 "which has so far marred every attempt at the introduction or extension of manufactures in this country has driven both English and Irish capital out of the market."[6] Again, in 1825—"With respect to combinations it must be remembered that the frequent combinations which unfortunately have taken place among the working people of Ireland in most of the branches of trade have been the most encouraging stimulus to English importation."[7] It was Nassau Senior's opinion that "no business requiring, as all great manufacturing operations must, that many hundred workpeople should obey a single capitalist ,could be carried on in Ireland."[8] Daniel O'Connell's views on the subject are well known.

In view of these expressions of opinion it is not surprising that the allegation that combinations were the dominant cause of the decay of Irish industry should have come to

[1] John Gough. *Account of Two Journies Southward in Ireland in* 1817; Martin, *Ireland Before and After the Union* p. 68.
[2] *Defence of the Court of Directors of the Grand Canal Company* Dublin 1815.
[3] *Fourth Report of Revenue Commissioners* 1822 App. 44.
[4] *Select Committee on Combinations of Workmen* 1838 vol. ii. p. 160.
[5] *Select Committee on Condition of Irish Poor* 1824; *Select Committee on Combination of Workmen* 1838 vol. ii pp. 5-6, 119.
[6] *Sketch of the Origin and Progress of the Merino Factory in County Kilkenny* Dublin 1817.
[7] G. F. Dalton. *Tria Juncta in Uno.* Dublin 1825.
[8] *Ireland Journals &c.* p. 113.

be accepted at the present day as an indisputable truth. We must always be careful, however, in estimating the weight to be attached to the statements of contemporary observers of historical events, to distinguish between statements of fact and expressions of opinion. It is because we regard the utterances which we have quoted as falling within the latter category that we have refrained from committing ourselves to complete agreement with them. It will be noticed that we used a very guarded expression above—"There is abundant evidence of a close connexion between the prevalence of combinations and the decay of industry in Ireland." This sentence does not suggest which of these closely related phenomena was the cause, and which the effect of the other; and it would seem rash to conclude, because two events happened simultaneously, that one was caused by the other, until all other possible causes have been eliminated. We do not wish here to pronounce a definite opinion as to whether the industrial decay of Ireland was caused by the combinations; all that we wish to do is to warn the reader against jumping to conclusions without a full examination of all the other possible causes of that industrial decline. The trade unionism of the early nineteenth century was defensive rather than offensive; it aimed rather at the retention of old privileges than at the acquisition of new. It is obvious that a movement of this kind, desperately anxious to preserve the workers' former advantages in the face of changing conditions, would tend to become more and more violent in proportion to the extent to which the maintenance of the old prosperity was assailed. It is not altogether unreasonable to suggest therefore that the activity and violence of the Irish trade unionists were the effect rather than the cause of the general decay of Irish industry.[1] We do not wish to have it understood that we agree with this argument our-

[1] The defensive character of the Dublin unions appears very clearly from a Petition to the Lord Lieutenant from the journeymen carpenters in 1820. *Official Papers Public Record Office Dublin* carton 304 no. 2220.

selves, any more than that we disagree with it; all we wish to do is to emphasize the necessity of keeping an open mind on this important question until all the other possible causes of the decay of Irish industry have been excluded.

As an example of the danger of jumping to hasty conclusions in this matter we may refer to the classic case of the Dublin shipbuilders. The opinion that this industry was driven from Dublin by combinations has become a commonplace. Yet Mr. Hall, a prominent solicitor ,gave the following evidence before the Select Committee on Artisans and Machinery in 1824:—"Do you know what has led to shipbuilding being discontinued in Dublin ?—There are many causes for it; want of capital and want of trade; the men are mostly gone away from it.—Are you able to state whether it has principally left Dublin in consequence of the disputes between the masters and men ?—Very much so; for there is a line of demarcation drawn between masters and journeymen generally; the masters will not treat with the men, they rely mostly on the combination law."[1] It will be noticed that this impartial witness did not regard disputes as a primary cause of the desertion of Dublin by the shipbuilding industry; and that, in so far as he regarded it as a cause at all, he attributed the blame, not to the men, but to the masters. Again, it must not be forgotten that the men always continued to aver that the industry had been ruined on account of the masters' insisting on employing unskilled workers, with the result that the work was so badly done that Dublin acquired an evil reputation amongst shipowners.[2] It was certainly on this issue of the employment of untrained and unqualified men that the disputes in the industry always turned, because the wages of shipwrights were fixed, under a statute of the Irish Parliament, by the Recorder and magistrates at quarter

[1] p. 466.
[2] *Evidence on Combinations Poor Inquiry Commission* Appendix C part 2.

sessions.[1] We must also refer in this connection to the remarkable evidence of a master calico printer, Mr. Osbrey, before the Revenue Commissioners, as showing how intimately the rise of the combinations was connected with the threatened decay of Irish industries from other causes—in this case, from the repeal of the Union duties. Mr. Osbrey was asked: "Do you not think that competition would be the best means of putting an end to the combinations; that if they raised their prices upon you, and you could bring in the manufactures of the other country, it would enable you to reduce them?"; and the reply was: "It would reduce them in one way, but very fatal to the Irish manufacture, as it would put down the manufacture along with the combination."[2]

We have said enough to show that the workmen who engaged in combinations should not be convicted without a hearing. There were moreover certain circumstances, some peculiar to Ireland and some common to the whole United Kingdom, which must be taken into account before pronouncing a general condemnation of their conduct. We must remember that, although the law regarded combinations of men and combinations of masters with equal disfavour, the latter were in practice connived at, while the former were ruthlessly suppressed. The following is the evidence of an employer before the Select Committee on Artisans and Machinery in 1824:—"From: what you understand of what you call the combination laws now existing, do you know whether they are considered equal between the masters and men?—I am persuaded that they are considered unequal; they provide against the workmen, but I think the masters may evade them without risk.—Do you think that the conviction that an inequality exists may not have produced a good deal of the irritation and increased the combinations and consequent outrages?—I should think so."[3] "The Dublin brewers, distillers, soap

[1] Ryan, *Irish Labour Movement* p. 65. [2] *Fourth Report* app. 35. [3] p. 442.

manufacturers and other traders", we read in a pamphlet written in 1831, "are avowedly in combination to maintain uniform prices, and, sanctioned by their example, the tradesmen and labourers demand uniform wages."[1]

The masters, moreover, entrenched behind the privilege given them by this partial administration of the law, frequently behaved with extreme harshness towards their employees. At the time of the amalgamation of the British and Irish currencies, many masters refused to pay their men in the new currency, thus reducing their real wages; wages were paid irregularly, often late on Saturday night, and sometimes in bad coin; cases were not unknown where government contractors, who received thirty shillings a week from the public purse on account of each man whom they employed, refused to hand over more than eighteen shillings to the workman to whom it was due; and the attitude of the masters to the men was oftener than not tyrannical and unconciliatory.[2] "A very general outcry of combination has been raised against the operatives, in some cases without cause, and in others with cause connected with every degree of aggravation."[3]

Compared with the attitude of the masters, that of the men does not appear unreasonable. They frequently consented to a reduction in wages. "In the winter after the late peace the masters asked a reduction when business was in a declining state, which was agreed to by the journeymen, with an understanding that, if trade got better, the masters should give the regulated rate."[4] "I think it was in September 1816, from the depression of trade, we thought our employers ought to get some fall of the prices, so we called a general meeting of the journeymen, and agreed to a reduc-

[1] *Commentaries on National Policy and on Ireland* Dublin 1831.

[2] *Evidence on Combinations, Poor Inquiry Commission* app. C. part 2; *Select Committee on Combinations of Workmen* 1838 vol. ii. pp. 113, 128, 143-4.

[3] George Home. *Suggestions for Giving Employment to the Manufacturers in the Liberty* Dublin 1826.

[4] *Select Committee on Artisans and Machinery* 1824. Evidence of Charles Graham, journeyman saddler, p. 447.

tion of 2/6 in the pound."[1] On the establishment of the Irish Board of Trades in 1839, the operatives issued an address to the public in which they stated:—"We promise solemnly to enter heart and hand into the views of the manufacturers when they tend to the encouragement of trade, and our motto shall be 'high wages is not our object, but the establishment of Irish patronage for Irish manufacture on a solid and permanent basis'."[2]

As we said above, the unions were defensive rather than offensive. Far more disputes seem to have arisen on account of attempts by the masters to break away from some established custom of the trade than on account of attempts by the men to introduce new ones. "In the tenacity with which we find tradesmen in Ireland adhere to the laws of combination, we have a most decisive proof that men who once possessed certain comforts will make every effort to retain them."[3]

The above circumstances applied to the whole United Kingdom at the time; but there were additional circumstances peculiar to Ireland which rendered strong trade union action necessary. The vast majority of the working class in the towns was composed of Catholics, who, although legally admissible into the guilds, were not so admitted in fact, and had to form new bodies to enable them to take corporate action in matters relating to their trade.[4] Again, on account of the consolidation of farms and the consequent evictions, vast numbers of unemployed workers flocked in from the country to the towns, and would have reduced the standard of wages, had not those already engaged in the trades been very jealous of their privileges.[5] It is to this latter cause that we may attribute the fact that the Dublin dock porters formed an effective combination much

[1] *Ibid.* Evidence of Christopher Leahy, cabinet maker p. 454.
[2] *Report of the Irish Board of Trades* Dublin 1840.
[3] *Present State of Ireland* by James Cropper, Liverpool 1825.
[4] Ryan, *Irish Labour Movement* p. 70; *Select Committee on Combination Laws*, 1825, p. 12.
[5] Hancock. *On Laissez Faire and the Economic Resources of Ireland.* Dublin 1847.

earlier than any workers of the same class in England.[1]

It was also this influx of cheap country labour that caused the remarkable disproportion between the wages of unskilled and skilled workmen in Ireland. This disproportion was noticed by several observers. "We find in the towns", we read in 1825, "the wages of Irish labour 12d. per day, and those of masons, carpenters, etc. about 3/-. In the inland parts, where the former are 8d to 10d, the latter are 2/- to 2/6. Thus these workmen get three times as much as the labourers, while in England they generally obtain but 50 to 70 per cent. more."[2] Five years later we read that, "In Ireland circumstances have contributed to create a most unreasonable disproportion between the extremes in the scale, and, while the mechanic has contrived to maintain a most immoderate rate of wages, the common working classes are obliged to rest content with a pittance."[3] "Skilled labour" according to Sir Robert Kane, "is certainly dearer in this country than in Great Britain, whilst unskilled labour is much cheaper."[4]

We must warn the reader to refrain from drawing the conclusion from the quotations we have given that the cost of labour in general was higher in Ireland than in Great Britain. It must be remembered that the disproportion to which we have referred was caused as much by the cheapness of the unskilled as by the dearness of the skilled labour; that the cost of living was said to be higher in Dublin than in English towns;[5] and that the cost of labour in general could only be ascertained by investigating the proportions

[1] *Evidence on Combinations, Poor Inquiry Commission* App. C. part 2. On the terrible conditions which prevailed in Dublin and other towns owing to the immigration of a large unemployed rural population, see, *An Address to the Public on Behalf of the Poor* Dublin 1815: *Report of Select Committee on State of Poor in Ireland* 1830 pp. 15-16; *Poor Inquiry Commission* app. C. pt. 2 p. 101; *A Letter to the Commissioners of the Landlord and Tenant Inquiry on the State of the Law in Respect of the Building and Occupation of Houses in Towns* Dublin 1844; *Report of the Dublin Sanitary Association* 1849; Two papers by W. Hogan in the first volume of the Proceedings of the Dublin Statistical Society, etc.

[2] *The Present State of Ireland* by J. Cropper. Liverpool 1825.

[3] George Grierson, *The Circumstances of Ireland Considered* London 1830.

[4] *Industrial Resources* p. 383.

[5] *Select Committee on Combinations of Workman* 1838 vol. ii. p. 173.

which skilled and unskilled labour bore to each other.[1] Another cause which probably operated to strengthen trade unionism in Ireland was the absence of a poor law. In England, if a worker lost his employment, he could fall back on the parish; whereas in Ireland he would be exposed to starvation in the absence of a legal provision for the poor.[2]

Another cause which undoubtedly tended to render Ireland a fertile soil for the growth of combinations was the long experience which Irish workers had had of conspiracies to resist oppression. Practically from time immemorial the Irish peasantry and small tenant farmers had formed a well organized and effective combination for their protection against the extortions and exactions of the landlords, and it cannot be doubted that the experience of centuries of combination in the country helped the formation of combinations in the towns. The connection between the two becomes still more indisputable when we recall the fact that the Irish land problem was in reality a labour problem. As we saw above, the essential injustice of the Irish tenant's position was that the landlord took the whole surplus of what the tenant produced. In the case of cottiers and small tenants the rent was paid, not in money, but in labour. Here therefore we have a state of affairs where landlord and tenant are strictly convertible terms with employer and workman. This aspect of the cottier system appears clearly from J. S. Mill's analysis:—"The produce on the cottier system, being divided into two portions, rent and the remuneration of the labourer, the one is evidently determined by the other. The labourer has what the landlord does not take; the condition of the labourer depends on the amount of rent."[3] Lewis saw this clearly: "Whiteboyism sets the rich against the poor, it sets the poor against the rich.... It is not the banding together of a few outcasts who betake themselves to illegal courses, and prey on the rest of the

[1] Kane, *Industrial Resources* p. 383.
[2] *Journal of Dublin Statistical Society* vol. ii. p. 456.
[3] *The Irish Land Question* p. 72

community; but the deliberate association of the peasantry, seeking by cruel outrage to insure themselves against the risk of utter destitution and abandonment. Its influence therefore, even when unseen, is general; it is in fact the mould into which Irish society is cast; the expression of the wants and feelings of the great mass of the community."[1] The suggestion that Whiteboyism was really a labour movement is corroborated by the fact that it only embraced the cottiers and poorest of the small farmers, and did not include the substantial tenants.[2] In this respect Whiteboyism is in striking contrast with the Land League; the latter included tenants of all descriptions and ranks, whereas the former included none but farmers who were also labourers. In other words, the Land League was strictly an agrarian, and Whiteboyism principally a labour movement.

This aspect of Whiteboyism was thoroughly appreciated by contemporary observers. "The objects of the Ribbonmen," wrote an Irish landlord in 1821, "are first to compel the landholders and middlemen to reduce their nominal rents; secondly to compel the farmers and others not to pay more than certain fixed rents; thirdly to compel farmers and others not to pay less than certain wages; and fourthly to compel the labourers not to receive less than certain wages."[3] "The unreasonable smallness of the remuneration for agricultural labour has enabled the designing wretches, who abound in some Irish districts, to band the peasantry into lawless associations, for the purpose of dictating the amount of remuneration which shall be given and accepted. It is the same system that prevails amongst tradesmen in towns."[4] Ebenezer Shackleton expressed the opinion that "the frequent bursts of insubordination in Ireland.... have mostly commenced in disputes con-

1 *Irish Disturbances* p. 306.
2 Lewis, *Irish Disturbances* p. 185
3 *Thoughts on the Report of the Committee on Agricultural Distress* by a Proprietor of Land Dublin 1821.
4 *Commentaries on National Policy and on Ireland* Dublin 1831.

cerning tithes, but have almost always ended in attempts to reduce rents or advance wages."[1] William Conner, whose writings on the Irish land question are very important, complained that the method by which the county roads were constructed by the labourers for the convenience of the landlords was precisely analogous to improvements in a factory being paid for by the operatives.[2] Lewis in his valuable book on Irish Disturbances emphasizes this side of Whiteboyism:—"The Whiteboy Association—which includes Rightboys, Threshers, Whitefeet, Blackfeet, Terry Alts, Captain Rock's men, etc.—may be considered as a vast trade union for the protection of the Irish peasantry; the object being, not to regulate the rate of wages or the hours of work, but to keep the actual occupant in possession of his land, and in general to regulate the relations of landlord and tenant for the benefit of the latter. Certain other objects are occasionally added, the chief of which is to prevent the employment of a stranger, the quantity of work being in the opinion of the labourers already insufficient."[3] Dr. Sigerson calls the Rockite insurrection an agrarian "strike"[4]; and James Connolly was of opinion that the Ribbon Conspiracy "was in effect a secret agricultural trade union of labourers and cottier farmers."[5]

Indeed the analogy between trade unionists and Whiteboys was at all points complete. The former insisted on minimum wages, the latter fixed maximum rents; the former sought to reduce the hours in the working day, the latter to prevent the increase in the days in the working year by strict observation of the customary holidays; the former resented the employment of untrained apprentices and men outside the union, the latter objected to the admission of strangers to the tenancy of lands in their district. The

[1] *Poor Law the Best Cure for Boyism in Ireland* Dublin 1832.
[2] *The True Political Economy of Ireland* Dublin 1835.
[3] p. 99. [4] *Irish Land Tenures* p. 159.
[5] *Labour in Irish History* p. 107.

grievances of the Threshers, as enumerated by Lord Buckingham in 1806, included "the letting of land to stranger occupants, the county rates, and wages."[1] In 1815 threatening notices were served on Kerrymen working in county Cork, and on Connaughtmen by King's County men. We have evidence of the existence of a combination in county Kildare "to prevent the hiring of strangers for the harvest works and to fix a rate of wages."[2] Combinations were formed amongst the road makers in county Cork to insist on a minimum rate of wages.[3]

The aptitude which the Irish showed in combining to protect their interests in the country cannot have been without its effect when they migrated to the towns. Beaumont remarked that the success of combinations in Ireland was owing to the fact that the workers applied the principles of Whiteboyism to industry [4]; and Nassau Senior said that "the insurrectionary law of the towns differs from that of the country only in its immediate object. It aims at influencing the relation between employer and labourer, instead of that between landlord and tenant."[5] The Irish carried their memories of Whiteboyism, not alone to the cities of Ireland, but to England and Scotland. They took a prominent part in organizing trade unions wherever they settled in Great Britain; in Glasgow and its neighbourhood the formidable union of the cotton spinners was first organized by the Irish immigrants.[6]

Considering the experience of the Irish in the matter of combination, and the great provocation which the Irish workers received from their employers, it is not surprising that trade unionism was active in the Irish towns during the early nineteenth century. At the same time we cannot help feeling that it was not quite so formidable as is some-

[1] *Fortescue MSS* vol. VIII p. 464.
[2] *Official Papers Public Record Office Dublin* carton 304 no. 2220.
[3] *Ibidem:* carton 304 no. 2146.
[4] *L'Irlande Sociale* 1834 vol. ii. p. 117.
[5] *Ireland Journals &c.* 1844 p. 34.
[6] Lewis. *Report on Irish Poor in Great Britain. Poor Inquiry Commission* p. xxiii.

times suggested. The general impression left on one's mind by a perusal of the evidence before the various committees that investigated the subject is that the Irish trade unions were neither so dangerous nor so violent as they were generally painted by their opponents. Some of the keenest observers of Irish life at the time expressed the opinion that the prevalence of trade unionism was much exaggerated. The Repeal Association reported that it was untrue that the Irish were more addicted to combination than the English[1]; and Sir John MacNeill, the well known engineer who constructed the Dublin and Drogheda Railway, said that the workers were on the whole tractable, and seldom struck.[2] But the most valuable authority we can quote on the subject is Sir Robert Kane, who devoted to it considerable attention, and stated his conclusions in a passage which we cannot refrain from quoting in spite of its length:—"No person really conversant with the progress of industry in the two countries would assert that there is more combination here than in Great Britain. The history of industry in England for the last century presents a series of the most violent outbreaks, riots, and combinations, murders of the most amiable employers, destruction of machinery and mills; in fact, such an array of illegal interference with the just rights of property and labour, as would, if judiciously worked up by an active editor, supply materials for a history of Great Britain that has not yet been written. But these events are lost sight of by the public in the vast extent of British industry. The ringleaders are punished; the general mass return to their work; in no case has the object of the strike been at all successful, for the unfortunate artisans, seeking to enforce from particular localities or employers what the general progress of industrial discovery opposes, must yield before the movement of the age, and by warring against, in place of moulding themselves to it, too often suffer under its evils, without being able to participate in its goods.

[1] *Reports* vol. i. p. 255. [2] *Devon Comm.* p. 506.

"In this country, however, cases of combination derive an extrinsic importance from causes quite independent of their true nature. Our industry is so limited in amount, that a disagreement, which in England would never be heard of, except by those immediately concerned, becomes a topic of universal comment, and, unfortunately, the organs of public opinion are too often hurried by the eagerness of political feeling into speaking of a quarrel between an employer and a few men, as if it were a general outbreak of the working against the employing classes. Thus some time ago a sugar bakery was erected in Cork, and the proprietor very properly brought over from England bricklayers conversant with the modes of setting the pans and other apparatus. For the rough work, to which only they were really competent, Irish bricklayers were employed, but these, finding that the Englishmen worked for lower wages than the Cork standard, refused to work with them. In this they were perfectly justified. The Irish bricklayers had a clear right to leave work and stay idle, if they preferred it to earning money. But they went further, and demanded that the English bricklayers should be dismissed ,and that none but the workmen at high rates of wages should be employed. Here they were totally in the wrong, and the proprietor very properly refused to comply. The idle workmen stood about the gates for a few days; their wives favoured the proprietor with a course of Munster billingsgate; but the intervention of a few policemen restored order, and the matter was really so unimportant that in a week it was forgotten in Cork.

"But it was not forgotten elsewhere. The journals took it up, and forgetting that the whole affair was a question of working for wages under the ordinary rate, they seized on the question of English and Irish, and poured out on the poor ignorant Cork workmen and their unhappy country, column after column of vulgar abuse and contumely. We were savages, brutal rioters; the whole was but one indication of the hatred we bear to Englishmen; of the stupid obstinacy with which our barbarism repels the introduction of intelligence and civilization from the sister kingdom; and, not only were such absurdities printed by the most eminent daily press, but the articles were reprinted in works pretending to be purely statistical, and it was inferred, that Ireland is in a state of social barbarism; that if mills were erected they would be burned; if masters gave employment their throats would be cut; that the means of earning wholesome food and healthful habitations, of dressing comfortably, and educating their children to useful trades, are looked upon in Ireland as objects sedulously to be avoided; that the native Irish have an indomitable and natural taste for rags and dirt, for sloth and hunger, for violence and murder. We can afford to laugh at such tirades now. After all the schoolmaster is abroad.

"Besides the fact of the importance of such strikes being magnified by the unwholesome appetite for political excitement which pervades this country, there is another, perhaps still more influential in its operation upon trade. Employers are in Ireland much less able to stand out against strikes than in the sister kingdom. They possess less capital; its rapid circulation is a matter of more pressing necessity, and hence any temporary interruption is more felt."[1]

Indeed, on a review of the whole subject, we are driven to the conclusion that what was so loudly condemned by the Irish public opinion of the day, as voiced by O'Connell, was not the combinations themselves so much as the violent and tyrannical methods of which they were sometimes guilty. There is no doubt that the trade unions, especially before the repeal of the Combination Laws, were frequently guilty of much cruelty and harshness, which were features of the trade unionism of that date elsewhere than in Ireland.[2]

[1] *Industrial Resources of Ireland* pp. 384-6.

[2] On the brutality sometimes employed in trade disputes in Dublin see *Select Committee on Combination Laws* 1825, and *Select Committee on Combinations of Workmen* 1838.

(c) *The Scarcity of Fuel in Ireland.*

The third alleged reason for the backwardness of Irish industry which we shall examine is the shortage of coal in Ireland. We shall in the first place give some account of the supply of coal in Ireland, and in the next place of the facilities that existed for obtaining it abroad.

Wakefield gives a good account of the Irish collieries in 1812. According to him there were two coal mines worked in Ulster, one at Ballycastle, the other in County Tyrone, between Dungannon and Stewartstown, and an unsuccessful attempt had been made to convey coal from these mines to Dublin. "In Connaught", we learn, "collieries have been worked at Arigna, one of which I visited in 1809 . . . These works belonged originally to a company of the O'Reilly's, who having failed, it fell by mortgage into the hands of the Latouches, who are said to have already lost in consequence of their interference with it £60,000. At present they are paying £500 per month and employ 253 men. Mr. Williams (the manager) comes from Staffordshire, and is apprehensive that the concern will never answer, partly on account of the difficulty he encounters in managing the working people, whom he describes as untractable, and given to laziness, intoxication, and quarrelling at patterns and fairs. Besides the coal is of a bad quality; and what has hitherto been raised is employed in the foundry. When I asked Mr. Williams whether he considered the colliery as likely to supply with fuel any considerable portion of the kingdom, he shrugged his shoulders in a significant manner without making any reply; but there appears to be very little hope that these works will ever turn out to be productive." The coalfields of Leinster were more advanced than those of Connaught. "Leinster possesses a large vein of coal" ,Wakefield continues, "which is worked near Castlecomer, and by the Grand Canal Company at Doonane. The coal here is a stone coal and is raised in immense pieces. A great part of it is conveyed to Dublin by the canal, and is sent to various parts of Ireland as back carriage for cars which go into that neighbourhood. It is used chiefly by maltsters and blacksmiths, for whose purposes it is peculiarly fitted." A certain amount of coal mining was also carried on in Munster. "A colliery, being a continuation of the vein from Castlecomer, is worked in Tipperary on the borders of Queen's County. In the county of Cork, Mr. Freeman has reopened a mine, which he is working with considerable spirit." Mr. Freeman also worked the valuable mines in the barony of Duhallow. "Some of the best pits are upon his estate to the southwest of Kanturk . . . Under the direction of an experienced artist, he has just erected at considerable expense a large water wheel to work the pump necessary for discharging the water of the pits."[1]

The Irish collieries do not appear to have made any noticeable progress in the years following Wakefield's visit. Mr. Griffith, in the valuable report which he drew up for the Dublin Society on the Leinster coalfields, reported that the annual produce of those fields was about 70,000 tons of coal and 100,000 tons of culm, the average price of the former being about 20/- and of the latter about 5/- per ton. "The collieries," adds Mr. Griffith, "have been, and are, conducted in a faulty and expensive manner in almost every department . . . . The mines have hitherto been conducted on so rude and unscientific a system, that the ruin of those engaged in them has been almost inevitable."[2] We have also an independent account of the state of the Tipperary coal field at the same date, from which we learn that all the adjoining towns were supplied for domestic purposes from the collieries. In many parts of the district the culm was so near the surface that it could be directly shovelled from the pit into the barrow. A rude

[1] Vol. i. pp. 613-8.
[2] Griffith, *Geological and Mining Report on the Leinster Coal District* Dublin 1814.

system of cooperative production or profit sharing seems to have been adopted: "When a pit is sunk and rigged, a crew of colliers will take it, work it to a certain distance on each side, pay a fine of from 5 to 20 guineas, and give one half of the coal and culm on the bank free of any expense to the proprietor." Good sinkers and colliers were enabled by this arrangement to earn about 2/6 per day.[1] At this period, the Munster coal fields would appear to have been the most advanced in Ireland. "The work (at Kanturk) has been carried on to a very considerable extent, and its annual supplies of coal and culm have materially contributed to the agricultural improvement of an immense tract of the counties of Cork and Limerick."[2] "Notwithstanding the present execrable state of the cross roads", it was stated four years later, "the produce of the Munster coal fields forces itself within nine miles of the city of Cork on the Mallow and Muskerry side, to the confines of the County of Waterford beyond Mitchelstown, and to the great public lime-kilns of Kilmallock, and that great district of the County Limerick in which it is universally used."[3]

A detailed account of the condition of the Irish collieries is contained in the report of the Railway Commissioners. From this source we learn that the Irish coal fields were not in a progressive state. The Tyrone mines had been acquired by the Hibernian Mining Company, and, though extensive workings had been made, the undertaking had not proved successful. No coal of any description was raised in the Antrim mines. The collieries in the neighbourhood of Castlecomer and Doonane produced about 120,000 tons of coal and culm annually, the coal being used for domestic purposes and for milling, and the culm for burning

[1] *A Description of the Collieries of Killenaule.* Dublin 1814.
[2] Griffith, *Geological and Mining Report on the Leinster Coal District.* Dublin 1814.
[3] Purdon, *Suggestions on the Best Mode of Relieving the Present Prevailing Distress in Part of the South of Ireland* Dublin 1818. In 1819 Sir Edward Newenham applied to the government for a loan to enable him to work his collieries at Killenaule. *Official Papers Public Record Office Dublin* carton 456 no. 1924.

lime. The price of coal at these collieries was about 20/- and of culm about 6/- per ton. The principal collieries in County Tipperary were situated at Colebrook and at Coolquil, near Killenaule. Their annual produce was about 20,000 tons. In Munster the production of coal was conducted on a small scale at Moy and Seafield, Co. Clare, Longhill and Newcastle, county Limerick, and in the neighbourhood of Tralee and Listowel. "The principal collieries are situated on the north bank of the river Blackwater; and at this moment extensive works are being carried on, particularly at Dromagh and Gurteen Collieries, ten miles west of Mallow." In Connaught the only colliery was at Arigna, where the annual product of about 2,340 tons was used for smelting iron.[1] One of the objects aimed at by the Railway Commissioners was to construct the railways in such a way as to utilize the Irish collieries for the provision of locomotive fuel, but this, in common with their other recommendations, was neglected by the government.

Sir Robert Kane devoted much attention to the Irish coal resources, and gave a very full account of the extent to which they were developed. He estimated the amount raised in the Leinster coalfield at 120,000 tons per annum, and the average price obtained at about 11/6 per ton for coal, and 4/- per ton for culm.[2] The same writer calculated that about 50,000 tons were raised annually in the Tipperary collieries, and expressed the opinion that the Munster coalfield was probably the "most extensive in the British Empire"! The collieries of the Tyrone district were worked, according to the same authority, partly by the Hibernian Mining Company and partly by private companies. "The industry of the latter has been and is profitable; the works of the former have been carried on at a loss." [3] The Antrim coal fields had been for the most part worked out, and the success of the Arigna mines had been jeopardized by

[1] *Second Report of Railway Commissioners* 1838 pp. 33-6 and App. B. no. 8.
[2] *Industrial Resources* p. 10.
[3] *Ibid.* p. 13.

speculation.[1] The following were the pitmouth prices of coal at the time:—

	Large coal	Culm
	s. d.	s. d.
Leinster*	11 6	4 0
Tipperary	12 0	5 0
Tyrone	12 0	5 0
Connaught	from 4 9 to 6 4	

* Kane *op. cit.* p. 49.

The output of the Irish collieries reached its high water mark in 1850, since when it has suffered a constant and gradual decline.[2] It is apparent that even at the zenith of its success the Irish coal mining industry did not suffice to meet the industrial needs of the country, and we must therefore direct our attention to the facilities which existed for obtaining coal from elsewhere.

In the first place, it may be remarked that the only possible external source from which coal could be obtained at the period was Great Britain, and that Ireland therefore depended on the latter for this very important factor in her industrial life. In spite of the duties to which we shall presently refer, English coal was able to undersell Irish in the Irish market. "In those parts of the south of Ireland, as at Ross and in the harbour of Waterford, to which places coal is brought by river and canal navigation from the coal mines in the County of Kilkenny and Queen's County, and coal is also brought by sea from Whitehaven, the sea-borne coal is at one half the price of the native coal of Ireland, the Whitehaven coals at the places of both meeting being on an average at about 4/- a barrel of $4^1/_2$ cwt. and the Irish being from 8 to 10 shillings the same quantity."[3] Wakefield remarked the large amount of British coal that was being imported into Ireland:—"The quality of the

[1] *Ibid.* pp. 14-19.
[2] *Report of the Coal Industry Committee* 1919.
[3] Fraser, *Gleanings in Ireland* 1802.

coal that can be obtained from the northern collieries is so bad that many persons who reside in the neighbourhood burn English coal in preference, through economy . . . From what I have heard and seen I will venture to assert that there is no vein of coal yet discovered in Ireland which can come into general consumption. This article is imported in great quantities from Workington, Whitehaven, Liverpool, North Wales, Swansea, and other places. Most of the vessels which carry corn to Liverpool, or which go with copper from Tralee to Swansea take in a cargo of coals when they return. Along the whole sea coast from Belfast to Cork, English coal is the general fuel used in gentlemen's houses, and it finds its way inland for the same purpose by the Boyne from Drogheda to Navan, and from Dublin through Kildare as far as Tullamore by one branch of the Grand Canal, and to Carlow by another. At the latter English coal is cheaper than that procured from the collieries of Castle Comer which are only at the distance of nine miles. These coals are conveyed also to Mullingar and as far as Enniscorthy. In Cork English coal is chiefly burned, and it is the kind generally used throughout the whole coast of that county. English coals are burned even in the remotest parts of Ireland."[1] Thirty years later Sir Robert Kane wrote that, "none of our districts come near enough to the coast to meet the competition of British coal."[2]

The dependence of Ireland for its coal supplies on Great Britain rendered it a matter of importance that the import of that article should be impeded by as few taxes and other restrictions as possible. The Act of Union provided that "coals on importation into Ireland from Great Britain shall be subject to burthens not exceeding those to which they are now subject." The burthen referred to was a duty of ten pence per ton. It would appear to the ordinary reader that this clause was intended to embody a permanent

[1] vol. i. p. 621.
[2] *Industrial Resources* p. 50.

and deliberate article of the treaty between the two nations; nevertheless it was flagrantly set aside four years later, when the duty was increased to 1s /9d per ton.[1] This duty, taken in conjunction with the high cost of transport before the introduction of steamships, operated to place the Irish consumer at a severe disadvantage compared with the English; Mr. Houghton, the owner of a large woollen manufactory at Celbridge, complained in 1822 that coal could be obtained in Yorkshire for 7/- a ton, but could not be obtained in Ireland for less than 28/-.[2] The injustice of the tax was aggravated by the repeal of the acts of the Irish Parliament which had made provision for the supply of coal at a cheap and uniform rate to the poor of Dublin.[3] Presumably with the object of guarding against the danger of the Irish collieries reaping any advantage, the duty was collected—with doubtful legality—on coal carried coastwise to Dublin from other ports in Ireland.[4] One cannot help noticing the fact that the enthusiasm of the Revenue Commissioners, which effected the repeal of the Union duties, did not extend to recommending the repeal of the coal duties at the same time, so that the Irish manufacturer was thus placed at a disadvantage compared with his English rival. "The woollen and cotton manufactures of Dublin", it was complained, "are at present engaged in the closest and most active competition with the woollen manufactures of Yorkshire and the cotton manufactures of Lancashire and Scotland. Everywhere coal is most extensively used in these manufactures. In Yorkshire, Lancashire, and Glasgow it costs 5, 6, or 7/- the ton, and it is consumed wholly free of duty; in Dublin, even if duty free, it would inevitably cost at present 12, 13, or 14/- the ton; but it is subject to the duty to the Crown and to local imposts which raise the price to 18, 19 or 20/-. This difference in price is to that

[1] 44 Geo. III c. 26.
[2] *Fourth Report of Revenue Commissioners* app. 23.
[3] 1 and 2 Geo. IV c. 68.
[4] *Report of the Dublin Chamber of Commerce* 1827.

amount a deduction from the profits of the Irish manufacturer, and it is in the same proportion a direct discouragement to manufacturers in Ireland. The manufactures of bottle glass, window glass, salt, refined sugar, and of several other articles in which coal is extensively consumed, are now, with scarcely an exception, abandoned throughout Ireland."[1] "It is in vain to think", reported the committee of 1830, "that the rude hand labour of Ireland can compete with the machinery of Great Britain. If the manufactures of Ireland are therefore to be sustained, it can only be by the application of machinery. But this is impeded by the duty on coals."[2]

The import duty was however but part of the burden that had to be borne by the Irish manufacturer, as the import of coal into Dublin and Cork was made the occasion of the exaction of many oppressive local dues. "A petition" we read in one of the reports of the Dublin Chamber of Commerce, "has been lately presented to Parliament praying for the repeal of the duties on coal. The direct relief from such a measure in the remission of duty must be far less considerable than that which must accrue from the consequent abolition of the local imposts and vexatious restrictions connected, in the port of Dublin especially, with the collection of the duty."[3] In addition to the import tax of 1/9, coal sold in Dublin bore a tax of 11d per ton paid to the Wide Street Commissioners, 6½d a ton to the Ballast office, and an illegal tax of 6d a ton extorted by the persons who superintended the measurement, the coal meters.[4] Year after year the Dublin Chamber of Commerce exerted itself for the abolition of these oppressive burthens.[5] The

[1] *Statement on Behalf of the Manufacturers of Ireland* Dublin 1830.

[2] *Report of Select Committee on State of the Poor in Ireland* 1830 p. 16. The duty on the import of coals is complained of in *A Short Inquiry into the Present Alarming Dearth of Coals* by a Friend to National Industry Dublin 1800, and in John Finlay's *Letters Addressed to the Irish Government* Dublin 1822, and see *Official Papers* 1790-1831 *Dublin Record Office* carton 456 no. 1950.

[3] *Report of Dublin Chamber of Commerce* 1825.

[4] *Statement of the Proceedings of the Society for the Improvement of Ireland.* Dublin 1828.

[5] See the annual reports 1821-3.

contrast between the positions of Dublin and Belfast, as coal importing centres, is demonstrated by the following list of the local dues collected in each:—

DUBLIN*

Improvement dues	11d a ton
Guild of Merchants' dues	3/6 a ship and 6d a ton
City dues: anchorage	3/1 a ship
shippage	11d a ship
Lord Mayor's fee	2/3¾d a ship
Water bailiff's fee	5/6½d a ship
Chapter & Guild fee	1/6 a ship paid over a year

BELFAST

Dues for metage	4d a ton
Dues for use of measures	3/9 „ ship
Dues for use of beams and weights	2/3 „ „

* *Parl. Pap.* no. 15 of 1831.

At length the import tax was repealed in 1831[1]. The amount of the duty collected between 1820 and 1830 was as follows:—

Year*	£.
1820	52,378
1821	52,635
1822	61,826
1823	54,456
1824	58,812
1825	69,571
1826	67,972
1827	55,704
1828	62,372
1829	74,050

* *Parl. Pap.* no. 207 of 1830.

In the following year the local exactions were abolished by two statutes, which made provision for the compensation of the existing coal meters by a tax of 4d per ton on coal landed in Dublin, except coal used for manufacturing purposes.[2] Thenceforward the Irish manufacturer was in a position to obtain coal on the same terms as the English, subject only to the difference in the cost of transport. The

[1] 1 and 2 Wm. IV c. 16.
[2] 2 Wm. IV. c. 21; 2 and 3 Wm. IV. c. 90.

Dublin manufacturers were however placed for some time at a disadvantage compared with those of Belfast and other centres, by reason of a conspiracy amongst the coal exporters and shipowners of Whitehaven, who agreed to keep up the price of coals in Dublin, and to prevent the Dublin merchants from obtaining their coals at the Whitehaven collieries and carrying them in their own ships. The result of this conspiracy was that the price of coal was thirty *per cent.* higher in Dublin than in Belfast.[1] Apart from an exceptional incident of this kind, the Irish manufacturer was, as we have said, on a complete footing of equality with his British rival. It is therefore important to inquire to what extent the increased cost of transport of coal brought to Ireland operated to create a preference in favour of the British manufacturer. In order to arrive at a satisfactory opinion on this matter it is necessary to answer two questions: how far did the cost of transport enter into the price of coal; and how far did the price of coal enter into the general costs of manufacture?

With regard to the first question, we may reply that coal was not an article into whose price the cost of transport entered very largely, especially after the introduction of steamships. "Coals are now carried to Ireland so rapidly and at so little cost from England, that manufactures cannot now be prevented from spreading in Ireland by want of coals"—such was the opinion of the Poor Inquiry Commission.[2] Sir Robert Kane held the same view.[3]

The part played by coal in increasing the cost of manufacture was also small. Sir Robert Kane devoted attention to the matter, and came to the conclusion that the difference in the cost of manufacture attributable to the cost of coal was extremely small—"Coals at a factory in Leeds cost 3/4d per ton. A forty horse-power engine burns three tons per

[1] *Select Committee on Commerce Manufactures and Shipping* 1833.

[2] *Third Report* 1836 p. 25. On the other hand the Railway Commissioners remarked that coal in Dublin cost from 16 to 18/- a ton, as against 5 or 6/- in Yorkshire. *Second Report* app. A. no. 8. [3] *Industrial Resources* p. 377.

day, which costs £200 per year. The wear of engine, oil and engineer's salary are £310, making total expense of power £510. The wages paid are £14,000 per year, and the total value of the produce £50,000. In Dublin coals are four times as dear, but the other charges of the engine being the same, the total cost of power for a similar factory is £1310. The total cost of power in Leeds is thus 1·2 per cent. of the value of the product, and in Dublin 2·62. The difference is more than balanced by the wages in Dublin. In Leeds wages form 28 *per cent.* of the value of the produce."[1] Kane's conclusion is as follows:—"There is no locality in Ireland where fuel for industrial purposes may not be had; and the cost of that fuel may not exceed, by more than half, the average cost of fuel in the manufacturing districts of England, and certainly need never be the double. The cost of fuel to generate steam power bears so small a porportion to the value of the produce of mechanical industry as to be totally unimportant in comparison with money wages and raw material . . ."[2] The Repeal Association came to the same conclusion:—"We may justly conclude that the price of fuel is very unimportant, compared with that of wages and raw material."[3] Twenty years afterwards Sir Robert Kane maintained the same opinion; in 1865 he stated that the proportion of fuel cost in production of steam-made goods was 1¼ *per cent.* in England and $2^2/_3$ *per cent.* in Ireland.[4]

It must also be remembered in considering the question of how far Irish industry suffered from the difficulty of obtaining coal, that the amount of steam-driven machinery in Ireland was very insignificant. It may be said that this was on account of the difficulty of procuring fuel; but we do not think that this was so, but that it was rather a symptom of the general industrial backwardness of the country, and of the slowness with which the industrial revolution

[1] *Op. cit.* p. 60. [2] *Ibid.* p. 64.
[3] *Repeal Reports* vol. i. p. 209.
[4] Murphy. *Ireland Political and Statistical* p. 434.

made itself felt. Steam engines were first introduced into Ireland in connection with brewing and distilling; the first steam engine constructed in Ireland was designed for the use of a distiller in Drogheda.[1] The following table illustrates the slow growth of steam as a motive power in Irish industry:

NUMBER OF STEAM ENGINES EMPLOYED IN FACTORIES IN IRELAND IN 1835.*

Town	No. of steam engines employed	Remarks
Belfast	50	earliest erected 1806, 2 in 1810, 1 in 1812, 1 in 1817.
Cork	28	earliest erected in 1815, 2 in 1817.
Dublin	29	earliest erected in 1833.
Galway	11	earliest erected in 1835.
Kilkenny.. ..	7	earliest erected in 1826.
Carrick	12	earliest erected in 1818.
Derry	8	earliest erected in 1815.
Waterford ..	7	earliest erected in 1817.

* *Second Report of Railway Commissioners* 1838 app. B no. 17.

The following table shows the extent to which steam power was used in 1850 :—

ACCOUNT OF MOTIVE POWER IN TEXTILE FACTORIES IN IRELAND.*

Type of factory	motive power	
	steam	water
	h. p.	h. p.
Cotton	353	526
Woollen	8	229
Worsted	0	36
Linen	2285	1095
	2646	1886

* *Parl. Pap.* no. 745 of 1850.

We are therefore driven to the conclusion that the scarcity of Irish coal was not an important factor in the retardation of Irish industrial development. Coal could at all times be obtained cheaper from England than from the existing Irish collieries; and the additional price that the Irish manufacturer had to pay for coal did not place him at a

[1] Curwen. *Observations* vol. ii. pp. 109 and 288.

serious disadvantage in his industry, because the cost of transport was but a small fraction of the cost of the article, the expense incurred for fuel was but a small part of the total expenses of manufacture, and the number of factories where coal was employed was but a small proportion of the factories in Ireland.

(d) *The Fiscal Policy of the Government.*

The Act of Union reduced and assimilated the duties on the importation of British goods into Ireland and of Irish goods into Great Britain. From the time of the Restoration the importation of Irish goods into Great Britain had been virtually prohibited by the high duties imposed, while, during the same period, no corresponding discouragement had existed on the importation of British goods into Ireland. The grant of free trade in 1780 did not affect the conditions of the cross-channel trade. One of the principal objects sought to be attained by Pitt's famous commercial propositions was the opening of this trade by the imposition of uniform duties in both countries; but the fear of the British manufacturers that the British market would become flooded with cheap Irish goods frustrated Pitt's attempt. In the next fifteen years the relative industrial condition of the two countries had changed; and the British manufacturers offered no opposition to the Act of Union, which contained practically the same provisions with regard to the cross-channel trade as the commercial propositions which they had so strenuously opposed. The Irish manufacturers, on the contrary, who approved of the commercial propositions, presented numerous petitions against the Act of Union. In both cases the wish of the British manufacturers was respected; the measure of which they disapproved was abandoned, and the measure of which they approved was passed.[1]

[1] For fuller details of the pre-Union fiscal policy see the author's *Economic History of Ireland in the Seventeenth Century* pp. 57-68 and 150-173 and *Economic History of Ireland in the Eighteenth Century* pp. 173-181 and 223-269.

The commercial clause of the Act of Union is so important that we reprint it at length:

"That it be the sixth article of Union, that His Majesty's subjects of Great Britain and Ireland shall, from and after the 1st day of January 1801, be entitled to the same privileges, and be on the same footing, as to encouragements and bounties, on the like articles being the growth, produce, or manufacture of either country, respectively, and generally in respect of trade and navigation in all ports and places in the United Kingdom and its dependencies; and that in all treaties made by His Majesty, his heirs and successors, with any foreign power, His Majesty's subjects of Ireland shall have the same privileges, and be on the same footing, as His Majesty's subjects of Great Britain:

"That, from the 1st day of January 1801, all prohibitions and bounties on the export of articles, the growth, produce, or manufacture, of either country, to the other, shall cease and determine; and that the said articles shall thenceforth be exported from one country to the other, without duty or bounty on such export:

"That all articles, the growth, produce, or manufacture of either country (not hereinafter enumerated as subject to specific duties), shall from thenceforth be imported into each country from the other, free from duty, other than such countervailing duties on the several articles enumerated in the schedule No. I A and B, hereunto annexed, as are therein specified, or to such other countervailing duties as shall hereafter be imposed by the Parliament of the United Kingdom, in the manner hereinafter provided; and that, for the period of twenty years from the Union, the articles enumerated in the schedule No. II. hereunto annexed, shall be subject on importation into each country from the other, to the duties specified in the said schedule No. II., and the woollen manufactures, known by the names of Old and New Drapery, shall pay, on importation into each country from the other, the duties now payable on importation into

Ireland; salt and hops, on importation into Ireland from Great Britain, duties not exceeding those which are now paid on importation into Ireland; and coals, on importation into Ireland from Great Britain, shall be subject to burthens not exceeding those to which they are now subject:

"That calicoes and muslins shall, on their importation into either country from the other, be subject and liable to the duties now payable on the same on the importation thereof from Great Britain into Ireland, until the 5th day of January 1808; and from and after the said day, the said duties shall be annually reduced, by equal proportions as near as may be in each year, so as that the said duties shall stand at ten per centum from and after the 5th day of January 1816, until the 5th day of January 1821, and that cotton yarn and cotton twist shall, on their importation into either country from the other, be subject and liable to the duties now payable upon the same on the importation thereof from Great Britain into Ireland, until the 5th day of January, 1808, and from and after the said day the said duties shall be annually reduced by equal proportions as near as may be in each year, so that all duties shall cease on the said articles from and after the 5th day of January, 1816:

"That any articles of the growth, produce, or manufacture of either country, which are or may be subject to internal duty, or to duty on the materials of which they are composed, may be made subject, on their importation into each country respectively from the other, to such countervailing duty as shall appear to be just and reasonable in respect of such internal duty or duties on the materials; and that for the said purposes the articles specified in the said schedule No. I. A and B shall be subject to the duties set forth therein, liable to be taken off, diminished, or increased, in the manner herein specified; and that, upon the export of the said articles from each country to the other respectively, a drawback shall be given equal in amount to the countervailing duty payable on such articles on the import thereof into the same country from the other; and that in like manner in future it shall be competent to the united Parliament to impose any new or additional countervailing duties, or to take off, or diminish such existing countervailing duties as may appear, on like principles, to be just and reasonable in respect of any future or additional internal duty on any article of the growth ,produce, or manufacture of either country, or of any new or additional duty on any materials of which such articles may be composed, or of any abatement of duty on the same; and that when any such new or additional countervailing duty shall be so imposed on the import of any article into either country from the other, a drawback, equal in amount to such countervailing duty, shall be given in like manner on the export of every such article respectively from the same country to the other:

"That all articles, the growth, produce, or manufacture of either country, when exported through the other, shall in all cases be exported subject to the same charges as if they had been exported directly from the country of which they were the growth, produce, or manufacture:

"That all duties charged on the import of foreign or colonial goods into either country, shall, on their export to the other, be either drawn back, or the amount, if any, be retained, shall be placed to the credit of the country to which they shall be so exported, so long as the expenditure of the United Kingdom shall be defrayed by proportional contribution: Provided always, that nothing herein shall extend to take away any duty, bounty, or prohibition, which exists with respect to corn, meal, malt, flour, or biscuit; but that all duties, bounties, or prohibitions, on the said articles may be regulated, varied, or repealed, from time to time, as the united Parliament shall deem expedient".

SCHEDULE I.

This Schedule contains the articles to be charged with countervailing duties.

SCHEDULE II.

"Of the articles charged with the duties specified upon importation into Great Britain and Ireland, respectively, according to the sixth article of Union:

Apparel	Ten pounds per cent on the true value."
Brass, wrought	
Cabinet ware	
Coaches and other carriages	
Copper, wrought	
Cottons, other than calicoes and muslins	
Glass	
Haberdashery	
Hats	
Tin plates, wrought iron and hardware	
Gold and silver lace, gold and silver thread, bullion for lace, pearls, and spangles	
Paper, stained	
Pottery	
Saddlery and other manufactured leather	
Silk manufacture	
Stockings	

The result of this provision of the Act of Union was greatly to diminish the protection which Irish industries had theretofore enjoyed, and of which they stood in such urgent need on account of their comparatively undeveloped condition. Irish industries were for all practical purposes exposed to the full strength of British competition, because, as we shall see, the ten per cent. duties were scarcely sufficient to counterbalance the many advantages of other kinds which the British manufacturer enjoyed, and were in no sense preferential. The attainment by the British manufacturer of this superior position may be approximately dated by the change of attitude to which we have called attention. So long as he felt that his Irish rival was in a position to produce as cheaply as he was, he bitterly opposed the opening of a free trade between the two countries on the ground that the British markets would be flooded with Irish goods; but, as soon as he felt convinced that the long period of preferential legislation he had enjoyed had secured him in a position where he could defy competition, he sought the opportunity to compete with the Irish manufacturer in the Irish market. The former danger was averted by the defeat of the commercial propositions; and the latter advantage was secured by the passage of the Act of Union.

From the time of the Union it was the deliberate policy of the British manufacturer to swamp the Irish market and to drive his Irish competitor out of business. Any circumstance which threatened to hinder this commercial invasion was bitterly resented. Thus, widespread alarm was aroused at the suggestion that the growing practice of raising public loans for Irish purposes in England would create such an adverse balance of exchange as to cause large quantities of Irish goods to be imported into Great Britain.[1] The fear was however unwarranted, as the carefully fostered superiority of the British capitalist enabled him to undersell the Irish in the Irish market. "In spite of the high duties", we read in 1804, "and the disadvantage of the rate of exchange, English manufactures of all kinds except linen are imported into Ireland, and sold there of a better quality and at a lower price than those of the country".[2] Ten years later Sir Henry Parnell complained in the House of Commons that, "in Ireland every effort that has been made to establish manufactures has been defeated by the cheapness with which English manufactures can be sold there".[3] The anxiety of the government at this time to remove every barrier to the free intercourse between the two countries is evidenced by a letter written by Lord Auckland to Lord Grenville in 1806: "The Committee of Council addressed yesterday a short minute to the Treasury, recommending a bill to be brought in to give a free intercourse and interchange respecting every species of grain between Great Britain and Ireland; and consequently to make

[1] Lord Lauderdale, *Hints to the Manufacturers of Great Britain on the Consequence of the Irish Union.* Edinburgh 1805.
[2] *The Real Cause of the High Rate of Exchange.* Dublin 1804.
[3] *Substance of the Speeches of Sir H. Parnell Bart.* London 1814.

a further and important step towards the completion of the Union"[1]

In the twenty years following the Union the complaints of distress amongst the Irish manufacturing interests were constant. "The present commercial distress of this country", it was complained in 1810, "and more particularly of this metropolis, afford ample and melancholy material for disquietude. In the memory of the oldest inhabitants of Dublin, a period of more general distress than the present can scarcely be recollected."[2] Six years later a member of the Dublin Society complained that the artisans of the city had been reduced to a potato diet, and referred to the great difficulty which the Dublin operatives in the textile manufactures experienced in finding employment.[3] In the following year 74,000 operatives were out of employment in Dublin alone.[4] Ireland obtained but a negligible share of the great commercial advantages that England derived from the Napoleonic War. "The chief gain" according to Dr. Cunningham, "which accrued to England during the Revolutionary and Napoleonic Wars was the monopoly which she practically secured of the shipping of the world. The United States was a real competitor; but England attained a position which she had never attained before. Ireland however had little or no mercantile marine; the profits of the carrying trade, and of the trade with distant countries, was not for her. What she could do was to provide for the victualling of vessels, as well as to furnish supplies of sailcloth; the Irish salt beef, which ships obtained at Cork, had a high reputation, but a certain new activity in these trades was almost the only advantage which accrued to Ireland from the great commercial monopoly by which England gained so much".[5]

[1] *Fortescue MSS* vol. viii p. 151.

[2] *A Short Inquiry into the Causes of the Present Distresses of the Irish Traders* Dublin 1810.

[3] *Suggestions Submitted to the Consideration of the Nobility etc. of Ireland* by a Member of the Dublin Society Dublin 1816.

[4] John McGuire, *A Plan of General and Perpetual Employment*, etc. Dublin 1817.

[5] *Growth of English Industry & Commerce* vol. iii p. 846.

Every year that passed accentuated the inequality that existed between the British and Irish manufacturers. "At the Union", it was stated in 1818, "the calico trade enjoyed a protecting duty of ten per cent. ad valorem, over and above twelve pence halfpenny a yard square; one penny a yard of the duty was to be taken off every year, the ad valorem duty remains; in 1800 we had in the vicinity of Dublin 19 printing calico manufactories employing 1200 persons; in 1818 there are four employing about 120 persons. In 1800 we made cloth of the finest and most durable kind; Balbriggan employed near two thousand persons; the sound of the shuttle was heard throughout the Liberty—in 1818 we make thin reduced cloth at five pence per yard; no furniture cloth: Balbriggan almost a desert, and the Liberty silent—its Protestant inhabitants have fled to America. Again in 1800 we had 17 paper mills employing 2000 people; we have now 5. Other manufactories have suffered in proportion. Nothing in fact can secure even our home consumption, but high protecting duties; large drawbacks and high bounties may give us an export."[1] "It is obvious" wrote O'Driscoll five years later, "that the Union destroyed all the weak and feeble manufactures of the country; all those which required the shelter of the walls of Parliament and the constant superintendence of a close and anxious concern. The Union stripped them of all this, and exposed them suddenly to the visitation of a rude and withering competition with the manufactures of England; or to what was quite as bad, a competition impending and in view. The Union also, by increasing the number of absentees, withdrew the consumer, and left the fruit of industry to rot upon the ground...... The Union destroyed the feeble manufactures of the south."[2]

Towards the end of the period indicated for the continuance of Union duties the Irish manufacturers displayed

[1] *A Freeman's Letter to the Rt. Hon. Robert Peel*, Dublin 1818.
[2] *View of Ireland*, vol. i. pp. 229-38.

considerable anxiety about their lapse. As early as 1817 the woollen manufacturers had seen Peel with a view to procuring their extension; and in 1819 a petition was presented to the government from the "manufacturers of the City of Dublin engaged in woollen, worsted, stuff, silk, cotton, iron and various other branches of trade", praying for the continuance of the duties. In the following year the "spinners, manufacturers, bleachers, and printers of cotton in the town and neighbourhood of Belfast" represented to the government that the abrogation of the duties would be "ruinous" to their interests; and the cotton manufacturers of the whole of Ireland petitioned in the same sense. The Dublin woollen manufacturers were anxious that the woollen industry should be "popularized", as the linen had been in the previous century.[1] These representations were not without effect; for in 1820 the government decided that the duties should not be immediately abolished, but should be gradually reduced. An act was accordingly passed providing that the duties should remain at ten per cent. until the 31st of December 1825, and that they should then be decreased by four equal quinquennial reductions, and should finally cease in 1840.[2] If this act had not been repealed, the Irish manufacturer would have had a reasonable period in which to prepare for the competition which he might expect to meet on the abolition of the duties; and, in fact, many manufacturers increased their establishments on account of the preference in the Irish market which the act apparently guaranteed. The feeling produced by the act in England was however very different; the English manufacturers felt that they had been cheated of the valuable Irish market which they had been anxiously preparing to flood with English goods; and the commercial and manufacturing classes commenced an agitation against the continuance of the duties. One of the first acts of the

[1] *Official Papers Public Record Office Dublin* 1790-1831 carton 457 nos. 2135 and 2228.
[2] 1 Geo. IV. c. 45.

newly founded Manchester Chamber of Commerce was to protest against what it considered the backward step of the legislature. It was the resolution passed on this occasion that gave the Manchester School its name.[1]

Consequently the subject of the Union duties was raised in the following session of parliament, when a commission was appointed to inquire into various matters connected with the revenue in Ireland. This commission received a great deal of evidence dealing with the protecting duties, and issued several bulky reports. It is interesting to examine the evidence which was given, as it shows that the commercial and manufacturing classes in Ireland were unanimously opposed to any departure from the provisions of the act of 1820.

Mr. Willans, the largest woollen manufacturer in Ireland, strongly urged that the removal of the duties should be gradual, as the industry was still only in its infancy; and Mr. Houghton, another large woollen manufacturer, stated that in his opinion the manufacture would be ruined by the removal of the duties. Mr. Wright, a hat manufacturer, stated that he thought the abolition of the duties "would entirely annihilate a great portion of the trade of the kingdom"; Mr. Leland, another hat manufacturer, stated that he had closed down the greater part of his factory in 1820 in the belief that the duties would be abolished the following year, but that he had reopened it on the passing of the act continuing the duties; and it was stated by other witnesses that the felt hat manufacture of county Wicklow could not survive if unrestricted English competition were allowed. Mr. John Duffy, a calico printer, had no hesitation in stating that his manufactory would be "totally abandoned" if the duties were removed, and that a great deal of fresh capital had been invested in the cotton industry in reliance on the act of 1820. This gentleman further said that Irish businessmen had no idea that the review which the Union duties

[1] Palgrave, *Dictionary of Political Economy*, art. Manchester School.

were to receive in 1820 necessarily entailed their abolition. "We never understood that the duties were to die a natural death at the end of the twenty years; we had always a different feeling.... The express conviction upon my mind, and that of many with whom I have conversed, is that at the period of twenty years from the Union the manufactures would be reviewed, and that it was expected they would require further protection." Mr. Orr, another calico printer, was asked whether, if the duties were abolished, he would be able to carry on his business; his reply was: "I would abandon it entirely, so completely convinced am I that it would be attended with the total destruction of our manufacture; when the duties are reduced to five per cent. it will not be worth while to follow the business; the present act allows us time to prepare for withdrawing our capitals". Mr. Williams, a glass manufacturer, stated that the repeal of the duties would "entirely annibilate" his trade, while Mr. Donovan, another glass manufacturer, complained that the trade generally were conducting their business in reliance on the continuance of the duties. Mr. Robinson, owner of the Phoenix Iron Works in Dublin, said, "I could never carry on the mill at any time in competition with the English without protection"; and told the commission that the abolition of the duties in 1820 was never contemplated by Irish business men:—"whenever the subject was started it was supposed that they would be either extended or modified."[1]

Equally emphatic opinions were expressed by the Dublin Chamber of Commerce. In 1821 the Chamber had presented a petition to the House of Commons, in which it was stated that a sudden removal of the protection afforded by the duties to the manufacturers of Ireland would be "productive of consequences deeply injurious, and in many cases ruinous to an important portion thereof."[2] Two years later the

[1] *Fourth Report of Revenue Commissioners* 1822.
[2] *Report of Council of Dublin Chamber of Commerce* 1821.

council reiterated the opinion: "Your council were not insensible to the various advantages of which the extinction of international duties and a freedom of commercial intercourse must be productive; they nevertheless conceived that those advantages, great as they confessedly are, might be too dearly purchased by such a sacrifice of our manufacturing interests, as an abrupt and unexpected discontinuance of protection would be likely to involve. The validity of the protection afforded by those duties could not be questioned by your council in defiance of the unanimous and concurrent testimony of the persons engaged in the principal manufactures of this country, who could scarcely be mistaken on a point essentially connected with their practical observations and immediate interests. The Irish manufacturer, excluded as by an impassable barrier from the British markets, ought not upon slight grounds at least to be deprived of the limited and temporary possession of his own, which he held by a legislative tenure."[1] In 1822 the Limerick Chamber of Commerce resolved that "it would not be prudent at present to make any further modification in the present protecting duties than those proposed by the late act."[2]

The general feeling in the country even outside commercial circles seems to have been in favour of the retention of the duties. "Take off the protecting duties", wrote Lord Blessington, "and Ireland will be filled with the manufactures of England."[3] "It has long been asserted and believed that the Irish manufacturers, not being able to cope with those of England, would be ruined by the influx of English articles if it were not for these protecting duties."[4] The only expressions of a contrary opinion were based on the fact that the duties were not high enough, and that, as they were ineffective to protect Irish industry against

[1] *Report of Council of Dublin Chamber of Commerce* 1823.
[2] *Fourth Report of Revenue Commissioners* 1822 App. 55.
[3] *Observations on the State of Ireland.* London 1822.
[4] *A Letter to Sir John Newport Bart.* by Hibernicus, Dublin 1821.

British competition, they might as well be abolished, as there was no hope of their being increased.[4]

It would appear surprising that a commission of inquiry could disregard such weighty and unanimous evidence, if it were not abundantly clear that the inquiry was conducted, not for the purpose of eliciting information, but of stating preconceived conclusions. It is quite plain to anyone who reads the verbatim account of the proceedings in the appendices to the reports of the inquiry that the Irish witnesses were not examined, but cross examined. The only witness who was not cross examined—and he was led—was the secretary of the Manchester Chamber of Commerce, whose opinions were subsequently adopted by the commissioners. When we remember that the Manchester Chamber of Commerce was the body which led the English opposition to the retention of the duties, it must seem somewhat unfair that the representative of that body should have been accorded exclusive consideration by the commission.

One example will suffice to illustrate the manner in which this important inquiry was conducted. The commissioners in their fourth report recommended the immediate cessation of the duties on all classes of goods that were not manufactured in Ireland. This was a reasonable recommendation, as the existence of a protective duty on a commodity not manufactured in the country simply had the effect of raising the price on the consumer without conferring any corresponding advantage on the producer. The commissioners were however unwise enough to draw up a schedule which purported to enumerate all the commodities that came within this class, and in this schedule they included the very important article of new drapery. The following extract from a memorial presented by the manufacturers of new drapery speaks for itself: "They have great cause to regret

[2] O'Driscoll. *Review of the Evidence taken before the Irish Committee* Dublin 1825. O'Driscoll *View of Ireland.* London 1823 vol. i. p. 56. *An Impartial Review of the True Causes of Existing Irish Misery.* Dublin 1822. The only Irish writer of importance who favoured the repeal of the duties was George Ensor in *A Defence of the Irish.* Dublin 1825.

that such recommendation was adopted without the examination of any persons immediately concerned in the manufacture of such articles, and that it did not come to your knowledge that several persons are resident in Dublin having considerable capitals embarked therein. Memorialists beg to state that the proposed measure, if carried into effect, would be tantamount to a total repeal of the duties on stuff goods, and would in a short time destroy that manufacture in Ireland.... Figured twills and printed stuffs being articles of recent introduction considerable efforts have been made in Ireland to establish the manufacture, which has been attended with heavy expense, and is now in a state of progressive advancement and improvement." The commissioners, in a supplement to their fourth report, admitted their ignorance of such a manufacture in Ireland, and recommended that it should be accorded the limited measure of protection that was recommended in the case of the manufacture of old drapery.[1]

Enough has been said to enable the reader to judge of the information and impartiality of this commission. We now pass to its actual recommendations concerning the protecting duties, which are contained in the second and fourth reports which it issued. The second report dealt with various minor matters relating to customs, and was on the whole unexceptionable. It recommended, for example, that all duties on the importation of foreign and colonial goods into Great Britain and Ireland should be equalized, and that such goods should be carried between Ireland and Great Britain as coastwise traffic. Various suggestions were also made regarding countervailing duties when the excise was different in the two countries. It was the fourth report that dealt directly with the Union duties. The commissioners recommended in the first place that all duties should be discontinued in the case of articles not manufactured in Ireland; this, as we said above, was unex-

[1] *Supplement to Fourth Report of Revenue Commissioners* 1822.

ceptionable. They then proceeded to deal with the case of goods manufactured in both countries, and recommended that existing duties should be reduced by annual steps until they were completely extinguished in 1829. In this they went directly against the wishes of the Irish manufacturers. We have seen for example the strong opinions expressed by Messrs Willans and Houghton, the two leaders of the woollen industry. This is how the commissioners dealt with that evidence: "The present state of the two establishments of Messrs Willans and Messrs Houghton convince us that a system of improvement has begun, and we are equally convinced that this tendency of improvement would be materially promoted by the operation of that incitement which can only be derived from competition."[1]

Parliament lost no time in putting the recommendations of the commission into effect. An act was passed in 1823, providing that the duties on all articles not manufactured in Ireland should cease on the 10th of October of that year, and that the duties on other articles should be reduced annually until 1829.[2] The anxiety of parliament to give effect to the recommendations of its advisers on this occasion is in singular contrast to the neglect with which it treated the innumerable recommendations of royal commissions and select committees that public money should be advanced for the reclamation of waste lands and other works of public utility in Ireland. But even this rapid reduction of the duties protecting Irish industry was not sufficient for a parliament obsessed with the idea of *laissez faire*. In the following session even the reduced duties were abolished, and the British-Irish trade put on the footing of coastwise trade.[3]

If the account we have given of the conduct of the Revenue Commissioners be correct, can it be suggested that

[1] *Second and Fourth Reports of Revenue Commissioners* 1822.
[2] 4 Geo. IV. c. 26.
[3] 5 Geo. IV. c. 22.

the following comment of John O'Connell, writing on behalf of the Repeal Association in 1843, was exaggerated or unjust? "In the twenty years that elapsed 'ere the commercial arrangements of the Union were reconsidered in 1821, the manufactures of Ireland may at the best be said to have dragged on a precarious and sickly existence rather than to have maintained, much less improved, the vigour that had marked their early growth before 1800. They were no longer formidable, yet the cruel spirit of commercial monopoly was not to be satisfied so long as any vitality remained; and, though the cries of the perishing artisans of Ireland did, by some strange chance, reach the ears of the English Parliament in 1820, and procure some extension of the time originally marked out for the duration of the Union duties, yet in the very next year a commission was appointed, as it would seem, to find excuse for getting rid of them, and on its report their doom was sealed, and they were got rid of with as much haste as decency at all allowed."[1]

One cannot help feeling that Irish interests were not sufficiently studied by this commission, and that this very important step in the commercial history of Ireland was hurried through in an unsatisfactory and unseemly manner. Whether rightly or wrongly, the Irish manufacturing and trading community believed that the duties would not be suffered to expire in 1820, and it was commonly rumoured that Castlereagh had promised in his speech on the Union that the duties would only be reduced when Irish manufactures were in a position to compete with British.[2] It cannot be suggested that this condition was fulfilled in 1824; indeed the evidence is unanimous that, owing to the greater capital at his command and to the superior processes which he had adopted, the British manufacturer was in a position to undersell the Irish in a free market. As early as 1814 it was complained that even with the aid of the protecting

[1] *The Commercial Injustices* Dublin 1843.
[2] *The Repeal Question* Dublin 1840.

duties the Irish cloth manufacturers could not sell their goods as cheap as the British.[1]

The fact is that the duties were protective in the strict sense, and were in no way preferential. So great was the superiority enjoyed by the British manufacturer over the Irish, that a nominal equality between them was tantamount to a real superiority for the former. Amongst other advantages which the British manufacturer enjoyed were more abundant capital, better facilities for the teaching of trades, the existence of supplementary employment for women and children which tended to lower the skilled workmen's minimum living wage, cheaper coal, and, above all, many years, or rather centuries, of protective and encouraging legislation. The opening of free trade between these two countries, which stood on such different industrial planes, operated simply to confer a preference on the more developed. As Beaumont remarked, "the industry, which despotism ruined so rapidly, does not always revive with freedom; for, if it cannot exist without freedom, it is not freedom which creates it, and, in order that it may be reborn and developed, many other conditions are essential."[2] It may be suggested that the recommendations of the Revenue Commissioners were dictated, not by industrial, but by financial considerations. Colour is lent to this view by the passage in the report of the commissioners where it is stated that "a large proportion of the business of the department of customs in Ireland arose from the collection of the Union duties, though they were not in a proportionate degree productive to the revenue."[3] It may also be suggested that the abolition of the cross-channel duties was, in the view of the framers of the Act of Union, the logical sequel to the Union of the British and Irish exchequers.[4] But this does not help matters; it rather impales us upon the horns of

[1] John Edward. *The Interests of Ireland* Dublin 1814.
[2] *L'Irlande Sociale* vol. ii. p. 113.
[3] *Fourth Report of Revenue Commissioners* 1822.
[4] *F. R. C.* p. 7.

a dilemma. If the duties were abolished for revenue purposes, it may be said that the financial productiveness or symmetry of a united kingdom should not be attained at the expense of the industrial decay of one of its parts; while if the duties were abolished for industrial purposes it may be said that the industry of the stronger contracting party should not be benefited at the expense of that of the weaker.

The predictions of the manufacturers in 1822 seem to have been justified by the result. We could quote innumerable opinions expressed by well informed Irishmen of the period that the manufactures of the country were grievously injured by the repeal of the duties; but we shall content ourselves with quoting a few representative ones. We read that in 1830, "Ireland imports from England fifteen nineteenths of the manufactures of all kinds consumed in Ireland, with the exception of leather and linen alone."[1] In 1831 the Lord Mayor, Sheriff, Commons and Citizens of Dublin presented a petition to the House of Commons in which it was stated that, "the decline in the state of manufacturing pursuits has rapidly increased within these few years, and particularly from the period when different legislative enactments took place, promoting the importation into this country of British and foreign manufactures generally; and your petitioners must therefore mainly attribute the effects which have followed to the causes which have preceded them."[2] In the same year the master manufacturers of Dublin appointed a committee to inquire into the industrial depression, and the committee, which examined many witnesses, attributed the manufacturing distress to "the sudden and unexpected repeal of the protecting duties, which by the act of 1820 were to have been progressively decreased and not finally to have ceased until 1840, so as to have given time to the Irish manufacturer

[1] W. Morris, *A Demonstration that Great Britain and Ireland have Resources &c.* London 1830.

[2] Quoted by Jonathan Sisson in *A Second Letter to Earl Grey*. London 1832.

to compete with Great Britain."[1] These expressions of opinion simply reflected those of the whole Irish public.[2]

A few years later we find a very important confirmation of the view that the repeal of the duties had proved the ruin of Irish industry. "Under the now exploded system of bounties and protecting duties", we read in the Second Report of Drummond's Railway Commission, "many new manufactures sprang up; but, not being the natural growth of circumstances favourable to their establishment, most of them gradually disappeared, as soon as the undue encouragement which had created and stimulated them was withdrawn."[3] This statement is important, as it is the utterance of those who, while profoundly disapproving of protecting duties, could not deny that they had in fact stimulated Irish industry while they were in force. The Second Repeal Prize Essay stated that "the repeal of the protecting duties . . . has unquestionably been attended with the ruin of a great number of our once prosperous establishments;"[4] and Isaac Butt lectured his students in Trinity College in favour of protecting duties for Irish industry.[5] A good example of the mentality of the orthodox economist is to be found in a pamphlet which, while admitting that free trade ruined Irish industry, rejoices in the fact, as an illustration of the economic law of the survival of the fittest.[6]

Of course the most direct and serious evil which the repeal of the duties inflicted on Irish industry was the power which it conferred on the British manufacturer to flood the Irish market. "Since the abolition of these duties the Englishman has had complete command of our market. The instances are many in which attempts in Ireland to restore some waning or perished manufacture have been crushed

[1] *A Letter to Earl Grey* by Jonathan Sisson. Dublin 1831.
[2] *Ibidem.*
[3] *Second Report of Railway Commissioners* 1837 p. 9.
[4] *Second Repeal Prize Essay*, Dublin 1845 p. 96.
[5] Isaac Butt. *Protection to Home Industry*. Dublin 1846.
[6] *Facts and Arguments for the Repeal of the Union Examined.* Dublin 1843.

by means of the temporary sacrifice of profit which the superior wealth of the English capitalist enabled him to make, to undersell his rash Irish competitor."[1] "Your legislature kept up commercial restrictions only till Irish trade and commerce were forcibly crushed, and the capital which ought to have sustained them effectually secured to England. Then, when the current of trade was established —Irish raw produce to England—English manufactures to Ireland—Englishmen offered us 'free trade'. It is not more free trade but less free trade that Ireland wants now. Your restricted trade made Irishmen bankrupt, but your free trade is sweeping them into their graves."[2] The repeal of the duties also operated to keep English capital out of Ireland. "There are some English capitalists who have mills here, but they settled here at a time when by a system of differential duties trade between England and Ireland was impeded . . . English capitalists will establish factories in France, Austria, and Belgium, because the tariffs of these countries secure them higher returns than English competition allows."[3] It is certain that the introduction of steam navigation greatly increased the advantages of the English manufacturers, and that these advantages were still further increased by the spread of the railway system.[4] Daniel O'Connell is stated to have said that the first measure of an independent Irish Parliament would be the imposition of protecting duties of 25 per cent.[5]

We shall not here consider the effect of the repeal on the particular industries to which we have already referred in the preceding section. We may perhaps remind the reader that we have adduced evidence to prove that the woollen, silk, and cotton manufactures suffered severely from the repeal of the duties. The greater part of the frames

[1] John O'Connell *An Argument for Ireland.* Dublin 1847.
[2] *The Nation* March 1847.
[3] Kane, *Industrial Resources of Ireland* p. 390.
[4] *Report of Select Committee on State of Poor* 1830 p. 15; *Second Report of Railway Commissioners* 1837 p. 8 ; Alton *The Evils of Ireland* Limerick 1841.
[5] *Debate on the Repeal of the Union* 1834 p. 62.

employed in the Dublin hosiery manufacture were thrown idle and sold as old iron;[1] the Dublin glass works and salt works were ruined; the paper manufacture was reduced to about one-third of its former extent; and six or seven sugar factories were abandoned.[2] The Poor Inquiry Commissioners received evidence that the removal of the duties had been most injurious from representatives of the following trades—calico-printers, soapmakers, soap-boilers, cutlers, glovers, hatters, ironfounders, housesmiths, livery fringe manufacturers, and silk manufacturers.[3] "The industrial history of Ireland during the nineteenth century", Miss Murray concludes, "shows how impossible it was for Irish manufacturers to compete with British, once the two countries were commercially united, and all custom duties on articles going from one country to the other gradually abolished. It also shows the advisability of a country possessed of little industrial development fostering and protecting its infant manufactures until they are firmly established, in order to prevent them being crushed out of existence by the competition of other countries. But union with Great Britain necessitated the application of the new free trade principles to Ireland just at the time when Irish industries should have met with encouragement and protection."[4]

(*e*) *The Difficulty of Accumulating Capital Under the Irish Land Laws.*

If the conclusions which we reached in the last section be correct, the repeal of the protecting duties played an important part in the decay of Irish industry. The evil

[1] *Report of Loyal National Repeal Association on Woollen Silk and Cotton Manufactures.* Dublin 1840.

[2] Jonathan Sisson. *A Letter to Earl Grey* Dublin 1831.

[3] *Poor Inquiry Commission App.* C. *part* 2 *Evidence on Combinations.* On the depressed state of industry in Cork in 1843 see the *Speech of Alderman Hayes on the Repeal of the Union* Dublin 1843; and in Dublin in 1840 see Locker Lampson, *Ireland in the Nineteenth Century* p. 183.

[4] *Commercial Relations* p. 351.

effects of the repeal of the duties were, we have seen, primarily owing to the great difference in the development of British and Irish manufactures; while the former had reached the point where they could successfully meet all competition, the latter were still in a state of comparative infancy. We must now prosecute our inquiry a step further, and endeavour to discover the reasons for this disparity. The first and most obvious reason was the oppression of Irish industry which had continued throughout the greater part of the eighteenth century. The effect of the hostile legislation of the English, and afterwards of the British Parliament, was that Irish industrial enterprise had been stunted and confined within narrow bounds. The greater part of the oppressive legislation had however been repealed before the Union; the colonial and foreign markets were thrown open in 1780; and, as we have seen, the British market was practically thrown open by the Act of Union itself. How was it then that Irish industry continued to be inferior to British? The answer to this question is twofold. In the first place, it was not easy for the industry of a country that had been artificially discouraged during a long period to recover its prosperity immediately after the removal of the discouragements under which it had suffered. The results of the oppression were cumulative; not alone had the operatives of the country lost their skill and experience, but the markets had been acquired by the manufacturers of the nation in whose favour the legislation had been enacted. This is so obvious that we need not labour it. In the second place, there were other independent causes which made it peculiarly difficult for Ireland to recover this lost ground. Possibly the most urgent necessity of a country that has suffered under a prolonged course of commercial oppression is an abundant supply of capital wherewith to build up new industries. Ireland however was sadly lacking in this important factor of industrial regeneration. We have already drawn attention to the extent to which the impossibility of accumulating capital under the existing land system prevented the introduction of improved methods of agriculture and the reclamation of waste lands; the same inability to accumulate capital was the foremost cause of the failure of Ireland to utilise her commercial liberty.

We demonstrated in a previous chapter that the landlord —or rather the landlords, as there were usually one or more middlemen—took the whole surplus product of the soil, and left to the occupying tenant nothing but the means of procuring a bare subsistence. Any small pittance that remained to the tenant after the payment of his rent was, as we shall see presently, devoured by the tithe or county cess. It is obvious that a tenantry so circumstanced could not accumulate any savings, and it follows that the establishment of industries in Ireland by the tenant class was impossible. The poverty of the tenantry operated not alone to diminish the supply of available capital, but also to lessen the demand for the finished products of industry. So long as the vast majority of the agricultural population was depressed, the demand for the comforts and luxuries of an advanced state of civilization must necessarily have remained negligible.[1]

It may be suggested that the impoverishment of the tenants led to the enrichment of the landlords; and that, if the former could not accumulate capital, there was nothing to prevent the latter from doing so. Such a suggestion, however, indicates a complete ignorance of the outlook and character of the Irish landlord class. In Ireland the landlords despised all forms of trade; those who were resident preferred to spend their revenues in high living rather than in the promotion of useful industry; and a very large part of the Irish land revenue was paid into the pockets of absentees, who had no interest in developing the industrial resources of a country in which they never resided.

[1] O'Flynn, *The Present State of the Irish Poor.* London 1835.

It is impossible to estimate the volume of Irish wealth which was annually drained abroad. In the next chapter we shall deal with the question of this drain, and shall show that the amount exported from Ireland to absentee landlords and to an absentee government amounted to several millions a year. The part of this huge sum which was devoted to capitalizing industrial enterprises in the localities in which the recipients resided may be accounted so much capital lost to Ireland. This colossal drain also operated to diminish the Irish demand for manufactured goods. Obviously, if the millions which were exported had been retained in Ireland, the demand for all kinds of goods would have been substantially increased; and it is not unreasonable to conclude that that increased demand would have been satisfied, at least to some extent, by the output of Irish manufactures. "The introduction and extension of manufactures' said Sadleir, "is rendered impossible by absenteeship. It is difficult to imagine how they could be introduced or encouraged without either capital or demand, to both of which that evil is fatal."[1] Thus, neither the tenant nor the landlord was in a position to contribute capital for the industrial development of the country. As Sir Robert Kane put it, "the lord was above industry; the slave was below it."[2]

The accumulation of savings is not in itself sufficient to furnish a supply of capital for industry. The amounts thus saved must be rendered available to those who require them. In Ireland, during the period under review, even the small savings which it was possible to amass were rendered sterile and ineffective on account of the defects of the banking system. We shall show in a later chapter how the law of banking oppressed the Irish manufacturer; how the repeated failure of the private banks tended to create periodical crises; and how the monopoly of the Bank of Ireland was abused. Several witnesses gave evidence before

[1] *Ireland, Its Evils &c.* 1829 p. 76. [2] *Industrial Resources* p. 322.

the Poor Inquiry Commission to the effect that Irish industry was grievously retarded by the lack of proper credit facilities. A carpet manufacturer testified: "I sell quite as cheap as the English carpets are sold, but I cannot afford to give the long credit that the English do, and consequently the preference is given to them;" a cutler: "Irish cutlery has always been considered at least thirty per cent. better than Sheffield manufacture, but many masters, for the sake of the long credit given, import Sheffield goods and put their own name on them and sell them as Irish"; a hosier: "the long credit which the English capitalists can afford to give causes excessive importation, and the manufacturers here cannot therefore compete with them"; and an engineer: "owing to the protecting duties having been withdrawn, and the credit given by English manufacturers, our trade has been gradually sinking."[1] The lack of adequate credit facilities was also stated before the Handloom Weavers Commission as one of the main causes of the decay of Irish industry.[2]

It may be suggested that the difficulty of accumulating capital in Ireland should not be urged as a reason for the non-development of Irish industry, because capital is fluid, and would have found its way to Ireland from other countries, if the return promised on its investment had been sufficiently attractive. Such was the argument of the classical economists. It must be remembered however that the assumptions of the classical economists were not invariably correct, that the flow of capital was not so fluid and free as they postulated, and that, in any case, the other causes which had operated to retard Irish industry had decreased the attractiveness of the country as a field for profitable speculation. "Suppose an Englishman", said Sir Robert Kane, "possessed of £50,000 and wishing to invest it in spinning cotton; he has the choice to go to

[1] *Poor Inquiry Commission, Evidence on Combination* app. C. pt. 2

[2] *Otway's Report* p. 630.

Manchester or Killaloe. In the former place he has coals cheap, workmen of every class at hand, machinery made at his door, markets established, and, if he wants to sell in Ireland, he has canal and railway to Liverpool, and steam to Dublin, canals thence to the Shannon. If he comes to Killaloe he has to bring his machinery, and all his higher workmen, to bring cotton, and to settle amongst a people concerning whom his ears have been stuffed with newspaper stories, some unfortunately true, but mostly false. His sympathies are at his home, and unless profits were considerably higher, he would remain at home, and such should certainly be his course. Now profits cannot be sensibly higher in Ireland than in England. There is therefore no inducement for him to come."[1] So long as the Union duties were retained, there was a temptation for English capitalists to settle in Ireland with a view to securing the Irish market, but, as soon as the duties were repealed, that temptation vanished. "But some English capitalists have settled amongst us, it may be said, and hence the above reasoning cannot be absolute. There are some, as the Willans, who have cloth mills here and in Leeds, but they settled here at a time when by a system of differential duties, trade between England and this country was impeded."[2] It would thus appear that one of the results of the repeal of the Union duties was to discourage British manufacturers from investing capital in Ireland.

It must also be remembered that the fact that several British companies that had attempted to carry on business in Ireland had failed—largely through their own fault—tended to discourage other speculators from an apparently unprofitable field. "Numerous companies", wrote Sir Robert Kane, "have been from time to time formed in England for the purpose of developing some branch of the industrial resources of Ireland. They have been almost universally failures, and Ireland, as a field of enterprise,

[1] *Industrial Resources* p. 390. [2] *Ibidem.*

has been hence at a discount in the English market. It is not difficult to see why they failed; the causes were ignorance of the country and want of economy."[1] Nor must it be forgotten that British capitalists were—naturally, according to the standards of the age—jealous of the growth of rival establishments in Ireland. It was urged as one of the arguments in favour of the Act of Union that British manufacturers would be more inclined to invest money in Ireland. We can judge of the justice of this argument by two passages from pamphlets written twenty years later. "Let us explore the whole island", wrote William Parker in 1819, "and we shall in vain endeavour to find out where British capitalists made any permanent and useful establishments in it. Indeed, near Dublin, an English woollen manufacturer settled with a large capital, but British jealousy of Irish industry urged his former partners in England to oppose every measure of his, and to do all they could to work his ruin. It is true that a few individuals in humble life, and with as humble means, came over, desirous to make and not to expend money."[2] Three years later we read: "Linen is the only branch of trade worthy the name of Irish manufacture; every effort that has been hitherto made to establish any other kind of manufacture has been immediately crushed by English capital, and, in one instance, when a spirited individual in the vicinity of Dublin had commenced a factory with every appearance of success, an immense subscription was entered into at Liverpool by merchants in the same line for the purpose of destroying it in its infancy, and I need scarcely add that it had the desired effect."[3] Smith O'Brien clearly realized the strength of English opposition to Irish manufactures. "I have turned aside", he exclaimed, "from this point of inquiry in utter despair, being convinced that nothing can be effectively done for the protection of manufactures

[1] *Industrial Resources* p. 392.
[2] *A Plea for the Poor and Industrious* Cork 1819.
[3] *An Impartial Review of the True Causes of Irish Misery* Dublin 1822.

in Ireland through the medium of a legislature in which interests predominate which are naturally adverse to the encouragement of this class of Irish industry."[1]

It would appear therefore that the growth of industry in Ireland was hindered by the impediments which were placed in the way of accumulating capital in Ireland, and of utilizing it if accumulated; and that this deficiency was in no way compensated for by any readiness on the part of British capitalists to invest money in Irish enterprises. As in the case of our discussion on the causes which retarded the progress of Irish agriculture, we are in a position to add weight to our conclusion by an application of the principle of *exceptio probat regulam.* If we can point to one district in Ireland where the practice of the landlord's taking the whole surplus produce of the land did not prevail, and if we can show that that district, at the time when the rest of Ireland was experiencing a period of industrial decay, was enjoying a period of industrial progress, we suggest that we have materially added to the evidence in support of our contention. Such an exceptional district was to be found in north-east Ulster.

It is true that Crommelin had settled in Lisburn, and that the linen industry had found its principal centre in the counties of Down, Armagh, and Antrim. The question nevertheless arises—why had that industry not spread throughout the south and west of Ireland? To this question we answer unhesitatingly that the true secret of the industrial success of Ulster was the prevalence of the Ulster custom of land tenure. For one thing, Ulster had occupied an exceptionally favourable position compared with the rest of Ireland during the eighteenth century; owing to the fact that the great majority of its inhabitants were Protestants, it had escaped the full rigours of the penal code. "The first question which will present itself is, why should one quarter of the island stand an exception to these

[3] *Reproductive Employment* Dublin 1847.

evils? Why should you find in Ulster enterprise, spirit, and energetic industry, manufacture, and the free circulation of capital? I answer, because it is for the most part exempt from the operation of the penal laws, being for the most part Protestant."[1] Thus, Ulster escaped the worst results of the eighteenth century penal laws; but in addition it was favoured by the Ulster custom, which enabled the tenantry—Protestant or Catholic—to reap the reward of their own industry, and to accumulate for investment in industry the fruits of their agricultural labours. "It may be said", wrote Mr. Sharman Crawford, "that there is here a combination of manufacture with agriculture, which is a cause of increased prosperity. It is very true that such a combination exists, but not to nearly as great an extent as it formerly did. But what laid the foundation of this manufacture? The security of tenure. What gave that energy to the people's minds which induced the industrial combination of agriculture and manufacture? I answer, the impulse acquired from the feeling connected with his occupancy of the soil, that he had the certain enjoyment of all his labour created."[2] Not only did less of the produce of the tenants' toil pass into the pockets of the landlords in Ulster than in the south and west; of what the landlord did obtain in that province a far smaller proportion left the country for payment to absentees. Generally speaking absenteeism was less widespread in Ulster than in the other provinces of Ireland.[3] The pressure of tithes moreover was less severely felt in the north; certain articles, the principal of which was the potato, which were tithable in the south, were exempt from tithes in Ulster.[4]

We find therefore that the people of Ulster were exempt from many of the disabilities that pressed so hard on the

[1] *Reflections on the State of Ireland* London 1822. This was clearly perceived and stated by Wakefield, vol. i. p. 700.
[2] *Depopulation not Necessary* London 1849.
[3] *The Causes of the Discontents of Ireland* Dublin 1823.
[4] Barry O'Brien *Fifty Years of Concessions* vol. i. p. 370.

people of the south. The burdens of the penal laws, rack rents, absentee landlords, and tithes weighed less heavily in Ulster than elsewhere. It is, we suggest, not unreasonable to infer that there was some connection between these exemptions and the comparative prosperity of Ulster. The localities where the accumulation of capital by the tenantry was not impossible progressed industrially, whereas those where such accumulation was discouraged presented the spectacle of industrial decay.

These causes doubtless operated to localize the linen industry in the north. The other industries which had shown signs of developing in the south under the protective system adopted by Grattan's Parliament had not, as we have already seen, attained sufficient strength to withstand the effects of unlimited competition from British goods. But the linen industry was in a different position; for over a century it had received the special attention and encouragement of the legislature; at the date when every other Irish industry was being suppressed, the linen industry was in receipt of large annual premiums and bounties. When, therefore, the period of fierce competition and of transition from small to large scale manufacture arrived, the linen industry was sufficiently developed to weather the storm which overwhelmed the less favoured industries. It must also be remembered that linen was the last of the textile industries to adopt machinery in place of hand-weaving, and that its period of transition did not therefore make the heavy demand for large capital that the woollen and cotton trades required. Ulster was consequently fortunate in possessing the one Irish industry that was in the best position to go safely through the trying years of the early nineteenth century; and it therefore occupied the lucky position in 1850 that its staple industry was flourishing and progressive, while the manufactures of the south had fallen into decay. Nor should it be forgotten that the happy accident which decided the founders of the

Irish cotton industry to open their establishments in the north greatly aided Ulster in attaining to her position of industrial supremacy. At a later stage the continuance of this trade was only rendered possible by the proximity of Ulster to the great cotton mills of Scotland—a geographical advantage of which Ulster was certainly entitled to reap the reward, but for the possession of which she is not entitled to claim any unique merit.

The remarkable progress made by Belfast in the first half of the nineteenth century was due to its being the most conveniently situated seaport of Ulster. "Let those" wrote Wakefield, "who look only at the dark side of the picture turn their eyes to Belfast. This town, which about a century ago scarcely deserved notice, is now in point of trade and consequence the fifth in the island."[1] "As we approached Belfast", wrote a traveller six years later, "the accumulation of riches by the profitable application of capital and productive labour to manufacture and commerce became visible, by the improvement which had been made on both sides of our path. This gratification kept increasing as we shortened our distance from the town .... The quays have been greatly extended and extensive docks are now making."[2] The population of the town grew by leaps and bounds from 8,549 in 1758 to 37,000 in 1821, 53,000 in 1831, 75,000 in 1841, and 103,000 in 1851.[3]

In addition to its favourable position as the most centrally situated port for the cotton and linen districts, Belfast also enjoyed some peculiar advantages which doubtless helped it to progress. The principal of these local advantages was the method by which the Chichester estate was managed. Owing to financial difficulties, the owners of this estate were forced at the end of the eighteenth century to grant many leases in perpetuity in consideration of large fines. The possession of such leases liberated the tenants from

[1] Vol. ii. p. 65. [2] Curwen, *Observations* vol. i. pp. 117-20.

[3] Godkin. *Land War* p. 382. For the number of factories, etc. in 1836 see *Poor Inquiry Commission* app. C. part 1. p. 5.

the pressure of Irish landlordism, and rendered possible the growth of an independent middle class who could accumulate capital.[1] Belfast possessed the further advantage of being able to obtain coal cheaper than Dublin. Prior to 1831 this difference in the cost of coal was caused by the oppressive port-tolls and dues which were collected in Dublin; but, even after the repeal of these dues, Belfast still enjoyed an advantage on account of the conspiracy in the coal trade directed against Dublin.[2]

But these local advantages would not in themselves have sufficed to produce the great industrial development of Belfast and of Ulster; they could at most but aid an already existing tendency. The ultimate cause that enabled Ulster to progress while the rest of Ireland declined was the freedom of the province from the worst burdens of the land system, and the consequent ability of its population to accumulate capital for manufactures. It must be remembered that the advantage which Ulster enjoyed in this respect, and the disadvantage under which the rest of Ireland laboured, were cumulative in their effects. In the one case the amassing of capital rendered possible industry, which in its turn enabled more capital to be saved; in the other case, the impossibility of starting industries through lack of capital closed the door to the only means by which large sums can be saved in modern times. We may say a word in conclusion about what we regard as a popular fallacy, namely that Ulster flourished while the rest of Ireland declined owing to some superior industrial capacity in her people. We have already discussed how far the libels on the industrial character of the Irish labourer are justified, and have suggested that whatever shortcomings in that respect he possessed were the effects rather than the cause of the industrial depression of the country. We now suggest likewise that, if the inhabitants of Ulster possessed any industrial virtues

[1] MacDougall. *A Treatise on the Irish Fisheries.* Belfast 1819. Godkin. *Land War* pp. 383-4. [2] Supra p. 412.

which were absent in the south, such a superior character was the effect rather than the cause of the long period of encouragement and success which their manufactures had enjoyed.

The only reason for referring to the exceptional position of Belfast and Ulster in the present section is to emphasize, by the application of the maxim *exceptio probat regulam*, what we have said about the relation between the land system and the non-development of industry outside Ulster. If our conclusions on this subject are correct, it would appear that the ultimate cause of the failure of Ireland to achieve industrial success in the first half of the nineteenth century was the impossibility of accumulating capital under the existing land system. The necessarily evil consequences of this disability were aggravated by the withdrawal of the limited protection that Irish industry enjoyed at the time when British industry was in a position of overwhelming competitive advantage. The shortage of fuel in Ireland was an unimportant or neutral factor in the situation; and the alleged indolent character of the Irish workers, and their readiness to enter into combinations, were the effects rather than the causes of the industrial backwardness of Ireland.

PART III.

PUBLIC FINANCE ETC.

CHAPTER XI.

Public Burdens.

Section 1. Imperial Taxation.

THE whole imperial taxation of Ireland in the nineteenth century was based upon the financial section of the Act of Union, which reads as follows:

(1). That it be the Seventh Article of Union that the charge arising from the payment of the interest, and the sinking fund for the reduction of the principal of the debt incurred in either Kingdom before the Union, shall continue to be separately defrayed by Great Britain and Ireland respectively, except as hereinafter provided:

(2). That, for the space of twenty years after the Union shall take place, the contribution of Great Britain and Ireland respectively towards the expenditure of the United Kingdom in each year, shall be defrayed in the proportion of fifteen parts for Great Britain and two parts for Ireland; and that at the expiration of the said twenty years the future expenditure of the United Kingdom (other than the interest and charges of the debt to which either country shall be separately liable) shall be defrayed, in such proportion as the Parliament of the United Kingdom shall deem just and reasonable, upon a comparison of the real value of the exports and imports of the respective countries, upon an average of the three years next preceding the period of revision; or on a comparison of the value of the quantities of the following articles consumed within the respective countries, on a similar average, videlicet, beer, spirits, sugar, wine, tea, tobacco, and malt; or according to the aggregate proportion resulting from both these considerations combined; or on a comparison of the amount of income in each country, estimated from the produce for the same period of a general tax, if such shall have been imposed on the same description of income in both countries:

(3). And that the Parliament of the United Kingdom shall afterwards proceed in like manner to revise and fix the said proportions, according to the same rules or any of them, at periods not more distant than twenty years nor less than seven years from each other; unless previous to any such period the Parliament of the United Kingdom shall have declared, as hereinafter provided, that the expenditure of the United Kingdom shall be defrayed, indiscriminately, by equal taxes imposed on the like articles in both countries:

(4). That, for the defraying the said expenditure according to the rules above laid down, the revenues of Ireland shall hereafter constitute a Consolidated Fund, which shall be charged, in the first instance, with the interest of the debt of Ireland, and with the sinking fund applicable to the reduction of the said debt, and the remainder shall be applied towards defraying the proportion of the expenditure of the United Kingdom to which Ireland may be liable in each year:

(5). That the proportion of contribution to which Great Britain and Ireland will be liable shall be raised by such taxes in each country respectively, as the Parliament of the United Kingdom shall from time to time deem fit; Provided always, that in regulating the taxes in each country by which their respective proportions shall be levied, no article in Ireland shall be made liable to any new or additional duty by which the whole amount of duty payable thereon would exceed the amount which will be thereafter payable in England on the like article:

(6). That if, at the end of any year, any surplus shall accrue from the revenues of Ireland, after defraying the interest, sinking fund, and proportional contributions and separate charges to which the said country shall then be liable, taxes shall be taken off to the amount of such surplus, or the surplus shall be applied by the Parliament of the United Kingdom to local purposes in Ireland, or to make good any deficiency which may arise in the revenues of Ireland in time of peace, or be invested by the Commissioners of the National Debt of Ireland in the Funds, to accumulate for the benefit of Ireland at compound interest, in ease of the contribution of Ireland in time of war; provided that the surplus so to accumulate shall at no future period be suffered to exceed the sum of 5,000,000*l*,:

(7). That all moneys to be raised after the Union, by loan, in peace or war, for the service of the United Kingdom by the Parliament thereof, shall be considered to be a joint debt, and the charges thereof shall be borne by the respective countries in the proportion of their respective contributions; provided that if at any time, in raising their respective contributions hereby fixed for each country the Parliament of the United Kingdom shall judge it fit to raise a greater proportion of such respective contributions in one country within the year than in the other, or to set apart a greater proportion of sinking fund for the liquidation of the whole or any part of the loan raised on account of the one country than of that raised on account of the other country, then such part of the said loan, for the liquidation of which different provisions shall have been made for the respective countries, shall be kept distinct, and shall be borne by each separately, and only that part of the said loan be deemed joint and common, for the reduction of which the respective countries shall have made provision in the proportion of their respective contributions:

(8). That if at any future day the separate debt of each country respectively shall have been liquidated, or if the values of their respective debts (estimated according to the amount of the interest and annuities attending the same, and of the sinking fund applicable to the reduction thereof, and to the period within which the whole capital of such debt shall appear to be redeemable by such sinking fund) shall be to each other in the same proportion with the respective contributions of each country respectively; or if the amount by which the value of the larger of such debts shall vary from such proportion shall not exceed one-hundredth part of the said value: And if it shall appear to the Parliament of the United Kingdom that the respective circumstances of the two countries will thenceforth admit of their contributing indiscriminately, by equal taxes imposed on the same articles in each, to the future expenditure of the United Kingdom, it shall be competent to the Parliament of the United Kingdom to declare that all future expense thenceforth to be incurred, together with the interest and charges of all joint debts contracted previous to such declaration, shall be so defrayed indiscriminately by equal taxes imposed on the same articles in each country, and thenceforth from time to time, as circumstances may require, to impose and apply such taxes accordingly, subject only to such particular exemptions or abatements in Ireland, and in that part of Great Britain called Scotland, as circumstances may appear from time to time to demand:

(9). That, from the period of such declaration, it shall no longer be necessary to regulate the contribution of the two countries towards the future expenditure of the United Kingdom according to any specific proportion, or according to any of the rules herein-before prescribed: Provided, nevertheless, that the interest or charges which may remain on account of any part of the separate debt with which either country shall be chargeable, and which shall not be liquidated or consolidated proportionably as above, shall, until extinguished, continue to be defrayed by separate taxes in each country: That a sum not less than the sum which has been granted by the Parliament in Ireland on the average of six years immediately preceding the 1st day of January in the year 1800, in premiums for the internal encouragement of agriculture or manufactures, or for the maintaining institutions for pious and charitable purposes, shall be applied, for the period of 20 years after the Union, to such local purposes in Ireland in such manner as the Parliament of the United Kingdom shall direct: That from and after the 1st day of January 1801, all public revenue arising to the United Kingdom from the territorial dependencies thereof, and applied to the general expenditure of the United Kingdom, shall be so applied in the proportions of the respective contributions of the two countries.

We do not propose to examine at length whether the proportion of two-seventeenths fixed for Ireland's contribution was just or unjust, which we have discussed elsewhere.[1] It is sufficient to state that the proportion was believed by the best Irish opinion of the time to be altogether excessive, and that, in fact, it afterwards proved exorbitant. It is only fair to state however that Mr. Childers, the most reliable authority on Irish financial affairs, inclined to think that the greater part of the injustice of the proportion arose from causes which could not have been foreseen at the time of its calculation. If this opinion be correct, we must pause before condemning the framers of the Act of Union. "The basis", said Mr. Childers, "of Lord Castlereagh's calculation was severely criticized in the final debates in the Irish House of Commons, and the leading arguments in proof of Ireland's inability to bear the pro-

[1] *Economic History of Ireland in the Eighteenth Century* p. 246.

portion of contribution assigned to her were summed up in a protest entered by twenty peers upon the journals of the Irish House of Lords. The forecast of the future contained in this protest proved, in the events which took place, to be more accurate than that made by Lord Castlereagh. We think, however, that the framers of the Act of Union must be acquitted of any intentional financial injustice towards Ireland. Supposing that the average expenditure of Great Britain had not exceeded during the fifteen years which followed the Union her average expenditure during the fifteen years that preceded it, the average expenditure of Ireland during the second period, compared with the first, would not apparently have been to any very serious extent increased. The miscalculation made by the framers of the Union was chiefly due, it is submitted, to their failure to foresee the future increase of the total expenditure of the United Kingdom, and for this they can hardly be blamed."[1] That the proportions arrived at were, in fact, excessive was subsequently admitted on all sides. Mr. Goulburn, afterwards Chancellor of the Exchequer, speaking in the House of Commons in 1822 said:—"The Union contribution of $^2/_{17}$ for Ireland is now confessed on all hands to have been unjust."[2]

It is possible that the continuance of the French war could not have reasonably been foreseen by the framers of the Act of Union; but the war did in fact continue, and Ireland was consequently called upon to meet an ever-increasing taxation. This is admirably put in the majority report of the Financial Relations Commission:—

"Whether the proportions of contribution fixed by the Act of Union were ever just appears more than doubtful, but that they became manifestly unjust shortly after the contract was entered into can scarcely be denied. This, in our opinion, has been proved beyond dispute in the evidence given before the different financial inquiries

[1] *F. R. C.* p. 142. [2] *Repeal Reports* vol. i. p. 61.

which have taken place since the passing of the Act of Union, and has been candidly and freely admitted by all the different witnesses examined on the subject, including those representing the Treasury. Mr. John Smith, the Treasury Officer in 1816, Mr. Chisholm, representing the Exchequer in 1865, and Sir Edward Hamilton, in the evidence given to ourselves, all admitted that whatever may be said as to the fairness of Ireland's proportion of two to fifteen in ordinary times of peace, it became absolutely too high under the circumstances which followed the Act of Union. In the sixteen years which followed the Union, the debts of Ireland were quadrupled, her taxation was increased fourfold, and at the end of the period she was nearly bankrupt."[1]

The result of this unprecedented and unforeseen increase of the expenditure of the United Kingdom, was that Ireland was quite unable to raise its contribution by revenue alone, and that resort had consequently to be made to loans. The question of how far the Irish contribution during the seventeen years after the Union was raised by taxation, and how far by borrowing, is thus discussed by Mr. Childers:—

> It must now be considered to what extent the expenditure of Ireland during the period which followed the Union was met by revenue and to what extent by loans. The loans raised for both countries after the Union till the amalgamation of the Exchequers in 1817 were treated as additions to the separate pre-Union debts. The total annual revenue raised in Ireland during the 16 years ending 25th March 1800, was 24,314,467*l*., or an annual average of 1,519,654*l*. The total annual revenue raised during the 16 years ending 5th January, 1817, was 77,844,194*l*., or an annual average of 4,865,262*l*. During the first of these two periods the total Irish expenditure was 38,487,908*l*., an annual average of 2,405,443*l*. During the second period the total expenditure charged to Ireland was 159,737,805*l*., or an annual average of 9.983,613*l*. Therefore, although the increase in Irish revenue during the second period, as compared with the first, was great, it was by no means so great as the increase of Irish expenditure. The average annual revenue in the second was 3.2 times as large as that in the first period, but the average annual expenditure was 4.1 times as large.

The relative proportions borne by revenue and expenditure in the two countries during the period 1801-17 are clearly shown by the table on the following page.

[1] *F. R. C.* pp. 5-6. [2] *F. R. C.* p. 143.

GREAT BRITAIN					IRELAND				
Year	Total Revenue applicable to Public Expenditure	Total Actual Expenditure	Proportion Per Cent of Revenue to Expenditure	Proportion Per Cent of Total Revenue of both Countries	Year	Total Revenue applicable to Public Expenditure	Total Actual Expenditure	Proportion Per Cent of Revenue to Expenditure	Proportion Per Cent of Total Revenue of both Countries
	£	£				£	£		
1801	35,262,508	64,277,348	55.	91.8	1801	3,186,929	7,628,066	41.8	8.2
1802	36,744,967	55,351,099	66.4	90.1	1802	4,022,248	6,595,240	60.9	9.9
1803	38,132,768	51,812,173	73.6	91.9	1803	3,373,489	6,577,761	51.2	8.1
1804	45,925,296	62,611,005	73.3	92.5	1804	3,733,950	7,845,120	47.6	7.5
1805	50,228,236	71,254,371	70.5	92.8	1805	3,901,917	7,707,244	50.6	7.2
1806	53,703,128	71,634,885	75.	92.3	1806	4,502,789	8,273,727	54.4	7.7
1807	58,972,487	72,720,761	81.8	92.2	1807	4,990,655	8,307,943	60.	7.8
1808	61,583,333	79,966,072	77.	92.27	1808	5,162,016	8,940,373	57.7	7.73
1809	63,489,738	82,620,629	76.8	92.7	1809	5,081,304	9,357,076	54.3	7.3
1810	68,573,702	85,721,364	80.	93.6	1810	4,687,491	10,426,028	44.9	6.4
1811	66,375,825	91,703,778	72.3	93.	1811	5,017,734	11,306,300	44.3	7.
1812	64,270,276	99,363,681	64.68	92.	1812	5,696,841	11,455,449	49.8	8.
1813	71,614,495	114,150,713	62.7	92.4	1813	5,891,588	12,845,452	46.	7.6
1814	72,577,562	117,612,837	61.7	92.	1814	6,432,184	13,277,268	48.4	8.
1815	76,869,272	102,456,858	75.	92.1	1815	6,598,773	17,057,036	38.6	7.9
1816	63,335,535	78,363,023	80.82	92.	1816	5,564,285	12,137,821	45.8	8.
Total of the 16 years	927,659,128	1,301,620,597		—	—	77,844,193	159,737,804		—
Annual Average Amount	57,978,695	81,351,287	71.6	92.25	—	4,865,262	9,983,613	49.	7,75

Mr. Childers remarks, commenting on this table:—

It will be observed that, as the general result of the whole period, while Great Britain raised 71 per cent. of her expenditure out of revenue, Ireland raised no more than 49 per cent. We are inclined to agree with the view expressed by Mr. Chisholm in commenting upon these figures that "The fact that, notwithstanding her large increase of revenue from year to year, she was enabled to provide by taxation for so small a proportion of her increased expenditure, in comparison with Great Britain, tends to the inference that her relative ability did not increase in the same proportion with that of Great Britain to contribute to the largely-increased expenditure, and that, although her proportion of $^{2}/_{17}$ may have been fairly estimated in 1801, it was too high a proportion in the subsequent years."[1]

During this period Ireland was overtaxed, not only comparatively with Great Britain, but absolutely in regard to its taxable capacity. The select committee appointed by the House of Commons in 1815 to inquire into public revenue and expenditure in Ireland reported that "for several years Ireland has advanced in permanent taxation more rapidly than Great Britain itself, notwithstanding the immense exertions of the latter country, and including the extraordinary war taxes; the permanent taxation of Great Britain having increased from 1801 in the proportion of 16½ to 10, and the whole revenue of Great Britain including the war taxes as $21^{1}/_{4}$ to 10, and the revenue of Ireland in the proportion of 23 to 10".[2] On the numerous additional taxes imposed on Ireland during the years following the Union Mr. Childers remarked as follows:—

It may be well to refer to some of the chief of the numerous taxes imposed upon Ireland during this period, and for this purpose it is convenient to compare with 1801, a single later year, in 1812. In the latter year the total revenue raised in Ireland amounted to 5,696,841*l.*, of which a little over one million was produced by non-tax revenue and by stamps, while the whole of the balance was raised in almost equal proportions by custom and excise. The duty on home-made spirits in Ireland was 2*s.*4½*d.* in 1801, and in 1812 it stood after a succession of rises at 5*s.* 1¼*d.* The duties on brandy and Geneva and on rum had, during the same period, been raised from 8*s.* 7½*d.* and 6*s.* 8¾*d* to 12*s.* 7½*d.* and 10*s.* 3½*d.* respectively. The duty on tea had been raised from 35 per cent. on superior teas and 20 per cent. on cheap teas, to 96 per cent. on all teas. The duty on malt was at 1*s.* 6¼*d.* in 1801 and at 2*s.* 6¾*d.* in 1812. An additional duty of 2*s.* 8*d.* per cwt. was placed on sugar in 1801, and 3*s.* 6*d.* in 1806. The duty on

[1] *F. R. C.* p. 144 [2] *F. R. C.* p. 146.

tobacco had risen from 1*s*. to 3*s*. 2*d*. in the pound. It appears from these instances that there was during this period a very considerable rise in the indirect taxation of Ireland. At the same time it appears from a study of the "official values" of imports and exports of Ireland during this period that the bulk and volume of trade had received a considerable expansion. The total exports and imports were in 1802 represented by the official figure, 10,316,327*l*., and in the year 1814 by the official figure 13,278,721*l*. It also appears from figures given in the return, C.—194, of 1834, page 9, as to the articles retained for consumption in Ireland at various periods that, as between 1790 and 1820, the consumption of spirits, tobacco, tea, and sugar altogether considerably increased, although that of wine had very much diminished. Increase of consumption as well as increase in rates of taxation seems therefore to have taken place in Ireland during this period.

It appears, however, to be clear in view of the diminishing receipts from increasing taxation and the inability to raise considerable loans in the country, that Ireland had during this period, notwithstanding her immunity from very large taxes which affected Great Britain only, been taxed to the extreme limits of her capacity. The result of the impossibility under the financial arrangement of the Union as affected by the war, of making the revenue of Ireland come within measurable distance of her expenditure, was the accumulation of a debt out of all proportion to her resources, a result which led to the consolidation of the Exchequers in 1817.[1]

The overtaxation of Ireland was bitterly complained of at the time. "Perhaps the taxes of an Englishman amount to three pounds, while those of an Irishman of the same rank amount not to twenty shillings; but certain it is the Englishman's means of paying those three pounds exceed the Irishman's means of paying his one pound in a ratio far more than proportional."[2]

The most conclusive test of the complete financial exhaustion of Ireland was that it was impossible to raise any loans in the country.

An important further proof of the complete exhaustion of Irish resources in the course of the great war is the fact that the power to raise money on the public credit in Ireland almost came to an end, so that it became necessary to raise the great bulk of the Irish loans in England. In the year 1801 the interest upon 16,739,521*l*. of unredeemed Irish debt was payable in Great Britain, and the interest upon 10,101,698*l*. of the debt was payable in Ireland. At the end of the war in 1817 these proportions had so far changed that the interest upon 92,144,904*l*. of the unredeemed Irish debt was payable in Great Britain, while the interest upon 21,535,254*l*. of that debt was payable in Ireland. In the year 1815 it was considered to be impossible to raise in Ireland so much as a single million by way of public loan.[3]

[1] *Ibidem*. [2] Rev. Henry Major, *Observations Demonstrative of the Necessity to Ireland's Welfare, &c.* Dublin 1815. [3] *F. R. C.* p. 145.

During the period 1800-1816 the British debt had increased by fifty per cent, while that of Ireland had quadrupled. This extraordinary increase was due to the fact that a far greater proportion of Irish than of British expenditure had to be met by loan, and that loans could only be raised in Ireland at considerable expense. The select committee of the House of Commons, which investigated the financial relations between the two countries in 1811-1815, found that in 1815 the Irish debt had become to the British as 2 to 13 or 12½, and was therefore in excess of the Union proportion of 2 to 15. One of the conditions precedent—subject to an important question of construction of the Act of Union, to which we shall refer presently—to the amalgamation of the British and Irish exchequers had therefore become fulfilled.

In order to save Ireland from the bankruptcy which appeared imminent, the House of Commons in 1816 passed resolutions, embodying the following recommendations of the select committee of the previous year:—

"1. That it is the opinion of this Committee that the values of the respective debts of Great Britain and Ireland, estimated according to the provisions of the Act of Union, have been, at a period subsequent to those Acts, in the same proportion to each other (within one-hundredth part of the said value) with the respective contributions of each country respectively, towards the annual expenditure of the United Kingdom; and that the respective circumstances of the two countries will henceforth admit of their contributing indiscriminately, by equal taxes imposed upon the same articles in each, to the future expenditure of the United Kingdom; subject only to such particular exemptions or abatements in Ireland and in Scotland as circumstances may appear from time to time to demand; and that it is no longer necessary to regulate the contribution of the two countries according to any specific proportion or according to the rules prescribed by the Acts of Union, with respect to such proportions.

"2. That it is the opinion of this Committee that it is expedient that all expenses henceforth to be incurred, together with the interest and charges of all debts hitherto contracted, shall be so defrayed indiscriminately by equal taxes to be imposed on the same articles in each country; and that from time to time, as circumstances may require, such taxes should be imposed and applied accordingly, subject only to such exemptions and abatements in Ireland and Scotland as circumstances may appear to demand.

"3. That it is the opinion of this Committee that such legislative measures should be adopted as may be necessary to carry into further effect the purposes of the said Acts of Union, by consolidating the public revenues of Great Britain and Ireland into one fund, and applying the same to the general services of the United Kingdom."

These resolutions having been agreed to, a bill was rapidly passed into law consolidating the debts and public revenues of the two kingdoms. This act provided that all revenues in Great Britain and Ireland should, after the 5th Jan. 1817, constitute one general fund; and that that fund was to be charged with, and indiscriminately applied to, (1) the services of the British and Irish debts, (2) the Civil List, (3) all other services previously charged on the separate consolidated funds of the two kingdoms, and (4) the supply services of the United Kingdom generally.[1]

We must now consider the difficulty of construction to which we referred above. On examining the Act of Union it will be found that the unification of Great Britain and Ireland for revenue purposes was only to take place on the fulfilment of two conditions; the first, "if at any future day the separate debt of each country shall have been liquidated, or if the value of their respective debts shall be to each other in the same proportion with the respective contributions of each country respectively;" the second, "if it shall appear to the Parliament of the United Kingdom that the respective circumstances of the two countries will thenceforth admit of their contributing indiscriminately by equal taxes imposed upon the same articles in each to the future expenditure of the United Kingdom." Those who afterwards complained of the heavy burdens laid on Ireland by the Consolidation Act argued that neither of these statutory conditions had been fulfilled.

Those who suggested that the former condition had not been fulfilled based their argument on the contention that the Act of Union contemplated the proportion of 2 to 15 being arrived at by the liquidation of part of the British debt, and not by the increase of the Irish. It was urged

[1] 56 Geo. III c. 98.

in support of this contention that the act did not contemplate any increase in the separate debts of the two kingdoms after the Union, but that all debts contracted after that date should be considered a joint liability. If this was the true construction of the act, there could be no doubt that the agreed proportion of the debts could be arrived at only by the liquidation of part of the British. What in fact happened was that the proportion of 2 to 15 was reached owing to the enormous increase of the Irish debt; and it was contended that this did not meet the requirements of the Act of Union.[1]

A glance at the Act of Union is enough to convince one that its construction on this point is by no means self-evident. Resort has therefore been had by controversialists to the utterances of the framers of the act. Such utterances, though admissible in parliamentary and political discussions to demonstrate the intentions of the legislature, are of course inadmissible in a court of law to help to construe a statute. It seems to be clear that the framers of the Act of Union contemplated that the reduction of the debts to the proportion of 2 to 15 would be brought about by the liquidation of part of the British debt; but they nowhere promised or suggested that it would never be brought about in any other way. Thus Lord Castlereagh said:—"Common taxes are not to take place till either the past and separate debts of both countries shall be liquidated, or till they shall come to each other in the proportion of their contributions. Before this can take place the taxes of Great Britain must be reduced by the amount of 10 millions a year."[2]

It must be mentioned here that there is some doubt as to the precise words that Castlereagh used on this occasion. The version of his speech printed by Rea, of Exchequer Street, Dublin, adds the following sentence:—"It may happen however that, if war should continue, and Ireland

[1] John O'Connell, *Argument for Ireland* Dublin 1847, p. 280, *Second Repeal Prize Essay* p. 56; *Repeal Reports* vol. i. p. 61. [2] *F. R. C.* p. 94.

fund her supplies, while England raises a great part of hers within the year, and mortgages her income tax to their rapid reduction in time of peace, that the proportion of the debt of Ireland may rise." The versions printed by Stockdale, of Abbey Street, and Milliken, of Grafton Street, omit this passage. John O'Connell was inclined to think the first version the most reliable.[1] Pitt obviously contemplated that the British debt would be reduced.[2] On the other hand, Foster clearly foresaw the possibility of the proportion being brought about by the increase of the Irish debt. "We owe 25 millions, they owe 361, but when we shall owe 50 and they not above 240, we are to lose the benefit; we cannot bear equal taxation now, but when we double our debt we shall be richer and more adequate to support it. Our increase of poverty and their increase of wealth are to bring us to an equality of condition."[3] It is probable that the framers of the act in speaking of this matter laboured under the same mistake as when they fixed the proportions of contribution, namely, they assumed that the French war would come to a speedy conclusion. In that case, the British debt would have been reduced as contemplated. The continuance of the war upset all calculations.

The following is what Mr. Childers says on the construction of this part of the Act:

The wording of the Act of Union in this respect appears to be ambiguous and its construction doubtful. The Select Committee on the taxation of Ireland in 1864 examined three barristers with regard to the construction of subsections 7 and 8 of Article 7 of the Act. Two of these witnesses maintained (one of them, Mr. Dillon, with some hesitation), that, strictly speaking, after the Union, no addition could be made to the separate debt of Ireland, except for local purposes, while Mr. Napier on the other hand, who had been Lord Chancellor of Ireland, gave it as his opinion that an addition to the separate debt of Ireland, under circumstances which took place, was distinctly contemplated by the Act.

The provisions in question seem to have been drawn in an obscure manner, and there is some reason for thinking that important words which should have been inserted in subsection 7, were accidentally omitted. The words in that section which form one of the recitals, viz., "provided

[1] *An Argument for Ireland* p. 309. [2] *F. R. C.* p. 4. [3] *F. R. C.* p. 148.

that if at any time, in raising their respective contributions hereby fixed for each country, the Parliament of the United Kingdom shall judge it fit to raise a greater proportion of such respective contributions in one country within the year than in the other," are not followed, in the operative part of the same sentence, by any words which relate to such a contingency. It was suggested in the evidence before the Select Committee of 1864 that this first contingency had been lost sight of by the draftsman in the consideration of a second contingency, viz., the more rapid liquidation of debt in one country than in the other.

It is, we think, clear from the speeches of Lord Castlereagh, and of Mr. Foster, that at the time of the Union, at any rate, both sides contemplated the increase of the separate Irish debt as one of the two modes in which the two debts might be brought into the ratio of 2 to 15. It is submitted that, in view of the fact that no question was raised as to the legitimacy of the increase of the separate debts by the Committees of 1811, 1812, and 1815, and as the House of Commons by its resolutions of 1816 implied the legitimacy of that increase, it is not now properly open to question. Even supposing that the terms of the Act of Union, taken literally do not expressly sanction the course of procedure which was in fact adopted the maxim of law "*fieri non oportuit ; factum valeat*" may well be held to apply to this case.[1]

It is a matter of doubt therefore whether the first condition requisite for financial unification had taken place; there is no doubt that the second had not. As Mr. Childers well puts it:

"Opinions may also differ as to whether Parliament was, in 1816, justified in considering that the circumstances of the two countries would thenceforth admit of uniform taxation, especially in view of the fact that for a long time subsequent to the war the systems of taxation remained very distinct, and are not even yet quite homogeneous. There is no evidence that any special consideration was given by Parliament to this question, or inquiry made."[2]

"Advantage was taken of that one single branch "the Repeal Association complained, "of the contingency contemplated in the Union Act, although the other branch of the contingency, viz., the nearer approach to equality of the respective abilities of the two countries, had not only not occurred, but by the confession of the English ministers themselves in 1816 the very contrary had occurred—namely Ireland had become poorer than before, while Great Britain had actually increased in capital and resources. Advantage was taken of that single branch of the contingency to consolidate the debts, to do away with all measures of propor-

[1] *F. R. C.* p. 149. [2] *F. R. C.* p. 149.

tionate contribution, and place the purse of Ireland, without restriction or limit, in the hands of the British Chancellor of the Exchequer."[1]

It is only fair to point out, as Mr. Childers has done,[2] that the immediate object of the Consolidation Bill of 1816 was, not to equalize taxation, but to avert Ireland's impending bankruptcy. Nevertheless, as we shall see in a moment, advantage was taken of the act by later Chancellors of the Exchequer to equalize British and Irish taxes, just as though the second condition precedent to consolidation had been fulfilled. The following extract from a petition presented to parliament by the Repeal Association sets out this grievance very clearly: "The Consolidation Act was introduced under the strange pretext of relieving Ireland from the theretofore excessive and exhaustive demands upon her; but while it nominally did so, it in reality utterly swept away and destroyed all species of protection which she had hitherto possessed from a further and monstrous increase of these demands; and in consequence of it she has, upon an average of twenty-six years since the passing of that pretended act of relief, been made to pay more in proportion than she did before; and in addition was by it, and still remains, mortgaged in every shilling and every acre for the whole of the enormous debt of Great Britain, as well that contracted since as that contracted before the Union."[3]

In view of the fact that the step taken in 1816 operated, not only to tide Ireland over her temporary difficulties, but permanently to regulate the financial relations between the two countries, it is not irrelevant to consider what should have been done at the time. There can be no doubt that the financial failure of Ireland was attributable to the injustice of the contribution fixed by the Union in the events which had happened, and it would therefore seem that the just thing to have done was to revise the basis

[1] *Repeal Reports* vol. i. p. 60. [2] *F. R. C.* p. 147.
[3] O'Connell. *An Argument for Ireland* p. 290.

of the proportions contributed by Great Britain and Ireland to the joint expenditure. The one objection to this course was that the Act of Union provided that no such revision should take place for twenty years. This objection was answered by John O'Connell:—"There was a difficulty indeed in the way of revision; inasmuch as the Act of Union ordained that twenty years should pass without revision, or any alteration, unless the contingencies under which consolidation was to be effected should occur in the interval. But when a greater difficulty, viz. that of carrying the consolidation against the spirit and meaning of the Act of Union, was so little thought of, a less degree of boldness would have sufficed to get over that which we have mentioned."[1]

As we have already said, although the financial unification of 1816 was designed rather to prevent Ireland from falling into a state of bankruptcy than to equalize the taxes of Great Britain and Ireland, nevertheless the consolidation was made use of to assimilate the taxes of the two countries. This was done by means of three devices:

(1) The abolition of taxes to which Great Britain was subject but which did not extend to Ireland.

(2) The equalization of lower rates, in certain cases, in Ireland, with the higher rates prevailing in Great Britain or in England.

(3) The extension to Ireland of certain taxes from which she had previously been exempted.[2]

The remission of taxes which applied to Great Britain but not to Ireland formed a remarkable feature of the fiscal legislation after the war. "In 1822 returns were presented to Parliament 'showing the taxes the collection of which ceased during the preceding ten years.' By these returns it appears that the relief extended to Great Britain up to 1822 was the following:

[1] *An Argument for Ireland* p. 325.
[2] *F. R. C.* p. 155.

Assessed taxes, diminished or repealed	£ 808,484
Property Tax	14,617,823
Customs	255,356
Excise	7,559,934
Taxes	347,762
	£23,589,359

"To this enormous sum more than two millions were added in 1822, and between three and four in 1830—so that the Duke of Wellington made no vain boast when he talked of a relief to the extent of about thirty millions. Now, what have been the operations of the Exchequer so far as regards Ireland ? One of the returns of which we speak professes to be a further and final account of all taxes, the collection of which ceased in Ireland during the ten preceding years, and it gives the following figures:

Customs	£ 55,273
Excise	312,600
Taxes	216,079
Stamps	24,368
	£608,320[1]

Tax after tax which affected Great Britain alone was repealed in this period; the property tax in 1816, the salt tax in 1820, the beer tax in 1830, the printed cotton tax in 1831, and the candle tax in 1832.[2] "We desire" said Mr. Childers:

"to note some of the chief remissions subsequently to the year 1830 of excise duties which did not extend to Ireland. The beer duty, producing about three millions in 1829, was repealed in 1830. The duty on printed cottons, producing over two millions in 1829, was repealed in 1831; that on candles, then producing 470,000*l.*, was repealed in 1832; the duty on starch, producing 117,000*l.* in 1833, was repealed in 1834; half of the soap duty was remitted in 1833. These changes in taxation, not extending to Ireland, immediately followed the first measure of parliamentary reform; at a later period, in 1853, the soap duty, then producing 1,170,000*l.*, was wholly repealed; the duty on bricks, then producing 456,000*l.*, was repealed in 1850; and the duty on hops, to the estimated amount of 250,000*l.*, besides 98,671*l* custom duty, was repealed in 1862."[3]

[1] Staunton, *Hints for Hardinge* Dublin 1830.
[2] *Second Repeal Prize Essay* p. 104.
[3] *F. R. C.* p. 156.

The following figures show the comparative relief from taxation experienced by Great Britain and Ireland respectively during the period 1800-45:*

	Relief of Taxation		Imposition of Taxation	
	Gt. Btn.	Ireland	Gt. Btn.	Ireland
From 1800 to 1815	—	—	30,000,000	4,450,000
From 1815 to 1845	£47,114,574	£2,664,090	10,620,000	1,060,000
Totals	£47,114,574	£2,664,090	40,620,000	5,510,000

* *Parliamentary Papers* 1842 No. 305, 1843 No. 573, and 1845 No. 652.

The following figures from the report of the Financial Relations Commission show the amount of taxes to which Great Britain was subject, and from which Ireland was exempt, in the years 1817-21 and in 1845.*

Revenue derived in the years 1817-1821 from taxation not imposed in Ireland.

Customs	£14,347,204
Excise	44,096,425
Stamps	13,126,966
Taxes	29,826,855
Total	£101,397,450
Annual average	20,279,490

Similar Account for the Year 1845.

Income Tax	£ 5,182,649
Land and assessed taxes	4,441,746
Hackney carriages	65,933
Stage carriages	431,371
Spirits, excess over rates in Ireland	2,350,304
Patent medicines	28,942
Soap	963,507
Bricks	561,867
Hops	257,447
Post horses	169,853
Total	£14,453,619

* *F. R. C.* p. 155.

The second method by which the assimilation of Irish and British taxation was brought about was by raising the rates in Ireland on articles which had been more heavily taxed in Great Britian. The tea, sugar, wine, tobacco, and foreign spirits taxes were assimilated in 1814, the malt tax in 1815, the hides and skins, and paper tax in 1825, the vinegar, cider, and perry tax in 1826, and the bottle and glass tax in 1828.[1]

The third method of assimilation, namely, the extension to Ireland of taxes which previously applied only to Great Britain, does not concern us in this period, as the first great example of such extension was the income tax in 1853.[2]

The result of the process of assimilation was that, after about 1825, Ireland was subjected to by far the greater number of taxes affecting Great Britain, and the "particular exemptions or abatements" which the Act of Union had provided for were few and far between. The following passage from a pamphlet written in 1830 by Michael Staunton, by far the best authority at that period on all questions dealing with Irish public finance, shows how far the process of assimilation had been carried at that date, and how insignificant were the Irish exceptions.

"The 'least taxed country in Europe' is by far the poorest, but it is compelled, nevertheless, to endure *nearly* all the the taxes of the richest. It endures *all* the taxes that press on the comforts and industry of the people. The principal articles in the schedule of British taxation are the following:

	Per Ann.		Per Ann.
Liquors, producing ..	17,761,573	Stamp Duties	7,317,602
Other stimulants	11,869,356	Post-Office	2,207,998
Food	937,622	Land and Assessed Taxes	5,162,873
Dress, &c.	2,573,604	Other resources	666,572
Household articles ..	2,711,557		
Miscellaneous	3,326,627		

"The 'liquors' are spirits, malt, and wine. All spirits but Irish pay as much duty in Dublin as London. A tax on Irish whiskey, most injurious, and unjust towards this

[1] *Second Repeal Prize Essay* p. 104. Staunton *Hints for Hardinge* Dublin 1830 p. 36.

[2] F. R. C. p. 9. The eagerness of British Ministers to assimilate the taxation of the two countries is shown by a letter written by Lord Auckland in 1806, in the *Fortescue MSS* vol. vii p. 347. The Excise Commissioners of 1835 recommended complete assimilation. O'Connell complained bitterly of this passion for assimilation. Fitzpatrick *Correspondence of Daniel O'Connell* vol. ii. p. 289.

country, adds to its price to the English consumer. This imposes no very perceptible burthen upon him, and so far from its being a sufficient reason for the postponement, or withholding, of a benefit claimed for Ireland, or for giving her an addition to her privations under pretence of 'assimilating' the taxes of the two countries, it is a ground on which she may seek to be recompensed or exempted. English monopoly has scarcely left her any manufacture but that of whiskey, and it is not the least of her grievances that the consumption of that article is restricted and discouraged amongst the people of England by heavy duties. As to all other spirits, and to wine, the Dublin and London consumer are quite on an equality.

"The 'other stimulants', are sugar, tea, coffee, and tobacco. They produce more than a fifth of the entire taxation of the United Kingdom, and they are exactly as burthensome to the poorest as to the richest of these kingdoms—to that which is supposed to be the 'least taxed country in Europe', as to the spot imagined to be the most loaded with taxes.

"The 'food' consists of butter, cheese, currants and raisins, and corn. The Englishman who makes his own butter has it on as good terms as the Irishman. If he import the article, it comes to him affected by a small duty, and in this respect he is not worse off than the Irishman. In the other articles under the head of 'food', with the exception of cheese, there is no difference between the two countries.

"The articles of 'dress, &c.' are cotton and wool, silks, printed goods, hides and skins, and paper. These form a considerable item in the schedule, and any taxes that affect them operate equally in England and Ireland. If there be a difference, it is one against Ireland, and not in favour of it. The duties on the coarser kind of paper are, we believe, unequal—the inequality is *against* 'the least taxed country in Europe.'

"The 'household' articles are soap, candles, tallow and

coals. We are burthened by a very heavy coal tax. We endure a coal tax from which that part of Great Britain called Scotland is exempt. The English soap and tallow tax does not affect this country, but its amount is not of great magnitude.

"The building articles are glass, bricks and tiles, and timber. We pay the English glass and timber duties. From the duties on bricks and tiles we are exempt, but they are not considerable.

"The other heads of taxation are auctions, licences, insurances, stamps ,post-office, and land and assessed taxes. In respect of auctions, licences, insurances, and post-office, there is no difference between the 'least taxed' and most taxed countries. Our stamp duties are lighter in many instances than the English, and though we have *some* 'land taxes' we have no assessed taxes. We do not undervalue our exemption from heavier stamp duties and the assessed taxes, but it comprehends nearly all the fiscal indulgence practised towards Ireland, and supplies the only foundation for the assumption that, in reference not only to England, but all other countries, our taxes are insignificant. The effect of this exemption is, that it relieves us from such contributions as we should, under other circumstances, make to the one-twelfth or one-thirteenth of the Imperial income. The amount of this contribution would be under 400,000*l* a year, if Mr. Goulburn was right in his estimate of the produce of the proposed stamp duties, for the assessed taxes, from which we have been relieved, produced only 297,000*l*. in the last year of their existence. We contribute our full quota to about 50 out of 54 or 55 millions, which form the total of the Imperial revenue. It is on the ground of the contribution not going farther than the fifty millions, and not reaching to the four or five additional millions produced by the assessed and other taxes, that we are pronounced 'the least taxed country in Europe'."[1]

[1] *Hints for Hardinge*, Dublin 1830 pp. 10-13.

"The coat which the peasant wears", said Mr. Spring Rice, "the blanket with which he is to cover his children, the few articles of furniture which he acquires, all contribute to the exigencies of the state before they can enter his cottage."[1]

"It is pretended", said the Report of the Repeal Association, "that Ireland has been more than compensated for all possible fiscal losses since 1800 by her continued exemption from several taxes to which Great Britain is subject. But your Committee find that the exemption of Ireland consists only as to the land tax, the income and assessed taxes, and a portion of the excise duties averaging about $^1/_{14}$th of the whole revenue of excise; and that the total sum paid by Great Britain under the four heads does not exceed, if it even approach to, twelve millions out of the average fifty-one or fifty-two millions of imperial expenditure."[2] The one tax for which all Irish opinion clamoured, namely the absentee tax, was the one which the Imperial Parliament consistently refused to impose.

The comparative advantages derived from the course of assimilation following the Consolidation Act by Great Britain and Ireland respectively may be judged from the following table:

	Period of 18 years 1800—17	Period of 16 years 1818—33	Period of 16 years 1834—49
	£	£	£
Average taxation of Great Britain*	58,000,000	51,000,000	48,000,000
Average taxation of Ireland	4,375,000	4,687,500	5,200,000

* *F. R. C.* p. 88.

It appears from the above figures that, while the annual taxation of Great Britain during the period 1800-50 tended to fall, that of Ireland tended to rise. The injustice of this

[1] *Considerations on the Present State of Ireland* London 1822.
[2] *Repeal Reports* vol. i. p. 61.

can be fully realized only if we remember that during the same period Great Britain was yearly increasing in wealth and resources, while Ireland was passing through a period of economic decline which culminated in the famine. The following table further demonstrates the same point, by showing that, until the actual deadly work of the famine had been done, Ireland tended to pay a gradually increasing proportion of the taxation of the United Kingdom, and that while the *per capita* taxation in Great Britain was reduced in a period of thirty years by 31.1 *per cent.*, that of Ireland was reduced by only 3.4 *per cent.*

Year	Taxation per head of population		Proportion of revenue raised in	
	Great Britain	Ireland	Great Britain	Ireland
	£. s. d.	s. d.	*per cent*	*per cent*
1819-20	3 10 3	14 3	91	9
1829-30	2 18 0	13 1	90·4	9·6
1839-40	2 7 5	12 5	89·6	10·4
1849-50	2 7 8	13 11	91·6	8·4

* *F. R. C.* p. 154.

It appears from the above figures that the amount paid *per capita* in Ireland was much lower than in England, and that the percentage of revenue contributed by Ireland was not so great as the percentage of her population, and it might be concluded that Ireland did not therefore pay her fair share of the joint burden. The answer to this suggestion is that the vast majority of the taxes were the same in both countries, and that Ireland's inferior contribution was simply an indication of her poverty. This is admirably put by Michael Staunton:

"The *amount* of our revenue, if it be really as small as is generally imagined, only proves that the consumption of taxed articles is limited by the poverty of the people, not that the imposts upon the articles which are used are light, or unfelt by the consumers. Our revenue is usually taken by public writers and speakers to be £4,000,000. As this forms not even a twelfth of the whole revenue, though the population of Ireland is at least the one-third of that of the United Kingdom, the conclusion is, that Ireland is an untaxed country, as compared with Great Britain. That this is fallacious is proved by the impossibility of adding half a million to the four, if every tax existing in England were paid by the Irish people. Let all the assessed taxes be revived, and there are only added 300,000*l.* to the four millions. The *amount* of the revenue, then, speaks only as to the number of persons capable of paying considerable taxes, and not as to the extent to which taxes press upon a single individual obliged to pay them. Though our revenue is small, wine, coffee, tea, sugar, tobacco, and other necessaries are as heavily taxed in Dublin as London. The difference is all in the number of the consumers, or their ability to consume. The customs' duties of Liverpool are above three millions, while the customs' duties of Bristol (a place of nearly equal population) are little more than one million. As well may it be held upon these data that the Liverpool merchant pays more than three times the customs' duties to which the merchant in the other port is subject, as that there is a material difference between the pressure of taxes in England and Ireland, because in one country the produce of revenue is only four millions, while in the other it reaches to fifty millions. The amount of the customs duty in Liverpool only shews that there are more merchants there, or merchants of a greater extent of business, than are to be found in Bristol, not that any merchant has to pay on his transactions more in proportion to the state than a person of his avocation in any other port of England, however insignificant."[1] "Ireland is indeed sometimes spoken of", it was remarked by the Grand Jury Commissioners of 1842, "as if its burdens were light because they are less than those of Great Britain; but unfortunately so are its means. The idea of the proportion which the property of the one country bears to the other may be formed

[1] *Hints for Hardinge* Dublin 1831 pp. 13-14.

from the amount which pays legacy duty in each; and the amount in 1840 in Great Britain was rather more than forty millions, in Ireland only about two."[1]

In view of the statistics we have quoted it is not unreasonable to conclude that Ireland was taxed beyond its resources in the fifty years following the Union. But the injustice did not end there. Overtaxation, though always a hardship, is not invariably an unmixed evil; and circumstances may be imagined in which taxation beyond the resources of a country would be amply justified by some ultimate benefit which it would produce. In Ireland however there was no such justification; on the contrary the revenue raised by the oppressive fiscal system was not alone not put to productive national purposes, but was, to a great extent, actually taken out of the country. The evil of the surplus revenue for which Ireland received no return is exactly analogous to the absenteeism of the landlords. In each case we see the exaction of extortionate payments from a community that can ill afford them, and in each case the evil of this extortion is intensified by the fact that these payments are spent in another country. Indeed it is strictly correct to describe the surplus revenue of Ireland devoted to imperial purposes as a kind of public, as distinguished from private, absenteeism; and in making up the account of how Irish absenteeism increased after the Union we must include this item, as well as the rents which were remitted to the landlords living abroad. We must further remember that this new form of absenteeism was a direct product of the Union; the evil of non-resident landowners had been complained of in the seventeenth and eighteenth centuries, and even earlier; but the further method of draining Ireland of its wealth by annually exporting some millions of its revenue was a device unknown before the legislative Union.

In attempting to estimate the extent of this drain, it is important to grasp the difference between the estimated

[1] *Report* p. xxvi.

and the true revenue of Ireland. After the abolition of the Union duties on the cross-channel trade, the only method of arriving at the amount of the Irish revenue was by taking account of the sum actually collected in Ireland. It is obvious however that this calculation could be but approximately correct, owing to the fact that taxes were frequently collected in Ireland on articles consumed in Great Britain—for example, spirits—and in Great Britain on articles consumed in Ireland—for example, tea landed in a British port. An attempt to correct this error was made by the Treasury; and the figures at which it arrived are probably the most correct estimate we shall ever possess of the true revenue of Ireland in the nineteenth century, although, owing to lack of *data*, they must not be taken to be exactly accurate. "They cannot be taken as giving more than a tolerable approximation to the actual facts."[1] These returns give reason for believing that during the first half of the century the export of duty-paid articles from Great Britain to Ireland greatly exceeded that from Ireland to Great Britain, and consequently that the Irish true revenue was in excess of the estimated revenue in that period. The following tables prepared by the Treasury show, as nearly as can be calculated, the estimated and true revenue of Ireland in the years 1820-50:

(1) Table showing Revenue as Collected in Great Britain and Ireland for every Tenth Year from 1819 to 1850*.

Year	Great Britain	Ireland	Total
	Revenue as Collected	Revenue as Collected	Revenue
	£	£	£
1819	52,605,508	5,253,909	57,859,417
1829	50,928,489	4,461,217	55,389,706
1839	47,286,842	4,574,150	51,860,992
1849	53,128,685	4,338,091	57,466,776

* *F. R. C.* p. 153, and see Cobbett, *Three Lectures on the Political State of Ireland* Dublin 1834; Staunton *Hints for Hardinge* pp. 25 sq.

[1] *F. R. C.* p. 152.

(2) TABLE SHOWING TRUE REVENUE, AS ESTIMATED BY THE TREASURY, OF GREAT BRITAIN AND IRELAND FOR EVERY TENTH YEAR FROM 1819 TO 1850.

Year	Great Britain	Ireland	Total
	Estimated true Revenue	Estimated true Revenue	Revenue
	£	£	£
1819	51,445,764	5,256,564	56,702,328
1829	49,637,892	5,502,125	55,140,017
1839	46,262,412	5,415,889	51,678,301
1849	51,870,866	4,861,465	56,732,331

Having now ascertained ,as accurately as we can, the true revenue of Ireland, we must next try to estimate how much of that revenue was spent in Ireland, and how much went away never to return. It is not an easy matter to establish an infallible criterion for distinguishing Irish from imperial expenditure; but probably Mr. Childers' test is as satisfactory as any:—"For the present historical purpose it is, we think, legitimate to take the 'Charge for Irish purposes upon the Imperial Exchequer' in the sense which is given to this expression in the recent Treasury returns, i.e. as comprising the Irish civil government expenditure i.e. the cost of the legal and police establishments, of the government offices whose operation is limited to Ireland, of prisons and education in Ireland, and the expenditure on postal services and collection of revenue so far as it is incurred in Ireland."[1] Taking this to be the proper test of local expenditure, and assuming that the Treasury returns of the true Irish revenue are approximately correct, we arrive at the following figures, as showing the amount of Irish revenue which was spent in Ireland in the years 1820-50:

[1] *F. R. C.* p. 165.

STATEMENT SHOWING THE ESTIMATED LOCAL EXPENDITURE INCURRED IN IRELAND, AND THE BALANCE OF TRUE REVENUE WHICH IS AVAILABLE FOR IMPERIAL SERVICES AFTER SUCH EXPENDITURE HAS BEEN MET.*

Year	Revenue as collected	Adjustment (+) or (—)	Estimated True Revenue	Estimated Local Expenditure	Balance available for Imperial Services
	£	£	£	£	£
1819	5,253,909	+ 2,655	5,256,564	1,564,880	3,691,684
1829	4,461,217	+1,040,908	5,502,125	1,345,549	3,691,684
1839	4,574,150	+ 841,739	5,415,889	1,789,567	3,626,322
1849	4,338,091	+ 523,374	4,861,465	2,247,687	2,613,778

* *F. R. C.* p. 165.

It appears, at the first glance, from the above table that the amount of Irish revenue spent abroad greatly exceeded that spent in Ireland. But the benefits conferred on Ireland and the other parts of the empire are not to be determined merely by ascertaining the locality where the revenue was expended. It is possible to imagine cases where a country may derive far more ultimate gain from public money spent abroad than at home—for example the case of prosecuting a successful war on foreign soil; and on the contrary it is equally possible to imagine cases where revenue spent at home is noxious rather than advantageous—for example money expended by a tyrannical government for the maintenance of an oppressive standing army and secret police. In view of this, we must not be content to judge of the benefits which Ireland derived from her revenue by a mere examination of the locality in which it was expended, but must pursue our inquiry further. In pursuing this further inquiry we are immediately struck by three considerations: (1) that much of the apparent Irish local expenditure was really imperial in aim and result, (2) that many local services were wastefully and uneconomically administered, and (3) that Ireland received a totally disproportionate share of the benefits derived from the expenditure of her surplus revenue for imperial purposes. Let us consider these in turn.

On the first point, that much apparently local expenditure was really imperial, we cannot do better than quote from the majority report of the Financial Relations Commission:—

> We cannot admit the justice of this mode of dealing with Imperial expenditure. Whilst the kingdoms are united under one Parliament, and Imperial expenditure is determined on Imperial grounds, we cannot but regard the maintenance of order, the enforcement of the laws, the collection and protection of the revenue, as subjects of Imperial concern, no matter in what part of the United Kingdom they take place, and the expenditure upon them must be regarded as a whole, and Imperial in its character. We cannot suppose that anyone will deny that these matters are Imperial in their character, yet by Sir Edward Hamilton's definition they are set down as local. It is true that in particular instances one part of the Kingdom may be more interested in attention being paid to them than another. The maintenance of order and the upholding of the laws in Ireland may be of more importance to its inhabitants than to those of Great Britain, but the latter, it cannot be doubted, are also interested in them, and the distinction which Sir Edward Hamilton endeavours to draw is in reality a distinction between different sorts of Imperial expenditure founded upon the supposed comparative benefits derived from it by one part of the United Kingdom rather than from another. If this principle be adopted its application cannot be stopped where the Treasury calculations leave off. If the Imperial expenditure necessary for the maintenance of Civil Government in Ireland is to be regarded as local because Ireland is mainly benefited by it, questions may be asked, and must be asked, why the Imperial expenditure on the army and navy should not be charged to Great Britain, because she is mainly interested in and benefited by the expenditure.
>
> If Ireland is to be hypothetically submerged in the ocean in order to ascertain what expenditure would be saved thereby to Great Britain, Great Britain herself must also undergo a similar operation, if we wish to ascertain what Imperial expenditure would be saved to Ireland under such circumstances. We believe that a large proportion of the so-called "local expenditure" in Ireland is due to her connexion with Great Britain, and if the latter country ceased to exist we see no reason for supposing that the revenue for carrying on the Government of Ireland need exceed that, for instance, required in Sweden where the population is about the same, and where the annual expenditure for all purposes is less than the "local expenditure" in Ireland.[1]

Another matter to which we should refer here, but which we shall treat more fully in the next section, is that many imperial services were paid for out of the proceeds of Irish local taxation.[2]

On the second consideration which we have suggested, we need only say that it must have been apparent to anyone who has read this book that Ireland was burthened with many boards and departments which did not render the

[1] *F. R. C.* p. 23. [2] *Repeal Reports* vol. iii p. 75 and *Devon Comm.* p. 945.

community any service commensurate with their cost. The observance of due economy in the public service is a matter to be observed by the government; if that economy is not observed, the unnecessary expense involved should not be debited against the taxpayers who are mulcted to support it. "Wasteful or extravagant expenditure does not justify excessive taxation."[1] Moreover it was the intention of the Act of Union that the cost of the civil administration of Great Britain and Ireland should be borne indiscriminately. Again to quote Mr. Childers:—

> It does not seem that because the cost of civil administration in Ireland is greater, relatively to population and wealth, than it is in Great Britain, this, by itself, is any reason why the people of Ireland should contribute to the public revenue a share in excess of their relative wealth.
>
> It was, in our opinion, the clear intention of the framers of the Act of Union, that, so far as related to taxation or the raising of revenue, Ireland should (whether contributing, as she did till 1817, according to a certain ratio, or whether, as subsequently, by way of indiscriminate taxation subject to exceptions) have a distinct position and separate consideration. But it was their equally clear intention that all expenditure, including no less that upon civil government in Ireland than that upon the army and navy, should be in common, or Imperial. It was never intended that the ratio of contribution or the extent of the exemptions and abatements (as the case might be) should be affected by consideration of the relative cost of administration in each of the three kingdoms.[2]

The third consideration is probably the most important, as it emphasizes the point we have already mentioned in dealing with Irish industries, that the interests of Ireland were during the nineteenth century habitually subordinated to those of Great Britain, and that, in fact, the whole imperial policy was designed with a view to benefiting the predominant partner. The small part of the advantages of British imperial development which Ireland enjoyed was well described by Mr. Murrough O'Brien in the memorandum which he presented to the Financial Relations Commission:—"Ireland, a very poor, purely agricultural and pastoral country, has no need of the costly army and navy which the commerce, foreign relations, and policy of Great Britain require, and which her wealth can maintain. Ireland should not be expected to contribute to these costly

[1] *F. R. C.* p. 25. [2] *F. R. C.* p. 191.

defence services, either in proportion to her population or her wealth; she derives but little advantage from them, and would scarcely be more in danger of invasion or aggression from other powers than Iceland is, but for her connection with Great Britain."[1] Mr. Childers proceeds to explain that "the obligation in question extends beyond the army and navy to other items of the expenditure usually termed 'imperal'; to the charges for instance in respect of the National Debt, which was mainly incurred in wars of which the main object has always been, according to one view taken of modern history, the extension and defence of commercial and trading interests. The allegation is also applied to the cost of the diplomatic services".[2]

It has been suggested by Mr. Childers that the repeal of the corn laws in 1846 made some difference to Ireland in respect of her dependence on the imperial forces for her subsistence in time of war. "Before the repeal of the corn laws Ireland exported wheat to England, but under the present circumstances of agriculture, her wheat area has greatly declined, and at present a large part of her own wheat supply comes from abroad."[3] It is possible that the result of the repeal of the corn laws may have operated to make Ireland more dependent on foreign foodstuffs than she formerly was; but this simply lends weight to the disapprobation of that measure which we have already expressed. It is simply another way of stating that Ireland was injured by the new free trade policy of England. "The reductions of 1844 were the corn duties, and those on certain articles of foreign import; chiefly those used in the production of manufactures. England is a larger consumer of bread stuffs, it is needless to say, than unfortunate Ireland; and, therefore, the relief in the respect of the corn duties must be more sensibly felt by her. The relief on articles of import subsidiary to manufactures must also be more beneficial to her, as she has so many and such various branches of

[1] *F. R. C.* p. 188. [2] *Ibidem.* [3] *F. R. C.* p. 189.

flourishing industry in that line; and Ireland has none save the linen, a branch not affected by those reductions. We are therefore entitled to say that the unjust disparity of taxation relief, existing at the end of last year, against Ireland has, if anything, been aggravated by the tax reductions of this year."[1] Mr. Childers says that "The change (from protection to free trade) is usually considered to have been advantageous to a population, the bulk of which had come not to depend upon agriculture, but upon manufacturing industry and commerce. It is, we think, evident that the change has not been so advantageous to Ireland, a country in which there is but little trade or manufacturing industry, as it has been to England; and that, although as consumers the Irish population may have gained in some cases by the abolition of duties on food stuffs, yet that on the other hand, as producers chiefly dependent on agriculture, they have lost in a far greater degree by the cheap prices in the British markets, produced, in part at least, by the free and untaxed supply of foreign corn, live-stock, butter, cheese, eggs, and other articles of food . . . ."[2] Even taking into account the increased reliance of Ireland after the repeal of the corn laws on the imperial arms for the supply of her necessary food, Mr. Childers draws the following conclusion:—"If, however, we look at the cost of the army and navy and other similar services as a national insurance paid for the protection of sea-borne commerce, or as a means of the extension of the Empire, and with it of trade, or as a means of preserving to this country the great field of trade and investment of surplus capital afforded by India and the minor dependencies of the Crown, it must seem that the benefits reaped from this outlay by Great Britain, looked at as a whole, are immensely greater than those which are reaped by Ireland."[3]

It is therefore the best opinion that, even in the period

[1] John O'Connell, *An Argument for Ireland* p. 356.
[2] *F. R. C.* pp. 159-60. [3] *F. R. C.* p. 189.

subsequent to the repeal of the corn laws, Great Britain derived by far the greater proportion of the benefit of the so-called imperial expenditure. How much greater then must have been the benefit which she derived during the period 1800-46, when she was principally dependent for her food supply on Ireland. If Ireland, as Mr. Childers showed, derived but little benefit from the imperial expenditure in the second half of the nineteenth century, how little must she have derived from that in the first half.

Having shown that a large part of the so-called local expenditure in Ireland was really imperial in character, that much of the local expenditure was wasteful and unproductive, and that Ireland derived but a small proportion of the benefits conferred by imperial outlay, we must now direct our attention for a moment to the allegation that an undue share of public money was advanced to Ireland by way of loans. The loans advanced to Ireland after the Union were undoubtedly large compared with those advanced to Great Britain, but we must not lose sight of the fact that the former country was undeveloped, and consequently more in need of governmental assistance than the latter. It must also be remembered that many of the grants of public money which the Irish Parliament had been accustomed to make were discontinued immediately after the Union.[1]

In attempting to arrive at an opinion as to how far the loans made to Ireland were an advantage or a disadvantage to the Treasury, we must distinguish between those that were repaid and those that were remitted. With regard to the former, it is difficult to see how their advance laid Ireland under a greater obligation to the Imperial Treasury than that which the private borrower incurs towards the ordinary moneylender. "Every loan which is fully repaid with interest until the date of repayment must in some degree be beneficial to a lender, like the State, precluded

[1] *Second Repeal Prize Essay* p. 74.

from speculative operations. Whether it is beneficial to the borrower depends upon the manner in which the money borrowed is expended. If it is spent in developing the latent resources of a business or country, the borrower may gain largely by the transaction. If on the other hand the money borrowed is spent in the relief of temporary distress or otherwise not in a reproductive manner, the borrower will in the end lose by the amount by which the interest paid and the capital repaid exceed the sum originally advanced"[1]

So much for the amount of loans repaid; the benefit to the lender is certain, while that to the borrower is uncertain. In the case of loans not repaid—or "remitted"—a further consideration must be taken into account, namely whether the lender gives an appropriate *quid pro quo* for the remission. In the case of the greater part of the Irish loans which were remitted, the *quid pro quo* given was the imposition of the income tax upon Ireland in 1853, which has in fact produced far more than the interest due on the loans.[2] It must also be considered whether the sum advanced was advanced for services which the lender was bound to perform. The larger part of the loans to Ireland which were afterwards remitted—in consideration of Ireland's shouldering the burden of the income tax—were loans intended to tide the country over the terrible crisis of the famine. "The advance of money to support existence in Ireland as the result of the famine was a matter of imperial necessity, and should have in the first instance been treated as extraordinary expenditure, to be defrayed out of current imperial revenue, and not as a loan to Ireland."[3]

In conclusion, it must not be forgotten that the so-called advances to Ireland formed but a negligible proportion of the surplus revenue which was raised in Ireland over and above the cost of the government of the country. In other words, the advances to Ireland were made not

[1] *F. R. C.* p. 163. [2] *F. R. C.* p. 161.

[3] *F. R. C.* p. 161. The justice of remitting the whole of the loans incurred in respect of the famine was strongly urged by a Select Committee of the House of Lords in 1852.

out of British but out of Irish money. "Will it be said", it was asked in 1815, "that Ireland should be satisfied with a grant now and then *out of her own money* from the bounty of Parliament for the purpose of enabling her to build a barrack, improve a harbour, construct a canal, assist a lazar house, and so forth ?"[1]

The advances to Ireland, therefore, fall into two classes, those repaid and those remitted. The former were of certain benefit to the lender, though of uncertain benefit to the borrower; while the latter were either repaid several times over by the consideration exacted for their remission, or else were advanced for services which the lender was obliged to perform. Finally, it must be remembered that the money advanced on such magnanimous terms was but a fraction of that contributed year after year by Ireland for the general purposes of the Empire in whose prosperity she enjoyed but a minor and precarious part.[2]

Section 2. Local Taxation.

The Irish taxpayer was loaded with local as well as national burdens. Indeed the taxes imposed by the county were almost as heavy as those imposed by the State. Like the national taxes, the local taxes increased grievously after the Union and were the object of much public attention. A select committee, which reported in 1816, recommended a general inspection of Ireland with a view to equalizing the burden of local taxation more equitably than theretofore;[3] and another in 1822 found that the powers possessed

[1] Rev. Henry Major, *Observations Demonstrative of the Necessity to Ireland's Welfare &c.* Dublin 1815.

[2] At the date of the remission, the outstanding Irish liabilities were as follows:

Debts due for the building of workhouses	£ 1.122.707
Debts due for temporary relief advances under 10 Vict. c. 17	783.228
Debts due for advances for works under 1 Vict. c. 21 and 9 Vict c. 1 ..	170.282
Debts due for advances for the relief of distressed unions under 13 Vict. c. 14	299.924
Labour rate advances under 9 and 10 Vict. c. 10	2.046.784

F. R. C. app. xix.

[3] *Select Committee on Grand Jury Presentments* 1816.

by the grand juries had "proved in very many instances burdensome to the occupying tenantry in an excessive degree."[1] In consequence of the very great attention given to the grand jury laws by witnesses before the Committee of 1824-5 on the State of Ireland, a further Select Committee on Grand Jury Presentments was created in 1826. The Spring Rice Committee of 1830 reported that "the county rates now constitute the heaviest burden to which occupiers of land in Ireland are subject."[2]

The local taxes increased greatly in the period following the Union, chiefly owing to the increased variety of purposes to which they might be legally applied. This increase of the burden of taxation attracted much attention; many parliamentary committees were appointed to investigate it; but, as was the general rule with committees charged to frame remedial measures, little attention was paid to their recommendations. Thus, the select committee of 1816 recommended that a fresh allocation of the burdens of local taxation should be attempted; and, although a bill was introduced in 1819 to give effect to this recommendation, it was not passed into law.[3] The recommendations of various select committees which had sat from 1815 onwards were partly given effect to in 1835,[4] and those relating to the City of Dublin a year later.[5] The Commission on Grand Jury Presentments in 1842 drew attention to the importance of the subject:—"The Committee appointed by the House of Commons to enquire into the state of agriculture in 1833 particularly mentioned the county rates in England as being 'a grievous charge borne principally by the land;' as being 'a grievous abuse' because 'placed under the control of authorities not personally responsible', and 'as requiring the early and deliberate attention of the

[1] *Second Report of Select Committee on Grand Jury Presentments* 1822.
[2] *Report of Select Committee on State of Poor in Ireland* 1830 p. 41.
[3] *Select Committee on Survey and Valuation of Ireland* 1824.
[4] 6 & 7 Wm. IV c. 116, amended by 7 Wm. IV c. 21, 1 Vict. c. 54, 2 and 3 Vict. c. 50 and 3 and 4 Vict. c. 70. [5] 7 and 8 Wm. IV. C. 106.

legislature'. If it were necessary to watch and restrict the charges upon land in England, it is certainly as requisite to do so in Ireland. We are satisfied that the whole system under which moneys are now applied and collected by Grand Jury Presentments requires essential change."[1] Nevertheless these grievances were not redressed till many years later.

The injustices connected with the county cess may be considered under three heads: its amount, its incidence, and the abuses attending its collection and expenditure. With regard to the amount of the cess, it increased steadily from the beginning of the century, and doubled in twenty years. This was due principally to the large number of additional functions which were entrusted to the grand juries. "The taxation of lands in Ireland", so ran the report of the Select Committee of 1822, "by presentments of grand juries, originally confined to the construction and maintenance of roads and bridges and provision for some other minor objects, has in the lapse of time been extended to the support of a great variety of establishments, expensive in their nature.... augmenting considerably the charge on the landholders of the counties, so as within twenty years to have nearly doubled the amount of these levies by a comparison of last year's levy with the average for three years return presented to the House of Commons in 1803, such average being £407,281, and the amount of the last year's levy being upwards of £720,000, of which latter sum by far the greater proportion was allotted to the great objects of later Parliamentary enactments."[2] Originally the funds raised by grand juries were limited to a very small number of purposes; but by a gradual process of extension they came to apply to a much wider field. A statute of 1823 directed returns to be made of the amounts raised by grand juries, classified under the following heads:—

1 *Report of Commission on Grand Jury Presentments* 1842 p. xxvi.
2 *First Report of Select Committee on Grand Jury Presentments* 1822.

(1) the construction of new roads, bridges, &c., (2) repairing roads, bridges &c., (3) the erection and maintenance of court and session houses, (4) the building and repairing of gaols, bridewells and houses of correction, (5) the other expenses of gaols &c., (6) the police establishment and the payment of witnesses, (7) salaries to county officers, (8) public charities, (9) the repayment of advances to the government, and (10) miscellaneous.[1] Many of the above purposes, for example the police and the provision of district fever hospitals and dispensaries, were matters altogether outside the discretion of the grand juries, for which the sums raised were not optional but compulsory. It was these compulsory presentments which formed the greater part of the money raised by local taxation; and it was felt as a grievance that sums, really destined for general imperial purposes, should be charged on the local taxpayer. "In consequence of the variety of matters provided for by grand jury presentment by this[2] and other statutes, the amount of grand jury cess is, in most parts of the country, very heavy, and in some cases even oppressive, and accordingly some step should be taken to lighten the burden."[3] In spite however of the numerous protests by the Repeal Association and other bodies representing public opinion, the amount of the county cess continued to increase; in 1843 it reached £1,140,000.[4]

Before we pass from the amount of the local taxation, which was generally complained of as excessive, we must add, in fairness to the grand juries, that by far the greater part of the taxes which they raised were completely outside their control. These were the so-called "compulsory" presentments, which were greatly increased by successive statutes, and accounted for the bulk of the increase of local taxation after the Union. The successive committees which

[1] 4 Geo. IV c. 33. s. 18. [2] 6 and 7 Wm. IV c. 116. [3] *Repeal Reports* Vol. iii p. 75.

[4] *Dev. Comm.* p. 975. Tables showing the amount raised annually by local taxation in the period 1800-1850 are to be found in *Parl. Pap.* no. 196 of 1830. *Devon Comm.* pp. 1002 sq. and *Thom's Directory* 1851 p. 190.

considered the grand jury laws were impressed by the importance of these compulsory presentments, and agreed in recommending their reduction. Thus the select committee appointed in 1826 drew attention to "the burden imposed by various Acts of Parliament upon the land over which the grand jury exercises no discretion, and to which they are no parties, except so far as the legislature has made them the instrument of imposing them upon the people;" and recommended that such compulsory presentments should claim the first attention of the legislature.[1] The Select Committee on County Cess, ten years later, made recommendations in the same sense, and prepared a very useful list of the matters in respect of which the grand juries were compulsorily bound to make assessments, from which we learn that they included such important matters as the police, district lunatic asylums, the expenses of witnesses and poor prosecutors, the expenses of surveys and valuations, and the militia.[2] These compulsory presentments were again complained of by the Commissioners on Grand Jury Presentments in 1842, and by the Devon Commission. "The custom", we read in the report of the latter commission, "which has obtained so much of late years of charging by act of Parliament, and, it may be, according to an ill-considered scale, large sums upon the respective counties, and over which the grand juries have no control, has created much discontent and is liable to serious objection. The greater proportion of county charge is thus removed from the reach of the ratepayers, and their power in regulating county expenditure becomes quite insignificant.... It will be seen from the return which we have prepared that, of the whole amount of money levied under Grand Jury presentments throughout Ireland, a proportion of about one-third alone is at the option and under the control of the grand jury at each assizes. The portion,

[1] *Report of Select Committee on Grand Jury Presentments, Ireland* 1827.
[2] *Report of Select Committee on County Cess Ireland* 1836.

amounting to nearly two-fifths of the whole, which is raised under presentments which these bodies are compelled to make, under the provisions of some Act of Parliament, enforced by the authoritative direction of the presiding Judge of Assize, is in fact a heavy tax for public purposes imposed exclusively on the occupiers of Ireland. This is a system which should be discontinued as quickly as circumstances will permit."[1] "The very circumstance of such presentments being compulsory—which by the way is almost a contradiction in terms—proves that it is but a clumsy mode of raising money by a machinery intended for wholly different purposes."[2]

The second way in which the county cess worked injustice was through its incidence. Previous to the completion of the public survey and valuation of Ireland, the local charges were applotted upon an antiquated and altogether inequitable plan. The county was divided into taxable units which bore no relation to their extent or value, and upon these units the county charges were raised. The injustice of the system was acknowledged by the Irish Parliament, which had on three occasions enjoined grand juries to proceed to the revision of their assessments; but these injunctions were never obeyed.[3] "The obscurity of the assessments", we read in 1815, "is such as to render them liable to the most unjustifiable abuses. The collections are applotted according to certain surveys which differ most materially from the actual contents of the land. The object of such survey was to bring the valuation of land to one uniform standard; and hence the contents of unproductive farms are calculated in reduced acres, diminishing their number as the quality of land becomes depressed. This system, however wise for a particular purpose, can be but temporary. The improvement of ground is far from being uniformly and proportionally progressive. It is therefore incapable

[1] *Dev. Comm.* pp. 1156-9.
[2] *Repeal Reports* vol. iii p. 75.
[3] 9 Anne c. 9, 1 Geo. II c. 13, 33 Geo II c. 8.

of being calculated by one unvarying expression. A scale which has not altered during a vast lapse of years must become the cause of vast irregularity."[1] In the following year a select committee of the House of Commons reported that the various modes of assessment adopted in different counties, on account of the inequity of pressure which they produced, required "immediate and complete alteration."[2] The Select Committee on the Survey and Valuation of Ireland expressed the same opinion. "In some parts of Ireland the assessment is made by the civil division of ploughlands, varying in size and value, but rated at an equal sum. In other cases, a division by townlands has been established, each townland contributing according to its assumed area, which bears no defined proportion to the actual contents. Gneeves, cartrons, tales, and other sub-denominations of land are recognized in other parts of Ireland: but, however the names may vary, the evil seems universally the same; and the inequity complained of in the middle of the last century (sic) by Sir Wm. Petty, continues without correction to the present times."[3] The Commission of 1842 reported that, in the counties where the public survey and valuation had not been completed, the assessments were made "according to the quantities set down in the county book, or according to the quantity of cess payable by each holding from time immemorial". The Commission added:—"This leads to much irregularity and injustice; some divisions are charged with more acres than they contain; some with less; some lands are not assessed at all; and value as between division and division is left out of account altogether."[4]

It was primarily with the object of correcting these many irregularities that the government undertook the survey and valuation of Ireland. The work of the survey took a

[1] Thomas Rice, *An Inquiry into the Effects of the Irish Grand Jury Laws* London 1815.
[2] *Second Report of Select Committee on Grand Jury Presentments* 1816.
[3] *Select Committee on Survey & Valuation of Ireland*, 1824.
[4] *Report of Commissioners on Grand Jury Presentments* 1842 p. vi.

great deal longer than was expected, and several counties were still unsurveyed, and others, although surveyed, remained unvalued, at the time of the report of the Grand Jury Presentment Commissioners of 1842 .The Commission recommended that, in the case of the counties still uncompleted, a rapid and approximate revision of the poor law valuation should be made the basis of assessment pending the conclusion of the national survey and valuation. In 1848, only five counties remained to be valued[1], and the valuation of the whole country was completed in 1853. While it was generally admitted that the valuation was universally more accurate than the poor law valuation, and while it was obvious that as a basis of assessment it was immeasurably superior to the old system,it was nevertheless complained that it failed to attain the perfect justice at which it aimed, owing to a lack of coordination between the valuators, and the adoption of different principles of valuation in different districts.[2]

The grievances arising out of the amount of the tax, and the method of its assessment, were aggravated by numerous incidental abuses in the manner of its collection and administration. The more important of these abuses arose in connection with road making. The tax, although imposed by the landlords, was paid by the tenants, and constituted a case of taxation without representation. "The gentlemen of this country are supposed to tax themselves, and if this were the case the matter might be left to them without check. It not infrequently happens that the majority of those composing the grand jury are little affected by the tax, while it is generally so contrived among them that each has allotted to him to expend a portion of the money levied; it is a land tax paid by the occupier, the poor miserable 40s. freeholder; it is in addition to his rent, and, though small compared with it, it is grievous.

[1] *Dev. Comm.* p. 944.
[2] *Dev. Comm.* pp. 707 sq.

If the horse be loaded to the utmost strength of his back an additional weight will break him down; and such is the recent charge on the Irish peasant that this additional grand jury cess is a grievous burden. The tax is levied in the same manner as rent is collected, by pounding and selling cattle, and by sale of effects &c.—the same people who collect the rents are generally employed, and the tax is enforced in the same way. In this case the charge of fees to the constable is an additional burden on the poor suffering peasant."[1]

The Committee of 1830 recommended that, in all future levies, a part or the whole of the grand jury assessments should be borne by the landlords; and the Committee on Townland Valuation of 1844 recommended that all tenants, whether under existing or future leases, should have the power of deducting a proportion of the county rate, as under the poor law. The Devon Commission however dissented from these recommendations. "The complaints before us were directed not more against the amount than against the time and mode of collection, the number and payment of county officers, and the extent of compulsory presentments; simply to charge one half of the tax upon the landlord would leave these subjects of complaint untouched . . . To transfer a burden from the yearly tenant, who had equitably engaged to pay it, to the landlord, who had not entered into such an implied contract, would, we consider, be a measure which would materially disturb the relations of the owner and occupier of such tenancies, whilst, after all, it could produce only a very uncertain and unequal relief to the tenants-at-will. To relieve the tenant holding under lease, by authorizing him to deduct from his landlord, would be to relieve him from a burden to the payment of which he had bound himself by covenant . . . Moreover the advantage of transferring all power over county works to the landlord—a necessary consequence

[1] *Lachrymae Hiberniae* Dublin 1822.

of making him the sole cess-payer—we consider to be very doubtful; for in most instances the resident occupiers, and not the proprietor, who may be absent, are the parties most interested in opening new roads, or constructing other works of immediate utility.... On the whole then we cannot advise the great change to which we adverted. We believe that it would in many cases create a very unnecessary embarrassment to the landlords; that it would greatly disappoint the tenants; and that it would sow the seeds of much future dissension and discontent."[1] We are not called upon here to express any opinion upon the wisdom or unwisdom of this pronouncement, but simply to record it; and to record the fact that during the period of which we treat the county cess remained a charge upon the occupier, as distinguished from the owner, of land.

It was much complained of that unfit persons were allowed to take part in presentment sessions; that the officers of the grand juries were frequently inefficient, and not infrequently overpaid; that much bribery took place in connection with contracts; that tenders were fraudulently "rigged"; and finally that the funds at the disposal of the juries were very extravagantly and wastefully employed. A full account of these and other abuses is to be found in the report of the commissioners of 1842. It was also alleged that the collectors of the cess frequently took advantage of the ignorance of the taxpayers, and exacted from them sums considerably beyond those legally due. The fact that one gale of the cess was collected in July was also felt as a hardship, as the small tenant farmers were invariably pressed for money at that time of year.[2]

Possibly the most grievous injustice in connection with the grand jury system was that the local taxes were devoted in some cases to imperial services. Thus, from the date of its creation until 1846, the Royal Irish Constabulary was paid one half of its maintenance by the counties.

[1] *Dev. Comm.* pp. 1155-6. [2] *Dev. Comm.* p. 945.

The Devon Commission recommended that this charge should be met out of imperial taxes, and this suggestion was adopted by parliament.[1] This reform not alone removed the principal example of local taxation being applied for imperial purposes, but also abolished the most striking instance of compulsory presentments. It must not be forgotten however that this reform was only granted to Ireland as a solatium for the much greater evil of the repeal of the corn laws.

Before passing from the subject of local taxation, we must remind the reader that, after 1838, Ireland suffered the additional burden of the poor rate. As we have dealt with this fully in an earlier chapter, we shall not refer to it further.

Section 3. Tithes.

Another public burden imposed on the Irish people during the nineteenth century was that of tithes; but this imposition, unlike those of which we have already treated, was considerably lightened during the period under review. We do not feel called upon to enter at length upon the injustices of the Irish tithe system, as they were in no way increased after the Union; and we have already dealt with the subject before the Union.[2] The only way in which the burden of tithes was increased, in law if not in fact, after the Union, was by the passing of the statute which legitimated the custom, universally followed in Ireland since the resolution of the Irish House of Commons in 1735, exempting pasture lands from the payment of tithes.[3] The impolicy, not to say the injustice, of this measure, was strongly denounced by Wakefield:—"That which before the Union was only a resolution of the Irish House of Commons, is now a formal act of the Imperial parliament. The tithes of Ireland there-

[1] 9 and 10 Vict. c. 97 *Dev. Comm.* p. 947.
[2] *Economic History of Ireland in the Eighteenth Century* pp. 141-52.
[3] 40 Geo. III c. 23.

fore fall only upon the tillage land, the greater part of which is held by cottier tenants. I know of no act more mischievous, more impolitic, and unjust. The rich are in this manner exempted from bearing their share of a burden, which is proved by the very exemption, and the whole weight is suffered to fall upon the poor, who are the least able to support it. The oppression is the more galling, as it increases with the increase of tillage; it will affect the great mass of the people as population is extended; and on the whole may be considered as one of the most serious of the difficulties which occur in considering the affairs of Ireland."[1]

One consequence of the incidence of tithes on tillage lands was, that the burden tended to grow more oppressive with the rise of prices occasioned by the war; and the Protestant clergy—or rather the tithe proctors, who were the real offenders—doing as did the landlords, refused to take into consideration the fall of prices which followed the peace. William Parker, an able pamphleteer who wrote in 1816, after quoting the famous speech on the tithe question which Grattan delivered in the Irish House of Commons in 1788, proceeds:—"Such was the situation of the tithe system when Mr. Grattan astonished the Irish House of Commons with his splendid oratory, and such has the system continued to this day, after a lapse of twenty-eight years. But these last few years it has become more unjust and oppressive than at any previous period, for the tithe farmers exact the same ratage as when the produce of land was nearly quadruple the price that can be obtained at present; in fact these vultures of society exact these last two years almost the entire value of the land."[2] The real grievance complained of, after as well as before the Union, was not so much the amount

[1] Vol. ii p. 486. The discouragement which tillage experienced from the existing system of tithes is well explained in Count de Salis. *Consideration on the Propriety of a General Drainage Bill* Armagh 1813.

[2] *Observations on the Intended Amendment of the Irish Grand Jury Laws* Cork 1816.

of the tithe as the oppressive method of its collection [1]

It must not be supposed however that the tithe was the main grievance of the Irish tenant; it was but a small matter compared with his rent. The landlords endeavoured to pit the peasant against the parson, in order to distract attention from their own extortion. They did not succeed in deceiving contemporary observers. "Some of our Irish landlords represent tithes as the principal grievance of this aggrieved country; they ought to be ashamed to hold up their faces in the British Parliament and say so; the grievance of tithes is to that of the rack rent as the lighting down of the grasshopper, which is felt to be oppressive when coming upon a body enfeebled, while rent is the millstone hanging on the neck."[2]

It is not necessary for us to recount the details of the organized opposition to tithes on the part of the Irish tenantry and peasantry. It is sufficient to state that this opposition was uninterrupted and effective. "From 1783 to 1830", according to Mr. Barry O'Brien, who has dealt with the "tithe war" more fully than any other historian, "resistance continued to be offered at various intervals to the payment of tithes by the Presbyterians of the north and the Catholics of the south of Ireland. In the north, the resistance was generally passive; in the south it was generally active. The northerners fought the system in the courts, the southerners in the field. The latter attacked it on principle, protesting against the payment of tithes to an alien and hostile Church from which they did not receive the slightest benefit; the former attacked it in detail, objecting from time to time to the levying of tithes on certain specified articles.... The clergy then took legal proceedings against the defaulters, with whom however the Ulster juries were frequently found to be in sympathy, and in whose favour they

[1] *The State of Ireland Considered* &c. Dublin 1810.
[2] *Lachrymae Hiberniae* Dublin 1822.

often returned verdicts against the weight of evidence. By thus attacking the system in detail, the Presbyterians succeeded gradually in having potatoes, flax, and other articles, tithable in the south, exempted from tithes in the north. With reference to the southerners, in fairly well-to-do times they paid the tithes under protest. In seasons of distress they asked for reductions; and when no reductions were made they refused to pay, and resisted the efforts of the parson to compel them. They did not dream of going to the courts. They had no faith in them. British law in Ireland was, they felt, the law of the parsons and the landlords—their enemies. By the landlords and parsons the law was made or administered, and they knew by experience how little they—mere pariahs unconsidered and despised—could expect from it. Their resistance to tithes therefore took the form of rebellion against the law; and with such instruments of warfare as in their state of enforced uncivilization they could grasp they went out to fight—literally to fight—against an unjust and iniquitous system. The 'resources of civilization' were used against them, but in vain; and in many a year between 1785 and 1830 the clergy, though backed by the civil and military forces placed at their disposal by the executive, were obliged to forgo their unrighteous claims. The manner in which the tithes pressed upon the peasants of the south, and the circumstances of desperation under which they fought against the system, will be understood when it is stated that the great tithable articles in the southern districts were potatoes—articles not tithable in the north, be it remembered—and that potatoes were the staple food, in fact the only food, of the people. It is indeed scarcely an exaggeration to say that, when the southern peasants waged violent wars against tithes in the eighteenth and nineteenth centuries, they did but fight for very existence."[1] This alliance between the Presbyterians of the north

[1] *Fifty Years of Concessions* vol. i. p. 370.

and the Catholics of the south was remarkable, and was especially noticed by Wakefield:—"In Ireland, a people unanimous only on this subject declaim vehemently against it, considering that they might be replaced by a more equal, certain, and satisfactory impost. I request the reader to attend particularly to this passage, because I can safely assert that the writer has not exaggerated, when he states that the people of Ireland are 'unanimous' in their execrations against tithes. The Presbyterians will go to law rather than pay them; the poorer people take up arms to revenge the exactions hereby practised upon them."[1]

The tithe question kept the country in perpetual disturbance. One of the primary objects of the Whiteboy agitation was the reduction of tithes;[2] and the Threshers' Society, founded in 1806, professed the same object, together with the regulation of the priests' dues.[3] While the Whiteboy agitation usually aimed at other objects as well as the reduction of tithes, this latter was the only object aimed at in the great agitation of 1831 and 1832.[4] The immediate causes of this spontaneous and national, as distinguished from sectional, agitation which broke out about 1830 are thus enumerated by Mr. Barry O'Brien:—"Three chief causes contributed to produce an agitation against tithes in 1830. They were; first, the public spirit created by O'Connell during the struggle for emancipation—a spirit whose existence injuriously affected the perpetuation of the unjust privileges and monopolies of the favoured Church; secondly, the operation of a proselytising association known as the 'New Reformation Society'—a society whose action much stirred up feelings of religious animosity and sectarian ill-will; and thirdly, the distress that prevailed in many parts of the country, and whose prevalence rendered it very difficult for the peasantry to pay the landlord, the

[1] Vol. ii. p. 483.
[2] *Economic History of Ireland in the Eighteenth Century* p. 150.
[3] Lewis, *Irish Disturbances* p. 210.
[4] *Ibidem* p. 120.

parson, and the priest, and to feed and clothe themselves."[1] It is not necessary to enter into details either of this acute agitation against tithes, or of the causes which provoked it; it is sufficient to note its existence, and to pass to a consideration of the remedial measures which it succeeded in exacting.

The first important act relating to tithes was Goulburn's Voluntary Composition Act of 1823, which was passed with the professed object of "further encouraging the industry and enterprise of owners, farmers, and occupiers of land, and rendering the incomes arising from tithes more certain in amount and more easy of collection". This act provided that, on the application of the incumbent, or impropriator, or five landholders of the parish occupying lands of the value of £20 a year each, commissioners might be appointed, whose duty it was to fix the amount of the sum to be paid as composition for all tithes, based on the annual average amount paid during seven years preceding the 1st of November 1821. The composition was not to be lower than that average, nor to exceed it by more than twenty *per cent*, and was to continue for twenty-one years, subject to triennial variations based on the fluctuations in the price of wheat and oats.[2] Two years later septennial were substituted for triennial revisions.[3] This act also abolished the exemption which pasture lands had enjoyed from tithes. The act was, as far as it went, a success.[4]

The next step towards the removal of the tithe injustice was taken in 1832, when, on the recommendation of a select committee appointed in that year,an act was passed making the composition compulsory and perpetual. It was further provided that tenants at will and tenants from year to year should be exempt from the pay-

[1] *Fifty Years of Concessions* vol. i. p. 377.
[2] 4 Geo. IV c. 99.
[3] 5 Geo. IV c. 63; the statute was further amended in minor points by 7 and 8 Geo. IV c. 60.
[4] Locker Lampson. *Ireland in the Nineteenth Century* p. 151.

ment of tithes in respect of the lands which they occupied, and that tenants under all future leases, except those made under an already existing clause of renewal, should also be exempted.[1] In the following year an act was passed providing that the tithes of 1833 and the arrears of 1831-2 need not be collected, but should be paid to the clergy by the issue of exchequer bills to be repaid by the respective parishes in five years.[2] In the same year many of the grievances which existed in connection with ecclesiastical leases were redressed.[3]

These measures did not however fulfil the aspirations of the country, as, except in the case of tenants at will, tenants from year to year, and "future" tenants, the burden of the tithe was not shifted, but remained on the small Catholic farmers. The resistance of tithe therefore continued, and grew in intensity.[4] The government made attempts in 1834 and 1835 to transfer the burden from the tenants to the landlords, but these attempts were frustrated by the action of the House of Lords.[5] At length in 1838 a satisfactory measure succeeded in passing both houses of parliament. This act recited in its preamble that it was "expedient to abolish compositions for tithes in Ireland, and in lieu thereof to substitute rent-charges payable by persons having a perpetual estate or interest in the lands subject thereto, a reasonable allowance being made for the greater facility and security of collection arising out of such transfer of liability from the occupier to the owner of lands;" and provided that all land subject to tithe composition should be charged with an annual rent-charge equal to seventy-five *per cent* of the composition, to be paid by the person having the first estate of inheritance in the land. It was further provided that the amount so paid

[1] 2 and 3 Wm. IV. c. 119.
[2] 3 and 4 Wm. IV. c. 100.
[3] 3 and 4 Wm. IV. c. 37.
[4] Barry O'Brien *op. cit.* p. 449 Locker Lampson *op. cit.* p. 161.
[5] Barry O'Brien *op. cit.* 460, 500.

might be recovered from the tenants by way of rent, and that the rent-charge should be varied every seven years in the same manner as compositions. The loan of one million pounds made to the clergy in 1833 was also remitted.[1]

This act is generally admitted to have been an unqualified success. "The measure", wrote George Lewis Smyth, "has worked so well that any explanation of its machinery would be uninteresting. Once a good result has been produced, mankind are singularly indifferent to the particular process by which it has been brought about . . . Whether the advantage of the Church or the pacification of the country, for an interval at least, are to be considered, the tithe act of 1838 is certainly entitled to the praise of having essentially contributed to both objects. There were many persons who contended then, and still maintain, that its provisions ought to have been carried much further; but it is impossible to deny that, as a settlement of the enormous difficulties of the tithe question, this law has proved in its operation decidedly beneficial and successful, and not to the Church only but to the country at large."[2] It is not too much to say that the act of 1838 was the one measure of the nineteenth century affecting Ireland which completely attained the objects at which it aimed.

Tithe was not the only tax which the Irish Catholic had to pay for the upkeep of the Protestant Church; in addition he had to pay the parish cess, which was a tax imposed for the maintenance of the fabric of the established church, and for meeting the expenses of religious service. "It was", in the words of Lord Althorp, "an uncertain tax which varied according to the purposes to which it was applied. It might be increased by abuses of management, or it might be diminished by frugality; but in neither case had the Catholic the means of exercising any control over

[1] 1 and 2 Vict. c. 109.
[2] *Ireland Historical & Statistical* vol. iii pp. 150-1.

the money so levied upon his property."[1] This outrageous imposition was abolished in 1832.[2]

In considering the burden under which the Irish Catholic laboured, it must not be forgotten that he was bound to contribute not alone to the maintenance of the established Church, but of his own Church as well. We need not here enter into details of the cost of the maintenance of the Catholic Church in Ireland in the early years of the nineteenth century, beyond remarking that it was a highly organised and widely diffused body, and that the support of its ministry formed a not inconsiderable item in the economy of the country. "With respect to the Roman Catholic clergy", we read in 1810, "Mr. McKenna seems to be of opinion that the number of Roman Catholic priests does not exceed 1000; that the emoluments of a priest in the north average from £30 to £50 *per annum*; in other parts from £60 to £90; in Munster, where perquisites are higher from greater liberality of marriages, that towns produce from £120 to £130 *per annum*, and in some few instances go so high as £200 *per annum*."[3] "I should suppose £150 per year", said Daniel O'Connell in 1824, "would be a high average for a parish priest independent of his curate. A curate, if he resides with the clergyman, has from £20 to £30 a year with his home kept for him; if he does not reside he has one third of the benefice of the parish . . . I should think £200 a year for a parish priest would be a sufficient sum to cover the expenses of priest and curate; and there are about 2500 parishes."[4]

Before passing from the subject of tithes and other payments made for the service of religion, we may draw attention to the changing position which Catholics were beginning to enjoy in the first half of the nineteenth century. As we

[1] Barry O'Brien *op. cit.* vol. i. p. 375.
[2] 3 and 4 Wm. IV c. 37.
[3] *The State of Ireland Considered* &c. Dublin 1810. p. 96.
[4] *Select Committee on State of Ireland* 1824-5. See *Lachrymae Hiberniae* Dublin 1822 p 16, G. L. Smyth, *Ireland Historical and Statistical* vol. iii p. 167.

showed elsewhere, one of the most remarkable features of the Irish social structure in the previous century had been the debasement of the Catholics to the meanest and poorest employments and occupations. Not alone were they debarred from exercising any of the learned professions, but they were deliberately prevented by law from growing prosperous by the cultivation of the soil. Before the Union however the greater number of the statutes which had been aimed at the economic, as apart from the political, degradation of the Catholics had been repealed.[1]

After the Union a certain number of lucrative positions were still closed to Catholics—for example, Judgeships, the Attorney and Solicitor Generalships, the offices of King's Counsel and Master in Chancery—but generally speaking there was no position which Catholics were debarred from attaining on account of their religion. The only disabilities in regard to the acquisition or use of property under which Catholics continued to suffer were a disability to exercise the privileges of ownership in advowsons or rights to presentation to benefices[2] and the inability to purchase any manor or borough, the freeholders or inhabitants whereof were entitled to vote for burgesses in Parliament.[3]

Although, however, the letter of the penal laws had been abrogated, their spirit was still enforced. The law which prohibited Catholics from taking any lease at less than a rack rent had been repealed in 1779; nevertheless this law continued as a "rent-rule" long after its abrogation.[4] The inferior position of the Catholics was more marked in the towns than in the country. In 1793 the office of director of the Bank of Ireland was thrown open to Catholics, but the Bank continued to tender to its directors an oath which no Catholic could take. Although this obnoxious

[1] *Economic History of Ireland in the Eighteenth Century* pp. 24-30, 394.

[2] 17 and 18 Geo III c. 49.

[3] 22 and 23 Geo III c. 24. *The State of the Catholics of Ireland* by a Member of Parliament London 1807.

[4] Sigerson *History of Irish Land Tenures* p. 173.

custom was abandoned in 1830, the exclusion of Catholics was adhered to in practice. In 1844, of 220 clerks employed by the Bank in Dublin only three were Catholics.[1] It was also said, with what foundation we cannot judge, that the Bank of Ireland used its monopoly to impede the progress of Catholic merchants.[2] "The thing in Ireland", Daniel O'Connell complained in 1824, "which is most grievous is not perhaps the letter of the law, but the spirit in which the letter is acted on. There are other instances besides the Bank of Ireland in which the Act of 1793 rendered the Catholics admissible to offices not immediately under the government to which they have never been admitted; such for example as the freedom of the City of Dublin."[3] The Dublin companies, admission to which was thrown open to Catholics in 1829, remained exclusively Protestant, with the exception of a few Catholics who forced themselves in by *mandamus*. The Commissioners appointed in 1838 under the Municipal Corporations Act found that the Dublin companies included only half a dozen Catholics.[4] This exclusion from the companies was productive of injurious commercial results. "In the toll system the most infamous partiality prevails, as in towns the Protestant traders, being all freemen, are exempt from tolls on their goods, while the Catholics and dissenters are charged, as they are not freemen."[5]

More important possibly than the actual commercial disabilities suffered by the Catholics was the general attitude of contempt of which they were the object. "It is melancholy to observe", we read in 1814, "the habitual and fatal prepossession of the Protestants of the lower class generally speaking against the Catholics, which has increased considerably since the Rebellion. This produces a certain overbear-

[1] *Repeal Reports* vol. i. p. 30.
[2] *Ibid.* p. 35.
[3] *Evidence before Select Committee on State of Ireland* 1824.
[4] Webb *History of Trade Unionism* p. 482.
[5] *Commentaries on National Policy and on Ireland.* Dublin 1831.

ing style of address, manner and conduct towards the lower Catholics."[1] "According to the penal system", wrote Lewis, "which has to a greater or less extent been acted on nearly up to the present day, every Irish Catholic was presumed to be disaffected to the State, and was treated as an open or concealed rebel."[2]

In spite of the discouragement which they received, the Catholics nevertheless succeeded in improving their position. A large part of the land of the country passed into their possession after the repeal of the disabling acts in 1780. "The extension of tillage has obviously and unquestionably tended in a most eminent manner to enrich and to augment the Roman Catholic population of Ireland."[3] The Catholics appear also to have amassed wealth as graziers. "The wealth of a Roman Catholic grazier", observes Wakefield, "has been the result of a rise in prices. A lease taken fifty years ago, even had the lessee made no exertions whatever, must have produced a fortune."[4] "The next order among the Catholic body are those who, by the possession of old leases, and the business of grazing, have acquired fortunes, many of those are to be met with in all the rich and fertile districts of Ireland. Some by the sale of their stock of dairy cows and by letting their lands to cottier tenants; and others by commercial pursuits in Dublin, Cork, Limerick, Waterford and other towns. have raised themselves to affluence. These people since the alteration of the law invariably vest their property in land, and are rapidly forming a powerful aristocracy in Ireland."[5]

Catholics seem to have taken an important part in the commerce of the towns, to which they had been driven by

[1] John Edwards *The Interests of Ireland.* Dublin 1814.

[2] *Irish Disturbances* p. 47; see Wakefield vol. i. p. 590. The insecurity of property arising out of the penal laws did much to prevent the introduction of capital and manufactures from England. *Evidence of J. R. McCulloch before Select Committee of* 1824-5 p. 816. For an example of how far religious bigotry continued to attribute the economic ills of Ireland to the prevailing religion, see Bicheno, *Ireland and its Economy* p. 217 and O'Rourke *The Great Irish Famine* p. 524.

[3] Newenham. *View* 1809 p. 235.

[4] Vol. ii. p. 75. [5] Vol. ii. p. 545.

the laws prohibiting them long leases in land. "Roman Catholics were by the operation of the penal laws driven out of the trade of agriculture, and compelled like the Jews to betake themselves to pursuits of merchandise; and this led to the accumulation of much wealth in their hands."[1] In 1824 Daniel O'Connell expressed the view that the Catholic commercial community of Dublin was richer than the Protestant.[2] "Much of the wealth that Dublin, Limerick, Cork, and Waterford, now possess, has been acquired by Roman Catholics engaged in commercial pursuits".[3] The lack of proper banking facilities gave rise to a large class of usurers in the country towns, and many Catholics amassed large fortunes in this way.[4]

We have abundant evidence that the condition of the Catholics generally improved after the Union in comparison with that of the Protestants. "Those who set their faces against any further extension of the privileges of Roman Catholics", wrote an Irish landlord in 1813, "are not aware of the wealth and influence which they have latterly obtained in Ireland. Since they have had the power granted to them of applying their money to the purchase of land, much property has passed from the hands of Protestants to Romanists. When we take into consideration that in three provinces out of four, the Roman Catholics are infinitely more numerous and much more frugal than the Protestants, we may without hesitation presume that they will shortly become the more wealthy of the two bodies."[5] "As to drawing any comparison between the state of Catholic property now, whether landed or personal, with what it was previous to the year 1778, I cannot do it. But it has increased enormously and is increasing every day."[6]

[1] O'Driscoll. *Views of Ireland* vol. ii. p. 157.
[2] *Evidence before Select Committee of* 1824.
[3] Wakefield vol. ii. p. 546.
[4] *Repeal Reports* vol. i. p. 42.
[5] *On the State of Ireland* by an Irish Landlord. Dublin 1813, and see *Upon the Nature and Effects of the Legislative Union*. Dublin 1811.
[6] D. O'Connell's *Evidence before Select Committee* 1824.

Section 3. Urban Tolls.

The tolls and customs exacted by the corporate and market towns pressed very heavily on the farmers, and resulted in raising the price of their produce. The history of this matter is almost inextricably bound up with that of the Irish municipal corporations, and it is difficult to treat of the former without also dealing with the latter. As however it is only the former which is of importance in Irish economic history, we must try to effect a separation. We shall therefore confine ourselves to a description of the tolls, without referring to any of the other abuses of the Irish municipal system.

The oppressive and illegal tolls exacted by the urban authorities were the subject of a very ancient grievance in Ireland. In spite of many remedial statutes passed by the Irish Parliament, the evil continued in the early years of the nineteenth century.[1] In certain towns, for example Cork, Waterford, Tuam and Wexford, the people resisted the illegal claims of the collectors in the courts, and in one town, Naas, the unjust impositions were at once discontinued. In Dublin the corporation and the toll farmers made it a practice to let such proceedings go by default, so as to avoid publicity. Nevertheless, the abuses of the system still continued in almost unabated strength; in 1817 it was said that toll was not legally payable in one instance out of twenty in which it was exacted; and the annual amount thus extorted was reckoned at £700,000.[2]

In 1817 an act was passed with the object of suppressing the illegal exaction of tolls, by which it was provided that boards specifying particulars of the rates of toll charged

[1] O'Brien, *Economic History of Ireland in the Eighteenth Century* p. 369. Gale, *Corporate System of Ireland* pp. 106-7. Lord Blessington, *Observations on the State of Ireland* London 1822 *Report of Select Committee on State of Poor in Ireland* 1830 p. 47.

[2] Cantwell, *A Practical Treatise on the Laws of Tolls and Customs.* Dublin 1817. This work was revised and brought up to date by W. C. McDermott in 1829. See also *The Toll Collector's Terror or Farmer's Guide.* Dublin 1814. The fewness of the market towns was also a subject of complaint. Much time was lost in bringing a small quantity of produce to a market town many miles distant. Trimmer, *Further Observation etc.* London 1812

should be erected in every city and town, and that a schedule of the charges demanded should be registered with the clerk of the peace of each county.[1] The provisions of this act were unfortunately widely disregarded.[2] "These remedial provisions", said Gale, "had not the desired effect, and the tendency to abuse which attaches to this description of demand, and that political importance which corporate bodies acquired in Ireland, cooperated in exempting them from the salutary restrictions of the law."[3] A select committee was accordingly appointed in 1826 to investigate the whole question of Irish tolls and customs.

The report of this committee discloses the widespread extent of unjust and oppressive exactions, in defiance of the remedial statutes. "It fully appears", the report states, "that notwithstanding the many existing laws, many most exorbitant and illegal charges are still made in markets, seaports, and fairs, in Ireland, all of the most injurious tendency in checking commerce and industry. Several of these charges appear to your committee to be so burthensome and oppressive as to produce the most mischievous restraint both on the sale and transit of commodities. It appears from all the returns, without exception, from one of the largest counties in Ireland, that the tolls invariably claimed on corn, oatmeal, potatoes, and fresh butter, amount to five *per cent ad valorem*, and that duties of equal amount are claimed on the sale of flannels, frieze and the coarse woollen and linen manufactures of the country. In other fairs and markets one-sixteenth in kind or in value is demanded on wheat, potatoes, and oatmeal, and the general charge upon woollen goods amounts to one shilling in the pound sterling. In some cases the charge is made not only on the sale, but the exposure to sale, and consequently may either expose the vendor to an improvident sale, or to a repetition of

[1] 57 Geo. III. c. 108.

[2] *Practical Views and Suggestions* by Hibernicus Dublin 1823. Finlay, *Letters to the Irish Government*. Dublin 1822.

[3] *Corporate System of Ireland* p. 107.

this outrageous and illegal demand. As these charges are capable of repetition upon every sale, they may be imposed both on the wholesale and the retail purchase, thus doubling the amount of a burthen in its simplest form of a nature the most oppressive. Such tolls would unquestionably be illegal, even though supported by express charter or patent, (a circumstance which your committee cannot consider very likely to be the case); but, collected as they are now, they afford decisive evidence of the practical abuses prevailing in this matter in Ireland, and requiring the most decisive and effectual remedies to suppress them, and to prevent their recurrence. 'Even were outrageous tolls granted with a fair or market', observes Lord Coke (2 Inst. 220), 'the grants would be void.' Nor are these examples of violation of the general principles of the common law the only abuses existing; the statute law has been violated in many important particulars. The House will have seen that by the statute 1 Geo. III c. 17 all turf, furze, and faggots are allowed to pass into and through every city and town free from all customs, tolls, and payments, claimed by any officer or member of a corporation ;yet in several cases claims of toll on turf and furze are specifically made, and a general charge upon wood and timber of all descriptions seems to pervade a majority of the returns. In like manner, though potatoes are freed from all charge for weighing, not only are general charges for weighing all commodities introduced, but specific fees for the weighing of potatoes are set forth. Thus the intentions of the legislature in exempting from burthen the food of the lower classes of the community have been defeated, and the violation of a positive act of parliament is advanced as the supposed foundation of a claim of right." The committee next details similar violations of the statute of 1717, which exempted flax, yarns, bundle-cloth, cottons, kelp, ashes, and flax-seed, as articles connected with the linen and cotton manufactures, from such local duties; and refer to many other cases in which express statutory enactments were openly violated. The evil custom of the administration of oaths by the toll collectors is also referred to: "It appears that in order to ascertain whether cattle have in point of fact been sold, the toll attaching to the sale only, the toll gatherers have administered illegal oaths to the peasantry. This act is in itself a felony; and in its practice it overfamiliarizes the peasantry with an habitual violation of the law and a disregard of the obligation of an oath."[1]

The great majority of the tolls demanded rested on no legal foundation, and could not for a moment be supported in a court of law. Apart from statute, the only methods by which the right to tolls could originate were by prescription or express charter. In order to maintain a prescriptive title, it was necessary to prove continuous possession from 1189, when the time of legal memory was deemed to begin. Obviously it would be impossible to claim any toll under this title on any article which had been used for the first time after that date, as, for example, potatoes. Moreover the amount paid must not exceed that paid when the custom originated, and the corporations were therefore not entitled to claim sums for toll, as they frequently did, which were larger than the total value of the goods themselves at the beginning of the custom. It was also found on examination that a comparison between the rates claimed by the corporations and those fixed to be paid by charter from time to time, which might be regarded as what was then regarded as a reasonable measure of toll, showed that the former in every case much exceeded the latter; it was arguable that they were unreasonable to a degree to render them illegal. The difficulties in the way of establishing the right to toll under express charter were almost as great as those attending their proof from prescription. If the grants adduced gave the right of toll only by general words, toll could be collected only at the rate or price paid

[1] *Select Committee on Tolls and Customs in Ireland* 1826.

at the date of the grant. The Irish corporations however demanded tolls proportioned to the selling price at the date of collection. If on the other hand the instrument relied on specifically mentioned the sums to be taken, it was usually found that such sums were extremely small, and in addition that such documents usually rendered the collectors of the toll liable to account for its due expenditure before some public officer. Invariably the early grants authorizing tolls were specifically made for public purposes, such as repairing the town walls, or building bridges; the right was coupled with a duty, the performance of which had long been neglected.

Assuming this statement of the law to be correct, it is doubtful if any but a very small part of the tolls levied by the Irish corporations in the nineteenth century rested on a legal right. "It might appear", wrote Gale, "if any inquiry were commenced, that few, if any, corporate cities or towns in Ireland could prove a legal right to any toll or custom now worth levying; prescriptive tolls levied in proportion to the value of articles in 1189 would not in this century repay the expenses of collection; while tolls derived under express grants when duly rated and collected under the healthy provisions of modern statutes would prove almost equally unprofitable. But in point of fact since the total abolition of town walls and other municipal fortifications one of the principal objects and considerations for granting or levying such dues has been for ever removed; and as to the other public purposes, namely paving, cleansing, lighting and watching, it will be recollected that an act of 1828[1] has empowered any twenty-one householders occupying tenements of £20 per annum each in any city, town corporate, or other town, to assemble and assess themselves for such objects without any reference to, or connection with, any corporate body happening to exist in such places. In this manner the legislature has swept

[1] 9 Geo. IV. c. 82.

away nearly the only plea or pretension for a continuance of such imposts...."[1]

In spite of the hostility of public opinion, nothing was done to abate the evils of the tolls, which were described as oppressive as ever before a parliamentary inquiry in 1830.[2] The Municipal Corporation Commissioners five years later devoted much attention to the subject. With respect to "tolls through", or tolls collected on the entrance into or passage of goods through a town granted in consideration of the performance of certain public services, the commissioners reported that, "the considerations for which they were given have been almost everywhere neglected, some long unperformed, some imperfectly attended to." The walls and fortifications had been razed or had fallen; and the other duties to be performed by the corporations were for the most part carried out by the grand juries or by self-constituted bodies under the act of 1828. The corporations found great difficulty in supporting their claim to these tolls in face of the constant legal resistance which they provoked; the corporations of Cork and Limerick had succeeded in establishing their title as tolls traverse; but most of the other corporations, including Dublin, had abandoned their claims in view of the opposition they aroused. The commissioners next proceed to consider tolls collected in fairs and markets, and these they found to be everywhere excessive, and productive of much violent opposition. Petty articles of common consumption among the poorest classes were frequently charged with tolls amounting to more than their intrinsic value. The commissioners recommended a "thorough revision by the legislative authority of the entire system."[3] The Municipal Reform Act of 1840 provided that no person should in the future be exempt from tolls unless he had been exempt on the 5th of June 1835; and empowered the

[1] *Op. cit.* pp. 128 sq.
[2] *Select Committee on Tolls and Customs in Markets and Fairs in Ireland* 1830.
[3] *Report of Municipal Corporations Commissioners* 1835 pp. 36-8.

commissioners of boroughs to abolish or purchase tolls.[1]

Another matter in connection with marketing which was felt as a burden by the tenantry was the want of uniformity in weights and measures, and the undue exactions made under the name of allowances for beamage.[2] Irish weights and measures were assimilated to English in 1824, but this was almost universally disregarded in Ireland, in spite of further statutes aimed at its observance.[3] In 1841 it was stated that the customs regarding weights and measures were not the same in any two places.[4]

Section 5. Absenteeism.

It may at first sight appear surprising that the subject of absenteeism should be included in this portion of the book rather than in that dealing with agricultural resources. As we shall explain lower down however the evil inflicted on Ireland by the non-residence of the landed proprietors was one which affected the public rather than the tenants of absentees. We therefore treat the subject as one of the public burdens to which Ireland was liable at the time.

One of the most fatuous arguments advanced in favour of the Act of Union was that it would decrease the number of absentees. Of course this was a prediction that could delude no sensible man, as the withdrawal of the legislature must manifestly cause the absence for a great part of the year of many of the principal noblemen and gentlemen of a country. The evil will not necessarily stop there, for not alone will those who are already engaged in politics migrate to the centre of political activity, but also those who are ambitious to embrace such a career.

[1] 3 and 4 Vict. c. 108 ss 3 and 132.
[2] *Dev. Comm.* p. 1162.
[3] 5 Geo IV c. 74 ; 4 and 5 Wm. IV c. 49; 5 and 6 Wm. IV c. 63.
[4] *Remarks on the Law and Present State of the Corn Measures and Weights in Ireland* by an Inhabitant of the City of Dublin Dutlin 1841.

The evil of absenteeism, moreover, is cumulative. While but one half of the members of a family may be non-resident in one generation, it is probable that three quarters will be non-resident in the next, and so on. Not only is it cumulative; it is, in addition, infectious. When several families of the land-owning class withdraw from a district, the temptation for the others to remain is sensibly diminished.

If any confirmation were needed of the truth of the above conclusions it would be found in the history of Ireland in the early nineteenth century. The extent of absenteeism is a matter on which it is not possible to adduce exact evidence, for the simple reason that no attempt was made at the time accurately to calculate the amount of absentee rents, and that it is not possible to compute them from any commercial or financial statistics at our disposal. All we can do, therefore, is to refer to the opinions of those contemporary writers who were most intimately acquainted with the circumstances of Ireland at the period. An examination of such authorities puts it beyond doubt that the amount of absentee rents annually remitted from Ireland increased substantially after—and, it is suggested, as a result of—the Union.

As we shall see in the next chapter, the year 1804 witnessed a remarkable controversy on the currency question, in the course of which many other economic topics were discussed. All the contributors to this controversy agreed that the Union had already had the result of increasing the number of absentees. "The Union in its effects", we read in one pamphlet, "by drawing over to England necessarily so many men of the first rank and fortune to attend their duty in Parliament, and swelling, by the allurement it holds out to others of profit, advancement, or pleasure, the band of voluntary absentees, contributes every year more and more to the impoverishment of this country."[1] "The Union with England", we read in another pamphlet of the same

[1] *A Word of Advice to the Trading and Monied Interests of Ireland.* Dublin 1804.

year, "added to the list of absentees, and that to a considerable degree. Besides the members elected to the Imperial Parliament a very great proportion of the noblemen and gentlemen who were members of the Irish Parliament and consequently spent their winters in Dublin now reside in London."[1] "The Union has increased the Irish absentee remittances to a considerable amount."[2] Five years later it was Newenham's opinion that, "the number of absentees has manifestly been much increased by the Union";[3] and George Ensor stated in 1814 that, "the deserted state of the tenantry and the people has been aggravated annually by the Union."[4] It was also remarked that the remittances to absentee mortgagees had considerably increased.[5]

A good method of estimating the numbers of landed gentry who resided in Ireland is to examine the number of members in the Dublin clubs. Luckily, we are in a position to give definite figures on this subject, as an Irish statute[6] had provided that the members of clubs were to make an annual payment to the Wide Streets Commissioners. The produce of this tax during the years 1815-21 was as follows:

Year ending 1st. Jan.*	1815	£1,324
do.	1816	1,224
do.	1817	1,130
do.	1818	1,023
do.	1819	870
do.	1820	644
do.	1821	255

* John Finlay *Letters to the Irish Government* Dublin 1822.

[1] *The Real Causes of the High Rate of Exchange.* Dublin 1804.
[2] *Observations on the Exchange between London and Dublin* by a Merchant of Dublin. Dublin 1804.
[3] *View of Ireland* p. 291.
[4] *Observations on the Present State of Ireland* Dublin 1814. and see Grattan. *Life of Grattan* vol. v p. 412.
[5] Wm. Jebb *An Inquiry into the Depreciation of the Irish Bank Paper* Dublin 1804; and see a very able pamphlet by the Rev. Henry Major entitled *Observations Demonstrative of the Necessity to Ireland's Welfare and to the Character of England of a Tax upon Absentees* Dublin 1815.
[6] 39 Geo. III c. 53.

O'Driscoll expressed the opinion in 1823 that "the Union has added considerably to the number of absentees";[1] and Sadleir expressed the same opinion.[2] Can there be any question, in the face of such a volume of contemporary opinion, that the evil of absenteeism increased after the Act of Union?[3]

It is quite impossible to calculate the annual value of the absentee rents remitted from Ireland. Various estimates were however made from time to time, which we shall give for what they are worth. In 1810 it was said to be £2.000,000;[4] in 1819 £4,000,000[5]; McCulloch put it at £3,500,000; and George Ensor at £4,000,000;[6] Daniel O'Connell in 1834 at three or four millions,[7] and in 1842 at £6,000,000[8]; *The Nation* at the same amount;[9] and John O'Connell at £5,000,000.[10] However these figures vary, they agree in one particular, namely, that the amount remitted increased greatly in the fifty years following the Union.

We have used the phrase "evils of absenteeism" several times. We must, however, warn the reader that there was a school of thought in the early nineteenth century, led by John Ramsay McCulloch, the well known economist, who refused to admit that absenteeism constituted an evil, or that Ireland was in any way injured by the non-residence of its landed proprietors. McCulloch explained his opinions at length before the Select Committee on the State of Ireland in 1825, and his evidence on that occasion aroused a storm of opposition and controversy, which, if it did not do much to solve the economic problems of Ireland at the time, at least succeeded in throwing a flood of light on the

[1] *Views of Ireland* vol. ii. p. 161.
[2] *Ireland its Evils etc* 1829 p. 53.
[3] The view that the Union had increased the number of absentees was combatted in Martin *Ireland Before and After the Union* pp. 278 sq.
[4] *The State of Ireland Considered.* Dublin 1810 p. 132.
[5] W. Parker. *A Plea for the Poor and Industrious.* Cork 1819.
[6] Staunton, *A Reply to Mr. Martin's Ireland etc* Dublin 1844.
[7] *Debate on the Repeal of the Union* Dublin 1834 p. 26.
[8] *Observations on Common Laws etc.* Dublin 1842.
[9] *The Nation* 27th. May 1843.
[10] *Argument for Ireland.* Dublin 1847 p. 351.

whole nature and effects of absenteeism. Apart from the evidence itself, the appearance of Mr. McCulloch as a witness was a remarkable innovation, as it marked the arrival of political economy at the position of an exact science on which expert evidence was admissible. Mr. McCulloch, according to Blackwood's Magazine, was "not a man of business, was neither an Irish landlord nor an Irish farmer, nor an Irishman of any kind, had actually never seen Ireland, and yet appeared before the Committee to dilate on the condition of the sister Kingdom."[1]

Mr. McCulloch's evidence, which Palgrave's Dictionary describes as a paradox, was so remarkable that it can only be conveyed by literal quotation. The first answer given by the witness sums up his whole position: "I am not aware that the residence of the landlords would increase the general and average rate of wages all over the country." Being asked, not unnaturally, by the committee further to explain this opinion, he proceeded: "The income of a landlord, when he is an absentee, is really as much expended in Ireland as if he were living in it . . . . . . His rent must be remitted, if an absentee, in money or commodities. As it cannot be remitted in money, owing to the limited quantity of specie in circulation, it must be remitted in commodities; and this I think would be the nature of the operation: when a landlord has an estate in Ireland and goes to live in London or Paris, his agent gets the rent and goes and buys a bill of exchange with it; now this bill is a draft drawn against equivalent commodities that are to be exported from Ireland; it is nothing more than an order to receive an equivalent amount in commodities that must be sent from Ireland. The merchants who get £10,000 or any other sum from the agents of an absentee landlord go into the Irish market and buy exactly the same amount of commodities as the landlord would have bought, had he

[1] Vol. xix p. 55. On the influence exerted by the classical economists on parliament at the time see Cunningham, *Growth of English Industry and Commerce* vol. iii pp. 737 sq.

been at home; the only difference being that the landlord would eat them and wear them in London or Paris and not in Ireland.... If the remittances to absentee landlords amount to three millions a year, were the absentee landlords to return home to Ireland, the foreign trade of Ireland would be diminished by that amount."

Mr. McCulloch was then asked: "Would not there be a beneficial local effect created by the residence of Irish gentry now absent ?" to which he replied:—"If the question be confined to particular spots, the expenditure of considerable sums of money in them may perhaps be of some advantage to their inhabitants; but when a landlord goes abroad the expenditure of his income, though not probably productive of advantage to that particular parish, will certainly be proportionally advantageous to some other part of the country, inasmuch as the income must be all laid out in the first instance on Irish commodities." Being pressed as to whether "the population of the country would not be benefited by the expenditure among them of a certain portion of the rent which is remitted ?" he replied: —"No, I do not see how it could be benefited in the least." On further examination he admitted that Ireland might suffer some moral and political injury through the non-residence of the landed proprietors, but that no economic injury could be experienced, with the possible exception of the loss of employment of a certain number of footmen and other non-productive workers. The committee next asked Mr. McCulloch to consider what the effects in England would be if the majority of the landowners were to take up their residence in France; but the philosopher was not to be shaken in his opinion, and boldly replied: "I think that if there were courts established in England like the sheriff courts of Scotland, and if the agents were men of as good character as in Scotland, England would rather gain by the absence of seven-eighths of her landed proprietors."[1]

[1] *Select Committee on State of Ireland* 1825 pp. 813-87.

This evidence, which was published broadcast at the time by the landlords, did a great deal of harm, as it provided a justification for a course of conduct, for which theretofore no justification had been thought possible. To a generation obsessed by the infallibility of political economists, the opinion of Mr. McCulloch was sufficient to outweigh all the evidence of facts and experience. "Formerly this ancient enemy of Ireland concealed its footsteps as much as possible, and when observed disguised itself under a number of specious pretences and apologies—health, safety, education and a variety of other reasons were always forthcoming, amounting on the whole to a kind of necessity; and necessity, as is well known, can have no law, whether of duty or gratitude. Now, however, fully absolved by political economy, and even invested with peculiar honours, it no longer seeks concealment, but boldly avows itself; affects the language, and assumes the pretensions of genuine patriotism, and perpetually stirs you with declamations concerning a country, which it personally deserts, and is constantly pillaging and oppressing by proxy."[1]

Needless to say the enunciation of these paradoxical and novel opinions called forth a mass of controversial publications. Possibly the most able refutation is to be found in an anonymous article in Blackwood's Magazine,[2] and they were also effectively dealt with in a number of pamphlets.[3] The argument against absenteeism was well put by O'Driscoll: "If a family live cheaply and are industrious they will probably become rich. So it is with a nation; if the Irish live cheaply upon potatoes, and export their corn, they ought to have more money, and more of what

[1] Sadleir. *Ireland its Evils &c.* p. 46. [2] Vol. xix, p. 55.

[3] See, for example, Lord Stourton, *A Letter to the Rt. Hon. George Canning*, London, 1827, Sadleir. *Ireland its Evils etc.* Dublin 1829. Staunton, *Hints for Hardinge* Dublin 1830 O'Rourke *The Great Irish Famine.* Dublin 1846 p. 583. Vereker. *Absenteeism considered in its Economical and Social Effects upon Ireland* Dublin 1848 *Ireland's Hour.* App. A. Dublin 1850, McCulloch's views were supported by Ebenezer Shackleton in *Thoughts on Reading Vereker's Paper on Absenteeism* Dublin 1850

money could purchase; but the money which they ought to have—that is, the difference between a corn and a potato diet—goes in Ireland to pay tithes, taxes, and rents. The effect however would not be so injurious to the country if so many of the landlords did not reside abroad."[1] Professor Hancock adopted McCulloch's views in a modified form. He divided absentees into three classes: (a) Those who live abroad on account of pecuniary difficulties or on account of their real income falling short of their nominal income so that they cannot maintain their position at home, (b) Those who, possessed of great wealth, reside abroad for the pursuit of pleasure, (c) Those who spend a portion of every year in London in consequence of the demands of political life. Hancock says that class (a) is injurious whether resident or absent, that class (b) "does not operate to lower wages in Ireland", and that class (c) is positively beneficial.[2] Of course another classification of absentees, not founded on the damage they inflicted on the country, but on the blame which they deserved, was whether they possessed English estates or not. Those landlords who possessed English estates were quite justified in spending a considerable portion of each year in England, whereas no such justification existed for absentees whose property was exclusively Irish.[3]

McCulloch was right in insisting that the landlord, whether resident or absent, was paid, not in money, but in commodities, which he exchanged for other commodities. But he failed to appreciate the importance of the difference between such an exchange being conducted in Ireland or elsewhere. If it were conducted in Ireland, it gave rise to the employment of numerous operatives engaged in the manufacture of the goods taken in exchange, whereas if it took place elsewhere, the Irish workers were deprived of so much employment. Even in the most unfavourable

[1] *Views of Ireland* vol. i. p. 188.
[2] *Irish Absenteeism.* Dublin 1850.
[3] *Commentaries on National Policy and on Ireland.* Dublin 1831.

case that could be imagined, when the landlord exchanged his rents for foreign manufactured products, a substantial amount of employment would be given to those engaged on their importation, such as shippers, merchants, carriers, and retail dealers.

As we saw above, McCulloch claimed as one of the benefits of absenteeism that it increased the exports of the country from which the rents were drawn. He seems completely to have lost sight of the fact that the mere volume of exports is no criterion of a country's prosperity, but that exports must be considered in relation to imports. Exports which are balanced by corresponding imports are no doubt indicative of an increasing wealth, but exports which are not so balanced are a sign rather of increasing poverty. In other words they point to a drain on the country's resources. But even McCulloch did not suggest that the imports of Ireland were augmented by the non-residence of its landed proprietors. The increased export therefore which he applauded was simply one sign of an increased drain on the already impoverished country. That was the whole evil of absenteeism; it entailed that Ireland shipped abroad a certain volume of wealth each year for which she received no return. In 1831 there were complaints of the "ruinous nature of Irish commerce to all but the persons actually engaged on it and the absentees."[1] It was admitted on all sides that this unpaid-for exportation conferred substantial advantages upon the countries to which it went; the accretion of so much unearned wealth afforded the means of considerable employment to the workers of Great Britain; could it be contended therefore it inflicted no damage on the country from which it departed ?

We have assumed so far that the landlords spent the

[1] *Commentaries on National Policy and on Ireland.* London 1831. In the years following the Union Irish imports exceeded exports on account of the large loans raised for Irish purposes in London. J. L. Foster *An Essay on the Principle of Commercial Enchanges* London 1804.

whole of their incomes, but in fact this was not so; they spent a certain part, and saved the rest. In other words they laid aside a certain amount for the purpose of the accumulation of capital. Surely it was a matter of importance to ascertain where that capital was invested. The economists of the more orthodox school argued that capital would be employed wherever the largest profit was anticipated, and that it was as likely to be invested in Irish industry by an absentee as by a resident, provided that the return promised by investment in Ireland was larger than that promised by investment elsewhere. No doubt this was theoretically sound, but it assumed the free flow of capital and labour, and the equal industrial development of Ireland and other countries; but we know that, in fact, the flow of capital and labour was not absolutely free, and that Ireland was in fact less developed than neighbouring countries. Besides, it was extremely probable—not to say certain—that capitalists would prefer to invest in the country where they resided, and where they could consequently watch the enterprises which they helped to establish. Can it be doubted that the withdrawal of so much potential capital from Ireland tended to render it extremely difficult for Irish industrial enterprise to find capital? "Ireland", according to O'Driscoll, "is enabled by her foreign trade to send abroad the rental of her lands to non-resident proprietors; it is that that has made her poor and kept her so. No capital can accumulate in a country subject to such an incessant drainage. The lancets of a thousand absentees are in her veins."[1]

One kind of industry, at any rate, stood to lose by absenteeism, namely the so-called "luxury" trade. Evidence, to the effect that business had been ruined by the increased non-residence of the landowners, was given before the Poor Inquiry Commission, by representatives of the following industries:- basket-makers, bookbinders, bricklayers, brush-

[1] *View of Ireland* vol. ii. p. 177.

makers, coachbuilders, paperstainers and painters, and stucco-plasterers.[1]

The absentees moreover succeeded in escaping from the principal taxes which they would have had to pay if resident in Ireland. The principal taxes payable by the Irish landlord before the extension of the income tax to Ireland were assessed on residents only. In view of the absentees' exemption from these taxes, it was not unreasonable to suggest that they should have been subject to some countervailing tax on their rents.[2] Their absence operated to inflict hardships on those who were liable to the same taxes. but could not live abroad. "The class of the population best able to contribute to the exigencies of the State continued to emigrate, and consequently the deficiency between the estimated and the actual produce of the duties on wines, windows, hearths, carriages, servants, &c. had to be made up by an additional impost to be collected from those who, through necessity, preference, or patriotism continued to reside in Ireland."[3] While more and more of the country's wealth was being exported, ever increasing taxes had to be met by those remaining at home. Thus the public revenue was raised by the oppression of those least able to bear it, while those who should have contributed the greater part escaped.

The general experience was that the estates of absentees were less efficiently managed than those of residents. This was the view expressed by the Devon Commisssion.[4] At the same time we must insist that the greatest evils of absenteeism were not those experienced by the tenantry of the absentees but those felt by the country as a whole. Many absentee estates were conspicuously well managed; and, if the grievances of the tenants were alone to be considered, equal complaint might be made of the landlord's

[1] *Evidence on Combinations, Poor Inquiry Commission App. C. pt.* 2.
[2] *Letter from the Rt. Hon. Denis Browne, M. P.*, London, 1822.
[3] *The Absentee*, by an Officer of the Customs in Ireland, London, 1820.
[4] pp. 1026-7.

residence in London and in Dublin. The real evil of absenteeism was not local but national. "The question is not between the absentees and their tenantry, but between the absentees and their country. In fact the question is between the absentees and the same classes of persons in Ireland as those to whom in England they now distribute the wealth of the country with which they are entrusted."[1] Palgrave's *Dictionary of Political Economy* distinguishes three possible kinds of absenteeism with different results. According to this classification, if the absentee were to become a resident and to consume nothing but foreign manufactured commodities, he would not bestow any benefit on the country by his residence; if his absenteeism causes the export of manufactured goods from the country from which his rents are drawn, he does not inflict any damage on that country; but, if his absenteeism causes the export of raw material, it tends to diminish employment and is consequently injurious. The case of Ireland is a perfect example of the last category; the exports from Ireland caused by absenteeism were without exception raw material; and we must, therefore, conclude that according to the theory quoted Irish absenteeism was injurious to the country.

But possibly the best evidence of the injurious tendency of Irish absenteeism is the universal agreement of all the best writers and thinkers on Irish affairs. "This year" said Ensor "we send as usual millions to be spent in England; and our people are supported by a small proportion returned by English charity."[2] "If the return of a percentage on the original transfer of revenue from Ireland", wrote the same writer three years later, "stayed a famine, what would be the prosperity of Ireland if its abundant produce, the

[1] O'Driscoll, *Review of the Evidence taken before the Committee on the State of Ireland* Dublin 1825. Wakefield vol. i. p. 290. Wm. Conner *The True Political Economy of Ireland*. Dublin 1835.

[2] *An Address to the People of Ireland.* Dublin 1822, see also *An Impartial Review of the True Causes of Existing Misery in Ireland.* Dublin 1825.

whole of its national opulence, was directly disposed to accumulate capital, to increase profits, refresh and invigorate industry and labour, by being freely changed among its people?"[1] Lavergne, the French economist, discussing the evils of absenteeism in the United Kingdom, does not consider the case of Ireland to admit of discussion:- "En ce qui concerne l'Irlande la question me parait tranchée par les faits."[2] We must in conclusion draw attention to the fact that our discussion has been confined altogether to the purely economic effects of absenteeism. The moral and social evils were universally admitted. We must remind the reader that we have already referred to a new form of absenteeism which appeared for the first time after the Union, namely the remission of large sums abroad by way of imperial taxation for which no return was received. The effect of this drain was precisely the same as that caused by the non-residence of the landed proprietors. Another analogous drain which we should not fail to mention, was the profit of the Irish export trade, which was for the most part secured by British shipowners.[3] A considerable profit was also derived from Irish trade by British merchants, who appointed factors to represent them in the Irish ports.[4] Each of these varieties of absenteeism helped to swell the total drain on the country.

[1] *A Defence of the Irish.* Dublin 1825.
[2] *Economie rurale de l'Angleterre* 1858 p. 383.
[3] On this subject see *Report of the Select Committee of the House of Commons respecting the Caledonian Canal with an Introduction etc.* Dublin 1805, *Practical Views and Suggestions* by Hibernicus Dublin 1823, *Report of Dublin Chamber of Commerce* 1827, Michael Staunton *Hints for Hardinge* Dublin 1830 and *Thom's Directory* 1851 p. 253.
[4] *Select Committee on Irish Currency and Exchanges* 1804.

CHAPTER XII.

CURRENCY AND CREDIT.

IN dealing with the question of currency it is well to remind the reader that in the early years of the nineteenth century the need for a circulating medium was so little felt by a great part of the people that practically no currency circulated in the country districts of Ireland. The vast majority of the population consisted of the families of cottiers and very small farmers, and such families were for the most part self-supporting. According to Wakefield, "a family spins, weaves, and manufactures its own linen and frieze; those who use candles make them themselves; and all these people at the same time cultivate a small piece of land and save food sufficient for their maintenance."[1] Coin was not needed even for the payment of rent; for, as we have seen, one of the distinguishing features of the cottier system was that rent was paid in labour. Such small necessaries as the peasantry were forced to purchase in the neighbouring towns were frequently paid for on the tally system without the intervention of any coin. "In places remote from towns the exchange of commodities is carried on by tally payments, a circumstance which forms a striking comparison between the state of Ireland and England. Under this system people purchase at the highest rate without knowing it, and, to use their own expression, are placed under the complete control of

[1] Vol. i. p. 676.

their masters .... I have reason to believe that payments by tally are much more general in Ireland than is to be concluded from the evidence which I have procured ... In the grazing counties it forms the entire mode of transfer amongst the common people ; it prevails throughout Connaught and a great part of Munster."[1]

The extreme scarcity of coin in country parts no doubt accounts for the ignorance of the first principles of money which was so common in Ireland. The story of the burning of Beresford's bank notes by the mob is well known; and the extraordinary practice of pawning money for less than its full value was not unknown. "In Galway", wrote J. C. Foster, "I was assured, so little do the people know the commercial value of money, they are constantly in the habit of pawning it .... I went to a pawnbroker's shop; and on asking the question the shopman told me it was quite a common thing to have money pawned; and he produced a drawer containing a £10 Bank of Ireland note, pawned for a shilling; a £1 Provincial Bank note pawned for six shillings; and a guinea in gold of the reign of Geo. III pawned for fifteen shillings two months ago."[2] The scarcity of coin produced the further result that the defects of the monetary system had practically no effect on the great majority of the people, but were confined in their effects to the landlords, the large farmers, and the inhabitants of the towns, especially the commercial and manufacturing classes.

At the beginning of the nineteenth century the condition of the Irish currency was far from satisfactory. The suspension of cash payments in 1797 resulted in a withdrawal of the greater part of the gold coin from circulation, a greatly increased issue of paper by the Bank of Ireland, and a correspondingly increased issue of paper and tokens by the irresponsible bankers who abounded throughout the country. The currency in circulation consisted in the

[1] Wakefield vol. ii. pp. 17 and 182; and see Butt *The Famine in the Land* p. 40 from which it appears that the same custom was common in 1848.

[2] *Letters on the Condition of the People of Ireland.*

first place of a quantity of gold coin estimated by the best judges to amount to about £2,000,000. In 1797, before the suspension of cash payments, the gold in circulation had amounted to £5,000,000. The next most important medium in circulation was the issue of the Bank of Ireland which amounted in value in 1804 to the sum of £2,986,999, having increased from £2,266,000 in 1801 and from £600,000 in 1797. The other banks followed the example of the Bank of Ireland. On account of the withdrawal of gold from circulation, and the fact that the Bank of Ireland did not establish any country branches, many irresponsible people were tempted to form private banks and to issue large volumes of notes. The number of private banks increased very rapidly during the years immediately following the Union; in 1797 there were 6 banks outside Dublin, in 1801, 23, in 1802, 29, in 1803, 30, and in 1804, 50. The issue of debased currency did not end with these professional, if incapable, bankers; hundreds of petty shopkeepers issued a species of I. O. U. called paper money, which circulated locally. In Youghal, for example, a town of less than 9,000 inhabitants, silver money was issued by twenty-three small retail traders. Needless to say these issues were not in all cases redeemed on demand, and it was a common experience, on presenting a quantity of silver money to the shopkeeper who had issued it, to be told that it could only be redeemed in an equivalent value of the commodity in which he traded. The country was flooded with every kind of forged note. Just as the over-issue of the Bank of Ireland had driven the gold out of circulation, so the issues of notes for small amounts drove the silver out of circulation as well, and the only description of silver coin to be found in Dublin was an exceedingly debased counterfeit. The copper coinage was said to be so defective that there was not a single genuine halfpenny in circulation.[1] "The circulating medium",

[1] *Select Committee on Circulating Medium* 1804, Smyth, *Ireland. Historical and Statistical* vol. iii 341-5, Gilbart *History of Banking in Ireland pp.* 27-31. Dillon *Banking in Ireland.*

it was stated in 1804, "in the southern provinces, with the exception of the metropolis, at this moment consists of a very moderate quantity of National Bank paper; a much larger proportion of Dublin private bank paper; an incalculable influx of country coinage in paper, for gold and silver; and an accumulated mass of counterfeited silver and copper, base beyond sufferance, description or example."[1] In Dublin, the evil of base silver had become so great, that these issues were suppressed by the action of the Irish Treasury, which did not however substitute anything in their place; and the city was consequently left without any circulating medium less than a pound.[2]

In addition to the very great inconvenience caused to Irish traders and merchants by this unregulated and unsatisfactory currency, serious injury was caused to Irish commerce as a result of the unfavourable rate of exchange which the depreciation produced. In normal times, owing to the differences between the English and the Irish pound, exchange between London and Dublin was considered at par when it stood at $8^1/_3{}^0/_0$, that is to say, when £100 British was reckoned equal to £108. 6. 8 Irish. Immediately after the suspension of cash payments the exchange began to turn against Ireland, until in 1804 it had touched $16^0/_0$ or $7^2/_3{}^0/_0$ above normal. If allowance of $^2/_3{}^0/_0$ were made as a sufficient price for the expense of remittance, it might be concluded that Irish currency had sunk in value $7^0/_0$.

The strange thing was that this adverse exchange was experienced only in the south of Ireland. The exchange between London and Belfast remained quite normal. In 1797 the United Irishmen in Belfast, wishing to embarrass the established government, refused to take Bank of Ireland paper, and consequently the practice of payment in specie was maintained in north-east Ulster, even when the currency of the rest of Ireland had reached the extreme

[1] *A Candid Cobbler's Cursory and Critical Conjectures.* Dublin 1804.
[2] J. L. Foster, *An Essay on the Principle of Commercial Exchanges* Dublin 1804.

state of depreciation which we have described.[1] While therefore the rate of exchange of Dublin on London was $16^1/_4$ %, that of Belfast on London was $5^1/_4$ %, and there was actually a rate of exchange of 11½ quoted at Belfast on Dublin.[2] "At Belfast, and in its immediate neighbourhood, Bank of Ireland notes have never acquired any general circulation. The currency is carried on either in specie or in the notes of private bankers payable in that manner. The differences between the currencies of Belfast and Dublin has produced an actual exchange between the two places in favour of the former. When payments are made at Belfast in Bank of Ireland notes, an additional amount is paid proportioned to the discount."[3] At Newry, situated midway between Dublin and Belfast, two rates of exchange were habitually quoted.[4] It must be recorded to the credit of the northern manufacturers that they were anxious to support the Bank of Ireland, and held meetings exhorting the landlords to accept its notes in payment of their rents. The landlords, however, refused, and the price of manufactured goods had therefore to be raised.[5]

There is no need to explain the evil effects produced by the existence of this adverse rate of exchange in the south of Ireland. The price of all imported goods was raised, and, as a consequence, the price of home manufactured commodities as well. The landlords, owing to the arbitrary powers which they possessed over their tenants, frequently insisted on being paid their rents in cash, but invariably paid what they themselves owed in the depreciated medium.[6] So critical did the situation become in 1804, that a select committee was appointed to enquire into the causes which had produced it, and the measures which were required to amend it.

[1] Parnell, *Observations on the State of the Currency in Ireland.* Dublin 1804. *The State of Ireland Considered* Dublin 1810. [2] Parnell *op. cit.* [3] Lord King. *Thoughts on the Restriction of Payments in Specie at the Banks of England and Ireland* London 1803.

[4] J. L. Foster *Essay on the Principle of Commercial Exchanges*, London 1804.

[5] Lord King *op. cit.*

[6] Wm. Jebb. *An Enquiry into the Depreciation of the Irish Bank Paper.* Dublin 1804.

The question of the adverse exchange gave rise to a large volume of controversial literature. "Exchange engrosses the public mind, there seems indeed some lowering cloud over our commercial atmosphere."[1] Certain apologists of the Bank of Ireland attempted to suggest causes of the unsatisfactory exchange other than the depreciation of the currency. It was argued, for example, that the real cause was the adverse balance of trade, but it was demonstrated in reply that the balance of trade was actually favourable to Ireland, and that consequently the adverse exchange must be caused by the value of the medium of payment. It was rejoined that the balance of trade was deceptive, inasmuch as a large part of the exports were really sent abroad in payment of absentee rents; it was rebutted that the absentee rents had not affected the exchange before the suspension of cash payments, that they formed a comparatively small proportion of the total volume of exports, and that, even if they had increased since the Union, they had not increased so rapidly as to produce such remarkable consequences.[2] The more the attempts to minimize the evil of depreciation, the more clearly did it appear as the real keystone of the situation.

The case against the Bank of Ireland was admirably put by Lord King, who pointed out that there were only two exceptions to the unfavourable exchange which since 1799 had generally prevailed between London and other parts of Europe, namely the course of exchange with Lisbon and with Dublin. Both Portugal and Ireland had suffered from a depreciated currency during those years.[3] Foster, in the following passage of his pamphlet, showed that Ireland exhibited all the symptoms of a country whose exchange had become adverse through a depreciation of its currency:—

[1] *A Candid Cobbler's Cursory and Critical Conjectures.* Dublin 1804.
[2] J. L. Foster *op. cit.* Parnell *op. cit.* Lord Lauderdale, *Thoughts on the Alarming State of the Circulation and on the Means of Redressing the Pecuniary Grievances of Ireland.* Edinburgh 1805 D. Beaumont Payne, *An Exposition of the Irish Exchange* Wells 1806.
[3] *Op cit.*

"The following appear to be the principal, if not all, the symptoms of the depreciation of paper through excess which it is possible for any country to exhibit. *First* a high and permanent excess of the market price above the mint price of bullion; *secondly* an open discount upon paper as compared with coin; *thirdly* an exchange unfavourable to the country when computed in bank notes,yet possibly favourable when computed in specie; unfavourable to those parts of the country where the circulating medium is paper; yet much less unfavourable to other parts whose circulating medium is specie; *fourthly* an exchange between different parts of the same country, whose circulating mediums are different; *fifthly* the entire disappearance of all the smaller coin, which had been in circulation along with specie, but which cannot continue in circulation along with any other circulating medium of less value; and *lastly and above all,* we should be led to expect that these different tests of depreciation nicely agreed with each other: these are all the tests of depreciation which can be expected; and they are all exhibited in Ireland."[1]

The select committee of the House of Commons endorsed the opinion that the adverse exchange was caused by the depreciation of the Irish currency. "In Belfast", we read in their report, "the bills of exchange are purchased by guineas and other bankers' notes; and if the exchange between Great Britain and Ireland be stated as it actually exists, where guineas are the circulating medium, your Committee would be inclined to think that the exchange is now, and actually has been, in favour of Ireland; but if it is to be estimated by the rate which prevails where paper is the circulating medium, the exchange appears to be now, and to have been since 1798, uniformly against Ireland, and to have arisen to a degree wholly unprecedented. The former they would call the real, and the latter the nominal rate; and the difference between them arises, as far as your

[1] *Op. cit.*

Committee can form a judgment, from the depreciation of the circulating paper." The depreciation of the currency was, in the opinion of the committee, the result of the suspension of cash payments, which "compelled the bank to refrain from sending into circulation gold, the only common medium between the two countries. It gave occasion to the great issue of paper which followed to replace the gold so withdrawn, and removed at the same time the best and most effective check against the depreciation of that paper, namely its convertibility into gold at the will of the holder; it tended to encourage an unlimited and over-abundant issue, by releasing the bank from performing their engagements; and, by taking away from them the former criterion, namely the diminution of their gold, which they were accustomed to look to for judging when their paper became excessive, it promoted an unrestrained trade in paper currency, and excited individuals to speculations which interfered with the steady national rates of exchange. The number of speculators so encouraged contributed to raise the price of bills on England, which being paid for in depreciated paper, the rate of exchange rose proportionally." The adverse exchange, the committee went on to state, was the cause of the debasement of the silver currency, as it produced the withdrawal from circulation of the silver coinage.

The committee expressed itself of the opinion that the repeal of the Restriction Act of 1797 would provide the most effective remedy for the evils complained of; but it did not recommend this step, as it understood there were various political considerations urged against it. The principal recommendations made were: that the Bank of Ireland should be compelled to pay its notes in Bank of England notes; that the currencies of the two countries should be assimilated; that the Bank of Ireland should establish a sufficient fund in London for drawing on; and that the loan raised in London for the purposes of the Irish government should be managed by the Bank of Ireland.

A motion to the effect that the Bank of Ireland should be bound to pay its notes in Bank of England notes was made, but negatived in the House of Lords.[1] The silver currency was amended by two statutes, one authorizing the Bank of Ireland to issue dollars of the value of six shillings each,[2] and the other declaring illegal the issue of "silver notes."[3] The latter statute was widely violated.[4]

In the course of six or seven years the exchange again became normal, "not by any reduction in the issues of the Bank of Ireland, but by the depreciation of the currency of England, which became as great as that of the Irish currency in 1810, when the exchange between London and Dublin settled again at about par."[5] In 1826 the currencies of Great Britain and Ireland were assimilated, and after that date no exchange problems between the two countries could arise.[6]

The best account of the chaotic state of the Irish currency in the early years of the nineteenth century is to be found in Wakefield's evidence before the Bullion Committee of 1810, which we quote at length:—

"I will endeavour to give you a list of the items that compose the circulating medium of the sister island, and the means by which transfers are effected without the intervention of that medium.

"1. *Issues of the National Bank*—which are partly paper, and partly tokens. The paper consists of notes payable to bearer on demand, and notes payable to order seven days after sight. The tokens are Spanish dollars stamped as tokens, for six shillings Irish currency, and amount to £200,000. This last issue is partly a credit medium, for the dollar is worth only about 4s. 3d. or 4s. 6d. and the

[1] Wakefield vol. ii. p. 184. [2] 44 Geo. III c. 71. [3] 44 Geo. III c. 91.
[4] Wakefield vol. ii. p. 173. [5] Parnell *State of the Currency Question* London 1818. The fact that the currency of Great Britain had been seriously depreciated by overissue was conclusively established by the Bullion Commission of 1810. [6] 6 Geo IV. c. 79.

difference between this intrinsic value and the sum of six shillings, at which they are issued, is completely a credit given by the public, and rests on the same foundation as an issue of paper.

"2. *Issues of Private Bankers.*—The banking-houses in Dublin, except those of Messrs. Latouche and Co., and Sir Thomas Newcomen and Co., issue notes payable to bearer as well as the country banks.

"The issues of private bankers are notes payable in bank of Ireland notes, and not in specie.

"Private bankers' post bills are likewise made payable in Bank of Ireland notes; and as they require acceptance ten days before they are payable, they are kept in a forced circulation.

"The Lurgan, Londonderry, and two Belfast banks, make their notes payable in Dublin as well as at their own house: but nearly all the other private bankers make their notes only payable at the place whence they are issued.

"The notes of both the Bank of Ireland and of private bankers are now for one or more pounds, not for a guinea, or £1. 2s. 9d. currency, as they were formerly.

"All private bankers in Ireland are compelled by the 29 Geo. II. c. 16. to take out a licence, and prohibited from trading, which has thrown the banking trade into the hands of a wealthier class of persons than it would otherwise have been in. The prohibition against bankers trading has deprived them of some of their means of forcing paper into circulation; but this obstacle has been more than overcome by the increased activity and use of those left.

"Private bankers have for a long time regularly collected the specie in circulation, but on no occasion voluntarily issued it, which has caused guineas to disappear from three provinces, and heightens the premium on them. The recent establishment of two banks at Belfast, threatens the same consequences in the north.

"It is common for private bankers to pay a commission

to butter-factors, corn-buyers, and other dealers, on the amount of the paper they can issue. Though the paymasters of regiments are prohibited from this practice, and are supplied with the Bank of Ireland notes, yet these notes are exchanged for smaller ones by the country bankers, and are thus withdrawn from circulation, and replaced by private paper.

"At Ballinasloe fair, all payments are made in bills on Dublin, at sixty-one days date; and although the business done there is immense, the Galway bankers attend, and are ready to exchange these bills at par for their own notes.

"The Bank of Ireland is restrained by their charter from taking a larger discount than five per cent.; and those Dublin bankers who issue paper discount at that rate in their own notes, but the two banking-houses which do not issue paper, charge the legal rate of discount, which is six per cent.

"Under this head of issues of private banks, I wish to add that there is in Ireland a circulation of forged notes, of which no one here can form an idea; and the amount of which it is impossible to guess, although it is known to be enormous; indeed, so large as to deserve a place in every calculation of the amount of the circulating medium of the sister island.

"In the city and neighbourhood of Dublin, Bank of Ireland and Dublin private bankers' paper constitutes the circulating medium.

"Kilkenny, Wexford, Waterford, Youghal, Clonmel, Fermoy, Cork, Mallow, Limerick, Ennis, Galway, and Tuam, have private bankers, whose paper is the prevailing, and in most instances, the entire circulating medium of their respective neighbourhoods. Each of these private banks have by them some quantity of Bank of Ireland paper, which, however, they never issue when they can avoid doing so. They all draw bills upon London at thirty-one days, which is a premium of one half per cent.: and one cause of their only paying their notes at their own banks, is to secure this profit.

"3. *Promissory Notes,* called *Silver Notes*—are in circulation in the counties of Kerry, Limerick, Clare, and Cork, in direct violation of the law which prohibits the issue of notes for small sums. But great art is used to evade the penalties to which the issuers of such notes are liable. They are drawn as if they were the weigh-bills of corn buyers, as I. O. U., or bearing a date previous to the act. The amount of this species of paper is inconsiderable.

"4. *Bills of Exchange*—greatly aid transfers, and supply the place of circulating medium, especially those drawn on Dublin, which pass from hand to hand till they fall due.

"5. *Tally Payments.*—There is a considerable transfer of property and payment for labour in various parts of Ireland, by tally between landlords and their tenants; the work of the latter being set against the rent and property of the former.

"6. *Guineas.*—It is a general opinion that guineas are hoarded, and there are some facts with which I am acquainted that seem to support it. I have been assured by several, that they always lay by every guinea they receive, looking upon them as a rarity; and I am sure that in consequence many affix an ideal value to coin. One person told me he had borrowed bank notes at an interest of twelve per cent., with which to pay his rent, though he had gold by him which he would not part with.

"In that part of Ireland in which guineas still circulate, two prices are put on every article offered for sale; and it is common to buy at the coin price, and pay in paper, when the buyer pays in addition what is called the discount, which however is the premium on guineas.

"The quantity of gold in the north of Ireland has been much over-rated. I have known the agents of absentee proprietors supply a shop-keeper with a few guineas to sell to the tenants at a premium, on the day that their rents are payable, which on the rents being paid, were again given to the shop-keeper to resell; and this operation to the profit of the agents and the shop-keeper, and to the delusion of the public, has been repeated with the same guineas several times in one day. I have not heard of this trick anywhere but in the north, where it is supposed guineas circulate, and the agents pretend that their employers insist on being paid their rents in gold.

"7. *Spanish Dollars*—are imported by individuals from Liverpool chiefly, and circulate without a stamp at an uncertain value, according to their weight and the market price of silver.

"8. *Bank Tokens*—are issued by the treasury to the Bank of Ireland, who issue them to the public: they are of silver, and are for five-pence, ten-pence, and thirty-pence. The act which makes it an offence to coin them directs them to be received at the exchequer, and thus secures their value to the public. They were stamped bank tokens, because the bank had previously issued dollars so stamped, and it was therefore deemed a less innovation. They were issued for the above sums, both as forming change for the stamped dollar, and to confine their circulation to Ireland. These tokens amount to £955,000 British. They are not current by the King's proclamation like mint coin.

"9. *Copper Coin*—consists of pence and halfpence. There was a new coinage of 600 tons since the year 1804. Thirteen of these pence represent a British shilling.

"10. *English Mint Silver*—is seldom seen, and not current, except in Cork and its neighbourhood, which I apprehend arises from the frequent communication with English shipping.

"11. In the King's County, Lord Charleville has issued a piece of copper about the size and weight of a penny piece, promising the payment of 13d. every Tuesday in

Tullamore, which is the currency of small payments in that neighbourhood."[1]

The system of banking in Ireland in the early nineteenth century was pregnant with danger to the credit as well as to the currency of the country. Under its charter "the Bank of Ireland enjoyed the right to prevent the establishment of any bank of issue, with more than six partners in any part of Ireland; still from the year 1783 to the year 1825 they confined their banking operations to the City of Dublin; and although repeatedly solicited by the merchants and traders of Cork, Limerick, Waterford, Belfast, and other great commercial towns to establish branches in those localities, they peremptorily refused to do so; the result was that a large number of private banks with less than six partners were established in the provinces."[2] Such a state of affairs was necessarily most detrimental to the growth of Irish industrial enterprise. In Dublin the Bank of Ireland possessed the virtual monopoly of financing large undertakings; but it was persistently complained that the Bank had abused its power to discourage the advancement of Catholic traders.[3] In the provinces matters were infinitely worse; for there, not only was the manufacturer or trader without the means of procuring financial accommodation, but he was in danger of losing his deposits and savings in one of the numerous, nay almost continuous, periods of banking failure. "It appears", wrote Wakefield in 1810, "that the whole number of registered banks in 1804 was 50, of which 19 now remain; the rest having disappeared, and, I believe, for the most part failed."[4] The year 1820 was notorious for the numerous banking failures that occurred. "Then began an accumulative series of those rapid failures which seem to be known to no other country, and which spread indescribable calamity

[1] For information relating to the coins issued in Ireland after the Union, of value to the numismatist rather than the economist, see Lindsay *Coins of Ireland* pp. 62-3. The last Irish coins were issued in 1822-3. Lindsay says that "the harp on these coins is peculiarly beautiful". [2] *Repeal Reports* vol. i. p. 27. [3] *Ibid.* p. 35. [4] Vol. ii p. 171.

and consternation over the whole surface of the island. In the month of June the banking firm of Roche & Co. of Cork failed; and on the same morning that of Leslie & Co. suspended payment in the same city. By the next Saturday, Messrs. Maunsell of Limerick had closed their doors. These embarrassments were quickly followed by the stoppage of Messrs. Riall at Clonmel; Sause at Carrick-on-Suir; Newport at Waterford; Loughnan at Kilkenny; Alexander at Dublin; until within a single month eleven banks had broken, and in the whole South of Ireland there remained open only three houses—Messrs. Delacour at Mallow, Redmond at Wexford, and Pike at Cork."[1] "In 1804", wrote Sir Henry Parnell in 1828, "there were in Ireland fifty registered banks. Since that year a great many more have been established, but the whole have failed one after the other, involving the country from time to time in complete distress."[2] The banking history of the period 1800-20 is summarized as follows by George Lewis Smyth—"The Bank of Ireland monopoly, copper and silver notes, I. O. U's. for all amounts; the panics of 1804, 1810, 1814 and 1820; the stoppage of fifty banks; and the loss of millions which it is impossible to calculate."[3]

In consequence of the failures of 1820, an important statute was passed, by which the Bank of Ireland was authorized to increase its capital by the additional sum of £500,000, to be advanced to the government. Bank notes were declared to be receivable in payment of taxes; and the Bank consented to a restriction of its privilege, so as to permit banking companies and co-partnerships, consisting of more than six persons, residing and having their houses of business at a greater distance than fifty miles from Dublin, to issue notes payable on demand outside that radius.[4] This act at first proved ineffective, as it was not clear from its wording, whether all the partners in such

[1] Smyth. *Ireland. Historical and Statistical* vol. iii. p. 348. [2] *State of the Currency Question*. London 1828. [3] *Op. cit.* vol. iii. p. 350. On the old Irish private banks see a series of articles by Mr. MacCarthy Tenison in vols 11 and 12 of the Journal of the Institute of Bankers in Ireland. [4] 1 & 2 Geo. IV. c. 72.

enterprises must not reside in Ireland; and legal opinions were given to the effect that persons resident in England were ineligible to become partners. This doubt was removed by a subsequent statute.[1]

In the interval between the failure of the majority of the private banks in 1820 and the establishment of the first joint stock bank, Ireland was practically without any credit facilities except those afforded by the Bank of Ireland. "At one period", Mr. Spring Rice wrote in 1822, "Ireland was a country of bankers. To readers whose abstract idea of a banker has been formed among the sleek well-fed inhabitants of Threadneedle and Lombard Streets the Irish country bankers would appear creatures of a very different genus. The circulating medium of the latter neither moved armies nor senates; it passed modestly as the representative of shillings and sixpences; and in some instances bore the value of three halfpence only .... Yet the failure of eleven out of fourteen banks plunged the entire of the South of Ireland into ruin and distress."[2] In 1823, there were twenty-six counties, and one entire province—Connaught—which did not possess a single bank.[3]

The year 1824 marked a turning point. From that year forward joint stock banks and their branches were established in every part of the country. The first joint stock bank to be established was the Provincial Banking Company in 1824, which was closely followed by the Hibernian and Northern Banks in 1825. These early joint stock banks provoked the hostility of the Bank of Ireland, which, seeing its monopoly in danger, did all it could to hamper their success. In the first place it offered all the resistance of which it was capable to the act of parliament which was proposed to get rid of the confusion regarding the need for residence in Ireland contained in the act of 1821. Having failed to prevent the passing of this measure, the Bank of

[1] 5 Geo. IV. c. 73 amended by 6 Geo. IV. c. 42.

[2] *Considerations on the Present State of Ireland.* London 1822.

[3] *Practical Views and Suggestions* by Hibernicus. Dublin 1823.

Ireland next proceeded to enter into active competition with the Provincial Bank in every town in which the latter opened branches. This indicated a remarkable change of policy on the part of the Bank. From 1782 until 1824, when it had possessed the monopoly of joint stock banking throughout the whole of Ireland, it studiously refrained from extending its operations outside Dublin; but, as soon as the credit needs of provincial traders were afforded some consideration by a rival bank, it showed an extreme solicitude to minister to them. "The moment the urgency of the circumstances invited others into the field; as soon as London capitalists published a prospectus, in which they promised to afford certain towns in the country parts of Ireland that accommodation which the Bank of Ireland had so long denied them, the Bank at once set up a determined opposition in those very towns, and resorted to every means within its reach to embarrass and defeat the new enterprise. It thus not only refused to do the good required, when it alone had the power, but it laboured to deter others from rendering it, even where the legislature had specially interfered for the purpose."[1] The Bank of Ireland was not satisfied merely with opening rival establishments in the towns where the Provincial Bank opened branches; it organized several heavy and keenly-timed runs on the latter.[2] The competition and the runs having failed, another course of action was adopted. The Provincial Bank, which, under the Act of 1821, was prohibited from issuing notes within fifty miles of Dublin, established an agency in Dublin for the payment in Dublin of its notes issued elsewhere. The Bank of Ireland thereupon instituted legal proceedings with a view to obtaining a decision that this was an infringement of its monopoly. Appeals to the highest courts were threatened by both sides; but fortunately the action was compromised; and the position contended for by the

[1] Smyth, *Ireland. Historical and Statistical.* vol. iii. p. 358.
[2] Smyth *op. cit.* vol. iii. p. 357. Gilbart *History of Banking in Ireland.* p. 81.

Provincial Bank received the sanction of the legislature in the following year.[1]

The opposition of the Bank of Ireland thus failed at every point; and the progress of the joint stock banks was one of almost complete success. The Belfast Bank was incorporated in 1827, the Agricultural and Commercial Bank in 1834, the National Bank in 1835, the Royal Bank of Ireland in 1836, the Ulster Bank in 1837, the Tipperary Bank in 1839, and the London and Dublin Bank in 1843. Of these the only failures were the Agricultural and Commercial and the Tipperary Banks. The Southern Bank, which was established on the ruins of the Agricultural and Commercial, only survived a few months. The London and Dublin Bank gave up business in 1848. All the other joint stock banks were conspicuously successful.[2]

The foundation of these joint stock banks was productive of an immediate increase in the credit facilities of Ireland. The Select Committee on the Condition of the Poor, 1830, reported that:—"The banking business of Ireland is now placed on a much better footing than in former times. Prior to the failure of the private banks, and for some time subsequent to that calamity, the rate of discount charged upon mercantile paper was 5 or 6 *per cent*, together with a double commission, postages, and incidental expenses. At present the same business is transacted at 4 *per cent* only by the Bank of Ireland and the joint stock banks. In 1820 the circulation of one entire province, and very nearly of another, was swept away in a single week. At present there exists in Ireland but one private bank issuing paper; and there prevails on the subject of the currency a feeling of great satisfaction and entire confidence. The rate of interest upon the securities is stated to have fallen at least one *per cent;* and in some cases in Ulster money has been lent on mortgage at 4½ *per cent.*"[3]

[1] 6 Geo. IV. c. 42. Smyth *op. cit.* pp. 359-60. Dillon *History of Banking in Ireland* p. 51.

[2] Full particulars of each of these banks is to be found in Smyth *op. cit.* pp. 350 sq. and Dillon *op. cit.*.

[3] p. 14.

In spite of this marked improvement on the former state of affairs, much still remained to be done. The Bank of Ireland continued to exercise its monopoly within a radius of fifty miles of Dublin—in other words in the richest and most important part of the country. Within this area the old evils of monopoly were still experienced. Although, owing to the pressure of competition, the Bank had been forced to open no less than seventeen branches outside the area of its monopoly, it had opened only six within that area; so that the number of branches of joint stock banks within that important area only amounted to one for every 217,000 of the population, as compared with one for every 60,000 in other parts of Ireland, and one for every 7,750 in Scotland. Even in the parts of Ireland where the Bank of Ireland monopoly did not prevail, the banking facilities were inadequate; as the banks were extremely conservative and unwilling to finance industrial and commercial enterprise. The Report of the Repeal Association, issued in 1844, from which we have taken the above facts, stated as follows:—"Referring to the six joint stock banks of issue, your Committee deem it advisable to state that their capability to afford legitimate banking facilities to a country like Ireland is at present totally inadequate. This belief is founded upon the fact that the aggregate amount of the paid-up capital of all the joint stock banks of issue in Ireland does not exceed £4,230,000, from which is to be deducted the paid-up capital of the Bank of Ireland lent to Government, leaving an available paid-up capita of only about £1,600,000. The amount of credit obtained by those banks from the public in Ireland appears to be as follows:—

Average circulation in 1841	£5.500,000
Deposits about	6.000,000
	£11.500,000
To which is to be added their paid-up capital of	4.230.000
	£15,730,000

"If these banks acted according to the rules adopted by well-regulated banking establishments in Great Britain, and elsewhere, they ought to have afforded to their customers in Ireland, discounts and cash-credits to the extent of two-thirds of the sum of £15,730,000 viz. about £10,500,000 sterling; whereas your Committee have good reason to believe, that the total average amount of Irish bills under discount at present does not exceed £4,000,000 sterling, and very little, if any, accommodation is afforded to the agriculturalist, merchant, or manufacturer in the shape of cash credits.

"In pursuing this enquiry your Committee feel no hesitation in stating that the decay of our manufactures, the annihilation of our commerce, and the backward and neglected state of our agriculture, is in part attributable to the contracted and vicious system of banking operations in Ireland; and, although considerable advantage has resulted from the modification of the Bank of Ireland monopoly in 1825, still the system is at present so totally at variance with the principles of enlightened legislation as to demand immediate alteration."[1]

In consequence of the unsatisfactory condition of the Irish banks, and the many complaints which were made that Irish industry and commerce were being hampered by the lack of credit facilities, a select committee was appointed in 1837. No action however was taken on its report until 1845, when Sir Robert Peel's famous banking act was passed. The most important provision of this act was that the Bank of Ireland's monopoly was taken away, even within the limited area to which it had been confined by the act of 1821. The issue of notes by the banks already possessing branches in that area was limited by the condition that no bank should issue notes to more than the average amount of its circulation during the year preceding 1st May 1845. For any excess over this

[1] *Repeal Reports* vol. i. pp. 28-33.

amount, gold and silver should be held by the bank in stated proportions. In the event of the union of two or more banks, the new bank so formed was authorized to issue notes to the amount of the circulation of the united banks; and on any bank's relinquishing its issue, the Bank of Ireland was authorized to increase its issue by the amount relinquished. The issue of notes for fractional sums, or for sums less than a pound, was prohibited.[1] The amounts of notes so authorized to be issued were as follows:—

Bank of Ireland	£3,738,428
Belfast Bank	281,611
National Bank	852,269
Northern Bank	243,440
Provincial Bank	927,667
Ulster Bank	311,079
	£6,354,494

This act gave general satisfaction. Writing in 1849, Mr. George Lewis Smyth, who had a thorough knowledge of the evils of Irish banking in the past, expressed the opinion that "there are perhaps no public institutions to be met with in Ireland which have given healthier signs of progress and improvement than the banks have done of late years."[2]

We have so far confined our treatment of the subject of credit to the facilities for borrowing that were afforded to the large trader or farmer; but before concluding this chapter we must say something about the facilities possessed by the small farmers and peasants. As we have already said, the use of any kind of circulating medium was by no means general among these classes, but occasions arose in which the alternative to obtaining credit was starvation, and in such cases the intervention of some measure of value was unavoidable. Every advantage was taken by the lender to reap profit on account of the borrower's ignorance of the

[1] 8 and 9 Vict. c. 37.
[2] *Op. cit.* vol. iii p. 370.

first facts about money, and exorbitant rates of interest for such loans were generally charged. "Agricultural credit has no more existence in Ireland than in France— it is only agricultural usury. The country is generally so divided and subdivided that a large proportion of the occupiers are of a class below that with whom the present great banking establishments usually have transactions; and the charges made by these banks on small bills are quite exorbitant — 7 to 20 per cent."[1]

Where any goods were obtained on credit from the shopkeepers in the neighbouring towns, the cottiers were forced to pay unreasonable rates of interest. "The cottier very often neither possesses the necessary seed, nor has he money to buy it. Recourse must then be had to buying on credit, and, ridiculous as it may appear, a grinding usury is one of the oppressions under which the Irish peasant suffers when driven to purchase without money."[2] The shopkeepers always charged double the market price when they sold on credit; and they frequently refused to sell for ready money, even when it was offered, so as not to lose their hold over their victims.[3] The practice was not unknown of landlords' agents participating in the profits of such usurers, or "gombeen-men", as they came to be called. "Many agents have sons or other relations settled as shopkeepers on some part of the estate to which they belong, and a tenant, unless he chooses to run the risk of incurring the displeasure of these harpies, cannot purchase a yard of tape or a pound of cheese in any other place. Nay, I have known agents, when they had no relations to provide for in this manner, dispose of a shop to a stranger, and exact from him a percentage on all his profits."[4]

In somè cases the landlord himself acted the part of gombeen-man. "The few necessaries", we read in 1818,

[1] Philip Reade. *Whig and Tory Remedies for Irish Evils* Dublin 1844.
[2] Ryan, *Practical Remedies for the Practical Evils of Ireland.* Dublin 1828.
[3] *Poor Inquiry Commission* 1834 App. A. p. 200; *ibidem* 3rd. Report p. 27.
[4] Wakefield vol. i. p. 299.

"which the cottier requires are supplied by his employer; the best prices are paid and demanded for the worst commodities; and, though he may have well-grounded misapprehensions of being overcharged, he has no power of controlling or checking his account, which is seldom adjusted more than once a year. Should he be even fairly dealt with, suspicion and dissatisfaction are the natural consequences of such a running account, the balance of which is never known till the day of reckoning."[1] It was also the custom for cottiers to buy their potatoes from the farmer during the winter and spring months, on the ruinous condition of paying the highest price that would prevail during the summer season.[2] The factors who bought the small farmer's produce were also frequently guilty of the most harsh exactions.[3] Of course these practices amounted to sheer usury, and would never have been possible if there had been in Ireland any general and proper provision for the advancement of small sums to the poor. As it was, the cottiers and small tenants who desired accommodation were driven to resort either to the pawnbrokers—who were of small assistance to borrowers who had in general nothing to pawn—or to the small local usurers, whose interest generally amounted to sixty *per cent.*[4] "There is probably no country in the world", according to Mr. Muggeridge", in which the pawning and borrowing of small sums is carried on to as great an extent as in Ireland, or on such disadvantageous terms. For loans of two, three or four pounds advanced in the months of May or June notes of hand will frequently be passed made payable after harvest, in which the interest is made to amount to half the sum borrowed; when such a ruinous course is attempted to be avoided, and persons get potatoes or other articles on

[1] Curwen. *Observations* vol. i. p. 221.

[2] W. L. Shouldham. *Remarks on the Small Loan Fund System* London 1839.

[3] Bicheno. *Ireland and Its Economy* p. 18. These gentry were known as sky farmers. *Fifth Report of Limerick Agricultural Associdtion* Limerick 1827.

[4] *The Present State of Tipperary*, by a Magistrate of the County, Dublin, 1842. On the pawnbrokers see the Poor Inquiry Commission App. E. pp. 93-102.

credit, they seem only to escape Scylla to fall on Charybdis."[1]

Several attempts were made to remedy this deplorable lack of credit facilities among the poor. The Irish Loan Fund, the origin of which is attributed to Dean Swift, received the recognition and encouragement of the Irish Parliament. In 1778 the Managers of the Dublin Charitable Musical Society were incorporated as a charitable loan society, and authorized to hold property and to issue loans in the manufacturing counties and market towns of Ireland. These loans were repayable by instalments, but no interest was charged. The assistance contemplated by this act was intended for urban rather than rural workers.[2]

During the early part of the nineteenth century various associations were formed in London with a view to improving the condition of the Irish peasantry. In the year 1823, following the severe famine of the previous year, a large sum was subscribed for the relief of the distress in Ireland. After the relief of the immediate distress, a surplus of £40,000 remained; and this sum, together with other sums remaining in the hands of some local relief committees, was administered, under a statute then passed, by county boards of trustees in Ireland, which issued loans through the medium of local associations in certain counties. These associations were called the "Irish Reproductive Loan Funds", to distinguish them from the existing loan fund society, and were primarily designed to benefit the agricultural population. The boards of trustees were subject to audit by the London board of directors; and this arrangement continued until 1848, when the whole organization was dissolved, the money in hand being placed at the disposal of the Lord Lieutenant for application to such useful purposes as he might think proper with the sanction of the Treasury.[3] The Irish Reproductive Loan Funds did not produce the maximum benefits of which they were capable, as their

[1] Muggeridge's Report p. 727.
[2] 17 and 18 Geo. III. c. 12.
[3] 11 & 12 Vict. c. 115.

affairs were managed in a very lax and wasteful manner.[1]

The law relating to charitable loan societies was put on a new footing in 1823, when it was provided by statute that any number of persons desirous of forming a charitable loan society might do so, and might charge interest on loans issued by them. It was provided that no loan exceeding £10 should be made to the same person within twelve months, but that loans of £100 might be made to a committee or committees of three or more solvent persons, upon their joint and several security, repayable in twelve months with interest. No trustees or managers were to be remunerated, but clerks were to be paid salaries and expenses; and any implements of industry lent by loan fund societies were to be protected from distraint and execution.[2] Many abuses arose in the administration of this act, in consequence of which an amending act was passed in 1836, creating an Irish Loan Fund Board with power to supervise the working of the societies.[3] The former *maximum* of £10 was continued; and the local societies were authorized to apply such part of their surplus profits as they thought fit to charitable purposes. In 1838 a further Act was passed exempting all the loan funds connected with the Irish Reproductive Loan Funds Institution from any control by the Loan Fund Board.[4]

Many abuses were prevalent in the administration of the local societies, which the Board confessed itself unable to correct. The chief of these were the payment of 6 *per cent* interest on large sums and of 4 *per cent* on small sums, whereas the converse should have been the case; the payment of large salaries to officers of societies; the high rents paid for offices; and the misappropriation of profits.[5] In 1842 the Board was so impressed by the prevalence of abuses that it drew up the draft of an act embodying the amendments which it judged necessary for the proper

[1] *Report of Select Committee on Loan Fund Societies Ireland* 1855 p. 46.
[2] 4 Geo. IV. c. 32, 10 Geo. IV. c. 42. [3] 6 and 7 Wm. IV. c. 55. [4] 1 & 2 Vict. c. 78
[5] *Report of Irish Loan Fund Board* 1840.

working of the system. The Board stated that the evils of the existing system arose principally from two causes:—(1) the want of a proper and vigilant inspection, and (2) the absence of adequate power being vested in the Board for the correction or eradication of evils when discovered.[1] "I have never conversed with a man", a correspondent wrote to Sir Robert Peel, "who had borrowed money from the Loan Fund that did not regret it. I have seen numbers 'canted' or ruined by them, and I have been told by every gentleman who manages them in the country towns that they do more harm than good."[2]

The government adopted the suggestions of the Board, and introduced an important measure in the following year, increasing the power of the central authority, and reducing the rate of interest which might be charged on advances.[3] The abuses nevertheless continued, possibly is an aggravated form, and the number of societies began to decrease. The remarkable decline of the system in 1847 was no doubt partly attributable to the famine, but other more permanent causes were also at work, as appears from the following passage from the annual report of the Board for 1848:—

"But whilst the Board notice the famine as the chief cause of the diminishing circulation of the Loan Funds, it appears to them that there are others in operation.

"In the first place, the tendency of the Board's own control has been to diminish rather than to increase the circulation, gradually closing institutions of doubtful character, which had been certified under the abrogated rules, and refusing to certify any new ones, without having endeavoured to satisfy themselves, in the first instance, of the respectability of the parties proposing to conduct the operations. Another cause of the gradual contraction

[1] *Report of Irish Loan Fund Board* 1842.
[2] *An Address to Sir R. Peel* by Juverna Dublin 1843.
[3] 6 and 7 Vict. c. 91. A summary of the provisions of this lengthy act is to be found in the *Report of the Select Committee on Charitable Loan Societies, Ireland,* 1897 p. 4.

of the circulation is to be looked for in the odium which has attached to the system generally in some districts where bad management, and the operations of uncertified societies, or pretended Loan Funds, have brought any sort of money loans to the humbler classes into disrepute. The 53rd section of the statute, which makes the formation of such institutions penal, does not direct this Board, or any other public authority, to take the initiative in suppressing the same."

The position of affairs continued so unsatisfactory that in 1852 the Board urged, "that some inquiry, parliamentary or governmental, is urgently required into the adequacy of the present machinery of local management, and of the existing legislative control over the institution."[1]

Banking institutions are as necessary for the reception of the savings of the thrifty as for the provision of credit for the indigent, and the Irish poor were as ill provided in the former as in the latter respect. The Irish peasant was naturally parsimonious, even to a fault, but, such was the rapacity of his landlord, that he was tempted to hoard his small savings secretly and unfruitfully. It was to give him an opportunity of reaping some advantage from his abstinence, and at the same time of securing that his savings might be utilized for the public benefit, that the savings banks of the early nineteenth century were established. So rapidly did these institutions spread, and so popular did they become, that the legislature felt bound to interfere in their regulation in 1817. Two statutes passed in that year provided that trustees of savings banks should not make a profit out of the banks; that they should remit to the office for the reduction of the National Debt all deposits exceeding £50 in the aggregate; that the Office of National Debt was to allow interest at the rate

[1] *Report of Loan Fund Board* 1852. Further information on the loan fund system may be obtained in the *Report of the Select Committee on Loan Fund Societies Ireland* 1855, the *Report of the Departmental Committee on Agricultural Credit in Ireland* 1914, and Dillon. *History of Banking in Ireland.*

of £4.11.3 per cent per annum; and that not more than £50 could be deposited by any person in any one year.[1] In 1824 a further act was passed, limiting deposits in the first year to £50 and in every subsequent year to £30, and providing that when the deposits of any one individual exceeded £200, no interest was to be allowed on the excess over £200.[2] In 1828 was passed an amending and consolidating act which provided that the rules of each Trustee Savings Bank must be approved by the National Debt Commissioners; that the rate of interest allowed by that office should be reduced to £3.16.0½ per cent, while depositors received from the Savings Bank interest at the rate of £3.8.5¼ per cent;-and that no depositor should be allowed to accumulate more than £150, though interest might be allowed to accumulate until the deposit amounted to £200.[3] Within five years after the passing of this act 76 Savings Banks existed in Ireland, with close on 50,000 depositors, and deposits amounting to £1,373,993.[4] These institutions were extremely popular, and were availed of extensively by the poorest class of the population. It is recorded that on one occasion the paupers in Killarney workhouse broke out in a body on hearing that the local savings bank was going to fail, so that they might recover the deposits which they had lodged.[5]

With these brief accounts of the loan fund banks and the savings banks, our description of the facilities provided for the credit and the thrift of the poorer classes in Ireland must end. It was not till many years later than 1850 that the idea of the application of the savings of a district to its agricultural improvement found practical expression in the credit societies founded by the cooperative movement.

[1] 57 Geo. III cc. 105 and 130.
[2] 5 Geo. IV c. 62.
[3] 9 Geo. IV c. 92.
[4] *Departmental Committee on Agricultural Credit in Ireland.* 1914 p. 40.
[5] Smyth *Ireland Historical and Statistical* vol iii p. 29.

CHAPTER XIII

MEANS OF COMMUNICATION.

Section 1. Roads.

THE construction of roads in Ireland was not vested in any single authority. Roughly speaking, the roads of the country may be divided into three classes, those constructed in the ordinary way by grand juries, those constructed wholly or in part at the national expense, and those constructed under the supervision of the Postmaster-General. The construction of roads by the grand juries was regulated by various statutes of the Irish Parliament,[1] which were amended in important respects by the Grand Jury Act of 1835. This act gave power to grand juries to enter into contracts for the repair of roads for seven years at a time to prevent the necessity of frequent presentments, and gave power to justices of the peace to authorize the expenditure of county money in case of urgent repairs.[2] The turnpike roads were made to a greater or less degree at the national expense, and had received considerable encouragement from the Irish Parliament. These roads were vested in trustees, who however fell heavily into debt, and in the last years of the Irish Parliament the plan of leaving the construction of main roads to the discretion of the postal authorities came into favour.[3] After the Union public money was frequently voted for the construction of roads in mountainous and remote districts, usually with the pro-

[1] O'Brien, *Economic History of Ireland in the Eighteenth Century* pp. 359-60.
[2] 6 and 7 Wm. IV. c. 116.
[3] Smyth. *Ireland Historical and Statistical* vol. ii. p. 348.

vision that the amount so advanced should be repaid by the counties benefited;[1] and in the great famine many roads were authorized as relief works.[2]

The construction of roads in the mountainous districts was accompanied by great benefits to the localities which they served. The Select Committee of 1819 reported that "the mountainous districts, whilst they are subject to their proportion of the expense of county works, have not had their due share of the benefits of the grand jury system. . . . among the positive evils arising from the want of employment and the impassable state of the mountain districts is the facility of illicit distillation."[3] Much advantage accrued to the agricultural prosperity of the districts served. "Before the new line in Kerry", it was stated in 1828, "ten horses were employed to carry twenty firkins or one ton of butter to Cork city, each horse carrying no more than two firkins of 56 pounds each; but since these new lines have been finished, it has been found practical to transport the quantity of butter stated by one horse drawing a Scotch car—from which the advantage has resulted that the nine horses not now employed for this purpose are employed in drawing to the mountain farms manuring sand from the sea coast."[4] Richard Griffith, in his reports on the public works in the south of Ireland, attaches particular importance to the good work done by the roads; and refers to the case of villages such as Castleisland, which had previously possessed no shops except those of small hucksters who could supply "a farthing's worth of candle or a pennyworth of tobacco" growing into substantial towns with good shops and a flourishing trade.[5] "As the roads advanced", said

[1] 6 Geo. IV. c. 101 ; 1 and 2 Wm. IV c. 33; 2 and 3 Vict. c. 50 ; *Parl. Pap.* no. 649 of 1831-2.

[2] 11 and 12 Vict. c. 51. At the end of 1849 £22,627 had been expended on roads under this act. *19th Report of Board of Public Works*. 1851.

[3] *Second Report of Select Committee on the State of Disease and the Condition of the Labouring Poor in Ireland* 1819.

[4] *Sketch of the Proceedings of the Society for the Improvement of Ireland*, Dublin 1828.

[5] *Report on the Southern District of Ireland. Parl. Pap.* no. 156 of 1829 and no. 119 of 1831.

Sir Robert Kane, "cottages and farmhouses sprang into existence along their sides; cultivation extended itself from their edges into the waste. The bad characters who had inhabited the district disappeared. . . . The whole organization of the locality has been changed."[1] The Devon Commission came to the same conclusion: "It appears from the evidence that the construction of roads in waste districts is absolutely essential to enable any improvement to take place in them; that new lines of road have caused considerable improvement in such districts; that the construction of new roads have (*sic*) in some cases much increased the revenue of such districts by the additional consumption of taxed articles; that obedience to the laws of police and excise is much promoted by the construction of roads in waste districts."[2]

That the opening up of waste districts had not been sufficiently accomplished, and that further efforts in that direction were still required was the opinion of Sir Robert Kane.[3] The Devon Commission came to the conclusion that the operations of the Board of Works in this respect were extravagantly and wastefully conducted:—"The scale of the Board of Works is too expensive in the construction of their works to admit of proprietors joining in such operations. . . ."[4]

Some of the best roads in Ireland were constructed by the Postmaster General, under the statute which conferred on him the power of improving existing and of constructing new roads. A statute of the Irish Parliament had provided that the Postmaster General might straighten and widen roads and lay out new roads, which were to be paid for by the grand juries of the counties through which they passed.[5] In 1809 power was given to the grand juries to appoint supervisors to inspect the condition of the post

[1] *Industrial Resources* p. 331.

[2] *Devon Commn.* p. 886. For an account of the sums advanced for this purpose see *Parl. Pap.* no. 140 of 1829 and the annual reports of the Commissioners of Public Works.

[3] *Industrial Resources* p. 330. [4] *Devon Commn.* p. 887. [5] 32 Geo. III c. 32.

roads[1], and in 1830 the powers of the Postmaster General were transferred to the Commissioners of Public Works.[2]

The system on which Irish roads were constructed by grand juries was pregnant with many abuses. In the first place, as we have pointed out in the previous chapter, the burdens imposed by grand jury presentments were very unequally distributed. "The money for roads", says Wakefield, "is collected according to some obsolete admeasurement, and falls very unequally. In some counties every 'plough land' and in others every 'carver' pays a certain proportion, some by the acre, but in many cases upon fifty acres. . . . The greatest objection which can be made to this mode of collection is that the assessment becomes an acreable tax, from which all housekeepers are exempted, so that the inhabitants of towns enjoy the convenience of good roads without paying a single farthing towards the expense."[3] The rule by which no presentment could be made for the repairs of a road until it had actually fallen into disrepair was also the cause of considerable inconvenience and unnecessary expense. "It is by never suffering a road to get out of repair that economy and comfort are combined. What is the effect of the grand jury laws? the reverse of the principle just laid down. No money can be appropriated to the public works till it has been proved by affidavit that they are already out of order."[4] Moreover, as the rule was that the road-works had only to be done immediately before the meeting of the grand juries, repairs were frequently scamped.[5] The Devon Commission was of opinion that "the present system of contracting for the repair of roads, and of delaying the payment to the contractors, is productive of considerable evil."[6]

In spite of these many drawbacks, the general impression in the early years of the nineteenth century was that the

[1] 49 Geo. III c. 84. [2] 1 and 2 Wm. IV c. 33. [3] Vol. i. pp. 657-8.
[4] Rice, *An Inquiry into the Effects of the Irish Grand Jury Laws.* London 1815.
[5] *Ibidem.* [6] *Devon Commn.* p. 887.

Irish roads were excellent. "There are few things in Ireland", said Wakefield, "which astonish a stranger more than the magnificence of its excellent roads. . . . In the majority of the counties the roads are not only excellent but numerous; this great advantage has arisen chiefly from the country gentlemen having a just opinion of their usefulness."[1] "Since Mr. Arthur Young visited Ireland", according to Newenham, "the roads have become much more numerous; and are in general in better condition. Sandy soils, so frequent in other countries, which render the roads so heavy, are nowhere to be met with in Ireland, except in a very few places near the coast."[2] "We travelled from Limerick to Dublin" a tourist wrote in 1810 "over as fine a road as any kingdom can boast of; we met with inns exceedingly good, and with horses excellent, which brought us on at a pace equal to the best English posting."[3] "It is undoubted that the roads are improved since Mr. Young's time".[4] "The roads of Ireland," said Mr. Nimmo, the famous engineer, "and especially the cross roads, are confessedly the finest in Europe; and her rapid progress in agriculture, though in the central parts perhaps much cultivated by her system of inland navigation, yet certainly is in a much greater degree owing to the excellence and facility of her land carriage. In this respect she vastly excels England."[5] "The roads of Ireland are the best in the world."[6] "While the traveller", said Bicheno, "witnesses on every side the appearance of begging and filth, he feels he is rolling over roads as well formed and made as any he may have passed over in more fortunate countries."[7] Many years later Sir Lucius O'Brien wrote, "our highways have been brought to a perfection even

[1] Vol. i. pp. 659-662.
[2] *View of Ireland* p. 31.
[3] *Journal of a Tour through Several of the Southern Counties of Ireland.* London 1810, and see Jeffreys, *An Englishman's Descriptive Account of Dublin,* &c. London 1810, and Barnes, *A Statistical Account of Ireland founded upon Historical Facts.* Dublin 1811.
[4] *Letters on Ireland* by a Citizen of Waterford, Waterford 1813.
[5] *Report and Estimates on Draining and Cultivating the Bogs,* Dublin 1818.
[6] *The State of Ireland Considered.* Dublin 1810.
[7] *Ireland and its Economy* p. 40.

greater than that of those in England";[1] and it was stated in 1851 that "the condition of the roads is excellent".[2]

Section 2. Canals.

The construction of canals and the improvement of inland navigation were encouraged by very substantial pecuniary assistance from the Irish Parliament. There was no object in which more public money was spent. Ireland in this respect presented a curious contrast to England, where the extensive system of canals and waterways came into existence purely as the result of private enterprise without any public assistance. It must not be concluded that all the money voted by the Irish Parliament was profitably spent; on the contrary, the construction of canals was a most fruitful occasion for jobbery and corruption.[3] In spite of these abuses however a considerable length of inland waterways was actually completed. It was the hope of the time that canals would improve the agriculture and industry of the counties through which they passed, by affording a cheap means of transport; and as late as 1819 Richard Griffith wrote as if he considered the construction of canals the panacea for all the economic evils of Ireland.[4]

In the year of the Union the original plan of the Irish Parliament of a central body charged with the superintendence of all the canals of the country, which had been abandoned in 1787, was reverted to, and a new body, the Directors of Inland Navigation, was appointed, and the sum of £500,000 granted for the improvement of the port of Dublin and of inland navigation. In these directors were vested all canals managed by local corporations which had been

[1] *Ireland in* 1848, London 1848.
[2] *Thom's Directory* 1851 p. 200.
[3] O'Brien *Economic History of Ireland in the Eighteenth Century* p. 362.
[4] *Practical Domestic Politics*, London 1819; and see Dawson, *Canal Extensions in Ireland*. Dublin 1819.

constructed entirely by public money; and they were given power to "order, direct, regulate, and appoint all matters and things relating to inland navigation." Their powers and their property were transferred in 1831 to the Irish Board of Works. Both the Directors of Inland Navigation and the Board of Works expended considerable sums on the completion of unfinished, and on the construction of new, canals and waterways.[1]

This large expenditure of public money was not accompanied by any adequate return. Not only were the canals themselves not profitable, but they failed to produce the good results to agriculture and commerce which had been predicted. In spite of the much greater cheapness of water than of land carriage,[2] the volume of goods transported by canal always remained negligible. "What has been the result", asks Wakefield, "of the expenditure of so enormous a sum? The conveyance of a few passengers by canal instead of by stage coaches from Dublin to Mullingar and other places in a country where intercourse between its inhabitants is still very much limited; and the supplying of Dublin with turf, a fuel much more expensive than Whitehaven coals."[3] "The Grand and Royal Canals," it was stated many years later, "are made use of principally for the conveyance of a very sorry description of fuel dug from the almost unprofitable bogs and morasses. This indifferent peat fuel is, with the exception of an occasional bark freighted with provisions and poultry, the only produce now seen to be borne on these splendid works of human skill."[4] Nor did agriculture noticeably improve in the neighbourhood of the canals. "When gentlemen ascribe so much benefit to canals, it is incumbent on them to show that the land in the neighbourhood of the two grand ones is better cultivated than that at a distance. After the fullest investigation

[1] *Royal Commission on Canals and Inland Navigation*, 1906 vol. xi p. 8.
[2] Kane *Industrial Resources* p. 335.
[3] Vol. i. p. 651.
[4] Beere, *A Letter to the King on the Practical Improvements of Ireland.* London 1827.

I cannot discover any improvement they have effected."[1]

We do not propose to enter in detail into the history of the various Irish canals after the Union, but only to indicate the main development of the principal ones in that period. The history of the Grand Canal may be briefly summarized in the words of the late Mr. Coyne:—

"The Grand Canal was commenced by the Commissioners of Inland Navigation, who received grants of public money, between 1753 and 1772, to the amount of £70,496. In the latter year the completion of the canal was transferred to a company. Between 1772 and 1800 the company received grants to the extent of £83,776, in addition to £18,231 to secure the completion of the Ringsend Docks. In 1798 the company obtained a loan of £27,692 of public money on the opening of the Athy branch of the canal, and a further grant of £138,461 was made as recommended by the Government and approved of by a Committee in the House of Commons in 1813, on the terms that the company should raise £46,154, to be applied along with the £138,461 in payment of their debts. The extension of the canal from the Shannon to Ballinasloe and the Mountmellick and Kilbeggan branches were subsequently made for the purpose of giving employment to the poor, and £98,524 was advanced to facilitate their execution. The extensions were opened in 1830. In 1844 the repayment of this sum was commuted by Statute for £10,000. By an Act of 1848 the original company, called 'the Undertakers of the Grand Canal', was reconstituted under the name of the 'Grand Canal Company'. The passenger traffic on the canal ceased on the opening of the railway system, but the company received a remission of its debt to the Government to the extent of £88,524. The total capital expenditure on the canal is put down at £1,137,680, out of which public grants amounted to £321,674."[2]

The Royal Canal, which had always been an unprofitable undertaking, was in 1813 vested in the Directors of Inland Navigation. It was by them completed, and handed over in 1818 to a company, and was taken over by the Midland Great Western Railway Company in 1845. The Suir Navigation was constructed by a company founded in 1836. The Lagan Navigation, which had been commenced by the Irish Parliament, was completed out of private funds by the Marquess of Donegall between 1809 and 1820, and was in 1843 vested in the present company. The Ulster Canal was constructed by a private company under an act of 1826, and completed in 1842; the greater part of the capital being supplied by loans which were afterwards remitted.

[1] Wakefield vol. i. pp. 653-4. [2] *Parl. Pap.* no. 1032 of 1902.

The Upper and Lower Bann Navigations were constructed between 1847 and 1849 by the Board of Works in connection with arterial drainage works, and were afterwards transferred to trustees. The Newry Navigation and Ship Canal were vested in 1800 in the Directors of Inland Navigation, and in 1829 transferred to a private company. The Ballinamore and Ballyconnell canal was commenced by the Board of Works in 1846.[1]

Section 3. Railways.

The first railway constructed in Ireland was that between Dublin and Kingstown, which was commenced in 1831 and opened in 1834. No other railway was opened till 1839, when the Ulster Railway was partially opened. Meanwhile the whole question of the future of the Irish railway system had engaged the attention of a very important commission, presided over by Mr. Thomas Drummond, which made some very valuable and far-seeing recommendations. This commission was instructed to inquire into the best means of promoting the construction of a general system of railways with a view to developing the resources of the country at the smallest outlay. The commissioners received a vast amount of evidence, and presented two reports. The first report stated that "the first and most important conclusion at which we have arrived is that the intercourse in Ireland is not at present, nor is likely, for many years to come, to be of that constant and active kind which would justify the expectation that railways spread over the country in distinct lines from town to town would prove remunerative;"—and recommended that a few great trunk lines should be selected for encouragement.

[1] *Royal Commission on Canals and Waterways*, 1906. vol. xi. pp. 23-29, Marmion, *Maritime Ports* pp. 117-127. Those desirous of more detailed information and statistics relating to the Irish canals after the Union can consult with advantage *The Report of the Commissioners on the Navigation which connects Coleraine Belfast and Limerick* 1882 (cd 3173). Many interesting statistics of the traffic on the Irish canals in 1850 are to be found in *Thom's Directory* 1851 p. 201.

In their second report the commissioners indicated what, in their opinion, would constitute the most suitable trunk lines. They proposed the formation of two lines, one to the south-west, the other to the north-west, of Dublin. The south-west line was to pass through Sallins, Monasterevan, Portarlington, and Maryborough, whence a branch should be thrown out to Kilkenny. The main line was then to proceed to Rathdowney, Templemore, Thurles, and Holycross, whence a branch to Limerick should diverge. The main line was then to proceed to Cashel, and a place called Marhill in County Tipperary, whence branches should be constructed on the one side to Limerick, and on the other to Clonmel and Waterford. The main line would then continue to Cahir, Mitchelstown, Mallow and Cork. The north-western line was to be laid to Navan, where it would bifurcate, one branch going west to Enniskillen, and the other north to Armagh, where it would meet the Ulster Railway, and thus afford direct communication between Dublin and Belfast.

Such were the trunk lines proposed by the commissioners, and the next question to be considered was, at whose expense and under whose supervision they would best be constructed. The first thing postulated was that each of these great systems should be placed under one management and treated as one concern. The commissioners expressed the opinion that, if large bodies of capitalists could be found to undertake these works, they should be permitted to do so, but, if no such private capitalists could be found, they expressed the hope, "that to avoid the evil of partial execution and to accomplish so important a national object as that contemplated in the completion of the entire system, we look forward to a certain degree of assistance from the state." They therefore recommended:—

(*a*) "That the Government should advance by way of loan a considerable portion of the amount of the estimates at the lowest rate of interest, and on the easiest terms of repayment, to be secured by a mortgage of the works. We think that many landholders may also be found to subscribe towards carrying into effect an object which in addition to its importance as a national concern, cannot fail to benefit and improve their own properties.

"As a further assistance in filling the subscriptions, perhaps powers might be given to the counties interested as well as to corporate towns, to become shareholders to certain amounts; the Government in such cases advancing the money on the security of presentments in the usual manner, and the return of such shares being available for the reduction of the county or other rates.

"Provision, however, will be necessary in this case to secure the co-operation of the whole of the districts interested, the approval of a certain majority having been obtained.

"(*b*) If these means be rejected, or fail to produce sufficient subscriptions to insure in the first instance the execution of the entire system, we would suggest that the work might still be allowed to go forward, beginning at Dublin or other fixed terminus, to any other determinate point, such portion, however, not to be considered as an integral line but only as part of the general system, and to be continued from that point towards the ultimate intended termini of the several lines and branches as new subscriptions are received. The subscribers to these continuations should be entitled to all the privileges and advantages arising from the whole portion of the line already executed, from the date of the payment of their respective subscriptions, equitably estimated according to the time when each subscription shall be made.

"(*c*) We would further venture to suggest that the Government should undertake either or both of the proposed combined lines on the application of the counties interested, the outlay to be repaid by small instalments at the lowest admissible rate of interest, and under the provision that in the event of the returns not paying the stipulated amount of interest, the counties shall supply the deficits by presentments."

It was pointed out that the grant of this assistance would have the incidental good effect of "affording present employment to vast numbers of the people, and of throwing open resources and means of profitable occupation."[1]

Public opinion in Ireland was strongly in favour of the Drummond report, but in spite of this the government refused to adopt its recommendations. Early in 1839 a great public meeting held in Dublin passed a resolution that, inasmuch as an adequate system of railways could not be constructed by private capital, the government should be urged to take the work into its own hands, thereby saving the cost of private bill legislation. Promises were also made that the lands necessary for railway construction would be given free of cost. Similar resolutions were adopted

[1] *Second Report of Railway Commissioners* 1838.

at another public meeting held about the same time in the north of Ireland. In addition, an address to the Queen was presented by a number of Irish peers, headed by the Duke of Leinster, praying that action might be taken on the Drummond report.[1] On this subject Irish opinion never wavered. Sir Robert Kane described the report as, "a masterpiece of physical and statistical investigation, which will connect the names of its eminent authors permanently with the records of Irish progress;" and expressed his complete agreement with its main conclusions.[2] The same view was taken by the Repeal Association, who resolved that, "on the subject of railways, as on all other means of social advance, we have to complain of the indifference, ignorance, or oppressive policy of England."[3]

The government at first made a feeble movement in the direction of putting the recommendations of Drummond's report into effect. A bill was introduced by Lord Morpeth providing for an advance of two and a half millions for the construction of lines between Dublin and Cork, with a branch to Limerick, as public works, for the execution of which the Treasury was to be empowered to issue exchequer bills; and providing further that the revenue of the projected undertakings should be appropriated as follows:

(1) to the maintenance and working of the railways,
(2) to the payment of interest at 3½ per cent. on the advances,
(3) to a sinking fund not exceeding 1½ per cent. per annum,
(4) to the reduction of rates or extension of the system.

The parliamentary history of this measure can be best described in the words of Mr. Locker Lampson: "Peel attacked the measure, but, in spite of his and other opposition, Morpeth's motion passed the Commons by a majority of 44. When it got to the Lords it encountered fresh oppo-

[1] *Vice-Regal Commission on Irish Railways* 1906 vol. vi. p. 5.
[2] *Industrial Resources* pp. 348-367.
[3] *Repeal Reports* vol. i. p. 249 ; Pim, *Irish Railways*, London. 1839, Humphrey Brown, *Irish Wants and Practical Remedies*, London 1848. The Devon Commission was also in favour of the Drummond Report. Contra. G. L. Smyth. *Observation on the Report of the Irish Railway Commissioners* London 1839.

sition, Brougham opposing it from mere hatred of the government. After this the question came up again in the lower house, but on three different occasions the house was counted out, and the scheme was eventually dropped from sheer lack of enthusiasm. The tendencies of the bill were too progressive, the practical vigour with which it grappled with difficulties too incomprehensible, for little minds and small men living from day to day; and its opponents, who intensely disliked the principle, were gratified to find economic and other obstacles in the way of unpopular reform."[1] The apparent apathy of the House of Commons on this occasion stands in striking contrast to its perseverance in passing coercion bills.

The construction of railways in Ireland was left therefore to private enterprise. But the government betrayed by its actions an appreciation of the fact that the conditions of Great Britain and Ireland were in no way similar, and the advance of money by way of loan to the Dublin and Kingstown Railway in 1836, and to the Dublin and Drogheda Railway in 1842, was a tacit admission that Irish railways could not succeed without State aid. The result of the reliance on private capitalists was that the progress of railway construction in Ireland was exceedingly slow. "In 1846 acts of parliament were in existence authorizing the construction of more than 1500 miles of railway in Ireland, and some of these acts had passed as long as eleven years previously, yet at the end of 1846 only 123 miles of railway had been completed, and only 164 were in the course of completion though arrested in their progress for want of funds. Almost in the same period 2,600 miles of railway had been completed in England .... The cause of the weakness in Ireland to prosecute these undertakings was the total want of domestic capital for the purpose, and the unwillingness of English capitalists to embark their funds in a country whose social and political position they viewed

[1] *Ireland in the Nineteenth Century* p. 246.

with distrust."[1] The construction of such a length of railway in England gave abundant employment, and completely removed the distress which had been felt about 1840; when the condition of Ireland began to go from bad to worse.[2] An opportunity for obtaining some state assistance for Irish railways arose when, during the famine, it was proposed to expend millions on useless undertakings; and the opposition so far pressed their views on the government as to induce it to lend £620,000 to the Great Southern and Western, the Waterford and Kilkenny, and the Dublin and Drogheda Railway Companies.[3]

THE FOLLOWING TABLE SHOWS THE PROGRESS OF THE IRISH RAILWAY SYSTEM DURING THE PERIOD 1836-50.

Year ending 30th June *	Miles open on 1st Jan. of each Yr.	Passengers		Goods Parcels Cattle &c £	Total Receipts £	Average per mile £
		number	amount £			
1836	6	1,237,800	35,316	105	35,421	5,903
1837	6	1,184,428	31,401	44	31,945	5,322
1838	6	1,243,972	33,318	270	33,588	5,598
1839	6	1,341,208	34,409	307	34,716	5,786
1840	13½	1,358,761	36,176	414	36,590	2,710
1841	13½	1,629,024	41,002	466	41,468	3,071
1842	13½	2,046,901	54,219	2,520	56,739	4,202
1843	31	2,074,444	56,548	6,802	63,350	2,027
1844	31	2,588,096	62,608	8,886	71,494	2,287
1845	65	3,481,707	104,712	14,636	119,398	1,836
1846	65	3,610,506	105,469	18,274	123,743	1,903
1847	120	3,866,294	149,581	35,000	184,581	1,528
1848	209	4,374,749	211,593	60,215	271,808	1,299
1849	361	4,963,856	283,481	121,694	405,175	1,120
1850	475	5,181,794	315,341	159,963	475,304	1,000

* *Thom's Directory* 1851 p. 205.

[1] Disraeli, *Life of Lord George Bentinck* pp. 342-4.
[2] *Ibid.* p. 339.
[3] *Vice-Regal Commission on Irish Railways* 1906 vol. vi. p. 5. O'Rourke, *The Great Irish Famine* 1847.

CHAPTER XIV

CONCLUSION.

In the foregoing chapters we have discussed the various branches of Irish economic life during the first half of the nineteenth century. We must now endeavour to supply an answer to the question which we suggested in the introductory chapter, namely, why Ireland continued to express dissatisfaction with the Act of Union and to agitate for its repeal. We fully realize that to deal with this question is to incur the risk of an accusation of writing propaganda rather than history. We nevertheless offer no apology for the inclusion of this subject in the discussion, which indeed would be essentially incomplete without it. We shall confine ourselves strictly to the economic grounds upon which the Union was assailed; and shall not attempt to express any opinion as to what form of government should have taken its place. We shall thus confine the political aspect of the subject within the narrowest possible limits; but in doing so we must not be taken as endorsing the view that the influence of political changes on Irish economic life was unimportant; on the contrary, the further study of Irish history which the preparation of the present volume has entailed has strengthened our opinion as to the intimate connection which has at all times existed between political and economic events in Ireland.

While it would be irrelevant to quote authorities to prove that there was from the very beginning of the nineteenth century a widespread and deep-rooted dissatisfaction with the Act of Union, it may be of interest to point out that the Union was attacked persistently on economic grounds, and that the greater part of recorded public opinion in Ireland during the first half of the century inclined to the view that the Union had proved economically disastrous.

The first evil effects of the Union were felt in Dublin, which suffered a severe loss owing to the disappearance of the resident parliament. The loss experienced by the capital city on the withdrawal of the legislature directed the attention of its merchants towards the possibility of making it a great centre of shipping, but none of the many projects framed to attain this object materialized.[1] Twenty years after the Union the value of houses in Dublin had fallen thirty per cent., and in the manufacturing quarter of the Liberties fifty per cent.[2]

The sufferings caused by the Union were not confined to the capital, but affected the whole of Ireland. In 1809 Henry Grattan wrote to his son:—"The Union has not given us new capital or new trade; the export trade is the old trade of Ireland, increasing from its nature, not from the Union. . . . The export trade that Ireland has is a legacy of the Irish Parliament. . . ."[3] In the same year Newenham expressed the opinion that, "in reference to commerce, the Irish people have no reason whatsoever to congratulate themselves upon the Union. The commercial prosperity of Ireland has visibly declined since that measure was carried into effect."[4] "In its result", it was complained in 1811, "the Act of Union has not produced any of the results which it was expected to have afforded. It has

[1] *A Letter addressed to His Excellency Philip Earl of Hardwicke upon the Improvement of the Harbour of Dublin.* Dublin 1804. *Observations on the Defects of the Port of Dublin.* Dublin 1804. *A Brief Statement of Facts respecting the Proposed Improvements to be made in the Bay and Harbour of Dublin.* Dublin 1804. Ball *Howth and its Owners* pp 145 sq

[2] *A Letter to Sir John Newport, Bart.* by Hibernicus, Dublin 1821.

[3] Grattan. *Life of Grattan*, vol. v. p. 400.

[4] *View of Ireland* p. 289.

only tended to impoverish Ireland. . . . Such is the impression prevalent in Ireland."[1] "The traders in particular", it was stated in 1810, "do not hesitate to impute their distresses to the absence of a Parliament which watched unceasingly over their interests. 'We are bereaved', they say, 'of the natural protectors of our industry. We are depressed and overpowered by the competition of our English neighbours, and we are shut out of every market by their superior capital and influence'."[2] "Instead of an increase of trade and capital, there has been decay of trade, a destruction of capital, and a defalcation of revenue."[3] "The evil effects of the legislative union", we read in a pamphlet published in 1815, "every day more severely proves; the nobility and gentry of Ireland now being resident in England think of this country only when their rents become due; their children born in England, their education no longer Irish, they despise the land of their forefathers, and deem the people turbulent, drunken, idle and ignorant."[4] In the same year Henry Major, a Protestant clergyman, who had been in favour of the Union in 1800, wrote: "The Union has now been tried more than ten years, and how has it served Ireland? Let its warmest advocates answer the question. As to myself, so much injury does this ill-fated country suffer from the increased number of absentees, the consequence of that measure, that, while nothing is done by the legislature to put an effectual termination to the grievance or to counterbalance its ruinous effects, I cannot avoid comparing the attachment of England to her sister island as the hug of the harlot who clasped her satiated wooer in her muscular embrace until he had thrown into her widely distended lap his last solitary shilling."[5] Three years later another Irish writer complain-

[1] *Upon the Nature and Effects of the Legislative Union.* Dublin 1811.
[2] *A Short Inquiry into the Cause of the Present Distresses of the Irish Traders.* Dublin 1810. [3] *A Sketch of the Present State of Ireland.* Dublin 1811.
[4] *Strictures on Bankruptcy Insolvency and on the State of the Nation* Dublin 1815.
[5] *Observations Demonstrative of the Necessity to Ireland's Welfare,* &c. Dublin 1815.

ed that "the highly flattering promises held out at the time of the Union have as yet produced nothing but disappointment, which must soon turn to despair, if the Imperial Parliament, through the influence of a benevolent and paternal government, does not endeavour to give to Ireland a substantial good, instead of the phantom which she has been constantly grasping."[1] The period 1800 to 1820 was described by G. L. Smyth as, "a period of severe trial to Irish interests. Native establishments disappeared by degrees, merchants retired from business, the products of English skill impelled by superior capital found new markets, and much of that decay and many of those losses occurred, which were subsequently relied on as facts and arguments to justify the Repeal Association."[2] "I consider", said Lord Blessington in 1822 "that the greater part of the misfortunes of Ireland had their origin in the Union;"[3] and an English traveller in Ireland observed in the following year: "I hastily reviewed the effects produced by the Union, and could not help coming to the conclusion, from what I had seen and heard since the Irish Parliament was dissolved, that, whatever advantage the empire may have derived from that measure, Ireland has not profited by it in the fair ratio of gain."[4] It was stated that the Union had deprived Ireland of a large part of the profit she would have derived from the war if she had remained independent. "Most part of the profit which that country might have made by the war she lost by the Union; she even lost the clothing of the army which had been upon her own establishment. The most insignificant military accoutrement was sent over ready made from England. Ireland furnished indeed the strong limbs; but she was not permitted to clothe or to equip them; she reaped nothing of the great

[1] Wm. Parker. *A Plea for the Poor and Industrious* Cork 1819.
[2] *Ireland Historical and Statistical* vol. iii p. 378.
[3] *Observations on the State of Ireland* London 1822.
[4] *Observations made during a Short Excursion to Dublin, Delgany &c.* by A. B. Liverpool 1823.

harvest of wealth which the war afforded. Britain gathered it all."[1]

One of the arguments advanced in favour of the Union had been that British capital would be attracted to Ireland on account of the superior security which the improved form of government would afford. This prediction was however not fulfilled. "When Mr. Pitt carried his favourite measure of the Union", Lord Blessington complained, "he held out to Ireland the prospect of advantages to be derived from English capital. About twenty years have passed, and but a small share of English wealth has been expended in speculation in that country."[2] George Cornewall Lewis remarked several years later that, "the insecurity of property in Ireland, whether real or supposed, assists in increasing the number of the Irish emigrants to Great Britain, inasmuch as it prevents the English and Scotch capitalist from transmitting materials to be manufactured in Ireland."[3] Any movement in the direction of the investment of English capital in Ireland, which was noticeable in the years immediately following the Union, was checked by the discontinuance of the Union duties in 1824.[4]

One blemish in the post-Union form of government which arrested attention was the inability of even the most well-meaning ministers to carry through any ameliorating measures owing to the short duration of their residence in the country. "The ministers for Ireland" wrote William Parker, "have been men of distinguished talents, but this country was unfortunately deprived of their services, just as they became acquainted with our general and local grievances, and before they had time to effect any great legislative measure. To this may be attributed the great defect in all the acts of parliament which have passed

[1] O'Driscoll, *View of Ireland* vol. ii. p. 253.
[2] *Observations on the Proposed North of Ireland Canal* London 1822.
[3] *Report of Poor Inquiry Commission on State of Irish Poor in Great Britain* p. xxviii.
[4] supra pp. 434, 440.

since the Union."[1] Jonathan Sisson complained of the constant change of administration as productive of neglect of Irish interests.[2]

Throughout the whole of the first half of the nineteenth century, the Act of Union continued to excite an acute feeling of dissatisfaction on economic grounds. The question naturally arises as to how far this feeling was justified. A perusal of the foregoing pages will to some extent enable us to answer that question. We have seen that the great mass of the agricultural population of Ireland were sunk in extreme poverty during the first half of the nineteenth century; that the labouring class were on the very margin of subsistence, that the farming class were not much better off, and that the landlords were for the most part hopelessly encumbered. We have also referred to the misery of the industrial section of the population, to the gradual decay of many manufactures, and to the appalling sufferings endured by the manufacturers in these decaying industries. If any further evidence of the increasing poverty of Ireland during the period be required, we can point to the decrease in the quantities of various commodities that were consumed in the country.

The increase in the volume of the Irish export trade after the Union is sometimes quoted as evidence of the beneficial effects of that measure. The amount of the external trade of a country is however a misleading and imperfect criterion of its prosperity. The amount of the export trade is a

[1] *An Essay on the Employment of the Labouring Classes* Cork, 1819.

[2] *A Second Letter to Earl Grey* London 1832. It is impossible to indicate completely the innumerable anti-Union publications of the early nineteenth century. Those who wish for further information on the contemporary strictures directed against its economic, as apart from its political, results should refer to Grattan, *Life of Grattan*, vol. v. pp. 187 and 399-400, Ensor, *Observations on Corn Laws*, etc. Dublin 1842. The opposite view is to be found in *Letters on Ireland by a Citizen of Waterford*, Waterford 1813. *A Conversation on the Repeal of the Union* by a Patriot, Dublin 1848. The great pro-Union publication was *Ireland Before and After the Union* by R. Montgomery Martin, Dublin 1843. Mr. Martin, who had published various previous tracts on the subject, was a hack pamphleteer, and his effusions were produced under Treasury favour. He was rewarded with the office of Treasurer of Hong Kong. *Second Repeal Prize Essay* p. 113. Mr. Martin's opinions were controverted, and his partiality exposed in *An Address to Sir Robert Peel* by Juverna, Dublin 1843, and *A Reply to Mr. M. Martin, etc.* by M. Staunton, Dublin 1844.

particularly fallacious test to apply, as the volume of exports is in itself a neutral fact. "It is to be borne in mind", we are warned by Mr. Childers, "that high exports may mean that there is a great 'economic drain' upon a country, and be therefore not a proof of its wealth but of its impoverishment. By an 'economic drain' is meant the fact of wealth leaving a country, not in exchange for other commodities which the country requires, but to pay, for instance, interest upon public debt held by foreign creditors, continuing even after the amount of interest paid has exceeded the sum of money originally advanced .... In another case, that of export to pay the rents of absentee landowners living outside the country, and in so far as those rents are not returned to the country for the improvement of estates, the economic drain is evident. In this case rent receipts are the only return for the wealth sent out of the country ...."[1] The latter case was the case of Ireland in the nineteenth century. Though the exports greatly increased, they were not counterbalanced by imports, and consequently pointed to the annual departure from the country of a great volume of wealth for which no return was received—the consequence of the growth of absenteeism, and of excessive taxation for imperial purposes.[2]

While the mere volume of external trade is a fallacious test of a country's prosperity, there is one special branch of that trade, an examination of which affords a satisfactory criterion, namely the trade concerned with the importation of those commodities, which, though not produced in, are very generally consumed in, the country. The application of this test to the twenty years of Grattan's Parliament led us to the conclusion that the quantity of such articles consumed in that period increased in a greater degree than the population of the country; from which we inferred that this was a period of increasing prosperity.[3] The application

[1] *F. R. C.* p. 167. [2] See *First Repeal Prize Essay* Dublin 1845; Smyth *Ireland Historical and Statistical* voi. lii p. 303; Marmion *Maritime Ports* p. 95.

[3] *Economic History of Ireland in the Eighteenth Century* p. 405.

of the same test to the post-Union period leads us to an opposite conclusion, as we find that the average annual consumption of such articles per head of the population tended to diminish rather than to increase.

The following figures show the annual average quantities of various articles retained for home consumption in Ireland at each decennial period from 1800 to 1840:—

Period*	Wine Imp. glns.	Tobacco pds.	Tea pds.	Foreign Spirits Imp. glns.
3 Years ending 1800	1,238,512	6,405,283	2,773,070	155,069
3 " " 1810	1,127,200	5,625,376	3,551,188	572,846
3 " " 1820	501,016	4,146,454	3,316,321	34,434
3 " " 1830	806,079	4,060,077	3,887,955	32,018
3 " " 1840	754,476	5,128,850	4,008,148	36,706

* *Thom's Directory* 1851 p. 251 and see Staunton *The Case of Ireland.* Dublin 1831, and the *First Repeal Prize Essay* p. 54.

If we assume that during the period 1800-1840 the population increased from 4,500,000, to 8,175,124[1], we arrive at the following figures:

INCREASE OR DECREASE PER CENT, OF POPULATION AND OF THE CONSUMPTION OF CERTAIN COMMODITIES IN IRELAND FROM 1800 TO 1840

	Increase per cent.	Decrease per cent.
Population	81·67	—
Consumption of wine	—	39·09
" " tobacco ..	—	19·09
" " tea	44·62	—
" " foreign spirits	—	64·33

These figures demonstrate that the average *per capita* consumption of certain commodities—two of which were luxuries and two articles of popular consumption—decreased in the first forty years of the nineteenth century. Having regard to the nature of the commodities we have selected for our test, this may be regarded as an infallible test of the economic progress or retrogression of the country

[1] O'Brien *Economic History of Ireland in the Eighteenth Century* p. 10; *Census of Ireland* 1851.

during the period to which it is applied; and, unless the accuracy of these statistics is challenged, it is impossible to deny that the condition of Ireland deteriorated after the Union. This increasing poverty was quite sufficient to render the Irish people dissatisfied with the system under which it occurred, especially as they attributed some share of the responsibility for it to the government of the time. The question arises how far this attribution of blame was justified by the facts. Was it correct to trace some causal connection between the misery of Ireland and the action or inaction of the United Parliament?

A brief recapitulation of the main conclusions arrived at in the foregoing pages may help to supply an answer to this question. In the first part of the book we saw that the central problem of Irish economic life in the early nineteenth century was the apparent disproportion between the population and resources of the country. While the former increased with unprecedented rapidity, the latter remained stationary. The pressure of the problem was greatly aggravated by the conduct of the landlords in consolidating the farms on their estates without any regard for the sufferings of those tenants who were ejected in the process. This action of the landlords was founded on two assumptions, that large farms were more economical than small, and that the country was overpopulated. We exposed the fallacy of both these assumptions, the former of which was contradicted by all the best economic and expert agricultural opinion of the time, and the latter by the fact that the available resources of Ireland had not been even approximately utilized. We next indicated what, in our opinion, were the true causes of Irish agricultural distress, namely the inequitable distribution of the produce of the soil, and the failure of those responsible to render available the unused resources of the country. The former of these causes was evidenced by the exorbitant rents paid for land and the confiscation of the tenant's improvements, and the latter by the existence of millions of acres of unreclaimed land. If these were the true causes of Irish distress, the correct remedies were, first, an adjustment of the relations between landlord and tenant, and, second, the reclamation of the waste lands. The former of these reforms would obviously not be introduced by the landlords and could not be achieved by the tenants, while landlords and tenants alike were unable or unwilling to effect the latter. As it was certain that these urgent and obvious reforms would not be attained by the efforts of private individuals, it was, we suggested, clearly the duty of the government to undertake them.

This conclusion led us to an examination of the question whether the government based its policy on the landlords' assumption that the country was overpopulated or on the correct assumption that it was underdeveloped. If the latter assumption had been accepted by the government, legislation would no doubt have been passed to rectify the existing inequality of the distribution of the produce of the soil, and to facilitate and encourage the draining of the waste lands. We found, however, that practically no such legislation was passed. Suggestions put forward by private members for remedial land legislation were rejected by successive parliaments; the only laws which passed dealing with the subject were designed to benefit the landlords exclusively; and, in spite of the emphatic and repeated recommendations of numerous commissions and committees of inquiry, only the most attenuated, meagre, and futile measures in aid of reclamation were introduced. The government therefore did not adopt the assumption of underdevelopment. How far did it adopt that of overpopulation? The long succession of statutes clearly designed to assist the landlords in their campaign of consolidation suggests that it adopted the latter assumption without reserve. These legislative aids to depopulation were the ejectment acts, the subletting act, the raising of the franchise, the poor law, the repeal of the corn laws, and the passive, if not active, encouragement of emigration. Moreover the relief measures adopted in the great crisis of the famine were grounded on the landlords' rather than on the correct assumption; and no use was made of this exceptional opportunity of permanently increasing the resources of the country.

When we passed from the consideration of agriculture to that of industry we found evidence of similar decay and distress. An examination of the causes of that decay led us to the conclusion that it was not the result of any inherent defect in the people or the country. The best and most impartial contemporary observers refused to convict the Irish of any industrial incapacity; and, in so far as the Irish working classes lacked skill as distinguished from industry, that defect was the effect rather than the cause of the stagnation of the country. The combinations of workmen were also the effect rather than the cause of the industrial depression, and the absence of Irish supplies of coal and other fuel played but an inconsiderable part in impeding the progress of manufactures. The real cause of the failure of Irish industry was its exposure to the full pressure of British competition before it was sufficiently developed to withstand it. The Union duties of ten *per cent.* were protective in the true sense of the word and in no way preferential, as they simply put the Irish manufacturer in a position of equal advantage with the British;[1] and the repeal of these duties in 1824, against the advice of the Irish mercantile and manufacturing interests, was attended by the most disastrous results. The superiority enjoyed by the British manufactures was the result of two causes, the first being the long period of encouragement which they had enjoyed, during which Irish industry had been retarded and oppressed, and the second the difficulty of procuring capital in Ireland owing to the land system and

[1] See Jervis. *A Brief View of the Past and Present State of Ireland.* Bath, 1813.

insufficient credit facilities. Thus, the nominal equality conferred by the repeal of the Union duties was a real inequality in favour of Great Britain; and this unfair competition was established precisely at the moment when it could produce the most injurious results, namely at the period of transition from small to large scale industry, when the possession of capital was of more than usual importance. The correctness of this conclusion may be confirmed by the application of the maxim *exceptio probat regulam.* The linen trade of north-east Ulster alone of all Irish industries survived the storm; and it is interesting to note that this industry was an exception to every other Irish industry in all the respects to which we have called attention. It had enjoyed a long period of legislative encouragement; it was situated in a district where the evil effects of the Irish land system were scarcely felt; and it was the last of the textile industries to be affected by the industrial revolution.

Turning to the public finance of the country, we found that the proportion fixed for Ireland's contribution under the Act of Union was probably unfair at the time it was calculated, and was certainly unfair in the event. The ordinary burden of taxation resulting from the continuance of the war reduced Ireland to the brink of bankruptcy, to avert which the exchequers of the two countries were consolidated. We demonstrated that the conditions precedent to this step provided by the Act of Union had not been fulfilled; and that the consolidation resulted, not in the relief, but in the further oppression, of the Irish taxpayer, as it was made the excuse for the gradual assimilation of the taxation of the two countries. This assimilation was achieved by abolishing duties which applied to Great Britain alone, and by raising the rate of duty on articles in Ireland, where the Irish rate was lower than the British rate. The result of this process was that, whereas the taxation of Great Britain *per capita* was reduced between 1819 and 1850 by 32 *per cent.*, that of Ireland was reduced by only 3 *per cent.* Thus, the period of decreasing *per capita* consumption was also one of practically unaltered *per capita* taxation. Of the revenue raised, by far the greater part was taken out of the country for expenditure on imperial purposes, from which Ireland derived comparatively little advantage, especially prior to the repeal of the corn laws; and a new form of absenteeism was thus created. Of the money retained in Ireland, much was extravagantly and wastefully spent, and much was spent on services really imperial in nature. The loans for Irish purposes made by the Treasury were of small benefit to Ireland. Those repaid were of more advantage to the lender than to the borrower; while those remitted were sums which had been advanced for imperial purposes which the Treasury was in any case bound to perform, and their remission was paid for by Ireland shouldering the burden of the income tax, which amounted to far more than the annual interest on the loans. In any event, the advances were advances of Irish, and not of British, money.

The imperial taxes were not the only burdens with which the Irish taxpayer was oppressed. The county cess was a matter of acute complaint on account of its large amount, its unfair incidence, and the many abuses in its collection and expenditure. Many really imperial services were financed by county taxation over which the grand juries exercised no control. The worst example of this was the case of the police, who were charged on the local taxes until 1846. Remedial legislation was, it is true, passed dealing with the tithes, parish cess, and urban tolls; but the value of this relief was more than counterbalanced by the establishment of the poor rate in 1838. Finally, the burden of absenteeism, which we demonstrated to be a public rather than an individual hardship, greatly increased as a result of the Union.

We are now perhaps in a position to suggest an answer to

the question which we proposed above; namely how far it is correct to trace some causal connection between the misery of Ireland and the action or inaction of the United Parliament. The period under review was characterized by four dominant features: the growth of population, the non-development of agricultural resources, the decay of manufacturing industry, and the increase of the public burdens borne by the Irish taxpayer. For the first of these phenomena—the growth of population—the government was not responsible; for the second—the non-development of agricultural resources—the government was to blame for refusing to act upon the recommendations of its own advisers, and for adopting instead a course of action calculated to facilitate depopulation; for the third—the decay of manufacturing industry— the government was clearly responsible, as the proximate cause of that decay was the fiscal policy of the United Parliament; while for the fourth—the increase of public burdens—the government was of course directly responsible. Thus, the industrial and the financial misery of Ireland were attributable to governmental action, and the agricultural misery to governmental action and inaction combined.

The attitude of the government towards Ireland requires some explanation. It cannot be accounted for by ignorance of the needs of the country, because expert advice on Irish matters was constantly being sought. Between 1800 and 1831 no less then 114 commissions and 61 committees reported on Irish affairs.[1] The failure of the government to adopt the recommendations of some of these bodies and its readiness to adopt those of others, would seem to indicate that it possessed some definite policy of its own. We believe it is correct to say that its policy was the assimilation of the institutions of Great Britain and Ireland as rapidly as possible. It was assumed that the political union of the two countries had

[1] Martin, *Ireland Before and After the Union* p. 33.

also unified their economic conditions and requirements.

Thus, in dealing with the great problem presented by the Irish land system, parliament completely ignored the fact that, while the land law in England and Ireland was substantially the same, the spirit in which the law was administered and the traditional relationship of landlord and tenant were fundamentally different. It was the ignorance of this essential distinction between the two countries that caused parliament to insist that the free contractual relationship between landlord and tenant should not be interfered with, as such an interference would amount to an infringement of the landlord's right to do what he liked with his own. The few measures passed dealing with the law of real property—such, for example, as the ejectment acts—were designed to facilitate the landlords in the unregulated management of their estates, and to hasten the conversion of their land into large holdings, which, because they were thought suitable for England, must also be suitable for Ireland. Similarly, the refusal to entertain any proposals for public assistance for the reclamation of the waste lands or the construction of railways rested on the assumption that private enterprise would succeed in doing in Ireland what it had done in England, quite regardless of the fundamental distinction between the circumstances of the two countries. Again, the poor law was extended to Ireland in defiance of the fact that the problems of England and Ireland in this respect were completely dissimilar. In England the problem was to make the unemployed work, and in Ireland to make work for the unemployed.

If we pass from agriculture to manufacture, we find the same assumption underlying the legislation of the period. For centuries the industries of Great Britain had been skilfully and successfully fostered and encouraged, while those of Ireland had been restrained and oppressed. Nevertheless it was apparently assumed that a removal of all restraints on the intercourse between the two countries would place their manufactures upon a footing of equality. In fact, of course, this nominal equality amounted to a real inequality. It is remarkable that both phases of English legislation operated to the benefit of England and the detriment of Ireland. The duties on the channel trade were retained in 1785, and abolished in 1824, in obedience to the wishes of the English, and against the wishes of the Irish, manufacturers. In each case the interest of England prevailed. The repeal of the corn laws twenty years later also rested on the assumption that the interests of England and Ireland were identical; whereas of course in this respect they were fundamentally opposed. "The government of Ireland", according to Lord Liverpool, "has been a system of short-sighted policy that sacrificed the real interests of Ireland to the supposed interests of Great Britain."[1] The great change in the official attitude towards the protection of industry simply reflected the revolution in the economic thought of the time: when the commercial propositions were rejected, protection was still favourably regarded by the mercantile classes; at the time of the Union, Adam Smith's ideas were gaining popularity; at the date of the repeal of the Union duties, the Manchester School was dominant; and the repeal of the corn laws signalled the triumph of Cobdenism. It is little wonder that the orthodox political economists were held in scant favour in Ireland, seeing that the application of their principles seemed to lead to the further impoverishment of the country. "I am aware", wrote Mr. G. H. Evans in 1829, "that, although Mr. McCulloch is a person of acknowledged merit and of first rate authority on subjects of political economy in other countries, there exists in Ireland an unfounded prejudice against him and all political economists."[2] The government policy at this time is well expressed in a letter

[1] Yonge, *Life of Lord Liverpool*, vol. ii. p. 278.

[2] *Remarks on the Policy of Introducing the System of Poor Rates into Ireland*, London 1829.

written by Sir R. Peel:—"The time is come when it is unnecessary any longer to pet Ireland. We only spoil her by undeserved flattery, and by treating her to everything for which she ought herself to pay."[1]

In the domain of public finance, also, assimilation was the keynote of the policy of parliament. Although the Act of Union clearly contemplated the continuance of preferential treatment for Ireland, the taxes of the two countries were gradually assimilated, with the result that, while the taxation per head in Great Britain was annually reduced, it remained practically stationary in Ireland. The assumption that the interests of the two countries were in all respects identical moreover committed Ireland to the financing of an imperial policy dictated almost altogether by the special needs and peculiar development of the other portions of the United Kingdom.

We may remark in passing that the strict observance of the indivisibility of the United Kingdom was relaxed in the case of one branch of legislation, namely coercion acts. Whereas, when it was a question of reforming the land laws or of providing money for the development of natural resources, the suggestion that Ireland was a separate unit was vehemently combated, the individuality of the country passed unquestioned when it was a question of applying repressive measures. "The opening of the Imperial Parliament", Mr. Spring Rice wrote in 1822, "took place on the 22nd of January 1801, and the first measure relating to Ireland discussed in the House of Commons was by a most ominous fatality the Irish martial law bill; since that period the discussion on Irish affairs has been confined in ninety-nine cases out of a hundred to questions of strong and coercive legislation; martial law, suspension of the habeas corpus act, insurrection acts, and bills for the preservation of the peace."[2] It was this aspect of parliamentary

[1] Parker, *Sir R. Peel*, vol. ii. p. 122.
[2] *Considerations on the Present State of Ireland*, London 1822.

history that led John Stuart Mill to exclaim that, "from the year 1800 down to 1829 it may be said though in some sense we treated Ireland as a sister, it was as a sister Cinderella."[1] Sir Robert Kane drew the following striking parallel between the action of the government in suppressing disorder and in encouraging the development of Ireland. "It is singularly illustrative of how little reflection was devoted to Irish subjects—of how slightly the true and only means of consolidating a people by giving them common habits of industry, of sobriety, of traffic, was thought about in relation to this country,—that the Shannon was for so many generations looked upon as a useful barrier and defence against the uncivilized tribes who dwelt beyond it. The cost of maintaining in good repair the various fortresses at what were called the passes of the Shannon was defrayed with pleasure, but the idea of rendering fortifications useless, of erecting the bulwark of the state in the hearts of the inhabitants by fostering their industry, by encouraging their commerce and agriculture, and promoting their education, did not occur to the statesmen of that epoch. Let us hope that a new era has arrived."[2] The result of this policy of treating Ireland as a unit for the purpose of coercion and as an undistinguishable portion of the United Kingdom for the purpose of economic development was that, in 1849, "the government had 50,000 armed men in the country to keep the people down; and were annually voting away large sums of money to keep them up."[3]

This reference to Irish coercive legislation is not irrelevant, as it demonstrates that the peculiar circumstances and needs of Ireland in one respect forced themselves upon the government's attention. In respect of economic legislation, however, the government refused to recognize the distinction between the two countries. In 1868 John Stuart Mill attacked in the House of Commons the suggestion that

[1] *Irish Land Question* p. 113. [2] *Industrial Resources* p. 335.
[3] Bennett Smith. *Life of John Bright*, vol. i. p. 260.

what was good for England was necessarily good for Ireland: "My right hon. friend thinks that a maxim of political economy if good in England must be good in Ireland. But that is like saying that because there is but one science of astronomy, and the same law of gravitation holds for the earth and the planets, therefore the earth and the planets do not move in different orbits. So far from being a set of maxims and rules, to be applied without regard to times, places and circumstances, the function of political economy is to enable us to find the rules which ought to govern any state of circumstances with which we have to deal—circumstances which are never the same in any two cases. I do not know in political economy, more than I know in any other art, a single practical rule that must be applicable to all cases; and I am sure that no one is at all capable of determining what is the right political economy for any country until he knows its circumstances. My right hon. friend perhaps thinks that what is good political economy for England must be good for India—or perhaps for the savages in the backwoods of America. My right hon. friend has been very plain spoken, and I will be plain spoken too. Political economy has a great many enemies; but its worst enemies are some of its friends, and I do not know that it has a more dangerous enemy than my right hon. friend. It is such modes of argument as he is in the habit of employing that have made political economy so thoroughly unpopular with a large and not the least philanthropic portion of the people of England. In my right hon. friend's mind, political economy seems to exist as a bar even to the consideration of anything that is proposed for the benefit of the economic condition of any people in any but the old ways; as if science was a thing, not to guide our judgment, but to stand in its place—a thing which can dispense with the necessity of studying the particular case, and determining how a given cause will operate under its circumstances. Political economy has never in my eyes possessed this character. Political economy in my eyes is a science by means of which we are enabled to form a judgment as to what each particular case requires."[1] Many years later Sir West Ridgeway observed that, "every measure must be marred and spoilt which is pervaded by the fatal delusion that what is suited to Great Britain must also be suited to Ireland."[2]

The assumption that the economic interests of Great Britain and Ireland were identical and were capable of being advanced by identical legislation was more than usually fallacious and pernicious in the first half of the nineteenth century, because at no time were the actual conditions and needs of the two countries more fundamentally different. The industry of Great Britain had for nearly two hundred years been systematically developed by every kind of artificial encouragement, whereas that of Ireland had been no less systematically harassed and oppressed. The result of this difference of treatment was that, whereas the industry of Great Britain had been brought to a point where it was sufficiently strong to dispense with further legislative encouragement, that of Ireland was still in the stage of infancy. Different stages of industrial development call for different industrial policies. Whereas the highly developed manufactures of Great Britain not only did not require artificial encouragement, but actually stood in danger of being impeded in their expansion by any legislative interference, the puny and neglected manufactures of Ireland cried out for the protection and encouragement which had been found so successful in England in the previous century. In other words, the manufactures of Great Britain had as much to gain as the Irish had to lose by a regime of legislative non-interference. The one promised still further to flourish and the other still further to decay under a policy of *laissez faire*.

[1] *The Irish Land Question* pp. 117-8.
[2] Shaw Mulholland. *The Predominant Partner*. p. 97.

Such was the condition of affairs in the two countries when *laissez faire* came to be adopted as the shibboleth of economic wisdom in England. Unquestionably this new policy was calculated greatly to benefit the England of the time. Centuries of the most jealous protection had brought British industry to the point where it craved for ever expanding freedom from legislative control. It was felt that all that was required to make England the richest of all nations was the removal of all artificial barriers which in any way hampered her manufacturers and merchants in their triumphant conquest of the markets of the world. As was always the case, the policy of the English government followed that of the English merchants, and the regime of *laissez faire* was inaugurated.

Unfortunately it was not recognized that the wisdom of this policy is not of universal application, and that circumstances may exist which render a course of legislative non-interference almost as great a hardship as the most tyrannical and meddling interference of the government in the domain of industry. While *laissez faire* may be an excellent motto in the case of a country whose prosperity is established, it is quite otherwise in the case of a country whose prosperity is on the decline. The food of the one may be the poison of the other. Ireland in the early nineteenth century was in precisely the position in which *laissez faire* was calculated to produce the worst possible results. A long course of the most oppressive behaviour on the part of the landlords, connived at, if not actually abetted, by the government, had plunged the mass of the people into a state of unexampled misery; while, at the same time, millions of acres of potentially fertile land capable of supporting a large population in comfort lay waste and unreclaimed; but any suggestion that these obvious evils should be remedied by the aid of the legislature was brushed aside as an infringement of the sacred shibboleth of *laissez faire*. In the department of industry the conditions were the same as in that of agriculture. Centuries of penal laws and restrictive legislation had resulted in the immaturity of some Irish manufactures and the decay of others. But no attempt must be made to nourish or revive them; the era of legislative interference in industry had passed away; and the motto of the day was *laissez faire*—which in its application to Ireland might be translated: "Having put a country into a most unsatisfactory condition, leave it there."

All the evils attendant on the application of the policy of *laissez faire* to Ireland were the result of the adoption by parliament of the fundamentally false assumption that the interests of Great Britain and Ireland were identical, and that the laws and economic institutions of the two countries should therefore be assimilated. It is obvious that, when a democratically elected parliament insists on applying identical legislation to two countries, vastly unequal in area and wealth, whose interests are not the same, it will in almost every case have regard to the interests of the larger and richer, rather than to those of the smaller and poorer country. The insistence on identical treatment for Great Britain and Ireland after the Union therefore had the consequence that, on every occasion on which the interests of the two countries were not identical, those of Great Britain prevailed. It is not too much to say that the parliament at Westminster consulted the interests of Great Britain in preference to those of Ireland as distinctly after as before the Act of Union; and that, in Dr. Cunningham's words, "the regime of ill-assorted companionship has been almost as baneful as the period of jealous repression and Protestant ascendancy."[1]

[1] *Growth of English Industry & Commerce* vol. iii. p. 849.

INDEX.

INDEX.

B.

INDEX.

INDEX.

INDEX.

INDEX.

INDEX.

INDEX.

INDEX.

INDEX.

INDEX.

INDEX.

INDEX.

INDEX.

INDEX.

INDEX.

INDEX.

INDEX.

INDEX.

INDEX.

INDEX.

M.

INDEX.

INDEX.

INDEX.

INDEX.

INDEX.

INDEX.

S.

INDEX.

INDEX.

INDEX.

INDEX.

INDEX.

INDEX.

INDEX.

INDEX.